D1104569

To Cynthia,
For those
sleepless nights
Love!
Rich

Imperial Germany and War, 1871–1918

MODERN WAR STUDIES

Theodore A. Wilson
General Editor

Raymond Callahan
Jacob W. Kipp
Allan R. Millett
Carol Reardon
Dennis Showalter
David R. Stone
James H. Willbanks
Series Editors

Imperial Germany and War, 1871–1918

DANIEL J. HUGHES
and
RICHARD L. DINARDO

UNIVERSITY PRESS OF KANSAS

Published by the University Press of Kansas (Lawrence, Kansas 66045), which was organized by the Kansas Board of Regents and is operated and funded by Emporia State University, Fort Hays State University, Kansas State University, Pittsburg State University, the University of Kansas, and Wichita State University

© 2018 by the University Press of Kansas
All rights reserved

Library of Congress Cataloging-in-Publication Data

Names: Hughes, Daniel J., 1946– author. | DiNardo, R. L., author.
Title: Imperial Germany and war, 1871–1918 / Daniel J. Hughes and Richard L. DiNardo.
Description: Lawrence : University Press of Kansas, 2018. | Series: Modern war studies | Includes bibliographical references and index.
Identifiers: LCCN 2018003390
ISBN 9780700626007 (hardback)
ISBN 9780700626014 (ebook)
Subjects: LCSH: Germany. Heer—History. | Germany. Heer—Organization. |Germany—Politics and government—1871–1918. | Germany—History, Military—20th century. | World War, 1914–1918—Germany. | BISAC: HISTORY / Military / World War I. | HISTORY / Europe / Germany. | HISTORY / Modern / 19th Century.
Classification: LCC UA712 .H84 2018 | DDC 355.40943/09041—dc23.
LC record available at https://lccn.loc.gov/2018003390

British Library Cataloguing-in-Publication Data is available.

Printed in the United States of America

10 9 8 7 6 5 4 3 2 1

The paper used in this publication is recycled and contains 30 percent postconsumer waste. It is acid free and meets the minimum requirements of the American National Standard for Permanence of Paper for Printed Library Materials Z39.48-1992.

For our friends

CONTENTS

Photo galleries follow pages 73, 236, 342, and 450.

ACKNOWLEDGMENTS

Writing a book is normally a solitary activity. A collaboration poses a unique set of challenges, especially when the two authors live a considerable distance from each other, even in the age of the internet and instantaneous communication. There are ways, however, to surmount these challenges. Therefore, I (RLD) would like to state at the outset that the principal author of this work is Daniel J. Hughes. Dan called me in 2014 and asked me to update what was already a massive work. My major contributions were made in chapter 8 and in the concluding remarks of each chapter. The conclusion was written jointly. The fact that we had already coauthored two articles made the process rather smooth.

I (DJH) wish to acknowledge the following individuals who were particularly important to the writing of this volume. First and foremost is my coauthor, Professor Richard DiNardo. The late Professor Donald Douglas of Wichita State University largely created my interest in German history. Two professors at the German Military History Research Office (then in Freiburg), the late Manfred Messerschmidt and the late Wilhelm Deist, guided my early ventures into the historiography of the Prussian army. The staff of the German military archives, especially the late Dr. Friedrich Christian Stahl, eased my early use of the archives. The late Dr. H. O. Malone of the US Army Training and Doctrine Command made immense contributions to my career. My former colleague and current friend Samuel J. Lewis, formerly of the US Army Command and General Staff College, generously shared his insights into the German army's institutions and ideas.

I (RLD) would like to express my gratitude to the following people and institutions. My friend Jack Tunstall was kind enough to provide material from the Austrian archives. The successive heads of the German military archives in Freiburg, and their respective staffs, made every research trip there a very productive experience. Likewise, the staffs of the state archives of Baden-Württemberg and the Bavarian military archives were tremendously helpful. I would also like to acknowledge the support of the Marine Corps Command and Staff College and the financial assistance provided by the Marine Corps University Foundation. And it is always a pleasure to work with the University Press of Kansas. Personally, two people who helped shape my professional career are Cynthia Whittaker, professor emeritus from Bernard Baruch College, and the late Professor David Syrett. I would also like to acknowledge my wife, Rita, for her saintly patience while I worked on this project. Finally, I would like to acknowledge Daniel J. Hughes. When Dan called me several years ago to be his coauthor on this volume, I was delighted to renew our collaboration and excited about the impact this work could have.

Although a great many people have been mentioned here, we alone are responsible for the work. We therefore accept responsibility for any errors of commission and omission.

PREFACE

From the wars of German unification (1864–1871) to the present time, the German army has been one of the most widely studied, criticized, and imitated military organizations in the modern world. In forging the united Germany that emerged in 1871, the Prussian army created new military and political realities in Europe. The new imperial German military establishment was really a combination of the militaries of Bavaria, Saxony, Württemberg, and Prussia, but the core of the organization was certainly provided by Prussia. Some authors still refer to the "Prusso-German" military system.[1] The Prussian War Ministry and the Great General Staff exercised considerable influence in domestic politics. War planning was almost exclusively the province of the General Staff.

The military effectiveness of the Prussian army system was beyond doubt in 1871, and other military establishments sought to imitate the Prussians, in form if not in substance.[2] Based on this reputation, the German army seemed equally formidable as the First World War began. The military collapse in 1918 brought the end of the German Empire but did not end the army's role in domestic politics, as it assisted in establishing both the Weimar Republic and Adolf Hitler's dictatorship. The army's reputation for military effectiveness, however, especially at the tactical and operational levels of war, remained. That reputation has been somewhat diminished by generations of careful study, both in Germany and elsewhere. Nonetheless, the image of the German army as a force capable of operational and tactical brilliance in both world wars remains strong, especially in the popular imagination and even in professional military circles.[3]

Because of the army's role in establishing one line of military theory and practice, scholars in a variety of disciplines from 1871 to the present day have addressed the German military experience from their varying perspectives. Military thinkers, historians, officers, and defense professionals have examined German systems in the context of the continuing need to prepare military forces for large-scale conventional warfare. German concepts of the conduct of warfare, leadership, command, combat effectiveness, organization, and other topics have been suggestive in shaping military structures and methods. The rise of airpower and the development of nuclear weapons had their effects on the conduct of land warfare, but they did not render the German system entirely irrelevant.[4]

This volume is an institutional study of the most essential components of the German system between 1871 and 1918.[5] It examines various foundational areas such as theory, doctrine, institutional structures, training, and the officer corps. The major focus of this work is adaptation and change. The army had to adapt and change in the face of rapid technological developments, while also trying to figure out what a future war would look like and planning for it. Doctrinal changes in the pre-1914 period were often manifested in subtle ways, usually in the form of slight revisions in successive editions of the manuals that shaped the army's tactics. A detailed examination of these modifications is necessary, as a series of minor changes over time can add up to a major change. In war planning, there was one major shift in German thinking about how to conduct a future war in the period between 1871 and 1914. After that, alterations in war plans and mobilization schedules were made subtly and to provide flexibility for the army.[6] The need for adaptation and change only increased after 1914, when theory and doctrine met the reality of modern warfare and was found wanting in a number of respects. Although this study considers battles and campaigns, occasionally in some detail, they are not the primary focus and are discussed mainly in the context of institutional adaptation and change.[7]

The German army in this period reflected the federal nature of the German Empire and thus consisted of four state armies—those of Prussia, Bavaria, Saxony, and Württemberg. The king of Prussia, who also held the position of German emperor, was the unifying individual under the German constitution of 1871. The Prussian army was by far the largest of the four state contingents and dominated all aspects of the army's training and doctrine. Domestically, the Prussian army remained what it had always been: a royal army dedicated to the Prussian state's conservative and monarchical social structure. These two fundamental aspects of the army's identity played important roles in determining its social and political place in modern Germany, but they also substantially influenced its internal workings in everything from officer selection and training to tactics and command from the lowest to the highest levels. The army was, in short, a bulwark against the emperor's internal opponents as well as Germany's foreign enemies and rivals.

As noted earlier, this volume focuses on theory and practice leading up to the First World War and on the variety of adaptations that became necessary as the war progressed. The army struggled to adjust to the dichotomous nature of warfare between 1914 and 1917. Trench warfare on the western front forced the army to abandon many of its fundamental prewar principles and practices. The almost constant presence of the German High Command on the western front introduced the practice of micromanagement to a degree that senior field commanders found severely constraining. On the eastern front and in the Balkans, however, traditional approaches in tactics, operations, and command remained relatively intact. More favorable force-to-space ratios and less capable enemies allowed the army to attain major (but not decisive) victories within its traditional methodological framework. In preparation for the desperate final offensives of 1918, the army's leadership faced the necessity of retraining its tactical units to return to the kind of mobile warfare (*Bewegungskrieg*) it had prepared for in 1871–1914. This was no easy task, as years of trench warfare (*Stellungskrieg*) in the west and massive casualties had robbed the army of leaders and units experienced in these traditional methods.

Ultimately, the purpose of this work can be stated simply: to provide a comprehensive examination of the army of the *Kaiserreich* as an institution. This aim is also reflected in the chronological scope of the work, which covers the entire history of the German Empire. Thus, although there are some allusions to them, there is no extended discussion or analysis of the wars of unification from which the empire arose.[8] Likewise, although some attention is paid to the empire's military institutions when they were still in an embryonic state in Prussia during the early nineteenth century, a detailed discussion of that period of Prussian history is beyond the scope of this work. We hope this work gains the attention not only of those with an interest in the Great War but also of those readers who are drawn to the broader history of Germany's imperial era.

Before beginning our examination, some explanation is in order. First, names in this volume are rendered in the German version rather than the English. Thus, the German emperor in 1914 is referred to as Wilhelm II, not William II. Likewise, this volume uses German place names as they existed in 1914. For example, the capital of Austrian Galicia is Lemberg, as opposed to Lvov (Russian), Lwow (Polish), or Lviv (Ukrainian). This practice applies to general officer ranks as well. Thus, a *Generalmajor* is equivalent to an American one-star general, and a *Generalleutnant* would have two stars if the Germans used such a system.[9] Other common German terms also appear in the text for the sake of simplicity and consistency with the documents and literature on which this study is based.

CHAPTER ONE

THE MID-NINETEENTH-CENTURY FOUNDATIONS

On 16 June 1871 the city of Berlin, capital of the new German Empire, played host to one of the greatest military parades in its history. The occasion was the end of the successful war against France and the creation of the German Empire under Prussian domination. This, the third of the wars of unification, was the historic high point of the Prussian army, which, over the next forty years, reaped the rewards of its great victories. The parade was a symbolic end of the old era in Prussia and the beginning of the imperial, or Wilhelmine, period of modern Germany. At the head of his glittering military machine rode Wilhelm I, king of Prussia and German emperor. Behind him came one of the most popular men in Prussia—indeed, in all of Germany: Helmuth von Moltke, chief of the Prussian General Staff and architect of the victorious campaigns in Bohemia and France.[1] Behind him marched the elite of the Prussian army—the guards infantry and cavalry—and many of the army's future leaders. In troubled cooperation with Bismarck, the army had created the new Reich in three victorious campaigns against Denmark (1864), Austria and its German allies (1866), and France (1870–1871). In addition to creating the military foundation of the new empire, Moltke's victories served to legitimize the Prussian army's theories and philosophy of war, elements of which endured in a variety of armies until the last decade of the twentieth century.

Bismarck's empire offered a political solution to the question of German unification, but only within a framework that by its nature resisted many of the forces that gave rise to Germany's growing wealth and power. This Prussian solution—unification from above rather than from below, and therefore conservative rather than democratic—created a federal state resting on the closely related foundations of monarchical government, military force, and the psychological consequences of the wildly popular victory over France. Prussia thus entered the new era in a manner that left its traditional social structure and its monarchical political structure intact. The aristocracy retained its power base and its ideology. The state therefore represented the powerful forces that sought to control or even destroy the forces of political and social modernization.

The Royal Prussian Army

The army remained a primarily royal institution under the new German Constitution. Its officers and men retained their traditional oaths to the king of Prussia, whose legitimacy as commander rested in the traditional power and authority of the Prussian monarchy rather than in the Prussian Constitution of 1850 or the German Constitution of 1871. In the entire army, only a single officer, the war minister, took an oath of loyalty to the Prussian Constitution. Military conventions concluded between Prussia and many of the other states of the German Empire incorporated the smaller contingents directly into the Prussian army or imposed its structural and doctrinal framework on them.[2] Although Bavaria, Saxony, and Württemberg retained their state armies, the Prussian system dominated in almost every aspect, especially in theory and structure of the armed forces.

The Prussian army's foundations lay in its traditional role in shaping and defending Prussia's monarchy and social order, dating to the days of the Great Elector (1640–1688) and King Friedrich Wilhelm I (1713–1740). The former made the army the fundamental pillar of the state, while the latter permanently drew Prussia's landed nobility into military service as officers.[3] The Prussian army thereafter served two major functions. It was, perhaps most obviously, the state's primary means of survival and expansion. Less obviously today, the army was the guarantor of the Hohenzollern monarchy's power and of the illiberal rule of Prussia's upper classes.

The army's organization reflected its aristocratic and monarchical character. Three institutions played key roles in shaping the army's structure, personnel system, and way of war. These were, respectively, the War Ministry, the Military Cabinet, and the General Staff. The strong and sometimes eccentric personalities that dominated the army from 1871 to 1918 did so within the framework of these three institutions.

The War Ministry

The Prussian War Ministry was created as part of the Stein-Hardenberg efforts to reform the Prussian state after its military defeat at the hands of

Napoleon in 1806 and its subsequent collapse.[4] The key military reformer was Gerhard von Scharnhorst (1756–1813), who led the Military Reform Commission established by King Friedrich Wilhelm III in July 1807. As part of the effort to introduce the principle of ministerial responsibility in the military arena, the commission gained royal approval to create what later became known as the War Ministry on 15 July 1808. Scharnhorst's goal was to centralize responsibility for all military affairs under the War Ministry, which accordingly had two main departments: the General War Department (*Allgemeine Kriegsdepartement*) and the Military Administration Department (*Militär-Oekonomie-Departement*). The War Ministry would thus unify administration, campaign planning, and personnel affairs under a single responsible cabinet secretary.[5]

The reformers immediately encountered the two enduring problems of bureaucratic rationalization of the Prussian military system. The first was the issue of the king's authority as supreme commander of the army (*Kommandogewalt*). No king was willing to compromise on this, either by creating a single official to administer all military affairs or, even worse from the royal point of view, by allowing any popular body to interfere in the exercise of this authority.[6] The royal edict of 1808 establishing the War Ministry thus did not give that office command of the field army during wartime, a responsibility that in theory remained a personal function of the monarch until the collapse in 1918. Friedrich Wilhelm III, faced with this problem, declined to appoint a war minister until 1814, when Hermann von Boyen, a relatively liberal reformer, became the first person to hold that office.

The second issue that remained problematic throughout the remaining century of Hohenzollern rule in Prussia was that of direct access (*Immediatvortrag*) to the king. Even as the war minister began to assume control over nearly all military functions, the commanding generals (corps commanders) retained the right to report directly to the king, and by 1900, several dozen high-ranking positions had acquired that privilege. As a practical matter, the army always lacked any unified control beyond the person of the monarch.[7]

The War Ministry's General War Department, headed initially by Scharnhorst, was in theory responsible for the most important matters related to command, while the Military Administration Department dealt with administrative affairs. The General War Department had three main subordinate sections for personnel affairs, general staff functions, and weapons and related issues.[8] The first of these departments was particularly problematic because it managed the most sensitive issue in the entire Prussian system. From the point of view of the monarch and the aristocracy, nothing was more critical than selecting, promoting, assigning, and dismissing or retiring officers.

The Military Cabinet

This office, initially known as the Section for the Administration of Personnel Affairs, was later officially designated the Military Cabinet, and it is known to history by that name.[9] The origins of this shadowy institution lay in the early eighteenth century and the king's *Generaladjutants*, who administered various official duties involving sensitive, important, or secret matters.[10]

From the beginning, the head of the Department for Personnel Affairs was also an adjutant to the king. He thus had direct access to the monarch, even though he was a subordinate of the war minister. For the period between 1814 and 1857, most correspondence and decisions related to personnel matters went through the various war ministers, who were unwilling to exert themselves in sensitive personnel decisions or to challenge the right of their subordinates to report directly to the king.[11] Following the Revolution of 1848–1849 and the creation of the Prussian Constitution of 1850, the struggle to emancipate the Military Cabinet from the War Ministry began in earnest.

This process originated in 1857 when King Friedrich Wilhelm IV (who ruled from 1840 to 1859) ordered that all directors of the Department for Personnel Affairs be chosen exclusively from his personal adjutants or from generals attached to his personal entourage.[12] Edwin von Manteuffel, who headed both the Department for Personnel Affairs and the Military Cabinet from February 1857 through June 1865, used his position as general adjutant to bypass the war minister, who gradually lost control over personnel actions. This continued until 18 January 1861, when a cabinet order gave the head of the department the right to conduct his business, issue orders, and render personnel decisions without the approval of the war minister, who thus formally lost all ministerial responsibility for these actions.[13]

Subsequent war ministers, especially Julius von Verdy du Vernois (April 1889–October 1890), attempted to rein in the chief of the Military Cabinet, but to no avail.[14] A very small number of individuals, usually fewer than ten officers and about a dozen civil servants, thus controlled the vast majority of the army's decisions related to officer personnel.[15] In 1861 the Military Cabinet received authorization to publish personnel actions without the formal approval of the war minister.[16] The Military Cabinet's responsibilities were defined as the execution of all highest (royal) orders in assignments, promotions, retirement, pay, punishment, granting of awards, permission to marry, and dismissals of officers and officer candidates.[17]

Only the direst circumstances could force the king to subordinate the Military Cabinet to any other military authority. In the spring of 1918 such a moment arrived when Erich Ludendorff's power was sufficient to cause the removal of the chief of the Military Cabinet, but not for reasons of personnel administration.[18] For all practical purposes, from 1860 until the end of the monarchy, the Military Cabinet made nearly all personnel decisions in a secret and frequently arbitrary manner with no oversight except by the king himself.

As a result, the chief of the Military Cabinet became the most powerful person in the army, second only to the king, and he was capable of intimidating officers at all levels, active or reserve. He was therefore the most feared person in the army, perhaps in all of Prussia or even all of Germany. The resulting witticisms and complaints about the cabinet's arbitrary decisions had no impact on the chief's authority. *Wie Gott will und Albedyll* (as God and Albedyll wills) was the saying used to describe the reign of terror when Emil von Albedyll held the office (April 1872–August 1888).[19] Another officer remarked that anyone who lacked personal "connections" with important men in the Military Cabinet had to trust his fate to the mercy of his beloved God.[20] In 1870 the chief of the Military Cabinet was powerful enough to assign officers to Prince Friedrich Karl's staff and subordinate units with complete disregard of the prince's desires.[21]

The Military Cabinet, which had no role in planning or conducting campaigns, made the appointments to key command positions, sometimes with the approval of the General Staff, but sometimes against its recommendations.[22] On the whole, however, the chief of the General Staff could assign his officers as he wished.[23] Nevertheless, even Count von Schlieffen could not prevail in making General Staff assignments if the Military Cabinet was determined to resist his requested appointments.[24]

Finally, in 1883, a royal order completely emancipated the Military Cabinet's personnel functions from the War Ministry.[25] This served to shield the Military Cabinet from both the Prussian parliament and the Reichstag. From 1893 onward, the Military Cabinet also had a very influential role in officer personnel affairs in Württemberg's army.[26] It was small wonder that the army's enemies in the Reichstag referred to the Military Cabinet as "antediluvian" and "absolutism in its clearest form."[27]

Despite consistent criticism from political parties in the Reichstag, the army made no secret of its desire to preserve royal control over all personnel matters.[28] In 1909 the war minister, the ultraconservative General Karl von Einem, vigorously defended the process in the Reichstag, thus formally and officially reversing the position taken by Scharnhorst and the Military Reform Commission. Despite the secrecy and arbitrary action inherent in the process, many officers regarded it as necessary in a royal army such as Prussia's.[29]

The General Staff

The third of the three key institutions of the Prussian army was the General Staff. Although the earliest origins of the Prussian General Staff can arguably be traced to about 1655, its modern history began in 1802. In January and November of that year, Colonel Christian von Massenbach proposed the establishment of a permanent staff that in peacetime would plan for various eventualities that might arise. Shortly thereafter, in 1803, King Friedrich Wilhelm III ordered the reorganization of the Quartermaster General's Staff into the General Staff and made Lieutenant General von Geusau its first chief.[30] As Geusau was nearly seventy years old and distracted by other duties, his three key assistants, the most notable of whom was Scharnhorst, did most of the work.[31] Although the General Staff was largely in place in 1806, it could not save the Prussian army from the French army under Napoleon. Nevertheless, many important figures in the future development of the General Staff performed well enough to survive with their reputations intact, including Scharnhorst, Müffling, Valentini, Rühle von Lilienstern, and Boyen.

In July 1807 the reform process began in earnest, and Scharnhorst became chief of the General Staff (then still called the Quartermaster General's Staff). He remained in that capacity until August 1813, when he was succeeded by August Wilhelm von Gneisenau, one of his close associates in the reform party. Massenbach, largely discredited as a field soldier by his actions at Prenzlau, had no opportunity to implement his ideas, which had always taken second place to those of Scharnhorst.[32] The latter's memorandum of 1808 established the wartime composition of the General Staff as one colonel, four majors, eight captains, and twelve lieutenants.[33] Both Gneisenau and Scharnhorst were thus key in establishing the basic features of the General Staff system, which lasted well into the Second World War. The General Staff officially received that designation on 20 June 1817.[34]

As previously noted, Scharnhorst successfully implemented his proposal that the chief of the General Staff become a subordinate of the war minister. He further proposed that the General Staff adopt a functional organization with four sections: strategy and tactics, internal administration, replacements, and artillery and munitions. Although opposition from conservatives prevented the full implementation of his plan, the General Staff played a key role in the final campaigns against Napoleon. Scharnhorst in those years established the fundamental principle that the General Staff officer, at whatever level he functioned, should remain in the background, giving the commander advice and support without limiting the commander's authority or tarnishing his image with subordinates and the troops at large. When Scharnhorst died of complications from a wound suffered at Gross-Görschen, Gneisenau took his place as chief of the General Staff.[35]

Gneisenau's contributions to the ethos and methods of the General Staff were nearly as important as Scharnhorst's. Gneisenau emphasized clarity in communications, brevity, and reliance on general directives rather than detailed orders. He also developed the concept of joint responsibility, which, though unwritten, remained one of the fundamental pillars of the General Staff system until Hitler abolished it in the Second World War. Under this principle, the General Staff officer assumed responsibility for his commander's decisions; thus, the officer's evaluation was in part dependent on the performance and fate of the commander he advised. Eventually, the army accorded its General Staff officers the right to register a dissenting opinion in the unit's war diary if they had strongly advised the commander against a particular course of action. Joint responsibility did not mean joint or shared command, however. The Prussian army, throughout its long history, recognized only a single commander in any given unit. So firm was the resolve not to dilute the authority of the commander that the Prussian army never established positions such as deputy or vice commander, as had been the practice in many other armies.

From 1815 until its growth in power and prestige during the wars of unification (1864–1871), the General Staff functioned in difficult circumstances but continued to establish the basic procedures that laid the foundation for its later glory. From the outset, the General Staff had two elements. The *Grosser Generalstab* (Great General Staff) in Berlin worked directly under the chief of the General Staff on the centralized functions assigned to it by the War Ministry. Other General Staff officers, collectively known as the *Truppengeneralstab* (General Staff in the units), served as chiefs of staff and primary advisers to corps commanders and, intermittently until 1853, division commanders. These officers worked directly for their units' commanders but remained General Staff officers in every sense. The two groups were part of the same select body of General Staff officers, and any individual might find himself in either group at any given time. Most officers rotated consistently but with substantial variation among the Great General Staff, the unit General Staff, and normal command assignments at levels appropriate to their rank. This practice had the dual purposes of providing trained advisers to large unit commanders and ensuring that the General Staff did not stagnate and become a military ivory tower out of touch with developments in the army.[36] This remained standard practice until the end of the Second World War.[37]

The General Staff was not a particularly important or vibrant institution for much of the period between 1815 and the arrival of Helmuth von Moltke in 1857. It lost much of its royal support and vitality as the reformers declined in influence or left the army. Its assigned officer strength declined from sixty-nine at the beginning of the postwar period to a mere twenty-four in 1824. The divisions lost their General Staff officers that year, creating a gap that lasted almost thirty years. For the next three decades, the General Staff performed its work in the shadow of the War Ministry.[38] Its chiefs accepted this subordinate position.[39] The General Staff had limited direct influence on the army's training, doctrinal manuals, weapons development, and related areas, and the war minister continued to exercise his authority through ad hoc commissions to deal with specific issues as they arose. The results of the mobilization of 1850 demonstrated that neither the army nor its General Staff was prepared to deal with a serious military crisis.[40]

Although the Prussian General Staff had several influential chiefs in the first half of the nineteenth century, the decisive personality in establishing the General Staff's position for the period covered by this study was Helmuth von Moltke.[41] When Moltke became chief of the General Staff in 1857, that body was but a minor element of the War Ministry, responsible for only a fraction of the duties and functions later associated with it. This quiet but effective chief gradually extended his involvement in these and many other areas. In 1858 the General Staff gained control over corps staff rides. In 1861 the king extended this authority to the maneuvers of large units. Of even greater importance, in 1858 Moltke ordered the General Staff to use railroads for large exercises in peacetime, and in 1859 he instituted the extensive coordination between the army and the Prussian railway system that became the foundation of Prussia's speedy and efficient mobilizations in 1866, 1870, and 1914.[42]

The size of the General Staff increased as Moltke extended its influence. When Moltke became chief, the General Staff had fewer than 65 officers, and only about 20 of them were in Berlin. By 1900, the General Staff had nearly 300 officers, more than 100 of whom served in the central staff in Berlin.[43] The number of fully qualified General Staff officers was greater, since at any one time some of them were commanding units at various levels or serving on special assignments. Between 1900 and 1914 the General Staff doubled its strength, growing to about 650 officers. About 150 of them worked in the main sections dealing with mobilization, strategic planning, intelligence, education and training, fortresses, military history, and so forth.[44]

Standing Army or Citizen-Soldiers?

The nature of the army's use of manpower and its unit structure were just as important as the High Command structures discussed above. The revolutionary changes in society and warfare brought about by the French Revolution forced Prussia to reduce its reliance on the lowest classes of society and foreigners to fill its enlisted ranks. To a limited degree, the monarchy had (unwillingly, but of necessity) enlisted the resources of the entire state in the final struggles against Napoleon after 1812. The military reformers had hoped, like the French, to create a revitalized nation of citizens rather than subjects and, in the military realm, an army of citizens who would support the state out of commitment rather than the coercion that had characterized the army of the *ancien régime*. To that end, Prussia emerged from the Napoleonic wars with a relatively small active army and a substantial body of citizen-soldiers, the *Landwehr*, with elected officers and relatively independent units of marginally trained civilians. The army's unit structure, like so many other aspects of its development, thus went back to the reforms of Scharnhorst and his colleagues.

The long struggle over the Prussian *Landwehr* and the effort to create a viable system of reserve forces illustrate the difficulties the Prussian army faced in reconciling the potentially conflicting demands of military effectiveness and political reliability. The *Landwehr* issue first arose during the dark days between the battles of Jena/Auerstädt and the final victories over Napoleon. The reformers hoped to combine the principle of universal military service with a reserve army of citizen-soldiers. Scharnhorst hoped to use these two innovations to bind the army more closely to the population and to preserve a democratic base within the army. Royal decrees established the principle of universal service on 9 February 1813 and instituted the *Landwehr* on 17 March of that year.[45] The latter decree broadened the similar steps already taken by the provincial Diet in East Prussia after General Yorck von Wartenburg deserted Napoleon and joined the advancing Russians to drive the hated French out of Prussia and Germany.

The *Landwehr* was not the only effort to draw the great mass of the population directly into the twin efforts to unite people and nation and to eject the French from Prussia. When mobilized, the *Landwehr* would be part of the regular army, with appropriate pay, discipline, and administrative arrangements. Scharnhorst also proposed a second line of reserves, the *Landsturm*, to be composed of all physically fit citizens. These reserves would engage in guerrilla warfare against the enemy, like the Spaniards had done in 1808. To be used only as a last resort, the *Landsturm* was not expected to have military discipline or administrative arrangements. Its members, moreover, would be organized and used without regard to social origins. A royal decree on 12 April 1813 officially established the *Landsturm*.[46] From the outset, the *Landwehr* and *Landsturm* were controversial because they threatened the layering of Prussian society and because many conservatives were fearful of the long-term consequences of arming the population.

In the spring of 1814 Hermann von Boyen became Prussian war minister and began the task of creating a long-term peacetime army, including reserve forces. Boyen soon came up with a plan that reaffirmed the principle of universal military service and assigned all able-bodied men to one of four sections of Prussia's armed forces: the active army, the *Landwehr* of the first and second levies, and the *Landsturm*. The *Landwehr* of the first levy was to conduct limited peacetime drills and serve alongside regular forces during wartime. The *Landwehr* of the second levy, consisting of veterans of the regular army and of the first *Landwehr* levy, was to perform garrison duties in wartime. The *Landsturm* was to be an emergency mobilization of all men between the ages of seventeen and fifty not serving in the other three military forces.[47] The new law also established the princi-

ple of the one-year volunteer, which became the backbone of the state's reserve forces and one of the main elements linking Prussia's upper classes
and educated middle classes with the army and the monarchy.

Boyen and the other reformers saw the *Landwehr* as an institution that
would bind people and army together and create a citizen-based officer
corps as a balance to the aristocratic and conservative officers of the active
army. Thus, the *Landwehr* was to consist of coherent and independent
units rather than serve as a source of individual replacements for the active army. Boyen wished to ensure that the *Landwehr* officer corps, in large
part elected by local units, would train its own units and command them
upon mobilization. The original plan called for mixing three *Landwehr*
and three active battalions in a wartime brigade.[48] Boyen's proposals became law on 3 September 1814. Unfortunately, the statute was very vague
and required additional implementing legislation and regulations, which
gave conservative opponents an opportunity to dilute its effects.[49]

The debate over the desirability and effectiveness of such a reserve
system continued unabated through the next several decades and foreshadowed many of the disputes over the great military reforms of 1860.
Conservatives attacked the idea of separating the line from reserve forces
on political and military grounds. Those who opposed universal military
service saw the *Landwehr* as an unreliable force of dubious value to the
active army in wartime and one that might turn against the monarchy
in a crisis. Prominent officers, from princes of the royal house to powerful figures such as Job von Witzleben, warned of the consequences of
Boyen's reforms.[50] Civilian liberals, in contrast, saw the *Landwehr* and its
middle-class officer corps as the "only counterweight to the noble officers
of the army." In a similar vein, others saw the *Landwehr* officer as the only
guarantee for the citizens' spirit in the army.[51]

In the years between 1815 and 1860, the *Landwehr* encountered many
difficulties in finding capable officers and forming effective forces, even
at the company level. *Landwehr* officers came almost entirely from very
poorly trained one-year volunteers, a problem made worse by the relatively small size of the active army and the departure of officers who had
experience in the wars of liberation.[52] Numerous observers warned that
the *Landwehr*'s officer-related problems naturally extended to the units'
overall capabilities. Prussia's failure to implement universal military service deprived the *Landwehr* of a sufficient number of experienced soldiers
to replace those who left.[53] Shortages of funds only made these fundamental problems worse.[54]

Between the end of the Napoleonic period and the Roon reforms of 1859–1860, the *Landwehr* had several opportunities to either prove its worth or demonstrate the correctness of its critics. In each case its performance confirmed that it was of marginal value as a military force. In 1831 Prussia mobilized part of its forces, including some reserves, because of the Polish uprising, and it did the same in 1832 because of the French invasion of Belgium. Each mobilization revealed numerous weaknesses, and the *Landwehr* was no exception. From the king's point of view, the *Landwehr*'s performance during the Revolution of 1848 was, if anything, even worse, and this was especially true of the officer corps. The *Landwehr* units, which turned out to be weak militarily, all too frequently were less than reliable politically.[55] The *Landwehr* made, in the words of one distinguished historian, a "lamentable" showing.[56] Further mobilizations in 1850 and 1859 showed little if any improvement.[57]

These weaknesses were related to both officers and units and to military as well as political issues. Many *Landwehr* officers were too old, even by Prussian standards. Some units had company-level officers who were up to forty-nine years old, and the average age in 1848 was forty-seven for captains and thirty-nine for first lieutenants, even in the combat units.[58] Despite their long years of reserve duty, many had not improved on their inadequate training prior to commissioning, a problem related partly to the government's unwillingness to provide adequate financial support, but also to the poor structure of training and the lack of practical exercises. The *Landwehr*'s noncommissioned officers exhibited tremendous shortcomings in training and capabilities.[59] The army found, as many conservative officers had warned during the reform period, that it could not rely on the *Landwehr* for use in either foreign wars or domestic revolution. By the end of these sobering experiences, Prussia had acquired a new king and an aggressively conservative war minister, both bent on a thoroughgoing reform of the army's basic structure and its officer corps.

The Roon Reform of 1860

In October 1858 Prince Wilhelm of Prussia assumed the regency in place of his brother, King Friedrich Wilhelm IV, who had suffered a complete mental collapse.[60] Though a royal prince, Wilhelm had been a real officer for decades. A die-hard conservative, he had been forced to flee to England during the revolutions of 1848–1849. He was determined to effect a major change in the army and in October 1857, while not yet officially the regent, he requested the War Ministry to prepare a proposal to deal with the deficiencies revealed by the recent crises and mobilizations.[61] The war minister, Count Friedrich von Waldersee, responded with a memorandum dealing primarily with changes in the conscription system, an expansion of the army, and a reduced reliance on *Landwehr* soldiers to fill out active units during mobilization, while maintaining the two-year service obligation for conscripts.[62]

Prince Wilhelm also asked for a reform proposal from his old friend Count Albrecht von Roon, then commanding an infantry division in Posen. Roon's reply, one of the most important documents in Prussian military history, became the basis of what is known as the Roon reforms of 1860.[63] Most historians have seen these reforms primarily as military efforts to improve the army's ability to mobilize its forces and to wage war, despite the fact that they clearly strengthened the monarchical and conservative nature of the army. Roon no doubt was equally interested in the external and domestic significance of his concepts.[64]

The essential features of these complicated proposals were a moderate increase in the standing army, the abolition of the *Landwehr* as established by Napoleonic era reformers, the creation of a new reserve system, and the introduction of a three-year term of service for most conscripts. Roon saw the *Landwehr* as one of the main roots of the army's problems. It was, he wrote, a "politically false institution because it no longer impressed foreign powers and was of doubtful significance for both external and internal policy." It was, he went on, equally false on military grounds because it lacked the "firm soldiers' spirit" and "the certain disciplinary control necessary in a dependable military organism."[65] Roon proposed a substantially new basis for the army by ensuring that the active army and its officer corps were firmly in control of the state's armed forces and that these forces possessed an organization that could effectively organize the nation's resources for war.

In 1860 the army enacted this great reform proposal as Roon became war minister.[66] New reserve units, up to corps size in wartime, became the primary second-line military force. The *Landwehr* as a semi-independent force primarily loyal to the middle-class strata of society disappeared completely. Roon replaced it with reserve units that were an extension of the active army. These new reserve units, commanded by regular officers from the rank of major upward, would take the field with the active-duty army. The younger groups of the *Landwehr* entered the new reserve units, while the older reservists became members of the downgraded *Landwehr*.

The latter, along with the *Landsturm*, consisting of the oldest men still eligible for military duty, was intended only to perform garrison duty in rear areas. Introduction of the three-year service commitment and an overall increase in the size of the active army produced more trained enlisted men for the reserve units.[67]

Although the Prussian parliament refused to approve the army's budget, the king continued to command the army independently of any parliamentary or other governmental limitations, ignoring the fact that, in theory, no funds were available. During the great constitutional conflict between 1860 and 1866, the king and his chancellor, Otto von Bismarck, ruled without a budget when the Prussian parliament refused to grant annual appropriations because of its hostility to Roon's reform program. Using his "constitutional gap" theory, Bismarck simply announced that the government would continue to collect taxes and provide funds for the army. After the victorious war against Austria, the parliament conceded the government's right to conduct the army's business in this manner.

The shadow of this confrontation, based on the king's right to command the army (*Kommandogewalt*), hung ominously over subsequent discussions of the military budget. After 1870, when the military budget became an imperial matter, the practice of granting multiyear appropriations, frequently for seven years in advance, effectively limited all but the most determined criticism of the army. While great controversies arose in subsequent years over the size of the army, neither the Prussian parliament nor the German Reichstag ever seriously challenged the king's right to command the army as he saw fit. As a result, many measures that would require parliamentary sanction in a democracy rested solely on orders of the king. The parliaments of Prussia and Germany had no voice in critical personnel matters or in internal army affairs such as doctrine and unit structure.

The Roon reforms changed the structure of the army in several less controversial ways. The final version increased the mobilized strength of the field army by some 32,000 officers and men, from about 335,000 to 367,000. Total wartime strength, including replacement and fortress units, rose from approximately 532,000 to 637,000. The active officer corps grew by about 1,200 to a total of 8,000. To overcome the resulting shortages, the army allowed selected *Landwehr* officers to join active units and shortened the courses of senior cadets and officer candidates in the war schools. At the end of the reform the active army had eighty-one regiments of infantry and forty of cavalry.[68]

Finally, it should be noted that, after the reforms, the active Prussian army was basically an army of cadre units, a mobilization base to bring substantial elements of the citizenry into existing units upon mobilization. Active units were not at full strength in peacetime; they relied on reservists, all of whom had previously served two or three years on active duty, to reach wartime strength. Active officers commanded the new reserve units above the company level and in some cases at that echelon. The highest reserve rank was captain, and all reserve officers and officers of the new *Landwehr*, a second-line reserve force relegated to rear-area duty, had previously passed through the active army. The old *Landwehr* officer corps ceased to exist. All officers therefore had active or reserve commissions conferred through the regular army.[69] All this put the officer corps on the path it would follow with few exceptions or changes until the outbreak of war in 1914.

Most historians agree that King Wilhelm I pressed for the reforms primarily to bolster his army and state against potential rivals in European power politics rather than to mount an attack against his internal political enemies.[70] However, the reforms certainly bound the bulk of Prussia's armed forces more closely to the monarch and promised to make the reserve officers and their units more reliable in case of a political crisis, a fact that the opposition political parties clearly recognized at the time.[71]

The Officer Corps

Ideology

The Prussian army proudly displayed its conservative ideology on numerous political and social questions. This basic orientation survived the fall of the monarchy and remained intact until the rapid expansion of the army prior to the Second World War, when the substantial influx of young officers with a strong National Socialist orientation reduced traditional Prussian conservatives to isolated segments of the high officer corps. This conservative worldview had a definite impact on the army's approach to war and its relation to Prussian and German society.

The key to this conservatism was the officer corps and its ideology, recruitment process, and social position. As previously mentioned, officers took an oath to the king of Prussia rather than to any written constitution or set of basic national values beyond those traditionally associated with the Hohenzollern monarchy. This link to the Hohenzollerns was the basis of the officer corps' homogeneity and exclusivity.[72] Prussian monarchs realized that the army and its officer corps were the ultimate guarantors of their positions. Friedrich Wilhelm IV stated this unequivocally when he said that his army was the necessary condition of the existence of the throne. In a similar, almost prophetic, vein, Bismarck once reminded Wilhelm II that as long as he had his officer corps he could do anything he wished, but should this cease to be the case, the entire situation would be different.[73]

The officer corps, for its part, developed an allegiance to the monarchy that transcended the temporary lack of respect that emerged when kings such as Friedrich Wilhelm IV or Wilhelm II seemed hesitant or less than royal in their conduct or strength of will. Many officers retained their personal loyalty to Wilhelm II even after the disasters of the First World War, when the kaiser became a passive observer in the shadow of the semidictatorship of Hindenburg and Ludendorff.[74] This loyalty to the monarchy began in the cadet corps, which, in the words of one admiring general, sought to instill feelings of awe and respect for the ruling houses not only of Prussia but also of other German states and some foreign nations.[75] In return for their unquestioned loyalty, officers were generously rewarded with the prestige reserved for the highest echelons of Prussian society. The army's social standing, moreover, rose substantially during the latter decades of the nineteenth century as it basked in the glory of the wars of unification.

The commissioning process was one of the primary means of ensuring the ideological basis of the officer corps. The army desired educated officers only to the extent that this would reinforce its social basis and produce a sufficient number of officers with the skills necessary to master advances in applied technology and mathematics. The Prussian officer corps was not an educated group by the standards of modern armed forces, although it made important concessions to education over the course of the nineteenth century. The army wished to establish educational standards that would exclude the sons of lower-class families while admitting the sons of landowners, officers, lower civil servants, and other social groups deemed desirable in the officer corps.[76]

Education

Although some have noted improved educational levels after the reform period, for at least the first half of the nineteenth century, the army was sorely lacking in real educational standards for its officer corps.[77] Even as late as midcentury, numerous sources attest to the presence of many poorly educated men in an army that profited from the presence of Clausewitz, Moltke, and other talented and literate officers. Count Wrangel's boast that he conducted war with the sword and not with the pen found wide endorsement in the army.[78]

Efforts by Napoleonic era reformers to establish rigid examinations to determine eligibility for commissions resulted in an 1808 regulation that affirmed the principles of knowledge and education as fundamental requirements.[79] Nevertheless, conservatives in the army frustrated all efforts to use educational requirements to transform the officer corps. In 1816 the army established "division schools" to provide rudimentary education for socially acceptable youngsters who aspired to become officers. The curricula of these schools consisted of simple mathematics, a little history and geography, and some German grammar. They had separate classes for students who wished to take the officer candidate examination and for those who hoped to pass the officer examination.[80]

Prince Wilhelm (later King and Emperor Wilhelm I) headed a commission in 1825 that recommended the elimination of these miserable excuses for schools and the use of scholarships to enable the sons of poor officers to attend *Gymnasia*. The government did not accept this proposal and allowed semiliterate officer candidates to join the army if they could find regiments to accept them. Subsequent efforts by Boyen to require that all officer candidates possess a certificate of eligibility for higher schooling also failed. The first major step in raising educational levels came in 1854, when the army abolished the division schools, notorious for their low standards. In place of the nine divisions schools, General Eduard von Peucker, the general inspector of military training and education, established the first three war schools at Neisse, Potsdam, and Erfurt. Not to be confused with the *Allgemeine Kriegsschule* (the old name of the War Academy), these centralized institutions remained key components of the commissioning process until 1914.[81]

By the mid-nineteenth century, those who argued for improved educational standards for commissions had begun to make some progress. Peucker's efforts in 1856–1857 to impose the *Primareife* (equivalent to a high school diploma) as the minimal educational requirement failed, but a few years later the Roon reforms nearly succeeded on that point.[82] In 1862 Wilhelm I accepted Roon's proposal in principle but balked at implementation.[83] This only delayed the inevitable, and in 1870 a cabinet order specified that, after 1 April 1872, only those who possessed the *Prima-reife* could take the officer candidate examination. The army continued to grant numerous exceptions, however, and many graduates of the shadowy military preparation schools joined the officer corps. In 1899 Wilhelm II ordered a strict enforcement of the *Primareife* requirement and a reduction in the number of exceptions granted. Nevertheless, between 1902 and 1912, more than 1,000 young men were exempted from this educational prerequisite.

In 1900 Wilhelm II, despite his sympathy for maintaining the social homogeneity of the officer corps, approved a regulation granting favorable treatment to young men possessing the *Abitur* (a nine-year diploma with examinations and theoretical eligibility to attend a university). Those who held the *Abitur* were exempt from the preliminary officer candidate examination and could bypass the war school course if they proved to be especially capable during the probationary period in their regiments. This caused a gradual improvement in the educational level of the officer corps, and by 1914, about 65 percent of officer candidates held the *Abitur*.[84] The army attracted a very respectable proportion of the total number of young men earning the *Abitur*, between 6 and 7 percent by 1900.[85]

Arriving at an overall assessment of the educational level of the Prussian officer corps is no simple matter. It is almost certainly wrong to argue that the educational level of the officer corps actually declined during the imperial period.[86] Rather, the argument for a gradual improvement seems well-founded, despite the officer corps' shortcomings.[87] The Prussian officer corps in this regard was in no way inferior to most of its European counterparts.[88] The Prussian army had many highly literate officers, and the proportion of its generals who wrote books and published articles in professional journals is one that few modern armies can match. Much of this intellectual activity, but by no means all of it, centered on the elite corps of the Prussian General Staff. Although the Prussian officer corps in 1914 was not highly educated by the standards of most professions in Germany or by the standards of most modern armed forces, neither was it composed of semiliterates at any rank. Still, education remained subordinate to social class and ideological conformity as a measure of a young man's military potential.

In this area, as in so many others, the attitude of the elder Moltke typified the army's predominant attitude. In 1871 he reminded the Reichstag that "more important than what is learned in school is the subsequent moral education (*Erziehung*) of the man—his becoming accustomed to order, punctuality, neatness, obedience and loyalty; in short, discipline. It is that discipline that placed our army in a position to win three campaigns."[89]

The Commissioning Process

The army's process of conferring commissions on its young officers clearly illustrated the fundamental social and institutional factors that gave the officer corps its unique position.[90] Most young men (with the exception of cadets, as discussed later) who wished to become officers had to find regiments that were willing to accept them as officer candidates. No central institution served as an induction or commissioning agent. If a regimental commander had vacant positions, and if he were satisfied that the applicant possessed the educational qualifications, social background, and personal characteristics required by the army and his regiment, he had the authority to accept the young man as an officer candidate. The applicant then had to take the officer candidate examination, administered by the *Ober-Militär-Prüfungskommission* at several sites throughout Prussia but normally at division headquarters. The candidate then joined his regiment and served as an enlisted soldier in a special rank between sergeant and sergeant-major. Although the candidate's duties were much the same as those of a typical enlisted man, his special position separated him from the lower rank and file.[91] Very few Prussian officers actually rose from the ranks. The most notable exception was Carl von Reyher, who served as chief of the General Staff from 1848 to 1858.

After several months of service in the regiment, the candidate went off to one of the division schools, which were later consolidated into a smaller number of centralized war schools. While there, the candidate took the officer examination and then returned to his regiment for an indefinite period, usually one to three months, until he received a commission. Before that could happen, the candidate was subjected to the officer's election, whereby all officers of the regiment voted on the candidate's suitability to become an officer. A single negative vote was sufficient to prevent the granting of a commission, although in theory, the corps commander had the final word.[92] So ingrained was the concept of the officer's election that it survived, at least in theory, until Hitler abolished it in 1943.[93] Finally, if the regimental commander approved, the young man, after approximately eighteen months of duty as an officer candidate, became a second lieutenant.[94] This was the commissioning process experienced by the majority of Prussian officers.[95] Only a few particularly privileged or well-connected men bypassed this system or the other route, the cadet corps.[96] Once commissioned, an officer could be dismissed only by an order of the king.

Cadets took a different road to obtain their commissions.[97] Cadets had no choice of unit and had to accept whatever assignment the Military Cabinet deemed appropriate, based on the needs of the army. Cadets who entered the army after their *Ober-Prima* (ninth year) had to follow the same path as non-cadets but spent fewer months in their units before and after their war school studies. They could receive a commission in about one year. The *Selekta* of the cadet corps, whose extra year gave them the equivalent of the war school diploma as well as the *Abitur*, entered the army as lieutenants.

Social Composition

The army that Moltke led to victory in 1866 and 1870–1871 was decidedly aristocratic in terms of the social composition of its officer corps, and it remained so at the highest levels throughout the imperial period. An understanding of the ethos of Prussia's military aristocracy is essential to an understanding of its way of war. The reformers had hoped to open the officer corps to all men of talent and education, regardless of wealth or social origin. After the end of the Napoleonic period and the demise of the reformers, reactionaries in the army attempted to restore the aristocratic exclusivity that had traditionally characterized Prussia's officers.

Efforts to reestablish the traditional reliance on nobles enjoyed partial success but were doomed to failure as the Prussian army expanded before and after the wars of unification. At the end of the Napoleonic Wars, the officer corps was almost equally divided between nobles and non-nobles. In 1817 the army had 4,138 noble officers and 3,367 commoners.[98] Efforts to purge the wartime officer corps of undesirable elements continued in the following decade but could not prevent a gradual growth of non-noble elements. In 1860 about 65 percent of all officers were nobles. As the army expanded under the Roon reforms and during the gradual increases between 1871 and 1914, the percentage of noble officers fell dramatically. In 1913 only about one officer in three possessed a title of nobility, while the overall size of the officer corps increased from about 17,000 in 1875 to 30,000 immediately before the outbreak of war in 1914.[99] Although certain regiments, particularly the guards and many cavalry units, remained bastions of the aristocracy, non-nobles increasingly dominated the middle and lower officer ranks as the decades passed.

Nevertheless, key positions remained in the hands of the aristocracy throughout the life of Bismarck's empire. For the entire imperial period up to the First World War (1871–1914), nearly 70 percent of all generals were nobles. Likewise, the highest positions in the General Staff remained in the hands of the aristocracy throughout the nineteenth century. More than eight in ten General Staff generals were nobles, a figure that showed no appreciable change from those appointed by Count Helmuth von Moltke to those appointed by Schlieffen and the younger Moltke.[100]

At lower levels of the General Staff, the picture was quite different. By 1913, about 70 percent of the men assigned to the *Grosser Generalstab* were bourgeois, including most of the officers holding key positions as section leaders. Some have cited this as an indication of the growing professionalization of the General Staff, a point of undoubted merit.[101] Yet the persistence of the aristocracy in the General Staff's highest ranks (not just in the *Grosser Generalstab*) seems to contrast starkly with the growing number of non-nobles among the General Staff corps as a whole. It could not have been an accident that so many generals of the General Staff, many of whom were also commanders of divisions and corps at some point, were drawn from the nobility.

Traditional aristocratic values permeated the intellectual, cultural, and social life of the officer corps. Officers policed their own ranks with courts of honor (*Ehrengerichte*) and continued to fight duels in spite of numerous official admonitions and orders to cease this antiquated practice. Officers were expected to maintain a lifestyle appropriate to their station in life, which was quite exalted. All officers, regardless of rank or social class, were eligible to attend court (*hoffähig*). This privilege was restricted to a tiny minority of the Prussian and German populations, normally nobles and very high-ranking commoners in the civil service.[102] The army carefully examined the backgrounds of officers' potential wives, demanding that their families' occupations, reputations, and, if necessary, wealth be appropriate. The officer corps, in short, was not open to all men of talent; it was open only to men of talent whose social background and personal characteristics were consistent with the army's image of what the king's officers should be.

As the nineteenth century progressed, suitability for the officer corps became primarily a function of a young man's social standing based on his family's occupational background. The Prussian army consistently tried to fill its officer corps with the sons of officers, landowners, and high civil servants. These "old Prussian" types were most likely to have the personal characteristics and political loyalties necessary for an army that was, after all, a royal institution rather than a broad-based entity that served the population as a whole. Precise determinations of officers' occupational backgrounds are not available, but Karl Demeter's research convincingly suggests that even as late as 1913, these old Prussian types provided the army with more than 70 percent of its officers.[103]

Promotions to the army's highest and most influential positions were even more narrowly confined to old Prussian types. For the empire as a whole, more than nine out of ten generals were sons of landowners, officers, or high civil servants or some combination of these groups. This dominance of old Prussian types was clearly evident among the non-noble generals serving between 1871 and 1914, as nearly eight in ten of them were drawn from the same social groups as the noble generals.[104] Among its highest and most influential echelons, the officer corps was remarkably homogeneous even in 1914.

Although much of the specialist and general literature describes the officer corps as "Junker," that expression must be used with caution in relation to the Prussian army in the nineteenth century. Imprecision is a major problem in using the term, which has become a pejorative expression to describe conservative officers and their sinister designs, of which most historians strongly disapprove. In its original meaning, "Junker" referred primarily to sons of noble East Elbian landowners; others have broadened the term to include any East Elbian noble.[105] Among the key intellectuals and commanders prominent in the development of the army's theory and doctrine, Junkers were in a distinct minority. Barely half of Prussia's generals were born in the provinces east of the Elbe River, and relatively few of them were sons of landowners. If one assumes a direct connection with the landed East Elbian nobility, fewer than one Prussian general in five was a Junker.[106] Most generals were sons of government professionals—that is, officers or civil servants—without landed connections and without other visible means of support. For the empire as a whole, nearly two generals in three (65.86 percent) fell into this category, a proportion that remained reasonably stable between 1871 and 1914.[107]

Wealth

The financial circumstances of the officer corps reflected the social structure of Prussia and the prestige of the army in society.[108] Until 1909 the army remunerated its junior officers at a minimal level, assuming that they would use their personal funds to make up the difference between their pay and the sums required to maintain an acceptable lifestyle. The amount of private income needed varied greatly from the guards units (especially the cavalry) to the regular infantry units. Even in 1914, some of the former required their members to provide hundreds of marks per month to support their horses and entertainment costs, while many officers in ordinary regiments had little or no private income. Young men of wealth and pedigree could find acceptance in the "wealthy" regiments, while others had to confine their early careers to regiments where the demands on private income were modest. Cavalry regiments were the most expensive, followed by some artillery and a few infantry regiments. Pre-1914 handbooks used the following as a guideline for the monthly requirements of a moderate lifestyle in a typical regiment: cavalry, 150 marks; artillery, 70; infantry, 45. In comparison, the average German industrial worker in 1913 earned about 25 marks per week.[109] Many officers had little or no private income and survived by living in "splendid misery" or by acquiring debt during their junior years. A few received special subsidies from the army, the so-called emperor's *Zulage*. The net result was that low pay in the junior grades excluded most men from the officer corps.

Wealth-based divisions survived even within the officer corps. A number of cavalry regiments became the preserve of wealthy playboys from prosperous aristocratic families. Other cavalry units attracted a mixture of wealthy commoners and aristocrats who could not find positions in the more prestigious regiments. The luxurious lifestyles in these elite units became a major target for the army's political enemies and a source of concern to many senior officers. In the final years before 1914 the War Ministry tried to control excessive monetary requirements by individual regiments, but it could not overcome the entrenched resistance and power of regimental commanders. It was thus no accident that the cavalry stubbornly clung to an outmoded vision of its role in warfare all the way onto the battlefields of 1914.

To generalize about a complicated issue, it is safe to say that most officers were not wealthy but had at least an upper-middle-class background. Most had private income of at least a few hundred marks per year, although there were exceptions. The expenses of acquiring the education needed for a military career were far less than those incurred to prepare for other professions in Germany. Young aristocrats in particular found that a military career was an affordable way to maintain their social standing, which could suffer greatly if they chose occupations that lacked respectability. Wealthy young men used their commissions to enhance their social standing far beyond what they might have achieved in most other occupations.

The Reserve Officer Corps

While the active army remained under the control of the aristocracy and other old Prussian types, the bulk of its wartime officer strength was in its reserve corps. Upon mobilization, these men constituted the majority of the officers in the reserve and *Landwehr* units, but they also served in active units in large numbers.[110] After the Roon reforms, the reserve officer corps consisted exclusively of men who had either been on active duty or served as one-year volunteers before becoming reserve officers upon leaving active duty. The one-year volunteer system, therefore, was one of the pillars of the entire military system. Prior to the Roon reforms, one-year volunteers went directly into the *Landwehr*, with little oversight from the active officer corps. This system had its origins in Boyen's invigoration of the *Landwehr* in 1813–1814. After the Roon reforms, the reserve officer system was much more closely bound to the active army and the oversight of the Military Cabinet.[111]

The reserve officer corps, like its active counterpart, was open only to men who possessed the proper social background, personal characteristics, and financial means to support their station in life. One-year volunteers had to belong to the "educated classes," defined as possession of the *Sekundareife* at a *Gymnasium* or *Oberrealschule*, a requirement that intentionally eliminated most sons of the working class and the peasantry. One-year volunteers also had to pay all their own expenses, estimated to be at least 2,000 to 3,000 marks; however, this could be much more in some locations and in the mounted branches. One-year volunteers paid for their uniforms, quarters, food, military equipment, enlisted servants, and, in some cases, horses and fodder.[112] At a time when an ordinary semiskilled worker might have an annual income of 1,000 to 1,300 marks, only the educated middle classes could afford to use the one-year system as a way to avoid duty as a common soldier. A very small number of especially desirable candidates, at most one-tenth of 1 percent in Prussia, received state support.[113] To continue service as a reserve officer, one had to possess an annual income of at least 1,200 marks; this figure rose to 1,800 marks for men who were married.[114] These requirements were beyond the means of the majority of even those with the requisite education.[115]

One-year volunteers made a substantial contribution to the strength of the army and saved it a lot of money. In the 1870s about 7,000 men served in that capacity in a given year, but by 1914 the number had risen to between 14,000 and 16,000. Most of this growth took place after 1899, as the army began to expand and a shortage of officers afflicted some of the active regiments.[116] Many other former one-year volunteers served as reserve noncommissioned officers and enlisted men. A reasonably reliable estimate is that 200,000 former one-year volunteers were still reporting for annual training in 1905.[117] One-year volunteers could choose their active-duty regiments, where they served in middle positions between normal enlisted men and noncommissioned officers. Here they enjoyed a leisurely year or suffered substantial abuse at the hands of their noncommissioned officers, depending on which account one chooses to believe. Their experiences could not have been too terrible, however, as many chose to attain reserve commissions and remain in the reserves in one capacity or another.[118] At the termination of his year of active duty, the volunteer's unit passed judgment on his eligibility to continue as an applicant for a reserve commission. Just prior to the First World War, the active army gave certificates of eligibility to just under half the one-year volunteers.[119] Those who were not eligible continued to serve as enlisted men in their reserve units until their service obligation was completed. Eligible men who were interested in receiving reserve commissions applied to District Commands (Bezirkskommandos), which oversaw reserve officers in their respective regions of Prussia. If accepted as officer candidates, they served for two periods of active duty over the following two years as noncommissioned officers and took a fairly rigorous examination on military subjects. If they passed, they served two additional periods of active duty, performing officer duties in their reserve or active units.

The district commanders and the reserve officers of the districts passed final judgment on a candidate's suitability to wear the king's uniform, although, of course, the Military Cabinet also had a voice. Between 1877 and 1909 a Prussian army order governed the factors to be considered in granting such commissions. In 1909 it was clear that the districts had been sufficiently rigorous in enforcing the army's social and military standards that such centralized supervision was no longer necessary. Acting on a request by the Bavarian War Ministry, the Prussian War Ministry withdrew the 1877 order.[120] District commanders carefully examined candidates' private lives and police records and questioned former school directors and other sources that would be useful in determining the acceptability of officer candidates who, in the words of a popular handbook for potential officers, had to possess a "stainless character."[121] The army took care to exclude those who had been active in the Social Democratic Party and, in most but not all cases, Jews.[122] Most reserve officers were sons of the educated middle class and had solid civilian occupations themselves; unlike their active counterparts, few were offspring of members of the officer corps.[123]

Once commissioned, reserve officers had to continue to meet the army's standards in both their private and public lives. This meant avoiding contact with undesirable social elements, including political parties opposed to the government or hostile to the army. The Military Cabinet reserved the right to dismiss anyone it deemed unsuited for continued service. Not even good political connections could compensate for shortcomings in this area. The most famous example of a reserve officer losing his commission was Prince Heinrich of Schönaich-Carolath, who was dismissed in 1885 after revealing that he had supported Liberal Party representative Eugen Richter when the latter opposed the army in the Reichstag on a budget matter. He was not alone in losing his commission, and the Military Cabinet's oversight clearly extended beyond active duty to nearly all reserve officers.[124]

Social Prestige

Officers willingly, even eagerly, accepted these arbitrary limitations because of the enormous social prestige attached to a reserve commission. Many high-ranking civil servants maintained their reserve ranks and wore their uniforms on numerous occasions because of the elite status it automatically conferred. Chancellors Bismarck, Bülow, and Michaelis wore their uniforms on occasion, as did some prominent members of the Reichstag. Upon retirement or attainment of a venerated age and status, some distinguished political and governmental leaders preferred to be acknowledged with reserve commissions (even honorary) rather than high civilian titles.[125]

The reserve officer system eventually became one of the most controversial aspects of the Prussian military system. Because the educated middle classes accepted the system and coveted their reserve commissions, a number of historians have seen the institution as the final surrender of

German liberalism to the militarism of the Prussian monarchy.[126] Some have cited the militarization of the middle classes, but this cannot properly be attributed to the reserve officer system, which simply did not involve a sufficient number of individuals to have this effect. Nevertheless, the reserve officer system, if compared to the circumstances in 1848 and other developments before the Roon reforms, certainly reflected the fact that much of the upper middle class was ideologically aligned with the king and his officer corps.[127]

Patriotism and Religion

Even in the increasingly secular intellectual climate of the nineteenth century, the Prussian monarchy continued to pay at least lip service to the old principle of the divine rights of kings. Wilhelm I, for his part, definitely continued to believe in this medieval concept, and officers frequently adopted attitudes of obsequious obeisance that, however appropriate in the days of Frederick Barbarossa, seem somewhat out of place in the days of Marx, Darwin, and Freud. Kissing the royal hand, whether gloved or otherwise, was a not uncommon occurrence, even on the part of such hard-bitten officers as August von Mackensen.[128] Of course, the practical aspects of using religion to support the established order were far more widespread than this ancient curiosity.

The "School of the Nation"

As a result of its sometimes blind loyalty to the monarchy, the army proclaimed its lack of involvement in politics. This was an entirely false front, however, even though many have fallen prey to this illusion.[129] The army's literature exhibited extensive efforts to promote the government's conservative political, social, and cultural values. This had not always been the case. The Napoleonic era reformers conceived the concept that the army should be the nation's school for values (*Erziehungsschule der Nation*).[130] They hoped that universal military service would enable the army to instill national consciousness and patriotism among the masses.

The liberal idealism of the reformers quickly gave way to the more pragmatic concerns of Prussia's increasingly conservative military and political leaders. The concept of a "school of the nation" increasingly meant instilling new recruits with loyalty to the monarchy and the Prussian state, respect for established authority and religion, and hostility to the ideas of democracy and, later, socialism. Hans von Beseler, an officer of middle-class origins who was later raised to the nobility, wrote: "Militarism is the spirit of obedience and discipline, self-denial and loyalty until death. . . . One of the most important and most serious tasks of the professional soldier is to transfer this soldierly spirit to the entire nation through the school of the army, and thereby expand and further the great work of educating the people."[131]

Although such statements have been subjected to harsh criticism and even ridicule among modern historians, many Prussian officers of all types, from the reserved intellectual Moltke to unsophisticated field commanders, took the idea very seriously. Helmuth von Moltke informed the Reichstag in February 1874 that it was not the schoolmaster who had won Prussia's battles but "the military profession as popular educator, which had for nearly sixty years trained the nation for bodily activity and moral health, to order and exactness, to loyalty and obedience, to love of fatherland and to manliness." Another officer, writing in 1888, informed his comrades of their obligation to serve as educator, to fill their recruits with "loyalty to the king, honor and duty, a sense of order, lawfulness, love of fatherland and respect for God."[132] The Prussian army made no secret of its goal of instilling conservative and patriotic values into its recruits and, through them, the entire nation. The concept was, as one author has argued, a battle concept, the answer to the middle classes' struggle against the standing army from the period after the Napoleonic Wars to the end of the nineteenth century.[133]

Christianity

Recently, scholars have cast doubt on the importance of religion in the army, arguing that the officer corps was more secular than previously portrayed by historians.[134] The evidence is equally strong, however, that many powerful and influential officers took religion very seriously. Wilhelm I was a devout Christian, as were numerous important officers.[135] Whatever the personal piety of officers, the army incorporated religious services and messages into its ceremonies on numerous occasions. Wilhelm II's speeches at the annual swearing-in ceremonies to administer the royal oath to the Guards Corps were virtual sermons.[136] The kaiser maneuvers typically had scheduled religious services, complete with prescribed uniforms.[137] The army had Protestant chaplains throughout the nineteenth century and Catholic priests from 1852.[138] Normal procedures required, at least in theory, that every soldier attend church services at least one Sunday per month, and the army instructed its officers to allow their men to attend as often as they wished, consistent with duty requirements.[139] Officers accompanied their soldiers to obligatory church services on Sundays and regarded religious activities as part of their official duties. There can be no doubt that the army aggressively used Christianity as a weapon against social democracy and as a tool, with questionable success, to increase the soldiers' devotion to the king, the state, and conservative social values.[140]

Anti-Catholicism

Despite a paternalistic interest in its enlisted Catholics, the Prussian army's officer personnel policy was strongly anti-Catholic. A cabinet order by Friedrich Wilhelm III had forbidden Prussian officers from promising to raise their children as Catholics, even though that was a condition of marriage to a Catholic woman. General Willibald von Arndt, the grandson of Ernst Moritz Arndt, was reputedly denied a corps command because he allowed his children to be raised as Catholics.[141] Hermann von Tresckow, who served as chief of the Military Cabinet from 1864 until 1871, was well known for his hatred of Catholics, who constituted about one-third of Prussia's population.[142] The Catholic political leader Matthias Erzberger estimated in 1912 that 16 percent of the officer corps was Catholic, a figure roughly equivalent to the percentage of Catholics occupying the important administrative position of *Landrat*.[143] Erzberger's estimate, though credible because of the source, was probably far too high.[144] Although the necessity of acquiring a large number of junior officers forced the army to commission Catholics, very few rose to high rank. For the empire as a whole, only about 5 percent of the army's general officers were Catholics.[145] Many of these men were special cases, coming from families with particularly good connections or long military traditions.[146]

The rise of the Catholic Center Party in the Reichstag gave Prussian officers, from the emperor down, new reasons to identify Catholicism with the enemies of Prussia and the new German Empire. Although Wilhelm I had attempted to avoid religious controversy in the officer corps during the *Kulturkampf* and had appointed Catholic *Freiherr* von Loe as an adjutant, he was deeply distrustful of Catholics.[147] His grandson was less reserved. In some of his tirades he questioned the loyalty of Catholic officers, a nearly unprecedented public act by the head of the ruling house.[148]

From chiefs of the General Staff to various field commanders, the surviving statements of many luminaries of the Prussian officer corps provide ample evidence that prejudice against Catholics was alive and widespread well into the twentieth century.[149]

Anti-Semitism

One aspect of the Prussian army's conservative Protestantism was its strong anti-Semitism. Although the army frequently gave commissions to young men whose family backgrounds were less than perfect, and it allowed strong personal attributes in one area to overcome deficiencies in other areas, there was one blemish that could not be overcome. With perhaps a single exception in the period 1820–1848, practicing Jews could not serve as officers in the Prussian army. The few baptized Jews who received commissions during the war against France in 1870–1871 were not fully accepted even during wartime and were ruthlessly and quickly eliminated after the war's conclusion.[150] The reaction of Ernst Baron von Amelunxen to the proposal to grant a battlefield commission to a Jewish noncommissioned officer was probably typical. Captain (later General) Amelunxen denied such a request because, as a Christian, he could not be responsible for placing a Jew in command of his soldiers.[151] Jews served, of course, as enlisted men and even as one-year volunteers, although the latter were rarely given commissions as reserve officers. Indeed, by 1900, Jewish spokesmen had given up their efforts to open the active officer corps to practicing Jews and concentrated instead on gaining access to reserve commissions. In this they enjoyed little success. Perhaps as many as 30,000 Jews served as one-year volunteers between 1885 and 1910, but hardly more than 300, all baptized, received reserve commissions. By 1914, there were no Jewish officers on active duty and probably very few in the reserves.[152]

Throughout the nineteenth century the army's anti-Semitism was primarily religious and cultural, although racial anti-Semitism made rapid inroads in some segments of German society around the turn of the century. The army on occasion gave commissions to men from Jewish families that had converted to Christianity. Numerous officers wrote comments in their memoirs and letters indicating their belief that Jews could not be full members of a Christian state or that their involvement in liberal, democratic, or socialist causes led to suspicions of disloyalty.[153] A few Jews whose families had converted to Protestantism may have received commissions and become generals. Probably the best-known examples were Reinhold von Mossner and Otto Liman von Sanders. Mossner's father, a wealthy banker and landowner in Silesia, had been a personal friend of Wilhelm I. Mossner married into the Uradel Wolffersorf family, gained a title of nobility as a major in 1890, and served as an aide to Wilhelm II. His personal connections to the Hohenzollerns and his personal background thus compensated for his Jewish origins, but few were in a position to duplicate his success. Sanders, famous for his exploits in Turkey, was also a special case. His grandfather had converted to the Evangelical faith, his father was a large East Elbian landowner, and his wife was the daughter of a Prussian officer. Sanders was therefore not a Jew by the religious or social definition of the Prussian army.[154]

Jews were occasionally present on the periphery of the Prussian army in two ways. Academics of Jewish background occasionally held teaching positions at the War Academy.[155] Wealthy Jewish women sometimes became military wives and thus rescued impecunious nobles from their financial straits in exchange for respectability.[156] One officer who acquired a Jewish wife for that purpose referred to her as his "change purse." Such marriages occurred in all kinds of units, from provincial artillery to Berlin guards regiments.[157]

Courts of Honor

Few institutions of the Prussian army better reflected its continuing aristocratic, some would say feudal, core than courts of honor and dueling. Both illustrated the officer corps' insistence that its sense of honor went far beyond that applicable to most segments of the population and that courts of honor and dueling were essential for proper gentlemen to protect their good names and reputations. In 1906 war minister Karl von Einem informed the Reichstag that as long as dueling was recognized by "wide circles" as a means of rehabilitating one's honor, the officer corps would not tolerate within its ranks anyone who was not willing to defend his honor "with weapon in hand."[158]

Special courts of honor for officers, the *Ehrengerichte*, formally came into existence early in the nineteenth century and continued until they were outlawed under Article 105 of the Weimar Constitution. Military reformers convinced the king to issue the "Regulation Concerning Punishment of Officers" in August 1808. That regulation made the officer corps responsible for policing itself in matters related to the honor of any individual officer or the entire officer corps. If any one officer had seemingly compromised the honor of the whole officer corps, the regulation called for the creation of a court of honor consisting of officers drawn from the subject's regiment. A new order in 1821 gave courts of honor more definite form and made the officer corps responsible for the conduct of its members. Each regiment subsequently established a standing commission to consider relevant cases.[159]

A new regulation dealing with courts of honor, revised in 1874, provided the essential feature of the system that existed through the First World War. Each regiment established its own court of honor, usually consisting of ten officers, as did corresponding naval units. Separate courts were established for company-grade and field-grade (staff) officers. General officers were not subject to courts of honor. Separate courts of honor governed the conduct of medical officers in the army and navy. Members of the courts were elected for one-year terms and were authorized to consider any matters that might compromise the honor of the officer corps or that might lead to a duel between officers. The authority of the courts of honor extended to all active and reserve officers, officers *à la suite* of the army, officers of the gendarmerie, retired officers, and any others holding commissions that allowed them to wear the uniform. The 1874 regulation extended the system to the armies of Bavaria, Saxony, and Württemberg.[160] In theory, regimental adjutants were the coordinating officers for courts of honor, but at the division and corps level, the senior General Staff officer was usually the chief person administering the regulation.[161]

Concluding Remarks

Armies do not spring into being overnight. In this respect, the army of the *Kaiserreich* was no exception. The army was based on Prussian institutions, some of which dated from the Napoleonic era; others went back to the eighteenth century, if not further. These institutions were incorporated into the imperial system for reasons both domestic and foreign. Domestically, the army constituted one of the pillars that supported the conservative social and political order envisioned by Bismarck and other founders of the empire.[162] Although in some cases almost archaic in appearance, these institutions proved remarkably flexible and adaptive, able to accommodate to some degree the societal changes that occurred in Germany during the prewar period.

Aside from the issue of monarchy, the army's principal purpose was to defend the empire against its foreign enemies. In the context of the imperial era, this meant France and possibly Russia.[163] Here also, some of the institutions that underpinned the army proved capable of adapting to the demands of modern war. The Military Cabinet and the General Staff were generally able to get the right commanders and chiefs of staff to the right place at the right time. The most famous example was the duumvirate of Paul von Hindenburg and Erich Ludendorff, although there were others. The reserve and *Landwehr* components met the test of war in 1914, achieving better results than their French and Russian opponents.[164]

Perhaps the greatest failure among the institutions of the imperial army was that of the emperor. He was the unifying force, vested with the power of decision or at least influence over military matters. The constitution that outlined the kaiser's powers had arguably been written with the tacit assumption that whoever occupied the office would have considerable military experience. This certainly applied to the first two rulers of the *Kaiserreich*, Wilhelm I and Friedrich III.[165] But Wilhelm II was lacking in this area. His only military experience was at the regimental level, and even that was laden with artificialities. Although not a stupid man, Wilhelm II lacked intellect. His intelligence and mercurial personality were not tempered by a combination of rigorous education and extensive experience at a variety of levels. Thus, although he was capable of the occasional shrewd insight, Wilhelm's statements and opinions too often left high civilian and military officials doubtful of his judgment. To everyone's relief, Wilhelm II promised that, in the event of war, he would remain out of military matters.[166] This ensured, however, that the head of the state and commander in chief of the army would be a passive wartime observer at best.

Although institutions are organizations, they are ultimately composed of people with a combination of different and similar experiences who share a common ethos and intellectual perspective. For the army of the *Kaiserreich*, the most important common intellectual perspective was its theory of war. This theory, underpinned by extensive historical analysis, was most fully developed by Carl von Clausewitz, the great Prussian theorist and Napoleonic era soldier. After Clausewitz's death in 1831, the torch was passed to Count Helmuth von Moltke in the 1850s. It is to these men and their concepts that we now turn.

CHAPTER TWO

THE PRUSSIAN THEORY OF WAR
FROM CLAUSEWITZ TO MOLTKE

The years from 1789 to 1815 saw important, indeed revolutionary, changes in Europe. The French Revolution transformed the social and political structure of France and introduced the germ of further radical change throughout the continent. Changes in social structure produced a vast transformation in warfare, while the "god of war," as Clausewitz called Napoleon, conducted spectacular but unsuccessful efforts to extend his dominion across Europe. Other powers, particularly Prussia, reluctantly adapted to these changes, usually after crushing defeats. The cabinet wars of the eighteenth century gave way to the first of the truly national wars as the surviving monarchs harnessed the full energies of their states to defeat the French threat. Important as this was, change in another field also had a significant impact.

These years were also a time of intellectual transformation. The Enlightenment, which had set European intellectual development on a new path blazed by the earlier scientific revolution, gave way, particularly in Germany, to a new age in philosophy and politics. This new movement was essentially a counter-Enlightenment, directed against the rationalism of the philosophes. In the military realm, this emerging mixture of romanticism, historicism, nationalism, and other elements provided new ways of looking at the state and its military forces. It was the genius of Clausewitz that molded this new intellectual outlook and changes in warfare into a new philosophy of war, which, however elusive in some respects and incomplete in others, laid the intellectual foundation of the emerging Prusso-German way of war.[1]

Although Clausewitz's classic book *On War* formed the basis of much of the Prussian theory of war throughout the period covered by this volume, other leading military intellectuals contributed importantly to the development of Prussian thought. This chapter begins with an examination of a few of these thinkers, both to establish the context and to indicate the nature of their important contributions. For instance, the ideas, battles, and writings of Frederick the Great occupied a prominent place in Prussian theory, even if he was questionably understood.[2] Adam Heinrich von Bülow (1757–1807) contributed numerous definitions that became prominent in later interpretations of Napoleonic warfare, even though he displayed no real understanding of the innovations of the French Revolution and Napoleon.[3] Gerhard von Scharnhorst (1755–1813), one of the key individuals in the reform of the Prussian state and its military system after the disastrous defeats at Jena and Auerstädt, contributed numerous basic ideas to Prussian military theory.[4] They are logical starting points.[5]

Bülow pursued brief and largely unsuccessful careers in the Prussian army and various business enterprises before becoming a writer on a variety of subjects, military theory being the most prominent. His most important work, *The Spirit of Modern Systems of War* (1799), laid out those ideas most relevant to this study.[6] Like most Enlightenment theorists, Bülow saw warfare largely in mathematical terms and was unable to escape the limits of this approach, even though he recognized some of the tactical innovations of his era.[7] Claiming to be the founder of military science, Bülow argued that his geometric system of the base and the ninety-degree angle guaranteed military victory to commanders who followed the scientific laws he had discovered. He even tried to explain Napoleon's early victories by reference to his formula. Ultimately, his argument that commanders should direct their efforts against the enemy's country rather than the army and his emphasis on fixed magazines could not be reconciled with Napoleon's methods, but Bülow stuck to his approach in an increasingly erratic and sometimes belligerent manner.[8] His most enduring contribution was in the area of terminology. He invented or at least popularized the concepts of the "base" and "objective," and he may have been the originator of the concepts of "strategy" and "tactics."[9] His definitions, now obsolete, gave way entirely to those of Clausewitz, discussed below. Bülow adopted Henry Lloyd's concept of "lines of operation" and, in combination with his own mathematical ideas, used it as the basis of his theory. These concepts, along with the idea of the base of operations, have endured.

Clausewitz first criticized this approach in 1805 in an anonymous article in the military journal *Neue Bellona*, and since then, most writers have regarded Bülow's writings as curious anachronisms associated with a bygone era.[10] Bülow became associated with what most German military theorists regarded as outmoded ideas of victory through reliance on maneuver and the mathematical forms of the late eighteenth century.[11] The Prussian government, enraged by Bülow's prediction of French hegemony in Europe, declared him insane and imprisoned him in Colberg and later Riga, where he came under Russian control. He died in prison in 1807, possibly from mistreatment.[12]

Scharnhorst, born of relatively humble origins in the Kingdom of Hanover, made a series of highly important contributions to the fundamentals of Prussian-German military thought and practice.[13] Widely known for his military writings while still a very young officer, Scharnhorst became the leading intellectual of the Prussian army immediately after his transfer from the Hanoverian army in 1801. Although he is best known for his contributions to the early establishment of the Prussian General Staff system, Scharnhorst's legacy in other areas is equally important. His emphasis on professional military education and his treatment of war as an art rather than a science became trademarks of the Prussian system. Certainly he inspired many of Clausewitz's ideas, even though the latter fundamentally rejected the broader theories of Lloyd, the man who had inspired Scharnhorst.[14] Scharnhorst's views on education, field manuals (regulations), military history, theory, strategy, combined arms, rotation of General Staff officers between staff and field units, and many other practical points were echoed in the later writings of Clausewitz, Moltke, and Schlieffen.[15] Perhaps his most important legacy in the realm of military theory was the impact he had on his most brilliant student, Clausewitz.

Carl von Clausewitz

Carl von Clausewitz, born in 1780 to the son of a former officer in the army of Frederick the Great, entered Prussian service at the age of eleven as an officer candidate.[16] He was captured by the French in the Jena campaign of 1806 and spent more than a year in genteel detention in France. Following his release in 1807, Clausewitz rejoined Scharnhorst and played an important if publicly unnoticed role in the reform of the Prussian army. He was the actual author of much of Scharnhorst's official correspondence over the next several years. He gained admission to the new General Staff, served as an instructor at the new General War School (*Allgemeine Kriegsschule*) from 1810 to 1812, and tutored the Prussian crown prince.[17]

Refusing to accept Friedrich Wilhelm III's complete capitulation to Napoleon, Clausewitz joined those officers who resigned their commissions. He gained admission to the tsar's service and served in a relatively minor position during the campaign of 1812. He returned to Germany in the service of the German Legion and played a key role in the rapid rearmament of Prussia's eastern provinces. Following Napoleon's final defeat, Clausewitz returned to Prussian service, but his subsequent career suffered from what the king and many others regarded as his disloyalty during Prussia's most desperate hours.[18] The remainder of his military career was relatively uneventful except for his writings, most of which were published after his death in 1831. The most important of these was *On War*, published in 1834. Although the manuscript was clearly unfinished, recent scholarship has argued that *On War* was much closer to a completed work than previously thought. Regardless of the status of its completeness when it was published, *On War* has become the classic study of war.[19]

Clausewitz's Influence

A vast literature on Clausewitz has dissected his views from every conceivable angle and arrived at widely divergent views about the extent and nature of his influence on Prussian and German theory and practice.[20] One book studied his reception in the English-speaking world.[21] Another historian argued that it is a "joke" to regard *On War* as a sort of bible in the Prussian army, even though several nineteenth-century German writers used precisely that term to describe Clausewitz's influence.[22] Peter Paret, one of the leading authorities, argued in 1965 (quoting German officer and historian Max Jähns) that *On War* had been widely read in the German army, but he seemed to back away from that conclusion twenty years later in an article in the revised *Makers of Modern Strategy*.[23] The issue here is not merely how many officers actually read *On War* but the extent of its influence on Prussian-German military theory and doctrine.

Maverick military writer Wilhelm Rüstow, writing in 1857, was perhaps the first to note that *On War* was frequently discussed but little read, a judgment that might fairly describe the general treatment of Clausewitz's writings up to the present day.[24] Substantial evidence indicates that, through the 1840s, Clausewitz was not widely known among the public, and his name was almost entirely absent from scholarly encyclopedias and lexicons.[25] But the evidence in the military literature is less definite. Greisheim's well-known published lectures on tactics (1861) clearly recognized Clausewitz's importance.[26] In three books published between 1841 and 1845, the now-forgotten Saxon officer Karl Pönitz used an imaginary posthumous exchange of letters with Clausewitz to argue points of military theory, and they elicited a reply by a Prussian General Staff officer. This would hardly have been possible if Clausewitz had been completely obscure in military circles.[27] The writings of Prince Friedrich Karl, dating to the period before 1860, show unmistakable signs of Clausewitz's ideas and even use some of his specific phrases.[28] By the end of the nineteenth century, numerous officers argued that Clausewitz was the basis of German theory and strategic thought.[29]

As several historians have pointed out, Clausewitz's actual influence is difficult to measure with any precision.[30] Others argue that Clausewitz's influence was limited to a few issues, including his emphasis on large-scale combat, the uniqueness of each situation, and the role of imponderable factors in war.[31] A few historians, notably Herbert Rosinski and Gerhard Ritter, reached the opposite conclusion. The former wrote of *On War*'s "immense influence," while the latter repeated the words of Sigismund von Schlichting and others, indicating that the work was a "bible" of German theory.[32] By 1914, a number of authors had begun to criticize various parts of *On War*, and some have used these cases to deny Clausewitz's influence. Yet, as one officer-scholar pointed out more recently, this may be seen as a sign of Clausewitz's continuing impact, since dissenting authors felt it necessary to single out *On War* to justify their departure from its views, a practice that continues to this day.[33]

A careful examination of the military literature after the publication of Clausewitz's major work reveals that many of Clausewitz's most important concepts entered the thought of the Prussian army in two ways. First, many of Prussia's most influential military writers incorporated some of Clausewitz's basic concepts into their writings, usually, but not always, with specific references. Second, the writings and General Staff work of Helmuth von Moltke, which provided the foundation for German doctrinal publications throughout the second half of the nineteenth century and beyond the First World War, incorporated basic Clausewitzian concepts into Prussian theory.[34] Here, it should be noted that many of the ideas of Clausewitz and Scharnhorst had become basic features of Prussian thought before being set forth in *On War*.[35] The following section examines some of Clausewitz's most enduring theoretical points, including some very important ones the Prussian army did not wholly accept but still occupied a central place in Prusso-German theory.

Sources of Clausewitz's Thought

Clausewitz seems to have been a product of one of the major intellectual and philosophical paradigm shifts of his day: the end of Enlightenment and the beginning of Romanticism.[36] Although many profess to see a dialectical process in Clausewitz's writings, the leading scholars deny that his intellectual methods can be traced to Georg Hegel or that he used the Hegelian method.[37] Many writers see much evidence of Immanuel Kant's philosophy and of Romanticism throughout Clausewitz's approach.[38] Clausewitz's writings stress the limits of reason and rationality in war—surely a sign that he favored Kant's critique of reason. Certainly Clausewitz had some contact with professors and others who popularized Kant's philosophy.[39] Nevertheless, as Hew Strachan warns, the link with Kant should not be taken too far, since many of the basic concepts of *On War* are not compatible with Kant's thought as developed in *The Perpetual Peace*.[40] The most convincing analysis is that of Paret, who points out that even in his earliest writings, Clausewitz partook fully of Kant's rejection of the illusion of rationalism and replaced it with a consideration of the realities of human activity, unforeseen events, and chance. In this sense, Clausewitz drew heavily on contemporary theories of art that stressed free (unsystematic) reasoning.[41]

The Nature of War

Using the analogy of a duel between individuals, Clausewitz defined war simply as "an act of force to compel our enemy to do our will." Physical force is the *means*, and the imposition of one's will is the *object*. Rendering the enemy powerless is the only *certain* means of attaining the object.[42] War is thus the "collision of two living forces." The contestants have two sources of power for this struggle, said Clausewitz: the total means at their disposal and the strength of their wills.[43] Clausewitz went on to point out that however extreme war might be in theory, in reality it can range from a struggle for extermination (*Vernichtungskrieg*) to simple armed observation, depending on the importance of the objectives being sought and the combatants' strength of will.[44] Later (book 1, chapter 2), Clausewitz emphasized that wars frequently end short of total victory for either side and that other reasons for terminating wars can emerge.[45]

In concluding his discussion of the nature of war, Clausewitz set forth his concept of the paradoxical trinity. War, in his view, has three primary tendencies that pull conflict in three directions, like three opposing magnets: (1) violence, hatred, and enmity; (2) chance and probability; (3) subordination to policy. These, in turn, are related primarily to popular passions, the military instrument, and the government. Numerous subsequent writers, particularly in the American military and security communities, have confused the basic trinity with the three related elements of a society at war.[46] In any case, the task Clausewitz set forth for the strategist was to find a theory that would balance these three tendencies.[47]

Although Clausewitz posited that war in theory consists of unrestrained violence aimed at the complete overthrow of the enemy, he realized that absolute war is rarely if ever attainable or even desirable. Napoleon waged such war, but Clausewitz warned that this cannot be a universal standard. Instead, theory must consider all those factors that prevent war from assuming its most extreme form. These include natural inertia, friction, human weaknesses, and contemporary ideas, emotions, and conditions.[48]

Above all, Clausewitz stressed political goals on both sides as the primary determinant of the level of force used. In most cases, a belligerent uses no greater force and adopts no greater military aim "than would be sufficient for the achievement of his political purpose."[49] Portrayals of Clausewitz as the philosopher of universal total war in a modern sense have little basis in the text of *On War*. Clausewitz always argued that war aims have to be commensurate with political goals, and he argued that these, not any inherent logic or requirements of military means, might push war toward its most extreme state—absolute war.

Policy and War

The strongest argument that Clausewitz exercised little influence in Prussian theory revolves around his argument that war is essentially a political act and that considerations of policy must always determine the goals and means of war. Clausewitz's original text argued that war is "not merely an act of policy, but a true political instrument, a continuation of political intercourse, carried on with the admixture of other means." In another passage he argued that war is *"only a branch of political activity; . . . it is in no sense autonomous"* (emphasis in original). He then pointed out that the political element remains the first consideration and that policy "will permeate all acts in war" and will "have a continuous influence on them." However, he warned that "policy is not a tyrant and that it must adapt to its chosen means [war], a process which can radically change it." He then made his famous statement that war may have its own grammar but not its own logic.[50] This insistence on the dominance of political considerations in all aspects of warfare runs throughout *On War* and Clausewitz's other works.

In defining the desired relationship between policy and war, German theory accepted the first part of Clausewitz's argument—that war is essentially a political act whose goals are set by the state—but rejected the second—that war therefore cannot be conducted according to the internal logic of military theory, that is, by optimal or preferred use of the military instrument. Numerous Prussian writers, from Scharnhorst and Reyher to von der Goltz, recognized that war is an instrumental act with goals established by the state's political objectives in going to war.[51] This fundamental point, entirely in accord with Clausewitz's views, appears in all kinds of Prussian military literature, from Moltke's broadest statements on the nature of strategy to Wilhelm Balck's widely read multivolume textbooks on tactics published in several editions in the decade before 1914.[52] The most authoritative overview of Prussian theory before the First World War, the 1910 edition of *Instructions for Large Unit Commanders*, stated, "The goal of war is the execution of policy with arms and the achievement of a peace that corresponds to the conditions of this policy."[53] Few if any Prussian theorists or practitioners prior to Ludendorff denied the Clausewitzian notion that policy determines the conditions and goals of war.

The role of policy considerations *during* a war is another matter entirely. Clausewitz argued that policy uses war as an instrument, establishes the amount of effort required, and permeates all military acts.[54] *On War* cautioned that policy is not a tyrant, cannot demand what is contrary to the nature of war, and has to adapt itself to its chosen means. The political aim remains the primary consideration.[55] In the final book of *On War*, Clausewitz cautioned that policy should not extend its influence to details such as the posting of guards or the use of patrols, but it is influential in the planning of wars, campaigns, and even battles. Unfortunately, the standard English translation has muddled the meaning of this passage.[56] The overriding theme of *On War*'s discussions of these and related matters is clearly the dominance of policy in all major aspects of war, a point recognized by virtually all serious studies of Clausewitz's writing.[57] For the most part, neither civilian nor military leaders in Germany accepted Clausewitz's views on the relationship between policy and war *during* a conflict. Instead, they relied on the views of Helmuth von Moltke, the most successful field commander of the post-Napoleonic period.[58]

Most Prussian military figures in the Wilhelmine period accepted Moltke's argument that policy dominates at the beginning of war in establishing its aims and at the end of war in determining the conditions of peace, but strategy is "fully independent of policy" during war.[59] Later, in an 1880 essay, Moltke went even further and, according to the Prussian General Staff, concluded that "strategy is independent of policy as much as possible," and "policy must not be allowed to interfere in operations."[60] Moltke was thus endorsing a view that held sway both before and after his time as chief of the General Staff. General Karl von Reyher, chief from May 1848 to October 1857, had expressed this same view in a letter to Friedrich Karl, cited previously. Numerous military authors subsequently attempted to minimize the influence of policy in wartime or to eliminate it entirely. As Wilhelm Scherff wrote in his introduction to the 1880 edition of *On War*, "The meddling of policy in war is and always remains a course of ruin."[61] This view endured even after the First World War, at least among some German officers.[62]

A related question of substantial importance involves giving advice to the head of state. Clausewitz addressed this clearly, but for a century, the second and subsequent editions of *On War* contained an important distortion. Clausewitz had argued that the supreme military commander should be a member of the cabinet, so that its members can "share in the major aspects of his activities." The second and subsequent editions contained an alteration by Count Friedrich Wilhelm von Brühl, Clausewitz's brother-in-law. Brühl reversed the reason for the military commander's being a member of the cabinet: "so that he may take part in its (cabinet's) councils and decisions on important occasions."[63] Some historians regard this as a significant reason for the troubled relationship between statesmen and military commanders in Prussian-German history.[64] This argument may have some merit, but it is questionable how much actual behavior or how many passages in the military literature were actually based on this section of *On War*. The conduct of Helmuth von Moltke during the wars of unification was far more important in setting the tone of civil-military relations in Wilhelmine Germany, as were his and other writings.[65] Even moderates such as Julius von Verdy du Vernois, who tried to find a middle ground, frequently sided with Moltke over Clausewitz and Bismarck.[66]

Twice during the wars of unification, after the Battle of Königgrätz in 1866 and during the siege of Paris in 1870, Moltke and Bismarck clashed over military strategy. Moltke, determined to have his way during the Franco-Prussian War, attempted to exclude Bismarck from all strategic discussions and virtually ceased conferring with the state's leading civilian minister. Moltke demanded, at a minimum, that the chief of the General Staff stand as an equal to the minister-president as an adviser to the king during wartime. Bismarck, of course, would not yield and insisted on the dominance of the civilian adviser and of his policy-based strategy in particular. Even those historians who accept the correctness of Moltke's position on the bombardment of Paris agree that his position was untenable in terms of political-military affairs and civil-military relations. Nevertheless, Moltke's point of view became the dominant paradigm in German military literature, which, after all, had a theoretical justification in the falsified passages of *On War*.[67]

In the matter of civil-military relations and tensions between civilian policy makers and military commanders, it can be argued that the German army institutionally departed from Clausewitz. In *On War*, Clausewitz suggested that a military commander, especially at the highest level, is both a "commander and a statesman." A wise commander remains attuned to policy shifts during the course of a war and adjusts his plans accordingly. Thus, in war, according to Clausewitz, there has to be regular, if not constant, communication between the military commander and the government.[68]

From Moltke on, imperial German military leaders took a position based more on Clausewitz's contemporary and rival Baron Antoine Jomini. He, like Clausewitz, agreed that war is, in essence, a political act. Once a government decides to go to war, however, policy issues, or what Jomini referred to as "political objective points," must be subordinated to military strategy, "at least until after a great success is attained."[69] Moltke and his successors ardently embraced this approach. Once the decision for war had been made, the political authority had to step aside and let the military go forth and achieve the desired victory. This approach was attractive to the military, which regarded any intrusion into military matters by civilian political authority as something to be avoided. This separation of the military leadership from its civilian counterparts, especially the Foreign Ministry, would only widen after Moltke and Bismarck left their respective offices.[70]

War as Art

Clausewitz argued that the conduct of war is an art, not a discipline (*Wissenschaft*), and certainly not a science in the mathematical sense developed by Lloyd, Bülow, and Jomini.[71] Clausewitz made this distinction on several grounds, some of which were related to the nature of war itself and some of which concerned the role of the commander. Unlike a science or a rigorous academic discipline, war to Clausewitz lacked a system of laws or principles. As noted above, Clausewitz's rejection of an established methodology was rooted in several elements: his general reaction against Enlightenment military thinking; the new intellectual currents of the counter-Enlightenment and Romanticism; and, probably, his embrace of eighteenth-century art theory.[72] Rejecting the Enlightenment's search for a general theory of war patterned on Newtonian physics, Clausewitz concluded that unlike science, which sought to *analyze*, the conduct of war sought to create through synthesis.[73] This creative art was, in Clausewitz's view, entirely dependent on circumstances, random events, chance, and the skill of the practitioner, rather than mathematical or geometrical formulas. Clausewitz understood, of course, that war is a unique kind of art, since it deals with a reacting object—the enemy—rather than an empty canvas or other artistic media.[74]

In creating this new interpretation of the essence of war, Clausewitz established several concepts that, regardless of their intellectual origins, became important, even critical elements of the Prusso-German way of war: (1) war is a free, creative activity, analogous to art;[75] (2) the essence of conducting war successfully is the ability to transform knowing (*Wissen*) into doing (*Können*);[76] (3) the commander, like an artist, synthesizes many elements of war and strategy into a unique, distinctive whole.[77] As a result, Clausewitz and his followers, especially Moltke, created a Prusso-German theory of war that was, by modern standards, hardly a system at all. Instead, Prussian theory embraced the concept of acting according to circumstances, with campaign planning, tactics, and leadership stressing the individual's initiative and creativity, independence of thought, and aggressive action. War, in short, was a free, creative activity with no preordained scientific laws. Proper conduct of war allowed commanders, from field army to platoon, extremely wide latitude to exercise their judgment.

Theory and Doctrine

Closely connected to this definition of war as an art was Clausewitz's position on the role of theory. Indeed, this new definition of the nature and purpose of theory is what most clearly distinguishes Clausewitz from his theoretical predecessors and his great contemporary Jomini. The function of theory, in Clausewitz's view, was to provide a way of thinking about problems, not a set of rules or maxims to be followed, as a scientist would discover and follow the rules of mathematics or physics. For Clausewitz, theory was a way of analyzing problems rather than determining a set of solutions. Theory should thus train a commander's mind. It was "not meant to provide him with positive doctrines and systems to be used as intellectual tools." He argued that it was "never permissible to use scientific guidelines to judge a given problem in war."[78]

Theory therefore had the primary purpose of clarifying concepts and ideas that would otherwise be confused and entangled.[79] Thus the critical thinker should never use the results of theory as laws and standards, but only as aids to judgment. This, of course, elevated tactical and strategic acts from the execution of predetermined rules to the exercise of individual judgment according to the commander's situation, talents, and purpose.[80] Therefore, in contrast to the Jominian tradition, theory should inform the commander's judgment but not guide his actions.[81] In Clausewitz's classic formulation, theory's goal "is to educate the mind of the future commander, or more accurately, to guide him in his self-education, but not to accompany him to the battlefield." As a distinguished historian pointed out, theory for Clausewitz had three broad areas of functional value: cognitive, pedagogic, and utilitarian.[82] It assisted in defining the terms of understanding the past, it taught fundamental approaches to the study of war, and it informed a commander's judgment in dealing with concrete cases. In a modern cliché, theory, according to Clausewitz, helps teach commanders *how* to think, not *what* to think.

Clausewitz's use of the terms "theory" and "doctrine" marked the beginning of a long German tradition that was quite distinct from that of modern armies. The German term *Lehre*—literally "teaching," but normally rendered as "doctrine" in English translations—lacks the authoritative connotations of the more rigid modern concepts of doctrine.[83] Clausewitz's ideas were not doctrine in the modern sense, whereas the Prussian army's field manuals certainly were. The Germans rarely described their official manuals as doctrine, however, because the German term *Doktrin* implies a certain rigidity and prescriptive quality that the Prussian army's regulations sought to avoid, at least from the time of Moltke forward.

This view of the nature of theory had several important results for the Prussian way of war. Prussian theory, both official and private, almost universally avoided lists of principles of war or other truncated aphorisms, which became attractive to modern armed forces after J. F. C. Fuller first invented the formal concept of principles of war in 1926.[84] Because the Prussians regarded their tactical regulations as broad statements of general recommendations, their education always stressed that the official manuals required broader personal study to be of any use.[85] Prussian and German manuals were, therefore, written in numbered paragraphs rather than in essay form, and they were devoid of the cartoons, pictures, and illustrations typical of modern doctrinal publications.[86] Prussian regulations were authoritative guidelines rather than rules or even rigid expectations of actions to be taken. Disregarding them was of no great consequence if doing so were appropriate to the circumstances.[87] Wilhelm Balck, perhaps the most influential and internationally respected author on tactics prior to 1914, argued that narrow regulatory forms were good only for those armies that had poor tactical training or doubted that the average officer could properly estimate situations and react accordingly.[88]

All these factors had an impact on German military education and training, subjects that are considered later. Commanders, and especially corps commanders, had the authority to create their own tactical theories and methods even if they were not in accordance with official regulations. This allowed for flexibility and initiative, but it also created the potential for local rigidity and eccentricities.

Moral Factors

In emphasizing the uniqueness of each war and its situations, Clause-witz was not merely rejecting the mechanistic view of warfare set forth by scientific military thinkers from Lloyd to Jomini. One of the bases for Clausewitz's new approach to war and the theory of conducting war was his great insight into the role of moral factors. Both of *On War*'s continuing analogies—comparing war to commerce and to a duel between two individuals—rest on the moral factors that Clausewitz saw as dominating warfare at all levels. Although Clausewitz wove these moral forces into the entire fabric of his great work, his chapter on strategy identified three as most important: the talent of the supreme commander, the martial spirit of the army, and the army's patriotic spirit (*Volksgeist*).[89] From these flowed many elements of the Prusso-German way of war.

Moltke spoke for many Prussian military writers when he argued that although the moral element is rarely of value in peacetime, it is a precondition of all success in war.[90] Numerous Prussian authors endorsed these views of Clausewitz and Moltke. Many, only partly correctly, attributed Napoleon's victories, as well as those of Moltke in the wars of unification, primarily to moral rather than physical factors.[91] Even those who disagreed on many issues, such as Generals Friedrich von Bernhardi and Heinrich Rohne, agreed that the will to win ultimately decides battles.[92] German writers looked to moral factors to overcome numerical inferiority, to compensate for high battlefield casualties, to identify and prepare the right kind of battlefield leaders, and to overcome the psychological strains of the modern, "empty" battlefield.[93] Even Schlieffen, sometimes accused of ignoring moral factors, actually built much of his system on the assumed German superiority in martial spirit and command at all levels.[94] One of the reasons for the German dislike of defensive strategy and tactics was that this form of warfare was injurious to the army's fighting spirit.[95] Although a few prominent writers warned against placing excessive emphasis on moral factors, the views of Clausewitz and Moltke, no doubt taken to extremes, continued to dominate in this critical area.[96]

Genius, Competence, and Character

Clausewitz's insistence on the dominance of imponderables and the limits of doctrinal solutions meant that commanders at all levels were the key to success in war. Clausewitz argued that high commanders need moral courage and balance (considered together, strength of character), boldness, an ability to improvise, creativity, and intelligence to deal with the realities of war. He linked these characteristics in his concept of "genius," which he used in a broad sense to describe the combination of attributes required in a successful commander.[97] Only such an individual, argued Clausewitz, can deal with the uncertainties of war. Returning to his theory of art, Clausewitz argued that genius is the innate talent that establishes the rules of the artist. In this, he departed from Scharnhorst but established the Prusso-German army's enduring belief that the keys to strategic success were commanders.[98]

Much of the chapter in *On War* devoted to genius centered on the challenges posed by ambiguity. Clausewitz cautioned that "a fog of greater or lesser uncertainty" clouded three-quarters of the factors on which military action was based.[99] This raised chance to a ubiquitous factor in war, since "all information and assumptions are open to doubt."[100] Later, Clausewitz warned that emotion created a psychological fog that became the source of indecision in commanders lacking character.[101] Taken together, these two sources of "fog" caused all action to take place in a twilight that distorted reality and forced the commander to "trust to talent or luck."[102]

Clausewitz devoted a short chapter to "Friction in War" and elaborated on this concept in the course of numerous other discussions. Friction in this view consists of the unforeseeable "countless minor incidents" that reduce the general level of an army's performance. Chance events play an important role in producing friction, which, as a whole, corresponds to the factors that distinguish real war from war on paper.[103] Friction, according to Clausewitz, "is the force that makes the apparently easy so difficult." The capable general knows about friction and does not set a standard of performance that friction makes impossible to achieve.[104]

Clausewitz's emphasis on the role of the creative leader at all levels, but especially in high command positions, naturally led him to stress execution in strategy and campaigns rather than elaborate designs created beforehand. This coincided with his view of the artistic nature of the conduct of war, since the individual ability to create is the essence of the artist. Clausewitz thereby originated an enduring dichotomy in German theory between knowing (*Wissen*) and doing (*Können*). This is why Max Schering gave Clausewitz the title "philosopher of action."[105]

In his reaction against the geometric models of Enlightenment thinking, Clausewitz stressed execution over formal design because the incalculable elements of war will inevitably frustrate any system or plan. In chapter 2 of book 2, he titled one section "Knowledge Must Become Capability."[106] He thought that basic concepts in war are simple, but executing them is another matter altogether. Hence, he formulated his famous proposition that "everything in war is simple, but the simplest thing is very difficult."[107] The intelligent and discerning commander quickly knows what to do; being able to do it is the hard part. Only the resolute commander, said Clausewitz, can carry out his plans in the face of the uncertainties and difficulties he encounters in their execution.[108] This concept of competence was closely identified with another enduring feature of Clausewitz's thought, the role of character in a supreme commander.

In the chapter of *On War* dedicated to genius, Clausewitz laid out the enduring Prussian view of character. This he defined as the ability to make a difficult decision and stick with it in the face of factors that would cause an ordinary person to vacillate and lapse into indecision or to make hasty and wrongheaded changes to his plans. In war, said Clausewitz, the torrent of events and diverse opinions can quickly cause an irresolute personality to lose his sense of balance and confidence. The commander who possesses character sticks to his first decision, the one most carefully thought out, and refuses to change it "unless forced to do so by clear conviction." In the case of doubt, those who possess character hold on to their convictions stubbornly. But, as Clausewitz warned, this stubbornness, if taken too far, can degenerate into obstinacy as soon as one resists change not because of superior insight or higher principle but because of instinctive objections.[109]

This definition of character, perhaps first set forth by Scharnhorst, found resonance in the Prussian theory of war in the First World War and beyond.[110] The 1912 manual for instruction at the war school, citing Schlieffen, also referred to character as the willpower of the supreme commander. General Paul von Holleben, writing in 1902, likened character to the ability to transform knowing into doing. Friedrich Immanuel, in his widely respected prewar handbook on tactics, argued that strength of character allowed a man to maintain his nerves, a cool head, and clear eyes while correctly estimating situations and focusing on the goal. "He who rules himself also rules his subordinates."[111] Likewise, General Karl Litzmann, in reviewing Freytag-Loringhoven's well-known book *The Power of Personality in War*, approvingly expressed his agreement that neither regulations nor rote training, but rather personality and character, were necessary to prepare the army for war.[112] The writings of numerous other officers, high and low, testify to the general acceptance of this Clausewitzian concept.[113]

"Character" came to have an additional and entirely different connotation as the nineteenth century progressed. By the 1880s at the latest, the concept of character had acquired dimensions beyond Clausewitz's definition; it came to be identified with the proper attitudes and class backgrounds desired to maintain the upper-class social content of the officer corps. Although it is true, as noted by one historian, that "character" subsumed various individual traits (sense of duty, obedience, honor, self-reliance, orderliness, and so forth), it is not correct to see this as a substitute for a patent of nobility.[114] Preferential treatment of nobles continued throughout the life of Prussia and its army.

"Character" eventually acquired another aspect with important implications for the officer corps, although this had some basis in Clausewitz if one adopts an entirely one-sided and limited view of some passages of *On War*.[115] Clausewitz's opposition to rationalism and his preference for "doing" over "knowing" as the measure of an officer's ability, though not representative of what he truly expected of intellectually capable commanders, found an influential counterpart in the officer corps: a reluctance to embrace education. Scharnhorst and other reformers had embraced higher educational standards for the officer corps, but after 1819, the push to enforce educational standards stalled (see chapter 1).

"Education" (*Bildung*) and "character" became slogans for the exclusion of those social and political groups that might not be entirely loyal to the conservative and monarchical values of the army because of their class backgrounds. Conservatives employed "character" as a means of closing the officer corps to undesirable social elements (peasants, workers, lower-middle-class individuals), while liberals embraced "education" as a means of broadening the army's social base.[116] Officer handbooks stressed that character became more important as one advanced in rank, while the Military Cabinet openly stated that it was not concerned about the educational shortcomings of officers and officer candidates if such persons had "character."[117] Use of the term thus became a tool in minimizing the value of education in the officer corps, a proposition largely at odds with Clausewitz's original formulation and intent.

Strategy

Few aspects of the German approach to war have been more controversial than strategy and its execution in twentieth-century wars. If there is a broad consensus on anything in German military history, it is that the German armed forces, however capable in battle, were failures in designing and executing strategy.[118] The question here is the theoretical foundation of the German approach to strategy rather than specific issues in the First World War, the subject of a later chapter. Three concepts and their relationships are central to an understanding of the place of strategy in the German way of war: strategy, operations, and tactics. Clausewitz and Moltke provided some, but not all, of the theoretical bases of Prussian-German thought in these areas. Interestingly, the 1910 *Instructions for Large Unit Commanders* did not define strategy or its relationship to tactics. An understanding of the Prussian army's view of such matters must rest on an examination of the theoretical writings of individuals.

As previously mentioned, Bülow was the creator of the terms "strategy" and "tactics," even though his definitions soon gave way to those of Clausewitz.[119] In giving these terms the broad military meaning that endured into the twenty-first century, Clausewitz used his usual motif of ends and means. Tactics, he concluded, is the art of planning and conducting combat, while strategy is the art of using battles to achieve the object of war.[120] Strategy, wrote Clausewitz, "decides the time when, the place where, and the forces with which the engagement is to be fought and through this threefold activity exerts considerable influence on its outcome."[121] The strategic means of exploiting a tactical victory, attainable only in battle, received extensive treatment.[122] Strategy, wrote Clausewitz, is a plan linking battles and campaigns to goals:

> Strategy is the use of the engagement to achieve the goal of the war. Strategy therefore must give the entirety of the military action an objective that corresponds to this goal. This means that strategy traces out a plan of war and links the goal to a series of actions which should lead to it. In other words, strategy creates the concepts for individual campaigns and within these arranges the individual engagements.[123]

Clausewitz extended his reservations about theory in general to strategic theory in particular. Strategic theory, in this view, deals with planning and attempts "to shed light on the components of war and their interrelationships, stressing the few principles or rules that can be demonstrated."[124] Ultimately, decided Clausewitz, victory does not reside primarily in the strategic concept.

Strategic success, in Clausewitz's view, depends on the exploitation of tactical victory. To some degree, Clausewitz prioritized tactics over strategy, one of his most controversial yet frequently overlooked concepts. Because tactical success is the basis of all strategic plans, there is no victory in strategy but only in the exploitation of a tactical victory. Success in strategy, he argued, rests in part on the timely preparation for a tactical victory and in part on the exploitation of success in such a battle.[125] As outrageous as this might seem to modern readers, the argument makes perfect sense within its overall context. Wars are won, in Clausewitz's view, by winning battles, and any strategic design, no matter how brilliant, will fail if an army cannot win the resulting battles. Only great tactical success leads to great strategic success.[126] From the opposite perspective, one side can frustrate all the enemy's strategic planning by winning the battles produced by his plan.[127] Strategy, in short, has the object of arranging battles in such a way as to achieve the war's objective and must assume that one can triumph on the battlefield.[128] Only when one has no fear of the enemy or of the outcome of the battle can one expect results from strategic actions alone. In another passage, Clausewitz argued that only great tactical successes can lead to great strategic successes, "or as we have said more specifically, *tactical successes* are of *paramount importance* in war."[129]

Prussian thinking, therefore, postulated that the main purpose of strategy is to create opportunities to fight battles on favorable terms, and these battles in turn create conditions for the favorable termination of the war. Colmar von der Goltz's important and influential book *The Nation in Arms*, first published in 1883, made this point along the same lines as Clausewitz and Moltke. Likewise, Balck consistently argued that tactics— that is, the preparation for and execution of battle—had primacy over the grander designs of strategy. Numerous prewar writers endorsed this view, primarily in the sense that substantial tactical victories often create new situations and enhanced opportunities, leading the strategist to consider changing the basic concept accordingly.[130] Despite Ludendorff's unfortunate experience in the battles of 1918, such a view was still widespread in the decade following the First World War. Hermann von Kuhl, in criticizing Hans Delbrück's contrary views, argued that every soldier knows that tactics must take priority over strategy.[131]

In this case as in so many others, Moltke translated the philosophical style of *On War* into simple, direct language but retained the essence of the original. He made Clausewitz's views available to the officers of the General Staff and senior commanders, to others who had access to his unpublished works, and to the Prussian army and public at large by 1900. In his 1871 "Essay on Strategy," Moltke acknowledged the views of writers before Clausewitz but accepted the latter's definition and usage. Although Moltke placed slightly more emphasis on strategy as opposed to tactics, he, like Clausewitz, concluded that "the demands of strategy grow silent in the face of a tactical victory and adapt themselves to the newly created situation." He argued that no plan of operations extends with certainty beyond the first encounter with the enemy. Moltke also provided the most succinct statement of the German view of the essence of military strategy ever written: "Strategy is a system of expedients. It is more than a mere discipline; it is the transfer of knowledge to practical life, the continued development of the original leading thought in accordance with constantly changing circumstances. It is the art of acting under pressure of the most difficult conditions."[132]

Two reservations are in order regarding the Clausewitz-Moltke definitions and evaluations of strategy. Although most Prussian military writers accepted these viewpoints and incorporated them into official and private publications, some exceptions arose.[133] Schlichting, the father of modern "operational art," took a different position on the relation between strategy and tactics. He openly criticized these views even as he argued that Moltke had correctly recognized the basic changes in warfare and had created a new method of conducting campaigns and fighting battles that Schlichting hoped to formalize.[134] Schlichting argued that Clausewitz's definition and use of strategy were outdated. He concluded that changes in warfare and armies, as well as Moltke's concept of campaigns, had changed the relationship proclaimed by Clausewitz, whose "outmoded picture of battle" had to be discarded.[135]

One of Moltke's closest associates, Julius von Verdy du Vernois, reviewed various definitions and theories of strategy and rejected Clausewitz's definition as one-sided because it did not allot sufficient importance to operations. He concluded that no truly comprehensive definition of strategy was possible and that the views of Archduke Charles, Jomini, Willisen, Clausewitz, Moltke, Schlichting, and others all had a certain justification.[136] His own definition was vague, convoluted, and lengthy.[137] Balck's far more modern and satisfactory definition had little impact on the German military establishment, possibly because it was based on the writings of Delbrück.[138]

Operations

Closely related to the Prussian concepts of tactics and strategy was the issue of "operations," a term used in German theory to describe the movements of large units or groups of units. Since 1983, the term has become part of the nearly ubiquitous division of war into three levels: strategic, operational, and tactical.[139] German theory, unlike Soviet and modern Western doctrine, did not divide warfare into hierarchical levels, although many recent writers have assumed this to be the case. Prusso-German theory rarely used the concept of "levels of war." Instead, Prussian writers maintained the traditional conceptual division between spheres or areas of strategy and tactics, based on the usages of Clausewitz and Moltke with some individual variations.[140] The terms "operational level of war" and "operational art" rarely if ever appeared in German theory. These terms originated in Soviet military theory and were adopted by the Americans and others in the early 1980s.

Unlike modern usage, in which "operation" describes all sorts of military activities from squad tactics and administrative activities to theater-level campaign plans, in Prussian thinking, the word had a very specific meaning. "Operation" conceptualized the movements of large units at division level or higher. Both elements are important to an understanding of the German concept. Without movement, there is no "operation," since the mere size of the force involved is not the issue. This usage, consistently adopted by nearly all German theorists from Bülow onward, reflected the

German view that the two essential categories of military activity are strategy and tactics, with operations as a subarea within strategy.[141]

The Prussian term "operations" meant the scheme of movement of large units. Again, without movement, there was no "operation," regardless of the size of the units involved. The *Allgemeine Militär Encyclopedia* of 1873 defined operations as "all movements and actions of the units which aim at victory of the field army over the enemy."[142] Poten's *Military Dictionary* of 1879 defined operations as "in the broader sense all movements of large military units; in the narrower sense those strategic maneuvers which strive for large decisions."[143] Accordingly, all operations ended in battles or in the creation of favorable situations for battles.[144] The most authoritative pre-1914 manual for large-unit commanders, a revised version of Moltke's 1869 document, used "operations" entirely in the sense of movements leading to battle throughout the text.[145]

Although Clausewitz used the term "operation" on a few occasions, it was not a central concept in his writing. This is not clear in the modern English translation, which contains the term or its variations at least 350 times, rendering at least forty German words or phrases as "operations" or "operational." *On War* actually used the term about half a dozen times, primarily in conjunction with lines of operations, operational bases, and so forth, but never as a level of war or as an intermediate concept separate from strategy and tactics.[146] Raymond Aron correctly attributed the dichotomy between tactics and strategy to Clausewitz's consistent theme of ends and means, tactics being the means of strategy.[147]

Annihilation

This brings the discussion to one of the most controversial aspects of the Clausewitzian and Prusso-German philosophies of war—the principle of annihilation. Clausewitz stressed annihilation of the enemy's armed forces (not of the state) as the primary—indeed, in most cases the only— means to achieve the goal of imposing one's will on the enemy. Destruction of the enemy's armed forces is, Clausewitz argued, the highest aim of warfare. All plans should be based on this, as an arch rests on its abutment.[148] By destruction, Clausewitz meant rendering the enemy's forces incapable of further resistance.[149] This, he said, was the goal of every major battle, particularly if it were unavoidable because of the configuration of forces and circumstances.[150] This definition of annihilation and Clausewitz's emphasis on it became basic to nearly all German military theory and doctrine prior to 1914 and beyond.[151]

Given this emphasis on annihilation of the enemy's fighting forces as the primary or even exclusive means of war, Clausewitz naturally stressed the centrality of battles over maneuvers or other activities. Although this has led many writers to criticize Alfred von Schlieffen for developing what some have called the "dogma of the battle of annihilation," the concept was definitely and quite logically founded in the writings of Clausewitz.[152] The latter's views were more complex than many subsequent German writers recognized.

In denying the validity of the formal theorists who preceded him—in this case, specifically, Archduke Charles of Austria—Clausewitz warned that it is very dangerous to attempt to gain the object of a war without fighting decisive battles, even though he recognized that this is a possibility in some cases. He warned that battles and annihilation, though important in almost every war, should not be raised to the level of a law. He argued that this is an "unreal" act when facing an enemy that possesses substantially greater strength. Overall, however, he clearly denied that marches or maneuvers can win wars without battles. Indeed, it was probably Clausewitz who first gave the term "maneuver" the pejorative connotation it subsequently acquired in nearly all German military writing.[153]

Clausewitz's views were not as one-sided in their emphasis on battles of annihilation as many German followers and foreign critics later concluded.[154] He recognized that wars with limited aims might be fought without the means of annihilating all the enemy's military forces or extending destruction beyond them. Real war, he said, "can be a matter of degree." Moreover, he argued, in some circumstances the threat of war or the threat of a battle might be sufficient to achieve one's objectives. This was, in part, the basis of Clausewitz's distinction between absolute war and real war. Clausewitz probably came to this realization late in life, and it is possible that a thorough revision of On War would have more thoroughly integrated this line of reasoning into the text.[155] The Prussian General Staff, in adapting Clausewitz to its perceived strategic requirements late in the century, stressed the principle of annihilation in its writings and teachings on strategic theory, military history, and practical doctrine.

The army's allegedly excessive emphasis on annihilation became the basis of Hans Delbrück's argument that the army failed to note Clausewitz's "second form" of strategy, one that did not call for the annihilation of the enemy in some circumstances. Eventually, Delbrück argued that there are two forms of strategy, annihilation (*Vernichtung*) and exhaustion (*Ermattung*); unfortunately, the latter has been translated as "attrition," with all the pejorative connotations of that term. Delbrück's efforts to apply this analysis to Frederick the Great set off a bitter dispute with a number of General Staff officers that lasted until the First World War.[156] Most historians now conclude that Delbrück was correct and that the Prussian General Staff distorted or ignored strategic alternatives to the "dogma" of annihilation, although one recent analysis of the controversy attributes errors to both sides.[157]

Unfortunately, the argument is based on a false interpretation of the annihilation principle. German theory restricted annihilation to campaigns and battles against the enemy's fielded armies; it did not address the larger political goal of destroying the enemy state. In this limited context, destroying the opposing armies made perfect sense, particularly if the implied alternative was to fight a battle without intending to render the enemy incapable of further serious resistance. Such would make another costly battle probable or even inevitable. German theory sought battles of annihilation to reduce the costs and duration of bloody wars. After 1871, when German strategists consistently had to consider the possibility of a two-front war, neutralizing the foe's resistance as quickly as feasible made perfect sense, assuming it were possible at all. Even Schlieffen, in his most optimistic projections, did not consider that a victory over the French would completely end French resistance and allow the entire German army to move to the eastern front.

Moltke seemingly adopted the extreme view of annihilation during the wars against Austria and France.[158] In 1866, however, his demands for annihilation extended only to the Austrian military forces, not to the Hapsburg state, a position entirely consistent with Prussia's overall policy objectives.[159] His intentions in the war against France extended to the full destruction of the enemy nation's powers of resistance, in part because he regarded France as Prussia's hereditary enemy, and in part because he recognized that the "people's war" that developed after the initial Prussian victories presented quite different problems than did the eighteenth-century cabinet wars.[160]

Under the direct influence of Moltke's writings and the official historiography of the Prussian General Staff, Prusso-German doctrine and theory between 1871 and 1914 accepted the need to annihilate the enemy's armed forces, but only in extreme cases did this extend to destruction of the enemy state. The 1869 and 1910 *Instructions for Large Unit Commanders* stressed annihilation, but only as the single way to attain the policy objectives of foreseeable wars with certainty. Numerous military authors struck the same chord, stressing annihilation of the enemy's fielded forces with the object of breaking his will to resist, but leaving the decision on total destruction of the enemy state to policy.[161]

Ironically, it was Napoleonic warfare, not German theory, that frequently strove for wars to annihilate the opposing state and replace its political and social structure. The Prussian army's approach to military strategy usually limited destruction to the enemy's army. Thus, the Clausewitzian-Prussian system concerned battles, not wars, of annihilation, a fact overlooked by many otherwise perceptive analyses.[162] Even Clausewitz recognized as early as 1804 that in striving for limited goals, one might and sometimes should strive for annihilation of the enemy's forces, and it is hardly surprising that Prussian theory held that the enemy's army should be defeated as completely as possible once war began.[163] Destruction of the enemy's army remained, as in Clausewitz's theory, only a means to an end—the most rapid and the only certain means, regardless of the scope of the objective.[164] The question was thus the relevance of the principle of military annihilation in any given set of circumstances.[165]

Defense and Offense

Given that war is a struggle to impose one's will and that annihilation of the enemy's military forces is the only certain way to achieve that goal, Clausewitz turned to the two forms of war—defense and offense.[166] He analyzed these forms in two ways: with respect to the object of war and in their relationship to each other. The former, with calculations of strength, determined the form to be adopted; the latter established the intellectual framework that provided the essential features, advantages, disadvantages, and reciprocal interactions of the forms of war. Clausewitz's theories on these points by no means found universal acceptance among Prussian military theorists, who, on the basis of the First World War, were generally condemned for failing to accept and act on *On War*'s admonitions.

Clausewitz began his presentation on the defensive form of war, the longest chapter in *On War* and one of the most thoughtful, by defining it as "the parrying of a blow." Anticipating Moltke's formula of the offensive defense, or the strategic defense conducted by using the tactical offense,

Clausewitz condemned "pure defense," by which he meant passively waiting for the enemy. Instead, he argued for returning or even anticipating the enemy's strikes within the theater. He then produced his famous formulation that the defensive form "is not a simple shield, but a shield of well-directed blows."[167] The object of warding off enemy thrusts with active defense was simple: preservation. *On War* went on to argue that defense is the stronger form of war, with the negative goal of preservation, whereas offense, though weaker, has the positive goal of conquest.[168] Because mere preservation cannot, in the long run, produce a decision in war, Clausewitz offered his famous formulation of the counterattack and counteroffensive, the "flashing sword of retribution," which he saw as the "greatest moment for the defense."[169] The irony, then, was that a successful defense should end in an offensive.

Clausewitz never argued that defense is the most *desirable* form of war.[170] On the contrary, he argued that defense "should be used only so long as weakness compels, and be abandoned as soon as we are strong enough to pursue a positive object."[171] Moltke was of the same opinion, as an examination of his writings reveals, but by the end of the nineteenth century, many Prussian theorists were emphasizing the opposite point of view.[172] Indeed, one of the most consistent points of criticism aimed at virtually all European armies in 1914 was an alleged "cult of the offensive."[173]

Clausewitz did not doubt the value of the offensive form of warfare in a variety of circumstances. Above all, it was essential because, as he noted, only the offense can produce positive and decisive results. In his chapter on defense, Clausewitz listed six conditions under which one might wish to act offensively, even if one were generally disposed to be on the defense, including if the enemy were widely dispersed, if the enemy were clumsy and vacillating, if the composition of one's own army made it particularly suited to the offensive, if the need for a decision was urgent, and if one or more of these factors worked together. Those who criticize various German thinkers and practitioners for violating Clausewitz's basic concepts rarely cite these passages, which indicate that even the great theorist thought offensive action was possible in a situation that might dictate a defensive stance.[174]

Clausewitz began his lengthy chapter on offense by pointing out that offense is a part of defense and that no defense is complete without at least one offensive concept: the counterattack. The offense, in contrast, is complete in itself, although considerations of time and space, which lead to pauses in offensive actions, "introduce defense as a necessary evil."[175]

In chapter 15 of book 7, Clausewitz discussed the most important characteristics and advantages of using an offensive across an entire theater of war to achieve a decision. He began this discussion by pointing out that the attacker can overcome all the advantages of the defense by his numerical or moral superiority, by the advantage of his position, and by his army's knowledge that it is on the advancing side. An attacker lacking greater numbers can make up for that shortcoming with moral superiority. Clausewitz frequently emphasized that numerical superiority, particularly at the decisive point of a campaign and a battle, is of fundamental importance. He then argued that while prudence is the "true spirit of the defense, courage and confidence" occupy that position for the attacker. The attacker, moreover, faces less uncertainty. In subsequent sections Clausewitz stressed the importance of obtaining real victory rather than merely occupying positions and of exploiting a victory once won.[176]

In the following chapter, Clausewitz elaborated on the characteristics of an offensive that does not seek a decision across the entire theater of war. Here he suggested that an attacker might wish to seize a piece of territory or an important depot or to capture an important fortress. These kinds of discussions, of which there are several in *On War*, became the basis for arguments that Clausewitz recognized two kinds of war as defined by unlimited or limited objectives. Even a small battlefield success might be the reason for launching a limited offensive.[177] Moltke's counterpart to this line of thought was his concept of combining offense and defense in different measures, depending on the demands of the strategic and tactical situations.

Later in book 7 Clausewitz discussed one of his most important concepts: the culminating point of victory, which he termed the "keystone for most plans of campaign."[178] This chapter was, in effect, a warning to a potential attacker that his strength must suffice to reach his goals and that attaining such strength would be difficult. Clausewitz pointed out that many factors gradually work to reduce the strength of the attacker. The attacker must therefore be prepared for the point at which he will become the defender. If the attacker's resources are insufficient to attain his objective, or if he continues beyond the limits of his resources, he "will cross the threshold of equilibrium, the line of culmination, without knowing it." The attacker thus takes on more than he can manage "and, as it were, go[es] into debt."[179]

Center of Gravity

With this in mind, Clausewitz was concerned about the attacker concentrating his efforts on the most important matters and focusing on defeating the enemy's means of resistance before declining resources produced failure. This led to one of Clausewitz's most interesting and important concepts: the center of gravity. This became a key concept of the Prusso-German military system and, after 1980, came to dominate modern American military thought. In fact, it became the single most important element of a wide range of military activities, from planning campaigns to selecting targets for air strikes. The two armed forces, however, arrived at very different interpretations and uses of this basic Clausewitzian concept.[180]

Clausewitz's precise meaning when using the term "center of gravity"—which he admitted was a limited analogy from physics—is difficult to determine. He used the phrase in numerous contexts that lacked any consistency. Another problem is that the standard English translation does not render all uses of the German *Schwerpunkt* as "center of gravity," and it occasionally inserts the term when it does not appear in the original text. A few examples should make this point clear. On page 71 (all references are to the Howard-Paret English edition) Clausewitz stated that the center of gravity is a turning point in a campaign, while on page 258 he argued that the main battle (*Hauptschlacht*—a very important term that has been lost in the English edition) is the center of gravity.[181] On page 485 he said that the center of gravity is an analogy and that the mass of an army is the center of gravity, which is struck by another such mass. On several occasions Clausewitz concluded that if there were no decisive battle, there could be no center of gravity. In several cases Clausewitz used center of gravity in a slang sense, simply to emphasize the most important point of an argument, a turning point in a campaign, or the most important branch of the army in a particular case. The one common element in most of these uses was the designation of where the main military effort should be made. Prusso-German military theory adopted this meaning and used center of gravity simply to designate the main effort of a wide variety of military undertakings. The term was used relatively rarely in Moltke's day but became increasingly important in subsequent years.[182]

On the one hand, Prussian theory did not fully accept Clausewitz's views on the superiority of the defense and the potential limitations of the offense in a balanced manner; instead, it chose to emphasize those factors that seemed to favor the attacker. German commanders often had good reason for these deviations, particularly in the strategic situation prior to 1914, but sometimes they were simply blind to Clausewitz's complex views and to the realities of their situations. On the other hand, Prussian theory hardly ignored the Clausewitzian concepts of offense and defense. Moltke made much of this, as discussed later in this chapter. Two examples from the mainstream of Prussian-German theory, Baron Hugo von Freytag-Loringhoven and Colmar *Freiherr* von der Goltz, illustrate the point. The former warned that almost every offensive aimed at destroying the enemy would lack the strength to see the effort through to the end, while the latter, using Clausewitz's own terms, repeated many of the reasons for the diminishing strength of a strategic offensive.[183] Other writers considered the issue, but General Friedrich *Freiherr* von Falkenhausen was probably representative in recognizing the danger but also confidently expecting that an intelligent conduct of the strategic offensive would succeed.[184]

In discussing the offensive, Clausewitz stressed the important advantages of superiority in numbers. He argued that in ordinary cases, superior numbers (particularly two to one) would prevail, "however adverse the other circumstances." Clausewitz thus argued that since the best strategy is *always to be very strong*, first in general and then at the decisive point, the highest law of strategy was that of "*keeping one's forces concentrated.*"[185] Clausewitz, indeed, thought the principle of concentration meant that all envelopments must be entirely within the realm of tactics and that coordinated strategic attacks by separated armies were unlikely to succeed.[186] In subsequent decades, German military thinkers agreed with Clausewitz's emphasis on numbers and superiority at the decisive point of a war. As Goltz wrote (following a paraphrase of Clausewitz's point about being superior at the decisive point), most German writers thought that "to dispute the value of numbers is equivalent to denying this universally recognized military principle."[187] When, for practical reasons, German thinkers after the wars of unification and the Franco-Russian alliance had to consider how to defeat a numerically superior enemy, they returned to the other part of Clausewitz's line of thought—concentration of forces at the decisive point or time.

A necessary corollary of Clausewitz's arguments on numbers and battles was the acceptance of heavy losses as a nearly inevitable by-product of any war, even a successful one. Clausewitz rejected the views of "kind-hearted people" who thought there might be some ingenious way to defeat the enemy without too much bloodshed. He went on to say in a later section of *On War* "We are not interested in generals who win victories without bloodshed."[188] Prusso-German theory from Moltke onward accepted this basic viewpoint, based on entirely reasonable grounds, as will be seen.

Intelligence

Clausewitz accorded intelligence great importance in book 1 (The Nature of War), although he devoted only two pages directly to the subject. Using the German word *Nachrichten* (literally "news" or "reports" of any kind), Clausewitz wrote that intelligence is "the basis, in short, of all our own concepts and actions."[189] The Howard-Paret translation renders "concepts and actions" (*Ideen und Handlungen*) as "plans and operations" and, unfortunately, drops "all" from the statement, thus considerably reducing the text's emphasis on intelligence. To Clausewitz, intelligence meant "every sort of information (*die ganze Kenntnisse*) about the enemy and his country." He emphasized, quite correctly, the unreliability of much of this information and the contradictory and false nature of intelligence received during a war. He warned that the commander should be guided by the laws of probability and should trust his own judgment while refusing to give in to the tendency to believe the worst among the flood of false and alarming reports. This was entirely in accord with his emphasis on the character and judgment required in senior commanders. Clausewitz listed intelligence as one of the elements that "coalesce to form the atmosphere of war and turn it into a medium that impedes certainty." Intelligence is thus part of the friction and the fog of uncertainty that impedes activity. The only remedy is combat experience in the commander and his army.[190]

History

Finally, in a view that remained at the center of Prusso-German concepts to the very end, Clausewitz suggested that the study of military history is the best way, outside of having combat experience, to learn about the nature of war and how to conduct it. Clausewitz argued that the study of military history helps one to understand friction and chance and that it therefore predominates over theory and principles. Subsequent chapters consider these concepts under the appropriate headings of institutional development and officer education, which fell more under the work and legacy of Helmuth von Moltke and his successors at the General Staff.

Count Helmuth von Moltke

"That is all well and good, but who is this General von Moltke?" Such was the question posed by Lieutenant General Albrecht von Manstein during the early stages of the Battle of Königgrätz when he received Moltke's order to halt a premature attack.[191] Helmuth von Moltke had been chief of the Prussian General Staff since 1857, but he had yet to place his imprint on wide sections of the Prussian army and its theory. All this changed with the victories over Austria (1866) and France (1870–1871). By the time of the founding of the German Empire in January 1871, he had become one of the most famous men in Europe. Over the next seventeen years, Moltke's ideas laid the practical foundations of the Prusso-German way of war.

Moltke in many ways seemed an unlikely candidate for both his high position and his role as the man who shaped Prussian military thought from Clausewitz to the end of the nineteenth century. Although he was a student at the *Allgemeine Kriegsschule* (War Academy) when Clausewitz was director of student affairs, they had little or no contact. *On War* had not yet been written, and Moltke seemingly concentrated on academic rather than military subjects.[192] Moltke had held no command position beyond a company and had seen no duty with units after 1835. Yet the pace of military life in those years allowed him time for reading and self-development, and Moltke broadened his education far beyond that of the vast majority of the officers of his day. Modest and unassuming, he wrote nonmilitary books; drew elegant topographic maps; composed profound essays on tactics, command, strategy, and other military subjects; created the foundations of operational art; and led his country's army to victory in three wars. He was one of the relatively few officers who claimed that Clausewitz's writings had been directly and importantly influential in shaping his views.[193] A recent author who placed him alongside Luther and Bismarck in German history may have exaggerated slightly, or perhaps he was correct.[194]

Although few if any writers question Moltke's importance both in his day and in the years up to the First World War, assessments of his influence and his overall contributions vary widely. Gunther Rothenberg concluded that Moltke was the most important and incisive military writer between Napoleon and 1914, while David Chandler called him the "ablest military mind since Napoleon."[195] Another historian, while acknowledging Moltke's importance in establishing the General Staff system and his role in developing the idea of deterrence, referred to him as the prototype of the "military mind," unable to see anything other than the military aspects of security problems.[196] Others, however, have disputed this, pointing out that Moltke's military planning after 1871 was in accordance with the political projects of the chancellor, Otto von Bismarck.[197]

Moltke's writings lacked the abstract philosophical approach of Clausewitz, and for that reason, as well as because of his position, they were more directly influential. On many points, Moltke's writings and teachings translated Clausewitz's concepts into the practical words and actions preferred by soldiers. On other points, his views marked new departures and approaches in conducting operations and waging battles.[198] The following sections concentrate on those areas in which Moltke made important innovations in Prussian theory or disagreed with Clausewitz.

From Cabinet War to People's War

Moltke's lifetime spanned the enormous changes in warfare that accompanied the industrialization and population growth of the nineteenth century. Over the course of the century, modern nations acquired the human and material resources to raise and equip mass armies that dwarfed even those of Napoleon and his enemies. Gradually, a host of technological changes, primarily in transportation, communications, and firepower, transformed the dimensions and nature of the battlefield. Popular passions, fired by nationalism and imperialism, gave war an increased intensity. Historians, using terms developed in the nineteenth century, have characterized these transformations as the shift from cabinet war to people's war.[199]

Although Moltke's victorious campaigns of 1864 and 1866 exhibited many of the technological and strategic changes of the period, they generally fell under the concept of eighteenth-century cabinet wars. This was primarily a result of Bismarck's limited goals and the strategic circumstances, which facilitated an early settlement after Prussia's battlefield victories. The campaigns of 1870–1871, however, witnessed a continuation of warfare after the annihilation of the French regular army and may be seen as a line of demarcation between cabinet war and people's war. The Germans soon found themselves struggling to defeat the popular uprising that followed the capture of Emperor Napoleon III and the emergence of the new republic. This new phase, a mixture of traditional combat, guerrilla war by small units, and individual resistance, strained the Prusso-German army to its limits. Although the German army prevailed, its leaders were relieved when the war ended.[200] The term "people's war" (*Volkskrieg*) soon entered the German military vocabulary as a monstrous alternative to cabinet war.[201]

In some respects, the final phase of the Franco-Prussian War reintroduced "absolute" war (Napoleonic warfare being the first in the modern era) along the lines Clausewitz had suggested as a theoretical possibility. Stig Förster has concluded that this experience turned Moltke, first, into an advocate or prophet of absolute war and, later, into an advocate of the use of military power as a deterrent to prevent war. There is, indeed, some evidence that in 1870–1871 Moltke wanted the total submission of the French nation, even if that meant occupying the entire country. He also desired a dictated peace that would preclude renewed French challenges to Germany's position.[202] After 1871 he regarded a new war with France as inevitable, and on at least two occasions he argued for a preventive war before the French became too strong. It should be noted that Moltke also considered a preventive war against Russia.[203]

Late in life, after his retirement, Moltke addressed the Reichstag in support of a bill to expand the army (14 May 1890) and set forth his final views on war. He pointed out that the costs, length, and consequences of a new European war were incalculable and suggested that war be avoided through deterrence based on strength. Only the sword, he argued, could keep other swords in their respective scabbards.[204] Moltke thus abandoned any idea of preventive war and, in effect, argued that the purpose of armaments was to deter modern war with its frightful if unforeseeable consequences.[205]

Annihilation

The political goals of or motives for war had relatively little impact on Moltke's theories about the conduct of war or those of his successors. German theory prepared for campaigns and battles designed to defeat the enemy's armies in wars of maneuver using the army's relatively unstructured system of conducting operations and battles. From this perspective, campaigns had the purpose of annihilating the enemy's forces (rendering them incapable of further resistance) as rapidly as possible. Even if the goal were limited to exhausting the enemy's will to resist and concluding the war with negotiations, specific battles normally had one of two objectives: to destroy the opposing forces or to contribute as a secondary effort while other battles achieved a favorable decision. As Dennis Showalter has argued, the fact that German theory and practice concentrated on battles of annihilation did not mean that Moltke and others sought total victory through destruction of the enemy state. Rapid and decisive victory was the means, regardless of the nature of the war. This made perfect sense for a state surrounded by potential enemies whose combined resources might be overwhelming in a prolonged war; it served the additional purpose of avoiding the kind of protracted conflict that had proved so frustrating and costly in 1871.[206] Some of Moltke's subordinates used the problems of the people's war to argue for total utilization of the nation's manpower. Goltz became the best-known representative of this concept of the nation in arms.[207]

Offense and Defense

In considering the relationship between offensive warfare and the defense, Moltke adopted a point of view that echoed much of Clausewitz's thought. He recognized that the tactical defense had many strengths, the most important of which were the ability to select the position and to use firepower to the fullest effect. However, he also recognized the value of holding the initiative and coined the phrase "laying down the law" of the battlefield to the enemy. He concluded, at least by 1882, that the defender had decisive advantages over the attacker. He also pointed out that it was often desirable for the enemy to attack first. Yet he recognized that only the offensive, even if it took the form of a counterattack, produced decisive results. If one's forces were equal to those of the attacker, Moltke recommended taking the initiative and thus the offensive. The strategic offensive, in short, was the direct way to the objective; the strategic defensive was the roundabout way.[208]

Moltke's solution was the defensive-offensive form of war. While maintaining the strategic offensive, one should, he argued, seek to use the tactical defensive wherever possible. The defender's advantage, he wrote, was decisive and remained important even if the attacker had the advantage of surprise and terrain.[209] From his earliest writings, Moltke recognized that the increased firepower available to defenders was a serious threat to any attacking force. His *Instructions for Large Unit Commanders* cautioned that "infantry has the power to repel any frontal attack," and "it should assure itself that it cannot be attacked from the front." In many cases, he argued, defending infantry "is invincible."[210] He recognized that in those days, before improvements in artillery range and the development of indirect fire, the defender was a threat even to the artillery.[211] He concluded that in many cases a commander might wish to restrain his units' offensive spirit and use the defense to weaken the enemy before going over to the offensive, a tactic that would be especially effective if, for reasons of policy or military circumstances, the opponent felt compelled to attack.[212] Nevertheless, Moltke agreed that a decision could be reached only through offensive action and that, sooner or later, the army would have to attack.

Despite his recognition of the power of the defense, Moltke placed no great faith in fortresses. As early as 1862 he argued that constructing large numbers of fortresses would decrease the military strength of Prussia. Instead, Moltke wanted to invest resources in the field army because it, above all else, decided the outcome of war. Since armies no longer relied on fortresses to serve as magazines that supported entire campaigns, they had lost even that function. Railroads, wrote Moltke in 1861, had become the primary means of provisioning armies, and every increase in a state's railroad system should be considered a military advantage.[213]

Tactics

Moltke wrote many essays and memoranda on tactics and discussed the issue in numerous historical studies produced by the General Staff.[214] He developed no grand scheme in tactics; rather, he stressed cooperation of the arms, reliance on artillery to support infantry attacks, exploitation of the power of the defense, and vigorous exploitation of victory. Overall, he tried to place his tactical teachings within the larger framework of large-unit battles and operations. Like Clausewitz, Moltke stressed tactical victory as the foundation of all other successes.[215] Nevertheless, he reminded his readers that "a tactical victory is decisive only if won at the strategically correct point."[216] Moltke argued, perhaps more forcefully than Clausewitz, that tactical success could dictate subsequent strategy. He wrote in his essay "On Strategy" (1871): "Strategy appropriates the success of every engagement and builds upon it. The demands of strategy grow silent in the face of a tactical victory and adapt themselves to the newly created situation."[217]

In resolving this problem of the offensive, Moltke developed two solutions—one traditional and in the area of tactics, and the other radically new and in the area of strategy. In tactics, Moltke stressed flanking attacks to avoid the main strength of the defender's fire. This was difficult to achieve under modern conditions, however, for two reasons: the increased range of rifles forced the attacker to maneuver while under fire, with attendant heavy losses and delays, and the size of the armies had vastly increased their combat frontages. In the days of Frederick and Napoleon, commanders could personally maneuver their units on the battlefield while outside the effective range of musket fire. This was no longer easily accomplished and, in some cases, had become impossible without suffering unacceptable losses.

Foundations of Operational Art

An additional problem arose with the increased size of fielded armies in the second half of the nineteenth century. Entire armies could neither move up to the battlefield in great masses nor move around the battlefield in the traditional manner. Moltke also warned that they could not remain stationary in a small area for a long period of time because of difficulties in arranging for provisions and quarters. The traditional method of uniting on the battlefield and fighting a relatively set-piece battle in a restricted area offered few prospects for rapid and decisive offensive success.

Moltke resolved these twin dilemmas in tactics and strategy by combining movement to the deployment area (*Aufmarsch*) with movement into battle in a single concept of the campaign, whereby deployments and movements were still under way as combat began. In most earlier cases, commanders feared defeat in detail if the battle began before their full forces had been united, so they deployed the great mass of their strength as densely as possible. They normally hesitated to begin serious fighting before completing their battlefield deployment. This was entirely in accordance with Jomini's concepts of interior lines and the concentration of forces. Clausewitz failed to develop a comprehensive theoretical position, but his writings suggested that he was suspicious of separating the army into distant subordinate elements and that he preferred interior lines to concentric movements.

Moltke first implemented his ideas in the campaign against Austria in 1866, although the much smaller scale action against Denmark in 1864 must have had an effect on his thinking. In moving against the Hapsburg forces, the primary Prussian field armies advanced into Bohemia toward Königgrätz; meanwhile, a second army under the crown prince deployed by railway to Silesia, nearly 200 miles away, and prepared to move through the mountains to strike the Austrian flank from the north.[218] As originally deployed, the armies were not within supporting distance, and each might have had to face the Austrian army alone.[219] In the event, the frontal battle opened in neither the place nor the manner Moltke had anticipated, and it began before the crown prince's army arrived; however, the latter came up just in time to deliver the decisive flanking attack. The same general concept—moving divided and uniting during battles to create flanking attacks—characterized the opening German strategy in the Franco-Prussian War in 1870.[220] Later, Schlichting used these concepts to create the foundation of what is now known as operational art.[221] Theorists of the imperial Russian army and the Soviet army eventually formalized this into the concepts that have now been universally adopted in Western military doctrine.

Many senior Prussian commanders failed to appreciate the subtlety of Moltke's approach to strategy, and as a result, neither campaign was a perfect example of what was, after all, a very general set of propositions that Moltke himself had declined to establish as a formal system or theory. Particularly in 1866 the execution was less than perfect. In an effort to improve his subordinates' understanding of his approach, Moltke wrote *Instructions for Large Unit Commanders*, which became a secret manual available to senior commanders and General Staff officers. With only slight revisions in 1883 and 1910, it remained the basic regulation on this topic through 1914. Much of this manual's approach carried over into basic German regulations after the First World War.[222]

The 1869 *Instructions* introduced the argument that every large assembly of units was inherently catastrophic, because such a force could not be supported, could not move well, and could not conduct operations. Such an assembly would have to advance to the attack, and that could not be done on a single road or even several roads. The solution, therefore, was to keep the masses separated for operations as long as possible and to assemble them in good time for the decision in battle. The fruits of victory, Moltke wrote, lay not on the battlefield but on the other side—in exploitation. Proper exploitation, the manual said, would prevent the enemy from reestablishing himself and would accomplish what had to be attained without a second battle. This paraphrased paragraph, from page 176 of the English translation of the *Instructions*, was the closest Moltke and the German manuals ever came to establishing what could be called a methodology or system of "separated armies."

Although the phrase "march divided, fight united" had been known in the Prussian army since Scharnhorst first enunciated it, Moltke gave it new meaning. He raised it from a means of moving and provisioning large armies to a new method of conducting campaigns and joining the campaign plan directly to the execution of the battle. This method remained controversial, even up to 1914. Maintaining substantial distances between deployed field armies exposed them to defeat in detail and made close coordination of their movements and actions difficult or impossible, given the relatively poor communications of those days. Although the means of communication were far superior to those of the Napoleonic period, there was only erratic contact with the far-flung commanders on whom victory depended.[223]

Directives and Orders

To overcome this communications problem, Moltke fostered the principle of subordinate initiative and developed the procedure of commanding by general directives (*Weisungen*), which became one of the hallmarks of the Prusso-German system until well into the Second World War.[224] By "directives," Moltke meant "such communications from higher to lower headquarters that do not give definite orders for momentary conduct so much as guiding viewpoints." Directives thus "serve as guidelines for the decisions the subordinate headquarters have to make."[225] The General Staff, in its history of the campaign of 1870–1871, defined directives as communications from higher to lower commands that gave only general guidance rather than definite orders for action. Directives thus served as the basis for independent decisions by subordinate commanders.[226]

In conducting his campaigns in this manner, Moltke was simply making a virtue out of necessity. Armies had to be separated to some extent in order to receive provisions and to move along Europe's road system in an orderly and timely manner. Allowing his subordinate commanders to conduct their own movements and battles with a minimum of direct and specific orders was necessary to exploit the unanticipated opportunities that were the basis of German theory. Moltke's statement that strategy is a system of expedients reflected the view that although the commander could outline his general intent, he had to depend on his subordinates' initiative and their ability to adapt broad plans to the changing situations of war. As long as they remained within the broad framework of his intent for the campaign, Moltke encouraged his commanders to exercise initiative and to act quickly and decisively to exploit opportunities. He was willing to tolerate the resulting disruptions because he believed that mistakes in execution were less of a problem than inaction produced by timidly awaiting instructions from higher commanders.

Moltke was willing to abandon this system, however, when the situation demanded that the commander give direct and specific orders to subordinates. His own writings illustrated that at critical moments in 1866 and in 1870–1871, his headquarters issued direct orders rather than general directives.[227] Still, reliance on general directives at high levels of command remained a central feature of German doctrine, even in the more restrictive days of Schlieffen's dominance, until the new realities of trench warfare forced changes. Moltke's principles soon reemerged in the early years after the First World War.

Moltke further enshrined the practice, stressed earlier by Reyher, that orders should be free of mandatory formats, should require as little as possible, and should be brief. His own orders in 1866 and 1870–1871 were models of clarity and brevity. Numerous subsequent writers and manuals stressed these same points, and the Prussian army steadfastly declined to use standard field order formats with numbered paragraphs in the modern sense.[228] The 1906 infantry regulations, the 1908 field service regulations, and the 1910 version of the *Instructions for Large Unit Commanders* set forth principles and procedures for writing orders along the lines outlined by Moltke thirty years previously.[229]

Auftragstaktik

Few Prussian concepts have captured the imagination of modern military writers and official doctrine more than that of "mission-type" orders.[230] The concept stems from the German term *Auftragstaktik* ("mission tactics"). Contrary to many accounts, Moltke never used this term, which saw relatively little German use prior to 1918.[231] Although Moltke's practice of giving his subordinate commanders wide latitude in conducting battles may be seen as the ultimate origin of the concept, this had little to do with tactics and even less to do with small-unit commanders.

Moltke's methods were controversial in his day and remained so for some time. Certainly, they were not in the mainstream of Prussian or German thought when they first emerged in 1866, so it is not surprising that many contemporary officers, including some in his own army, found them too radical to serve as the basis for doctrine.[232] Moltke himself apparently felt obliged to defend his methods in *Militär-Wochenblatt* in 1867. Heinrich Friedjung's well-known study of the 1866 war, *Der Kampf um die Vorherrschaft in Deutschland*, included a strong attack on Moltke for dividing his armies and losing control of them at critical points. In the same vein, J. F. C. Fuller harshly criticized Moltke for unleashing his subordinate commanders and abdicating his own responsibilities.[233] As several writers have pointed out, Moltke's unwillingness to limit the initiative and aggressiveness of his subordinate commanders contrasted sharply with the practice of his opponent in 1866, Austrian Ludwig Benedek, who closely and excessively regulated his subordinates.[234] In the tactical realm, the question of mission orders produced a protracted debate between 1883 and 1914 and is examined in the following chapter.

Risk

Moltke's system of separating his field armies and allowing subordinate commanders great independence involved accepting risk in the tradition of Clausewitz, if not in the exact way Clausewitz envisioned. Replying to those who criticized the risks he took by dividing his forces in 1866, Moltke replied that those who wish to act with complete security will find attaining the goal difficult.[235] Numerous subsequent writers endorsed the concept of taking risks, to the point that it became a fundamental ingredient of the Prussian way of war. The 1910 *Instructions for Large Unit Commanders* reached the same conclusion in its discussion of large and separate movements: "Great successes in war are never to be attained without great risks."[236]

The main pillars of Prusso-German theory prior to the onset of war in 1914 were established by Clausewitz and Moltke. Clausewitz's influence, however, was much more indirect. In that regard, Moltke was critical in disseminating Clausewitz's ideas across the army. Moltke was a prolific writer; his collected military works alone run to some seventeen volumes. In addition, from the standpoint of readability, Moltke's writing was much more accessible than Clausewitz's.[237]

Unlike Clausewitz, who was attempting to develop an overarching theory of war applicable at any time and in any place, Moltke's writing was far more focused on practical military efforts. Moltke, like Clausewitz, embraced the idea of war as a nonlinear phenomenon. Also like Clausewitz, Moltke endorsed the idea that tactical outcomes drive operational and strategic decision making. Moltke could take this view because, during the Franco-Prussian War and in the immediate aftermath, the size of armies and the amount of open space available allowed field armies to engage in relatively nimble maneuvers. After 1890, however, changes in the conduct of warfare, an altered strategic situation, and many other factors challenged these theoretical foundations. Of these factors, two of the most important were advances in weaponry, especially artillery, after 1890 and the increasing size of the armies fielded by the European powers. The institutions and tactics of the Prusso-German army had to respond to these changes and sought to modernize and grow accordingly. It is to these developments within the imperial German army that this study now turns.

German military history imagined—Wilhelm II and his key commanders. Perhaps the two oddest people pictured are Bethmann-Hollweg (civilian) and Tirpitz (navy). The placing of Falkenhayn and Ludendorff next to each other shows either a high degree of naïveté or an ironic sense of humor. (Bain Collection, Library of Congress)

Theobald von Bethmann-Hollweg. Imperial German chancellor in 1914, he was ousted from his position by Ludendorff in 1917. (National Archives)

German army commanders in the west in 1914. The only one not pictured is Seventh Army commander Josias von Herringen. (National Archives)

Generaloberst Josias von Herringen (slightly off center, with the white beard), commander of German Seventh Army, and his staff. (National Archives)

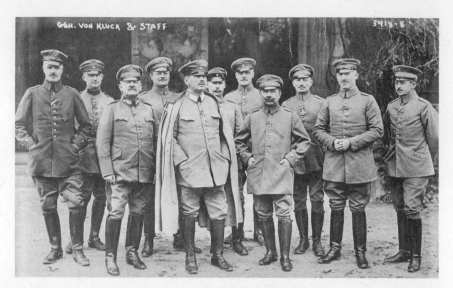

*Generaloberst Alexander von Kluck (*with coat draped over his shoulders*), commander of First Army, and his staff. Immediately to Kluck's right is Generalmajor Hermann von Kuhl, his chief of staff. (Bain Collection, Library of Congress)*

*The heroes of Tannenberg: Hindenburg (*center in lighter coat*) and the staff of Eighth Army. To the left of Hindenburg is Ludendorff; to the right of Hindenburg is Max Hoffmann, the perpetually grumpy staff officer who later became the* Ober Ost *chief of staff, after Hindenburg and Ludendorff took over the OHL. (National Archives)*

Erich von Falkenhayn. War minister in 1914, he succeeded Moltke as chief of the General Staff late in 1914 and headed the OHL until his fall in August 1916. He then commanded Ninth Army with great success in the Romanian campaign. (National Archives)

Wilhelm II (left) with one of his favorite commanders, August von Mackensen, in 1915. Between Mackensen and the kaiser is Mackensen's chief of staff, Hans von Seeckt. (Bain Collection, Library of Congress)

Max von Gallwitz, one of Germany's ablest field commanders. (Bain Collection, Library of Congress)

August von Mackensen, pictured here as a Generalfeldmarschall. An able commander, he was also a popular figure in Vienna and Sofia. (National Archives)

Crown Prince Rupprecht of Bavaria. Although not the best tactician, he often showed considerable insight on operational and strategic matters. (National Archives)

Generalfeldmarschall Colmar von der Goltz. A prolific writer and theorist, Goltz later headed the German Military Mission to Turkey. He was, along with Mackensen, one of Germany's ablest practitioners of coalition warfare. (National Archives)

Erich Ludendorff. By early 1917, he was the driving force at the OHL and was effectively the dictator of Germany. (National Archives)

Paul von Hindenburg, the most popular war hero in Germany and head of the Third OHL. By 1917, he was effectively the front man for Ludendorff. (National Archives)

Germany's military masters. Wilhelm II (center) flanked by Hindenburg (left) and Ludendorff (right). (National Archives)

Hindenburg and Ludendorff. (National Archives)

CHAPTER THREE

INSTITUTIONAL DEVELOPMENTS, 1871–1914

Between the wars of unification (1864–1871) and the outbreak of the First World War, the Prussian army and those of the other states of the empire increasingly formed a unified, truly German army, even though the peacetime force consisted of four contingents.[1] Prussia's army was the largest by far (accounting for about 75 percent of the force throughout the life of the empire), but Saxony, Württemberg, and especially Bavaria maintained some important vestiges of military independence, with separate units, command structures, and administrative organs. The largest non-Prussian contingents of the German army increasingly cooperated with the Prussians in training, officer education, doctrine, and so forth as the years passed.[2] Nonetheless, some regional and religious tensions remained. These bubbled up in the recriminations that followed the miscarriage of the Schlieffen Plan in 1914 and, later, the unsatisfactory conclusion of the war.

The German Constitution unified budgetary matters and required Reichstag approval for appropriations, although the legacy of the constitutional conflict and the royal powers of command hung heavily over the entire life of the empire. Since Germany was almost totally lacking in federal administrative organs, the imperial chancellor (normally the minister-president of Prussia) represented the government in parliament in theory. In practice, the Prussian war minister also had extensive and sometimes highly contentious dealings with the budget committees and the chamber at large. For the most part, the Prussian army's administrative branches, particularly the War Ministry and the General Staff, developed the army's strategic planning, theory, doctrine, training and education, force design, and the like, free of external interference. Eventually, however, and particularly after 1898, parliamentary and other forces began to exert more influence as modernization and expansion seemed to threaten the army's basic principles.

Size, Structure, and Funding of the Army

The German Constitution established the peacetime strength of the standing army as 1 percent of the population; in 1871 (based on the 1867 population) this was about 401,000. The constitution foresaw annual budgets but allowed multiyear appropriations. The first army law, passed in 1871 before the formal legal establishment of a fundamental army bill, was effective for three years. It was a transitional measure until passage of the Imperial Military Law of 2 May 1874. This law, representing a compromise between parliament and the government, established the army's strength from January 1875 until December 1881 and served as the fundamental legal basis for the army through July 1914.[3] Wilhelm I issued royal orders subjecting military administration to the new law's guidelines, although in theory, much of this fell under the king's traditional powers of command. The law also established that actual military strength would depend on parliamentary appropriations rather than the 1 percent principle of the constitution.[4] Subsequent multiyear appropriations were modeled on the 1874 law.

The army that Moltke had commanded in 1870–1871, and its active component for nearly two decades during his time as chief of the General Staff, was a relatively simple force consisting of the four combat arms (infantry, cavalry, artillery, and engineers) and limited supporting branches. Table 1 shows the traditional army and its strength under the 1874 law.[5] Special units included one railroad repair battalion, the palace guards and police, and a few labor formations. The regional commands (*Bezirskskommandos*) administered reserve affairs and some mobilization functions.

Table 1. Force Structure under the Army Law of 1874

Unit Type	Officers	Enlisted Men	Battalions, Squadrons, or Batteries
Infantry	9,123	269,969	469
Cavalry	2,357	65,498	465
Field artillery	1,627	30,702	300
Foot artillery	681	15,002	29
Engineers	346	9,051	18
Trains	243	5,051	18 (companies)
Special units	89	1,656	2
Regional commands	570	4,728	275

Table 2. Summary of Force Structure, 1874–1913

Date	Infantry	Cavalry	Field Artillery	Foot Artillery	Pioneer	Verkehr (Transport)	Train (Logistics)
2 April 1874	469	465	300	29	18	—	—
6 May 1880	503	465	340	31	19	—	18
11 March 1887	534	465	364	31	19	—	18
15 July 1890	538	465	434	31	20	—	21
3 August 1893	624.5*	465	494	37	23	7	21
25 August 1899	624	482	574	38	26	11	23
15 April 1905	633	510	574	40	29	12	23
28 June 1909	624	465	494	37	23	7	21
27 March 1911	634	510	592	48	29	17	23
14 June 1912	651	516	633	48	33	18	25
3 July 1913	669	550	633	55	44	31	26

Note: Numbers represent battalions for infantry and engineers (pioneer units), squadrons for cavalry, and batteries for field artillery, foot artillery, *Verkehr*, and train units.

* This number includes 538 full battalions and 173 half battalions, an increase of 173 half battalions from 15 July 1890. The number for 25 August 1899 shows an apparent net loss of half a battalion.

The Reichstag passed ten additional appropriations bills before the outbreak of war in 1914. Table 2 reflects the army's growth from 1874 until the final prewar law, passed in July 1913.[6]

As mentioned earlier, although the Prusso-German army possessed a large number of standing formations, it was actually a cadre force whose numbers more than doubled upon mobilization. Active units' wartime authorized strength was nearly twice that of their peacetime strength, as they took in large numbers of reserves, including officers. Active units also dispatched officers and noncommissioned officers to activated reserve units. When the process was completed, the army had four basic kinds of units: active, reserve, second-line reserve (*Landwehr*), and militia (*Landsturm*). In 1875, for example, mobilized strength would have risen from about 401,000 to 1.4 million.[7]

The army laws were some of the most contentious legislation in the brief history of the empire. These disputes frequently spilled over into questions of tax reform, imperialism, abuse of soldiers, and other issues in which socialist and democratic groups demanded reforms. Debates about the army's size, raising issues of quality versus quantity, created rifts between the government's civilian officials and the army, as well as within the army itself, especially between the War Ministry and the General Staff.[8]

Later on, especially after 1898, the army had to compete with the navy for funding. The breakneck pace of German naval expansion demanded enormous amounts of money and material. By 1911, the German navy's budget was almost 55 percent of the army's budget. Although the growth of naval armaments fell off a bit after 1912, there was still a finite number of reichsmarks to be disbursed to the army and the navy. Army leaders frequently had to deal with a fractious Reichstag in obtaining appropriations.[9]

Another important factor was a radical new form of nationalism, quite distinct from the traditional Prussian patriotic monarchism and the limited German nationalism of the Bismarck era. It manifested in the rise of political pressure groups such as the Army League, the Navy League, veterans' associations, and similar organizations for reservists. These groups emerged as a powerful force, demanding radical increases in armaments beyond what the War Ministry was willing to propose to the Reichstag. Although some voices in the legislature quailed at these financial demands for armaments, the appropriations were approved. Thus, the older interpretation, prevalent in the post-1918 accounts of many officers—namely, that the struggle over the size of the army was between the patriotic Right and the left-wing Reichstag—is now untenable.[10]

Army Organization and Staff

Divisions

The battalions of infantry, squadrons of cavalry, and batteries of artillery listed in table 2 were the basic tactical and organizational building blocks of the Prusso-German army. Upon them rested the remaining hierarchical unit structure of the fighting forces. The largest infantry unit was the division, actually a combined-arms formation with two infantry brigades. Each brigade had two regiments, and in most cases, each regiment had three battalions, giving a division twelve infantry battalions. In addition, each division had three to six squadrons in its attached cavalry brigade and, by 1914, twelve batteries of artillery, most with 77mm field guns. A division also had four machine gun companies, one per regiment. In 1914 a German division had about 563 officers and civil servants, 17,000 enlisted men of all ranks, 4,600 horses, and 600 wagons of various sizes.[11] A reserve division was of comparable strength, but with a weaker artillery element and fewer horses.

Cavalry divisions, except for the Guards Cavalry Division, existed only in wartime. They were much smaller than infantry divisions, with about 300 officers and civil servants, 5,300 enlisted men, and 239 wagons.[12] Their major subelements consisted of three brigades, each with two regiments (some had three) of four squadrons. By 1914, most also had a field artillery regiment (three batteries), a machine gun unit (six guns), a light infantry (*Jäger*) battalion, and one *Abteilung* (battalion) each of engineers and signals personnel.[13]

Corps

The army corps, consisting of two divisions, two field artillery brigades, and three squadrons of cavalry and supporting elements, was the combat element above the division. It, too, had a standard organization, although there were some deviations from the norm for various reasons.[14] In the German army, unlike in most European armies, the corps rather than the division controlled the major logistics and transportation functions.[15] Most active corps had about 1,500 officers and civil servants, 43,300 enlisted men, 17,000 horses, 3,000 horse-drawn wagons, 35 to 40 trucks (most from private sources), and 144 pieces of artillery.[16] By 1914, many also had aviation, hospital, and telephone units.[17] This reflected substantial growth since the first military bill, which had established an active corps strengths of about 840 officers, 35,250 soldiers, 10,600 horses, 1,300 horse-drawn wagons, and 96 guns. Reserve corps were smaller, with about 1,100 officers, 33,200 enlisted men, 6,600 horses, and 1100 horse-drawn wagons.[18] A corps marching on two roads extended almost eighteen miles (thirty kilometers) from its advance guard to the end of the trains and needed about eight hours to pass a given point.

Staffs

These large, complicated formations had, by modern standards, astonishingly small staffs, consistent with Moltke's insistence on keeping them as limited as possible. A division commander, a two-star general (Generalleutnant), had no deputy or vice commander and fewer than ten officers in his headquarters.[19] His main assistant was his chief of staff, a General Staff officer and frequently a lieutenant colonel, who directly supervised the staff of six or so officers and about eighty enlisted men and civil servants.[20] This staff structure reflected the army's emphasis on decentralized command of tactical units and the division's focus on combat at the cost of administration. The army's contentment with small staffs was an enduring feature of the Prussian system and was not merely a matter of resources. The elder Moltke had warned against surrounding commanders with too many sources of advice because this could lead to indecision at critical times.[21]

The corps commanders were some of the most powerful officers in the army, and many decisively influenced their subordinate units and officers. Corps were the basic elements of large-unit operations, training, administration, and so forth. Nevertheless, the General Staff had no role in selecting their commanders. Appointed by the Military Cabinet, corps commanders had no peacetime superior. They reported directly to the kaiser and enjoyed the right of direct access. They normally outranked the war minister and had virtually complete freedom in commanding the units in their geographic areas, to the point that a recent historian characterized them as "small war ministers."[22]

Their powerful positions, first established in 1816, grew during the long rule of Wilhelm I. In case of domestic emergency, the Prussian siege law of 1850 gave them virtually dictatorial political and police powers in their districts. Several, notably Count Gottlieb Haeseler, August Lentze, Sigismund von Schlichting, and Karl von Bülow, became famous throughout the army for their personalities, their exercise of power, and the personal stamp they put on their units' tactics and training. On occasion, a stubborn corps commander would simply refuse to adapt to important doctrinal changes or regulations.[23] Not even the army inspectors could coerce determined corps commanders, who had to bow to the will of only the kaiser and the chief of the Military Cabinet.[24] Corps commanders could arrange the forced banishment of officers in their commands or even, in rare cases, of royalty.[25] These were precisely the kinds of personalities the Prussian army wished to have in important command positions in wartime.

Even in 1914, corps commanders had remarkably small staffs to support them. The corps headquarters had an authorized strength of 66 officers and mid- to high-level civil servants and 245 enlisted men and lower civil servants. The corps General Staff section included five officers under the direction of the chief of the General Staff. His direct subordinates held the following positions: Ia, operations and tactics; Ib, rear affairs; Ic, intelligence; and Id, assistant to the Ia. The corps staff had the following other major sections: II, adjutants with various responsibilities; III, justice; and

IV, medical and veterinary matters. Other staff officers supervised head-quarters security, police, mail, weapons, logistics, engineers, and communications (telephones). A special representative of the High Command handled secret matters. A handful of other officers dealt with munitions, files, and medical supplies.[26]

Preparing for Modern War

The General Staff

The central institution for preparing the Prussian army's commanders for the intellectual demands of war was the General Staff. From its origins in the Napoleonic era to the end of the empire in 1918, the General Staff remained very small by modern standards. It gradually acquired a wider range of responsibilities, developed a separate career path for its officers, assumed the tasks of planning and conducting ground warfare, and populated many of the army's highest command positions with its members. The main element of continuity through these years was adherence to the General Staff's fundamental principles, although no single document or regulation defined them in any systematic or formal sense.[27] These principles were elitism, self-selection and autonomy in education and assignments, independence of judgment, maintenance of a particular organizational ethos, personal self-development, rigorous practice and study of strategic problems, and intellectual leadership in the army.[28] Of course, these were ideals that the General Staff rarely attained.

Most officers entered the General Staff system through the War Academy and a subsequent probationary period with the Great General Staff in Berlin.[29] At the conclusion of the latter, the chief of the General Staff or his delegate passed final judgment on each individual's suitability for a General Staff career. A few others gained admission to this select group through direct appointment by the chief. All future War Academy students served in regular regiments until they were senior second lieutenants or first lieutenants; this period varied somewhat, but by 1900, it generally entailed at least five years of commissioned service, and often much longer. Interested officers voluntarily took the entrance examinations to the War Academy with the approval of their regimental commanders. The General Staff then admitted about 10 to 15 percent of these applicants, who in any given year constituted less than 4 percent of the entire officer corps. After three years of study at the War Academy and examinations at the end of each, the General Staff accepted between 10 and 20 percent of the third-year class; these individuals then went on to an additional probationary year or two in Berlin. An indeterminate proportion of these officers, personally approved by the chief, became full-fledged General Staff officers. The General Staff was thus entirely in charge of its own recruitment and personnel selection policies; it had no bureaucratic constraints or quotas or any other limitations beyond its own decisions, assuming the chief of the Military Cabinet raised no objections in individual cases.

For the most part, the General Staff career pattern involved rotations between designated General Staff positions and unit commands appropriate to rank. The vast majority of General Staff positions were in Berlin at the Great General Staff or at division and higher headquarters. Each division had a single General Staff position, while corps headquarters had one or more. General Staff officers returned to battalions, regiments, and larger formations as commanders but normally did not otherwise serve in units or headquarters staffs. Beginning in 1858 at the latest, they routinely received accelerated promotions and were able to reach the rank of Generalmajor (a one-star rank) ahead of their contemporaries.[30] Many reached the highest levels of the officer corps, where they commanded corps or army inspections or the equivalent. Even among the army's generals, however, they were a minority.[31]

In other ways as well, the General Staff was an institution within an institution. It had its own line of communications. The Great General Staff communicated directly with General Staff officers in units, and unit General Staff officers could communicate directly with their General Staff superiors without going through their commanders. General Staff officers in charge of operations had the right to dissent from their unit commanders' decisions and record their views in writing in the units' war diaries. Once the commander had rendered a decision, however, it was the General Staff officer's duty to execute it without hesitation. At division level and higher, the senior General Staff officer served as either chief of the General Staff or operations officer (Ia), who was the primary staff officer at division headquarters.

General Staff officers were not co-commanders, deputy commanders, or even vice commanders in the modern sense.[32] The Prussian army always rejected the idea of sharing command. Nevertheless, the General Staff officer shared responsibility for the actions of his commander if he agreed with them. As Bronsart von Schellendorff's semiofficial handbook noted: "The officers of the General Staff do not occupy a command position. The commander alone gives orders and bears the responsibility."[33] Janson's semiofficial guide for General Staff officers in unit positions made the same point.[34] A General Staff officer whose advice proved unsatisfactory in the view of his General Staff superiors, regardless of the views of his unit commander, could be held responsible for his recommendations and suffer relief as a consequence.

The relationship between a commander and his chief of staff had a long and distinguished history in Prussia. The elder Moltke used army chiefs of staff in the wars of unification to keep obstreperous commanders like as Karl von Steinmetz, an old comrade of Wilhelm I in the Napoleonic Wars, from going completely rogue.[35] Likewise, an experienced chief of staff could backstop a commander from the royal family, whose competence might be regarded as questionable. This was apparently the case in 1866, when Crown Prince Friedrich Wilhelm was assigned Generalleutnant Carl Constantine *Graf* von Blumenthal as his chief of staff. The duo performed so well, however, that they were reunited in 1870.[36] This approach was employed once again in 1914, when three of the armies in the west would be commanded by Crown Prince Wilhelm (the kaiser's son), Crown Prince Rupprecht of Bavaria, and Duke Albrecht of Württemberg. Each was assigned a highly regarded chief of staff: Schmitt von Knobelsdorf for Wilhelm, Conrad Krafft von Dellmensingen for Rupprecht, and Walter von Lüttwitz for Albrecht. In all three cases, the royals' performance exceeded expectations.[37]

The practice of pairing a commander and a chief of staff has also been subject to misinterpretation. Less careful historians and authors have extrapolated entirely too much from the coupling of Paul von Hindenburg and Erich Ludendorff. Based on the conduct of that duumvirate, many writers have portrayed commanders as ornamental front men, mere ciphers for their chiefs of staff. B. H. Liddell Hart, for example, typified this when he referred to Hans von Seeckt, August von Mackensen's chief of staff for the 1915 campaigns, as Mackensen's "guiding brain."[38]

This image of German commanders and chiefs of staff is in equal parts insulting and inaccurate. Commander generals, like their chiefs of staff, were professionals who had spent many years in the service and had filled both staff and command billets at a variety of levels. Some were even *Kriegsakademie* graduates or former members of the faculty. All these activities required commanders to use their brains. A look at contemporaneous sources reveals the true nature of this relationship. For example,

Alfred Jansa, the perceptive if perhaps overly sensitive Austrian officer attached to Mackensen's operations staff for the Serbian campaign, saw Mackensen and Seeckt work at close quarters. In his estimation, although the decisions were made behind closed doors, it was clear that Mackensen was the ultimate deciding authority.[39]

Another important point here is that a "military marriage" between a commander and his chief of staff was not permanent. In this regard, the Hindenburg-Ludendorff coupling was the exception, not the rule. Mackensen, for example, had several chiefs of staff, including Seeckt, Richard Hentsch, and Gerhard Tappen. After Krafft moved on to take command of the Alpine Corps, Rupprecht was paired up with Hermann von Kuhl, a brilliant staff officer. There are many other examples.[40] Although the commander alone bore responsibility for results, be they positive or negative, the commander and his chief of staff often shared a common fate. If a commander was relieved for poor performance, the chief of staff was relieved as well. The most famous example was the relief of Eighth Army commander Max von Prittwitz and his chief of staff Georg von Waldersee in 1914 after the Gumbinnen defeat.

The army educated and trained its officers for General Staff duties in three broad ways beyond the normal duties associated with their assignments. Most, but not all, future General Staff officers attended the War Academy. General staff officers participated in war games, staff rides, and exercises designed to enhance their skills in dealing with problems of tactics and strategy. Finally, the army assumed that all officers, especially General Staff officers, would pursue private study to enhance their skills. It sponsored a substantial publishing empire to enhance opportunities for individual self-development.

The War Academy and Beyond

The army selected officers to attend the War Academy based on annual examinations prepared by the General Staff. They were open to senior lieutenants and captains who desired to take them and whose regimental commanders certified their good character and suitability. These examinations became very competitive after the Franco-Prussian War. By 1914, more than a thousand officers competed each year for the approximately 170 positions available in each first-year class. These examinations, which lasted about thirty hours in 1906, covered history, mathematics, a number of military subjects, and at least one foreign language.[41] Those whose marks fell short could take the examinations again the following year, and many who failed on the first attempt were successful on the second.[42]

Although outright favoritism apparently played little if any role in grading the examinations, the army's regimental system made its presence felt in this area, as in so many others. Candidates from regiments stationed in or near large cities and those with surpluses of junior officers were more likely to have the time and opportunity to prepare for the tests. In some units, particularly the guards infantry regiments, commanders encouraged their officers to compete. Some army corps conducted official courses to prepare their lieutenants for the examinations.[43] Many provincial regiments, which were frequently short of officers, lacked these advantages, and their officers had to study entirely on their own. In either case, successful preparation usually lasted for months.[44]

The result was that the socially elite guards units were disproportionately represented at the War Academy, based on the careers of Prussian generals. The same evidence does not indicate a strong bias in favor of nobles over commoners among the War Academy graduates who eventually became generals.[45] Historians' assessments of the role of nobility and privilege in the General Staff differ sharply. Some have argued that the General Staff and the War Ministry were the two places in the army where the nobility's dominance had been broken. Others, including some of the army's sharpest critics, have pointed out that the General Staff remained predominantly aristocratic. One of the latter historians argued that "feudal criteria of qualifications were worth more than accomplishments."[46]

While at the War Academy, officers studied tactics, military history, geography, and foreign languages, along with a variety of minor subjects. Classes lasted until about noon. Many officers attended classes at the University of Berlin, and some of that institution's professors taught at the War Academy. At the end of each year, the faculty eliminated a substantial portion of the class, sometimes as much as one-third. These decisions rested entirely on the judgment of the primary faculty members of the small groups into which the students were divided for classes. No numerical scores or test grades were used to make these decisions, and for the most part, students had no avenue of appeal. Those who were dismissed returned to their units, where they could continue their careers in a successful manner, much like those officers who had never attended the War Academy. There was thus no penalty for trying and failing. On the contrary, senior officers valued such individuals, and the army frequently placed them in important staff or instructional positions in the army's school system.

Most of those who completed their third year were allowed to join the Great General Staff for a probationary year or two, after which the chief of the General Staff made a final determination of their suitability. According to one graduate, typically about half of each year-group survived to finish the third year, and about half of these won an assignment to the General Staff.[47] Many graduates who did not gain admission to the General Staff went on to have successful careers, and some became generals.[48]

Although Hermann von Boyen and some early reformers had tried to turn the War Academy into a military university that provided a general education, by 1860, it had become a professional school concentrating on military subjects. Many historians have seen this as evidence of an increasingly narrow focus by the General Staff and the army, as broad education at the War Academy allegedly gave way to purely military training.[49] There is an element of truth in this, but it should not be taken too far. The following courses were taught at the War Academy in both 1827 and 1891: mathematics, physics (1891, choice of chemistry or physics), tactics, artillery, field fortifications, history, military history, military geography, general geography, chemistry, General Staff affairs (third year only). The following subjects were taught in 1827 but not in 1891: strategic-tactical considerations (one hour per week in the second year), French language, German literature, logic. The following subjects were taught in 1891 but not in 1827: military law, supply, government administration. In 1891 students could choose either French or Russian as their language.[50] Perhaps the most important differences in the curriculum were the disappearance of "strategic-tactical considerations," which was gone by 1836, and the elimination of historical studies for periods prior to 1848.[51]

This comparison may be misleading, however, as a basis for evaluating the nature of the curriculum. First, officers studying at the War Academy in 1891 and later almost certainly had a better general education than did officers studying in the early decades of the century. Uneducated officers could not have passed the highly competitive entry examinations after 1871. An increasing number of these officers had completed either the humanistic or "real" *Gymnasia* and did not need as much basic instruction as their earlier counterparts. In 1891–1892, for example, 162 of 312 students had the *Abitur*, while another 71 were *Selektaner* of the cadet corps.[52] In such circumstances, courses in government administration, military law, and supply (taught every week throughout the third year) may have been as appropriate as courses in literature and logic. Second, the absence of a course titled "strategy" poses a different question and illustrates why it is problematic to take this as a sign of curricular narrowing toward tactical or operational subjects. It is difficult to ascertain exactly what was taught in the course on "strategic-tactical considerations" earlier in the century. During Count von Moltke's tenure as chief of the General Staff (1857–1888), history became the primary means of studying a variety of military subjects, including both operations and strategy. Moltke's use of history to illustrate basic concepts and lessons of warfare at all levels is well known, and there can be no doubt that military strategy was an important element in the historical literature read by the students. They certainly read Clausewitz or other authors reflecting his influence, as well as a number of other important authors discussing the nature of warfare and its relationship to policy.

Compared with professors of history, Prussia's General Staff officers might have been narrowly educated. Compared with other groups of officers, however, they emerge in a better light. The literature produced by General Staff officers demonstrated knowledge of military and general history that exceeds what is normally found in contemporary officers who have completed several levels of "professional military education," even if that knowledge was frequently applied primarily to confirm theoretical propositions. No one has successfully argued that modern senior military leaders are collectively more literate (especially in history, philosophy, or literature) than were Prussia's senior General Staff officers. The willingness of German military writers to enter into controversies with Hans Delbrück (covered in the previous chapter) certainly shows a scholarly disposition. German military writers, including active and retired generals drawn mostly from the General Staff, produced a vast number of books and articles between 1871 and 1914 beyond the large official publishing program. Though perhaps limited in their perspectives, these works consistently illustrate a level of historical knowledge beyond that found in the comparatively rare publications (usually autobiographical in nature) of today's senior American officers.[53]

Although few if any important General Staff officers of the imperial period passed through the War Academy just prior to 1914, a glance at the instructional program between 1912 and 1914 illustrates the nature of the institution on the eve of the war. Listed below are the subjects, hours per week, and years offered in the three-year curriculum:[54]

Tactics: four hours first year, six hours second and third years (linked with General Staff service)

History: three hours first year

Military history: four hours all three years

Math/geography: one hour first year, two hours second year, three hours third year

Languages: six hours first year, four or six hours second and third years

Arms/ordnance: one hour first year

Naval warfare: one hour first year

Military hygiene: one hour first year

Military justice: one hour first year

Fortifications/siege warfare communications: two hours second year

Map preparation: one hour second year

Government: two hours second year (constitution, civil law, finance, administration)

Surveying: four hours third year

The real shortcoming was that the Prussian army limited "strategy" to what we now call "military strategy" and largely avoided what most modern armed forces define as "national" or "grand strategy." This was no doubt a serious shortcoming that became obvious during the planning and preparation for the First World War. The absence of a course with the title "strategy" late in the nineteenth century, however, does not necessarily indicate a narrowing of the army's approach from earlier decades.

After completing the War Academy, General Staff officers participated in what would today be termed "professional development." As previously mentioned, these men pursued careers that involved assignments exclusively in General Staff positions, except for tours as unit commanders or instructors in schools. They did not, therefore, spend years in assignments that were only distantly related to their main career fields. Beyond their day-to-day work, General Staff officers participated in a series of war games, exercises (on maps and in the field), and staff rides. These activities allowed them to develop their skills in planning and conducting war and to examine concepts related to strategy, mobilization, and so forth. Although these exercises were not necessarily directly connected with the General Staff's actual mobilization and war plans, they frequently involved concepts closely connected with them. Especially under Schlieffen's influence, gaming exercises were reoriented toward contemporary strategic issues rather than the use of historical cases as educational tools.[55] They were, nevertheless, primarily educational in nature.[56]

The most important of these simulations were map exercises, war games (*Kriegsspielen*), and General Staff "rides" conducted personally by the chief.[57] War games—pitting groups of officers against each other in battles or campaigns conducted on sand tables or maps—had their origins in the late eighteenth century. By 1900, they had become sophisticated exercises with formal rules, attrition tables, and umpires or directors. The Great General Staff ride took a number of General Staff officers on a three-week trip to a campaign area to study large-scale problems of strategy in one or more scenarios. Officers played the roles of commanders on both sides, studying the situations in the scenario, proposing solutions, and preparing orders to implement their decisions. This combined the advantages of map gaming with physical presence in the chosen theater. After 1891 the chief of the General Staff normally conducted two such staff rides each year. The army assigned a few line officers to these rides, and occasionally one of them performed well enough to earn a direct appointment to the General Staff without attending the War Academy.[58]

Other kinds of staff rides provided analogous training for General Staff officers and others holding key staff positions: corps General Staff rides, conducted for seventeen days each year by corps headquarters; fortress General Staff rides, with two corps participating each year for twelve days; and administrative rides of two weeks' duration to address issues of logistics, rail movements, and so forth.[59] Schlieffen also conducted a number of less formal evening exercises for selected officers drawn from the departments of the Berlin General Staff.

The General Staff also expected its officers to continue their military education on their own, beyond their duty assignments. Although the attitudes of a few senior officers may have reflected Waldersee's alleged suspicion of military authors, the General Staff produced many important authors whose works were widely available in regimental and other military libraries. General Staff officers and others certainly had a great diversity of military literature available if they chose to use it in their self-development.[60] A survey of German military literature based on a 1909 bibliography revealed that more than 300 active and retired officers who were still alive had produced books on military subjects. At least 500 officers wrote books between 1871 and 1918. Many others wrote articles in various official and private journals.[61] Although these publications varied widely in quality and intent, they confirm that officers who wished to continue their educations through private study had many opportunities to do so. On the negative side, the Prussian army had a long history of censorship, preventing the publication of works considered too critical of authorities or too sensitive in their subject matter. After 1871 the army mounted several efforts to prevent officers from publishing works critical of its performance or its equipment, but much of the discussion became public anyway.[62]

In 1897 the army gave its writers more freedom to express dissident views, although some limitations remained.[63] Although attacks on past leaders and other dignitaries were still problematic, officers had always felt free to question doctrine and established practice across a wide range of subjects. Recent research has confirmed the assertion of Baron von Freytag-Loringhoven, himself a noted author, that vigorous discussions of military subjects had been possible throughout the imperial period.[64] A pair of examples illustrates that this was true, even among the generals. In 1908 General Heinrich Rohne criticized a previous article by General Heckert on marksmanship. In the same year General Reisner *Freiherr* von Lichtenstern sharply criticized the 1906 infantry regulations.[65] Such examples can be found in great numbers, and the army's literature was filled with debates over tactics, organization, weapons, and the like, perhaps exceeding that found in any other military organization.

The army sponsored a number of periodicals to supplement and reinforce its official doctrine and way of war. The most important of these was *Militär-Wochenblatt*, established by the General Staff in 1816 but controlled by the War Ministry throughout the imperial period. Schlieffen established *Vierteljahrsheft für Truppenführung und Heereskunde* in 1904 to consider issues of large-scale operations and topics considered important by the General Staff, whose officers also contributed much of what appeared in *Militär-Wochenblatt*. Many other official, semiofficial, and private journals, some of which reflected the social tensions in Germany, considered questions of armaments, technology, personnel matters, and so forth.[66]

Training

Even before their induction into military service, some German youths were subjected to limited military training. The "scout" (*Pfadfinder*) movement emphasized physical fitness, and the Bavarian *Wehrkraftverein*, founded in 1909, likewise staged sporting events, hikes, and other activities. The Bavarian effort attracted the attention of Prussian military authorities, most notably Field Marshal Colmar *Freiherr* von der Goltz, who founded the *Jungdeutschlandbund* (with the kaiser's blessing) in 1912. This organization provided military training to boys of premilitary age.

The Prussian army maintained a highly decentralized training system. Because training was his greatest peacetime responsibility, the corps commander controlled the training of individual soldiers and units within his command.[67] Decentralization prevailed even within individual corps, as company commanders exercised responsibility for training within their units. Recruits thus received their basic training and socialization into the army in the units in which they served. The infantry regulations of 1906 precisely characterized the spirit of the Prussian system in paragraph four: "Every unit commander, from company commander upward, is responsible for the training of his subordinates according to the provisions of the regulations. He may be limited in the choice of means as little as possible. Superior officers are duty-bound to intervene as they note mistakes and failure to attain standards."[68]

By 1914, specialization in functions and the increasingly technical aspects of most branches of the military led to the creation of specialized schools and armywide programs in various areas. As a result, each of the main branches except the infantry fell under the general authority of "inspections," which exercised limited authority in weapons development, personnel programs, training standards, and so forth. These were:

Inspection of *Jägers* and marksmen
General inspection of cavalry (plus three cavalry inspections)
Inspection of field artillery
Inspection of foot (heavy) artillery
General inspection of combat engineers
General inspection of engineers and fortresses
Train inspection (logistics)
General inspection of military education and training
Field army inspections

These designations reflected the structure of the army and the priorities of its system of training and commanding units. "General inspections" had direct access to the king. Infantry, being the primary branch, had no such inspection; corps headquarters, officially titled *Generalkommandos*, served in that capacity, and most corps commanders were from the infantry. The designation *Generalkommando* or *Generalinspektion*, as opposed to the lower *Inspektion*, drew the traditional sharp line between corps-level authority and prestige on the one hand and lower functions on the other. Cavalry and engineers had general inspections because many of their functions related to the field army level of command. Field and heavy artillery had "inspectors."

The army inspections and their chiefs were to assume command of field armies in war. Their peacetime authority, however, was limited. Army inspectors commanded no units in peacetime and did not supervise corps commanders in the areas of training and officer development. Beginning in 1913, they exercised authority over corps commanders for the purpose of conducting corps-on-corps maneuvers at the end of the training year (September). To maintain the peacetime superiority of corps commanders, the army did not bestow the official designation "army headquarters" on the army inspections. In peacetime they had no chief of staff but only a single General Staff officer.

Maneuvers

Large-scale maneuvers were one of the primary means for the army to expand its tactical training within a framework of large-scale scenarios. The gradual process of individual and unit training, which began every October with the arrival of a fresh cohort of draftees and volunteers, culminated in the final training event of the year, the corps-level maneuvers in September. Each corps had ten days to exercise its subordinate units, usually with reinforced brigades maneuvering against each other, followed by division exercises and, finally, corps-level problems against enemy positions and forces simulated by flags.[69] The corps maneuvers offered the commanding general the opportunity to observe the state of training of his subordinate elements. From at least 1861 onward, the General Staff used the regulation on large-unit maneuvers to influence training at all levels.[70]

Each year a few corps also participated in the so-called kaiser maneuvers, a grand spectacle involving the emperor and several corps, accompanied by a vast entourage of participants, spectators, foreign dignitaries, and administrators. These maneuvers, especially during the time of Emperor Wilhelm II (1888–1918), have been the subject of great ridicule because they seemed to be staged for the emperor's entertainment and to be devoid of any training value.[71] Wilhelm II demanded to lead the final event or even command one side, resulting in some ridiculous cavalry charge or other tactical absurdity.[72] Foreign observers, especially the retired English colonel Charles Repington, frequently commented on the lack of tactical utility of the kaiser maneuvers.[73]

These criticisms, regardless of their merits in the realm of tactics, miss the real point of both the kaiser maneuvers and the other large-scale exercises conducted at the corps level. Their purpose was not to provide tactical training for small units or for individuals. That had already taken place within the units during the preceding months. The objective of the autumn maneuvers was to give large-unit (division and corps) commanders and their staffs experience in handling their units within the framework of large scenarios. As the instructions for the kaiser maneuvers of 1911 stated: "The Kaiser maneuvers primarily serve the schooling of senior commanders. Combat training of individual units cannot be considered in the same measure as is the case in smaller maneuvers." This had been the case since a royal order of Friedrich Wilhelm III in 1830.[74]

These maneuvers also served an important function in furthering the army's public image. Soldiers mustered and paraded with great pomp and ceremony as they departed for the kaiser maneuvers. The public observed the exercises from afar and participated in the nighttime festivities. Indeed, the maneuvers turned into a great festival in whatever province they happened to take place. In this respect, the maneuvers were comparable to air shows, firepower displays, and open houses of various kinds that modern states use to build popular support for expensive military forces.[75]

In 1905, even before he succeeded Schlieffen, Moltke brought a halt to the worst of Wilhelm's abuses.[76] During his tenure the kaiser maneuvers became more realistic and began to reflect the improvements in German capabilities that were evident after 1906. Like Waldersee, who publicly judged that the kaiser's side had performed poorly in 1890, Moltke earned the respect of many General Staff officers and others for standing up to Wilhelm II and insisting on improvements.[77] Actually, the maneuvers were never as worthless as some have portrayed. Schlieffen allegedly allowed Wilhelm to "win" in order to convince the kaiser to rely on his advice in the event of war.[78] In any case, as Schlieffen told Hermann von Stein, if the kaiser were to lead one of the sides, he would have to win.[79] The maneuvers also provided useful practice for some parts of the railway mobilization plan.[80]

Regardless of disagreement over the value of the kaiser maneuvers during Schlieffen's tenure, there is ample evidence that Moltke improved both the kaiser maneuvers and other large-scale exercises between 1907 and 1914.[81] In 1912 he overcame the War Ministry's objections to allowing the army inspections (which would be field army headquarters in wartime) to conduct their own corps-on-corps maneuvers. He hoped to use such exercises to improve strategic cavalry reconnaissance and to give commanders at the army and corps levels more experience in commanding large bodies of troops. Such maneuvers took place for the first time in 1913.[82] In that year the army inspectors directed eight Prussian corps in maneuvers against "flag" enemies, an equal number against each other, and five in mixed situations.[83]

The kaiser maneuvers revealed the difficulties of maintaining communications when high headquarters had to move frequently, a peacetime lesson that found its battlefield analog many times in 1914. The 1910 and 1911 maneuvers revealed problems in using radios to send orders. The maneuvers between 1909 and 1911 showed breakdowns in communications among various staffs, not unlike those encountered in 1914.[84] The 1912 report on the 1910–1911 kaiser maneuvers warned that cavalry reconnaissance was poor, while in 1913 the scenario denied one commander the use of his cavalry to force him to learn to use improvised cavalry divisions, their commanders, and even their General Staff officers. Several maneuver reports warned of the need to improve combined-arms cooperation and of the potential shortcomings of artillery munitions.[85] In 1913 the scenario intentionally forced commanders to fight with limited maneuver room so that they would have to consider frontal attacks.[86] The 1912 maneuvers further demonstrated that such events were not perfect, but they were far from worthless.[87] The final prewar maneuver tested airplanes.[88]

The General Staff's reports on these maneuvers reveal their purposes and results. The goal was to train corps commanders to command their units in accordance with the intentions of their respective field army commanders and to train the corps for large-scale combat. The reports emphasized understanding the higher commander's intent, using frontal attacks to fix the enemy in conjunction with flanking attacks, preparing full and clear orders at the army level, avoiding both hasty attacks and excessive caution, and a variety of tactical conclusions.[89] Moltke had directed the preparation of separate manuals to enable umpires to better judge the performance of airplanes and intelligence officers at the kaiser maneuvers.[90] At a lower level, procedures established for the 1913 division maneuvers (directed by their corps) instituted better procedures for training commanders and staff, as well as increased emphasis on combined-arms cooperation.[91]

Finally, it should be remembered that the Prussian army had limited resources to support large-scale maneuvers. Political leaders complicated matters by lobbying to have or not to have maneuvers in particular locations.[92] Land available for corps maneuvers was always limited. Germany had a total of about thirty large maneuver areas in 1911, but these were by no means sufficient. Financial barriers were the major hurdle to acquiring more space for large-scale training.[93]

Branches of the Military

Infantry

The infantry was the main branch of the Prussian army, and it was at the core of the army and the officer corps both in peace and in war. The 1906 infantry regulations correctly captured this essential principle: "The infantry is the main arm (*Hauptwaffe*). In conjunction with the artillery it defeats the enemy with its fire and breaks his last resistance. The infantry bears the main burden of combat and makes the greatest sacrifices. It therefore enjoys the greatest glory."[94] Although the various active regiments bore old designations such as infantry, fusilier, grenadier, or musketeer, they all had the same weapons and organization.[95] The infantry produced about two-thirds of Prussia's generals throughout the imperial period, a proportion that varied only slightly between 1871 and 1914.[96]

The same social divisions that characterized the officer corps as a whole were present in the ranks of the infantry, but to a much lesser extent. The guards infantry units were among the army's most prestigious socially, although most stood below the guards cavalry on the social desirability scale. They were, however, the military elite of the army and, in many ways, its intellectual core as well. Some regular regiments were regarded as better than others because of their locations in or near large cities. Despite this, the infantry as a branch was a thoroughly serious fighting force, struggling with the challenges of surviving and winning the next war. The resulting debates over tactics and command (discussed in a different section) revolved around the infantry battle but also determined much of the wartime activities of the other branches.

In 1914 an active infantry regiment had three battalions and a machine gun company. The regimental headquarters had a staff of four officers, about fifty enlisted men, and seventeen horses. Reserve and *Landwehr* regiments frequently had only two battalions and no machine gun company. A battalion had four company commanders, eighteen lieutenants, a paymaster, a doctor, and about 1,050 noncommissioned officers and enlisted men. It also had an authorized establishment of fifty-eight horses and nineteen wagons.

Cavalry

Cavalry, more expensive and exclusive than the other branches, was the favorite of young men of wealth and social aspirations, but it faced constant criticism as doubts about its utility on the battlefield grew. Many, perhaps most, young cavalry officers were wealthy playboys who sought the dashing lifestyle of the branch but otherwise showed little enthusiasm for rigorous preparations for war.[97] Cavalry officers needed substantial private income to supplement their salaries and were substantially underrepresented in the War Academy.[98] Reformers criticized the cavalry for its social exclusivity and for what many regarded as its limited value in modern war. Nevertheless, the cavalry had an aggressive approach to combat that rivaled that of the infantry, and it frequently recited the alleged admonition of Frederick the Great: Prussian cavalry never awaits an enemy assault—it goes over to the attack first.[99]

Despite many individual and unit acts of sacrifice and bravery, the cavalry had proved inadequate in the wars of unification. It had failed to accomplish much in terms of deep raids or exploitation, was inadequately armed for dismounted combat with firearms, and proved unskilled in overcoming terrain obstacles. Commanders frequently deployed cavalry poorly and used it piecemeal in battles.[100] The real question, raised years earlier by Moltke, concerned the cavalry's place on the modern battlefield. Since 1858, Moltke had warned that the days of massed cavalry attacks were over, especially against infantry, and the cavalry's primary task would be reconnaissance.[101] During the war against Austria in 1866, however, the Prussian cavalry proved indifferent in conducting reconnaissance and equally incapable of launching a pursuit after Königgrätz.[102]

As part of his postwar reform of the Prussian army, Moltke sought to improve the mounted arm, as well as clarify its role. He did this in an 1868 memorandum to King Wilhelm I. Although he still mentioned the need for cooperation with the infantry and artillery, Moltke downplayed the battlefield role of the cavalry. Instead, he emphasized screening and reconnaissance as the riders' true roles. In *Instructions for Large Unit Commanders* (1869) he made the famous statement that cavalry would find its main use in the beginning and end of a battle, adding that it would no longer be decisive.[103] Moltke's urging that the cavalry change its outlook had little effect on its performance in the Franco-Prussian War, although it has been credibly argued that cavalry leaders adapted reasonably well to the circumstances produced by the improvement in firearms and the continuing need for battlefield mobility at a speed greater than that of marching infantry.[104]

"But gentlemen, do not forget that these are Hussars—Hussars!" These words of General Adolf von Deines, imploring umpires at maneuvers not to judge that the old-fashioned attacks of his cavalry had failed, fairly represent the attitude of at least some cavalry leaders even on the eve of the First World War.[105] The years between 1872 and 1909 saw numerous efforts to modernize the basic cavalry regulations, which dated to 1855, with mixed results. The first effort began in March 1872 and produced little more than a reprint with marginal changes by June 1873. A highly respected and temperamental cavalryman, Generalmajor Karl von Schmidt, worked on further revisions the following winter but failed to produce any improvements under field tests in 1874. Another revised edition appeared in 1875, but it too proved unsatisfactory. A new commission headed by Baron Karl von Willisen convened in March 1876 and produced yet another edition that summer. This version only produced more complicated maneuvering without fundamentally addressing the question of the cavalry's battlefield missions.[106]

The 1875 regulations brought no stability to the branch, and in 1886 a new commission headed by three distinguished cavalry generals, Haeseler, Rosenberg, and Krosigk, produced new regulations. The main result was a return of cavalry maneuvers to the simple forms of Frederick the Great. This proved less than fully successful in modernizing the cavalry's view of battle, given that all cavalry units received a new kind of lance in 1890.[107]

The revised regulations of 1895 marked no real improvement in tactics. They maintained a balance between firearms on the one hand and the lance and saber on the other, tried to limit the use of dismounted combat, and insisted that mounted combat remained the main form of cavalry fighting. They accepted Moltke's old emphasis on the cavalry's role in exploitation of a battlefield victory.[108] Schlieffen was no friend of the cavalry, believing that even its function of strategic reconnaissance would soon give way to aviation.[109] He had little impact on the cavalry's doctrine and training.

The final prewar cavalry regulations appeared in 1909 and created a theoretical balance between mounted combat and fighting on foot with firearms, even addressing combat against an enemy armed with machine guns. They still envisioned mounted battles between large cavalry formations and argued that the cavalry should use its carbines only when the lance was not appropriate. Though an improvement, these regulations looked backward as much as forward and, like most Prusso-German manuals, allowed commanders great leeway in emphasis and interpretation. The question, then, is how the cavalry's leaders and spokesmen saw the functions of their branch in the last years before 1914.[110]

The army's prewar literature shows considerable controversy over the role of cavalry. While some officers defended the continuing emphasis on traditional mounted combat, defiantly commenting that their branch was "no life insurance company," many recognized that the glory days of cavalry charges were over. Nevertheless, even the most respected writers seemed to take equivocal positions. Wilhelm Balck's *Taktik* stated that cavalry attacks could succeed against infantry, arguing that "the cavalry works by the moral impression brought forth by the surprising appearance of a rapidly attacking mass of riders, by the weight if its shock." He argued, somewhat inconsistently with his other writings, that cavalry could succeed even against cohesive infantry if employed in sufficient numbers, and if necessary, it could substitute speed for surprise. Yet he also admitted that cavalry was only an "assisting arm" to the infantry and artillery.[111] Colmar von der Goltz likewise continued to take a middle position. Friedrich Immanuel's influential books on tactics stressed that cavalry could succeed only against disrupted infantry. He bluntly warned that "the time when masses of cavalry, as at Hohenfriedeberg, Leuthen, and Zorndorff, could overrun the enemy infantry and decide the battle, even against a semi-effective infantry, belongs to the past."[112] Jacob Meckel's book on the conduct of battle had delivered similar warnings years previously.[113]

Iconoclastic maverick Friedrich von Bernhardi, in contrast, denounced his fellow cavalrymen for training their units for close combat rather than strategic reconnaissance missions.[114] Junior officers also joined the fray, sometimes mocking those who would restrict the cavalry to raids on enemy lines of communication with the argument that one would not find a Murat or Seydlitz away from the main battlefield.[115] More authoritatively, the official manual for training junior officers at the war schools cautioned against attacking infantry and warned that cavalry attacks no longer played a decisive role in battle.[116] Overall, Dieter Storz is probably correct in his criticism that too many cavalry leaders took comfort in the hope that they could find a demoralized and disrupted enemy infantry formation to attack. But as Dennis Showalter has pointed out, the cavalry was hardly useless in the days when motor vehicles were still road bound or where, as in eastern Europe, conditions were more favorable.[117]

The roles of combat and reconnaissance were definitely in conflict, and the reformers could not prevail in favor of the latter. As Showalter has observed, the stronger the emphasis on dismounted fighting, which many demanded, the less capable cavalry would be for its screening mission.[118] Schlichting stressed the reconnaissance mission in his writing, calling for mixed units advancing at least a day's march ahead of the main bodies, which brought him into conflict with some cavalry leaders.[119] Even those who stressed combat roles for cavalry agreed that the destruction of enemy cavalry and aggressive reconnaissance were the most important missions.[120] The previously cited manual for instruction at the war schools emphasized reconnaissance as the main task of cavalry, and on occasion, corps commanders such as Karl von Bülow bitterly criticized the cavalry for its failure to perform this mission in maneuvers.[121] Schlieffen did not place much reliance on strategic cavalry reconnaissance, in part because he felt that aviation would increasingly fulfill that mission.[122] The last two prewar general inspectors of cavalry opposed this view, but to no avail. The scenario for the 1913 kaiser maneuvers required one party to use its cavalry for brushing aside enemy screens and disrupting deployments, while airplanes performed long-range reconnaissance missions.[123] The cavalry actually performed this function with some success in 1914, exhibiting a strength that most foreign observers, fascinated by the large-scale traditional attacks that characterized the kaiser maneuvers, had not expected.[124]

The exploitation mission remained largely theoretical prior to the outbreak of war in 1914. Bernhardi criticized high commanders for holding their cavalry as battlefield reserves rather than using it for exploitation, but the nature of the peacetime maneuvers made this difficult. Most writers recognized this mission as important, particularly within the German framework of mobile warfare. Schlieffen certainly stressed this in his comments on cavalry, but in the practical world of peacetime training, other matters took priority.[125] The peacetime organization of the cavalry, moreover, was not conducive to training for large-scale reconnaissance.

After 1890 the German army had no peacetime cavalry divisions, with the exception of the Guards Cavalry Division.[126] Instead, cavalry units were assigned to corps and divisions, with plans to form ten ad hoc divisions (of six regiments each) for use as "field army cavalry"; the rest would remain in their divisions as "division cavalry" for local battles and reconnaissance.[127] Schlieffen attempted to create ten "cavalry inspections," which would form command elements for the newly created divisions upon mobilization, but the War Ministry's opposition left the army with an unsatisfactory half measure. In 1913 the general inspector of cavalry warned that the only way to enable the cavalry to perform its missions was to create peacetime divisions and incorporate them into corps.[128] Even the younger Moltke was opposed to establishing more peacetime cavalry divisions, despite the importance of both reconnaissance and exploitation in his campaign concepts on both fronts.[129]

The cavalry's organization for war reflected these divergent views of its major functions. The army divided its 547 cavalry squadrons into two fundamentally different groups. Upon mobilization, each regiment assigned as "division cavalry" joined an army corps, which usually assigned each of its two squadrons to a division for local tasks of reconnaissance, security, or combat. The remaining regiments, the "army cavalry," formed independent divisions within ad hoc corps. Their anticipated missions were strategic reconnaissance and exploitation. Sharp disagreements arose between those who wanted more division cavalry and those who wanted to form more and stronger formations in the army cavalry.[130]

In 1898 the army established two additional cavalry inspections and a *Generalinspektion* of cavalry to oversee peacetime training.[131] Beginning in 1909 the army conducted large cavalry exercises annually, usually with five or six ad hoc divisions, despite the general inspector's urgent argument that only the peacetime establishment of both divisions and corps would allow proper training. In theory, a full-strength cavalry division would have had 1,000 to 1,200 rifles (about the same as an infantry battalion), twelve guns of light artillery, and one mounted machine gun battalion. But because so many regiments remained with the divisions, the branch lacked the forces to fill up even the ad hoc formations in 1914.[132] Some regiments thus entered the war with only four squadrons rather than the six that should have been available, and overall, the branch lacked the skill in large-scale operations that many thinkers, from Schlichting onward, thought necessary.[133]

Some of the blame can rightly be laid at the feet of the first general inspector, General Edler von der Planitz, but clearly a much larger institutional pathology was at work, and not even those who planned Germany's future wars could overcome it.[134] As it turned out, the army went to war in 1914 with four ad hoc "high cavalry commands," lacking the usual array of corps support elements and continuity of experience in training for the tasks anticipated. Not even this inadequate measure was available in the east.[135]

Upon mobilization in 1914, the army had 110 active, 33 reserve, and 19 *Landwehr* cavalry regiments. Each active regiment took four squadrons into the field and left one in garrison to provide and train replacements. The six exceptional regiments had six squadrons. The reserve and *Landwehr* regiments had three squadrons each. A regiment of four squadrons had 36 officers and 709 enlisted soldiers. In addition to its individual mounts, a regiment had sixty horses to pull its nine wagons carrying bridges, communications equipment, medical support, food, and fodder.[136]

Artillery

The third major arm, the artillery, has attracted numerous criticisms for its alleged unwillingness to adapt to the challenges of new technology and for a bureaucratic emphasis on imitating the mounted maneuvers of the cavalry.[137] But careful scholarship has shown that such facile generalizations, however pleasing to those who would like to find fault with the Prussian army, must be balanced by a recognition of the more practical considerations confronting a branch in which technology produced decisive change and dangerous foreign competition between 1871 and 1914.

The Prussian artillery had a checkered history prior to the foundation of the German Empire. Scharnhorst had led the effort to revive the branch during the wars of unification, producing a handbook for artillery and establishing the *Artillerie-Prüfungs-Kommission* (Artillery Examination Commission), a fundamental innovation in the long-term development of the branch.[138] In subsequent years the search for artillery with sufficient mobility to move with the infantry led to increased emphasis on the horse artillery, until, as Showalter states, the so-called cavalry spirit in the artillery turned the guns into "useless ballast."[139]

Social factors may have strengthened this tendency. Normally, only noblemen could hope to have careers in the cavalry. Aspiring bourgeois men, able and willing to cope with the mathematical and technical challenges that allegedly discouraged aristocrats from enlisting in the artillery, joined the branch and attempted to attain what was unavailable to them in the mounted arm. Exceptions existed, of course, and such notables as Prince Friedrich Karl and Count Alfred von Waldersee made their careers in the artillery.

The performance of the Prussian artillery in the war against Austria (1866) left much to be desired. Its smoothbore guns could not counter the Austrian rifled cannon, and its commanders frequently employed their guns piecemeal or saw their batteries decimated by enemy fire.[140] The Prussian artillery was slow to deploy, slow to fire, and slow to move up to the battlefronts. As a whole, officers lacked initiative and exhibited an unwillingness to accept responsibility for action when orders were lacking.[141] Moltke addressed some of these problems in his 1869 *Instructions for Large Unit Commanders*, and the army modernized its artillery's weaponry by 1870. The army established the Artillery Gunnery School in 1867, and by 1870, the field artillery's ability to maneuver and fire had improved greatly.[142] Even then, however, the artillery lacked a doctrinal manual to govern its tactical use and training.

The artillery redeemed itself in the Franco-Prussian War. Krupp's new generation of rifled cannons proved superior to those of the army's French opponents, while more effective deployment in massed lines contributed substantially to a number of Prussian victories. Commanders accepted Moltke's admonition to place their artillery among the forward units as their corps advanced, allowing artillerymen to employ their guns in a more timely manner.[143] Artillery leaders concluded that long-range duels against the enemy were a waste of time and began to concentrate their efforts on direct support to the infantry, a doctrinal point that became a major source of disagreement by the turn of the century. Generally speaking, although the artillery emerged from the war with the same glittering reputation the infantry had earned in 1866, its leaders recognized that some improvements were necessary.[144] The heavy artillery, however, showed little if any improvement in attacking fortresses, despite a substantial increase in numbers since the war against Denmark.[145]

At this point, the two preliminary lessons converged around the perceived need for improvements in artillery and munitions. The *Prüfungs-Kommission* recognized that forward batteries, sometimes threatened by enemy small-arms fire, needed a longer-range cannon to suppress enemy infantry fire. Increased velocity would improve accuracy in this mission, but it would also assist in the engagement of enemy artillery. The artillery branch decided that this mission could be more productively pursued by attempting to kill or wound crews than by attempting to destroy or damage their guns. Thus, improved shrapnel and muzzle velocity, along with an improved ability to keep pace with the infantry in mobile battles, became the desiderata stemming from the wars of unification. The problem was that better accuracy depended on better gunnery.[146]

The most important change immediately after the wars of unification was the separation of the artillery into two branches. Prior to this separation, which took effect between 1872 and 1874, the field artillery and the fortress artillery had constituted a single branch.[147] Henceforth they became separate branches for all practical purposes, and the fortress artillery was given the somewhat denigrating name "foot artillery." The branches initially maintained a single general inspector to provide some lingering if minimal unity. In 1887 the foot artillery received its own general inspector, and the last vestiges of unity disappeared. This separation has attracted the criticism and ridicule of historians, and although it may have been a mistake, given the vast changes in artillery after 1900, there were solid reasons for adopting this measure in 1872.[148]

As artillery became more technical and sophisticated, and as siege artillery and field artillery equipment and methods changed, officers and men found it increasingly difficult to move back and forth between the field units and the fortresses and to master the tasks of both. Moreover, the Prussian siege artillery had been anything but impressive in 1870–1871, being a mixture of amateurism and improvisation. The highly respected inspector of artillery, General der Artillerie Gustav von Hindersin, had argued as early as 1870 for separating the branches, partly because of his experience at Düppel in 1864.[149] In proposing a separation in a 24 January 1870 memorandum, Hindersin argued that the "field and fortress artillery had increasingly gone down separate paths," a conclusion that the experiences of 1870–1871 seemed to validate.[150] Although historians have concluded that the separation was a mistake, officers at the time were by no means unanimous in their views.[151]

The real problem was that Hindersin's successor as inspector of artillery, General der Kavallerie Theophilus von Podbielski, tried to convert the field artillery to a branch of the cavalry. Podbielski, who held the position until 1879, was even opposed to having a common general inspector. He emphasized cavalry-like formations and stressed movement over gunnery and fire support, even for artillery units whose crews rode wagons rather than horses. As a result, the field artillery lost much of its effectiveness during his lengthy tenure as general inspector. He was particularly known for rushing the artillery into firing configurations too quickly in maneuvers, so even though their formations were splendid and resembled those of the cavalry, they were frequently in no position to provide useful fire support to the infantry. Podbielski's sudden death in 1879 offered prospects for improvement but did not save his reputation.[152]

This excessive emphasis on movement and drills over shooting continued under Podbielski's immediate successors. The various editions of the field artillery regulations, which did not deal with tactics—that is, linking movements, firing, and use of terrain with various kinds of combat missions and support—failed to resolve the problem. The new regulations that appeared in 1873, 1876, and 1881 had much to say about battlefield movements but nothing about cooperation with the infantry or support of the battle, even though, in theory, support of infantry, rather than artillery duels, remained the primary mission.[153] The 1887 edition began to incorporate tactical considerations, such as choosing firing positions that offered protection and using surprise in firing.[154] As was frequently the case in Prussian history, relatively junior officers played important roles in gradually improving the quality of these regulations and in producing the important professional literature that supplemented them and provided the usual body of unofficial theory.[155]

In 1889 field artillery units came under the direct control of corps commanders. Most artillery officers welcomed this, since it meant that their branch would be fully integrated into the army's fighting units on an equal basis with the infantry. Henceforth the inspector of field artillery was limited to technical questions, while corps commanders assumed responsibility for field training, exercises, and personnel matters.[156]

The field artillery received its final prewar regulations in 1907, and by that time, the branch had begun to recover from the effects of the cavalry school of artillery. Ironically, the regulations adopted some of the firing principles of the foot artillery, particularly a return to the massed use of artillery, now using indirect fire from covered positions. They also drew on recent French developments.[157] The branch vigorously updated the 1907 regulations to keep pace with technology and the theoretical debates under way in the literature. The field artillery by then had also acquired a new version of its basic field gun to compete with the famous French 75mm. By 1912, the regulations had undergone 152 formal modifications, rising to 209 by 1914. These were sent to the units individually and discussed in the military journals.[158] During these years the foot artillery also developed a number of technical regulations on firing, munitions, and so forth, but these did not deal with tactics or combined arms.[159]

In the meantime, the foot artillery struggled to improve its capabilities and standing in the army, with limited results at first. The branch's lack of horses restricted it to purely defensive actions, despite the theoretical need to support sieges in offensive campaigns. Without mobility, the branch lost all connections with the field army, even in training. Perhaps the only positive development was that the branch and its regiments used their independence to build a more technically proficient officer corps than might have been possible had the separation not taken place.[160]

Advances in weapons and the army's recognition of the need for mobile heavy firepower to deal with enemy fortifications gradually led to improvements. One of the innovators, a Major Leydhecker, won the artillery essay prize in 1887, but when the army rejected his proposal to incorporate the foot artillery into the field artillery, he left the army. Nevertheless, the concept of integrating the foot artillery into mobile warfare training eventually took hold.[161] In 1887 the General Staff began experiments to provide mobility to 150mm and 210mm guns. In the same year the foot artillery received its own general inspector, who, in contrast to his counterpart in the field artillery, had direct access to the king. In 1888 batteries of the foot artillery took part in the autumn corps maneuvers for the first time.[162] In 1893 the branch received horses and equipment to pull its guns, although it was still dependent on the logistics units (trains) for much of its support. In that year the foot artillery found its place in the field army's mobilization plans for the first time, a development closely linked with Schlieffen's strategic planning.[163] Finally, in 1896, the foot artillery was given the name "heavy artillery of the field army," in recognition of its role in mobile warfare.[164] In that year it also acquired telephones, becoming the first branch to do so.[165]

By 1907, the field and foot artillery had begun to move closer together, as the heavy artillery became more mobile and a more integral part of the field army, and as the field artillery placed more emphasis on realistic tactics. The two branches first trained together in 1909, and exchanges of officers in their respective schools and units began to close the gap. The field artillery even started to lose some of its notoriously anti-intellectual image, as more officers participated in the branch's annual competition for articles on the employment of artillery. In addition, General Heinrich von Rohne's new journal, *Artilleristische Monatshefte*, encouraged both discussion and cooperation.[166]

In the meantime, the heavy artillery gradually became the premier arms of its kind worldwide, although until 1908 it possessed regulations only on the technical aspects of firing. By that time, the new heavy and mobile guns had become an integral part of German training and campaign planning, especially for the western theater. In 1900 competitive firing on the maneuver area at Münster in the kaiser's presence produced a complete victory for the heavy artillery over the field artillery.[167] The branch had become more modern than the field artillery in some respects.[168]

In another development consistent with its expanded role in mobile warfare, in 1908 the foot artillery received its first tactical manual.[169] As one officer wrote in *Militär-Wochenblatt*, with this manual the foot artillery finally emerged from the aura of the "black art" that had enshrouded it, achieving parity with the field artillery. The manual clearly established the foot artillery's place in mobile warfare and recognized that it had become part of the mainstream of combat.[170] It should be noted that moving the heavy guns and munitions of the foot artillery, and heavier artillery in general, was no easy task in the days before motorization and advances in metallurgy came to the rescue.[171]

The branch's organization, particularly upon mobilization, remained less than optimal. The general inspection of foot artillery supervised the branch as a whole, while the two foot artillery inspections functioned in peacetime as a headquarters for the brigades. All headquarters above battalion level were dissolved in wartime, and the battalions became more or less independent, except for tactical employment by the corps or divisions to which they were assigned. As casualties mounted, these battalions acquired inexperienced commanders, sometimes captains or even lieutenants, who lacked experience in their branches.[172]

A number of artillery issues remained under discussion as 1914 approached. Artillerymen of both branches, with the field artillery more prominent, debated the importance of covered positions, indirect fire, command procedures, cooperation with infantry, the artillery duel, and the advantages of shrapnel versus high-explosive munitions. Some of this was related to the increased importance accorded artillery under Schlieffen, some was a result of observation of the wars in South Africa and Manchuria, and some stemmed from advances in technology and weaponry.

The field artillery entered the final twenty years before 1914 armed with a single type of gun: the obsolete field cannon C73/88. It was a compromise based on the need for mobility, the size of the horse team, the desirability of improved range, and power. Its black-powder rounds lacked sufficient explosive effects to destroy field fortifications, but increased reliance on shrapnel made them dangerous to enemy gun crews and infantry in the open. It was, of course, a direct-fire weapon, dependent on rapid movement to carefully chosen positions.[173]

A number of technical developments had made the need for a new gun and new tactics imperative by 1896. Cordite replaced black powder and removed the vast clouds of smoke that had traditionally masked batteries. This improved the artillerymen's fields of vision but also their own visibility to the enemy. New mechanisms, still based primarily on springs and spades, had reduced recoil, although the process of getting such devices approved was difficult. Konrad Haussner, an engineer working for Krupp, devised a recoil system for field artillery pieces in 1888, but it took almost a decade of tests and litigation over patents before the Haussner system was accepted.[174]

To modernize the field artillery, the *Prüfungs-Kommission* adopted a new gun in 1896: the field cannon C/96. But this 77mm piece was utterly obsolete by the time it arrived in the units, primarily because the French had introduced the famous "75," the first truly rapid-fire gun. Its hydraulic recoil system allowed an unprecedented rate of fire, while its range offered an improved ability for massed batteries to blanket areas with suppressive fire. Its purpose, in fact, was precisely that, rather than the destruction of entrenchments. The new French gun was, in the words of one officer-historian, "an astonishing advance in armaments."[175] With the Haussner system still tied up in patent litigation, there was no immediate German response. As a result, much of the army's mobile artillery support became obsolete almost overnight.[176] On the plus side, a new light howitzer, introduced in 1898 and equipped with a recoil mechanism in 1909, greatly improved the artillery's ability to conduct indirect, high-angle fire.[177]

In 1905 the German army produced its answer to the French 75, a modification of its basic gun known as the FK 96 n.A. (field cannon 96 new type). It was nearly equal to the French 75 in ballistics and at least equal in most other respects, except for rate of fire. Its protective shield was better, as were its fire direction equipment and its brakes, based on the Haussner recoil system. The FK 96 n.A., moreover, required a smaller supporting crew. Most scholars now agree with contemporary German artillerymen that by 1914, the basic German field gun was the rough equivalent of the French 75, giving the French at best a marginal superiority in this element of field artillery.[178] The main advantages of the French 75mm gun over the

German 77mm were a slightly heavier round (16 pounds versus 15) and a slightly greater velocity (1,735 feet per second versus 1,525). These were marginal advantages, however. Direct-fire cannons using shrapnel as their main munitions were quickly passing into obsolescence, as indirect fire using howitzers and high-explosive rounds against field fortifications became more important.

The Germans were superior in the area of field howitzers from 1898 onward. Discussions of the superiority of the French 75mm field gun over the German FK 96 n.A. should not obscure the other part of the German field artillery in 1914—the light howitzer model 98/09. Whereas the 75mm gun was virtually the only equipment available to the French, about 20 percent of the German field artillery inventory consisted of howitzers, superior weapons for the bombarding of fortifications and indirect fire. After 1899, each corps and eventually each division had a battalion-sized unit equipped with the light field howitzer 98, 105mm caliber, with a range of 6,300 yards. It was particularly suitable for engaging field fortifications with high-angle, indirect fire from covered positions. Known later as the light field howitzer 98/09, it proved to be an excellent weapon in the positional war of 1914–1918.[179] In 1914 the Germans went to war with 1,260 of these howitzers, far greater than the number of similar weapons in their opponents' inventories. Between 1905 and 1913 the Germans also improved their fire control, developed the panoramic telescope, and improved their use of telephones.[180]

German artillery had three kinds of munitions by 1914: high explosive, shrapnel, and the so-called common round, which was a mixture of high explosives and shrapnel. The common round proved to be less useful, and the Germans soon found themselves with too much shrapnel and common rounds and not enough high-explosive ammunition.[181] While the Germans used batteries of six guns, the French used batteries of four, which proved superior, particularly in the period of mobile warfare in 1914.[182]

The German artillery was even more superior in the area of heavy field howitzers. The foot artillery began to acquire the heavy field howitzer 02 in 1903. This 150mm howitzer had a range of 7,450 yards, an explosive shell of 90 pounds, and remarkable mobility for such a heavy weapon. With some modifications, it too proved to be a workhorse of the First World War. In 1914 each active army corps had sixteen of these weapons organized in four batteries of four guns each. A small number of the heavy mortars, in calibers of 210mm, 305mm, and 420mm, were also available in 1914. The Germans had 256 of the 210mm mortars available in 1914, with 112 available for the field army; these were organized into battalions of two batteries with four tubes each. The 305mm, disguised by the name "heavy coastal mortar," became available in 1909, but only 12 were available in 1914. To deal with modern fortifications of the French eastern defensive system, the foot artillery also developed the 420mm mortar, with a range of 14,000 yards, deployed by railroad; a smaller version with a range of 9,300 yards was moved by trucks. Seven tubes were available in 1914, and they were one of the prewar period's best-kept secrets, not even being mentioned in the classified *Taschenbuch des Generalstabsoffiziers* of 1914.[183]

The primary debate on firing positions just before 1914 was not the desirability of using covered positions but whether all artillery should use them in every case. The prewar field artillery regulations gave open positions (direct fire) somewhat more emphasis, particularly where rapid fire in support of the infantry was necessary, as would be the case in a war of movement. Moreover, as the friendly attack advanced, the artillery would have to give up the advantage of its cover and move forward to open positions.[184] Many German artillerymen questioned whether covered positions would be available and doubted that reserve artillery units would have the skill needed to bring indirect fire to bear quickly enough.[185] Some corps commanders simply refused to allow their units to train to fire at distances greater than three miles (five kilometers). Instead, they placed an excessive emphasis on direct fire, mobility, and proximity to the infantry.[186] An effort to define and develop doctrine for "almost" covered positions proved abortive, and even the most vocal advocates had abandoned that position by 1910.[187]

Those who doubted the efficacy of total reliance on covered positions, which included the army's foremost artillery expert, General Heinrich Rohne, doubted that aerial observers would always enable the adjustment of fire rapidly enough to support the infantry.[188] Linnenkohl is probably correct that many artillerymen failed to fully consider the lessons from the Russo-Japanese War, where uncovered artillery suffered grievous losses, although advocates of covered positions cited the Japanese use of indirect fire.[189]

A related issue that divided leading writers was the old one of the artillery duel. As previously mentioned, most German artillerymen had concluded at the end of the wars of unification that the classic artillery duel was a thing of the past. Considering the heavy infantry losses in 1870, they stressed that the artillery's main task was to attack the enemy's infantry.[190] The 1907 drill regulations recognized for the first time that the artillery's main object was to support the infantry rather than to gain fire superiority over the enemy artillery.[191] The classic artillery duel, in this view, was obsolete.[192] The French army had long accepted that point of view.[193]

By 1910, numerous officers argued to the contrary. Even the inspector of the field artillery seemed to take an equivocal position, arguing in his 1910 report on gunnery that destruction of the enemy artillery, not neutralization, was the best way to assist the infantry.[194] These officers cited the equivocal portions of the regulations and pointed to the increased availability of howitzers, whose indirect fire could engage enemy artillery. In effect, some wanted the direct-fire guns to engage the enemy's infantry while the howitzers worked against his artillery.[195] Their warnings—that the artillery must be prepared to do both—were reasonable and were not that far from the positions of Rohne and Bernhardi. As the war began, both official doctrine and actual expectations allowed commanders the flexibility to direct their artillery according to the local situation.[196] This, of course, was related to the traditional Prussian reluctance to dictate to the local commander, but in this case, it also raised the question of who actually commanded the artillery in combat.

In 1899 the Germans abolished the concept of corps field artillery and subordinated the regiments to the divisions. This did away with any lingering concept of an "artillery reserve," which seemed to be a waste of assets, a view broadly in accordance with modern artillery thought.[197] The local commander of the combat units, usually the division commander, thus assumed overall command of the artillery formations assigned to him. In effect, the division commander was supposed to assign missions and priorities to the artillery as he planned the battle, and he was supposed to control them as the battle developed, without interfering in the details of their firing. Eventually, many senior officers came to believe that this control must become tighter in order to maintain fire on critical points.[198] Many artillery officers and others maintained that once the battle began, the commanders of the artillery should be responsible for lifting and shifting fires and for moving their batteries.[199] Bernhardi and Rohne once again found themselves on opposite sides, with Bernhardi demanding more independence for the artillery commanders and Rohne proposing to solve the problem by collocation.[200] A 1912 revision of the artillery regulations seems to have tightened control under the infantry commander.[201]

Technology and Modernization

Shortly after the First World War, several officers criticized the army's alleged reluctance to incorporate technological advances into its weapons and equipment. Karl Jüstrow's *Feldherr und Kriegstechnik* (The Supreme Commander and the Technology of War) broadened the early criticism into a major and enduring indictment of the Prussian army. This became a staple of subsequent criticisms of the army, as historians blamed the alleged reluctance to adapt to modernity on the aristocratic ethos of the officer corps, the stubbornness and bureaucratic behavior of the General Staff and the War Ministry, and a long-term overvaluation of moral over material factors extending all the way back to Clausewitz. There is an element of truth in all these accusations, but they, too, can be taken too far.[202]

Two historians have convincingly argued against the stereotype, concluding that the Germans were in no way inferior to other European armies in their willingness to embrace proven technology, particularly in the years during and after Karl von Einem's tenure as war minister. The Germans moved somewhat more slowly than the French, but they were more thorough in testing and more careful in adopting expensive changes.[203] Prussia's leaders cautiously adopted innovations when their addition to the army's combat capability was worth the cost and when they fit within the broad outlines of the army's philosophy of war fighting. Arden Bucholz was certainly correct in his argument that the General Staff, with only limited authority in this area, generally favored changes in equipment directly related to transportation, weapons, and communications, while the War Ministry and some field commanders were "more reticent."[204] The following sections discuss some of the areas in which the Prussian army moved to adapt to technological changes prior to 1914.

During the last decade before the war, the army adopted several types of new equipment and weaponry to enhance its combat power, mobility, and ability to direct its forces over the extended battlefields of a future war. These included substantial advances in airplanes, a modified rifle and upgraded cartridge, improvements in artillery, development of the first modern heavy and light mortars, wire communications, radios, motorized vehicles, optical devices for artillery, mobile field kitchens, improved binoculars, low-visibility uniforms, grenades, and light-based signaling equipment. Some of these innovations resulted from observations of the wars in South Africa and Manchuria, while others came out of the widespread discussions of technical developments in the military literature across the continent.[205] In

1903 the army established the Military-Technical Academy to further the knowledge and skills of officers from various branches. Students came from Prussian, Saxon, and Württemberg contingents.[206] By 1914, the *Militär-Wochenblatt* had a regular section devoted to technology.[207]

Communications

The Prussian army recognized the importance of communications in directing the large-scale operations inherent to modern war. Even though the army's theory held fast to the elder Moltke's concepts of commanding by directive and trusting subordinate initiative, its substantial but deeply flawed communications system had been developed along the lines envisioned in Schlieffen's essay "The Supreme Commander."

The first step toward creating modern communications for conducting operations and fighting battles was taken in 1896. That year the army converted a company of the Guards Combat Engineer Battalion into a telegraph company to develop that branch, which officially came into existence on 1 October 1899. The first such battalion had contingents from Saxony and Württemberg. The Bavarian army created its first communications unit in 1901. The branch grew rapidly thereafter, acquiring its own inspector in 1913. At the outbreak of the war, the communications units (*Nachrichten Truppe*) mobilized a total strength of about 550 officers and 5,800 enlisted men. By the end of the war, these numbers had risen to about 4,400 and 185,000, respectively.[208]

In 1914 the army's communications network had three key elements: telegraph, telephone, and radio.[209] Its intertheater communications depended on the empire's well-developed telegraph system, a more limited phone system, and its six main radio stations located in Cologne, Metz, Strassburg, Posen, Thorn, and Königsberg. The telegraph and phone systems ended at the empire's frontiers and were dependent on the seizure or repair of enemy lines and the local laying of new wires to extend their capabilities as the German army advanced.

The field army was dependent on telephones and radios to bridge the gaps between theater and field army commanders and their combat units. After years of attempting to develop specialized units to lay telegraph wires from headquarters to field units, continuing problems in maneuvers convinced the army to abandon its tactical telegraph system in 1910.[210] In its place, the army prepared to rely on field telephones and radios, a transition that was well under way when the war began in

1914. The field telephone units showed great promise, but in 1914 both the limitations of early technology (lack of amplifiers) and the rapidity of movement rendered continuous and effective communications very problematic. Prewar maneuvers, especially those between 1909 and 1911, had offered clear indications that the communications system could not meet the demands placed on it. The army realized it would have to use staff officers to deliver at least some messages in the traditional manner.[211] Field radios suffered from limited range, marginal reliability, and cumbersome encryption systems.

The communications system was lacking in quantity as well as quality in 1914, considering the nature of the impending campaign. Each field army had a radio detachment, as did each corps and division headquarters. Each corps also had a telephone section of twelve sets of equipment and about 62 miles (100 kilometers) of wire.[212] The cavalry divisions had a single radio station each. The army had about sixty radio sets available upon mobilization, a number that, in retrospect, was clearly insufficient but was at least the equivalent of all other European armies. Field telephones had a maximum effective range of about 25 miles, while the field radios had ranges of 150 to 180 miles. The French and British, however, had the benefit of the French civilian telegraph and telephone networks.[213]

Conceptually, the German process of communicating from the front units to higher headquarters was seriously flawed. Lower headquarters were responsible for maintaining communications and contact with higher headquarters. This left the initiative in the wrong hands, particularly since the key combat leaders—the corps commanders—were famously independent and reluctant to tolerate supervision. Acting in a narrow interpretation of the army's traditional principles of subordinate independence and initiative, high commanders seldom welcomed the continuous oversight offered by modern communications systems. In addition, German doctrine placed too little emphasis on lateral communications at the army level, where the all-powerful commanders were frequently reluctant to surrender any of their freedom of action. The entire system required a highly capable, energetic, and strong-willed commander at the top.[214]

Mobility

By 1900, the army had recognized the potential significance of motorized vehicles for mobile warfare. The transportation units received their own *Inspektion* in 1899 and, reflecting an increase in numbers and status, a *General-Inspektion* in 1911. The 1909 kaiser maneuvers had provided further evidence of the importance of both automobiles and trucks, despite continuing doubts about off-road capabilities. The Germans hoped to solve the financial problem of prewar purchases by combining regular motorized transport units and private vehicles. This was the origin of the "voluntary automobile corps" of 1914. By that year, the army had about 200 officers, 8,000 enlisted men, and 4,000 motorized vehicles in its inventory. It also hoped to use 5,000 private vehicles in case of war. The branch published its first modern manual in 1913. Here, as in other areas, the war found the army in a state of transformation, not one of blind resistance to technological and industrial developments.[215]

Aviation and Antiaircraft Defense

The emergence of aviation as another important element of war fighting came late in the period before the First World War, but the pace of its progress between 1908 and 1918 was more rapid than in any subsequent period of its history. The Prussian army demonstrated its usual cautious pragmatism in expending limited resources on a new technological development and moved forward decisively only when a new device clearly had an important place in the framework of its way of war. Although the German army had maintained balloon units since 1870, this equipment had failed to produce the spectacular results predicted by enthusiasts.[216] Nevertheless, the army maintained a small number of tethered balloon units for aerial observation, photography, and early experiments in radio telegraphy. In 1914 the army had such units available for each field army and one for use in Schleswig-Holstein. Eleven of the larger fortresses also had tethered balloon detachments.[217]

Around 1900, the early experiments of Count Ferdinand von Zeppelin—whom Emperor Wilhelm II called the "most important German of the twentieth century"—seemed to offer a new solution.[218] Zeppelin's early designs for dirigibles offered the best prospects for improvements in reconnaissance and transport until 1910.[219] The Prussian army invested moderate amounts in these "flying ships" and gave them the bulk of the available procurement funds until just before the First World War began. When the airplane emerged as a more capable instrument after 1909, the army placed sufficient emphasis on it to acquire a rough parity with the French by 1914.[220]

The French were the first to acquire a military dirigible (1906), and the Germans soon followed suit. From then until 1914, all the European armies continued to improve their airships and gradually acquired more of them.[221] The continuing German interest, sometimes an object of ridicule, was thus neither illogical nor backward. The Germans soon took the lead in developing dirigibles, but their efforts in this area had mixed results. The French, probably spurred by their rival's progress, began to acquire airplanes and took a wide early lead in that field.[222] The Germans' success in improving their dirigibles probably slowed the army's turn to heavier-than-air aviation, and the great popular enthusiasm for dirigibles in Germany may have made it difficult to interest civilian firms in airplanes. The army thus turned to its own internal resources to design and develop its first aircraft.[223]

The dazzling French performance at the Reims air show in 1909 may be seen as the turning point for German interest in military airplanes.[224] Nevertheless, the army continued to develop and use dirigibles, even though their shortcomings became more obvious over time. In October 1909 a General Staff report on technical developments noted the successful performance of dirigibles in that year's kaiser maneuvers but also cautioned that they could not fly above 3,000 feet, which made them vulnerable to ground fire and thus not ready for war. The same report noted the disconcerting results of the Reims air show and the French lead in the development of airplanes. It warned of the certainty that airplanes would soon have military utility but also cautioned that this should not be overestimated.[225]

Of course, the Germans were well aware, even as early as 1909, that the French were far advanced in fielding military aircraft. The General Staff followed these developments carefully and produced detailed reports on aviation in the French maneuvers in 1911, 1912, and 1913.[226] Beginning at least in 1913, German observers also prepared reports on the English army's aviation and kept track of other foreign developments through press articles of various kinds.[227] In September 1912 Moltke warned the War Ministry that Germany could overcome the great French advantage in this area of "greatest importance" only through extraordinary means. He apparently thought the War Ministry, not the Reichstag, was the chief obstacle, since he expressed confidence that the latter would provide the funds if requested.[228]

Between 1909 and 1914 the dirigible and the airplane competed for resources, even though the unit cost of the former was several times that of the latter. Many factors, including the much larger ground crews and the other required infrastructure, further increased the costs of dirigibles. The long-term trend was clear in the procurement budgets for those years: in 1909 airplanes consumed only about 1 percent of the total annual appropriations for aircraft acquisitions of all types, but by 1914 their share exceeded 50 percent of what was still a modest if rapidly increasing amount.[229] Additional support came from a cooperative effort by the government and private industry in the form of the National Aviation Fund. This semiprivate institution, headed by Prince Heinrich of Prussia, raised substantial amounts of money to purchase airplanes for the army. The fund provided sufficient support in 1912 to underwrite about half the army's total airplane purchases. Although it may have hindered the development of the civilian aviation industry in the long run, the fund was a significant boost for the army. Another semiprivate agency, the German Research Institute for Aviation, assisted in answering technical questions.[230]

By the end of the autumn maneuvers of 1911, both the French and the Germans had come to recognize the advantages of airplanes over dirigibles for reconnaissance. Although dirigibles could remain aloft for much longer periods, cruise great distances, and carefully observe because of their low speed, they also had significant drawbacks. They were very vulnerable to artillery used in the antiaircraft role. Airplanes were less dependent on weather, especially unfavorable winds. They were cheaper to maintain and support and could be deployed more easily to the fighting fronts. Airplanes were, at the time, nearly invulnerable to ground fire and could fly very low over enemy positions. Finally, the airplane had strong backers on the General Staff. Major Erich Ludendorff, chief of the Mobilization Section, forcefully recommended to the War Ministry in early 1913 the expansion of the army's air arm. The die had thus been cast, although dirigibles remained in limited service through much of the First World War.[231]

By 1914, Prussian doctrine envisioned that the primary role of aircraft in warfare would be reconnaissance, a particularly important function in the kind of war anticipated in German theory and strategy. The doctrine by no means ignored other potential missions for airplanes, but these were realities only in embryonic form.[232] Even in 1913, evidence indicated that dirigibles might be better than airplanes for dropping bombs. Hans von Beseler, one of the army's most intellectual General Staff officers, raised the possibility of using dirigibles to drop bombs on vehicle parks, concentrations of soldiers, and harbors. According to another officer, the

Italian army's use of bombing attacks by airplanes in North Africa suggested that not much could be accomplished by such missions. Dirigibles
were better for bombing, he argued, buttressing his arguments with fulsome praise for Zeppelin and his work.[233]

A General Staff study of the 1911 kaiser maneuvers reported that the
airplane had redefined deep reconnaissance (*Fernaufklärung*) and that
even mediocre aerial reconnaissance was better than that conducted by
the best cavalry.[234] The 1912 *Guidelines for Instruction in Tactics at the Royal
War Schools* emphasized the role airplanes would play in reconnaissance
and enumerated their advantages over dirigibles. The same guidelines
recognized that both airplanes and dirigibles had become more effective
than cavalry for strategic reconnaissance.[235] By 1913, the revolutionary
possibilities of aerial reconnaissance had begun to be noted even in Germany's nonmilitary periodicals, a certain sign of its ascendance over the
cavalry. Still, some cavalry leaders clung to their traditional if almost completely outmoded combat role.[236]

During the final three years before the war began, the army's literature began to examine other roles for airplanes, as well as the need to
develop measures to counter the effects of enemy aircraft. These roles
included spotting for artillery fire, communications, and aerial photography.[237] Since 1912, the army's air arm had been developing the art of
aerial photography, and by 1914, each aviation unit attached to the major
fortresses had cameras for this purpose.[238] In the fall of 1912 the general
inspector of foot artillery and the inspector of field artillery agreed that aircraft would be indispensable for adjusting fire. Moltke used their reports
to convince the War Ministry of the "urgent necessity" of permanently attaching airplanes to the artillery for additional research and to improve organizational arrangements.[239] In the fall of 1912 the army formed a special
command at Jüteborg for the systematic study of adjusting artillery fire
with aircraft, an area in which the French were still ahead.[240] The subject
of aerial combat also attracted interest, but machine guns were too heavy
for most prewar aircraft.[241]

The army's key responsible institutions, the General Staff and the War
Ministry, initially reacted very differently to aircraft. The General Staff was
much more enthusiastic about aviation than was the usually more conservative War Ministry. In 1908 Moltke established a technical section in the
General Staff to study progress in airplanes, but he had to convince the
War Ministry because it controlled the army's budget.[242] In 1910, possibly
in an effort to stir the hesitant War Ministry into action, Moltke raised

a number of fundamental questions about the use and development of aircraft, including the kinds of armaments to be placed on airplanes; the weight of munitions that could be dropped, and with what accuracy; problems encountered in night flying and landing; and how to enable aviators to distinguish friendly ground units from the enemy (use of flags).[243] In a letter to the war minister dated 2 March 1911, Moltke warned of the vulnerability of dirigibles to antiaircraft fire and of their persistent shortcomings.[244] By March 1912, the War Ministry had decided to increase financial support for airplanes, and from then until the summer of 1914, the Germans quickly made up ground previously lost to the French.[245]

In June 1913 Moltke developed a plan for the long-term development of the army's air arm, with the goal of having 528 airplanes of various kinds by April 1914 and nearly 1,800 by April 1916. Previous plans had established that the following headquarters elements would employ and control aircraft units: field armies, corps, cavalry corps, and important fortresses.[246] The most obvious shortcoming was the failure to provide the High Command with dedicated airplane squadrons for centralized strategic reconnaissance. Instead, the General Staff proposed to rely on the flying units of the field armies and corps. Although this was consistent with the army's customary principle of the decentralization of plan execution, it proved to be a serious problem in 1914, especially in light of the lack of communication between field armies and the High Command.[247]

The result of this growing awareness of the importance of airpower was that the Prussian army and, by extension, the German army entered the war in 1914 with a fully competitive air arm, approximately equal in number and quality to any single potential adversary. German industry had overcome the worst of the engine problems by 1914, although its motors were still somewhat inferior to those of the French. Prussia went to war with 450 airplanes, at least 250 of which were intended for active field service. The French had fewer pilots and aircraft available for active duty, but they had a better reserve system. It seems reasonable to agree with the most distinguished historian of early German airpower that the Germans and French were roughly equal in 1914.[248]

The army in 1914 had thirty-three tactical flying squadrons (*Abteilungen*), with six aircraft each, assigned to the army commands and corps. Each squadron had fourteen officers (including seven aircraft commanders and six observers) and about 120 enlisted men. Most of the squadrons had Albatross biplanes with a speed of about 60 miles per hour, an altitude limit of about 3,600 feet, and fuel for about four hours of flight.[249]

On the opposite side of the airpower equation, the Prussian army did not neglect antiaircraft defenses. The army's first serious efforts in this area began in 1905 with the employment of artillery pieces to bring down French observation balloons. Krupp developed a special gun, the balloon defense cannon, for this purpose, but by 1910, attention had started to focus on airplanes. As the war began in 1914, the army had plans to equip each field army with four such guns mounted on trucks and each division (active and reserve) with a battery of four horse-drawn guns. Only about thirty such guns were actually in the units when the war began, and the army assigned them to corps in particularly important areas.[250] The army also attempted to develop antiaircraft defenses by having regular ground units fire their rifles and machine guns, but this was pointless and simply alerted enemy aircraft to the presence of German soldiers. Another factor in imposing fire discipline (only officers could give the order to fire) was the assumption that soldiers and officers generally could not distinguish between enemy and friendly aircraft.[251] A doctrinal manual of 1913, *Guidelines for Instruction of Units on Airplanes and Fighting against Them*, laid out the basic principles.[252]

Preparations for Industrialized Warfare

The German armaments industry was a mixture of governmental arsenals and private enterprise. Its arsenals and shipyards produced rifles, artillery, munitions, ships, and the like. The arsenals contributed about 40 percent of the army's total requirements for weapons before the war began. Krupp, the largest private firm in the armaments business, was one of about a thousand private companies active in this sector. Such business enterprises were only a small part of the German economy and workforce and were not always particularly profitable. The unanswered question was whether the industry could sustain an expanded and prolonged war if that should come to pass.[253]

Concern about the economic and social consequences of a prolonged conflict had been the basis of Schlieffen's doubts that modern states could fight protracted wars with armies of millions and budgets of billions. One aspect of the related "short-war illusion" that allegedly afflicted most European armies prior to 1914 was the lack of comprehensive preparations for a lengthy war. Although peripheral to the German way of fighting wars, this factor merits a closer look. Developments and problems in this area, moreover, illustrate the shortcomings of the German military system. The author of the most comprehensive study of the subject argued that there were three broad questions about German economic preparations for war prior to 1914: How long would the war last? How dangerous would an enemy naval blockade be? What could an effectively blockaded state accomplish economically?[254]

Before addressing these fundamental questions, we must consider the impact of the German Empire's constitutional structure on long-term planning. The empire's fragmented state apparatus had no institution to coordinate either strategic or economic issues among military and civilian agencies. Serious as that was, it was only part of the problem. Bismarck's constitutional structure was highly dependent on personalities, and after the men who were active during the years of unification were gone, their successors, from the emperor on down, were unable to cope with the bureaucratic chaos of the political system. The East Elbian base of the Prussian government further hindered any willingness to involve the Reichstag in questions that might interfere with national political or military strategy.[255] This complete lack of coordination is clear, regardless of which aspect of preparations is examined.

The General Staff, though allegedly a bastion of the short-war illusion, was the only important military or political agency that made even sporadic efforts to address economic preparations. Results, however, depended on the War Ministry, which had sole responsibility for implementing such programs.[256] The War Ministry in turn had to deal with the practical questions of how to organize and fund various programs to prepare for a long war. It had to consider issues of foreign policy, relations with other government agencies, and political relationships with the Reichstag. All these issues made the War Ministry's task a difficult one. This was particularly true because some of these government agencies were notoriously uncooperative and because the last war minister prior to August 1914, Erich von Falkenhayn, shared the confidence of many that any future war would be brief.[257] In a state such as Prussia-Germany, only the emperor could have provided the impetus for coordinated and effective strategic preparations, economic or otherwise.

The military clearly recognized that an effective blockade would have economic and social impacts, particularly in terms of food. In 1874 Justus Scheibert, who had been the Prussian army observer to the American Civil War, noted the vulnerability of the German coast, like that of the Confederacy, to a naval blockade.[258] After 1883 both the General Staff and, later, the War Ministry began to consider this potential problem. The navy, however, used this fear of an effective blockade to buttress its demands for budget increases and to avoid alternative courses of action. In 1911 War Ministry reports examined the food situation and concluded there was no great problem. By 1913, various conferences produced a new sense of urgency but did not result in significant improvements. By then, the War Ministry and the General Staff were trying to act in concert to develop alternatives to overseas imports, but the Imperial Budget Office and other agencies (Prussian and German) declined to make preparations before war had actually begun. The Budget Office even dredged up an 1873 statute that seemed to make such preparations illegal. Equally irresponsible were the beliefs by some that Article 71 of the London Declaration on Sea Law would protect food supplies from British blockade.[259]

In the area of raw materials, it is clear that even the General Staff was relatively disinterested in creating war reserves, even though Moltke certainly had doubts about a short war. Germany had a two- to three-month supply of many kinds of raw materials on hand in August 1914, but shifts in production priorities, protected access to some continental sources, and reductions in exports meant that the crisis was not as immediately serious as older accounts have portrayed. Although Moltke acted much less energetically on this issue than on food supplies, historians still disagree about whether military or civilian agencies are primarily to blame for the lack of preparation. In any case, the Germans went into the war with serious potential shortcomings in many materials and managed to cope with the blockade only by a combination of rapid scientific development of alternatives, production shifts, extreme discipline, and recycling.[260]

Finally, there is the question of financial preparations, another area in which the military had an important interest but only a minor direct role. Most observers recognized that war would disrupt the nation's financial institutions and budgets, but even the most pessimistic cost estimates were but a fraction of real expenditures. Last-minute efforts in 1913 to expand cash reserves to support the first few months of war were unimportant. The empire's gold reserves in 1913 were about 936 million marks, while the actual costs of the war averaged 45.7 billion gold marks annually.[261]

Concluding Remarks

As an institution in the prewar period, the imperial German army presents an interesting mixture of old and new. Although the army expanded considerably over the period 1874–1913, ultimately becoming a cadre army capable of generating a mass force, the practices related to command echelons were quite different. The highest levels of the German army leadership consisted of a small group of people who were connected by background, marriage, and common experience. Thus the selection of commanders and their pairing with chiefs of staff had an almost eighteenth-century quality. Since officers were well acquainted with one another, the Military Cabinet could pair a commander and a chief of staff on the basis of compatibility and personality rather than strict adherence to criteria such as rank and seniority. Although this system had an almost archaic aspect, it nonetheless produced some of the most successful military marriages in military history.

In many other ways, however, the German army had to confront change that was proceeding at a bewildering pace. Change was also occurring in ways the German army had never needed to consider before, especially after 1890. Internally, the army's position at the top of heap with regard to monetary resources was challenged. This was especially true after Wilhelm II's decision to pursue *Weltpolitik* and the rise of Alfred von Tirpitz as a skilled bureaucratic infighter. Although the navy's budget never got beyond 55 percent of the army's budget, the army found itself in the unaccustomed position of having to fight for its share of finite resources.

Militarily, the combat branches of the army likewise wrestled with the challenges of modernity and rapid technological change. Of the three traditional branches, only the cavalry remained wedded to what were widely considered outmoded forms of combat. The artillery, especially after 1890, found itself involved in an arms race with the French, while also dealing with arcane patent procedures that slowed the development and fielding of new weapons systems. Ultimately, the artillery lagged slightly behind the French in field artillery, while forging well ahead in heavy artillery. The infantry also embraced technological change. Adopting a bolt-action rifle did not separate it from other European armies, but the German army's embrace of the machine gun put it well ahead of its most likely opponents.[262]

With regard to the emerging technologies of the early twentieth century, the army took an approach marked by reasonable caution, making it no different from its continental rivals. The Russian Second Army in the Tannenberg campaign, for example, had 350 miles of telephone wire available for its five corps, or an average of 70 miles of wire per corps; this was comparable to the 62 miles for a German corps.[263] It is fair to say that while the German army recognized the potential of both the telephone and the radio, it had not yet figured out how to fully exploit that potential. The army took the lead in the development of aircraft, and both Moltke and Ludendorff, then a rising star in the officer corps, were prescient in recognizing the possibilities. The airship, however, was already a successful technology, and it was not apparent in 1914 that the airship had reached its apex as a technology. The most accurate appraisal of the possibilities and limitations of these emerging technologies would come through the experience of combat. Absent that, a certain degree of plausible speculation was a necessity.

As the German army wrestled with these developments, it also expanded to three times its size in 1870. This had impacts far beyond those of testing, production, and fielding. The German army, like its European counterparts, had to figure out what war would look like while using these new weapons systems on a mass scale. This led to extended arguments among officers, conducted both in private and in public. These arguments are examined in the next chapter.

CHAPTER FOUR

GERMAN THEORY AND DOCTRINE
TO 1914

The imperial German military establishment inherited a rich intellectual tradition from its Prussian predecessor. The work of the reformers of the Napoleonic era and its aftermath, spearheaded by Gerhard von Scharnhorst and especially Carl von Clausewitz, had provided the Prussian army with a comprehensive theory of war. The intellectual torch of Clausewitz was taken up by Count Helmuth von Moltke, whose intellectual productivity continued into the first two decades of the imperial period. As time marched on, however, two things were certain—namely, that the pace of technological changes was having a considerable impact on the conduct of warfare and that the aged Moltke and his considerable intellect would soon pass from the scene.

The towering figure and teachings of Count Alfred von Schlieffen dominated Prussian military strategy during the period between Moltke's retirement (1888) and the outbreak of the First World War. Schlieffen served as the chief of the General Staff from 1891 until his retirement at the end of 1905. The fulsome praise of his admirers after 1918 has found its opposite counterpart in the criticisms leveled by recent historians.[1] Also of great importance, however, was Schlieffen's great rival, Sigismund von Schlichting. While Schlieffen left his mark on the history of strategic planning, Schlichting was crucial to the long-term development of modern military theory. Both of them substantially shaped German military thought throughout the period of this study.[2] Schlichting, known only to a few specialists today, was the most creative Prussian theorist in the years after Moltke's retirement.[3] Schlichting's work in revising Prussian tactics set the framework for the discussion of that basic problem throughout the decades between 1880 and 1914, while his theories on strategy formalized Moltke's teachings on the broader conduct of war.[4]

Alfred von Schlieffen

Count Alfred von Schlieffen came into the world on 28 August 1833 in Berlin. His father had risen to the rank of major in the Prussian army and was a landowner in Silesia. His credentials of eligibility for a commission, presented to the Second Guards Uhlan Regiment in 1853, were impeccable. His paternal grandfather had been a Prussian officer, while his mother's father had been a civil servant. The Schlieffen clan, raised to the rank of count in 1812, was a distinguished *Uradel* family whose original title, of Danish origin, dated to at least 1444.[5] The military tradition dominated Alfred's generation as well as those of his predecessors. Two brothers became Prussian generals, and a third was killed in the Franco-Prussian War. His wife, a cousin, was the daughter of a Prussian officer. The Schlieffen family retained its membership in the Lutheran church, which may have been significant in shaping his personality. Remaining outside the official Evangelical church apparently did no harm to his career. As some historians have noted, his background of Hutterian Pietism may have had a major impact on his personality.

Schlieffen received his early education in a private school in Niesky and then attended a well-known humanistic *Gymnasium* in Berlin and the University of Berlin, rather than joining the cadet corps, which provided so many officers for the army.[6] He entered the army as a one-year volunteer, possibly out of a reluctance to face any future war as an officer in the *Landwehr*. Even after receiving his commission, he doubted his prospects for a military career, in part because of his shortsightedness and in part because such careers were too dependent, as he put it, on luck and personality. Nevertheless, he persisted, perhaps because he had no enthusiasm for the legal profession, which seemed the only alternative for a person of his social class and background. He attended the War Academy (1858–1861) and gained regular admission to the General Staff.

Although his early career was reasonably typical for a cavalry officer in the Guards Corps, Schlieffen had some interesting experiences during the wars of unification. He was within ten miles of Vienna when the cease-fire was signed in 1866.[7] In the Franco-Prussian War he served as a General Staff officer with the Grand Duke of Mecklenburg. The duke's mediocre performance resulted in the relief of his General Staff chief, an episode that temporarily cast a long shadow over Schlieffen's own performance and raised questions about his initiative and ability to make difficult decisions.[8] In his official evaluations of Schlieffen's performance, Moltke repeatedly noted that although Schlieffen was an excellent officer, he lacked the initiative and ability to make decisions. This, according to Moltke, made him unfit for high General Staff service and more suited for duty in the units. By 1875, Moltke had reversed his position, concluding that Schlieffen was entirely acceptable for high positions in the General Staff.[9]

Following the death of his wife in 1872, Schlieffen turned his full attention to his military duties with a relentless determination that was remarkable even for General Staff officers.[10] Most contemporaries agreed that Schlieffen became fanatically devoted to his work, that he drove his subordinates to the limits of their abilities, and that he showed no regard for the finer aspects of life such as family and holidays. Schlieffen became equally famous for his keen intelligence and memory, his biting sarcasm, and his vicious intolerance of shortcomings in officers unfortunate enough to be subjected to his critiques after maneuvers or exercises.[11] Gerhard Ritter's image of Schlieffen as a narrow military specialist, interested only in the technical details of his profession, ignorant of the broader political issues, and devoid of other aspects of culture, has dominated the scholarship.[12] Others, particularly Schlieffen's admirers, have attempted to modify this one-sided image by pointing out Schlieffen's tenderness toward his daughters and his readings in philosophy (especially Nietzsche).[13] Nevertheless, even admirers in the old General Staff sometimes unwittingly reinforced the stereotype while defending their former chief.[14]

In most respects, Schlieffen's concepts of preparing the Prussian army for what he saw as the inevitable conflict with France and Russia were consistent with the principles of Moltke and Schlichting, even though the latter became one of Schlieffen's most vocal critics. Schlieffen's writings paralleled the course of his life following his appointment as chief of the General Staff. Prior to his retirement, Schlieffen's main products were campaign plans and staff training exercises of various types, none of which were published until later. After his retirement, he produced a number of historical studies designed to prove the correctness of his theoretical views.[15] Most of these studies represented his efforts to convince the officer corps, and perhaps posterity, to accept his ideas on strategy, although some served more mundane and immediate purposes.[16] Ironically, Schlieffen left no theoretical work on strategy. Instead, his writings focused on practical problems and specific cases. Schlieffen clearly accepted Clausewitz's view that war must serve the goals of strategy, but he apparently agreed with Moltke that military necessity had to take priority in campaign planning and execution.[17]

Encounter Battles and Flanking Attacks

German theory under Schlieffen accepted the traditional Prussian view that warfare consists of two basic types of battles: the large-scale meeting engagement (*Begegnungsgefecht*), in which advancing armies move directly and immediately from the march into large battles, and the battle against an enemy that had had time to deploy and develop a defensive position.[18] Schlieffen thus also accepted (perhaps excessively) the concept, originated by Moltke and refined by Schlichting, that the entire process of the conduct of war—mobilization, deployment to the campaign area, initial large-scale movements (operations), and battles—should be linked in a single concept of the campaign.[19] Schlieffen sometimes used the potentially misleading term *Gesamtschlacht* (whole or all-inclusive battle) to characterize his concept of a single integrated campaign.

During the years he was formulating his ideas on flanking attacks and turning movements, Schlieffen drew his inspiration and examples primarily from the experiences of Frederick the Great. Frederick's brilliant victory at Leuthen seems to have been his primary historical inspiration.[20] In 1909, long after his retirement, Schlieffen encountered the first volume of Hans Delbrück's *History of the Art of War*. He seized upon the Battle of Cannae as the perfect example of annihilation and shifted his emphasis from the single to the double envelopment. During the last years of his life, the old general cited this maneuver as the universal secret of victory, even though he recognized that such a victory required a brilliant commander and a mainly incompetent opponent.[21]

The goal of all major battles—a point that Schlieffen constantly emphasized—is the annihilation of the enemy's field forces. Only this, in Schlieffen's view, could prevent the enemy from regrouping and forcing additional costly struggles. Unlike Schlichting, Schlieffen regarded the great Prussian victory at Königgrätz as only an "ordinary" victory because large parts of the Austrian army had escaped destruction and might have fought another day.[22]

Turning Movements and Annihilation

Schlieffen used the term "annihilation" in the Clausewitzian sense of destruction of the enemy army's ability to continue to resist. Merely defeating the enemy army was not enough; its fighting strength had to be eliminated. Schlieffen argued that two elements were essential to achieve this goal.

The first was a deep strategic envelopment of the enemy's flank or flanks and rear. The second, frequently overlooked, was immediate and aggressive exploitation of tactical victories. He sometimes argued, based on his experiences in 1866, that only exploitation could assure the annihilation of a defeated enemy. Much of Schlieffen's historical writing was an effort to prove that all great commanders sought this goal with these methods.[23]

Schlieffen does not entirely deserve the harsh criticism he has received for his allegedly excessive emphasis on battles of annihilation and his exaggerated emphasis on flank attacks.[24] While stressing turning movements and flanking attacks, Schlieffen also warned that breakthrough battles would sometimes be necessary to create conditions for maneuver and mobile warfare. He particularly recognized that the extended battle lines that characterized the Russo-Japanese War showed that breakthroughs were both necessary and possible under some circumstances. Although Schlieffen warned that commanders must conduct their battles according to the dictates of local circumstances, his didactic exercises and his subsequent writings sought to train Prussia's officer corps to look for what he regarded as the ideal solution: assaulting the enemy's flanks. This was not as one-sided as it might seem. He stressed that successful attacks usually required frontal assaults to fix the enemy so that flanking attacks could be successful. Despite Schlieffen's emphasis on the turning aspects of his great plan, it would be a substantial injustice to conclude that he thought the army could entirely ignore other forms of campaigning and fighting battles.[25]

Schlieffen's emphasis on strategic turning movements (*Umgehung*) and tactical flanking attacks (*Umfassung*) reflected his recognition of the clear superiority of defensive firepower and the likely costly failure of frontal attacks.[26] He agreed with Schlichting that the extended nature of the modern theater of war required the commander to keep his reserves on the flanks, where the decision was expected, rather than in a central position, as conventional wisdom, with its strong emphasis on interior lines, required.[27] Schlieffen and others were trying to avoid the bloody frontal attacks of 1870–1871. In all fairness, they can hardly be blamed for eschewing the very types of frontal attacks that proved so costly and futile between 1914 and 1918.

Frontal Attacks

Although Schlieffen's view of the conduct of a campaign was more rigid than that of Moltke or Schlichting, the Prussian army did not entirely ignore the breakthrough battle or frontal assault. On the contrary, frontal assaults to fix the enemy's center were always a feature of the army's theory on flanking attacks.[28] Nor, contrary to popular opinion, did the army's training of junior officers ignore the difficult problems of frontal attacks when they proved unavoidable.[29] The Prussians, particularly Schlieffen, were convinced (probably correctly) that the French placed too much emphasis on frontal attacks in the alleged style of Napoleon.[30] Schlieffen recognized that if both sides attempted to outflank the other, fronts would be extended and thinned out, making a breakthrough possible. The army's manual for large-unit commanders concluded that breakthroughs were possible if fronts became too extended. Nevertheless, Schlieffen's main point—that any attempt to achieve a frontal breakthrough should be a last resort and that frontal attacks were unlikely to be decisive—was a sensible one.[31]

Command and Control

In devising a solution to the challenges of commanding the large armies fielded by industrialized nations, Schlieffen at first accepted the position of Moltke and the long Prussian tradition of independent subordinate commanders, but he eventually adopted a different position, at least for large units. In his concluding remarks to the 1899 eastern General Staff ride, Schlieffen said the great expanse of a modern theater of war would prevent a commander from directly controlling his subordinates with "calm orders," as was the case in war games. "The execution of movements thus rests largely in the hands of subordinate commanders. They therefore have the duty to understand fully the intention of the supreme commander and to consider the entire situation not just that of their own units. They must conform and subordinate their decisions and orders to the higher intent." He concluded that independence was necessary in decision making and action, but subordinates could carry out their tasks only if they subordinated their actions to the higher intent.[32]

In his famous and controversial essay "Der Krieg in der Gegenwart," published after his retirement, Schlieffen predicted that the supreme commander of the future would control his campaign in a well-appointed headquarters far in the rear, where he would use modern means of communication to monitor developments and issue orders for battles as they developed.[33] Schlieffen thus jettisoned Moltke's faith that subordinate commanders could be relied on to keep their actions within the overall plan of a campaign. He felt that the many misunderstandings and cases of outright disobedience that had occurred in 1866 and 1870–1871 would ruin a campaign in the modern age. Historians and some contemporaries have thus stressed his desire to limit subordinate initiative rather than regard it as an asset to be exploited.[34] It should be noted that these limitations applied primarily to commanders at the field army level. There is no reason to believe that Schlieffen wanted to limit subordinate initiative on the part of tactical commanders. Indeed, throughout his time, army doctrine and the writings of the General Staff continued to stress the need for subordinate initiative in conducting battles and engagements.

Schlieffen's views apparently became more rigid as time passed. In his closing remarks on the General Staff ride in the east in 1894, he said that modern conditions would require local deviations from the overall plan in the absence of orders from the supreme commander. In such cases, the responsibility for "an independent decision" rested on the subordinate commander, who nevertheless had to remain within the overall framework of the operation.[35] But as his plan continued to take shape, Schlieffen gradually became more critical both of Moltke's methods and of his subordinates, and he eventually came to fear the potential failures of his subordinates as much as the actions of the enemy.[36] Indeed, the strategic situation that had given birth to the plan seemed to provide an absolutely compelling reason to prevent modern subordinate commanders from acting as Moltke's had done.[37]

Two factors should be noted on this point. Schlieffen blamed some of Moltke's problems on the fact that he was merely the chief of the General Staff and not a supreme commander (*Feldherr*) and thus lacked full authority. Schlieffen, moreover, did not concern himself with such questions in discussions with senior commanders. He did little if anything to restrict the independence of commanders at the lower levels, a principle deeply if perhaps imperfectly embedded in the army's doctrinal manuals during his years as chief of the General Staff and one that has been largely overlooked.

Schlieffen's somewhat ambiguous teachings on subordinate independence reflected the difficulties in reconciling conflicting views at a time when radios could not provide reliable and timely communications. Although many have seen his "plan" as demanding rigid adherence to strict guidelines, Schlieffen often spoke of the necessity of encouraging independent-minded subordinate commanders and even repeated Moltke's admonition that no campaign plan lasted beyond the first encounter with the main enemy force. German doctrinal manuals published during and after Schlieffen's tenure as chief of the General Staff consistently called for independent action at all levels, not just in tactics.[38]

The problem, seemingly an impossible one to solve, was how to allow subordinates freedom to react to changing local situations and to exploit momentary advantages without endangering the larger plan. In this respect, both Schlichting and Schlieffen warned that Moltke's demand that commanders always march to the sound of the cannon thunder no longer applied. German doctrine in 1914 thus relied on commanders to use their judgment in adhering to their assigned tasks (*Aufträge*) while remaining within the overall intent of the directives or orders of their superiors.[39] This was entirely consistent with the long tradition of relying on the judgment of senior officers, which went back at least to Scharnhorst.[40] The problem, as Prussian theorists stressed, lay in execution and in educating commanders to reconcile conflicts as local conditions and individual situations demanded. Although many historians have harshly criticized Schlieffen's emphasis on central control, his views and the theory of the Prussian army in 1914 were less restrictive than the doctrines of most modern armies. His views on campaign planning were certainly less detailed and prescriptive than those held in current practice.

Although Schlieffen is most famous for his strategic campaign plan of 1905, he by no means ignored developments in weapons and tactics. The General Staff carefully studied the wars of German unification and subsequent conflicts and recognized that great changes had occurred since Moltke's writings on the power of the defensive form of fighting. Schlieffen fully understood that the growth of armies and the range of modern firearms had extended battlefronts substantially since the days of the wars of unification. He recognized that tactics would have to become more open than ever before and that merely sending out large numbers of skirmishers in front of closely packed columns would be of no avail. Although not directly responsible for tactical manuals and training, Schlieffen's role as chief of the General Staff meant that he had considerable influence, and he generally supported reform efforts. Some of Schlieffen's opponents, particularly Friedrich von Bernhardi, argued that Schlieffen's ideas on tactics were outdated and too mechanical. This was a dubious proposition. Schlieffen's ideas on campaign concepts in particular rested on the most realistic appraisal of modern tactical issues available prior to August 1914.[41]

Historians should not be deceived into thinking that a single "Schlieffen school" dominated military thought, tactics, command methods, or other aspects of the Prussian army between 1891 and 1914. Although a Schlieffen school composed of his adherents definitely existed both before and after the war, this group was by no means dominant.[42] Schlieffen knew that not all Prussian officers accepted his ideas on strategy, command methods, or tactics. This knowledge undoubtedly influenced his growing dogmatism and his concern that the officer corps lacked the single vision of war necessary to implement his concepts.[43]

Opponents there were between 1891 and 1914, but they by no means formed a unified or entirely progressive group. Many of their works received serious study in the army, and many of their ideas were present in official German theory in 1914. In the realm of strategy and operations, the most influential of these rivals was Sigismund von Schlichting, a man whose name is largely unknown today but whose significance in the area of military theory has far outlived that of Schlieffen.[44]

Sigismund von Schlichting

Born in Berlin on 3 October 1829, Wilhelm Lorenz Sigismund von Schlichting had a nearly ideal background for a nineteenth-century Prussian officer. The scion of a Silesian *Uradel* clan, Schlichting's noble ancestry was traceable at least as far back as the year 1280. His father and grandfather had been Prussian officers, the former a general. His mother, Emilie von Warburg, was the daughter of an East Elbian landowner, and his wife, Marie Countess von Zieten, was the daughter of a distinguished civil servant. Only in its religion did the Schlichting family show any variation from the typical background of Prussia's imperial-era generals. Schlichting belonged to the branch of the Lutherans that had refused amalgamation with the official Evangelical church of Prussia early in the nineteenth century.

Educated in the cadet corps, Schlichting joined the elite Seventh Grenadier Regiment as an officer candidate in 1847 and, after being commissioned in 1848, saw combat against Polish insurgents. He later commanded a company in the Third Guards Grenadier Regiment for five years, including the campaign against Austria in 1866. He served as a battalion commander in the Franco-Prussian War and received the Iron Cross Second Class. He later commanded a regiment, a brigade, a division, and, finally, XIV Corps (1888–1896). During those years he was also a General Staff officer and one of the leading intellects of the army.[45]

After the war against Austria, Schlichting's career took a turn when he was assigned to a General Staff position in the newly formed 18th Division in Flensburg. His selection to the General Staff without having attended the War Academy was somewhat out of the ordinary, but he was by no means unique in this regard.[46] However, assignment to a position with the *Truppengeneralstab* (General Staff of the units) without a probationary period with the General Staff in Berlin was most unusual.

Schlichting's career followed the normal pattern for General Staff officers, with alternating assignments between General Staff positions in Berlin or with units and command at the level appropriate to his advancing rank. He had the opportunity to observe the great Russian maneuvers near Warsaw in 1875 and later did the same in Italy. He attended lectures at the University of Berlin and read widely in the classics; he was familiar with Shakespeare and Goethe.[47]

Schlichting eventually became widely recognized in the General Staff for his incisive and elegant reports, and his views became known to wider audiences through his presentations to the Military Society in Berlin. Schlichting's reputation was sufficient to allow him to withstand a critical report by *Generalquartiermeister* Count Alfred von Waldersee, who disagreed with some of his views on military issues.[48]

Schlichting's contributions to the history of the Prussian army were manifold. His lengthy efforts to reform combat procedures reached a successful conclusion in 1888 with the publication of the Prussian army's first modern infantry regulations.[49] Schlichting was thus one of the fathers of tactical flexibility and initiative on the part of junior leaders, which, rightly or wrongly, became one of the most respected hallmarks of German combat performance in both world wars. He later extended his views to the sphere of strategy and sought to explain how commanders should conduct warfare under modern conditions. Between 1879 and 1909 he emerged as the chief spokesman for a substantial group of officers who sought to address the changes wrought by technical advances and the growth of mass armies.

Most Prussian theorists realized that fundamental changes had occurred at least since midcentury and particularly since 1871. Despite the continuing hope for a short war, most writers recognized that massive armies could not be defeated in a single battle. The criticism that Prussian officers failed to accept that the single decisive battle was no longer feasible has some foundation in the army's theory, but it should not be taken too far. Many realized that decisive battles would have to give way to extended and lengthy campaigns with many engagements and battles.[50] The 1910 manual for large-unit commanders made that point quite clear.[51] Armies of millions had replaced the preindustrial armies of Frederick, Napoleon, and even Moltke. From Goltz to Schlieffen, the question of the *Millionenheer* dominated discussions on the nature of warfare. This was also the essence of Schlichting's writing on strategy.

The Distributed Battlefield

Schlichting insisted that the Prussian army must abandon its reliance on the study of Napoleon and earlier commanders. Instead, he said, the study of war should turn to the campaigns of Helmuth von Moltke, who, in Schlichting's view, had overturned the Napoleonic model entirely.[52] Moltke had seemingly resolved the twin problems of improvements in weapons and the growth of armies by a series of theoretical breakthroughs that he then successfully put into practice in the wars of German unification. Moltke had linked mobilization, strategic deployment, and the initial moves toward the anticipated point of battle, combining all three fundamental elements into a single strategic concept. Of equal importance, Moltke had developed the idea of separate and largely independent armies whose movements (operations) would effect the final strategic deployment during the course of the major battle rather than before it. Although Moltke's methods seemed to violate the basic principle of concentration, subjecting the separated parts of the army to defeat in detail, Schlichting argued that they had created a new paradigm of warfare.[53]

Tactical envelopments (*Umfassung*) had become much more difficult during the nineteenth century as the range of weapons increased and the size of armies grew. As Moltke had written, conducting a flanking movement and a resulting flank attack within the range of modern weapons was exceedingly difficult. Extension of fighting fronts, caused by both the greater tactical width of formations and the increase in the number of units, created an additional barrier to traditional flank attacks. Large armies using weapons with extended ranges were able to extend their fronts into long defensive lines and thus avoid being outflanked or encircled. The result was that battles had lost much of their decisiveness. Even if defeated in a frontal battle, the defender could usually retreat in good order to another defensive position. There, the attacker might have to pay the same steep price for yet another partial victory.

The purpose of annihilating the enemy force was to reach a rapid decision and avoid subsequent costly battles. To achieve this, Prussian theorists were willing to take great risks and suffer substantial casualties, which would likely be fewer than those suffered in a second battle or a series of battles. As noted earlier, this concept of annihilation, which had its roots in Frederick the Great and Clausewitz, did not imply destruction of the enemy state.[54]

Schlichting argued that Napoleon, maneuvering with much smaller armies and fighting on more limited battlefields, had nearly always concentrated his forces before the battle and outside the immediate reach of the enemy. As had normally been the case with Frederick the Great, movements to the battlefield and conduct of the battle itself were quite different and separate acts in Napoleon's day, according to Schlichting. Relying on Napoleon's own writings and careful analyses of his campaigns, Schlichting skillfully argued that regardless of how Napoleon moved his armies through the theater of war to the battlefield, he always tried to unite his forces before the battle began. This frequently enabled him to defeat the enemy in detail and avoid suffering the same fate himself.[55]

Schlichting believed that several factors had rendered this approach to movement and combat obsolete. The improved range, accuracy, and rate of fire of modern weapons had expanded the battlefield and made flanking movements within the range of enemy fire extremely costly or impossible. Schlichting concluded that frontal assaults had little prospect of success against an enemy that had deployed his forces, and even if they were successful, as in 1870, the attacker would suffer excessive casualties. At the same time, expansion of the armies on both sides, combined with widening frontages of individual units, had extended the battlefield's breadth and depth to an extent undreamed of in Napoleon's time or even in the days of Moltke. This produced the problem of what Schlichting called the "parallel battle," in which long lines of units on both sides fought indecisively for days or even weeks, producing heavy casualties and indecisive results.

Schlichting concluded that, by combining the strategic movement of the separated parts of the armies with the initial engagements, Moltke's methods offered the prospect of making battles decisive again. Moltke, in arguing against concentrating the army prior to the battle, had concluded that the armies of the late nineteenth century could neither move effectively nor provision themselves if they were concentrated before the decision was at hand. A premature concentration, he said, was a disaster in and of itself. Instead, Moltke had developed his idea of "separated armies," in which the original mobilization led to an initial deployment of widely separated parts of the entire field army. These parts, usually consisting of field armies of two or more corps, used different roads and railroads to converge on the enemy from different directions. This final concentration was completed only during the battle, not on the prior day or at some earlier time. A properly executed campaign, using wide separations between independently moving field armies, allowed the attacker to engage the enemy in the flanks and rear, thus forcing him to fight with reversed fronts under disadvantageous circumstances. By avoiding purely frontal attacks against the enemy's chosen line of defense, such a procedure could achieve quick and decisive results.[56]

Schlichting attempted to turn this concept into a new and more clearly defined system than had Moltke, who was always reluctant to create any kind of formal theory. This concept differed from what many Prussians regarded as those of Napoleon in two fundamental ways, both of which seemed fraught with danger. First, a conscious decision not to concentrate one's entire army was both new and risky. An army attempting such a maneuver without substantial numerical superiority could be outflanked or have its weak center crushed by a counterattack. Second, because of the great distances involved and the primitive nature of communications, the separated field armies were beyond the direct control of the High Command. The latter therefore had to entrust the fate of the campaign to the field army commanders. This raised Schlichting's demands for tactical independence to the highest levels of large-unit command. Since Moltke, not Schlichting, originated the basic idea, perhaps it would be more accurate to say that Schlichting's theories extended Moltke's ideas on strategy to the lowest tactical unit—to the individual rifleman.

Schlichting took his analysis to its logical conclusion by arguing that these methods reflected fundamental changes in the nature of war itself rather than the personal concepts of an individual that might be accepted or rejected by others. He argued that some of these characteristics had been obvious as early as Solferino, even though neither party had recognized what was really taking place. Since these changes were inherent in the nature of warfare, Schlichting concluded that the antiquated picture of battle based on Clausewitz's interpretation of Napoleon should be discarded.[57]

Schlichting combined these ideas into a sketchily outlined view of war in which large field armies, moving separately and with only limited contact with one another and with the High Command, met the enemy in a series of encounter battles. He placed great faith in the telegraph as a means of communications with these far-flung armies, but he was also quite willing to trust local commanders' ability to win their battles while remaining within the framework of the overall concept. Europe's improving road network gave commanders more flexibility to move divided and fight united at the end of concentric movements. Schlichting's theory maintained the Prussian army's traditional division of war into two kinds—positional (*Stellungskrieg*) and mobile (*Bewegungskrieg*)—but he warned that an army conducting mobile warfare might encounter new problems in the modern era.[58]

Schlieffen accepted much of Schlichting's interpretation of the relationship between individual battles and the campaign as a whole, but his terminology has misled many subsequent writers. Because German theory had not developed the modern concept of "levels of war," Schlieffen used the dual idea of the "entire battle" (*Gesamtschlacht*) to characterize the large campaign (operational) framework and "partial battles" (*Teilschlachten*), where actual combat took place. The former, in essence a campaign concept, gave meaning and direction to the latter.[59]

Schlichting argued that an army conducting a war of movement under modern circumstances had to be prepared to make two very different kinds of attacks. Usually, he thought, armies would encounter each other in a series of meeting engagements in which advance guards would fight the opening round while commanders rushed one or more columns forward in such a manner as to strike the enemy in the flank or rear, while fixing his front with another column. This type of combat would typify battles in which neither side had an opportunity to prepare extensive defensive positions.

Schlichting warned that a second kind of combat was also possible, even likely, under modern conditions: attacks against prepared positions. Such attacks would be fundamentally different from those resulting directly from the strategic movement of armies. A prepared defense could be overcome only by a prepared attack. Schlichting warned against excessive haste in attacking prepared positions and cautioned that a successful attack would require careful preparations, a gradual reduction of the strength of the defense, and an assault theory quite different from the constant search for rapid action that was desirable under other circumstances. He further predicted that wars between armies of approximately equal size, skill, and leadership would produce many such battles, since both sides would maneuver and position themselves to counter hostile flanking movements. The Prussian army, he argued, should study the "parallel battle," because this type of combat was very likely in the congested areas of the potential front along Germany's western border.[60] Whereas an encounter battle united the attack with the strategic deployment and movement, an attack against a prepared position required a division of these two acts into separate undertakings. Schlichting criticized Schlieffen for the General Staff's excessive emphasis on turning movements and flanking attacks and frequently cited the massive "parallel battles" of the Russo-Japanese War in support of this argument.[61] Schlichting, joined on this issue by Friedrich von Bernhardi, argued that Schlieffen's one-sided views had distorted both his and the General Staff's writings on military history and its studies of war and training exercises.[62]

Schlichting rejected Schlieffen's idea that the commander should remain in his headquarters far to the rear of the advancing armies. Instead, he argued, the commander should go forward to the decisive point of the campaign. Schlieffen had feared that the commander would lose control of the larger course of events if he moved away from the army's communications center. Schlichting argued that the commander could best remain in control and prevent arbitrary action by subordinates by going forward with the advance elements. Both realized the danger of field army commanders departing from the overall intent of the campaign plan if left entirely on their own.[63] Schlichting, reflecting Moltke's earlier statements, had less faith in the telegraph and telephone, fearing that they would reduce subordinates' initiative. His views were entirely in line with those of Moltke, who was both suspicious of modern means of communication and willing to tolerate the independence of subordinate commanders if it were not taken to excess.[64]

Several of the Prussian army's most distinguished writers challenged Schlichting's strategic theory with great vigor. The ensuing debate, which lasted into the First World War and beyond, reveals the complexities that confronted military men everywhere during those decades of great change and conflicting evidence. Opposition to Schlichting came first from another now-forgotten Prussian general, Albert von Boguslawski.[65] A respected thinker and commander, Boguslawski denied the existence of any fundamental differences between Napoleon and Moltke.[66] He insisted that the basic foundations of strategy had remained unchanged from the time of Frederick the Great to the modern day. He denied that Napoleon had always tried to unite his forces before beginning a battle and argued that Napoleon's campaigns of 1813–1815 were quite similar to Moltke's of 1866.[67] He argued that Schlichting's view was too one-sided, an interesting accusation against the officer who was primarily responsible for creating the less formal procedures of the Prussian infantry regulations published from 1888 to 1914.[68]

Soon others joined the fray. The illustrious Colmar von der Goltz agreed with Schlichting that Moltke's methods were quite different from Napoleon's, but he denied that they reflected any fundamental change in warfare. Instead, Goltz argued, either method might be used with modern armies, an ironic position for the man whose book *The Nation in Arms* did more to popularize the mass armies of the late nineteenth century than any other single piece of literature.[69] Goltz's second book, which attracted much attention just before the turn of the century but is largely overlooked today, contained his own theories on the conduct of war.[70] Goltz made few if any references to the dispute over Schlichting's views, but he consistently illustrated his theoretical hypotheses with examples drawn from Napoleon. In his section on the planning of operations, Goltz assumed in passing that an army would effect "concentration prior to battle."[71] In a subsequent chapter on offensive action, Goltz argued that either method, Napoleon's or Moltke's, could produce favorable results in modern war, depending on the circumstances.[72]

Friedrich von Bernhardi and Baron Hugo von Freytag-Loringhoven, who otherwise had little in common, entered the ranks of those opposed to Schlichting on this issue.[73] Some of those who had previously objected to Schlichting's reform of the army's infantry tactics now argued that his concepts at all levels destroyed discipline and reduced the battlefield to confused chaos, a criticism of Moltke later made popular by J. F. C. Fuller.[74] Schlichting's views, they argued, created a formalism and rigidity in the same measure as the alleged methods of Napoleon, whom Schlichting had so strongly criticized. General Wilhelm von Scherff, one of the Prussian army's most prolific and illustrious theoreticians, had previously criticized Schlichting's insistence on open-order infantry tactics, and he now strongly attacked Schlichting's strategic views as well.[75]

Command and Initiative

In constructing his interpretation of Moltke's methods of conducting operations, Schlichting had extended his tactical concepts of subordinate independence and initiative to the commanders of field armies. Relying on the writings of Clausewitz, Moltke, and Scharnhorst, Schlichting stressed that modern command required general directives rather than detailed and inflexible orders in the execution of plans. Too much detail, he argued, was dangerous, since circumstances could not be foreseen.[76] Indeed, in a view that became commonplace before the First World War, he argued that the independence of subordinate commanders at all levels was the noblest German characteristic in war. No one, he stated, would want to return to the practices of strict control that had typified the methods of Frederick and Napoleon.[77]

This point proved to be less controversial than the issue of separated armies. Even Freytag-Loringhoven, critical of Schlichting on other issues, endorsed the view that the encouragement of initiative in commanders, which Moltke had made the basis of tactics and strategy, was a vast improvement over Napoleon's failure to develop his subordinates.[78] Despite some reservations expressed by people such as Goltz and Boguslawski, the principle of independent subordinate commanders had become one of the fundamental pillars of the Prussian approach to war by 1914.[79] Although one can argue the merits of this idea in either its past or its present application, it was definitely a major step toward modern warfare as it evolved in the West. Few slogans have become more generalized in modern armed forces than that of the decentralized execution of broad directives.[80]

One must consult a number of official and semiofficial sources to find this theory in any detail. No single document set it forth, and no combination of official regulations or publications was intended to be sufficient for officers to learn the theory and understand it.[81] The army taught its officers that they must read the tactical and historical studies of many privately published authors to develop proficiency in this area.[82] Among those books required for reading at the War Academy were Schlichting's *Taktische und strategische Grundsätze der Gegenwart*. The key challenge was commanding the far-flung field armies in a manner that would keep them within the framework of the theater-wide campaign yet allow them to conduct local battles as circumstances required.

Origins of Tactical Theory

Turning to the Prussian army's system of tactics and command going into the First World War, one must bear in mind that three related but distinct streams of tradition and thought had come together by 1906. The first was based on Moltke's theories of strategy and large-scale movements (operations). The second was the emerging tactical thought as outlined in the evolving infantry manuals, which sought to create a tactical system within the larger framework that was consistent with developments in warfare since the wars of unification. The third was the more narrow and specific military strategy developed by Schlieffen and continued by the younger Moltke.

The first drew on the traditions of Scharnhorst and Clausewitz, as modified by changes in firepower and army size. It was essentially a broad theory of the nature of war. The second was an extension of the first, reflecting not merely the tactical implementation of the larger theory of war but also the education and training of the officer corps, the army's force structure, and the ethos of the entire army. The third reflected a vision, perhaps too narrow, of the strategic requirements of the German Empire under the political circumstances created by the emergence of the two great power blocs in Europe after 1895. No single doctrinal manual or official publication laid this out in the manner of some modern Western manuals. Indeed, the German army assumed that its official regulations were a mere starting point, an introduction to the theory of war; officers had to study on their own in order to apply their judgments in the great varieties of war. Reproducing that theory today is a very complicated matter.

At the outset, it is important to note that the Prussian army considered the issues of tactics and command to be inextricably linked. The Prussian army thus did not develop a separate theory of leadership, which has been so firmly established in modern practice. Indeed, Prusso-German theory, from Moltke through the Second World War, defined tactics as the art of commanding units in battle (*Truppenführung*), and it defined command as the art of conducting battle.[83] In a broader sense, the German definition, which went back to Bülow and Clausewitz, defined tactics as the conduct of battles, as opposed to strategy, which was the art of leading armies or conducting war.[84]

The Prussian army's system of command and tactics rested on three fundamental pillars: the perceived realities of the battlefield, Prussia's (and later Germany's) strategic situation, and the army's preferred style of war. The last was closely related to the structure of the army, the social composition and ethos of its officer corps, and a host of other considerations. Although the Prussian army emerged victorious from its wars against Austria in 1866 and France in 1870–1871, its more insightful leaders realized that the tactical system of those wars, founded in part on the infantry regulations of 1847, had outlived its usefulness. Those regulations had provided more flexibility than earlier manuals and had defined the company column preceded by skirmishers as the primary tactical formation.[85] Many commanders were unwilling to use the more dispersed formations called for in the regulations and to risk the accompanying loss of control.[86] Changes ordered by Prince Wilhelm (later King and Emperor Wilhelm I) in 1853 and 1854 made the first efforts to allow individual infantrymen and squads to adapt to the requirements of the needle gun and subsequent improvements in rifles, but they were in fact a retreat from the most progressive notions of the regulations.[87]

The great losses suffered by Prussian infantry regiments in the victories of 1870–1871 provided the impetus to adapt the army's tactics to the firepower of modern weapons, which Moltke had advocated many years previously. Little real progress was made, and the Prussian army spent the next seventeen years clinging to the outmoded forms of 1847. Thoughtful officers recognized that the army's training suffered, as even the best commanders had difficulty adapting their tactical training to the demands of the old regulations.[88]

Schlichting became the chief (but by no means the only) spokesman for those who wanted to make radical changes in the army's offensive tactics. He wanted to abolish the battalion column and other standard formations and allow commanders at all levels to rely on their own judgment in determining the forms to use in any given attack. He warned that the costly attacks of 1870–1871 could not be repeated and feared that any frontal attack that depended on the attacker's infantry firepower would fail, especially against entrenched defenders. He wanted to require infantry commanders to prepare their attacks carefully by adapting their plans to the infinite varieties of terrain and other circumstances, rather than to attack immediately in a manner predetermined by regulations. He also stressed a careful search for vulnerable flanks. Schlichting trusted relatively junior officers to determine the methods to be used on the battlefield. Tactics, he wrote, are determined by commanders, not by regulations.[89]

Because this approach empowered, even obligated, commanders to adapt their tactics to their assigned tasks (*Aufträge*), it acquired the now-famous term *Auftragstaktik*.[90] The army's regulations rarely used the term, while private and semiofficial writings used it only occasionally. Giving small-unit commanders a substantial degree of freedom of action in the tactical realm was a new concept for the Prussian army. It sprang not from the army's long-established principles of initiative for subordinate commanders leading large units but rather from reformers' reactions to the improved firearms and extended battlefields that emerged in the mid-nineteenth century.

The opposing tactical concept also acquired a slogan, *Normaltaktik* (standard tactics). Its most prominent advocates were Albert von Boguslawski and, above all, Wilhelm von Scherff, both prominent writers and generals. Neither wanted to retain the outdated formations of the pre-1870 infantry manual. Instead, they advocated a greater reliance on the infantry's offensive firepower (as opposed to the shock of the traditional infantry charge), reliance on company (not battalion) columns in movements to the front line, and masses of riflemen in extended formations for the firefight and close assault.[91] Scherff and his supporters wanted to establish a few standard formations to achieve fire superiority for frontal attacks against both prepared and unprepared enemy defensive positions. Boguslawski and Scherff were less concerned with a commander's exploiting terrain than with his maintaining control over his men.[92]

The common ground shared by the two schools of thought was the recognition that firepower, either offensive or defensive, would dominate future battlefields and that, as a result, the army would have to improve its individual training and change its infantry tactics. The two most important differences involved whether the defender (in Schlichting's view) or the attacker (in Scherff's view) would actually have the fire superiority that both regarded as essential, and the feasibility of extending the principles of initiative and independence of action to junior infantry commanders. One author characterized this debate as a contest between reformers and "old Prussianism," which stressed the army's traditional reliance on authority and discipline.[93] For nearly twenty years, the army's official and semiofficial literature brimmed with discussions of these and related questions.

Finally, in 1888, Emperor Friedrich III ordered the corps commanders to submit proposals for changes, a clear recognition of their potentially decisive role in training. He subsequently commissioned a committee headed by Schlichting to produce the final product. Following Friedrich III's untimely death after a reign of only ninety-nine days, Wilhelm II (1888–1918) came to the throne and continued to support the reformers. Wilhelm's introduction to the manual warned the officer corps against resisting the new procedures and threatened retirement for those who did. The new manual was particularly timely, since it appeared in the same year that the introduction of smokeless powder and smaller-caliber rifles increased the need to adapt tactics to the evolving weaponry of the battlefield.[94]

1888 Infantry Regulations

The central feature of the 1888 infantry regulations was the abolition of all drills not directly relevant to tactical situations and all preordained forms (described with the pejorative term *Schema*).[95] The manual became the first to define the differences between meeting engagements and planned attacks against a deployed enemy force. It extended freedom of tactical action and form through the companies and platoons down to the individual soldier. This became a permanent feature of the army's theory (lasting until the end of the Second World War), and many came to see the mobile warfare described in the manual as the unique preserve and specialty of the Prussian army. This confidence became the basis of a variety of concepts and of a willingness to embark on campaigns even in the face of undoubted enemy numerical superiority.

The regulations required open-order tactics at all levels, as had previously been the case for skirmishers, and this became the first of the army's regular infantry manuals to apply to *Jäger* and *Schützen* battalions.[96] The regulations stressed fire superiority rather than massed assault as the basis for attacking the enemy's defensive position. In the attack, a battalion deployed a strong forward line of skirmishers, followed by companies in column until further directed by their commanders. Reserves followed to strengthen the forward line of riflemen as it deployed for the final assault. The regulations recommended flexibility in the density of the infantry firing line, with a company front of about 100 yards (or meters) in the attack. A company, however, should not deploy its full strength along its front; it should keep one or more platoons in reserve.[97] Infantry formations, then, would be much less dense than a simple comparison of company or battalion fronts with total manpower strength might suggest.

On the question of command, the regulations applied Moltke's principles of large-unit command to the smallest tactical elements.[98] The sections on regimental combat instructed commanders to assign individual tasks to battalions and leave the type and form of combat to them. Recognizing that the battalion commander lacked both the time and the means to control individual companies as they moved into combat, the regulations directed him to give the companies clear tasks (*Aufträge*) but to leave the means of accomplishing them to their commanders. Company commanders were thus responsible for deciding the place and time of the final phase of an engagement, neither of which could be determined in advance. Within the dispersed tactical formations, companies, platoons, and even squads must be capable of the independent execution of assigned tasks. Within this framework, the regulations recognized the problem of control and the possible contradictions between maintaining effective control and allowing independent action. The solution lay in formulating clear orders, immediately restoring unit cohesion and control after the confusion created by combat, and keeping the common goals in mind. Such problems were the price of tactical success in modern battle. The regulations adopted Moltke's older wording in the 1869 *Instructions for Large Unit Commanders* in admonishing leaders that omissions and neglect were graver errors than mistakes in the means chosen.[99]

The new infantry regulation did not find universal favor within the officer corps. Scherff, continuing his criticism of Schlichting's approach, condemned the 1888 manual for its excessive grant of freedom of action to lower-ranking commanders. Boguslawski criticized the lack of standard forms. Scherff and others demanded a renewed emphasis on the concept of a "normal attack," which would provide a few basic procedures as frameworks for engagements. They criticized the "individualized attack" of 1888 and claimed it would not bring decisive strength to bear at the proper time and place. Some senior commanders stubbornly clung to the tactics of 1870 and refused to adopt the provisions of the new regulations. By 1891, serious opposition had become apparent, even in the emperor's maneuvers.[100]

Various high-ranking officers joined in the defense of preordained standard tactical formations.[101] Some feared that the army's junior officers would simply be unable to master the complicated tactics outlined in the regulations and pointed out that great differences arose even with a single corps.[102] Others, including such luminaries as Baron Hugo von Freytag-Loringhoven and August Keim, objected that the new regulations did not go far enough in liberalizing tactical forms.[103] This debate reflected the essential issues that endured in 1914: conducting battles with extended tactical formations and maintaining control of subordinate units and commanders by brigade and battalion commanders. Schlichting's retirement in 1896 gave his opponents renewed opportunities to return to the older, more formalized tactics in use before 1888.[104]

Over the next eighteen years, the Prussian army grappled with the changes in warfare and the continuing contradictions outlined above. Gradually, a loose and uneasy consensus developed on many of the points at issue, and the arguments began to center around the increasingly dominant question of defensive firepower and the "crisis of the battle"—that is, how the attacker was to advance the final 300 yards or so to a final close assault on the enemy's defensive positions. Eventually, the Prussian army had to face the prospect of reconsidering the 1888 regulations.

Accordingly, in 1905 King and Emperor Wilhelm II authorized a new commission to revise the army's infantry regulations. The royal order establishing the commission instructed it to improve infantry combat training by considering (1) previously approved changes to the 1888 regulations, (2) progress in weapons, and (3) lessons of recent wars and peacetime experiences. The commission was led by a former commander of the Guards Corps, General Max von Bock und Polach, and two officers who later achieved prominence in the First World War, Karl von Bülow and Emil von Eichhorn.[105] All three were General Staff officers, and two (Bock and Eichhorn) were graduates of the War Academy.

Ascertaining the main lessons of the two most recent conflicts, the Boer and Russo-Japanese Wars, was no simple matter, as the conclusions seemed to be in conflict. The commission rejected the most extreme form of open-order swarms of skirmishers, the so-called Boer tactics, in favor of the more formal and drill-based methods used by the Japanese in Manchuria. Many German officers favored this approach because the Japanese had relied on Jacob Meckel's interpretation of the German regulations of 1888 and because their attacks usually possessed sufficient energy and self-sacrifice to succeed. Bülow was the driving force behind this view. He favored more drill in tactical training than did some of the others, although he was less committed to prescribed formations than were Meckel and others.[106]

The commission drew a number of basic lessons from the Russo-Japanese War. These included reliance on the infantry as the main arm, cooperation of infantry and artillery as a prominent feature of combat, attacking prepared positions only after greater preparation than had previously been prescribed, making reconnaissance an unconditional requirement, shedding of soldiers' backpacks before combat, use of sandbags by attacking infantry for protection under some circumstances, and finding more effective ways to fight in built-up areas.[107] In 1906 these and many similar concepts found their way into the new regulations.

1906 Infantry Regulations

The new infantry regulations were something of a landmark, in that they combined elements from the 1888 version with topics normally reserved for the field service regulations, the instructions for large-unit commanders, and the marksmanship regulations. There were also new sections on combined arms within the framework of the infantry attack.[108]

Like its predecessors, the 1906 regulations stressed offensive warfare in broad terms and devoted the bulk of tactical discussions to the attack. They identified three basic forms of the tactical offensive: encounter engagements, attacks on an enemy deployed for defense, and attacks on fortified positions, either field positions or fortresses. In all cases, the regulations strengthened the 1888 prohibition on preordained templates for tactical action with the oft-quoted conclusion of the section on the attack: "Every schematization of the methods of attack is forbidden."[109] Paraphrasing Clausewitz and Moltke, the manual cautioned that only the simple produced success, and it forbade all artificialities (*Kunsteleien*).[110] Numerous prewar handbooks stressed this need for tactical flexibility, citing both the 1888 and the 1906 regulations.[111]

On the critical issues of extended formations, advances by small groups, and command, the 1906 regulations continued in the tradition of the 1888 regulations and may be seen as a victory by the disciples of Schlichting over those of Scherff.[112] In the infantry firing line, the regulations allowed the commander to establish intervals according to circumstances but defined firing lines with intervals of two paces or less as "dense" and those with intervals of more than two as "loose."[113] In open formations, the regulations established the platoon as the basic unit for fire and movement but gave the commander the flexibility to move his unit forward in half platoons or squads if necessary, and they called for an advance by individual crawling when circumstances warranted.[114] A more complete change from the formal tactics of 1812 and 1847 could hardly have been envisioned. Above all, in a clear if subsequently disregarded presaging of the 1918 regulations, the 1906 manual recognized that the platoon, rather than the company or the battalion, would usually be the unit responsible for movement and fire in open-order formations.[115]

On the issue of command and subordinate initiative, the regulations emphasized both discipline and independence, while extending the principle of initiative down to the platoon, the squad, and even the individual rifleman.[116] The Prussian system of orders stressed brevity in content, speed in transmission, and flexibility in form. Orders below division level were to be verbal and were supposed to reflect the same flexibility allowed commanders in choosing their tactical formations.[117] The Prussian approach stressed speed in evaluating situations and the rapid transmission of very brief orders, a principle inculcated into officer training from the War Academy downward. At the lower levels, therefore, the army's command system was entirely consistent with its tactical doctrine.[118]

The publication of the 1906 regulations did not end the debate on infantry tactics.[119] Critics soon objected to the new regulations, sometimes on opposite grounds. General Gottlieb von Haeseler, one of the army's most illustrious corps commanders, criticized the new manual because its definition of the three kinds of basic attacks marked a retreat from the more flexible approach of its predecessor. He warned that training to that model would leave the army unprepared for the myriad variations a real war would produce.[120] Bernhardi, ever the critic, attacked the manual for its underlying emphasis on flanking attacks and warned that its methods would not work against an enemy that knew the German methods.[121] Others, continuing in the tradition of Meckel and Scherff, criticized the manual on the grounds that it relied too heavily on free forms and firepower and not enough on prearranged maneuvers and the moral power of the massed use of the bayonet.[122] Freytag-Loringhoven also warned that the imagined encounter battles simply would not develop in the manner the regulations predicted.[123]

Others, then and later, have defended the 1906 regulations because they attempted to eliminate drill-like movements from the battlefield, spread out the firing lines, and incorporate the results of the recent wars in South Africa and Manchuria.[124] General Friedrich *Freiherr* von Falken-hausen, one of the army's more prolific writers on training, defended the manual against its critics on the unintentionally prophetic grounds that, like all modern regulations, it was meant to be a general set of guidelines to be adapted, like orders, to prevailing local circumstances. He stated: "A simple literal following of a regulation no longer suffices. That would be like blind obedience. Just as an order must be understood by its sense, and its execution undertaken in accordance with the situation, so is the case of the regulation's *Bestimmungen und Ausführungen*."[125] *Freiherr* von Gayl was no doubt correct that the regulations were a continuation and, indeed, a triumph of Schlichting's ideas in the realm of infantry tactics. Controversy over details continued in the pages of the German army's literature until the eve of war in 1914. Nevertheless, the manual signaled the emergence of a broad consensus on the nature of future combat and the most reasonable approach to mastering its problems. Even Freytag-Loringhoven quickly embraced much of the 1906 infantry regulations.[126]

Some historians have criticized the regulations because they dropped some of the warnings in the 1888 manual stressing the defensive effects of modern firepower. The 1906 manual instead stressed flexible tactical forms and ruthless aggressiveness on the part of the attacker. Some considered its emphasis on attaining fire superiority a poor replacement for the more moderate approach of 1888. Certainly, the regulations of 1906 extended tactical freedom down to the platoon or even squad and stressed subordinate initiative in the sense of Moltke and Schlichting. It placed greater emphasis on the training responsibilities of battalion and higher commanders, thus allowing variations and mistakes. Modern historians have not reached a consensus on the true value of the tactical methods outlined in the 1906 manual, even though some contemporaries regarded it as ending the confusion over tactics.[127]

Theoretical Foundations of Prussian Warfare

Concentrating on the related issues of tactics and command, the following were the most important fundamental principles of the German approach down to 1914, although it must be emphasized that the army's literature was rich in alternative viewpoints and commentary, both positive and negative:

1. Annihilation of the enemy army (defined in Clausewitzian terms) is the military goal of war, both on offense and defense.
2. Germany's strategic situation is consistent with this and requires a rapid decision.
3. Only offensive action produces a decision, both in tactics and in strategy.
4. Decisiveness and risk taking are characteristics of successful offensive warfare.
5. An army trained for attack can also defend.
6. The objective of defense is to create favorable conditions for counterattacks and counteroffensives.
7. Maintaining the initiative is the key to success.
8. Enabling subordinate initiative is the basis for all timely action in warfare.
9. Orders and directives must preserve this initiative by leaving execution to subordinates, as long as they remain within the framework of the higher commander's intent.

10. Delay is worse than mistakes, which are the price of having aggressive local commanders.[128]
11. Local commanders must sometimes (though rarely) act in disregard or even in violation of outdated orders.
12. Maneuver is still possible in strategy and tactics—that is, in movement to and on the battlefield.
13. Defensive firepower has the potential to dominate the attacker.
14. The attacker can achieve fire superiority over the defender through concentric fire and the use of combined arms.
15. The attacker will succeed at heavy cost through a combination of frontal and flanking attacks.
16. The army must be trained and educated for offensive warfare.

This approach has attracted substantial criticism from historians for decades and from scholars in security studies over the last twenty years or so. The central question is whether this approach was a blind and unreasonable cult of the offensive or a rational calculation of the circumstances in the years from 1906 to 1914.[129]

Despite all the criticism of offensive doctrines in 1914, the Prussian army emphasized offensive action for reasons that appeared to be well-founded at the time and with which most military organizations in the modern era have agreed. The oft-repeated arguments that the German army, as well as most of its contemporaries, emphasized the offensive in a mindless enthusiasm for past glories and intentionally overlooked lessons from previous wars are without foundation. As one historian has noted, most European armies expected, despite their observations of the Russo-Japanese War, that highly capable and motivated infantry could capture trenches defended by barbed war and machine guns.[130]

Most Prussian generals accepted Clausewitz's dictum that only the offensive form of war would allow the army to achieve the nation's political goals. They further believed, perhaps wrongly, that Germany's strategic situation demanded rapid offensive action to end any war quickly. They held this belief on the sensible grounds that only a rapid decision would prevent repetitive and costly battles and that the fabric of German society might not withstand a prolonged war. Indeed, much of the emphasis on offensive action was based on fear of the results of a long war rather than blind faith in the feasibility of a short one.

Prolonged War

Contrary to what is commonly thought, in the years before 1914 the Germans were fully aware that a future war might be prolonged and that it could lead to social and economic ruin along the lines laid out in Bloch's *The Future of War*. It was for this reason (though not for it alone) that European military thinkers so assiduously sought ways to end wars quickly. This meant, of course, aggressive actions in both strategy and tactics.[131] Not all German officers believed that a short war was possible, particularly against Russia, but they all agreed that the only rational means of waging a war was to seek a rapid decision, since a long war might be tantamount to defeat.[132] Certainly the perceived necessity of avoiding a protracted war if at all possible was one of the foundations of Schlieffen's thought.[133]

In the realm of tactics, this required an army that was prepared to make aggressive attacks and willing to accept short-term losses to avoid greater losses in the long run. All the European armies accepted the necessity of suffering great losses. They knew the power of their weapons. The Germans frequently reminded themselves of their great losses in 1870–1871 but also insisted that their forces could take such losses and continue until they achieved victory.[134] German tactical doctrine thus made good sense, in that it was well integrated into the army's view of warfare and into Germany's overall strategic situation.[135]

This belief in the necessity of fighting offensively led the army to emphasize aggressive and independent action in commanders at all levels. The aim was to recognize and exploit opportunities before the enemy could react and thus maintain the initiative—in Clausewitz's words, to "set the law of the transaction." The fragile state of communications, both between higher headquarters and the scattered units and within units at the battalion and even company level as combat developed, logically led to a system of command that, in theory, allowed commanders great latitude in interpreting their orders and adjusting their assigned tasks to local circumstances. Speed and aggressive action in combat allowed no other approach before the era of effective tactical radio systems.

Auftragstaktik

Auftragstaktik is a much misunderstood aspect of the Prussian command system. Under this concept, the commander gave his subordinates clear orders or directives that contained specific tasks (*Aufträge*). The subordinate commander in turn decided how to carry out these tasks within the framework of the commander's intent. The emphasis was on giving the subordinate commander the freedom to act according to local circumstances, which would frequently be beyond the knowledge of higher headquarters or outdated orders.[136] Otto von Moser's widely read handbook (reprinted in four editions) contained one of the clearest statements of the purpose and method of this approach: "I term '*Auftragstaktik*' that command method, first stated in full clarity for junior commanders in the Infantry Regulations of 1888 and maintained in the same sense in the Regulation of 1906, by which the higher commander gives the lower commander not a binding order, but more a selection of his own train of thought in which he requires a common mental effort in fulfilling the combat assignment."[137]

Moltke's writings had consistently encouraged subordinate commanders to disregard their assigned tasks if the overall situation warranted such serious and potentially dangerous decisions. Numerous doctrinal manuals, semiofficial publications, and private works on military theory had repeated this point over the years.[138] The 1906 infantry regulations specifically stated that it was the duty of a subordinate commander to change or disregard his orders if events had rendered them obsolete. Of course, this was a serious matter not to be taken lightly, and the commander who did so had to assume full responsibility for his actions.[139]

German doctrine faithfully reflected this philosophy of command, even though it carried the danger, recognized decades earlier in Moltke's writing, that subordinates who exhibited excessive zeal or poor judgment might act contrary to the overall framework. Nevertheless, as previously noted, the army's doctrine and theory accepted that risk as the necessary price for encouraging commanders to act aggressively and to maintain the initiative in battle. Delay, after all, was worse than inaction for whatever reason.[140] Act, said Moltke, lest the enemy dictate "the law of the battlefield."[141]

Some military writers eventually came to see subordinate independence as the basis for the past success of what they regarded as a uniquely Prussian system.[142] In the years prior to 1914 numerous authors stressed the need for initiative at all levels of the army, from staff officers in the headquarters to the lowest combat levels.[143] In tactics, this came to be linked to what many authors argued was the inborn offensive spirit of the German soldier and his system.[144]

At the same time, of course, authors recognized that independence and initiative could be dangerous if they disrupted the overall plans of campaigns and battles. Examples from the experience of Frederick the Great (Manstein at Kolin) and Moltke (Steinmetz in 1870) illustrated the pitfalls of excessive independence. The army thus sought to strike a delicate balance between strict obedience to orders and the need to react quickly and decisively at all levels of command.[145] Schlieffen was well known to be suspicious of the entire concept, although he was primarily concerned with strategy rather than tactics.[146] All this brings the discussion back to the question of Prussian tactics on the eve of 1914. The basic assumption was that the German army, regardless of how the war began or the strategic situation on either front, would conduct offensive mobile warfare and attack whenever possible, even if on the strategic defensive, as anticipated in the east. The most essential tactical issue, therefore, was execution of the tactical offensive. As previously noted, the major European armies were, in most cases, politically committed to rapid offensives and unable or unwilling to wait passively for their enemies to take the offensive. Thus they shared the essential assumptions of Prussia's military leaders.

The Prussian army's doctrine clearly recognized that the power of the defender presented a difficult problem. Nearly all the major military writers cited previously, as well as the army's training literature, recognized that neither the mere weight of the attacking force nor the power of its enthusiasm would overcome modern defenders.[147] The Boer War had emerged as an example of how even thin defensive lines would probably prevail against traditional attacks or would at least inflict terrible losses.[148] Yet that conflict also offered evidence that advances in thin lines offered some protection against defensive firepower. Experiments with various densities and formations produced no conclusive results, except that Schlichting's flexible tactics had given way to excessive reliance on relatively dense skirmish lines and lengthy, unified rushes.[149]

The Prussian army taught its commanders that the power of the defense could often be overcome by a combination of factors that favored the attacker, as well as by linking a frontal attack with flanking attacks once the defender was pinned down. The main point was to use movement to bring superior numbers and combined-arms effects to bear against a portion of the enemy's front.[150]

The Prussian army's alleged assumption that a flanking attack was always possible was a major feature of the most extreme criticisms of prewar doctrine. If true, such an assumption would have been a major weakness in prewar theory. Prussian doctrine, however, made no such assumption. The official and semiofficial literature recognized that flanking movements were not always possible. However, it is true that a number of dissenters within the officer corps had warned for many years that the army, particularly during Schlieffen's tenure, placed too much emphasis on flanking attacks to the exclusion of considering the frontal attack or the breakthrough battle (*Durchbruch*).[151]

The other problem, noted by both Jacob Meckel and Wilhelm Balck, two writers on the opposite poles of many tactical issues, was that at the lower end of tactics all attacks were frontal. Enemy corps and divisions, even if forced to fight with reversed fronts, could usually turn at least a portion of their forces to face the enemy. The attacker would then have to confront companies and battalions deployed in hastily prepared defensive positions.[152] Virtually all of the Prussian army's thinkers recognized that the infantry would ultimately have to make such frontal attacks, regardless of the overall situation. By 1911, even the official literature had begun to reflect this realization.[153]

Confusion over this point is one of the reasons that so many writers have condemned the army for failing to devote sufficient time to studying the breakthrough battles that became the basis for all offensive action on the western front in 1914. It is true that the Germans devoted little space in their literature to breakthrough battles under that rubric, but it is false to conclude that they never studied the problems of the frontal attack. As a matter of fact, many German authors discussed the problems of attacking prepared positions.[154]

The 1906 infantry regulations discussed four types of attack situations, three of which were assumed to be primarily frontal: (1) attacks from the march, the "encounter engagements" anticipated in mobile warfare; (2) attacks against a deployed enemy; (3) attacks against prepared positions; and (4) attacks against an enemy flank. Regardless of the overall strategic situation, an advancing unit might stumble into battle against any of these situations without knowing in advance the extent to which such a situation prevailed. The basic procedures would be the same unless the attacker knew in advance that the defender was well dug in. The prewar semiofficial literature took this seriously. Most discussions of infantry tactics and combined arms centered on frontal attacks conducted under difficult circumstances.[155]

The Germans believed—wrongly, as it turned out—that these frontal attacks would be the product of a war of movement, not an insuperable barrier to mobile warfare. The German army's tactical literature probably devoted more effort and space to this issue than to any other. The problem is that too many historians and others have accepted the clichés rather than carefully examining that body of writing. Goltz had outlined this view of battle a number of times, most recently in the 1906 edition of his widely read *The Nation in Arms*.[156]

Simply stated, the German army hoped to deliver successful frontal attacks by means of combined-arms action, fire and movement, infantry fire superiority, aggressive and independent commanders, offensive use of machine guns, speed of execution, and finding and exploiting weak points in the enemy's defensive lines. The army's thought was in many ways surprisingly modern, although the execution in 1914 was frequently very deficient. Numerous handbooks, relying on the first section of the 1906 regulations, stressed combined-arms actions. As Moser's handbook on tactics from battalion to brigade stated, the three arms—infantry, cavalry, and artillery—fought shoulder to shoulder, and their tactics stood in the closest relationship to one another. One means to improve mutual understanding and cooperation was the summertime exchange of officers among the arms. Another general, writing in 1910, warned that the army had not yet done enough of this cross-assigning.[157]

One finds in both the doctrinal manuals and the supporting literature a strong emphasis on combined arms, especially cooperation between artillery and infantry. Paragraph 443 of the 1906 infantry regulations pointed out that infantry "will seldom be so placed that it must carry on combat alone." The next paragraph stated, "in battle the actions of the infantry and of the artillery must be exercised conjointly."[158] Goltz argued that the essence of the art of command was to bring about effective combined-arms action.[159] Meckel, frequently cited for his conservative views on modern tactics, was also in the forefront of those advocating cooperation among the various arms.[160] Balck concluded that while combined-arms action in a comprehensive sense had originated in fortress warfare, in the modern era (1908) it required equal emphasis in a war of movement.[161] The challenge was to coordinate infantry and artillery on a confused battlefield where time was of the essence and communications both to the side and to the rear were difficult. Most European armies recognized this on the eve of 1914; the problem was achieving effective coordination in the days before radios made this feasible in mobile warfare.[162] A General Staff report of 1912 warned that combined-arms cooperation was inadequate.[163]

The regulations produced after 1900 contained sections on cooperation among the various branches of the army.[164] This was not limited to the main manuals—the field service regulations and the infantry regulations.[165] The 1906 manual on field fortifications stressed infantry cooperation with artillery, while the manual for the training of junior officers at the war schools also emphasized cooperation between these arms.[166] In the years before the war, numerous lesser-known writers in *Militär-Wochenblatt* called for more practice in this area in peacetime training. In an attack, the infantry planned to rely on its own firepower, machine guns, and mobile light and heavy artillery.[167] By 1913, all corps commanders who were not artillerymen by career were able to attend an annual course at the artillery gunnery school.

The army's heavy field artillery, the best and most numerous in the world, seemed to offer the greatest chance of breaking the enemy's ability to resist at specified sections of the front and thus enabling the infantry to assault the enemy's defensive lines.[168] The 1906 infantry regulations termed the artillery "the skeleton of the battle" on which all else depended.[169] Confidence in the ability of the attacker's artillery to suppress defensive fire was widespread in Europe in 1914.[170] Indeed, one respected author argued that developments in artillery had actually improved the attacker's prospects.[171]

The army undertook some efforts to encourage better cooperation in training, with mixed results. On occasion it encouraged officers to serve in branches other than their own and granted corps commanders the authority to make such temporary transfers within the units under their command, but few officers were willing to do it. Ironically, the Guards Corps may have been the most progressive in this regard.[172] Commanders sometimes tailored their maneuvers to stress combined-arms exercises.[173] Freytag-Loringhoven argued that the subordination of much of the field artillery to division commanders in 1899 was an important step in furthering effective cooperation. Eventually, the divisions acquired a single commander of artillery to integrate fire planning into the scheme of maneuver.[174] Many shortcomings remained in 1914.[175]

The 1906 infantry regulations' picture of future attacks was straightforward and relatively simple. Every attack should begin with the deployment of skirmishers, who should not open fire until they were as close as possible to the enemy position. The manual recognized that many defensive positions would require the attacker to pass over broad tracts devoid of cover, in which case reconnaissance would be difficult, and the deployment of large forces might be impossible. In that situation, the attack should proceed with loose, unconnected firing units (not dense lines of infantrymen, as so often cited in subsequent criticisms). Reinforcements should come forward as possible. In the attack itself, no method could be prescribed in advance, as terrain and conditions would vary too greatly. Infantry combat exhibited "varied formations" at different points of the battlefield. Any unit, squad, section, platoon, or company should advance at every opportunity. Regularity should be avoided. Subsequent paragraphs stressed cooperation with the artillery. Companies attacking on a front with a breadth of 150 yards (a recommended norm) should usually deploy no more than one and a half platoons at a time along their sectors of the front. Units must act on their own initiative, rather than waiting for "nonsensical" orders from the rear, as long as they did so in accordance with the plan of the higher commander. The manual specifically cautioned against peacetime training conducted with unrealistically excessive speed.[176]

Exploitation of weak points in the enemy's line was another way the Prussian army hoped to overcome the firepower of the defender. The army planned to rely on its reconnaissance units—cavalry divisions at the field army level and regiments at lower levels—to locate such weak spots. Each active infantry division had a cavalry regiment for local reconnaissance. The army also had a fully developed method of constituting combined-arms advance guards while moving. They had the mission of developing the tactical situation and assisting the commander in deciding where to make his main effort. In most cases, this would be at the enemy's weakest point or where friendly fire could most effectively be brought to bear.[177]

Overall, however, the army's practice probably lagged behind its theory and doctrine; it is almost always possible to do more than is actually accomplished.[178] The anticipated speed of infantry attacks and the requirement that lower commanders act quickly and independently meant that synchronization in the modern sense, which relies on highly capable communications and enormous staffs, was contrary to the Prussian army's capabilities and method of waging war. Ironically, when it became very good at this synchronization in 1918, the circumstances of war had substantially, though temporarily, changed.

Frontal Attacks

In the realm of tactics, all these questions came together on the issue of frontal attacks against a deployed defender. One school of thought argued that the attacker could use the effects of his artillery and massed infantry fire, supported by machine guns, to achieve fire superiority at the point of attack. Under cover of this fire superiority, the attacker would use successive rushes by entire companies or platoons to close with the enemy and seize a section of his forward lines.[179] This would pave the way for disruption of the enemy's front and would enable the attacker to roll up the enemy lines and destroy enemy units by exploiting the breakthrough against an enemy forced to fight with reversed fronts or while in retreat. This concept required relatively dense firing lines (one- to two-yard intervals) so that a large number of riflemen in the attacking units could bring their fire to bear against the defender.

The opposing school of thought argued that the attacker should use extended front lines with greater intervals between riflemen to minimize losses to the defender's fire. The debate that took place between 1906 and 1912 in the pages of *Militär-Wochenblatt* illustrates the complexities of these issues, even though both sides accepted the proposition that the attacking infantry might suffer losses of up to 40 percent without sacrificing its ability to execute the assault.[180] It should be pointed out that the army did extensive testing on marksmanship and the probabilities of hits at various distances. It expected, for example, that an average rifleman had a 70 percent probability of hitting a man-size target at 200 yards and a 25 percent probability of hitting a prone target at that distance. The question was how to overcome this rifle fire, which the Prussians respected, even though they thought their marksmanship training was superior to that of other armies.[181] Between 1906 and 1914 this led to an extensive debate over measures to deal with infantry fire when moving up to the final assault positions and making the final assault (*Sturm*).

Major Walter von Hülsen, a battalion commander in the Third Foot Guards Regiment, opened the debate by arguing that fire superiority as usually understood was not a proper goal for the attacking infantry. Indeed, he argued, the attacker could not achieve fire superiority at all, given the advantages of the defender in fighting from stationary, protected positions. He argued that fire superiority, though critical for the defender, was not a main objective of the attacker. The latter's primary effort, he said, should be maintaining forward movement of the assaulting infantry until it closed with the defender's front line. This required relatively thin lines of attackers and movement by platoons, squads, or even individual riflemen. Hülsen and others stressed that the attacker's best chance was to make the advance as rapidly as possible; this was the only way to reduce losses and bring the assaulting infantry into the enemy's position.[182] Halting to engage in a protracted firefight would merely increase the attacker's losses and play into the defender's hand, since a lengthy exchange of rifle fire worked to the latter's advantage.[183] Indeed, that was exactly what the defender hoped for.[184]

Hülsen's proposal on the close assault stressed short rushes by small units to reduce the time and the number of targets available to the defender. This movement, rather than the attacker's rifle fire, would neutralize the defender's firepower. This was clearly at odds with the 1906 infantry regulations, which recognized that short rushes by small units might be necessary but preferred long rushes by platoons.[185] The key difference, perhaps, was that the regulations still linked individual advances, even by platoons, with fire superiority, whereas Hülsen stressed rapid movement over fire superiority. The challenge of balancing fire and movement was a serious problem in peacetime training and became a critical point of failure in 1914, even before trench warfare gripped the western front.

Other officers, defending a narrow interpretation of the 1906 infantry regulations, took issue with Hülsen. They argued that the attacking firing line must be as dense as possible (one-yard intervals); that in an infantry firefight, two riflemen were better than one; and that it would be foolhardy to intentionally attack with inferior numbers. These authors were willing to concede that denser lines would suffer heavier losses but concluded that only dense firing lines could create enough firepower to overcome the enemy's advantages.[186] This, of course, assumed that the infantry would be able to call in effective artillery fire and that commanders would wait for the effects of a combined-arms firefight that would eventually provide the attacker with fire superiority.

Defensive Concepts

The 1906 infantry regulations devoted a relatively brief section to defensive tactics, but even this was an improvement over the 1888 manual, which virtually ignored the defense. These defensive concepts were quite modern and did not, as is sometimes assumed, call for the mindless holding of every foot of ground along a single linear position, regardless of costs.[187] The regulations stated that defenses should be arranged not in continuous lines but in groups, with reserves ready for counterattacks. It stressed using the firepower of the defense, including artillery and machine guns, to allow the placement of fewer soldiers in defensive positions, thus making them available for counterattacks and flank protection. The point was to use the power of the defense to contain the enemy attack while preparing for a defensive counterattack. Holding ground as a matter of principle was not part of this scheme.[188]

This view of defensive combat was in accord with German theory in both tactics and strategy from Clausewitz forward, in that it saw offense and defense as inherently linked and held that a good defense should aim at annihilating the enemy with successful counterattacks. The supposedly innovative manuals of 1917 and 1918 (discussed in chapter 10) were, in actuality, a return to basic Prussian theory and to the concepts of the 1906 infantry regulations.

Concluding Remarks

From this brief overview, it should be clear that the Prussian army had a coherent and comprehensive view of infantry tactics going into the First World War, despite imperfections on some points and disagreements within the officer corps on others. The army's literature provides ample evidence of a lively debate on important issues of tactics and command, probably more so than any other army of the day, and certainly more so than the official and semiofficial literature of today's American military forces. Active and retired officers participated in freewheeling debates in the pages of publications that were available to the public.[189]

Perhaps the most critical development was recognized only tacitly. Given the size of the forces relative to the maneuver space available in the day of Clausewitz or Moltke, a tactical success *anywhere* could have operational or even strategic consequences. An examination of the opening phases of the Franco-Prussian War suggests that Moltke, taking advantage of some initial tactical victories and aided by abysmal French decision making, turned them into operational and strategic success.

The German army expanded considerably after Moltke's retirement. Although the size of the cavalry component remained relatively static, the number of infantry battalions increased by about 75 percent between 1874 and 1893. Likewise, the field artillery, foot artillery, and other ancillary parts of the army increased in size by varying amounts (see table 2 in chapter 3). By 1913, the German army had 200 more infantry battalions than it had in 1874, and there had been an almost exponential expansion of both field and foot artillery branches, not to mention logistical elements. With the available maneuver space being filled up, the relationship between the tactical and higher levels of war changed. Although, as argued above, Schlieffen was not as dogmatic as he is often portrayed, his approach to the relationship among tactics, operations, and strategy was different from that of Clausewitz and Moltke. For Schlieffen, tactical success had to occur at a *specific* point or points, which would enable the plan of campaign to unfold. For Schlieffen and for the younger Moltke (at least initially), tactical success had to be attained on the right flank of the German army's advance into the Low Countries and France. Warfare, however, has a way of confounding doctrines and plans, and there is no disguising the fact that the Prussian army's theories bore limited and bitter fruit in 1914, at least on the western front. It is to the issue of strategic planning that we now turn.

CHAPTER FIVE

THE SCHLIEFFEN ERA STRATEGIC PLANNING, 1890–1905

In an address to the assembled officers of German army headquarters on 19 May 1919, the army's First *Generalquartiermeister*, Wilhelm Groener, began the process of building the legend and counterlegend of Schlieffen and his grand concept for war. Of all those who came after Bismarck, Groener claimed, only Schlieffen had seen Germany's continental situation clearly.[1] This theme, extended to argue that Germany had lost the war because various persons and agencies had failed to follow Schlieffen's strategic concept or had failed to execute it properly, became a staple of the post-1918 military literature in Germany.[2] General Hermann von Kuhl revealed some of the details of the 1914 concept of operations in his book *The German General Staff in the Preparation and Execution of the World War* (1920), which was among the first into print, and he soon found strong support. Over the next decades, works by Wilhelm Groener, Wolfgang Foerster, and others denounced Schlieffen's successor for abandoning the plan, for watering it down so much that it could not succeed, or for simply performing so poorly in 1914 that certain victory gave way to certain defeat. Even harsh critics of the prewar army concluded that Schlieffen's masterpiece should have led to victory in the west. This, as one author wrote after the Second World War, was the "Schlieffen legend."[3] This discussion was clearly tied to the desire of various generals, scholars, and official historians to avoid blame or to insulate the General Staff from responsibility for the failures of 1914. The best summaries of this labyrinth of accusations and rationalizations are Terence Zuber's provocative study *Inventing the Schlieffen Plan* and the chapters in Hans Ehlert's edited volume *Der Schlieffenplan* (2006), which is now available in English.[4]

After the Second World War, as historians undertook a more critical examination of Schlieffen's concepts and impact, a new sort of anti-Schlieffen legend developed.[5] This began in earnest in 1956 when the distinguished historian Gerhard Ritter published the text of Schlieffen's 1905 memorandum and concluded that it was the basis of the German war plan of 1914.[6] Ritter and a host of other scholars identified a wide range of shortcomings in the plan, from its political weaknesses to its failure to appreciate logistics problems and the tactical superiority of the defense. Others linked the plan to Germany's aggressive drive for "world power" and attributed its alleged narrowness to the increasingly technical orientation of the General Staff, which could not cope with the demands of industrialized warfare. The plan and its author came to represent the larger shortcomings of German strategy, and at least one distinguished author attempted to extend Schlieffen's responsibility to the failures of the Second World War.[7] All in all, these scholars mounted an impressive and convincing attack on Schlieffen's ideas and methods, while more moderate views found little favor.[8] Ultimately, the plan came to symbolize the much criticized and allegedly irrational "cult of the offensive" that some believe characterizes most military organizations.[9]

One of the most important events for students of World War I was the collapse of the Soviet Union and its satellite governments in eastern Europe in 1991. The disintegration of the East German communist regime meant the opening of the East German archives. What emerged was a veritable treasure trove of documents regarding World War I that were long thought to have been destroyed. From the standpoint of the conflict over Schlieffen's plan, the most important was an analysis written by Wilhelm Dieckmann, an archivist in the German Reichsarchiv. Fragments of deployment plans and some maps were also recovered.[10]

Armed with new sources, Zuber touched off a fresh round of controversy by claiming that both views of Schlieffen's "plan" were wrong because they rested on a fundamentally flawed assumption. Zuber argued that the "Schlieffen Plan" is a myth, as the first public accounts of planning for the 1914 campaign made no mention of any such specific plan.[11] He alleged that a few former General Staff officers created the concept to absolve that institution of responsibility for the failures of 1914 and to transfer the blame to those who had allegedly failed to execute the plan properly. Their chief targets were three deceased men who had played central roles in 1914: Helmuth von Moltke, the chief of the General Staff; Karl von Bülow, the Second Army commander; and Lieutenant Colonel Richard Hentsch, a General Staff officer.[12]

In challenging the entire historical approach to Schlieffen and the campaign of 1914, Zuber has called into question nearly a century of historical writing and much of the interpretive basis of both subjects. He has also used this line of analysis to reduce Germany's responsibility for starting the First World War, concluding that the Germans planned counterattacks rather than the aggressive invasion of neutral states. Critics have rushed to challenge his arguments, which sometimes seem as tendentious as those he rejected.[13]

The Elder Moltke's Strategy for a Two-Front War

In the years after 1871, Moltke's approach to the problem of a two-front war stressed a balanced effort between east and west, use of the advantages of defense, and moderation in objectives. He doubted that wars between industrialized powers could be decisive in the same way they had been in the days of Napoleon or even in the limited manner of 1870–1871. He thus hoped to defeat French and Russian field armies but made no plans for deep exploitation or decisive advances to achieve a dictated peace. With only a single exception during the Balkan wars of 1876–1877, he steadfastly relied on the defensive in the west, using the favorable terrain Germany had acquired in Alsace and Lorraine, and he was prepared to retreat to the Rhine if necessary. In the east, he hoped to use limited offensives in cooperation with Austria-Hungary to defeat Russia's main armies without lengthy advances into the interior of the country.

In both cases, he intended to rely on negotiations to restore the status quo. He sought decisive battles as quickly as possible, but only within the framework of limited goals and a defensive overall conduct of the war. He feared excessive dependence on Austria-Hungary and hoped to use substantial German forces in the east both to conduct mobile warfare and to ensure an active Austrian participation.[14] Although his overall concept anticipated Schlieffen's logical conclusion that a nation with inferior forces faced with a two-front war must defeat first one foe and then turn the bulk of its forces against the other, he declined to adopt a one-sided or extreme emphasis on offensive warfare on either front. Thus, those who argued a basic similarity between his approach and Schlieffen's were substantially off the mark.[15]

Moltke influenced German war planning in another, often forgotten way. He had written on several occasions about the limits of long-term campaign planning, concentrating instead on a careful deployment (*Aufmarsch*) for the opening movements of the first battle. Campaign plans, he argued, did not survive the first major encounter with the enemy. From this he derived the proposition that strategy is a system of expedients, and although the commander should have a general concept of the war, he cannot follow a single detailed plan throughout the entire campaign. Only a layman, he said, believed that to be possible. This tradition of doubting the value of detailed, long-term planning went back to at least Grolman's time as chief of the General Staff and continued to 1914, with the limited and partial exception of Schlieffen.[16]

Moltke's final plans (1887–1888), accepted with only a few changes during Waldersee's short tenure, sent about two-thirds of the German army to the west in a defensive stance, while the remainder would be conducting a limited offensive against the Russian positions in the Polish salient.[17] These alterations reflected the influence of Waldersee, changes in political circumstances, and the calculation that even with a deployed force of about 350,000 German soldiers, Austria-Hungary and Germany would have only a slight superiority over the Russians. Some have seen in these memoranda a precursor of the later massive western deployments by Schlieffen.[18] This is true in terms of the division of Germany's forces, but not in the underlying concepts of campaigns that followed opening deployments. In these sketchy concepts and in a series of subsequent memoranda, Moltke continued to think of a western campaign based on a strategic defense, culminating with massive counterattacks primarily in the area around Nancy.

Schlieffen's Early Concepts, 1891–1892

Schlieffen became chief of the Prussian General Staff on 7 February 1891, succeeding Count Alfred von Waldersee, who had served in that capacity since the retirement of Count Helmuth von Moltke in 1888. Most historians regard Schlieffen's accession as a watershed in German strategic planning, concluding that his views of strategic problems and planning were so fundamentally different from those of Moltke and Waldersee (who made few significant changes) that he ushered in a new era.[19]

The sources available for the study of Schlieffen's concepts of strategic planning are numerous yet disappointingly incomplete. The army published a substantial amount of material from his staff rides and war games. Many of his contemporaries produced accounts of their experiences working with him. His surviving papers in the German Military Archives contain much useful material, most of which is also available on microfilm. Numerous studies, some very dubious, were based on archival materials before they were destroyed in the Second World War, and some of these are considered close to primary sources today. The most prominent source from the former East German archives is known as the "Dieckmann manuscript" (described below). In addition, historians have recently found relevant material in a variety of state archives in Germany.[20]

Schlieffen at first accepted the broad outlines of Moltke's cautious approach to a two-front war, but he soon began to question his predecessor's basic assumptions, in large part because of changes in the military situation in the east and a desire for more decisive action. Schlieffen's memorandum of April 1891, cited by Ritter, expressed regret that the existing deployment deprived the Germans of a choice between offense and defense in the west, and it clearly indicates that he would have preferred even then to make the major effort in the west rather than against Russia.[21] Given the strong Clausewitzian belief in the German army that only the offensive can produce a decision, Schlieffen's reluctance to surrender the initiative to the French is understandable.[22] In the same memorandum Schlieffen noted that a decision in the east had become much less likely because of improvements in Russian fortifications. Nevertheless, he apparently made no significant changes to the deployment plans and continued to rely on deployments leading to counteroffensives to achieve a decision against the French.

In an August 1892 memorandum Schlieffen returned to the basic question of a two-front war and began to seriously consider making the primary effort in the west. He raised the possibility that the Germans could bring the French to a decisive battle before the Russians (or the Austrians, for that matter) could complete their deployments. Schlieffen doubted—correctly, as we now know—that the French planned an early offensive, the lack of which would upset the fundamental premise of the plans of Moltke and Waldersee.[23] In these years the General Staff had excellent intelligence on French deployment plans but not on their concepts for subsequent operations.[24]

In a second memorandum in December 1892 Schlieffen noted that intelligence reports on the Russian deployment had rendered the General Staff's old plan even more obsolete. According to "certain reports," the Russian army's main effort would be against Germany rather than Austria-Hungary, and its deployment would be farther to the northeast, rendering the old General Staff plans ineffective. A decisive battle against the Russians seemed highly unlikely under these circumstances. This memorandum was not directly linked to a change in the deployment plans, and it did not mean that a shift of the main effort to the west would lead to abandoning all offensive action in the east. On the contrary, Schlieffen wanted to undertake offensive action even while on the strategic defensive, both for military reasons and for the political-military objective of ensuring active Austrian participation.[25]

Deployment Plans, 1893–1897

Schlieffen produced memoranda on the strategic problem of a two-front war at irregular intervals throughout his time as chief of the General Staff, but the first actual deployment plan that reflected his ideas was that for mobilization year 1893–1894, which, according to the regular schedule, was prepared by 1 April 1893 and remained in force until the end of March 1894.[26] This deployment plan sent about three-quarters of the German army to the west, a slight increase over the two-thirds allotted to that front by Moltke's final plan. While Ritter was correct in saying that the bulk of this force was on the right wing, identifying this as a prefiguring of the 1905 memorandum is misleading. None of these forces were north of the Metz-Diedenhofen area, and there were no units north of the Mosel River or in the Aachen area. It was, as Zuber argues, merely a continuation of the last plans of Moltke and Waldersee, the primary difference being a greater concentration for a more immediate and more powerful counterattack against the expected French attack on the German right.[27]

As was normal, the deployment plan was designed to move the field armies and corps to their positions of readiness for operations, but it did not contain a detailed design for the campaign. Schlieffen prepared a memorandum in July 1894 in which he discussed several options for a German offensive. The memorandum concluded that any flanking attack north of Verdun would be dependent on a successful breakthrough between Toul and Verdun and another around Nancy, which would be beyond the army's strength. The Germans, Schlieffen concluded, "must renounce any turning movement north of Verdun."[28] The key to any action, Schlieffen wrote, was a successful attack on the fortifications around Nancy. In discussing French options, Schlieffen decided to meet the expected French advance south of Metz with a preemptive German attack. He thus shifted the emphasis from a purely defensive approach followed by a counterattack to a version of Moltke's offensive-defensive approach.[29] Schlieffen, however, doubted that the Germans could depart from their essentially defensive plans unless they could be certain that their mobilization and deployment would be completed before that of the French, a doubtful proposition in 1894 and 1895.[30]

The 1894 memorandum, like all other deployment plans, was not a campaign plan. Its purpose was merely to deploy the army, which the High Command could then employ according to circumstances. The memorandum was important because it considered the necessity of an attack on Nancy, which was part of the basis of Schlieffen's interest in transforming the army's foot artillery into a mobile arm to deal with enemy fortresses in a timely manner. Schlieffen apparently made few changes for the 1894–1895 mobilization year, although definitive information is no longer available.[31]

Schlieffen's eastern deployment plans for the mobilization years 1894–1895 and 1895–1896 continued the earlier concepts involving strength allocation but also demonstrated the fundamental questions raised by national policy considerations and coalition planning. The 1894–1895 deployment divided the eastern force (increased slightly from fifteen to eighteen active and reserve infantry divisions) into two field armies, with eleven divisions deployed to cooperate with the Austro-Hungarian forces in an attack from Silesia and south of Posen and four divisions (plus one cavalry division) deployed to defend East Prussia. The following year, Schlieffen prepared two entirely separate deployment plans. The first (*Aufmarsch* A) deployed the entire eastern-front force in the north into West and East Prussia, with a force of four reserve divisions to cover the right flank. This would allow movement either to the east to defend East Prussia or to the south to cooperate with the Austrians, but it was essentially a compromise. Schlieffen's actual intentions are no longer known. The second (*Aufmarsch* B) sent the main body of the eastern force to Silesia and Posen to advance into Russian Poland in cooperation with the Austro-Hungarians.[32]

The eastern deployment for 1896–1897 reflected renewed conversations and Schlieffen's attempt to cooperate with Feldmarschall Friedrich Baron von Beck-Rzikowsky, the Austro-Hungarian chief of the General Staff. Schlieffen prepared a single eastern deployment plan, with a total of fifteen infantry divisions. The army was to assemble on the southern frontier of East and West Prussia for a flank attack against the Russian forces in the Warsaw area. This was a clear return to the plans of the elder Moltke and Waldersee and a major concession to the principle of cooperating with Germany's alliance partner.[33]

During the years 1895–1896 and 1896–1897 Schlieffen apparently made no major changes to the western deployment and left no memoranda indicating any change in fundamental thinking about a campaign against the French.[34] During those years, therefore, Schlieffen's planning reflected a compromise solution to the problem of a war on two fronts. The deployments for 1895–1896 and 1896–1897 sent sixteen and eighteen active corps to the west, respectively. The eastern front was to have three active corps in each year.[35] For political reasons, Schlieffen considered an offensive strategy in the east to be necessary, but he did not believe it could be decisive. In considering the western front, Schlieffen feared and resented leaving the initiative to the French. However, he was unable to find an offensive solution beyond a flanking counterattack against French forces advancing either north or south of Metz. The prospects, therefore, were for lengthy campaigns in both theaters rather than decisive action against either major opponent. The essential western dilemma remained that of Moltke's day: even a successful counterattack would allow the French to retreat behind their fortifications and avoid a decisive defeat.[36] Leaving the initiative to the French was equally unattractive, particularly since they might disrupt and divide a German army weakened by major deployments to the east, where the prospects for decisive action seemed slender regardless of the size of the deployed forces.

These difficulties emerged in an important memorandum that came to light only through Dieckmann's manuscript—the Köpke memorandum of August 1895. Its author was Generalmajor Ernst Gustav Köpke, then an *Oberquartiermeister* in the General Staff. Köpke was a fairly typical General Staff officer, largely unknown outside the army but very experienced in both staff and unit assignments.[37]

Köpke warned of the dangers that an attack on the fortifications around Nancy would entail. Further, he cautioned, even a successful assault on Nancy would lead nowhere. At best, such a partial victory would produce only a "slow, laborious, and bloody advance, at times in the manner of siege warfare." Even a gradual victory could not be counted on with certainty, and rapid victories of decisive significance could not be expected. He further warned that the Germans must conduct a "positional war on a larger scale, a battle along lengthy fronts with fortified field positions and the besieging of large fortified areas." There was, he argued, no other way to achieve victory over the French. Hopefully, he concluded, the Germans would not lack the intellectual and material preparations for such an action, and they would be trained and equipped for this form of combat.[38]

Köpke's memorandum shows that a recognition of the problems inherent in attacks against fortified field positions, so prominent in the German army's literature on infantry tactics, had found its way into the strategic thinking of the General Staff. Within a few years, as previous sections of this study have shown, this discussion came to dominate a substantial portion of the army's literature. Although a direct link between Köpke's memorandum and a basic change in Schlieffen's concepts cannot be proved, the possibility of a connection cannot be dismissed. Regardless, the memorandum is important in clarifying the General Staff's understanding of the nature of war around the turn of the century. Schlieffen's developing concepts should be seen as a recognition of these problems and as a search for both a tactical and a strategic answer to the problems of a two-front war.

The Concept of Invading Belgium, 1897

Schlieffen apparently first expressed his belief that the German army must consider enveloping the entire French fortress system by going through Belgium in a memorandum of August 1897.[39] This is a pivotal document in understanding both Schlieffen's evolving thought and the nature of the General Staff's campaign planning. The memorandum, known in detail only from the Dieckmann manuscript, shows that Schlieffen began to seriously study great flanking movement in 1897, but it also illustrates that there was no necessary or immediate connection between Schlieffen's memoranda and the wartime deployment plans.[40] The 1897–1898 deployment plan, completed in April 1897, prohibited any violation of Belgian territory and sent no large forces to the north of Luxembourg.[41]

The memorandum, in contrast, was more aggressive. It began with the premise that any German offensive had to avoid French fortifications and concluded that this was possible only north of Verdun. The problem was that the five roads leading through France and Luxembourg between Montmedy-Longwy and Verdun (to the south) were insufficient to move the forces needed to cut off Verdun and support a powerful offensive. Any force that moved beyond the Meuse River would be insufficient to achieve important results. The result was that "an offensive that wishes to go around the flank must not fail to violate the neutrality, not only of Luxembourg, but also of Belgium."

The memorandum then proposed a right flank envelopment with two field armies (First and Second) of eight corps moving between St. Vith and Diedenhofen, using the latter as the base of its turn. An additional force of six reserve divisions would assemble around Aachen to protect the turning movement against the Belgian army on its north (right) flank.

Another field army (Third) of eight reserve divisions would cross the Mosel River between Diedenhofen and Metz and invest the fortress of Verdun from the north and northwest on both sides of the Meuse.

The memorandum envisioned that the two right-wing armies would swing sharply south and engage the mass of the French army on the heights of Verdun. At that point, the Germans would be in dire need of assistance. This would be provided by Fourth Army's four corps, which would cross the Meuse between Verdun and Toul. In doing so, Fourth Army would have to take at least two important forts, overcome French resistance on the heights on the far bank of the river, and cope with possible threats to its left flank from forces coming from Toul and Nancy. To deal with this threat, and to tie down any French forces that might otherwise be sent to the French left flank, Fifth Army's four corps would move through Pont-a-Mousson and advance on both sides of the Mosel against Nancy. To assist this force, and to further immobilize other French forces, Sixth Army would attack between Nancy and Luneville. Finally, Seventh Army, consisting of five active corps and three reserve divisions, would defend the left flank and then join Sixth Army when Nancy was taken. One of the active corps and the reserve divisions were to defend upper Alsace and join Seventh Army when it advanced.

These armies constituted more than the entire force actually available to the German army and included three additional ad hoc corps to be formed from various supernumerary formations upon mobilization. The memorandum also foresaw the creation of one or two reserve armies consisting of reserve divisions formed from ad hoc reserve divisions and the deployment of all available *Landwehr* units to protect lines of communication, primarily in the rear of the two right-flank armies. The eastern frontiers would be left almost entirely undefended, a possibility to be embraced only if Germany could avoid the long-anticipated war on two fronts.

Schlieffen's memorandum gave no explanation for its disregard of the eastern front. Dieckmann, who had wide access to Schlieffen's writings, suggested that Schlieffen thought the recent accession of Nicholas II (1894–1917), coupled with Russia's shifting emphasis to the Far East and the Ottoman Empire, offered the prospect of improved relations between Germany and Russia. If this were the case, a two-front war was, at least temporarily, no longer certain. This speculation may be correct, or it may be that Schlieffen's thinking had an entirely different foundation. If Dieckmann is correct, Schlieffen was once again basing his strategic calculations on the Reich's political circumstances rather than, as usually alleged, on "technical" military considerations.

Schlieffen took two other actions to accommodate his plans to political circumstances and perhaps even to support the German government's efforts to improve relations with its eastern neighbor. While he was working on the memorandum, Schlieffen dropped his insistence on improved defensive measures in the eastern provinces, which included arming the civilian population for local self-defense. He was careful not to inform the Austrians that he had abandoned all cooperative efforts for an offensive in the east, and he virtually cut off contact with his Austro-Hungarian counterpart.[42]

Regardless of the reasons for its one-sided assumptions, the August 1897 memorandum, like many of Schlieffen's memoranda, had little if any immediate impact on his deployment plans. The 1897–1898 plan, prepared before the memorandum was written, was nearly the same as that for 1898–1899, which was prepared about eight months later. In 1897–1898 the deployment plan sent forty-eight infantry and six cavalry divisions to the west and sixteen infantry and five cavalry divisions to the east.[43] The 1898–1899 deployment plan called for forty-six infantry divisions in the west and twenty-two infantry divisions in the east; cavalry deployments remained the same.[44] The 1898–1899 plan thus increased the eastern deployment, whereas the memorandum had considered stripping the east of all large forces.

The first of Schlieffen's memoranda on the invasion of southern Belgium and the swing behind Verdun was thus a purely academic exercise and largely unrelated to the actual war deployment plan. Both mobilization plans forbade any violation of Belgian neutrality, and in neither year would the army have been in a position to perform a turning movement through Luxembourg and Belgium.[45] Instead, it would have been in a position to counterattack a possible French thrust south of Luxembourg and deal with a possible French attack south of Metz.

Planning for a Two-Front War, 1898

Schlieffen's memorandum of October 1898 returned to the question of a two-front war with renewed vigor. By then, it was clear that the army increases proposed by Schlieffen but opposed by the war minister would not take place. Worse, Russo-German relations would not obviate the need to prepare for war against both France and Russia, which in any case had continued to be the basis for all mobilization and deployment plans.[46] Another fact remained unscathed by recent developments: French mobilization and deployment required only about three weeks, while that of Germany required four weeks. In this memorandum Schlieffen once again assumed that the French would take the offensive immediately. Combined, these two factors rendered an early German advance beyond the line of the Saar River "inadvisable," in Schlieffen's words.[47]

In this same memorandum Schlieffen examined the likely French courses of action.[48] He concluded that a French attack on the German left flank was doomed to failure, but the French might advance through Luxembourg and Belgium to attack the German right flank. This meant that the Germans should be prepared for a French attack north of Diedenhofen, south of there, or even south of Metz. The last option would be best for the Germans, as it would give them an opportunity to make "an extremely favorable counterattack in the flank of the enemy." Schlieffen concluded that the Germans must therefore "make our right flank strong and extend it to the west as far as possible. This would not be possible without violating the neutrality of Luxembourg and possibly that of Belgium." The main thrust of the memorandum thus continued Schlieffen's long practice of relying on an offensive-defensive approach in the west to deal with the French, especially in the case of a two-front war.

If the French declined to attack, the memorandum went on, the Germans would make an inexcusable mistake if they did not seize the initiative and instead waited inactively until the enemy decided to advance. The danger in the east, moreover, worked against such a waiting strategy, just as waiting for the Italians would be an illusion. The solution, then, was a turning movement through Luxembourg and Belgium. This turning movement, however, "must not be too extended," since it had the "double task" of being a counterattack in case of an enemy advance and an offensive in case the enemy remained behind his fortifications.[49]

An annex to the memorandum gave further details on the concept of operations associated with this plan. Schlieffen discussed two concepts— one assuming that the French would launch an early offensive, and the other assuming that the French would not attack at all. In the case of a French offensive, Schlieffen argued that the right-wing armies should immediately counterattack the French left, while Sixth Army, deployed as stated above, would do the same against the French right. If successful, this would produce a widely separated pincer movement supported in the center by Third, Fourth, and Fifth Armies, which would stand on the defensive to engage the main French attack.

If the French remained behind their fortresses, the October 1898 memorandum called for the two right-wing armies (First and Second) to advance through Luxembourg and the southernmost finger of Belgium and to cross the Meuse River between Donchery (about three miles west of Sedan) and Stenay (about nine miles to the west, southwest of Montmedy). This force would then turn south to advance against the rear of the French fortifications from Verdun southward. Seventh Army, consisting of six reserve divisions, was to cover the southern flank of the turning forces, while Third Army (four active corps and two reserve divisions) was to cover the left flank of the crossing and then follow over the Meuse once the turning movement had succeeded.

Three field armies would then attempt to envelop the entire French left flank, forcing the French to turn and fight with reversed fronts and separated from their main lines of communication. This was a concept of maneuver and combat that had long dominated German theory. The remaining armies were to make supporting attacks to the south, overcome the French positions around Nancy, and advance in the direction of Toul and Epinal. The memorandum apparently contained no phase lines or day-to-day objectives, although this is not certain.[50] Overall, the memorandum discussed a concept of operations consistent with both the August 1897 memorandum and Schlieffen's belief that the Germans would ultimately have to attack by going around the French fortresses, either as part of a counterattack or on their own initiative.[51]

Multiple Deployment Plans, 1899–1900

Uncertainties in the political situation caused Schlieffen to prepare several deployment plans for mobilization year 1899–1900. The first two were finished in April 1899, thus following the October 1898 memorandum just discussed. Case I assumed a war against only France and sent the entire German army to the west. Case II prepared for a two-front conflict.[52] According to Dieckmann, the surviving archival material provided no information on where the western-front forces would have been deployed, but there was much information on a two-front war. This dual deployment sent forty-five infantry divisions and five cavalry divisions to the west and twenty-three infantry divisions and five cavalry divisions to the east. The western deployment (with two-thirds of the German army) remained largely as it had been in the days of Moltke and under Schlieffen's earlier deployment plans. It thus abandoned the turning movement through Belgium and reverted to the old idea of an attack against Nancy. The units that would have formed First and Second Armies in the event of a single-front war were deployed to the east under case II. Schlieffen apparently planned to adopt a largely defensive stand in East Prussia.[53]

The 1899–1900 deployment planning illustrates several problems in analyzing the development of German concepts. Friedrich von Boetticher, who had access to much of the archival material used by Dieckmann, described the deployment concept using the memorandum of October 1898 and thus included details that were not actually part of the deployment plan. His account entirely neglected case I (a single-front war), making both the memorandum and the deployment plan more one-sided than they actually were. Worse, the large-scale sketch he used to demonstrate the strength of the various armies implied a movement north of Luxembourg and through a large portion of Belgium south of the Meuse. But neither case I nor case II suggested such a northern movement. In fact, it is not certain that either deployment would have violated Belgium at all.[54] Dieckmann, in discussing the memorandum and the deployment plan, concluded that, like the 1897 memorandum, neither document would have led to a wide right-wing movement.[55] Boetticher, who provided the most detailed published account of the 1899–1900 concepts, confused the memorandum with the deployment plan and failed to mention that in the event of a two-front war, the General Staff planned to revert to the old concept of attacking around Nancy.

As Russian-German relations worsened over the issue of German policy in Turkey, Schlieffen modified the 1899–1900 deployment.[56] This new deployment plan, which became effective on 1 October 1899, modified case I (war against only France) and assumed that Russia might adopt a hostile attitude that required measures beyond protecting the eastern frontier. This would make it impossible to send the entire army to the west. The new deployment sent ten infantry divisions and three cavalry divisions to the east, with the mission of defending the area beyond the Vistula.[57] The right-wing armies retained most of their front-line strength, while the center grew stronger and the left-wing armies (Alsace-Lorraine) became weaker. Schlieffen apparently planned a close turning movement along the lines of his October 1898 memorandum, an aggressive counterattack but not a wide envelopment.[58] The northernmost army (First) was to deploy between Malmedy and Dasburg, with its cavalry initially assigned to Second Army in the Bitburg-Wasserbillig area. The deployment instructions forbade any movement into Luxembourg until the French had done so, and they made no mention of Belgium.

If the Russians actually participated, and if the Germans expected a Russian attack, the modified deployment plan sent an additional twelve divisions to the eastern front. These reinforcements came at the expense of the German right flank on the western front and would have meant the end of any turning movement. As Dieckmann concluded, this indicated that Schlieffen had not reached a final decision about a turning operation by the end of the century.[59] This contingency planning retained a largely defensive stance on both fronts if they both saw active hostilities.

In November 1899 Schlieffen produced a new memorandum addressing possible German courses of action in the case of a two-front war. He discussed sending the majority of the army to the east, apparently assuming that the French would not take the offensive as war began. In this scenario, the war in the west would consist of mutual "observation," with the Germans unable to take the offensive because of the limited forces available. A second discussion addressed the results of a French offensive, which Schlieffen thought would come north of Metz or Diedenhofen. He proposed massing the limited German forces on the German right to counterattack the French left. If the French main effort was south of Metz, Schlieffen proposed holding the main forces back and making preparations to move them to the area between Prüm and Saarbrücken, presumably for a counterattack against the left flank of a French attacking force.[60]

A few months later Generalmajor Hans Beseler, an *Oberquartiermeister* in the General Staff, prepared another memorandum proposing a solution to the problem of the western deployment. In its own way, Beseler's memorandum was as radical as Schlieffen's consideration of sending the bulk of the army to the eastern front. Beseler, one of the leading intellectuals of the prewar army and later a controversial figure for his activities during the First World War, submitted his memorandum on 18 January 1900, too late for full consideration in developing the 1900–1901 deployment plan.

Beseler argued for a turning movement through Luxembourg and Belgium. Because he recognized that the French would learn of the massing of the main German strength on the Belgian-Luxembourg frontier, he stressed the use of all available strength in a rapid offensive to achieve a decisive victory in the first battles.[61] Beseler's memorandum was extreme in both its proposals and its optimism, but it produced no immediate results.

Deployment Plans, 1900–1901 and 1901–1902

The deployment plans for mobilization year 1900–1901 illustrated the often tenuous relationship between Schlieffen's memoranda and the actual plans for war.[62] They also showed another example of a deployment alternative based on the assumption of greatly changed political circumstances, rather than military factors considered in isolation from the international environment.

Case I for mobilization year 1900–1901 was a continuation of the basic concepts in the revised deployments prepared in October 1899, with the major effort in the west. A total of fifty-eight infantry divisions were scheduled to be sent to the western front, and ten to the east. According to Dieckmann, case I assumed that Belgium and England would join the French. The plan was essentially the same as the October 1899 deployment plan, except that the turning flank included Third Army, which had abandoned the attack across the Meuse between Verdun and Toul. This did not mean a wider swing to the north; on the contrary, the turning flank extended farther to the south, with Diedenhofen becoming the pivot point.[63] This increased the turning flank to encompass a total of twelve corps, although its task remained the same as in previous years: passing through southern Belgium and Luxembourg, crossing the Meuse north of Verdun, and attacking in the rear of the line of French fortifications. Although the deployment directive did not mention Belgium, the northernmost army could have advanced through the southernmost tip of Belgium. First Army was to deploy with its right flank moving along the road from Montjoie to Malmedy. This deployment plan lacked the previous order not to violate Luxembourg's territory until the French had done so. The left wing was reinforced at the expense of the center armies (Fourth and Fifth), which probably signified abandonment of the attack on Nancy beyond a demonstration to fix some French forces. The deployment under case I did not assume a substantial Italian presence on the far right wing of the German forces. The eastern deployment under case I remained that of previous years. A total of ten infantry divisions and three cavalry divisions were entrusted with defense of the eastern provinces.

Case II (two-front war) for mobilization year 1900–1901, unlike previous plans, made the major effort in the east, sending forty-four divisions there and retaining only twenty-four in the west.[64] This represented a major new alternative, allowing the army to choose major offensives in either theater, depending on circumstances. Although the deployment plan lacked a definite outline of operations, Dieckmann assumed from the units' positions that the 1900–1901 deployment prepared for simultaneous offensives toward the Narew and Niemen Rivers.[65]

The western deployment for case II sent four field armies with ten corps and twenty-four active and reserve divisions (plus five cavalry divisions) to the French and Belgian borders for a strategic defensive. Dieckmann's manuscript indicates that this would probably be conducted offensively, with a counterattack against an anticipated French attack. This is not certain, however, since the deployment plan did not address this directly, and Dieckmann relied on Schlieffen's memorandum of November 1899, discussed above.[66]

The German deployment plans for 1901–1902 were based on the same assumptions as in 1900–1901. Case I assumed a two-front war with the main effort in the west and with Belgian and British participation. Case II also assumed a two-front war, but with England in alliance with Germany and the main effort against Russia. The case I deployment was basically the same as in 1900–1901, with a total of fifty-eight active and reserve infantry divisions and eight cavalry divisions ready for an offensive based on the limited turning movement of previous years.[67] The records used by Dieckmann contained no indication of an Italian presence on the western front. The Ehlert documents, however, indicate a vague assumption that an Italian force of unknown size would assemble near Breisach and Strassburg.[68] The eastern deployment had ten divisions, as in previous years, with the same assembly areas and tasks. Schlieffen created a supplement to the eastern deployment of case I, outlining plans for when substantial reinforcements began to arrive from the west. The second General Staff ride of 1901 was based on this situation, which in turn followed the situation played out in the first General Staff ride of 1901. This staff ride abandoned an enveloping movement through Luxembourg and Belgium and instead assumed that the Germans would launch a counteroffensive and produce a decisive victory "on the left bank of the Rhine near the Belgian frontier."[69] The latter was expected to produce a decisive German victory within four weeks, allowing nine corps to be transferred to the eastern front. In the meantime, the weak German forces would withdraw to Königsberg and behind the line Allenstein-Osterode-Rosenberg. The war games ended without a decisive outcome.[70] Here, it should be noted that Schlieffen recognized that even a decisive defeat of the French would not end the war and that thirteen corps would have to remain in the west. If there was any illusion in this memorandum, it was that of a short initial campaign, not a short war.

Case II for 1901–1902 sent about forty divisions to the east for the major effort, but a substantial twenty-seven would be sent to the west. The mission of the western armies was to stand on the defensive until they had an opportunity to counterattack one of the flanks of the attacking French army.[71] As a result, the western forces would not be deployed in forward areas until the direction of the French offensive became clear. The western armies had their initial headquarters far to the rear, in Jükerath, Koblenz, and Mainz.[72] The precise intentions for the eastern front are no longer available, but the assembly areas indicated a major effort first against the Russian Niemen Army, with a holding attack against the Russian forces on the Narew River.

Deployment Plans, 1902–1903: Counterattack

The flexibility that remained in both Schlieffen's thought and his planned deployments becomes clear when one considers mobilization year 1902–1903. No memoranda exist for the fundamental operational concepts behind the deployment plan for that year, but the Dieckmann manuscript contains detailed information on the deployment. The overall concept assumed a two-front war. As was normal, the General Staff prepared two cases, both of which now assumed a two-front war.

The overall deployments in case I remained as in 1900–1901 and 1901–1902 (major deployment in the west, with English and Belgian participation), and this discussion considers only the western plan.[73] It sent sixty divisions to the western front but contained important variations from the previous year's plan. Field armies two through six (eighteen corps) were to deploy close to the Luxembourg-French frontiers between Echternach (about eighteen miles northeast of Luxembourg City) and Champeny (in Alsace, about thirty-one miles southwest of Strassburg). First Army (four corps) was deployed between Eupen (about eleven miles south of Aachen) and Neuerberg (opposite central Luxembourg and about twelve miles north of Echternach). Second and Third Armies were deployed north of Diedenhofen, with the remaining four to the south. The right flank thus had slightly more strength in the north than had been the case in previous plans. Schlieffen apparently assumed that the French had learned of the planned German turning movement and would deploy strong forces on the French left and thus be the first to invade Belgium and Luxembourg. In that case, German First Army would be in a position to envelop the French left flank as it moved against the normal position of the German right flank.

According to Dieckmann, Schlieffen expected the German left wing to launch an offensive between Verdun and Toul. He thus hoped to entice the French into attacking the right flank of this group of German armies. The German right wing would then attack these outflanked French forces as they advanced. Such a concept was "an exceedingly surprising alteration of his operational intents" and was "in strong contradiction to his previous views."[74] This would have produced a classic illustration of the old Prussian military saying: he who would outflank can be outflanked.[75]

A General Staff ride of 1902, probably conducted before the 1902–1903 deployment plan was completed, considered the possibility of a French attack in anticipation of movement of the German right wing. The General Staff ride posited that the Germans had obligated themselves (through a treaty with England?) not to enter Belgium and Luxembourg unless the French had already violated their neutrality. The study also concluded that the Germans would defeat the mass of the French army deployed between Metz and the Vosges Mountains but that much of it would retreat behind the line of fortifications. The Germans would thus be faced with a costly campaign to attack the French fortress system.[76] First Army's separated deployment south of Aachen would put it in a position to move against the flank or rear of a French force deployed to defeat the German right wing if it were deployed according to previous years' plans.

Accordingly, the scenario of the staff study provided that three of the armies positioned along the Lorraine frontier south of Diedenhofen (Fourth, Fifth, and Sixth) were to attack the Maas front along the line Verdun-Toul. Schlieffen had apparently reversed his previous view that the fortified French positions between Toul and Epinal could withstand a German attack, concluding that such an attack, if linked with the turning movement north of Verdun, could succeed.[77] These deployments, which had a foundation in the French plan XIV, thus considerably altered the options open to a western-front commander by splitting the right flank, anticipating two flanking actions on the right, and assuming that the turning movement would improve the chances for making frontal assaults on the French center positions. As the study developed, the Germans met the main French forces in the Vosges and Lorraine and failed to achieve a decisive victory.[78]

The information on case II for 1902–1903 is somewhat contradictory. The Ehlert documents suggest that the eastern forces would have fourteen active corps, two reserve corps, and seven reserve divisions (thirty-nine total). This case also sent First Army to the Rhine province, where it would be in a position to attack a French army that tried to outflank the German right wing as it turned around Verdun.[79] According to Dieckmann, case II for 1902–1903 planned for forty-four divisions to be sent to the west and twenty-four to the east. Case II in 1901–1902 had sent only twenty-seven divisions to the west.

The decrease in the strength of the eastern force from four armies with forty-four infantry divisions to three armies with twenty-four active divisions allowed for only a limited offensive against the Russians. Although Dieckmann lacked documentary proof, he surmised from the concentration areas that one army would make the major attack toward the Niemen River, supported by a second army; meanwhile, the third army would attempt to fix the Russian forces deployed along the Narew.[80]

These relatively small eastern deployments in both cases for mobilization year 1902–1903 did not mean that Schlieffen had finally decided against any major offensive in the east. A memorandum of December 1902 addressed an eastern deployment of thirteen corps, with nine making the major effort consisting of an attack toward the Narew in conjunction with an Austrian attack from the south. The remaining four corps were to advance toward the Niemen River to fix the Russian forces deployed in the north and thus protect the flank of the main effort. Counting reserve divisions, the total forces sent to the east under this scenario would have been thirty-six divisions.

The deployment plan of 1902–1903 and the related memoranda are a further indication of the difficulties in identifying a single approach to warfare on either front in Schlieffen's thinking. His memoranda and deployment schemes reflect a flexibility of approach usually denied him by historians. The question remains whether his basic concepts became more one-sided and rigid in the last years of his term as chief of the General Staff, as is often assumed, and whether his legacy of apparent inflexibility was his creation or that of his postwar admirers.

Deployment Plans, 1903–1904

The 1903–1904 deployment plans reverted to the old formula of two very different cases: one sending the greater part of the army to the west, and the other sending a large majority to the east. In case I, the western forces would have sixty-five active and reserve divisions and the eastern forces a mere ten, along the lines of the plans from 1899 and 1900. The major difference from previous western plans was that Sixth and Seventh Armies on the western front were stronger, reflecting the increasingly obvious probability that Italian forces would not be available to defend the upper Rhine River area. The deployment also abandoned the separation of First Army and returned to the traditional close massing of the turning wing on the German right flank.[81] First Army would be deployed substantially to the north, with its original headquarters located at Montjoie rather than at St. Vith, about eighteen miles to the south. The 1903–1904 deployment thus placed three armies north of Metz and one north of Luxembourg. This deployment clearly anticipated an advance through southern Belgium, although the deployment instructions forbade any violation of Belgian territory without an explicit order of the High Command. German units could cross into Luxembourg only after the French did so, and then only to cover the German deployment. The eastern forces, reduced to their traditional ten divisions, also returned to the basic concepts that had prevailed in previous years.

No reliable information is available for the case II deployments. The documents in Ehlert's *The Schlieffen Plan* suggest that the General Staff never fully developed case II because it seemed "the less likely case."[82] Dieckmann surmised, on the basis of the first General Staff ride for 1903, that about half the forces would go to the west and be deployed for an attack on the French left, but aiming for only a partial victory. In this staff ride the weakened western armies attempted to overcome a French flanking attack through Belgium or Luxembourg by transferring forces from those deployed south of Metz. Dieckmann also surmised, based on the December 1902 memorandum cited above, that the major effort of the thirty-six active and reserve divisions would be against the Russian forces along the Narew River in conjunction with an Austrian offensive from the south.[83] Not too much should be made of this, however, since virtually no directly applicable documentation is available from either Dieckmann or other sources.[84]

For reasons unknown, the Dieckmann manuscript ends with this sketchy information on the 1903–1904 deployment plan. The historian is thus on less certain ground from this point forward.[85]

Deployment Plans, 1904–1905: No Right-Wing Sweep

The 1904–1905 deployment plan had the usual two variants. Case I assumed a war against France alone. It sent the entire force of twenty-six active corps to the west, leaving only two cavalry divisions and four reserve divisions in the east. Case II assumed a war against France and Russia. It sent twenty-three active corps, nine cavalry divisions, and fifteen reserve divisions to the west. The forces available in the east were limited to three active corps, two cavalry divisions, and four reserve divisions. The western armies had the same general deployment areas in both deployment schemes. The three active corps sent to the east in case II came from First, Third, and Fourth Armies.

These western deployments of 1904–1905, which varied substantially from a General Staff ride in 1904, limited the deployment's northern flank to the Bitburg area.[86] No field armies deployed the bulk their strength north of Luxembourg. This meant the German right would sweep south of the Meuse as it passed through Belgium, posing no threat to Namur, Liege, or Brussels. Ritter agreed that, under this plan, the right wing would pass through only the southern tip of Belgium, toward Mezieres and Stenay, with an anticipated battle near Verdun. Overall, the forces on the right flank were weaker than those in Lorraine. This reflects Schlieffen's continuing concern about holding attacks in the Nancy area, but it also raises the possibility that Schlieffen was again considering a genuine counteroffensive breakthrough around Nancy if the right wing were successful in drawing large French forces away from that sector.[87] In that case, of course, the fabled sweep through Belgium and northern France would have been a secondary undertaking, a large-scale supporting attack. Even Zuber's critics recognize that this plan is an illustration of the continuing flexibility in Schlieffen's thinking.[88]

The 1904–1905 deployment plans were not consistent with the deployment tested in the 1904 General Staff ride mentioned above. That exercise sent First Army across the Meuse around Liege; it then turned south as it passed between Namur and Charleroi and prepared to move against the flank of a major French attack toward Cologne. The staff ride also played out a major French advance between Metz and Strassburg. The result was an eventual German double envelopment of the French in Alsace and an indecisive battle on the German right. Apparently, Schlieffen was satisfied with this result, as Zoellner concluded that throughout the course of the exercise Schlieffen "sought to produce proof that an attack against the flank of the German army marching through Belgium was not to be easily executed."[89] This may be true, but in the staff ride, First Army was in a very different position than it would have been in according to current or past deployment plans. It seems that Schlieffen anticipated that the French left wing would move directly against the German right wing south of the Meuse but would be outflanked itself if First Army advanced near Namur.[90] What is most interesting is that Schlieffen accepted a result that was inconsistent with any desire to achieve a decisive envelopment of the French right flank if the French attacked north of Metz.[91]

Ritter tried to make this consistent with prevailing ideas by arguing that Schlieffen did this to illustrate that the Germans could "strengthen the right wing without undue concern for the left."[92] That is possible, but the results could also be seen as confirmation that the main battle would be in Lorraine and the choice of location might not be up to the Germans. The explanation may rest in the fact that Schlieffen, at least up to this time, regarded the great turning movement not as an end but as a means. The real goal, consistent with German theory and with the content of nearly all his studies and exercises, was destruction of the enemy's main force. The 1904 General Staff ride produced this on the German left flank rather than on the right, but the strategic result would have been the same. In any case, this instance underscores the difficulties of directly linking the General Staff exercises, which had both educational and testing functions, with any particular deployment plan.

Final Deployment Plan, 1905–1906

Schlieffen's final deployment plan, for mobilization year 1905–1906, is known only by documents recently discovered and published in Ehlert's The Schlieffen Plan.[93] Case I sent the entire army to the west, while case II sent thirty-three corps to the west, as in the previous years. The minor differences allow a common discussion based on case I.

This scheme sent a large part of the western army farther north than any previous plan, and it clearly laid the basis for an invasion of Holland as well as Belgium. The plan did not automatically produce such a result, however. It forbade violations of Holland and Belgium until the High Command (*Oberste Heeresleitung*, or *OHL*) had given the order, until the enemy had entered those nations, or until those states had engaged in hostilities. Cavalry reconnaissance in those countries was to begin only "if the advance into Holland and Belgium takes place."

The opening deployment of the armies, which reflected both campaign decisions and the requirements of railway movement, reflected this shift to the north and a stronger turning movement on the right flank. Five field armies would be deployed north of Metz, three north of Luxembourg, and one to the north of Aachen. This deployment clearly envisioned a movement of at least three field armies (eleven active and seven reserve corps) through Belgium and Luxembourg and an additional two through southern Luxembourg.

The surviving information concerns the usual case I, a single-front war in the west, with virtually the entire army deployed there. The plan sent fifty-two active and eighteen reserve divisions to the west; these would be deployed in six armies between Diedenhofen and Aachen, a seventh around Metz, and an eighth between Metz and Saarburg. It is not clear whether the right wing was prepared to advance across Holland or north of Liege, but it was clearly in a position to sweep across Belgium south of Liege along the southern bank of the Sambre. No forces were deployed in the far north position where First Army began in August 1914.[94]

Exercises and General Staff Rides

Beyond the various memoranda and deployment plans discussed above, there were two other kinds of General Staff activities relevant to this discussion. The first, mentioned briefly above, were the annual General Staff rides, usually two in number. These took groups of officers to the eastern and western frontiers, where they participated in large-scale map-based exercises. The second were the tactical and strategic problems presented to General Staff officers during the winter.[95] These exercises had no direct connection to war plans but served the purposes of training young General Staff officers in large-unit operations and testing concepts related to the General Staff's strategic concerns.[96] Of course, these bore the stamp of Schlieffen's intentions and, though useful from his perspective, were subject to manipulation and distortion to support the emerging orthodoxy of flanking attacks and turning movements.[97]

Schlieffen conducted staff rides primarily for the education and training of his General Staff officers. They were not designed to familiarize future army commanders with Schlieffen's campaign concepts. Indeed, he refused to conduct any war games to prepare future field army commanders for anticipated campaigns because he thought they would resent any such efforts and because he doubted their ability to keep secrets.[98]

As it has been pointed out, staff rides were widely distributed within the General Staff (in Berlin and in the units) and were classified merely as "secret," not "top secret" (*streng Geheim*). In the interests of secrecy, the General Staff routinely destroyed old versions of deployment plans but regarded the results of staff rides as entirely different kinds of documents.[99]

Overall, the surviving records of Schlieffen's exercises portray his early commitment to a combination of frontal holding attacks and flanking attacks in tactics and turning movements in strategy, yet they reveal substantial flexibility in strategic situations and concepts. In his 1892 western General Staff ride Schlieffen allowed a German advance through Belgium and Luxembourg only after an initial French violation of these countries' neutrality. In 1894 and 1898 the eastern General Staff rides closely resembled the actual situation in 1914; the latter even involved two of the key German commanders of 1914—Hindenburg and Prittwitz.[100] In 1895 Schlieffen noted in his closing remarks that both French and German players had limited their advances through Belgium to the area south of the Sambre, thus avoiding the crossings around Liege and Namur. In the 1897 eastern staff ride (which was not based on the 1897–1898 deployment plan) Schlieffen's scenario had the Germans driving the French back to their line of fortifications. The Germans then moved four corps and reserve divisions temporarily to the eastern front, where the staff ride took place. Meanwhile, the war with France continued. The scenario recognized that France had not been defeated and that the eastern army would soon have to send units back to the west.[101] Even in 1898 the German commander waited for the French to violate the neutrality of Belgium and Luxembourg.[102]

In the western General Staff rides of 1901 and 1902 Schlieffen continued to stress counterattacks as the solution to the problem of dealing with the French. In 1901 the ride concluded with a decisive battle along the German-Belgian border. Likewise, in 1902 the decisive battle was a German counterattack on the left wing of the French forces advancing to the west of Metz. Schlieffen, in effect, also defined what he meant by a decisive battle, since at the conclusion both staff rides he transferred only nine corps to the east, leaving thirteen active corps and twelve reserve divisions in the west, where the war against France would continue. These scenarios, as Zuber points out, had the advantage of allowing the Germans to eliminate the immediate French threat (but not the entire French army) close to the German railheads, thus facilitating the rapid transfer of forces to the eastern front.[103]

Schlieffen conducted two western General Staff rides in 1904, with the first probably taking place in June, although this is not certain.[104] Neither fit into the framework of what came to be called the "Schlieffen Plan." Both resulted in movements and battles far from those envisioned in the 1905 memorandum. In the first, a German counterattack destroyed the French force attacking into Lorraine through a double envelopment from Metz and Strassburg, while other German forces fought an indecisive battle north of Metz. The German right wing entered Holland and Belgium (which was allied with France) but achieved little. The entire affair lasted only until the twenty-first day of mobilization. The most noteworthy elements of this staff ride, aside from its departure from a wide right-wing sweep deep into France and Belgium, were its reliance on nonexistent German forces, a successful major breakthrough battle, and a decisive battle in Lorraine.[105]

The second western staff ride of 1904 began with the same general situation, except that the opening movements were not completed until the twenty-second day of mobilization. The Germans in this scenario did not have a large number of additional forces. The French, however, had several hypothetical reserve and active units. The French attacked north of Metz and into Alsace-Lorraine. They crossed the Rhine with eight corps but achieved little of strategic significance. The German First Army, which invaded Belgium, failed to envelop the French right flank, thus contradicting Schlieffen's own assumption that a broad advance would force the French to turn and defend the approaches to Paris. Instead, the German player proposed—and Schlieffen allowed it, despite his disapproval—a complete abandonment of the wide turning movement around the French left wing. The Germans instead moved south to confront the main French forces in Alsace-Lorraine. Due to faulty moves and the commander's failure to keep his focus on annihilating the French left wing, the latter defeated the German right wing north of Metz, while the French right wing threatened to complete an encirclement of the great mass of the German army. The exercise ended there, at mobilization day thirty-one.[106]

These two staff rides show that Schlieffen created games that conflicted with his emerging deployment concepts and that he allowed his officers to play the games out to unfavorable conclusions. Schlieffen's main teaching point seems to have been that forces must be massed against one or the other wing of an opposing army in order to achieve a decisive victory. This principle, rather than achieving victory through a wide swing through Belgium and Holland, was the basis of Schlieffen's teachings.

The right turning movement was not an end in itself; it was merely one means to achieve the goal of annihilating a major portion of the enemy army.[107] Ritter thus missed the point when he argued that Schlieffen used the staff ride of 1904 to demonstrate the necessity of "strengthen[ing] the right wing without undue concern for the left."[108] The irony is that Helmuth von Moltke, Schlieffen's successor, may have arrived at his concept of the double envelopment, which he hoped to achieve in 1914, from Schlieffen's exercises.[109]

Schlieffen's Final Staff Ride

Schlieffen conducted a staff ride in the summer of 1905 on a scale that dwarfed all previous efforts. Three groups of General Staff officers developed plans for the French, while Schlieffen himself acted as the German player for each group. The overall scenario sent nearly the entire German army to the western front, since Russian participation seemed unlikely under the circumstances. The three French solutions were:

1. Offensive between Metz and Strassburg against the southern flank of the German forces in Lorraine.
2. Attack on both sides of Metz.
3. Combined French and Belgian offensive with the French left wing extending to Maubeuge.[110]

In playing against the first French solution, Schlieffen abandoned the turning movement through Belgium and engaged the mass of the French army in Lorraine. In moving against the second French player, who attacked on both sides of Metz, Schlieffen executed the right turning movement while retaining three field armies in the Strassburg area to strike the French army in the flank and rear after it advanced beyond the Saar River. Counterattacking a French attack north of Metz had been the basis of Schlieffen's plans for years, as indicated by the previous discussion of his deployment plans.

The third case, in which Hugo von Freytag-Loringhoven led the French side, is the most important in light of subsequent developments. In this case, the French, allied with Belgium, advanced from the Maubeuge area through Luxembourg toward Namur and Brussels. Schlieffen, after first determining that there was no danger of a major French attack in Lorraine, moved the mass of the German army to the right wing and enveloped the French left flank short (east) of Paris, while a major assault from Metz attacked the French right. As Boetticher remarked, this final exercise demonstrated that even as late as 1905, Schlieffen by no means intended to advance to the west of Paris.[111] That, indeed, was an expedient to be adopted only if the effort to make a shorter turning movement into the French flank and rear was unsuccessful. Following a discussion of the results, the players repeated all three scenarios, with much the same results. In one case, Schlieffen moved the German far right wing around Paris and crossed the Seine near Rouen.[112]

Ritter's account of this staff ride, based on Zoellner, has misled subsequent historians. Paraphrasing Zoellner, Ritter argued that Schlieffen "put his cards on the table for the first time, showing those taking part in the ride that he meant to cut through neutral Belgium in great breadth."[113] Ritter thus ignored Schlieffen's very different actions in the first two scenarios and created the false impression that the turning movement under the third scenario was similar to that allegedly laid out in the 1905 memorandum. In fact, most of the staff ride's movements and battles took place far from Paris, as Zoellner's account makes clear.[114] Even Wolfgang Foerster, one of Schlieffen's most prolific defenders and Moltke's most bitter critics, admitted that this "astonishing" solution was difficult to reconcile with the 1905 memorandum. Foerster also noted that the records of Schlieffen's staff rides were not among the holdings of the Reichsarchiv when he was researching Schlieffen and the 1914 campaign.[115] Foerster was wrong, however, in believing that knowledge of the details of the solution to the first scenario would make a great impression among experts and would portray the 1914 deployment in an entirely new light.[116] Instead, the Schlieffen school continued to ignore evidence contrary to its dogmatic approach.

Schlieffen's Last War Game

The final item in establishing the planning context of the Schlieffen memorandum of December 1905 is Schlieffen's famous last war game of November–December 1905. The bulk of the material relating to this war game (*Kriegspiel*) has been lost, but Schlieffens's concluding discussion, containing many details of the action, has survived in his papers and is now available in a published translation.[117] Only recently, however, has it begun to attract the attention of scholars. Interestingly, Schlieffen's concluding remarks were dated 23 December 1905, indicating that they were written before he finished the December memorandum, which was actually completed early in 1906.

The scenario placed Germany in a two-front war against Russia, France, and England, with Belgium, Holland, and Italy remaining neutral. Schlieffen divided the army about equally between the eastern and western fronts and had the Germans go on the strategic defensive on both fronts. He stated that it was "impracticable to abandon the entire left bank of the Rhine and the whole left bank of the Moselle to the enemy and to stand by while a large area of German territory was laid waste by the enemy." In this scenario—unrealistically, in light of the two subsequent world wars—the French and English invaded Belgium, while the latter allowed German forces to join in the defense of Antwerp. A secondary French force advanced into Germany south of Metz, while a smaller force advanced to the Rhine above Strassburg. While the campaign in the west developed, Germany's eastern forces defeated the Russians and were available for redeployment by the fortieth day of mobilization. The Germans surrounded and destroyed the Anglo-French army in Belgium as well as the main French army south of Liege, with the assistance of a few corps from the east.[118]

Clearly, this war game offered little direct support for the basic strategic concept of the 1905 memorandum and can hardly be seen as a confirmation of its emphasis on the primacy of a quick defeat of the French. Indeed, some of its assumptions were directly in conflict with what has become known as the "Schlieffen Plan." Schlieffen's closing comments indicate that the real object was to show that a smaller army could defeat a larger one if it exploited the enemy's weaknesses and mistakes, accepted risks, attacked the enemy's flanks and rear in order to make him fight with reversed fronts in a confused manner, and made rapid decisions executed by a commander with "an iron character" and "a determined will to win."[119] All these factors were, as previous chapters have noted, fundamentals of German theory from the days of the elder Moltke forward. As Foley notes, Schlieffen was attempting to teach his General Staff officers "to fight intelligently" in a variety of circumstances.[120]

Likewise, the war game offers no support for those who accused Schlieffen of a simplistic and one-sided dependence on turning movements and flank attacks as the solution to every problem. The Anglo-French forces were defeated in large part because their own efforts to turn German positions set them up for envelopment.[121] Schlieffen's concluding remarks on the game's eastern campaign were equally balanced. At one point he used an example from the Russo-Japanese War to warn that excessive concern with flanks created the danger of defeat through a frontal breakthrough.[122] He warned his subordinates that in the future they would have to deal with "armies arrayed in long positions. The possibility of holding off a superior enemy from even somewhat strengthened field fortifications will result in more instances of trench warfare (*Positionskrieg*)." The Russo-Japanese War, he wrote, showed that it was possible for both sides to fight "for months at a time from unassailable positions."[123] At that point, Schlieffen repeated his frequent warning that this was unacceptable in Europe, where "one cannot move from position to position for a year or two with twelve-day battles until the combatants (*Kriegführenden*), entirely used up and exhausted, both sue for peace. We must attempt to defeat and destroy the enemy quickly."[124]

The answer, wrote Schlieffen, lay in finding gaps and breaking through the long fronts. He cited the battle on the Shaho River in the Russo-Japanese War and one case from the war game as examples. In general, however, Schlieffen warned that one must rely not on mere flanking attacks but on wider turning movements that threaten the enemy's rear as well as flanks. Such an enveloping maneuver, Schlieffen concluded, cannot be conducted without a powerful frontal attack, even if the desired strength is not available, and it must be followed by relentless exploitation.[125] All these concepts had been well entrenched in German theory for many years.

The "Schlieffen Plan"

Following the conclusion of his last war game, Schlieffen began to write his most important memorandum, known to history as the famous "Schlieffen Plan" of December 1905.[126] Nearly a century of historical writing has regarded this memorandum as the official war plan of 1914 (as modified in execution by Moltke), and much of the literature has equated it with a mobilization plan. Both these viewpoints are erroneous. The memorandum was not a deployment plan as conceived by the German General Staff from the days of Moltke onward. The Reichsarchiv's concept of equating the 1905 memorandum and the subsequent campaign plans should no longer be regarded as authoritative or valid.[127]

As this chapter has indicated, the deployment plans were entirely different documents from the various memoranda produced by the chiefs of the General Staff. Moreover, there is little evidence that the 1905 memorandum served as the basis for any deployment plan in any year.[128] It was merely the last of Schlieffen's preretirement essays on a war with France alone. It considered only one of the two cases usually laid out in a typical mobilization year. Thus the younger Moltke, who succeeded Schlieffen in January 1906, maintained the alternative plan for Germany's great eastern deployment (*Grosser Ostaufmarsch*) until 1913. Nevertheless, the Schlieffen memorandum of December 1905 remains a fundamentally important document for a number of reasons.

The plan allegedly contained in Schlieffen's memorandum of December 1905 has been the subject of an immense literature, beginning in 1920 and continuing beyond its first publication by Gerhard Ritter in 1956. The memorandum is clearly a discussion of Germany's strategic situation in 1905 and of a broad operational concept that involved sending the right wing of the German army through southern Holland, Belgium north and south of the Sambre, and Luxembourg, with the hope of turning the French defensive positions that had been the source of German concern since the days of the elder Moltke. The academic discussion of alternatives and difficulties rested on a series of optimistic assumptions mixed with a recognition that Germany's strength was insufficient for such an undertaking. It was not a mobilization plan for the entire army, nor did it contain, contrary to most views, any deployment or employment instructions for any of the field armies that were supposed to implement it. In 1914 each army had an individual deployment instruction (*Aufmarschweisung*) for the upcoming campaigns, but there was apparently no overall written concept; certainly none was contained in the 1905 memorandum. A comparison with an actual deployment directive makes the differences clear.[129]

Although the broad outline of the concept contained in the 1905 memorandum has been recognized for decades, a few qualifying points need to be made here. The memorandum assumed that, based on the circumstances of 1905, France would fight alone, and the French army would probably remain on the defensive as long as it could not count on Russian support. After considering the strength of the French fortification system and the terrain along the Franco-German border, the memorandum clearly indicated that the German army would have to circumvent these fortifications by advancing through Belgium, Luxembourg, and Holland, although Schlieffen hoped the latter would not resist.

To execute this great turning movement, Schlieffen's memorandum proposed to send twenty-three and a half active corps, twelve and

a half reserve corps, and eight cavalry divisions through the three otherwise neutral states. Schlieffen discussed swinging the far right wing
as far northwest as Abbeville and enveloping Paris to the west, forcing
the French back toward the Swiss frontier. This is the "Schlieffen Plan"
that is known to history. A careful reading of the memorandum, however,
reveals that there is both more and less to Schlieffen's concept than is
usually suggested.

Contrary to the arguments of many of Schlieffen's defenders and critics, the memorandum did not unconditionally call for a sweep to the west
of Paris.[130] The memorandum's assumption was that the French would
remain on the defensive and would retire behind their river lines after
initial battles along the Franco-Belgian frontier. The memorandum referred to a sweep west of Paris on two occasions. In the first instance,
the memorandum stated that the French might choose to withdraw and
defend behind the Somme-Oise line, which "would lead to a march of the
German right wing on Amiens or even on Abbeville."[131] But Schlieffen
doubted the French would do this; he believed they would instead make
a stand behind the Oise between La Fere and Paris. This, too, would necessitate an advance to the south and west of Paris. The memorandum
then went on: "One thing is clear. Unless the French do us the favor of
attacking," the Germans would have to move around Paris.[132] The long
turning movement around Paris was thus only a contingency, a reaction
to the worse and less likely case.[133]

The memorandum did not elaborate on the other contingency—that
the French would take the offensive—except in a single section toward
the end. Here, the memorandum acknowledged that the French might
choose to counterattack in the south, but it concluded that a French attack
in the south would be acceptable to the Germans. It stated that the Germans should change their plans as little as possible and refers readers to
maps 5 and 5A (now in the Schlieffen papers in Freiburg).[134]

At this point, the contradictory nature of the memorandum and
its maps emerges clearly. Maps 5 and 5A, titled "Deployment against a
French Offensive into Lorraine," actually abandoned the wide sweep near
the coast and instead depicted a right-wing turn south at La Fere, about
seventy miles northeast of Paris. The far-right corps thus made an even
shorter turning movement than was the case in 1914. The text hinted at
this truncated turning movement by stating that if the French did attack,
the Germans would advance to the line La Fere–Coblenz, with reserves
on the right, and would attack with the right. The text and map 5A, which

Ritter's book did not reproduce, make it clear that although Schlieffen preferred a turning movement in all the circumstances discussed in the memorandum, he did not unconditionally demand an advance west and south of Paris.[135] The main point, as always in Schlieffen's writing, was to bring the French army to battle in the open field under the most favorable possible circumstances.[136] The sweep around Paris was merely a contingency, not an end in itself, nor was it a requirement regardless of what the French did.

Even the maps, then, indicate that the 1905 memorandum, far from being a plan of campaign, was merely a discussion of contingencies, and it may have been intended for purposes other than those usually assumed. One historian recently argued that it was basically a paper demanding an expansion of the army. This argument has the merit of being based on the fact that the memorandum assumed a much larger army than actually existed in 1905–1906.[137] This point is by no means new, and a number of authors have recognized that army expansion was at least one of the memorandum's purposes.[138]

Another problem concerns the authenticity of the maps surviving in the Schlieffen papers and used as the basis for much of the traditional view of the 1905 memorandum. Schlieffen's handwritten drafts mention a single map, while the typewritten and other later copies refer to nine maps at various points in the text. Ritter's published version lists these references in the footnotes and prints amended versions of six maps, but in a different scale, thus creating an illusion of consistency in the originals.[139] The Schlieffen papers contain twelve maps, but several of these are obviously later additions with no direct connection to the 1905 memorandum.[140] The single map mentioned in Schlieffen's handwritten drafts had a scale of 1:300,000, but the maps in the *Nachlass* range from 1:300,000 to 1:1 million. The authenticity of some of the maps is thus open to question.[141] The maps, moreover, have different labels. Some have the imprint "Chief of the General Staff of the Army. Memorandum of December 1905." Others, notably map 3, which depicts an advance south and west of Paris with an eventual advance toward Langres, have those same words but apparently in Hahnke's handwriting. Other maps in the file have no General Staff markings at all, while two others, marked 10 and 11 by the Bundesarchiv, are not mentioned in the memorandum.[142] According to Wolfgang Foerster, Hahnke told him that Schlieffen finished the memorandum in January 1906 and that he (Hahnke) prepared the maps at an unspecified later date.[143]

Historians have assumed, largely on the basis of his other writings, that Schlieffen anticipated a decisive victory over the French by about the fortieth day after mobilization. This idea is well founded in the underlying reason for the plan and in the war games and General Staff rides conducted prior to 1905, but it has little basis in the memorandum and its maps. The maps concern primarily what Schlieffen expected to be a largely unopposed advance through Belgium to the French-Belgian frontier. Schlieffen apparently anticipated that this movement, as outlined in the maps (but not in the memorandum), would take twenty-two days from the beginning of mobilization. Map 3, "Further Advance," indicated an advance by the right wing to the line of Amiens–St. Quentin by day thirty-one of mobilization. At that rate, the swing around Paris before the decisive battle took place along and behind the Oise would have required another two to three weeks. In discussing this decisive struggle, the memorandum anticipated a series of battles lasting days.[144] These would be followed by exploitation, as the German army pushed the French army toward final destruction, perhaps up against the French border.

The maps, in short, are very problematic when placed in the overall context of the memorandum and its alleged role as a detailed campaign plan. The most important maps outline a campaign inconsistent with Schlieffen's fundamental objective of fighting a decisive battle within the time available in view of Russian mobilization capabilities. Yet, contrary to most accounts, neither the memorandum nor the maps contain a rigid timetable. Indeed, the only dates and phase lines on any of the maps are the expected lines of the forward corps on the twenty-second and thirty-first days of the advance, before the main battle had begun. The maps provide only the most general information about the French army and are not nearly as detailed in forecasting the place and nature of the battles as were the maps for staff rides and war games.

Concluding Remarks

The memorandum, in short, was never a campaign plan or a substitute for the annual deployment plan. It was merely the last of Schlieffen's official academic discussions of alternatives and the first of his postretirement efforts to convince Moltke and others that his views offered the only hope for winning a brutal multifront war against superior forces. Rather than a new deployment scheme, it was merely one way of using the traditional

Aufmarsch I as a basis for the scheme of maneuver, in this case, during a time when the French could count on little Russian support.[145] Regardless of their contents and intents, Schlieffen's memoranda, including that of 1905, did not constitute the German war plan in any of his years as chief of the General Staff or thereafter. Throughout his tenure, Schlieffen declined to prepare even general war plans along the lines of those prepared by the elder Moltke. The Military History Section of the General Staff, writing in 1919, concluded that neither Schlieffen nor the younger Moltke ever prepared such a comprehensive war plan, relying instead on the deployment plans prepared by April of each year. The section concluded that from these it was impossible to determine with any certainty the manner in which Moltke and Schlieffen would have conducted operations. There was no written planning in those years, the section concluded, only verbal discussions among key General Staff sections. In 1919 the Military History Section specifically rejected the idea that the Schlieffen memorandum of 1905 was the basis of campaign planning, since the document could not be found in the General Staff's records.[146] It definitely found its way into the holdings of the Reichsarchiv at some later date.[147]

Later, after extensive searching, the Reichsarchiv concluded that the German High Command had not provided the field armies with a single, unified order containing its intentions for operations in 1914. It pointed out that the field armies had complained about this at the time.[148] Hermann von Kuhl, one of the closest associates of Schlieffen and Moltke and chief of the General Staff of First Army (far right wing) in 1914, wrote after the war that he had never seen the Schlieffen memorandum of 1905. A copy of the memorandum that was given to Moltke early in 1906 remained in the cabinet of his first adjutant. From there, it found its way into the archives. Of course, the general concept of the memorandum was well known within the General Staff, as Kuhl noted.[149] Friedrich von Boetticher, a staunch advocate of the postwar Schlieffen school, admitted that only a few senior officers ever saw the memorandum.[150]

All these are indications of what should be obvious from the text itself: the memorandum was not a carefully prescribed and detailed campaign plan. It was merely a thought piece, and it never was the exclusive basis of any German deployment or campaign plan. In addition, it is worth noting that eight years passed before a mobilization and deployment plan was needed for an actual war—years that were marked by critical changes in the international situation. Thus we must now consider the outlook, methods, and intents of the man who was chief of the General Staff when the memorandum was completed and who remained in that position until his dismissal in September 1914: Generaloberst Helmuth von Moltke, nephew of the victor of 1866 and 1870 and known in history as the younger Moltke.

CHAPTER SIX

GERMAN STRATEGIC PLANNING,
1906–1914

Schlieffen was nearly seventy-three years old when he performed his final official duties and wrote his December 1905 memorandum. The question of his successor had been percolating since 1902. Finding a replacement was no easy task, given his years of domination of the General Staff. As one officer later remembered, the feeling prevalent after Schlieffen's departure was that no one could take his place: "The chair of the master was empty."[1] A number of possible replacements had surfaced in various quarters over the years.[2] It was not a simple matter of choosing the individual most capable of shaping Germany's strategic planning and leading the army into war if the need should arise. The person selected had to be an experienced General Staff officer who had few if any enemies among the most powerful aristocrats in the army and the bureaucracy and who possessed the confidence of the emperor. Given the army's fractured bureaucratic structure and the continuing role of aristocratic and royal connections at the highest levels of the officer corps, it is hardly surprising that the choice was controversial.

Schlieffen attempted to influence the decision, but with little result. His initial preference had apparently been Colmar *Freiherr* von der Goltz, a highly capable General Staff officer and an internationally famous military writer. Eventually, however, Goltz's views on fortresses and various tactical questions caused him to lose Schlieffen's favor. Goltz returned to the "front," served a lengthy tour in Turkey, and eventually became one of the more famous "mavericks" of the Prussian army.[3] Schlieffen then turned to Hans von Beseler, another prominent General Staff officer and chief of the Engineer and Pioneer Corps.[4] Despite the support of Count Dietrich von Hülsen Haeseler, chief of the Military Cabinet, Beseler found no favor with Wilhelm II. His many drawbacks as a candidate nullified his undisputed abilities. He had never been in the kaiser's entourage, had come up in the engineer branch, and had influential opponents in the Guards Corps. In addition, Beseler's title of nobility had been very recently acquired.[5] Several others were reportedly candidates at one point or another, including Paul von Hindenburg, but in 1906 Helmuth von

Moltke, a nephew of the hero of the wars of unification, became the new chief of the General Staff.[6]

If Moltke's own account is to be believed, the kaiser had assigned him to the General Staff in 1904 so that he would be prepared to succeed Schlieffen at some future date. Schlieffen was, in one general's words, "completely surprised" and not at all pleased when Moltke became a *Generalquartiermeister* in 1904.[7] The kaiser allegedly told Moltke that he did not want Goltz and "did not know" Beseler. The kaiser stated that the position of chief required a man of character rather than genius and that Moltke had his full confidence. So the kaiser rendered his fateful decision, although he probably had Moltke's traits exactly backward, since the younger Moltke certainly possessed more intelligence than strength of will.[8] Moltke and Wilhelm II remained friends until the crisis of August 1914, but they were probably not as close as some have argued.[9]

The decision was controversial from the start. Criticism of the younger Moltke mushroomed in the postwar literature, in part based on second-guessing and the repetition of secondhand tales, but there can be little doubt that many officers considered Moltke unsuited for his post from the outset.[10] Friedrich von Bernhardi, citing a letter of 1904, said he was "astounded" that Moltke had been appointed *Generalquartiermeister*. The Bavarian military attaché, writing in January 1906, reported widespread dissatisfaction with Wilhelm's choice. Others reported that the opposition included several prominent military leaders.[11] The key issues were Moltke's inexperience in General Staff work and his inability to lead the army under the great responsibilities of a European war, since under the Prussian system, the chief of the General Staff was the de facto overall commander of the field army during wartime. Many raised this issue, perhaps even with Wilhelm II. Jehuda Wallach has produced evidence that the chief of the Military Cabinet at one time had the kaiser's approval to replace Moltke should war break out.[12] Another chief of the Military Cabinet made no secret of his belief that Moltke was unsuitable for the position.[13] Even some of those who remained sympathetic to Moltke after the war recognized the opposition to his appointment.[14] Certainly a cloud hung over Moltke from the outset.[15] Some of this criticism found its way into the press.[16]

Moltke's relationship to Schlieffen has remained a point of controversy. Many of those who attacked Moltke after the war also argued that Schlieffen had recognized his successor's shortcomings and opposed his appointment. As Holger Herwig has pointed out, this is difficult to reconcile with Schlieffen's last fitness report (January 1905) on Moltke, although the source is indirect.[17] There is evidence that Schlieffen did not anticipate Moltke's appointment and that the two did not work closely together. Moltke's letters to his wife from 1904 and 1905 indicate disagreements with Schlieffen about the organization of maneuvers and the solutions to strategic problems during a staff ride, the latter leading Moltke to comment that he could not imagine greater differences in points of view than those between him and Schlieffen.[18] In 1905, while Schlieffen was recovering from a riding accident, he seemed very reluctant to allow Moltke to conduct business and went for long periods without speaking to his chief subordinate.[19] Wilhelm von Hahnke, who had a close professional and personal relationship with Schlieffen, insisted after the war that the two men were never close and that that the chief of staff had no confidence that Moltke accepted his theories or would be able to implement the concept of his 1905 memorandum.[20] Hahnke, of course, was a highly partisan participant in the attack on Moltke's failure to conduct the 1914 campaign according to the semiofficial and one-sided version of the "Schlieffen Plan" that arose after the war.

On one point there is agreement: the two had little if any contact after 1906.[21] Members of the postwar "Schlieffen school" derided the deceased Moltke for failing to consult with Schlieffen after the latter's retirement, citing this as evidence of a fundamental difference in outlook between the two men.[22] It seems reasonable to conclude that although the two men were not intimates, Schlieffen's doubts about Moltke were exaggerated to some extent by former officers who wanted to blame Moltke for what went wrong in 1914.[23]

Moltke was an unusual officer in a number of ways and something of an aberration in the high officer corps. Regarded by some as a religious dreamer, he was inclined to doubt biblical literalism. Under the influence of his strong-willed wife, he became familiar with the brand of theosophy propagated by Rudolf Steiner, although the extent of his beliefs and their influence is still open to debate. He disliked Catholicism, which he regarded as pagan, and he saw the influence of the modern sciences, not to mention socialism, as a deadly threat "to the poor fatherland." He heard the anti-Semitic diatribes of Adolf Stoecker on at least one occasion but seems to have been less hostile to Jews than many of his fellow officers were. His health was such that by 1914, the tall, portly Moltke required periodic visits to various clinics. The state of his physical and mental health thus added to the controversy over his suitability for the position of chief, particularly under the stresses of war. There can be little doubt that he was ill suited for the great physical, intellectual, and emotional demands of the political and military crises of August and September 1914.[24]

Criticisms of Moltke's performance have centered around four main issues: his personality quirks, his lack of preparation for his exalted position, his role in the 1914 crisis as an advocate of preventive war, and his actions in August and September 1914.[25] Comments on his personal failings and weaknesses abound in nearly every account of prewar planning and the conduct of the 1914 campaign, although, as one historian has noted, the primary sources "are few in number and poor in quality."[26] Most of his fellow officers who wrote about him after the war argued that Moltke lacked the most essential quality of a leader in wartime: an iron will. Some used examples from his prewar experiences to demonstrate this weakness.[27] Although one distinguished historian has denied it, strong evidence suggests that Moltke was to some degree unwilling to become chief of the General Staff, feeling that he was not up to the task.[28] Once in office, however, Moltke worked energetically to improve the army in areas that Schlieffen had been unable or unwilling to address.[29]

Helmuth von Moltke's career was unlike that of any of his predecessors, and in the eyes of many, this left him poorly prepared for the position he assumed on 1 January 1906. He was the son of Count von Moltke's younger brother Adam and thus had impeccable social qualifications for service in the Prussian officer corps. He inherited neither of the higher ranks of nobility (baron and count) awarded to his illustrious uncle. Born in 1848, he was close to sixty when he became chief of the General Staff and was a relatively elderly man when he led the army into the First World War.[30] He had spent most of his career in the guards infantry regiments and as an aide to his uncle, although he had also served as a personal aide to Wilhelm II for a number of years. He had a solid record in the Seventh Grenadier Regiment during the Franco-Prussian War and soon thereafter was transferred to the First Guards Regiment zu Fuss, the army's most elite infantry regiment and the first unit established for royal princes. He attended the War Academy and was appointed to the General Staff but spent most of his time until 1882 in the Guards Corps. He received high praise for his performance as a regimental and divisional commander, but from 1882 onward he performed few if any General Staff duties.[31] While serving as an aide to his uncle he took little part in General Staff exercises, planning, and so forth. Moltke's critics have attributed some of his alleged shortcomings to his privileged career path and his resulting inexperience.[32]

Equally important, perhaps, is the controversy over Moltke's intellectual outlook and its effect on his attitude toward a future war. Numerous authors have concluded that Moltke was by nature a pessimist, an inclination made worse by an addiction to spiritualism and a fatalism that may have sapped his energy in a crisis.[33] At one point, in a moment of discouragement, he compared the German army to a rabbit that pursuing dogs would eventually catch. When a subordinate countered that dogs could not kill a lion, Moltke replied that some dogs could accomplish even that. This comparison of the German army with an ill-fated rabbit pursued by hounds was, as one officer wrote, remarkable for the chief of the General Staff.[34] How this affected Moltke's planning and his mental state in 1914 remains uncertain. One of his close associates, Gerhard Tappen, wrote after the war that Moltke expected a decisive victory against France and that his staff exercises and war games showed this.[35] But recent scholarship has concluded that inwardly, at least, he was very pessimistic about Germany's long-term strategic prospects and far from confident in a quick victory.[36] As will be seen, the surviving evidence from his staff rides and war games shows that he was anything but excessively optimistic about the chances for a rapid victory.

One recent scholar has returned to the arguments of the Fischer school of interpretation on the origins of the First World War, claiming that Moltke aggressively pushed Germany toward what he and those around him confidently expected to be a victorious war. This argument, while not dismissing Moltke's interest in the occult, reduces it to relative insignificance, at least in the 1914 crisis.[37] On balance, the most reasonable judgment seems to be that of Gerhard Ritter, who posits that Moltke and others were pessimistic about Germany's long-term situation and believed that, when war inevitably came, only rapid offensive campaigns offered any hope for success.[38] Moltke's questionable health may have had an impact, but it became obvious only during the Marne campaign (discussed in the next chapter). The question here is Moltke's impact on Germany's planning for war from 1906 to 1914.

Many of his colleagues as well as historians have attributed Moltke's shortcomings, both as a planner and as field commander in 1914, to incompetence, inexperience in General Staff matters, physical ailments, or weaknesses of character.[39] Moltke was no doubt an intelligent man with broad interests and considerable learning.[40] Some contemporaries as well as a number of historians have argued that his career left him unprepared for his position because he had spent too many years as an aide-de-camp to the kaiser and as an officer in the guards units.[41] A recent scholar extended this to war games, arguing that Moltke had "only a vague notion of their real value."[42] This is no longer a tenable position, as the evidence shows that Moltke's General Staff rides were in no way inferior to Schlieffen's; in fact, they were remarkably similar.[43] Hew Strachan is no doubt correct that Moltke lacked Schlieffen's self-confidence and that he failed to "stamp his doctrine on the minds of the General Staff."[44] The problem with this line of thought is the assumption that Moltke's views on the nature of war, its problems, and the solutions to them (doctrine) differed fundamentally from those of Schlieffen.

Until recently, discussions of Moltke's role in war planning have assumed that Schlieffen's memorandum of December 1905 was the German plan for deployment and the conduct of the campaign. Most writers have therefore analyzed the extent of Moltke's changes, their bases in his thought, and their consequences for the war and for political-military relations in the empire.[45] Both those who thought Moltke adhered closely to the Schlieffen "plan" and those who regarded his changes as marginal have proceeded on these assumptions, for the good reason that the available evidence seemed to indicate their validity.[46] Those who wished to blame the failures of 1914 on Moltke's faulty execution of the Schlieffen concept reinforced this view, since it was an essential part of the campaign to make Moltke the scapegoat for the failure on the Marne. But, as has been argued, there is now good reason to doubt that the 1905 memorandum was ever the basis for German deployment planning, and Moltke's own record seems to reinforce this.

Here it is useful to distinguish between Moltke's view of the nature of warfare and his planning for the conduct of the campaign he envisioned in 1914. His views of tactics and operations were quite in line with mainstream German doctrinal thought during his period as chief of the General Staff. His concepts for the conduct of a campaign were different from those of the Schlieffen memorandum of 1905 but were well within the general streams of Prussian theory from the elder Moltke onward. He made no major innovations in the Prussian approach to infantry tactics, artillery employment, and so forth. His war games and exercises were quite similar in their broad framework to those of Schlieffen.[47] He made significant improvements in the army's training and preparations for a future war and laid more stress on adapting to technological change than is usually recognized. He certainly understood that breakthrough battles and frontal attacks would be necessary in a future war. By August 1914, he had been in office long enough to have undertaken major reforms had he desired to do so, but such was apparently not the case. He had more confidence in the command methods of his illustrious uncle than had Schlieffen, but he was quite aware of the danger that subordinate commanders would stray from the High Command's conceptual framework.[48]

In planning for the specific case of a war on two fronts, Moltke's views varied from those of Schlieffen, but not greatly. He accepted the primacy of the western front and the risk of trying to defend East Prussia with minimal forces if Germany had to fight both France and Russia simultaneously. He accepted Schlieffen's basic ideas on using an offensive defense against the Russians. In the west, he accepted the possibility that a war with France could require an envelopment with the right wing of the German armies, but like Schlieffen, he studied other possibilities. He was, however, more willing to consider that the major battle might be on the German left wing, that a breakthrough against the French frontier fortifications might be feasible, and that a double envelopment might be possible.

The two streams of thought—preparing a general way of fighting and designing a particular strategy and subordinate campaigns—came together in Moltke's General Staff exercises and war games. His conduct of these exercises was remarkably similar to Schlieffen's approach.[49] Moltke, however, had a highly flexible view of the western campaign and was just as willing to fight the anticipated decisive battle in Lorraine as on the German right flank.

Moltke's General Staff Rides, 1906 and 1908

As evidence from the Dieckmann manuscript indicates, there was not necessarily a direct connection between the deployment plans and concepts of campaigns on the one hand and the General Staff exercises, war games, and staff rides on the other. Nevertheless, the latter usually provides some insight into the thinking of the chief of the General Staff. The 1906 western General Staff ride, for example, bore little resemblance to the recently finished Schlieffen memorandum of 1905; instead, it was similar to earlier deployment plans and war games. It shows that from his earliest days as chief, Moltke was in no way wedded to the extreme case outlined in much of the 1905 memorandum.

The scenario in 1906 posited a two-front war and a corresponding division of the German army, with six active corps and nine reserve divisions (twenty-one divisions total) deploying to East Prussia and twenty corps to the western theater.[50] The scenario assumed that Belgium would resist a German passage through its territory and that Holland would remain neutral. No British participation was evident. The German player correctly assumed a French offensive, and the game director gave the French player an order to implement a Franco-Russian agreement on an immediate advance into Germany. The Germans deployed three field armies (fifteen corps) along the frontier between Diedenhofen and Montjoie (twenty-eight miles southeast of Liege), two armies (four active and three reserve corps) east of Metz (twenty-two to thirty-seven miles east and northeast of the city) along the Saar, and one active corps in Alsace. Two reserve corps were in a rear position north of Strassburg. The German right wing was thus not deployed to invade Holland or to advance across Belgium north of the Sambre. Its purpose was to envelop the flank of the main French force and engage the French army in the open field.[51]

As the game progressed, both armies executed their broad concepts. The French advanced into upper Alsace and reached the Rhine but could not force a crossing. A French offensive into Lorraine drove deep into German territory south and east of Metz, while the Belgians unsuccessfully attacked the northern flank of the German army. The German right wing, anchored on Diedenhofen, enveloped the weak French left wing and turned south as anticipated. The French, though defeated, successfully retreated to a position behind the Aisne River. The Germans defeated the Belgian army in a counterattack south of the Sambre, forcing the Belgians to retire to Namur. The major battle took place in Lorraine, since the German right wing had failed to engage the main body of the French army. The German player's actions seemed torn between the desire to adhere to the original plan of the right-wing envelopment and the need to abandon it to meet the needs created by the French offensive into Lorraine. The Germans therefore sent most of Third Army to Metz to assist in the critical battles around that fortress, but they maintained First and Second Armies on the right flank in an advance that failed to engage the mass of the enemy. The French scored a victory in Lorraine, nearly enveloping the weaker German forces, but by no means achieved a decisive result. At the conclusion of day twenty, both sides' campaigns ended without victory. The war would continue.

This may seem entirely inconsistent with Schlieffen's view of a western campaign.[52] But this is true only if one maintains the standard and one-sided view of the 1905 memorandum. Schlieffen's great swing through

Holland and Belgium north of the Sambre and around Paris assumed that the French would remain on the defensive. If they attacked, the 1905 memorandum called for a much shorter envelopment, along the lines of a number of Schlieffen's previous studies. Moltke's first General Staff ride was, therefore, consistent with Schlieffen's thinking in this kind of scenario. It was thus inconsistent not with Schlieffen's basic ideas but with the later distortions created by Moltke's postwar critics. Kabisch, for example, cited Schlieffen's idea that the primary goal is to destroy the enemy's main forces, then criticized Moltke's 1906 staff ride for doing precisely that in transferring forces from the right wing to Lorraine for the main battle. Kabisch thus ignored Moltke's argument throughout the closing remarks that destruction of the main enemy force, not the right-wing movement itself, was the critical factor. Kabisch had good knowledge of the 1905 memorandum but, like most of his fellow officers, failed to mention Schlieffen's alternative course of action if the French attacked exactly as posited in the 1906 staff ride. Foerster, in his *Gedankenwerkstatt*, managed to square the circle in his brief discussion of the 1906 staff ride; he cited Moltke's reasons for approving the movement of forces to fight the main French army yet criticized him for abandoning the right wing, even though it could have accomplished little in this situation.[53]

Moltke stated in his concluding remarks that the results confirmed Schlieffen's basic teaching that "only a grand operation with unified command" can lead to strategic and tactical pincer movements against the enemy and to a decisive victory. He then cited Schlieffen's statement that such an operation must have central control, as in a battalion exercise. The problem, he stated, was that the German commander lost control of his forces, just as a battalion commander can lose control of his companies. "One must always seek a coherent, unified operation."[54]

Little is known of Moltke's exercises for 1907, but the German archives now contain a lengthy summary of the 1908 western General Staff ride.[55] It, too, had little in common with the 1905 memorandum, if one limits the latter to an all-out offensive by the right wing, regardless of French actions. The staff ride scenario posited a war between Germany and France in alliance with England and assumed that the French would launch a major offensive similar to that of 1914. The situation required large forces in the east in case Russia intervened, but the Russians played no direct role in the exercise. The game's situation also delayed full German deployment by partial destruction of the Rhine bridges.

The German player's basic plan was flexible, although the deployment allowed a wider movement of the right wing than had the 1906 staff ride. Four armies deployed between Metz and Duisburg (fifty-six miles north-west of Aachen), one (Fifth) in a reserve position behind Metz, one in Lorraine, and one in Alsace. If the French attacked through Luxembourg and Belgium, the German player planned to fight the major battle along the line Liege-Verdun, where First Army would be in position for a flank-ing attack, with a possible breakthrough against the French line by Fourth and Fifth Armies attacking to the north. If the French player attacked be-tween Metz and Strassburg or along the upper Rhine, the German player planned to move his forces to the south to engage the enemy as he ad-vanced. The main effort would therefore be with field armies three to six, with First and Second Armies, on the right wing, covering the flank of the German forces as they turned to counterattack southward from the general direction Coblenz-Metz. If the French remained on the defensive, the German player planned to execute the wide movement broadly, as suggested in Schlieffen's 1905 memorandum, with the right wing pass-ing north of Liege-Namur.[56] The major point was to find the French main forces and seek a decision in mobile battles wherever they were.

At this point in his summary of the staff ride, Moltke rendered his anal-ysis of the German deployment and strategic concept. He stressed that the value of such a game was to get the commanders accustomed to han-dling large masses and adjusting to changing circumstances within the overall framework. He approvingly noted that the German concept was simple—to seek a decision against the main enemy force. He noted that "a good plan of operations is usually simple." He cited the elder Moltke's 1870 plan to march against Paris because the French army would have to defend the capital and, in doing so, would have to engage the Germans in the open field. He then paraphrased his uncle's famous statement: "It is not possible to plan beyond the first battle."[57]

Moltke allowed the French offensives to proceed on both sides of Metz, forcing the German player to decide how to deal with these attacks against his center and left flank. The German player rapidly moved his right wing to the south, rather than to the west. The French drove into Lorraine and Luxembourg but achieved no decisive results; they were then forced to withdraw behind their fortifications. Moltke concluded that the Germans would face "a new, difficult campaign" and that the failure of the French attack in Lorraine, despite a substantial superiority in infantry strength, demonstrated once again that one could not expect victory with a purely frontal attack. Overall, the staff ride was an effort to teach commanders the need for flexibility in planning and how to react to events during the campaign and to familiarize them with the problems of controlling the mass armies of the day.[58]

The relationship of the 1908 staff ride to the overall theory and doctrine of the German army is clear, but its relationship to the Schlieffen memorandum or actual German deployment plans is less so. The game's details were clearly based on German theory of the late nineteenth century, as sketched in previous sections of this study. This exercise's scenario disrupted the German mobilization-deployment timetable and created a very active opponent in its efforts to emphasize flexibility and reaction to events. It stressed destruction of the enemy rather than a preplanned maneuver as the key to victory. It followed Schlichting's interpretation of Moltke's methods of conducting a campaign by emphasizing that commanders must maintain a theater perspective. The staff ride offers little evidence that the wide swing through Belgium outlined in the Schlieffen memorandum of 1905 had become strategic dogma, so it can be seen as being in conflict with the alleged main thrust of the memorandum. Indeed, Moltke's postwar critics made precisely that point in condemning his staff rides and exercises.[59]

The problem with this interpretation is that Moltke's scenario was different from the one that dominated the 1905 memorandum, as had been true of the 1906 staff ride. In this case, the French decided to launch a double offensive rather than remain on the defensive, as the 1905 memorandum had assumed. In condemning Moltke, advocates of the Schlieffen legend once again ignored the fact that the 1905 memorandum also discussed abandoning the extended sweep of the right wing if the French came out to fight. The 1908 game stressed decisive battle, turning movements, flank attacks, and annihilation—all central elements of German theory from the elder Moltke to Schlieffen. The object of the 1905 memorandum and the 1908 staff ride were the same: engage the French army in the open field and defeat it. The 1908 staff ride also demonstrated, if only in the inherently limited fashion of an exercise, that the basic deployment of German forces on the right flank between Diedenhofen and Aachen provided the flexibility for a number of campaign alternatives.

Deployment Plans, 1906–1907 and 1907–1908

In April 1906 the General Staff completed the first deployment plan of Moltke's era, that for 1906–1907.[60] Much of the conceptual and implementation work for this deployment plan must have been finished during Schlieffen's last months in office, so the mobilization plan for 1906–1907 might be seen as that of Schlieffen, not Moltke. The latter was nevertheless responsible for it. The surviving records provide details on two variants for western deployment: *Aufmarsch* I for war against France alone, and *Aufmarsch* II for war against France and Russia. The former sent the entire army, twenty-six active and twelve reserve corps, eleven cavalry divisions, and twenty-six and a quarter *Landwehr* brigades to the west. The second variation sent three active corps, four reserve corps, two cavalry divisions, and seven *Landwehr* brigades to the east. This discussion considers case I, which assumed that Holland would be "friendly" and Belgium would be hostile.

This deployment was quite consistent with one of the contingencies discussed in the 1905 memorandum and should be seen as confirmation of a close relationship with that document, even though much of the work had been completed before Schlieffen finished his manuscript. The discovery and publication of this deployment plan should terminate the debate on whether the army ever planned to execute part of the 1905 memorandum. The army planned to do exactly that in 1906–1907, but not the extreme turning movement based on a defensive French strategy.

Seven of the eight armies were to "execute the leftward turning movement through Belgium." First Army, composed of five reserve corps, deployed to the far northern sector of the front and behind Second Army. First Army had the tasks of protecting the advance of the German right wing and advancing toward Antwerp if necessary. It was also to relieve Second Army's units from security and garrison duties as the advance proceeded. Second, Third, and Fourth Armies (twelve active and two reserve corps) were to move through southern Belgium and northern Luxembourg. Fifth Army was to move through Luxembourg toward Givet and maintain contact with the right-flank armies as they turned to the south and west. Sixth Army was to advance just north of Metz. Seventh Army was to defend the area south of Metz against an anticipated French offensive, tie down enemy forces, and be prepared to reinforce the right flank. Eighth Army was to deploy behind Sixth and follow it toward Verdun, while maintaining the army's anchoring position at Metz.

This deployment plan, which contained no detailed statement of the overall concept of the campaign beyond deployment and the direction of opening movements, is clearly in accord with the second part of the 1905 memorandum. As discussed in the previous chapter, it contemplated a short swinging movement to turn the French left flank as the mass of the French army attacked in the areas south of Metz. There is no indication of a lengthy move toward or around Paris, and First Army, composed only of reserve corps and thus short of artillery, was in no position to attempt any such movement.

The 1907–1908 mobilization plan retained the basic scheme of 1906–1907 but reflected a slight change in emphasis away from the far-right flank. While First Army was much stronger than in 1906–1907, the right-flank turning armies as a whole were not. First Army's deployment gave it the ability to go through the Maastricht appendage, but the actual intent is not known. Its opening movements were to be such that its right flank (reserve corps) cut off Antwerp, while the left flank advanced on Brussels. The deployment plan assumed that the Germans would lay siege to the Belgian fortress at Liege and that Second Army would advance north and south of the city. This suggests, but does not prove, that Moltke intended to cross the Maastricht appendage and thus violate Dutch neutrality, regardless of political circumstances.

The remainder of the deployment plan suggested a short turning movement similar to that of 1906–1907. Fourth Army, advancing to the Sedan-Bouillon line and then moving toward the Meuse River below Verdun, formed a pivot for the right-wing turning movement. Fifth Army was to defend against French advances between Metz and Verdun, while Sixth was to attack toward Nancy to fix French forces and deceive the French about the overall German intent. This also implied a campaign concept similar to Schlieffen's short turning movement. Five of the eleven available cavalry divisions were to conduct reconnaissance south of Liege and toward the line Sedan-Verdun, a further indication that Moltke anticipated a relatively short turning movement.

Deployment Plan, 1908–1909: The Coup de Main on Liege

The deployment plan for 1908–1909 is noteworthy for both continuity and change from those of the previous two years.[61] The surviving documents strongly emphasize that Holland's neutrality was to be respected. This plan was the first to incorporate a surprise attack on Liege, which might eliminate the need to invade Holland by opening a route through Belgium at an early stage in the campaign. For years, historians praised Moltke for this apparent subordination of campaign considerations to those of policy and economic issues in a prolonged war. While there is some truth in this, Moltke's attitude was still that campaign considerations took absolute priority. If the coup at Liege failed, he planned to move forces through Holland, despite the fact that "German interests demanded" its neutrality. Accordingly, the deployment plan included preparations for invading both Belgium and Holland if necessary.

First Army, as in previous years, deployed north of Aachen, but it was to move south and advance through the Liege area after Second Army had captured the Liege fortresses and opened the door to Belgium north of the Sambre River. If the coup at Liege failed, both armies would move through southern Holland. Moltke, in short, subordinated all economic and political concepts to achievement of the military goal of a rapid movement on the right flank.

The remainder of the opening movements were similar to those of the previous two years. First Army was to secure the German right flank by advancing on Brussels, Second was to advance with its right flank on Wavre and its left north of Namur, and Third was to move toward the Meuse River between Namur and Givet. Fourth and Fifth Armies were to advance to the west and then turn south toward the Meuse. Sixth Army served as a pivot, charged with maintaining the link between Fifth Army and Metz. Seventh Army was to defend and feint south of Metz, but the plan anticipated that it would not remain in southern Lorraine.

The plans for an eastern deployment in case of war with both France and Russia were unchanged from the previous year. The plan called for the detachment of some units from the western field armies if Russia entered the war. First Army was to dispatch one active and one reserve corps; Second Army, half a reserve corps; Third Army, one active corps; and Sixth Army, one active and one reserve corps. This clearly shows that First Army, on the far-right flank, was to contribute merely a supporting effort and that two-thirds of the eastern front's forces would come from the turning wing.

Moltke must have been confident that the right-flank armies, especially First Army, were more than sufficient to turn the French left flank. He was willing to weaken the very forces that would be needed to widen the war to Belgium and extend the conflict to Holland should the coup at Liege fail. As a practical matter, since war against France or Russia alone appeared increasingly unlikely, *Aufmarsch* I (France alone) seemed an obsolete concept even in 1908–1909. Over the course of that mobilization year, events related to the Bosnian annexation crisis further aggravated Russo-German relations.

Deployment Plan, 1909–1910

The surviving documents for 1909–1910 allow a broader look at Moltke's concepts of deployment than was the case for earlier years.[62] The deployment plan stipulated that Germany had to prepare for wars "against France *or* Russia, and for a war against *both*," in which England would participate. Moltke assumed that Italy would not join Germany. The overall plan prepared for two possible deployments in each theater, depending on Russian participation, and for a possible French entry after an eastern campaign had begun. Strength allocations were generally the same as in previous years. If Russia remained neutral, the entire army would deploy against France. If France remained neutral in a Russo-German war, the deployment plan would send fifteen (of twenty-six) active corps, seven reserve corps, and six cavalry divisions to the eastern front.

With regard to the western deployment, as in the previous year, respect for Dutch neutrality was dependent on the success of the early assault on Liege. The plan assumed a neutral Holland, an active English intervention, a neutral Switzerland, and a doubtful Belgium. First Army was to deploy as in previous years, situated to invade either Holland or Belgium as circumstances demanded. If Russia participated in a Franco-German war, the forces sent to the east would be as follows: First Army, one active and one reserve corps; Second Army, one active and half a reserve corps; Third Army, one active corps; Fifth Army, two reserve corps. This marked another case of weakening the far-right wing rather than the two defensive armies deployed south of Metz.

The eastern plan deployed the eastern forces for an offensive campaign in the northern sector of the front. If France remained neutral, First Army (two active and two reserve corps) was to deploy and move across the Vistula to provide protection from Russian forces mobilizing in the Warsaw area. Three remaining armies (thirteen active and five reserve corps) were to attack to the east. There is little evidence that Moltke planned to fulfill his recent and emerging agreements to cooperate directly with Austro-Hungarian plans for coordinated offensives against the Russians.

Deployment Plans, 1910–1911 and 1911–1912

The planned deployments for these years contained no important changes from the previous two years. The General Staff prepared for large and small deployments in both theaters, intending in each case to take the offensive in the theater with the larger forces. An invasion of Holland was again dependent on the results at Liege. Neither deployment offered the prospect of any direct assistance to Austria-Hungary. The General Staff estimated that the British Expeditionary Force would arrive with about 120,000 soldiers and that it would deploy in the line Antwerp-Calais after the fourteenth day of mobilization or in Denmark after the sixteenth day. English intervention was rated as "probable." Plans for an eastern deployment in case of war with both France and Russia remained as in the previous year.

Deployment Plan, 1913–1914: The End of Flexibility

Contrary to previous mobilization plans, that for 1913–1914 abandoned the long-established assumption that war against either France or Russia alone was sufficiently likely to warrant contingency planning.[63] The plan directed preparation for a single deployment under the traditional case I, war with France allied with Russia, with the main effort to be in the west. The basis of this approach was that, "because of popular opinion in France, one cannot anticipate that Germany would be in a state of hostilities with Russia or England alone. If Russia or England nevertheless declared war *alone*, German diplomacy must *force* France to definitively take a position." The General Staff therefore prepared a single option, deploying the vast majority of the army opposite France. Regardless of the nature and origins of a war, the General Staff planned to send twenty-three active corps, twenty-two reserve divisions, seventeen and one-half *Landwehr* brigades, and ten cavalry divisions to the west.

The plan assumed that on the day of mobilization, Germany would demand rights of passage through Belgium and Luxembourg. A decision on Holland would await events. The assault on Liege was to begin on the night of the fourth day of mobilization, and a second assault was possible with larger forces on the tenth day. If the Germans had not taken the Liege forts by the twelfth day, First Army would advance through Holland. While all this was under way, a single army—the Eighth, with three active corps, one reserve corps, and one cavalry division—would deploy in the eastern theater. With this plan, the General Staff reversed the old Clausewitzian view of the relationship between policy and war and made German diplomacy the tool of the army. The agent had become the principal.

Deployment of the seven field armies in the west was roughly the same as in previous years. First Army was to move toward Brussels and secure the right flank. Second Army was to advance across the line Wavre-Namur, while Third Army moved forward between Bastogne-Fumay and Metz. Both would be ready to turn south at that point. Sixth and Seventh Armies, south of Metz, were to defend the turning wing and tie down French forces opposite them. The plan also noted that Sixth Army might be called on to launch an offensive in the area around Metz or to the south. Each army's opening movement instructions required it to maintain contact with its right-wing neighbor. This was a harkening back to Schlieffen's oft-quoted admonition to keep the lines closed up, as in battalion drill. The point was to avoid the development of any gaps in the front, which would threaten the cohesion of the turning movement.

The eastern deployment documents for 1913–1914 offer a revealing glimpse into Moltke's campaign concepts, but they could not have been reassuring to Germany's eastern ally. The "Special Instructions for the Supreme Commander of the Eighth Army" gave that person the two main tasks of defending Germany's eastern provinces and offering support to Austria-Hungary's planned offensive. This was a hollow gesture, however, since the plan assigned only three *Landwehr* brigades and a few replacement (training) units from VI Corps to accomplish that task. Germany, the instructions noted, could best support the Austrians by tying down Russian forces in the north. Whether the Russians attacked or not, Eighth Army was to actively engage the Russian forces opposite East Prussia, and in some circumstances it might launch an offensive to the southeast behind Warsaw. The intent was clear: unless the Russians remained passive in the north, Austria-Hungary was on its own.

The 1913–1914 deployment plan is often seen as a fundamental turning point, beyond which the General Staff's planning deprived the government of any flexibility in a crisis. The army no longer had an updated plan for deploying large forces for a major campaign in the east because it assumed that any war would involve both France and Russia and that any war, regardless of its origins, would have to begin with a German attack on France through Luxembourg, Belgium, and, if militarily necessary, Holland. The surviving documents indicate that the General Staff revised both case II west and case II east as "studies" rather than full-scale plans and thus did not entirely neglect this front.[64] This was the basis of the postwar claims that the army could have executed an imperfect version of the *Grosser Ostaufmarch* in 1914 if absolutely necessary.

Comparison of Deployment Plans, 1900–1914

A comparison of the mobilization plans for the years 1900–1914 offers some basis for comparing Schlieffen's and Moltke's visions of a future campaign. The elder Moltke had warned that a mistake in deployment could not be corrected during the course of a campaign, a view that was confirmed in 1914. Table 3 presents a comparison of the deployments of Schlieffen (1900–1901 through 1906–1907) and Moltke (1907–1908 through 1914–1915). Of course, as noted earlier, one might regard the 1906–1907 plan as Moltke's, since he was chief of the General Staff at the time of its completion (1 April 1906).

Table 3 lists the field armies, active corps, and reserve divisions allocated to sectors of the front. It shows that the General Staff drastically changed its deployment allocations in the 1905–1906 mobilization year, but thereafter the changes were marginal. The far-right wing (First and Second Armies deployed around Aachen and slated to move north of Namur in most cases) varied only slightly in strength and was just as strong during Moltke's tenure as during Schlieffen's. If the right wing is defined as all the armies north of Luxembourg, the figures show a small reduction from 1906 to 1914. In 1905–1906, for example, the three field armies consistently deployed north of Luxembourg (including its northernmost area) had eleven active corps (twenty-two divisions) and fifteen reserve divisions. The corresponding numbers for 1907–1908 were eighteen active and twelve reserve divisions, but in 1914–1915 this increased to twenty active and twelve reserve divisions. Considering all forces north of Metz, the totals for 1905–1906 were thirty-four active and twenty reserve divisions. From this perspective, Moltke's deployment for 1914–1915 (thirty-four active and twenty reserve) showed a slight decrease from 1905–1906 (forty-two active and fifteen reserve) and a larger decrease from the most extreme case in 1906–1907 (forty-four active and nineteen reserve). These reductions seem modest, given the overall number of divisions involved and the fact that the figures for 1913 and 1914 reflect the forces assigned to the eastern front, which is not the case for previous years.

The figures for major units deployed in the areas around Metz and to the south indicate a similar pattern. The deployment plans assigned very strong forces to the southern part of the front prior to 1905–1906 and made substantial reductions thereafter. They showed no great increase in strength for the area south of Metz. Moltke's plans for 1909–1910 and the following years deployed the same number of active corps as had

Table 3. Field Armies (FA), Active Corps (AC), and Reserve Divisions (RD) by Deployment Area, 1900–1915

Year	Total	North of Metz	North of Luxembourg	Aachen Area	South of Metz
1900–1901	21	3 FA/11 AC/6 RD	1 FA/4 AC/4 RD	—	10 AC/6 RD
1901–1902	22	3 FA/11 AC/5 RD	1 FA/4 AC/3 RD	—	12 AC/3 RD
1902–1903	21	3 FA/13 AC/10 RD	1 FA/3 AC/6 RD	—	10 AC/10 RD
1903–1904	23	3 FA/11 AC/9 RD	1 FA/4 AC/4 RD	—	14 AC/4 RD
1904–1905	26	3 FA/10 AC/10 RD	1 FA/4 AC/4 RD	—	15 AC/6 RD
1905–1906	26	5 FA/21 AC/15 RD	3 FA/11 AC/15 RD	2 FA/7 AC/10 RD	6 AC/12 RD
1906–1907	26	6 FA/22 AC/19 RD	4 FA/12 AC/15 RD	2 FA/4 AC/10 RD	4 AC/12 RD
1907–1908	26	5 FA/21 AC/21 RD	2 FA/9 AC/12 RD	2 FA/4 AC/13 RD	5 AC/10 RD
1908–1909	26	5 FA/19 AC/17 RD	3 FA/12 AC/13 RD	2 FA/8 AC/8 RD	7 AC/4 RD
1909–1910	26	5 FA/20 AC/23 RD	2(+) FA/8–10 AC/8 RD	2 FA/8 AC/8 RD	6 AC/4 RD
1910–1911	26	5 FA/20 AC/21 RD	2(+) FA/8–10 AC/9 RD	2 FA/8 AC/9 RD	6 AC/4 RD
1911–1912	26	5 FA/20 AC/18 RD	3 FA/12 AC/11 RD	1(+) FA/6 AC/6 RD	6 AC/4 RD
1913–1914	23	5 FA/17 AC/18 RD	3 FA/11 AC/10 RD	2 FA/6 AC/8 RD	6 AC/4 RD
1914–1915	23	5 FA/17 AC/20 RD	3 FA/10 AC/12 RD	2 FA/7 AC/10 RD	6 AC/4 RD

Sources: Based on Hans Ehlert, Michael Epkenhans, and Gerhard P. Gross, eds., *The Schlieffen Plan: International Perspectives on the German Strategy for World War I*, trans. David T. Zabecki (Lexington: University Press of Kentucky, 2014), 346–525 (a few numbers do not add to the proper totals); Reichsarchiv, *Der Weltkrieg 1914 bis 1918*, 14 vols. (Berlin: E. S. Mittler, 1925–1944), 1:664–685.

Note: Information for 1912–1913 is not available. Although a few reserve corps had only one division, reserve corps are counted as two divisions. This slightly exaggerates the reserve division totals in a few cases for earlier years, but not for the last five years. Nearly all active corps had two divisions; two had three divisions in 1901–1902. The totals for "Aachen Area" and "North of Luxembourg" are included in the "North of Metz" column. Hence, one cannot add the totals horizontally to obtain the total number of corps available. The Guards Reserve Corps appears to have been counted as an active corps on rare occasions.

Schlieffen's more radical turning-movement concepts of 1905–1906 and 1906–1907. However, Moltke planned to send substantially fewer reserve forces to the south. These units were deficient in armaments, particularly artillery, and were substantially less capable of conducting offensive actions against prepared defenses.

By these measures, Moltke did not drastically reduce Schlieffen's emphasis on the right flank. These figures, of course, reflect only opening deployments and do not necessarily indicate any other campaign concepts such as depth of the turning movement on the right flank or an intellectual commitment to execute that concept regardless of French actions or the results of the first battles.

According to the majority of sources, Moltke retained the important elements of Schlieffen's deployment plans until 1908, when he began to alter the ratio of forces between the left and right wings.[65] The deployment plan for 1914–1915 (discussed below), executed in August 1914, demonstrated that Moltke's plan had deviated substantially from the concepts of the 1905 memorandum. This evidence, however, does not show that the 1914 deployment was different from the plans in effect in 1906–1913. A dubious comparison of Schlieffen's memorandum with Moltke's actual deployment plans was the basis of the Schlieffen school's subsequent condemnation of Moltke's planning.

The Reichsarchiv's official history, written by members of the Schlieffen school, stated that Moltke's first changes occurred in mobilization year 1908–1909 and consisted of sending one corps to defend upper Alsace. According to the same source, in mobilization year 1909–1910 Moltke gave Sixth and Seventh Armies the new task of defending the area between Metz and Strassburg. This is the basis for the conclusion that Moltke changed the strength ratios of the right and left wings from 7:1 under Schlieffen to 3:1 under his own plans after 1909–1910. According to the Reichsarchiv, Moltke left no memoranda explaining the nature of his thinking in making these changes, and the only major source on this topic is a memorandum in which Moltke discussed Schlieffen's 1905 concept paper.[66] It is worth noting that the deployment plans of 1906–1907 and 1907–1908 refer to a substantial Italian presence on the German left. After 1908, that was no longer the case.

Moltke's memorandum, attached to the surviving copies of Schlieffen's concept paper, offers a reasonable if incomplete picture of Moltke's view of the strategy that should be followed in a war against France and Russia, even though the date of its composition is unclear.[67] Moltke's main point was that the Germans should not invade Holland, even though a rapid victory over the French was imperative, because of the danger of a two-front war. In order to move large forces through the Liege area without violating Dutch territory, the German army would have to seize the fortress and the city rapidly, at the outset of the campaign. Moltke's memorandum thus approved a strong right wing, with important limitations and without addressing the question of strengthening the defense of Alsace-Lorraine.

Moltke's commentary also raises some questions. The entire purpose of the campaign, he argued, was to obtain a rapid victory over France so that forces could be sent to oppose the Russians. Yet he clearly did not think this would end the war in the west, since the primary reason for preserving Dutch neutrality was to maintain German access to imports and supplies. He was to some degree hedging his bets, even though this would be inconsistent with the concept of an aggressive offensive campaign in the west. In endorsing the strong right wing and the advance through the Liege area, Moltke seemed to imply that he expected the French to remain on the defensive behind the fortifications of their eastern frontier.[68] The next sentence, however, deftly posited that the main point was to defeat the French army in the open field, so the fortifications had to be circumvented.[69] The memorandum went on to say that the reconnaissance related to a rapid seizure of the Liege fortifications, especially the city itself, had already been completed. This surely indicates that his comments were not written immediately after he received the Schlieffen memorandum in February 1906. Since other evidence indicates that the plan to seize Liege was in place by 1910, it appears that Moltke's memorandum was written between 1907 and 1910 rather than in 1911, although this is by no means certain. Foley reasonably argues that the General Staff drew up the Liege plan in 1908.[70] The documents in the Ehlert volume offer substantial support for this view.

In any case, Moltke's concepts contained in his mobilization and deployment plans by 1910 significantly departed from the Schlieffen memorandum of December 1905 in several ways. Strengthening Sixth and Seventh Armies did not reduce the number of corps available on the right wing, since more reserve forces were available in that sector of the front. Moltke directed that empty trains be deployed behind the front in Alsace so that units could be transferred to the right wing if necessary. Moltke thus did not fundamentally alter Schlieffen's concept of placing overwhelming emphasis on the right wing if the French did not attack.[71]

Abandonment of the automatic invasion of Holland was a major change, with advantages and disadvantages, even though Moltke planned to execute this course of action if the Liege assault failed. Respecting Dutch neutrality forced the Germans to seize the Liege fortress immediately upon mobilization, and it reduced the roads and railways available to move the right wing quickly into French territory beyond the French-Belgian border.[72] This certainly made the campaign more of a gamble, since failure to seize the Liege fortresses immediately upon the opening of hostilities would threaten the speed of the right wing and give the French and Belgians an opportunity to deploy more effectively. The necessity for the coup de main at Liege also restricted the government's freedom of action in international politics, since it reduced the time from the beginning of mobilization to the beginning of actual fighting.[73] The General Staff apparently did not inform the civilian government or the emperor of its plans for the attack on Liege, although this is not certain.[74] Finally, Moltke wished to defend Alsace-Lorraine rather than abandon it to the French, and he may have intended for the German left wing to launch a counteroffensive and create a double envelopment of the enemy. For all these changes, Moltke earned the scorn of the Schlieffen school.

A secondhand account of Moltke's war games of 1909 lays out his thinking more clearly than his comments on the Schlieffen memorandum.[75] Moltke apparently used the staff rides to study the concept of mounting an offensive in Lorraine. In both rides, Moltke used German forces for a major counteroffensive against the flanks of the French and, using the fortress of Metz to divide the French forces, actually sought an offensive victory on both flanks. Moltke again made the point that if the main French forces were deployed south and east of Metz, the major battle would have to be fought there. Moltke assumed French offensives into both Luxembourg and Lorraine, and the solutions that arose in the staff rides bore a remarkable resemblance to Schlieffen's counterattacking strategy of previous years. It should also be remembered that the possibility of counterattacking a French attack was an option in Schlieffen's 1905 memorandum, even though that contingency was rarely mentioned in postwar accounts of prewar planning.

Deployment Plan, 1914–1915

The General Staff based the 1914–1915 deployment on the same assumptions used the previous year, and it employed much the same wording. The single mobilization could produce only a single deployment, with little variation from 1913–1914. Upon mobilization, the General Staff issued each field army headquarters a dossier of documents to facilitate movement from the deployment areas to the frontier and beyond. These included estimates on enemy armies, the army's own order of battle, initial locations of headquarters, and a variety of documents on logistics and communications. Also included were maps and a brief statement of the deployment plan.[76] They apparently did not include a detailed statement of Moltke's intent for the initial campaign. According to the Reichsarchiv, Moltke was so confident that the chiefs of the General Staffs of the field armies understood his overall concept through war games and exercises that he felt no need to conduct personal conversations with army staffs or commanders.[77]

The mobilization plan assumed, and virtually required, that on the second day of mobilization the government would demand that Belgium and Luxembourg immediately agree to allow the German army free passage and surrender control of the fortresses and railways to assure the execution of the planned movements. The plan also stated the overall intent of the opening moves of the campaign but did not discuss any concepts beyond the advances toward the first major battles.

The instructions went on to state that if Belgium refused passage through the area in and around Liege, Second Army would begin its preplanned assault. If that did not succeed by the twelfth day of mobilization, reserve units and heavy artillery would take over the attack while the flank armies moved on. In that case, First Army would advance through Holland, but only on the explicit orders of the High Command. German success at Liege in August 1914 was the only factor that spared Holland extended combat and foreign occupation during the next four years.

The specific instructions for the individual field armies and the cavalry units remained largely unchanged from the previous year. The main effort of the right-flank cavalry reconnaissance would be to maintain knowledge of the surviving Belgian units, locate the British Expeditionary Force, and identify any French units in northern Belgium. A second cavalry unit was to conduct reconnaissance in the direction of Dinant.

The instructions to Sixth and Seventh Armies were similar to those of previous years and hinted at a fundamental problem that arose during the 1914 campaign. The deployment order gave these armies, under the combined local command of the senior commander, their usual missions of defending the German left flank and tying down German forces, but they also ordered these armies to be prepared to go over to the offensive either north or south of Metz if they did not encounter superior French forces. These vague instructions, following in the tradition of Prussian command methods, offered wide leeway for the senior commander to remain on the defensive or to attack, depending on his estimate of the local situation.

As previously discussed, deployment plans were not intended to convey the full concept of a forthcoming campaign, nor did they discuss alternative courses of action once the campaign began. The 1914 instructions nevertheless gave some insight into Moltke's overall concept of movement toward the first major battles and a general sense of how he intended to use the strong right wing of the army. This section of the general instructions read as follows:

> The main strength of the German army will march through Belgium and Luxembourg into France. Its movement to contact, as far as the available intelligence on the French deployment is accurate, is understood as a turning movement around the center position Diedenhofen-Metz. The right wing is decisive for the progress of the turning movement. The movements of the inner field armies will be so arranged that the coherence of the army and the link to Diedenhofen-Metz will not be lost. The portion of the army deploying southeast of Metz and the fortresses of Metz and Diedenhofen will provide security for the left flank of the main forces of the army.[78]

After printing this section, the Reichsarchiv history gave its overview of the deployment directive. It admitted that this did not indicate that Moltke had abandoned the external form of the western deployment of Schlieffen's time, but it argued that a change in emphasis could be seen in the former's closing remarks in the General Staff rides. The volume concluded this discussion by citing Moltke's frequently repeated argument that the right wing's advance through Belgium into northern France would have no purpose if the French sought the main decision in Alsace-Lorraine.[79] For this willingness to abandon the allegedly firm German intention to place almost everything on the right wing and to sweep to the west of Paris, Moltke earned the opprobrium of most of his former colleagues, based on the accusation that he had "watered down" the Schlieffen Plan.

Moltke's Philosophy and Performance

Moltke's philosophy of war and his view of military strategy were clearly within the mainstream of German theory from 1871 to 1914, despite the criticisms of the Schlieffen school. His actual role in the war in 1914 remains controversial.[80] He was fatalistic about Germany's future and probably calculated that if war were inevitable, the sooner the better for Germany.[81] His staff rides and war games indicate a deep lack of confidence in a rapid victory, even though he accepted the necessity of seeking a rapid decision in the west before the Russians could fully employ their numerical superiority in the east.[82]

In a memorandum written early in 1913, Moltke laid out his analysis of the strategic situation confronting Germany. He rejected the primacy of the eastern front established by his uncle, concluding that Russian strength and deployment plans made a rapid victory in the east impossible.[83] He rejected the idea of a defensive war on both fronts because this would give the enemy the initiative. He thought this could be avoided only by placing the major effort in the west. He was convinced that Belgium would resist and that England would immediately join Germany's enemies. This burden had to be accepted because the "only chance" for a quick campaign against France involved violating Belgium's neutrality. The difficulties of the situation made aggressive offensive action even more necessary: "The more difficult is the problem which we have to solve, the more important is a rapid and energetic offensive." He made this argument with the full knowledge that the French expected the Germans to move through Belgium. Overall, the memorandum was a sober analysis of the problems of waging a two-front war against two enemies whose combined strength exceeded Germany's and who would be reinforced by the forces of Belgium and England. It closed with a point he had made repeatedly during staff rides and war games: the army must in all cases make flanking attacks if possible, using Metz as the anchor of its left flank.[84]

Moltke was not confident that a future war would be short, regardless of the outcome of the initial campaign.[85] His planning, like that of Schlieffen, assumed that a victorious campaign against the French would lead not to peace but to a redeployment of much of the army and another, even more difficult campaign against Russia. In memoranda to the War Ministry in January 1909, February 1911, and November 1912, he warned that many great battles would be required, and he feared that there was insufficient ammunition for those battles. In the last memorandum he became more specific, warning that the army was not strong enough to gain a rapid victory. Instead, the army had to expect "a protracted campaign with many difficult, lengthy battles, until we defeat *one* of our opponents." He warned that the army might be out of artillery munitions by the seventh or eighth week. Beyond this, the available munitions would not suffice, "since soon after the first great battle further difficult combat will follow."[86] This was not merely a tactical ploy to increase the army's supply of ammunition. Long before he had warned the kaiser that modern wars could not be won rapidly. Instead, he predicted, a future war would be a long, hard struggle against a country that would not be subdued until its "entire national power would be broken."[87] As Lothar Burchardt has pointed out, although Moltke may have wavered in this view between 1905 and 1911, by the latter date he could hope for a short war only against France, whereas a war against Russia had no foreseeable end.[88] In his military planning, Moltke could not escape the wishful thinking that the army could attain a rapid victory over the French.[89]

Moltke's concept of the western campaign and his associated deployment plan in 1914 rested on a number of questionable assumptions and may be criticized for this reason, but not on the grounds presented by his detractors over the years. The most obvious logical problem in his thinking was that it was internally inconsistent, not that it differed from Schlieffen's ideas. Given Moltke's entirely correct assumption that the French army would mass in the southeast for an offensive into Lorraine, an initial advance into Luxembourg and Belgium and an early attack on Liege were entirely illogical. If his action was substantially dependent on early French offensive moves, there was no reason to assume that the logical countermove would be the politically disastrous invasion of Belgium. Worse, the necessity of seizing Liege at the earliest stage of the campaign, which robbed German diplomacy of time and flexibility, was based on the same Schlieffen-like assumption that Moltke had already questioned in his war games and staff rides. If, as he stated repeatedly, the main point was to find the French army and defeat it in the open field, and if, as he assumed, the French army would be found in Lorraine, then the massive invasion of Belgium north of Liege-Namur made no sense at all. It was, of course, an insurance policy, offering the kind of campaign in open terrain and war of movement for which nearly all German officers thought themselves and their units especially well prepared.

Although some are harshly critical of Moltke's performance as chief of the General Staff, he accomplished much in preparing the army for war by 1914.[90] He received high praise from contemporaries for his training of General Staff officers, and it is now clear that his exercises and training programs were equal to Schlieffen's.[91] Moltke's training program also covered the most important problems encountered in commanding large field armies. His closing tactical problems, given to graduates of the War Academy and a few other officers, were also of high quality.[92] Moltke had a generally good relationship with the kaiser, at least until the famous crisis over a possible eastern front deployment in 1914.[93] Moltke restrained the kaiser from being a disruptive figure in annual maneuvers and worked for a variety of other improvements.[94] He established a Technical Section in the General Staff, incorporated more training in attacking entrenched positions, championed the use of airplanes, and attempted to modernize cavalry tactics, with limited success.[95] He also had only limited success in fostering cooperation with Austria-Hungary, but he was certainly more active in that area than Schlieffen had been.[96] In addition, Moltke was both more aggressive and more successful in working with other government ministers.[97]

While historians disagree over the extent to which Moltke revised the main concepts in Schlieffen's 1905 memorandum—that is, whether his changes were fundamental or merely minor variations—there is no doubt that the termination of any plan for a massive eastern deployment was a fateful step.[98] The elimination of *Aufmarsch* II, an option in most years during both Schlieffen's and Moltke's terms as chief of the General Staff, may have reflected a more realistic view of the international situation in April 1914, but it represented a massive restriction of the government's flexibility, as the events of 1914 demonstrated. Just before ordering the mobilization, the emperor raised the question of sending the army to the east rather than initiating a war against France. Moltke felt compelled to reply that any effort to send the bulk of the army to the east would produce chaos, prompting Wilhelm's devastating reply that Moltke's uncle would have given him a different answer.[99] Whether Moltke's inability to plan for and then attempt the great eastern deployment in 1914 shows his simplistic faith in the Schlieffen Plan, an inherent weakness of character, or sound judgment regarding the hopelessness of achieving a rapid victory in Russia is another question.[100]

The German Concept of Operations, 1914

While the general course of the western campaign of 1914 is well known, much uncertainty remains about what the Germans actually planned to do.[101] Despite the images created by the postwar Schlieffen disciples, it is now apparent that the German army went into the campaign of 1914 without a written plan outlining clear strategic objectives or any sort of timetable allegedly connected with the Schlieffen memorandum of 1905.[102] The oft-repeated allegations that the army had "scripted the entire campaign" or that it possessed a detailed plan down to the hour for each road, wall, and town are massive exaggerations.[103] For decades, historians and others have speculated about a document that was never meant to exist. Such a document would have been contrary to long Prussian traditions of planning for field operations.

The General Staff itself concluded in 1919 that neither Schlieffen nor Moltke had ever set forth a detailed campaign plan in written form, a fact confirmed later by the Reichsarchiv. The latter concluded, on the basis of extensive and unsuccessful searches for such a written plan, that no such document ever existed.[104] Although Moltke and many General Staff officers had a concept of operations in mind, the German army, in the tradition of the elder Moltke, entered the war without a unifying written directive or set or orders. Regardless of how clear Moltke's intentions may have been in his own mind, the Reichsarchiv was correct when it stated that these ideas "were not brought to the attention of the field army commands in the form of a unified army order," even in the moments of crisis and decision that began on 20 August 1914.[105] So secret was the overall concept that corps commanders, even after arriving in their jumping-off areas, did not know in which direction they would advance.[106]

Even before the war, the younger Moltke had frequently confirmed the old principles that detailed planning was beyond the scope of the deployment plan and that the concept of the campaign did not extend beyond a few basic ideas leading to the first great battle. In his memoirs, Gerhard Tappen confirmed that this principle had governed planning in 1914.[107] This was no departure from the army's basic approach to campaign planning, as its own prewar literature had made clear.[108] Moltke's memorandum of 1913, cited by Ritter, made the same point.[109] Tappen, indeed, insisted that he had never seen the Schlieffen memorandum of 1905.[110] The real concept of operations must therefore be gleaned from fragments of the directives given to the field armies, from Moltke's statements and actions during the early days of the campaign, and from the memoirs of the few officers who wrote about this subject after the war.

The deployment plan of 1914 departed from the extreme alternative in Schlieffen's 1905 memorandum in a number of ways that indicate a very different conception of the forthcoming campaign.[111] The concept behind the *Aufmarschplan* may or may not have been very different from Schlieffen's concept of planning, but to project the latter forward to 1914 requires a leap of faith usually discounted by historians. Little if any evidence exists for the postwar assumptions that First Army, on the far right wing of the German advance, was to move beyond Paris and envelop the French left wing in the manner suggested in the most radical case of the 1905 Schlieffen memorandum. The *OHL*'s directive to First Army, the details of which apparently extended only to the advance to the Namur-Liege area, does not suggest such a wide envelopment, which, in any case, would have merely removed Kluck's forces from the main battle. Even Hermann von Kuhl, one of the founders of the Schlieffen orthodoxy, did not originally argue that the great master would have gone to the west of Paris regardless of circumstances. In his first book on the campaign (1921) he attributed no such intent to Schlieffen's plan when he compared it with the actual events of 1914. On the contrary, he emphasized Schlieffen's desire to turn the French left flank. By 1930, Kuhl had changed his story somewhat, stating in his overview of Schlieffen's concept that if the French had defended behind the Marne or the Seine, then the German right wing would have gone around it to the west and south of Paris. But in discussing the actual plan of 1914, he stressed turning the French flank regardless of where it made a stand.[112]

Kluck's account, written in the winter 1914–1915 and published in 1920, provides the First Army commander's anticipation based on a 2 August 1914 conference. Kluck was of the opinion that the right flank army (his First Army) would make a wide turning movement through Belgium and Artois "and perhaps into Picardy." Had he intended from the outset to cross the lower Seine to the west of Paris, advancing into Picardy would have been an established objective, not just a possibility. Kluck's account makes no mention of a Schlieffen Plan or any of Schlieffen's memoranda, which he probably had never seen.[113] Indeed, several General Staff officers holding key positions in 1914 later stated that they had not seen the 1905 memorandum.[114] Conversely, strong evidence indicates that Moltke and his flank commanders anticipated that the right wing would swing sharply to the southwest and fight the main right-flank battle no farther west than was actually the case in 1914. One of the other earliest postwar accounts (1919) by Friedrich Immanuel, a well-respected military author even before the war, stated that the intent had been to fight the main battle between Paris and the Argonne, north of the Marne.[115] Even the Reichsarchiv acknowledged that First Army's deployment directive gave it the mission of guarding the right flank, not of conducting the decisive maneuver or waging the decisive battle.[116]

Moltke may have intended to attempt a double envelopment from the outset of the campaign. As late as July 1914, the General Staff had updated a plan for a breakthrough of the French fortifications between Toul and Verdun.[117] As early as 15 August, long before the initial battles with the French and British in Belgium, Moltke had decided to dispatch the six and a half *Ersatz* divisions to Strassburg and Bracken rather than to the right wing, despite the objections of the Operations Section.[118] Although the mobilization plan had placed sufficient vacant railway capacity behind Sixth and Seventh Armies to move much of their forces to reinforce the right flank, Moltke made no effort to execute this concept, even after initial victories in Alsace-Lorraine made it clear that the French offensive there had failed.[119] Instead of using these forces to reinforce the right wing, Moltke approved a counteroffensive, apparently hoping to break through the French forces and turn what seemed to be a successful envelopment of the French left flank into a double envelopment by Sixth and Seventh Armies attacking from the south.

This method of conducting the campaign had ample precedents in pre-war General Staff exercises and war games.[120] As discussed previously, Schlieffen had been willing to conduct the main battle in Alsace-Lorraine if the French had attacked in that direction, and even in the 1905 memorandum he had assumed a much shorter turning movement on his right flank if the French took the offensive. Moltke was prepared to place more emphasis on the German left wing, especially since he had essentially reverted to his uncle's basic concept of finding the main French army and conducting the battle wherever it was. Indeed, as he recognized, the basic strategic assumption of the two-front war—the necessity of defeating one enemy quickly—required the Germans to place the main effort wherever the French were encountered, since any delay threatened to open eastern Prussia, Silesia, or even Berlin to a Russian advance. In the event, the developments of the campaign soon rendered the prewar plans impossible to execute, if not irrelevant.

Concluding Remarks

In many ways, the younger Moltke's tenure as chief of the General Staff marked a continuation of the Schlieffen era. Moltke's staff rides and exercises provided as rigorous a preparation for war as possible. He minimized the kaiser's role in maneuvers, making them distinctly better than those in Schlieffen's time. In terms of strategy, Moltke continued the emphasis on defeating France first and as quickly as possible. His concept of operations (there was apparently no formal plan) was also similar to Schlieffen's, at least initially.

In some other respects, Moltke departed from Schlieffen's thinking. Some of this was unavoidable. Schlieffen had the advantage of not having to worry about Russia during his final years as chief. From 1904 to 1906 Russia was embroiled in a losing war with Japan and torn by revolution, effectively eliminating it as a major power in Europe. By 1908, however, Russia had recovered sufficiently to once again be a factor in European international relations.

The position of Italy also changed. As noted earlier, some of the deployment plans during the tenures of the elder Moltke and Schlieffen made reference to an Italian presence on the German left flank. After 1908 it became more obvious that Italy was backing away from its participation in the Triple Alliance. As early as 1908, Moltke anticipated that Italy would remain neutral. Even though Italy was not a major factor in the German calculus, it had to be dealt with.[121]

Moltke also departed from Schlieffen's approach in terms of where the decision against France would be sought. While Moltke still generally wanted the decisive battle to be fought by the German right wing, in the last few years before the war he was willing to consider attaining the desired result in Lorraine—in other words, anywhere the French army could be fought successfully. Arguably, this was one of the ways in which Moltke sought to re-create his illustrious uncle's approach to war and its conduct.

Perhaps the most critical departure from Schlieffen was the decision in 1913 to dispense with the idea of an eastern deployment in case of war against Russia alone. This, in effect, locked Germany into a single concept of how the war would be conducted. The army, as noted previously, severely limited the government's diplomatic flexibility. Moltke's decision here, however, can also be seen as one more illustration of the ongoing process of divorcing diplomacy from war planning, especially with regard to coalition warfare.[122]

Finally, there were two issues for which no preparation was available. The first was the lack of general officers with actual combat experience. None of the German generals in 1914 had commanded large units in combat. Some had combat experience from 1870–1871 as junior officers or as one-year volunteers, but even these were becoming a rare breed in 1914. Most had either retired (Hindenburg) or were nearing retirement (Mackensen and Gallwitz). While staff rides, maneuvers, and war games prepared generals as well as possible, the actual experience of command in combat is always something different.[123]

The other critical issue was the unknown impact of scale. Generals and staffs that had participated in annual maneuvers would now have to assemble, supply, and maneuver troops on a far larger scale than they had ever done before. That alone could be a daunting task.[124] And now it would have to be done against a thinking and reactive enemy. The campaign of 1914 is the focus of the next chapter.

German order for mobilization. This order would have been publicly posted in every town and city in Germany. The men pictured are Chancellor Bethmann-Hollweg (left) and Moltke (right). (National Archives)

German field kitchen, 1914. One can see why the field kitchen was popularly called the "goulash cannon." (Bain Collection, Library of Congress)

German bridge train, circa 1914. (Bain Collection, Library of Congress)

This rather naïve depiction of a German sharpshooter shows the innocence with which both sides approached war in 1914. (National Archives)

German heavy artillery devastated fortresses like this one at Przemyśl. (Bain Collection, Library of Congress)

German field artillery battery in action in Galicia, 1915. (Bain Collection, Library of Congress)

German ground crewman attaching a bomb to a plane, circa 1915. The size of the bomb and the nature of the attachment illustrate airpower in its embryonic stage. (Bain Collection, Library of Congress)

German raiding party on the Somme. By 1916, the German army was using the coal-scuttle steel helmet. Note the presence of pistols and hand grenades, especially the common German stick grenade popularly known as the "potato masher." (National Archives)

German trench destroyed by British artillery during the Battle of the Somme. (Bain Collection, Library of Congress)

German soldiers manhandling a 150mm howitzer forward. (National Archives)

German heavy howitzer. (National Archives)

German field headquarters on the western front. Once the lines had become fairly static, considerable retraining and a change of mentality were required to get the army in the west accustomed to mobile warfare. (National Archives)

German infantry engaged in a training exercise, practicing cutting barbed wire. Training of this kind was essential in trench warfare. (National Archives)

German heavy artillery battery in firing position. (National Archives)

The German army nearing the end. German prisoners in France, circa 1918. (Bain Collection, Library of Congress)

CHAPTER SEVEN

THE TEST OF 1914

During the afternoon of 1 August 1914, the populations of towns and cities across Germany read placards informing them that the kaiser would provide millions of men with free train rides, available upon the presentation of any piece of military paperwork, to sometimes distant destinations within the country. This offer was not to be refused. The placards informed readers of the mobilization of all of Germany's armed forces and warned of strict punishments for those who did not immediately report to their assigned stations. Thus, 2 August 1914 became the first day of mobilization under the imminent danger of war.[1]

Responsibility for the War

The "guns of August" touched off more than a world war; they initiated an ongoing historical debate (the war-guilt question). Article 231 of the Versailles settlement forced the new government in Germany to accept full responsibility for the war. This did not settle the question, however; instead, it inflamed the debate for the next two decades. Partly political (as governments sought to exculpate their countries) and partly historical (as numerous journalists, historians, and retired military and political leaders joined the fray), the controversy continued until the Second World War engulfed Europe. No real consensus developed from the hundreds of publications, but most scholars (especially in Germany) agreed that all the great powers shared responsibility in some measure.[2]

The second phase of the debate on responsibility for the war began in 1961, when distinguished German historian Fritz Fischer published his spectacular study *Germany's Aims in the First World War*. Fischer condemned the German government for deliberately starting the war as part of an effort to dominate the continent and combat domestic opposition. In two subsequent volumes Fischer expanded and defended his thesis.[3] He also raised troubling questions about continuity in German foreign policy from Wilhelm II to Hitler. The impact of his efforts was such that the war-guilt question became known as the "Fischer controversy." Numerous distinguished scholars rushed to defend the Second Reich against Fischer's accusations, while a substantial group of younger scholars, including some of Fischer's students, began to reconsider numerous aspects of Germany's domestic and international policies from Bismarck to the collapse of 1918.[4]

A third group of historians attempted to reach a synthesis by studying the war's origins in a broader international context and by investigating a host of military, political, and social topics. The opening of numerous archives after the Second World War gave these new studies a much firmer foundation in primary documents than had been possible prior to Fischer's first book. The entire question, in the words of one of the most prominent participants, became "one of the most complicated and bewildering in modern history."[5] The question of responsibility for the war is beyond the scope of this study, but some of the issues have relevance in establishing the strategic context of the army's preparations for war in 1914 and in evaluating its approach to strategy once the war began.[6] The best recent reviews of this topic are in the books by Hew Strachan and David Stevenson.[7]

One of the most important issues involves the army's expectations about the nature of a future war. The army was not obsessed with the idea of a short war. As discussed in chapter 2, the elder Moltke had long realized that any future war would be lengthy. German theory had for many years prior to 1914 considered that war would consist of more than a single decisive battle and that multiple phases or campaigns would be required. Many European military commanders agreed that a long war was possible, but they were reluctant to openly discuss this question with their political leaders.[8] Even Schlieffen had realized that a rapid defeat of France would not end the war in the west and that large forces would have to remain there during a second campaign in the east. A related issue was the army's expectations about the capabilities of its potential enemies and its estimate of Germany's chances against a coalition of France, Russia, and Great Britain. Circumstances had changed greatly between 1905 and 1914, and as a result, a discussion of these issues must center primarily on the views of the younger Moltke and, to a lesser degree, other German military leaders in the years just prior to 1914.

As the crisis of July 1914 deepened with the delivery of the Austro-Hungarian ultimatum to Serbia, the leaders of the Prussian army, in close cooperation with the leaders of other state armies, prepared to execute the plans the General Staff had finalized at the beginning of April. Those who argue that primary responsibility for the war rests with Germany have concluded that the army's key leaders pressured the government for a preventive war, using the assassination crisis as a pretext. Others have stressed the broader responsibility of other powers in starting a local war in the Balkans and allowing it to engulf the entire continent. In any case, the army's leadership seemed to get caught up in the national jubilation and patriotism that characterized some of the public reaction in Germany and throughout Europe. Although several scholars have mounted impressive attacks on the conventional wisdom that the people of Germany and Europe rushed headlong into the war in a fit of boundless enthusiasm, the rush to volunteer may be seen as a sign of broad patriotism. The nation's intellectuals, writers, and even artists joined in the "exuberance of the moment."[9]

The Mobilization of 1914

The Prussian War Ministry and General Staff executed the mobilization declared by the kaiser on 1 August with an efficiency that most modern military forces would envy. Millions of men, including a large proportion of reservists, mustered in their scattered garrisons, boarded trains, and moved to their assembly areas along Germany's eastern and western frontiers, accompanied by thousands of pieces of artillery and hundreds of thousands of horses. Active units sent officers and men to reserve units while incorporating large numbers of reservists into their own ranks. Reserve units arose from their cadres of active officers and mobilized with the same efficiency that characterized their active counterparts.[10] Assembling the dense concentration of units along the German frontier around Aachen was a particularly noteworthy example of the nearly flawless transition from peacetime to wartime organization, but it was by no means unique. The army's careful prior planning with the German railway system, an inherent part of the mobilization plan, ensured that the units, along with their supplies, horses, ammunition, and a wide variety of equipment, arrived at their destinations ready for the next phase: deployment (Aufmarsch) to their starting positions.[11]

Consistent with the strategic situation that had given birth to the various plans for mobilization, deployment, and campaigning since the days of Schlieffen, the 1914 concept required an exceptionally rapid preparation for war. The mobilization schedule called for Germany's western forces to be detrained and ready for foot movement on the thirteenth day of mobilization, 14 August, and to be ready for full offensive operations on 18 August, while Eighth Army in East Prussia was to be ready by 10 August.[12]

Mobilization was an immense and extraordinarily complicated undertaking.[13] In 1914 the army mobilized nearly 6 percent of the entire population—almost 4 million men already in units, plus an additional 1 million volunteers, thousands of wagons, and around 700,000 horses. The approximately 30,000 officers of the active army welcomed nearly 90,000 reserve and *Landwehr* officers and acting officers.[14] In the space of twelve days, the strength of the German field army (including its Bavarian, Württemberger, and Saxon components) jumped from 808,280 to 3,502,700 officers and men. The army's school system virtually shut down. Retired officers created new structures to replace the departed active corps.[15] These figures clearly show the degree to which the Prussian-German structure was a cadre system in which only one-quarter of the officers and an even smaller proportion of the enlisted men were regulars. Each of the twenty-five active corps required 140 trains, while reserve corps used 85 trains and cavalry divisions (ten in all) needed 31. Between 550 and 650 trains crossed the Rhine every day during the mobilization; this produced extremely heavy traffic on the dozen or so major bridges, such as the one at Cologne, where a west-moving train crossed every ten minutes for more than two weeks. Wilhlem Groener, head of the Railway Section of the General Staff, was so confident in his section and in the plan that he told his staff not to bother him with any problems short of the loss of two Rhine bridges.[16] Even the army's critics concede that the mobilization was a masterpiece of planning and execution.[17]

Mobilization, combined with the subsequent declaration of war, automatically activated a number of measures in Prussia and in most of the empire. As each of the active corps commanders prepared for departure, his place was taken by an acting commanding general, usually a retired general of the appropriate rank. The duties of the acting corps commanders were actually broader than those of their peacetime predecessors, particularly in Prussia, where the Siege Law of 4 June 1851 went into effect. This law gave the acting commanding generals a wide range of civil powers, nearly dictatorial in some respects, while the mobilization system required them to perform a variety of military functions. The staffs of the acting commanding generals eventually became substantial as they assumed responsibility for such duties as mail (and censorship), care of invalids, replacements (individual and unit), and routine peacetime matters. Mobilization exacerbated the question of the kaiser's control, since it increased the number of officers with theoretical direct access to him to sixty-two.[18]

For Moltke, the first crisis occurred before mobilization began, when the emperor briefly thought the war could be limited to Russia.[19] Wilhelm II thus proposed a mobilization based on the traditional deployment case II, with the bulk of the German army moving to the east. Moltke reminded the kaiser that the General Staff had dropped the *Grosser Ostaufmarsch* in 1913 and warned that sending the army to the east would produce a disorderly mob rather than a military force ready to attack. Jolted by this unwelcome dose of reality, Wilhelm responded that Moltke's uncle would have given a different reply. The crisis soon passed, as the hope that the British would remain neutral and restrain France proved ephemeral, but the effect on Moltke's fragile emotional state may have been serious.[20]

Historians and others have disagreed on whether Moltke was correct in dismissing any possibility of sending large forces to the east. He apparently gave his response without consulting Groener, head of the Railway Section. Groener later stated that it would have been possible to send the bulk of the army to the east, although his private comments indicate that he really thought otherwise.[21] After the war, Hermann von Staabs, one of the army's experts on railway movement, convincingly argued that the eastern deployment could have been accomplished in about two weeks, a verdict that has convinced some recent writers.[22]

The German Command Structure

The command structure for the upcoming campaigns reflected the monarchical nature of Prussia and the German Empire, as well as the inability to develop effective bureaucratic structures to deal with a war on two fronts. Here one must distinguish between the General Headquarters and the Army High Command, or *Oberste Heeresleitung* (*OHL*). The former was led by the emperor and included his entourage as well as the General Staff, representatives of the navy, the civil administration, dignitaries, and others.[23] As its head, the emperor offered the only prospect of coordinating the military, political, and economic aspects of the war.

Wilhelm II only occasionally exercised his powers as head of state and supreme commander (*Oberster Kriegsherr*). Indeed, he receded so far into the background on most matters that some historians have mockingly called him the "shadow kaiser." This is not an entirely accurate characterization of the kaiser's role. Although Wilhelm II, in accordance with his promise not to interfere, almost always deferred to the recommendations made by Moltke, Falkenhayn, and Ludendorff, the military leadership felt obliged to obtain his approval on nearly every important decision.[24] He exercised an important influence on the conduct of the war through his power to control appointments to high-level civilian and military positions. By supporting Falkenhayn until August 1916, for example, he maintained the primacy of the western front. Overall, he was, as one scholar has argued, "anything but insignificant."[25] His failure to show any sustained judgment in matters of policy and strategy meant that coordination of the nation's war effort and even its military strategy was sporadic and ineffective. Few modern great powers have embarked on a major war with less competent leadership at the highest levels, and the ultimate responsibility must be his. Despite his shortcomings, the mass of the officer corps remained loyal to him to the last.

The most important part of the General Headquarters was the *OHL*, which controlled the land war on both fronts. At its head was Moltke, who, as chief of the General Staff, served as the de facto commander of the overall land war as well as the western front commander. He had only a small number of General Staff officers on his staff. The *Oberquartiermeister*, General Hermann von Stein, was theoretically Moltke's highest-ranking deputy, but he remained in the background and dealt primarily with administrative matters. As chief of the Railway Section, Lieutenant Colonel Groener was the key person in charge of executing the mobilization. Lieutenant Colonel Gerhard Tappen served as chief of the Operations Section, perhaps the key subordinate post. Tappen had many critics who regarded him as mediocre.[26] Lieutenant Colonel Wilhelm Dommes, chief of the Political Section, also performed important duties in a variety of areas. The talented officer who headed the Intelligence Section, Lieutenant Colonel Richard Hentsch, also undertook a wide variety of duties.[27] Numerous other officers holding supervisory positions over various branches also accompanied the headquarters, although they worked primarily with the chief of the General Staff. It should be noted that the *OHL* underwent many changes during the war and increased greatly in size as its control over the army groups and field armies expanded.[28]

The French Plan

French planning was simpler and less subtle than either Schlieffen's scheme of 1905 or Moltke's of 1914. Giving wide latitude to the French supreme commander, Plan XVII deployed the mass of the French army so that it was capable of, but not committed to, conducting immediate offensives into Germany, north and south of Metz, and in Lorraine, where the French concentrated their largest forces.[29] Although the French expected a German advance through Belgium, they underestimated its strength and scope, relying on their left-flank army (Fifth Army, under Lanrezac), with assistance from the Belgians and the British. Fourth Army, in strategic reserve, would be available to either support Fifth Army or join the offensives. The main point of Joffre's plan, contained in his Order No. 1 of 8 August, was an immediate offensive thrust into Germany, precisely what the Germans expected.[30] Both sides thus had a reasonable idea of what the other would do, but neither was able to execute its plan.

Liege and the Advance through Belgium

The first phase of the 1914 campaign began while the bulk of both armies were just beginning their mobilization and initial deployments. As the main body of the German army completed its movement into its final deployment positions, other elements began the effort to seize the Belgian fortress at Liege and its important bridges and railway junctions.[31] The attack failed at first, in large part because Belgian troops managed to prepare field positions between the major forts. However, the energetic, even heroic intervention of Erich Ludendorff turned a potentially catastrophic defeat into victory by inducing the main garrison to surrender. The new 420mm howitzers pulverized the remaining fortresses, and the way through the critical Liege bottleneck was open.

Some writers have continued to portray the Liege attack as a failure because the original coup de main did not work. This is surely expecting too much of a force that was attacking under very difficult circumstances. Ludendorff's action enabled First and Second Armies to advance through the critical area with only a minor delay. The assault, conducted at first by a force of six infantry brigades maintained on a permanent wartime footing for this purpose, began on 4 August, while the rest of the army was just beginning to mobilize.[32] Although the Germans were disappointed and alarmed when the attack did not proceed as rapidly as planned, Kluck's First Army began to move through Aachen (not Liege) on 13 August, so the bulk of the right wing was delayed for only one or, at most, two days. Liege was, in short, an important victory, largely justifying Moltke's confidence that the bottleneck could be forced in a manner consistent with the planned envelopment of the French left wing and without invading Holland.[33]

The subsequent rapid advance across southern Belgium was accomplished with only sporadic contact with weak opposing forces during the first few days, giving the impression that the right wing of the German army was achieving a great victory. German intelligence estimates of the numerical strength of the French army, its general dispositions, and its intentions proved largely correct.[34] The Belgian army retreated into Antwerp, which German First Army invested with two reserve corps. This excessive diversion of force was the first visible consequence of sending available second-line formations to Alsace-Lorraine.[35] The British Expeditionary Force (BEF) remained a largely unknown factor until August, when its collision with First Army at Mons settled the question of its initial deployment. In a series of bloody but victorious engagements, First, Second, and Third Armies pushed rapidly forward, and by 27 August they had reached the approximate line St. Quentin–Hirson–Mezieres. Maubeuge was invested, and by then it was eighteen to thirty-seven miles behind the front lines. A false sense of victory—indeed, an entirely unjustified euphoria—briefly engulfed much of the German High Command.[36]

The French Attack in Alsace

In the meantime, south of Metz the anticipated French offensive had advanced about nine miles into Alsace and about twice that far in the southern area near Freiburg and the Swiss border. German Sixth and Seventh Armies halted the French attacks in a series of bloody encounters and prepared to launch a major counteroffensive that would push the invaders off German soil. These battles raised the question of theater-wide strategy, and the High Command had to make a choice of potentially decisive importance.

The deployment instructions for Sixth Army placed its commander, Crown Prince Rupprecht of Bavaria, in command of Seventh Army and in charge of coordinating the operations of the two armies.[37] The directive gave Rupprecht a clear but difficult primary task. The two field armies, acting in close conjunction and cooperation, were to protect the left flank of the main body of the army along the Nied River between Metz and the Saar. The crown prince was further instructed to engage the French army southwest of Metz but to withdraw if threatened by a superior enemy force. In particular, the two armies were to tie down the greatest possible number of French forces but avoid any defeat that would threaten the Nied position or lead to an easy French victory.[38] The mobilization instructions did not tell Rupprecht to be prepared to move part of his forces to the German right wing if they were not needed in Alsace-Lorraine, even though the railway mobilization plan apparently deployed a sufficient number of empty trains to the rear of Sixth Army to make such a move possible.[39] One General Staff officer concluded that this was evidence that Moltke had abandoned this basic idea, even though it had been a subject of much prewar discussion.[40] Such a transfer of forces was, of course, an allegedly critical part of Schlieffen's operational concept.

On 6 August the chief of the General Staff of Sixth Army, Conrad Krafft von Dellmensingen, submitted a proposal to Crown Prince Rupprecht that outlined their portion of the campaign. This report stressed three elements: (1) to fix enemy forces and prevent their transport to the decisive flank; (2) to be prepared to protect the Nied position by a retreat if the main enemy strength advanced to the east beyond Metz; and (3) to be prepared to attack through and south of Metz toward the west bank of the Mosel if no strong enemy forces were encountered.[41] This varied somewhat from the wording of the deployment directive, which stated that a retreat would be necessary if "superior" enemy forces appeared and that an attack might be necessary only if the Germans did not encounter "superior" enemy forces.[42] Krafft clearly recognized that Sixth and Seventh Armies were supposed to make a sort of demonstration, but he also thought the French might force the main battle in Lorraine, in which case the German right would move directly to the south to join a decisive counterattack.[43] Overall, Krafft and Rupprecht were anxious to launch a major offensive.[44]

Crown Prince Rupprecht's Counteroffensive

Although Rupprecht clearly recognized that his primary mission was to tie down French forces by making a demonstration that would prevent their transfer to the main front, his actions soon reversed the intentions of his instructions.[45] As early as 9 August, the impulsive attacks of Seventh Army threatened to create a gap between the two armies and jeopardize united action, even though the deployment instructions specifically ordered them to remain closely linked.[46] By 13 and 14 August, this had apparently become a serious problem, as intelligence reports indicated (to an exaggerated degree) that the main French offensive would take place in Alsace-Lorraine and that Sixth and Seventh Armies might have to retreat as suggested in the deployment instructions.[47] Despite this, Rupprecht, supported by Krafft von Dellmensingen, was not inclined to remain on the defensive for long. The crown prince repeatedly noted in his diary his dislike of a long-term defensive posture because he thought it was a mistake to leave the initiative to the enemy; in addition, such a course of action would damage the offensive spirit of his soldiers. Unless prohibited by a direct order, he noted, he would fulfill his task offensively.[48] Rupprecht's operations officer later argued that Sixth Army, which had control over Seventh, was simply too strong to remain on the defense. This would have been a waste of resources, and, as he pointed out, no glory would be gained by standing passively opposite the French fortifications.[49] The latter opinion was apparently based on regional and dynastic concerns. Sixth and Seventh Armies were composed largely of Bavarians and were commanded by Bavarian officers, most notably Rupprecht. There was some concern that Bavaria's standing would suffer if Sixth and Seventh Armies played the role of bystander while the Prussians grabbed the glory by winning the decisive victory.

This position, seemingly insubordinate from the outset, was consistent, at least in concept, with German theory from Moltke onward. Under that approach, laid out in numerous regulations, a local commander should (except in extraordinary circumstances) enjoy freedom of action to accomplish his assigned task either offensively or defensively, based on the local situation. The deployment directive was merely a starting point, and every senior commander in 1914 had been educated to exercise his own judgment and initiative as the campaign progressed. Conversely, Prussian theory also warned that the local commander must remain within the framework of the overall intent of the plan and do nothing to endanger the larger concept.

In addressing this serious issue, Moltke's conduct was all too typical of his own actions and those of the *OHL* in general in August and September 1914. Just before Crown Prince Rupprecht's offensive began, the High Command abrogated its responsibility to maintain the overall framework by repeatedly declining to give definite orders. Instead, the High Command retreated to the formalism that Sixth Army would have to accept full responsibility if it decided to launch an offensive. Ultimately, in the words of the Reichsarchiv, "the High Command gave the Sixth Army Command full freedom of action and full responsibility."[50]

Rupprecht adopted a liberal interpretation of the extent of his freedom of action. On 20 August, despite cautions from the *OHL*, Sixth and Seventh Armies launched a major counteroffensive against the advancing

French forces. In a series of costly battles, Rupprecht's forces stopped the French and then pushed them back toward the original borders.[51] The High Command, it must be noted, made halfhearted efforts to prevent this attack once it learned of the crown prince's intentions. Moltke sent one of his closest associates on the General Staff, Lieutenant Colonel Wilhelm von Dommes, to Sixth Army headquarters on 17 August. Both Rupprecht and his chief of the General Staff declined to be swayed from their determination to attack. The crown prince of Bavaria simply refused to follow his instructions, which apparently were not delivered with the decisiveness of a direct order. He commented that the *OHL* should "either allow me to act on my own or give me direct orders." But strict control of highly placed subordinates was not in the spirit of Moltke's personality or his method of command. Nor was it consistent with Rupprecht's position as heir to the throne of Bavaria, which could be overcome only by appeal to the emperor. So Sixth Army moved to execute its ill-considered offensive.[52] The exact source of Rupprecht's royal but seemingly unmilitary behavior is unknown, but most historians regard the decision as disastrous, particularly given the later actions of Moltke and Rupprecht.[53]

The blame for all this cannot be laid exclusively on the shoulders of the crown prince. On 22 August Sixth Army apparently asked the *OHL* if it should prepare to send forces to the right flank. Instead of approving this move, Tappen, the chief of the Operations Section, instructed Sixth Army to continue its offensive by exploiting its victory in the direction of Epinal. The *OHL* had apparently been misled by Sixth Army's optimistic reports and believed that a major breakthrough was possible on the left flank, something that Moltke may have wanted from the outset of the campaign.[54]

Moltke's war games and staff exercises had anticipated these events and had already worked out a possible course of action. He had always maintained that the main battle would take place wherever the main French forces were found, and his games had repeatedly considered not merely a major counteroffensive in the south but perhaps a shifting of the main effort there, if doing so offered the prospect of defeating the French army "in the open field." Moltke thus had to make a fateful choice around 20 August: transfer elements of Sixth and Seventh Armies to reinforce the right wing, or attempt a major breakthrough in the south, thus threatening the French with a gigantic double envelopment.

Moltke chose the southern offensive, hoping to achieve a massive strategic double envelopment. He did so based on the false confidence that his forces had already achieved a great victory on the right wing, which was then advancing rapidly through southern Belgium and into France. This decision, to continue the attack rather than transfer forces to the right wing, earned him the nearly universal condemnation of the Schlieffen school, which argued that this was further proof of his theoretical and practical departures from the Schlieffen Plan.

The perceived prospects for a successful breakthrough in the Epinal-Nancy area turned out to be without foundation, and Moltke's hopes for a double envelopment soon collapsed. The French halted Sixth Army's offensive by 24 August, and the next day they launched a major counterattack, supported by the guns of the fortifications around Nancy. Moltke, by then deeply committed to the offensive in Lorraine, demanded that Sixth and Seventh Armies renew their attacks and break through the French lines between Toul and Epinal. The *OHL* sent another emissary, Major Erich von Redern, to Rupprecht's headquarters to emphasize the need for a renewed offensive, a feat the crown prince thought impossible.[55] A specific order followed on 26 August, and another officer journeyed from the High Command to Sixth Army on 30 August to overcome the united opposition of Rupprecht and his General Staff officers.[56]

The end result was that the costly fighting continued without any important contribution to the overall German effort. The German left wing thus neither made a successful effort to achieve a breakthrough around Nancy nor dispatched significant forces to the German right-wing armies, all of which were in need of reinforcements by the end of August.[57] On the latter point, it should be noted that strong evidence exists that Moltke had decided against sending forces to the right flank as early as 22 August, probably because of excessively optimistic estimates of the successes already attained by First and Second Armies and because he doubted such a transfer could be completed in a timely manner.[58] Moltke was so certain of a successful breakthrough around Nancy that the emperor visited the front there to witness the anticipated victory.[59]

Developments in the Central Sector

In the meantime, developments in the area of German Fourth and Fifth Armies, deployed north of Metz, were equally lacking in decisive results. The Germans had correctly expected a French advance in this area, and both their prewar General Staff games and their intelligence estimates made this assumption. As noted previously, Schlieffen had occasionally conducted General Staff studies that envisioned a decisive victory by counterattacking a French force advancing in this area. In theory, the greater the proportion of the French army that became involved in a battle here, the shorter the decisive turning movement of the right wing and the better the prospects for a successful counterattack from Metz. But here, too, decisive results were elusive for both sides.

In a less serious replay of the events on the German left wing, the commander of Fifth Army, Crown Prince Wilhelm of Prussia, began a premature attack on 22 August.[60] Once again, the *OHL* had failed to provide clear orders, leaving local commanders on their own.[61] The Germans quickly advanced through Luxembourg and deep into the Ardennes, where they encountered French Third and Fourth Armies. In a series of bloody frontal encounters, the Germans pushed the French back to approximately the line Fumay-Sedan-Montmedy-Verdun by 25 August 1914.[62]

The Advance on the Right Wing after Liege

Returning to the right flank of the German advance, one can now see clearly, more so than in German headquarters in 1914, that the German army, though victorious everywhere, had been unable to bring the French to a decisive battle. The French, though battered, retained freedom of action and successfully extricated themselves from every major danger of large-scale envelopment by the Germans. This produced precisely what the elder Moltke had feared: indecisive and costly battles, where one bloody action led only to another. Schlieffen had emphasized turning movements to avoid these kinds of victories, which he described as "ordinary" because they did not produce decisive results.

After Liege fell, the bulk of King Albert's army retreated into Antwerp as the German right wing moved quickly through Belgium, probably in a manner generally anticipated in Moltke's prewar concept. Some civilians resisted the advancing Germans, provoking the sharp reprisals that seriously besmirched the German army's reputation in Europe and the United States.[63] Namur, a Belgian city whose fortress complex had been the cornerstone of the French army's defensive plans and positions on its left flank, quickly succumbed to the German army's siege artillery.[64] This, combined with increasing evidence of a massive German movement through Belgium north of the Sambre River, forced General Charles Lanrezac, commander of Fifth Army on the extreme left wing of the French forces, to turn part of his forces to the north to face German Second Army.[65]

German First Army, weakened by the detachment of forces to invest Belgian garrisons, advanced to the southwest, on Second Army's right flank, in an effort to envelop the French left as it deployed to face Bülow's forces.[66] Unaware of the location of the British Expeditionary Force, Kluck intended to make a wide sweep to outflank both the British and the French left flank in one turning movement. This raised the possibility of a sizable gap between First and Second Armies and the attendant danger of both being vulnerable to counterattacks on their open flanks. German theory had always warned that he who outflanked could be outflanked, and it had concluded that such risks were the price of great success, so this situation should not have come as a surprise. Nevertheless, neither the German command system nor the commanders themselves were able to deal with the dangers and maintain a sensible if risky command of the right-flank forces.

Moltke lost control of the situation on the crucial right flank for a number of reasons, and the events of 20–21 August were just the first sign of this failure. The *OHL* remained in Coblenz during this period, primarily because Moltke had to maintain good telephonic and telegraphic contact with the very uncertain campaign unfolding in East Prussia and Galicia, but in part because the staffs needed at least a minimal degree of order in the local area.[67] The institution of army group commander did not exist in 1914, and Moltke imposed on the right wing the same expedient he had employed in Lorraine: he subordinated Kluck's First Army to Bülow's command. He would have subordinated Third Army as well, but the latter's commander, the Saxon Baron von Hausen, was senior to Bülow.[68] This subordination of First Army to Second Army lasted until 27 August, despite Kluck's efforts to have it terminated earlier.[69] Moltke reinstated this measure on 10 September, during the retreat from the Marne.

Bülow and Kluck had very different ideas on tactics and strategy. The former was well known for his opposition to the army's emphasis on flanking attacks and turning movements in the Schlieffen manner, and the latter worked under the influence of Hermann von Kuhl, perhaps the most highly respected General Staff officer in the field in 1914. By 20 August, the views of the two army commanders and their staffs had become irreconcilable, and their attitudes toward each other turned bitter.[70] The result was that the German right flank faced its first real challenge on 21–23 August with only the vaguest of directives from the *OHL* and with a local command arrangement that fueled disagreement rather than cooperation.[71]

As the German right-wing armies advanced across the Meuse and into Belgium, the army's supply system began to show signs of severe strain. The forward corps, slowed only briefly by the battle at Liege, were in constant danger of outrunning their logistics. Considerable destruction of the Belgian railway system's infrastructure, including bridges, tunnels, and rolling stock, placed great burdens on the German railway construction units. By the end of August, the right-wing armies were much farther from their railheads than anticipated. Motorized transport, partly military and partly drawn from the voluntary associations, could not fully compensate for the gaps between the end of the functioning rail lines and the units.[72]

Beyond its railheads, the army depended on horse-drawn heavy transport units to carry supplies of all kinds to the field units beyond those few areas where motorized transport could be concentrated. Schlieffen had anticipated that the field units could largely live off the land as they advanced through Belgium into France. By the middle of August, many divisions were doing precisely that. The most critical shortage was fodder for the horses. The forward cavalry divisions, in particular, were unable to provide their horses with sufficient grain to maintain their strength. Making matters worse was the High Command's failure to implement a system for the collection and treatment of sick and exhausted horses. Thus the army suffered high losses in horses, many of which were entirely avoidable.[73] Despite numerous problems, the cavalry divisions covered great distances and fought many engagements, all of which consumed their fodder and mounts more rapidly than they could be replenished and rested.

Infantry forces also experienced great difficulties in moving sufficient munitions forward as the front advanced to the west and south. Among the many expedients adopted to ensure that the fighting units had sufficient ammunition and food—and one of the most immediately productive—was battlefield recovery. As early as the Battle of the Marne, First Army organized a program to recover unspent cartridges and iron rations from the dead and wounded.[74] First Army also drew on the resources of a voluntary automobile association from Aachen, which contributed nearly 300 trucks and autos for transporting food, ammunition, and wounded soldiers.[75]

Kluck's Turn to the South

Bülow, excessively concerned with protecting his right flank as he prepared for a major battle against Lanrezac's forces along the Sambre River, ordered Kluck to turn sharply south rather than continue his southwest-wardly march. Bülow hoped that this would put First Army in a better position to protect Second Army's right flank and reduce the gap between the two forces. Kluck protested but obeyed, although the larger consideration of enveloping and turning the entire Allied left flank might have dictated adherence to his original intent.[76]

As Kluck moved to the south, his forces stumbled upon the British Expeditionary Force at Mons on 23 August, touching off the sharp if brief battle known by that name. Joffre had requested the British commander, Sir John French, to move the BEF as far northeast as Namur to participate in French Fifth Army's attack in that area. Fortunately for the Entente, he declined Joffre's request to attack toward an enemy whose presence was suspected but whose strength, dispositions, and intentions were unknown. Instead, the British occupied a temporary defensive position, where the Germans encountered them in an engagement remarkably similar to those foreseen in German prewar theory. After a bloody day of indecisive fighting that was costly to both sides, the British withdrew when they learned of events to their right. Namur had fallen, German Third Army had crossed the Meuse, and the French were falling back before the advance of Bülow's Second Army. The BEF's own position, moreover, was threatened by the larger forces Kluck could bring to bear in the forthcoming days. Though a British defeat, Mons was by no means decisive, and it marked the debut of the legendary power of the massed rifle power of the British infantry.

Had Kluck remained true to his original intent, or had the British advanced as Joffre desired, First Army probably would have fallen upon the flank of the BEF, perhaps in the midst of an extended forward advance, with potentially catastrophic results.[77] Historians generally agree that First Army lost a great opportunity to outflank the BEF and perhaps deal it a crushing defeat, but they do not agree on who is to blame.[78] Events on 23 August in any case marked the final collapse of the French army's Plan XVII, and Joffre ordered a general retreat the next day.

Kluck's First Army pursued the British beyond Maubeuge until the actions of one of the BEF's subordinate commanders forced the British to stand and fight at Le Cateau on 25 August. Once again, the British found themselves in hastily prepared defensive positions, and the Germans came upon them without a firm idea of the strength or nature of their opposition. Again, after a day of heavy fighting and substantial losses on both sides, the British retreated and avoided a decisive defeat. German First Army, unable to organize a coordinated pursuit, lost contact with the main body of the BEF, in part because Kluck elected to resume his southwesterly movement, unaware that the British had withdrawn almost directly south.[79] First Army's failure to envelop the BEF led to bitter postwar accusations by Kluck and the defenders of Bülow.[80] The recriminations of the Entente side were immediate and substantial. Sir John French, feeling deserted by the French, proposed a British withdrawal beyond the Seine west of Paris and even to the new British base of operations in Normandy and Brittany.[81]

While Kluck was pushing the British back, farther to the east and north, Bülow's Second Army began a successful but indecisive battle against Lanrezac's Fifth Army south of Namur on 21 August. After a series of costly attacks by both sides, the French felt compelled to withdraw on 24 August, since they were being threatened by Bülow's advance from the north and Hausen's advance from the east. This battle, known to the French as the Battle of the Sambre and to the Germans as the Battle of Namur, was a clear German victory, but it was by no means as decisive as the Germans had hoped or as prewar planning had foreseen.[82]

Moltke's Directives, August–September 1914

These actions concluded the "battles of the frontier," as the Germans called them. At this point, Moltke had the opportunity to reconsider the strategic situation. His evaluation, contained in a general directive sent to the armies on 27 August, offered both an assessment of the frontier battles and instructions for what the OHL desired in a pursuit of what it considered a defeated (though not destroyed) enemy.[83] By 26 August, the German army had been partially victorious nearly everywhere along the front, but it had hardly destroyed the French and British armies, which retained substantial powers of resistance, as Moltke recognized.[84] He did, however, assume that the French were in "full retreat." On 27 August the OHL received the first news of the victory at Tannenberg, which may have contributed to what turned out to be excessive optimism.[85]

Moltke's directive for the armies reflected the conviction that the French were withdrawing toward Paris, and it emphasized a rapid pursuit, a cardinal feature of German theory from Clausewitz onward. Some have seen his directive as a complete abandonment of the Schlieffen concept for the right wing, while others have concluded that it was generally written in accordance with Schlieffen's scheme of maneuver if not its apportionment of strength.[86] It assumed that the next French position would be a defensive line along the Marne, with its left flank anchored on Paris. The directive instructed First Army to advance north of the Oise River in the direction of the lower Seine, but it did not mention any passage around Paris. It instructed First Army to be prepared to join Second Army's battles and to protect the right flank of the entire German army. Thus, even at this early stage, Moltke had already abandoned any slavish emphasis on the far right wing of the German offensive. A later, more general paragraph told the right-wing armies to be prepared to turn south if the French offered strong resistance along the Aisne or the Marne.[87] The direction of First Army's march, along the Oise toward the lower Seine, reflected the use of the former as a dividing line between First and Second Armies.

At this point, the Germans' initial campaign in the west began to lose any semblance of coherence. The ensuing gradual deterioration paralleled the army's failure to achieve a rapid victory and revealed a number of shortcomings in its approach to warfare. The Schlieffen school subsequently blamed the failure to achieve a rapid victory on Moltke's unwillingness to plan or execute the master's concept exactly as Schlieffen had set forth, as well as on the Reichstag's alleged failure to institute a full prewar mobilization of Germany's manpower resources. Both arguments are distorted oversimplifications, as recent research has shown. Failures of strategy were important, though not precisely along the lines raised by Moltke's critics. A careful examination of the course of events shows that other fundamental problems were also to blame.

As argued earlier, Moltke placed his primary emphasis on meeting and defeating the French army in open battle, regardless of where it was encountered, even if this meant surrendering much of the strategic initiative. This was also the main point of Schlieffen's thought, but that fact has been obscured by his postwar admirers, who raised the advance around Paris to the southwest from a means (conditional in Schlieffen's own writing on a defensive French strategy) to an end in itself.[88]

After 27 August, First and Second Armies pushed the French and English back more or less along the lines envisioned in Moltke's directive, but the victory was more apparent than real. The Germans had not annihilated any large French or British units, nor had they captured large numbers of artillery or prisoners. The battlefield, though still relatively fluid, had not produced the large-scale (or even smaller-scale) successful flanking attacks or turning movements on which German combat was based.

Following the Battle of Le Cateau, First Army advanced to the southwest, attempting to envelop the left flank of the British and French forces—a general line of advance that anticipated Moltke's 27 August directive. This had the effect of confirming Kluck's decision. By 28 August, however, Kluck was considering altering his line of advance and turning sharply south, thus moving his army across the Oise to complete the turning movement against the Entente's left flank.[89] A continued southwesterly movement would allow the enemy to retreat and avoid a decisive defeat.[90] Kluck did not consider such a move to be in violation of the intent of Moltke's directive, since it stated in part that First Army must be prepared to participate in Second Army's battles; more importantly, it specifically stated that strong resistance "along the Aisne and Marne may necessitate a wheel inward of the armies from a south-western to a southerly direction."[91] On 29 August Kluck received an urgent request for assistance from Second Army, which seemed to be locked in a serious battle against allegedly superior forces.[92]

Kluck, acting in accordance with the old Prussian principle of marching to the sound of the guns, turned First Army to the south, hoping to destroy French Fifth Army and any elements of the BEF that might be caught up in his movement.[93] Kuhl wrote a memorandum to Second Army on 28 August outlining his thinking, perhaps the most comprehensive communication between the two armies during the campaign. Kuhl argued, in the tradition of Clausewitz and the elder Moltke, that the concept of the overall operation had to recede to the background in the face of what he saw as an opportunity to achieve a turning movement against the entire enemy left flank, including the English.[94] Kluck left part of his forces facing in a southwesterly and westerly direction to provide a flank guard for the rest of the right wing.[95] First Army informed the High Command of its decision in the early-morning hours of 31 August.[96]

After receiving favorable reports from field armies one through four on 30 August, Moltke dispatched a series of individual orders that, in effect, endorsed Kluck's decision to move to the south in support of Second Army. This was before the OHL was aware of Kluck's decision. The Reichsarchiv concluded that the High Command ordered First Army's move to the south before Kluck made the same decision, or at least before it was known to the OHL. The OHL also concluded that there was no serious threat to Kluck's right flank.[97] Accounts that stress Kluck's disobedience fail to consider that such a decision was entirely in consonance with German theory, so it should not be surprising that both Kuhl and the General Staff came to the same conclusion.

On the one hand, Moltke may have regarded this as a temporary expedient. On the other hand, in further instructing First and Second Armies to cooperate with the attacks of Third Army, he changed the focus of the campaign from the far-right flank to the center area of Third Army. He apparently wanted First Army to follow Second Army in echelon, rather than implementing a more sweeping movement on or in front of Bülow's right flank. He sent such a message on 2 September, but in another case of failure to issue orders of sufficient clarity and decisiveness, his intentions did not determine the course of First Army's movements. He also apparently believed that the German center—Fourth and Fifth Armies—were on the verge of a decisive victory. He placed his emphasis there and thus absolutely ended any concept of pushing the right-wing forces to the Seine below Paris.[98] It should also be remembered that at this point, Moltke was urging Sixth Army to attempt a breakthrough of the French right wing in the Nancy area, apparently in the hope of forcing a double envelopment of the main French armies.

Over the course of 1–2 September, Bülow slowed his advance, partly to rest his soldiers. Kluck feared losing the opportunity to achieve a decisive turning movement that would, in the grand manner of Schlieffen, result in the annihilation of the French left-wing armies. Accordingly, despite Moltke's very specific orders of 2 September, Kluck sent his forces rapidly to the south, crossing the Marne and leaving an extended right flank reaching from directly east of Paris (where French Sixth Army was beginning to form up) to south of the Marne in the area of Montmirail.[99] Bülow was opposed to this move from the outset.[100] In Kluck's defense, it should be pointed out that the order also outlined the general plan to push the French to the southeast, away from Paris. He thought this was the main effort and that moving in echelon behind Second Army contradicted that attempt. As one scholar points out, returning to the formation prescribed in Moltke's orders would have required Kluck's army to halt for up to two days while Second Army caught up.[101]

Had he achieved a decisive victory, Kluck no doubt would have been a hero, and his actions would have been regarded as a splendid example of subordinate initiative.[102] For decades, German theory had emphasized that outdated or irrelevant orders should be disregarded if local circumstances so demanded. Ironically, Kluck himself was the victim of perhaps excessive subordinate initiative. During a critical point in this movement, the audacious advance of a corps commander forced Kluck's hand, just as he had forced Moltke's on more than one occasion.[103] All this took place beyond the sight of the *OHL*, as communications with headquarters had become increasingly fragmentary, and delays between sending and receiving messages extended to as much as twenty-four hours.[104] Moltke, for example, did not learn of Kluck's moves to disregard his instructions until midafternoon on 4 September.

Kluck's decision effectively divided his army into two parts: one along the Ourcq River opposite Paris, and the other across the Marne to the south. They were too distant for immediate mutual support, but Kluck was willing to accept this risk. He later claimed that he recognized the danger of his exposed flank but accepted the assurances of the *OHL* that no serious threat had yet emerged.[105] The Reichsarchiv later established that the High Command had not kept Kluck informed of intelligence indicating a growing French presence in the Paris area.[106] Kluck also claimed that he had urged the *OHL* to release part of the reserve corps at Brussels and to use *Landwehr* units to replace all active units along the lines of communications so that they could move to the right flank of First Army.[107]

By this time, the French had recognized a developing opportunity to defeat, or even annihilate, the German right wing, and they started to redeploy accordingly. By 3 September, the *OHL* had learned of the transfer of large French units from Alsace-Lorraine and the increasing French strength around Paris.[108] Late in the day on 4 September, upon learning of Kluck's true situation and position, Moltke reached a critical conclusion and jettisoned the entire concept of the great turning movement. In its place, he created a new strategy for the entire western front. This decision was truly the end of anything like a Schlieffen Plan.[109]

On the evening of 5 September, the High Command sent a new general directive to the western armies.[110] The document had the usual two parts: an assessment of the overall situation, and specific instructions for each field army. The former recognized that the French had escaped envelopment and maintained contact between their field armies and Paris. In addition, the French had sent forces from their right flank to their left, threatening the German right wing. The assessment concluded that "forcing the entire French army against the Swiss frontier in a southeasterly direction is thus no longer possible," and it warned that the French had assembled powerful forces around Paris. As a result, the directive ordered First and Second Armies to remain opposite Paris in a defensive mode to oppose French offensives from that area.[111] Fourth and Fifth Armies were to continue to attack to the southeast, while Sixth Army forced a crossing of the Mosel River between Toul and Epinal. Third Army was to support

Battle of the Marne.

whichever effort to its right (First and Second Armies) or its left (Fourth and Fifth Armies) that seemed appropriate.[112]

By this date, the *OHL*, despite the optimistic tone of much of its correspondence and internal reactions, had recognized that the right-wing armies needed reinforcements. First and Second Armies and, to a lesser degree, Third Army had lost nearly 50 percent of their strength before the Battle of the Marne began. Moltke had dispatched two corps to the eastern front, and two corps were engaged at Maubeuge and Antwerp. In addition, nearly every unit had suffered severe losses from combat, marching disabilities, sickness, and so forth. One estimate is that as the battle began, the French had a superiority of almost 200 battalions of infantry and 190 batteries of artillery. Realizing some of these problems, on 5 September the High Command instructed Sixth Army to make two corps available to reinforce the right wing. This was arranged, but only against the stubborn resistance of Krafft von Dellmensingen and Crown Prince Rupprecht.[113] None of these reinforcements were available in time, but they eventually included the headquarters of Seventh Army, which Moltke reconstituted in Belgium. Astonishingly, at the time of this decisive battle along the Marne, Moltke prepared to use the new Seventh Army for defense of the German rear and long flank in Belgium, rather than rushing it to the front as quickly as possible.[114] On 9 September he finally ordered Sixth Army to break off its attacks in the Nancy area.[115]

The Battle of the Marne

The opposing armies were soon fighting the Battle of the Marne, a series of engagements extending first from Paris to Château-Thierry and then all along the front. As Kluck turned south and continued to face west toward Paris, a wide gap developed between his forces and those of Bülow.[116] On 4 September Joffre issued his famous General Instruction No. 6, ordering his forces to attack the German right wing on both flanks in an attempt to exploit the gap between German First and Second Armies and destroy the former in a double envelopment. The BEF was to participate by attacking Kluck from the south.[117] Over the period 5–8 September, Kluck's army fought a series of battles, defending its positions along the Ourcq River to the east of Paris against the attacks of French Sixth Army (then under the direct command of Joffre) and its southern positions across the Marne against French Fifth Army and the BEF. The Entente forces had an overall superiority of about three to two, with fifty-six infantry divisions and 3,000 pieces of artillery massed against forty-four German divisions with about the same strength in guns.[118] Kluck's effective strength and the energy of his soldiers had been drained by the lengthy marches and numerous engagements fought along the advance. He decided to stand firm on both flanks, hoping to defeat both Entente attacks without a major withdrawal to the north of the Marne and to thwart the British and French attempt to separate his forces from Second Army and defeat them in detail. In fact, Kluck conducted both battles with vigorous offensive moves, a course of action that astonished some but was quite consistent with German theory, which frequently stressed offensive solutions to defensive problems.[119]

Kluck and his advisers, especially Kuhl, regarded the French offensive as an opportunity as much as a threat. The whole point of the German campaign was to engage the mass of the French army in open battle as soon as possible, and now Joffre seemed to offer such a possibility. Reverting to a defensive posture would have surrendered the initiative, which, under German theory, was the key to victory. So Kluck ordered two of his corps to move back to the north to join a counterattack along the Ourcq.[120] The resulting offensive solution was entirely representative of forty years of General Staff thinking and war games.

The *OHL* remained a largely passive observer of these events, which it could follow only at a distance, and there were crippling delays in receiving and transmitting information.[121] Moltke and his staff had a clear view of Anglo-French intentions, as German Fourth Army had captured a copy of Joffre's order even before all the French units had received theirs.[122] While Moltke's pessimism seemed to grow, others at the *OHL* actually welcomed the Entente's counteroffensive because it offered what had been lacking throughout the campaign: an opportunity to strike the main French forces in a decisive engagement. "Finally, we have come to grips with them," was Tappen's response.[123] Moltke still declined to intervene, perhaps owing to the communications problems, and he remained content to allow the commanders at the front to wage the battles themselves. From 6 to 8 September the *OHL* sent no orders to the field armies and struggled to keep abreast of events.[124] Commanders of the three right-wing armies made major decisions on their own, as Moltke refused to go forward himself or to use the accepted practice of establishing a forward battle command post.[125]

On the morning of 8 September Moltke convened a meeting with at least three of his principal advisers to discuss the overall situation on the western front. The news received the previous evening and in the early morning was mixed. Third, Fourth, and Fifth Armies reported generally good results from their sections of the front. From Belgium came the welcome report that the areas extending along the coast and into the center of Belgium and northern France were clear of enemy forces, so the re-forming Seventh Army would be available for use on the right flank. Its commander was moving elements of three corps forward to St. Quentin. First and Second Armies reported progress in reacting to French efforts to envelop the right wing. On the downside, the *OHL* had overheard a radio message from Cavalry Command One to Second Army indicating an enemy advance into the gap between First and Second Armies. The latter information confirmed Moltke's fear of a serious breakthrough in the area. He had been very pessimistic about the right-wing armies for some time, and on the previous day he had even discussed a possible retreat with the kaiser, who forbade it.[126] The pressure of events had already begun to damage Moltke both physically and emotionally. Crown Prince Rupprecht, who visited the *OHL* on 8 September, wrote in his diary that Moltke looked like a sick, broken man.[127] Members of Moltke's entourage later denied this, but their accounts are not convincing.[128]

The predominant opinion at the *OHL*, at least among Moltke's close advisers, was more positive. Tappen and Dommes were much more optimistic in their belief that First Army could deal with the crisis, and their arguments apparently reassured Moltke somewhat. The outcome of the discussion was the decision to send an emissary to the front, an expedient employed on several previous occasions, to clarify the situation, especially in First Army's area. Dommes offered to go, but Moltke selected Lieutenant Colonel Richard Hentsch, whose mission to the front became one of the most controversial episodes of the war and led to the German retreat from the Marne.

Hentsch's Mission

Hentsch seemed to be a curious choice for the mission. A Prussian by birth, he was an officer in the Saxon army. His brilliant performance at the Prussian War Academy had earned him a position on the General Staff, where his universally recognized abilities soon led to an assignment as section chief.[129] Hentsch's normal assignment during the war was chief of the Intelligence Section, a duty that had little or nothing to do with the assignment he was about to embark on.[130] Numerous persons who knew Hentsch during the war regarded him as extraordinarily pessimistic about the campaign, an allegation that is supported by some of the evidence but cannot be confirmed.[131] Some were critical of Moltke's choice. General Hermann von François, for one, argued that a number of more senior officers were available, including Tappen, Groener, *Generalquartiermeister* General von Stein, and various others. Any of these men would have been more appropriate, given their experience, rank, and regular assignments.[132]

The exact instructions Moltke gave to Hentsch were as controversial as they were obscure. Moltke issued only verbal instructions, and neither Hentsch nor the others made any record of the conversation. The basic question was whether Moltke had given Hentsch plenipotentiary authority (a *Vollmacht*) to issue orders on the authority of the High Command. Hentsch insisted that he had been granted such authority, in this case to order a retreat if he judged it necessary. He used this claim repeatedly in his dealings with First and Second Armies. Both Dommes and Tappen, who were present during Moltke's discussion of Hentsch's mission, later denied that Hentsch had been granted a *Vollmacht*.[133] Dommes later used Hentsch's lack of written instructions as proof that his mission was an ordinary one and that he lacked a *Vollmacht*—a reasonable argument, in view of the fact that Moltke had already sent several officers, including Hentsch, on simple fact-finding visits to the front.[134]. Hentsch, a highly respected individual, certainly believed he had a wide-ranging *Vollmacht* when he proceeded to the front, with two junior officers, at around 11:00 a.m. on 8 September 1914.[135]

The trio went to Fifth, Fourth, and Third Armies, in that order, and, after receiving generally favorable reports, arrived at Second Army headquarters at around 7:45 p.m.[136] Hentsch spoke with Bülow and his staff until nearly midnight. He repeatedly told the Second Army staff that First Army's situation was so serious that the *OHL* had to consider a retreat. Such an action, he stressed, would be absolutely necessary if the enemy broke through between the two right-wing armies. Several participants concluded that Hentsch had already made up his mind that Kluck's position was hopeless and that a retreat would be necessary.[137] He certainly told them that he had the authority to order a retreat.

Much confusion reigns about Hentsch's conversations with Bülow and members of his staff. The Reichsarchiv concluded that Bülow admitted that Second Army had lost much of its strength and that it could no longer deliver the decisive blows the situation demanded. At least two of the participants, however, reported that Bülow said no such thing. According to officers of the Second Army staff, Bülow referred to his reduced combat strength and lack of reserves but insisted that the units' combat power remained intact.[138] It is possible, but unlikely, that some officers, including Bülow, described First or Second Army as being reduced to ashes, but at least one of Hentsch's companions denied that he used this phrase. In any case, Bülow and his staff certainly did not portray their situation or their prospects as necessitating an immediate retreat.[139]

The relentless Hentsch was no doubt deeply convinced that the right wing stood in the midst of a great crisis. He stressed to Bülow—a legendary personality in his own right, and not one to be intimidated by a lieutenant colonel—that he had a *Vollmacht* and could order a retreat if necessary. At the time, neither Bülow nor Hentsch were aware of Kluck's successes in defending his positions, but Bülow steadfastly opposed a premature retreat. The two apparently agreed that a retreat would be necessary if strong enemy forces crossed the Marne and advanced into the rear of First Army.[140] Hentsch concluded his evening by sending a deceptively negative radio message to the High Command: "Situation of Second Army is serious, but not hopeless."[141]

Hentsch had a final round of conversations with Lauenstein and Matthes on the morning of 9 September before departing for First Army headquarters.[142] The overnight reports indicated no deterioration in the situation from the previous evening. Lauenstein indicated that Second Army would hold its position unless the enemy advanced, as discussed the previous night.[143] As Hentsch left, Second Army headquarters prepared to launch local offensive thrusts to parry the blows of the French. There was no serious thought of retreating at the time of Hentsch's departure.[144]

Hentsch's journey to First Army headquarters took him through the army's very disorganized rear area, which was burdened by a rapid wheeling of units to the north and the strains of combat on two sides and was in the midst of securing itself in case of further disruptions. The roads were cluttered with columns of wounded soldiers and retreating or otherwise moving supply units, resulting in traffic jams. This made a distinct impression on Hentsch, although his companions thought he later exaggerated the problems they observed. For whatever reason, it is clear that Hentsch was in a determinedly pessimistic mood when he arrived at the town of Mareiul, the location of First Army headquarters.[145]

Unfortunately, the discussions between Hentsch and First Army staff, which astonishingly did not include Kluck, did not produce contemporary memoranda on the content of these conversations.[146] Hentsch and the First Army chief of Staff, the highly respected Generalmajor Hermann von Kuhl, came away from their meetings with very different versions of what was said. Others agreed that Kuhl surprised Hentsch with a favorable estimate of the situation in First Army's area and that Kuhl initially refused to be intimidated by Hentsch's claim to have a *Vollmacht*.[147] When Kuhl declined to prepare an order for a retreat, Hentsch replied that such a move was essential, since Second Army had already begun to fall back and would be across the Marne by the next morning, 10 September. When Kuhl expressed astonishment that Bülow had ordered a retreat, Hentsch replied: "The decision to retreat has been very sour for old man Bülow."[148] Hentsch expanded on this falsehood by claiming that Second Army had not been withdrawn but had actually been thrown back. He then used the infamous argument that Second Army had been reduced to burned-out cinders.[149]

Kuhl finally gave in, conceding that if Second Army were retreating, First Army would have to do so also. He then proposed a withdrawal of First Army so that its left flank would be anchored at Soissons, to which Hentsch apparently agreed. Kuhl thus yielded to Hentsch's famous powers of persuasion and his claimed authority to speak on behalf of the *OHL*. Kuhl informed Kluck of the decision in what seemed to be a remarkably brief discussion. Kluck accepted his chief of staff's recommendation, no doubt under the impression that Hentsch spoke with Moltke's authority and was basing his decision on accurate information. As Kuhl moved to implement the order, the Battle of the Marne ended, the German retreat on the right wing began, and the hope for a rapid victory in the west disappeared.

Neither Kuhl nor Kluck distinguished himself in this episode, although both enjoyed splendid reputations for the rest of their long lives. Generaloberst Kluck did not speak to Hentsch, and he later attempted, quite inappropriately, to blame this on the latter.[150] Kuhl, for his part, did not try to verify Hentsch's report with Second Army headquarters, either by radio or by sending a General Staff officer to make an inquiry.[151] The results were that a Generaloberst and a Generalmajor, who for weeks had not hesitated to disregard or disobey undoubtedly legitimate directives or orders from Moltke and the High Command, quickly gave in on this decisive occasion, which had the effect of reversing most of their previous efforts. Moreover, they acceded to a lieutenant colonel who lacked written authorization to give orders. Kuhl's own summary of Hentsch's visit, written on 10 September 1914 but not used by the Reichsarchiv, reported his disagreement with Hentsch and indicated that he accepted Hentsch's claim of a *Vollmacht*.[152] Two of the most aggressive and independent senior officers in the Prussian army thus meekly abandoned their life's work without serious objections. General Hermann von François, noted for his independent and even insubordinate actions in the east, later suggested that Kluck should have disregarded Hentsch's order and held his position. François argued that, based on German regulations and officer education, a commander had the duty to use his judgment in such a situation.[153] He was correct, but the responsibility for a possible catastrophe would have been Kluck's alone.

While Hentsch completed his journey, concerns at the *OHL* increased. At this critical moment, as was the case throughout the campaign, headquarters lacked even the most basic information about developments at the front. In his daily report to the kaiser on 9 September, Moltke, caught in another of his mood swings, proposed a general retreat of the five right-wing armies. Wilhelm II, supported by Generals Plessen and Stein (a subordinate of Moltke), refused to authorize such a withdrawal until more information was available. Moltke told Tappen to prepare an order for a general withdrawal but delayed sending it to the field.[154]

Hentsch arrived in Luxembourg at around 3:00 p.m. on 10 September, leaving a highly anxious *OHL* in the dark while he made a leisurely journey back. On his return trip he stopped again at Fourth Army headquarters, where, according to the commander, Crown Prince Wilhelm, Hentsch tried unsuccessfully to order a retreat.[155] Upon finally arriving at Luxembourg, Hentsch immediately gave a verbal report to Moltke, with several others in attendance. He blamed everything on First Army and reported that it had already ordered a retreat before he arrived. Moltke, in a very excited and worried state, apparently overlooked First Army's radio message stating that it was withdrawing because of the *OHL*'s order.[156] Hentsch then described the lines to which First, Second, and Third Armies should retreat and concluded that Fourth and Fifth Armies could remain where they were. Moltke was apparently pleasantly surprised, noting that if First Army retreated to a point where its left flank was at Fismes, the gap between it and Second Army would be closed. Hentsch then convinced Moltke to visit Third, Fourth, and Fifth Army headquarters to verify these decisions. Moltke agreed, and for the only time in the campaign he ventured to the front to judge the situation personally. Before doing that, he sent another set of directives to the armies, establishing the positions they were to hold and again subordinating First Army to Bülow's Second Army.

The optimistic mood lasted only until around midnight, when bad news from both East Prussia and the armies on the western front arrived. First Army reported that it had retreated so that its left flank was at Soissons, as Hentsch had instructed Kuhl, not Fismes, as he had told Moltke. Thus, a twenty-five-mile gap between First and Second Armies remained to be closed, although the danger of an immediate breakthrough by the French and British had passed.

The conversation between Moltke and Hentsch offers useful insights into the question of the latter's authority to order a retreat, and a careful analysis suggests that he did not have such authority.[157] Hentsch claimed he had not ordered any retreats, a strange statement for one whose order to Kuhl began First Army's retreat, as attested to by several members of the First Army staff. Kuhl may have later exaggerated his initial resistance to Hentsch in an effort to exonerate himself, but there can be little doubt that Hentsch appeared to be issuing an order in Moltke's name.[158] Hentsch's written report, prepared on 15 September, stated, "The Chief of the General Staff gave me the authority (*Ermächtigung*) to order a withdrawal of armies one through five behind the Velse [River] and to the heights of the northern Argonne if necessary." Moltke later wrote a commentary on First Army's war diary, stating, "Lieutenant Colonel Hentsch had the task only to say to the First Army, if its retreat should be necessary, that it should withdraw to the line Soissons-Fismes, in order to re-establish contact with the Second Army. In no case did he have the task to say that the retreat was unavoidable."[159]

Although Hentsch certainly based his conversations and instructions at Second and First Armies on the claim of a *Vollmacht*, when he reported to Moltke, he was careful to emphasize the direction of the withdrawals and, in effect, to deny that he had ordered them against the will of the field commanders. This, of course, would have been in keeping with Moltke's understanding of the task he had given Hentsch, regardless of how misleading the latter's statement was.

By 1917, widespread rumors that Hentsch had improperly interfered in the command prerogatives of First and Second Armies caused Hentsch to request an official inquiry, to which Ludendorff agreed. The subsequent report, which Ludendorff sent to all staffs down to division level, only added to the confusion. On the one hand, Ludendorff exonerated Hentsch of the charge that he had exceeded his instructions, stating that only history could judge whether the decision had been the correct one. On the other hand, the report concluded that Hentsch had ordered First Army to retreat and, worse, it repeated Moltke's account of his instructions to Hentsch. Thus, the report found that Hentsch had the authority to coordinate a retreat already in progress but not to initiate one. "Under the assumptions," Ludendorff wrote, "Lieutenant Colonel Hentsch was empowered to give binding directions in the name of the High Command." The first of these findings concluded that Hentsch had misled Moltke or even lied to him upon his return to the *OHL*. The second meant that although Hentsch possessed plenipotentiary powers, he had exceeded them substantially.[160]

In any case, the retreat did not go as Hentsch envisioned. At Second Army, the nature of the retreat was attributable to confusion as much as to Hentsch's specific orders. By noon, Second Army's commander had become increasingly alarmed by aerial reconnaissance reports of enemy columns moving forward into the gap between First and Second Armies. Concerned that there had been no word on Hentsch's visit to First Army, Bülow prepared an order for his army's retreat and sent it out around noon, with a start time of about 1:00 p.m. Finally, at around the same time, a message arrived from First Army announcing the withdrawal of its left flank to the area Montigny-Gandelu. This message, which seemingly confirmed First Army's anticipated general withdrawal, was in fact notification of a purely local adjustment and had been sent before Hentsch's arrival at First Army. Since this seemed to be a general retreat, and since this would make Second Army's position untenable, Bülow notified the *OHL* of his army's retreat. Bülow's retreat, in short, had little to do with Hentsch's visit to the front. Once again, the failure of clear communications reached astonishing proportions.[161]

Moltke's Final Acts as Chief

Moltke, in the meantime, accompanied by Tappen and Dommes, departed for his visit to army headquarters on the morning of 11 September. He found Fifth Army headquarters in good spirits after a successful night assault and concluded that no withdrawal in that area was necessary. The three then visited Third Army headquarters at Suippes and Fourth Army headquarters at Courtisols, where they also found no great cause for alarm. Moltke therefore decided that these three armies should hold their ground.

While still at Fourth Army headquarters at Courtisols (east of Chalons), Moltke learned of a radio message from Bülow warning of a major enemy attack on the right and center portions of Third Army. The French, it appeared, were attempting a breakthrough that would push Fourth and Fifth Armies back against the French fortress system at Verdun, threatening them with annihilation. On the afternoon of 11 September Moltke ordered a general retreat of Third, Fourth, and Fifth Armies to more defensible positions.[162]

Moltke concluded his journey with a visit to Second Army headquarters at Reims, arriving late in the afternoon on the eleventh. Bülow and Moltke conferred and agreed on the measures to be taken. Moltke, as always placing great faith in Bülow, subordinated the reconstituted Seventh Army (then taking its position around St. Quentin) to Second Army, ensuring at least a measure of unity of command on the right wing of the German forces. That accomplished, Moltke returned to Luxembourg as the armies continued to execute the general withdrawal he had ordered. At this point, he still hoped to resume the offensive once the lines had been shortened and the new deployments completed.[163]

By all accounts, Moltke returned from his visit to the front a physical and emotional wreck. Since he was unable to make a second visit to the front on 13 September, Tappen and Stein went to Third, Fourth, and Fifth Armies to observe preparations for the retreat and battlefield conditions. They issued an order that day in the name of the *OHL*.[164] Moltke's condition during the daily briefing to the emperor on 14 September forced the issue of his suitability.

Encouraged by Plessen, General Moritz *Freiherr* von Lyncker, chief of the Military Cabinet and the officer responsible for all army personnel decisions, proposed to replace Moltke with the war minister, Erich von Falkenhayn. When the kaiser approved, Lyncker had the unpleasant task of informing Moltke, which he did on the afternoon of the fourteenth. Moltke remained in the position to maintain public appearances, while Falkenhayn assumed the actual duties of the chief of the General Staff. Moltke, who regarded himself as a martyr, accepted his humiliating fate with courageous resignation in public, while privately hoping for rehabilitation.

Between 11 and 14 September the German armies conducted an orderly withdrawal to their final positions, which they largely held until the great offensives by both sides in 1918. For the most part, the British and French failed to mount an aggressive pursuit, partly because their units were exhausted and partly because their cavalry did not act aggressively.[165] The main issue was arranging the armies to close the gaps between them, a feat rendered less difficult by the arrival of reinforcements from Belgium and by the transfer of several corps from Alsace-Lorraine. This ended the decisive Battle of the Marne—a great series of encounter battles similar to those envisioned in prewar German theory and doctrine. Its course and the controversy over it have obscured the brutal fact that by 6 September, nearly all the western front had become static.[166]

The Eastern Front

On the eastern front, in the meantime, the campaign had taken a circuitous path to a result that had emerged in a number of prewar staff studies and war games and that had important consequences far beyond local circumstances. Since the events surrounding the epic battles at Tannenberg and the Masurian Lakes are well known, the briefest of overviews will suffice for this presentation.

Moltke's instructions for the commander of German Eighth Army, General Max von Prittwitz und Gaffron, laid out several tasks to be accomplished.[167] The deployment instructions directed him to (1) defend East Prussia against an anticipated double-pronged Russian advance; (2) use offensive advances to tie up Russian forces, thus supporting the Austrian offensive in Galicia; and (3) maintain the line of the Vistula River as a basis for further action. The directive gave Prittwitz wide latitude to use his own judgment, but it also instructed him to conduct an offensive if the Russians did not attack. If the Russians attacked in great strength, the directive authorized Eighth Army to retreat behind the Vistula, thus surrendering much of East Prussia, but only in the direst of circumstances. Although the directive urged him to cooperate with the Austro-Hungarian forces to the south, this was clearly secondary.[168] Moltke's verbal instructions to Prittwitz and additional communications from the OHL provided no clarity. Moltke apparently told Prittwitz not to allow his army to be forced away from the Vistula and to preserve Eighth Army at all costs. A retreat was authorized only in the most extreme emergency, said Moltke, who was confident that superior German leadership would overcome Russian numerical superiority. To accomplish that, Moltke urged Prittwitz to attack wherever possible.[169]

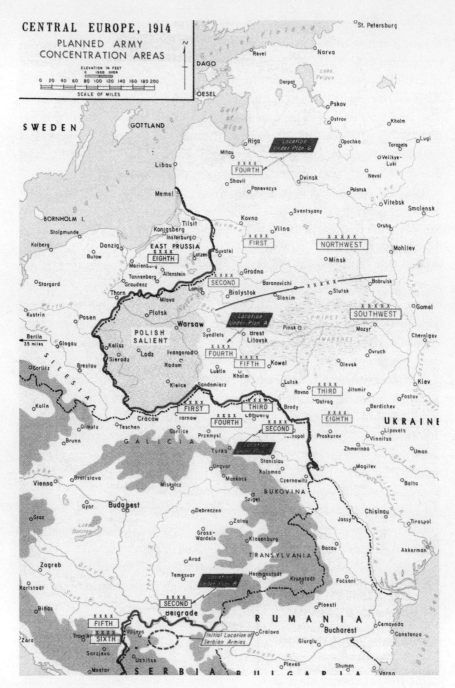

Eastern Deployments, 1914.

Substantially outnumbered, Prittwitz's task was extremely difficult from the outset. Eighth Army had very limited forces: a total of three active corps (XVII, XX, and I) and one reserve corps (I Reserve), a separate reserve division, and a cavalry division. It also commanded a number of *Landwehr* brigades, as well as the eastern fortresses and their garrisons. The total was about thirteen divisions. Except for the active units, these disparate formations lacked artillery, machine guns, supply and medical units, and even maps. Eighth Army faced about nineteen active Russian divisions, two reserve divisions, and ten cavalry divisions.[170]

In East Prussia the campaign began on 17 August, before Eighth Army had completed its deployment along the Angerrap River. The forces of Russian First Army attacked forward elements of German I Corps, which had deployed about twenty-five miles farther east than Prittwitz had directed. The corps commander, General Hermann von François, had deceived Prittwitz about his deployment and had maintained his primary headquarters, including his first General Staff officer, in Gumbinnen while he went forward to direct the battle. François, contemptuous of the Russians, did not hesitate to engage an enemy force of unknown size, even though no other German units were close enough to provide support. Upon learning of the nature of the engagement, Prittwitz sent a message ordering François to retreat. This allegedly evoked a defiant refusal, accompanied by François's comment that he would retreat when the Russians were defeated. The initiative of 2nd Division's commander saved the day, and Prittwitz finally forced François to retreat. Overall, Stalluponen was a demonstration of German tactical superiority over the Russians, even though it ended with a German withdrawal.[171]

Falling back to Gumbinnen, François not only prepared his corps to undertake a new attack on the advancing Russians but also convinced Prittwitz, possibly against his better judgment, to intervene with the other available elements of Eighth Army. The resulting Battle of Gumbinnen (20 August), the first large-scale battle on the northern section of the eastern front, was costly and inconclusive, although a second day of attacking Russian First Army might have produced a more clear-cut victory. As Dennis Showalter has pointed out, Gumbinnen showed that the Russians could be deadly on the defensive and that German soldiers were not immune from panic, whether caused by rumors or the actual results of battle.[172]

On the evening of 20 August, while considering whether to continue the effort to strike First Army from both flanks, Prittwitz learned that Russian Second Army (Samsonov) was advancing from the south, threatening to cut off and destroy the entire German Eighth Army. In a confusing welter of internal discussions, temper tantrums, and premature messages to the *OHL* at Coblenz, the Eighth Army staff struggled to decide what to do. There seemed to be three options, all of which were fraught with danger. Prittwitz could continue the battle at Gumbinnen, while attempting to delay Russian Second Army; he could try to delay Russian First Army while moving the main body of his forces to engage Russian Second Army, which seemed more of an immediate threat; or he could withdraw behind the Vistula. As the staff devised an embryonic form of the third course of action, Moltke came to believe that Prittwitz had lost either his nerve or his judgment and had decided on the third alternative. Possibly in reaction to the confusion, or possibly in an effort to save himself, Moltke relieved Prittwitz of his command, the first such case in modern German history.[173]

Moltke turned to one of his most trusted confidants and the hero of Liege: Erich Ludendorff. Thus, the General Staff officer who would be responsible for saving the situation was chosen before a new commander was identified. After considering several options, Moltke decided on retired general Paul von Beneckendorff und von Hindenburg, then living in Hannover.[174] Although neither Hindenburg nor Ludendorff was in favor with Wilhelm II, the kaiser accepted both and made the best of an awkward situation by personally awarding Ludendorff his *Pour le Merite* before he left for the east. Thus began the legendary team of Hindenburg and Ludendorff, which saved East Prussia but eventually contributed mightily to the nature and timing of Germany's eventual defeat in 1918.[175]

The remainder of the well-known Tannenberg campaign can be summarized briefly. Hindenburg and Ludendorff, who arrived independently at the same basic concept worked out by Max Hoffman and others on the Eighth Army staff, shifted their forces to the south against Russian Second Army. Several days of confused fighting produced a double envelopment of almost the entire Russian force, resulting in its near-total annihilation.[176] By 27 August, the battle was over except for rounding up prisoners and counting and distributing the trophies of war. Hindenburg then turned his forces north and pushed Russian First Army out of Prussia entirely, inflicting a costly but not total defeat on Rennenkampf's forces on 9 and 10 September.[177]

Together, these victories, though not as spectacular as the myth surrounding them, removed the immediate danger of a great Russian victory in East Prussia. Ironically, the two corps sent to the east arrived only after the conclusion of the battles, which confirmed the earlier judgments of Moltke and Schlieffen that a small force would suffice to protect East Prussia from the Russians. The long-term consequences were far in the future in August and September 1914. Hindenburg and, to a lesser extent, Ludendorff became the heroes of the war, the only command team that produced an important and clear-cut victory in 1914. Unfortunately for the Central Powers, that was not enough, even in the east.

Elsewhere, in the southern portion of the eastern front, the failure to develop a coherent plan in conjunction with Austria-Hungary, along with that country's inability to deal with the great mass of the Russian army, had important long-term consequences for the war. From the outset, the very weak bonds of trust and cooperation that had existed since the 1908 staff talks virtually collapsed. Worse, the Austro-Hungarian army never really recovered from the very heavy losses it suffered in Galicia. However successful the German way of war had proved in the northern sector of the eastern front, its fundamental failure to address the issues of coalition war exhibited a strategic shortsightedness that both limited the options in 1914 and continued to bedevil the war effort everywhere but on the western front.

The "Race to the Sea"

In France, the final chapter of the war before the onset of trench warfare was the improperly labeled "race to the sea." Falkenhayn, in an effort to renew the great turning movement, transferred substantial forces from the German left wing to the far-right wing and inserted a variety of new formations created on an emergency basis. He remained optimistic about the possibility of a rapid decision in the west and was willing to undertake a large-scale withdrawal to regroup the German forces. On the advice of Tappen, he instead sought a renewed envelopment of the French left flank.[178] Each German effort to outflank the British and French failed, and by November, the front armies faced each other in a largely continuous line of improvised field fortifications from the French frontier to the coast. The most spectacular part of this effort—the attempt to create a breakthrough in the Ypres sector—resulted in the tragic Battle of Langemarck, where a large number of Germany's most capable and educated young men (including many potential officers who would be desperately needed later) met their deaths in improvised and poorly trained units.

By 8 November, Falkenhayn realized that his effort had failed and that there was no hope of any great victory in the west. He also reluctantly concluded that the old means of mobile warfare no longer offered the prospect of a decisive victory. On 18 November his pessimism caused him to urge Bethmann-Hollweg to seek a diplomatic solution to the war, preferably based on peace with Russia.[179]

Absolute Failure or Mixed Results?

The inability of the German army to defeat the French in a short campaign created a golden opportunity for critics of all sorts to blame whatever culprit they desired, and the historical literature and other writings proceeded largely along this line for the rest of the twentieth century. Moltke blamed the emperor. Schlieffen's die-hard supporters blamed Moltke for watering down and then abandoning the largely imaginary Schlieffen Plan. Others, including the Reichsarchiv historians, blamed Hentsch and Moltke for losing their nerve and breaking off the Battle of the Marne, thus losing the campaign.[180]

If the campaign in the west is judged by its primary goal—the rapid defeat of France—then its failure is unequivocal. If, however, one considers the larger strategic issue facing the German army—how to avoid being overwhelmed by superior enemies while fighting on two fronts— the outcome of 1914 seems less a total failure: the army warded off both enemies, avoided a decisive defeat in both theaters, and robbed the most dangerous enemy, France, of much if its valuable industrial area.[181] If the military objective in 1914 had been to stand on the defensive and deny the enemy victory until negotiations could end the war, in the manner of the elder Moltke's plan, then the campaign in the west might have seemed, in retrospect, to be less of a failure. Nonetheless, especially given the basic tenets of the "German way of war" and the desired outcome of the army's prewar planning, a failure it was. The reasons for that failure can now be considered.

The Nature of the Failure

The leaders of the German army entered the war in 1914 with an imperfect understanding of the nature of the impending conflict, but they were not alone. All the great armies of Europe failed to fully appreciate the consequences of advances in weapons technology, particularly with regard to defense, as well as the impact of scale. European military leaders could foresee the dangers of lengthy positional warfare, but they did not understand that it might be unavoidable, given the force-to-space ratios of the western front and the marginal differences between the opposing sides. In retrospect, one can recognize that the search for rapid victory was rooted, at least in part, in the well-founded fear that wars could be disastrously long.[182] As Dennis Showalter has argued, the Germans sought battles of annihilation not merely to follow tradition but also to avoid wars of annihilation without victors.[183] The army, however, acquitted itself well in 1914, and although victory was in doubt from the start, failure in the opening campaigns can hardly be regarded as inevitable. The specific reasons for the failure to win in 1914 can be found in the battlefields and in the armies on both sides.

Molktke's Failure, or Schlieffen's?

In assessing the German failure of 1914, even the best scholarship lacks consensus. Sewell Tyng, author of perhaps the best one-volume account, concluded that the course of the campaign demonstrated "in striking fashion the soundness of the dying Schlieffen's injunction, 'make the right wing strong.'" Tyng then endorsed the Schlieffen school's condemnation of Moltke for weakening the right wing.[184] More recently, Holger Herwig, no believer in the Schlieffen recipe for victory, concluded his discussion by faulting both Moltke's personal characteristics and the Prussian General Staff system's failure to coordinate the right-wing armies.[185] The most recent study of Moltke dismissed the idea that the Battle of the Marne was decisive, arguing that if the Germans had been victorious there, they would have lost somewhere else.[186] That might be true for the war as a whole, but it sheds little light on the western campaign and the Marne battle.

Two schools of thought link the failure to Schlieffen's theories, but on opposite grounds. The Schlieffen school had no doubt as to why the campaign of 1914 failed. Wilhelm Groener wrote in 1927 that the official history demonstrated beyond question that the campaign failed because the Germans did not follow the advice of Schlieffen, especially that provided in his articles "Cannae" and "Der Krieg in der Gegenwart."[187] Others, far more critical of the old army, also cited the failure to follow Schlieffen's teachings on turning movements and flank attacks.[188] Jehuda Wallach, in an interesting reversal, blamed the defeat on the Marne to the fact that

Schlieffen had "hammered into the heads of his pupils and subordinates" an excessive fear of gaps in the line and "preached indefatigably the ultimate necessity of closing the ranks of the company-like front of armies of millions." He blamed Moltke for sticking "too much to the letter of the Schlieffen Plan."[189] Careful examination shows that numerous factors were involved in the outcome of the campaign, regardless of whether one believes it was doomed from the outset.

Moltke's decision to support a major offensive on the German left wing in Lorraine was very problematic. Although he rejected Schlieffen's apparent willingness to abandon much of Alsace-Lorraine to the French in order to mass forces on the German right wing, he recognized that the German left wing had to tie down sufficient French forces to create a German superiority if the primary battles were to be fought farther north and west. Moltke's major emphasis, like that of his uncle in 1870, was to fight the main French army wherever it was found, and by 14 August, it appeared that the battle would take place in Lorraine.[190] The continuation of Crown Prince Rupprecht's counteroffensive long after it was clear that the main French forces were not in Lorraine represented a return to Moltke's prewar concepts of a breakthrough in Lorraine and a potential double envelopment of the French.[191] Moltke stubbornly stuck to this approach long after all prospects for a decisive victory were gone.[192] As a result, the Germans tied down more forces in fruitless attacks against fortified positions than did the French in defending against them, and numerical superiority at the decisive point passed from the Germans to the French.[193] For this, Moltke has been the target of both those who blame him for abandoning the Schlieffen Plan and those who criticize him for following it too closely. By 10 September, the French had moved twenty infantry and three cavalry divisions from their right flank to the center and left sectors of the front. Indeed, Moltke continued to press the offensive in Lorraine when it was clear (by 16 August) that the mass of the French army was to the north. Moltke thus abandoned his own most basic principle of the campaign: that the mass of the German army must engage the mass of the French army wherever it was found.[194]

If one accepts the premise, advanced by the official history, that the Germans had actually won a victory by the time the retreat began, the logical conclusion is that the campaign failed in the way it did because various individuals lost their nerve. Most authors in this camp blame Second Army commander Karl von Bülow and Lieutenant Colonel Richard Hentsch, whose actions touched off the retreat.[195] Some histories have portrayed a French army that was much weaker than the German High Command believed, arguing that the Germans could have won if they had persevered.[196] This view found wide acceptance in the Reichswehr, where its implications that commanders should take great risks bore both good and bad fruit in the Second World War. Even the highly respected General Walther Reinhardt seemed to believe that the Marne retreat was the result of moral weakness rather than objective conditions on the battlefield.[197] The German retreat from the Marne can easily be seen as unnecessary, but it was more of a reflection of the failure of 1914 than its cause.[198]

Shortcomings of Command

Clearly, the German army's methods of command, and particularly the specific practices of Moltke, were a major factor in the outcome of the campaign. As noted earlier, Prussian theory from Count Moltke onward stressed subordinate initiative within the overall framework of the campaign concept. Schlieffen foresaw the difficulty of commanding large armies and was the first to create the image of the commander in the rear, using modern means of communication to control and direct an army of millions. In 1914 Moltke wrestled unsuccessfully to reconcile three potentially divergent factors in commanding the campaign: (1) the army's established tradition of subordinate initiative, thoroughly integrated into training and exercises of all kinds; (2) modern means of communications that, however imperfect, offered the prospect of commanding multiple armies and even fronts from the rear; and (3) his own personal reluctance to assert his authority over army-level commanders.

Historians are in almost universal agreement that Moltke declined to intervene in the decisions of his army commanders and that this had unfortunate results.[199] Instead, Moltke usually gave only the broadest of directives, from the opening deployment instructions to those of August. Only occasionally did he issue direct orders that he expected to be followed without question. He followed this procedure in part because he believed in his uncle's system; in part because he trusted the army commanders, especially Bülow (who became a sort of right-wing commander); and in part because the primitive state of communications limited what could be accomplished, regardless of one's intentions.[200] In addition, he may have felt that General Staff exercises, coupled with the directives in the deployment instructions, were sufficient guidelines for the army commanders.[201] Moltke's refusal to visit the front or move his headquarters forward left him at the mercy of his army commanders, especially because the intermediate level of army group commander did not yet exist and because he had to monitor the war in East Prussia.[202]

Compared with his counterpart Joffre, who traveled thousands of miles while visiting the front, Moltke was a desk-bound bureaucrat, possessing neither the ability to influence events with long-range communications, as envisioned by Schlieffen, nor the energy to visit the front in the dynamic manner of the French leader.[203] Moltke may have feared that going forward would give the kaiser an opportunity to exercise personal command or that his absence would give his enemies an opening to unseat him.[204]

Questions about German generalship do not end with Moltke. Some have argued that the German seniority system placed too many elderly generals in key command positions.[205] In addition, the ability of many high commanders has been called into question, although this is by no means a universal allegation.[206] Both issues merit investigation.

Although Prussian generals of the imperial period were old by modern standards, this criticism applies only partly to the higher commanders. Of the eight field army commanders in August 1914, three were royal princes, one was a Saxon, and four were Prussians.[207] All of the Prussians were colonel generals, the equivalent of a modern American four-star general, and along with Moltke, they were among the most senior active officers.[208] Both Alexander von Kluck and Karl von Bülow were sixty-eight years old, having entered the army in 1866. Max von Prittwitz und Gafffron was sixty-seven, and Josias von Heeringen, at sixty-four, was the youngest. Although all seem old by modern standards, only Bülow encountered contemporaneous criticism on the grounds of age and health. It should also be noted that some of Germany's most successful field commanders during the war, such as Paul von Hindenburg and August von Mackensen, were about the same age to these officers.[209] After the Battle of the Marne, the German army replaced more than thirty generals for various reasons. Joffre, by contrast, relieved many more general officers. Over the course of August and the first week of September 1914, for example, Joffre relieved two army, ten corps, and thirty-eight division commanders, mainly on the basis of poor performance. A similar rate of relieving commanders was experienced in the Austro-Hungarian army as well.[210]

The army commanders in 1914 demonstrated both the strengths and the weaknesses of the argument that the imperial army had to assign exceptional General Staff officers to high commanders. In many cases, the latter had attained their positions because of social standing or connections rather than ability, or they were line officers without the War Academy or General Staff preparation for high command. Three army commanders, the princes of royal houses, clearly needed experienced General Staff officers as their primary advisers.[211] Baron von Hausen, an experienced Saxon officer of substantial reputation, was, if anything, too deferential to his peers.[212] Of the four Prussian army commanders, three were General Staff officers themselves; Kluck, perhaps the most capable of the group, was the only exception.

These four Prussian army commanders had a remarkable range of experience to prepare them for their positions. Karl von Bülow, a brother of the former imperial chancellor Bernhard von Bülow, had served in numerous General Staff positions, headed a key department in the War Ministry, commanded a corps for nearly ten years, and helped write both the field artillery regulations of 1889 and the infantry regulations of 1906. Though not without his peculiarities, he had acquired nearly every imaginable qualification during his forty-eight years of commissioned service prior to the war.[213]

Josias von Heeringen, who commanded Seventh Army in Alsace in 1914, was also well connected and highly experienced. His brother was a prominent admiral. Heeringen, a War Academy graduate, was a General Staff officer and had commanded at every level; he had also served as war minister (1910–1913). He had nearly forty-eight years of commissioned service when the war began. Only a few senior commanders on either side could match his military qualifications and experience.

Alexander von Kluck, of more humble origins than the others, was the son of a civil servant (an architect) and had risen entirely by his own merits. Ennobled in 1909 while commander of I Corps in East Prussia, Kluck had attended a *Gymnasium* but was neither a graduate of the War Academy nor a General Staff officer. His chief adviser, Hermann von Kuhl, was widely regarded as one of the best General Staff officers in the army.

Most problematic in some respects was Max von Prittwitz und Gaffron, commander of the critical front held by Eighth Army in East Prussia. He was well educated, a graduate of the War Academy, and a career General Staff officer with considerable experience in high-level war games and exercises.[214] Moltke had apparently opposed his appointment as Eighth Army commander and tried to compensate for Prittwitz's shortcomings by assigning a close associate, Count Georg von Waldersee, to be his chief of staff. Prittwitz was known for his corpulence and his competence as a front soldier, but also for his lack of interest in any higher intellectual pursuits. He delighted the emperor with his anecdotes and storytelling and was a favorite of the Military Cabinet. There were apparently no allegations that Prittwitz's shortcomings had anything to do with his age or military experience.[215]

The campaign of 1914, particularly on the right wing, also illustrated the need for an intermediate headquarters between the OHL and the field armies to direct the latter. The General Staff, unable to move forward because of communications failures and a lack of imagination, was in no position to exercise proper command of the most important part of its western campaign. Moltke's expedient of subordinating one army to another was a failure. The practice bred resentment on the part of the army commander who was being subordinated to essentially a peer. The scale of operations made it impossible for an army commander such as Bülow and his staff, already overtaxed by exercising command over their own force, to direct the operations of another as well. The repositioning and increased size of the field armies in October made the problems of the OHL's excessive span of control even greater.

Arguably, the first army group command was created in the east with the establishment of Ober Ost in November 1914, discussed in the next chapter. In the west, the solution was the creation of three numbered groups of armies, each under the most senior army commander in the group. In January 1915 the OHL created a fourth group, centered around Fifth Army near Metz. These ad hoc army group headquarters consisted of the headquarters of the field armies and were, at best, a modest change in the arrangements in effect at the opening of the campaign. In 1916 the OHL regularized these army group commands, henceforth known by the names of their commanders, who were usually royal princes but sometimes other senior generals.[216]

Eventually, these army group headquarters acquired an authorized strength more appropriate to the scope of their responsibilities. Although variations continued, an army group headquarters generally had the following staff to assist its commander: The General Staff included a chief (a two-star position), usually an Oberquartiermeister (one star), a primary staff officer (colonel), and five lower-ranking field General Staff officers. The headquarters also had around ten adjutants; seventy-eight enlisted men serving as clerks and the like; seventy-two enlisted men working as drivers; and specialized officers for guard duty, medical care, military police, and so forth. Such a headquarters also had two small printing presses, bakeries, twenty-four autos, and a dozen or so trucks.[217] Although these developments were welcome, they obviously came far too late to impact the campaign in 1914. The advent of the army group headquarters also highlights the naïveté of Moltke's notion (once again, the underestimation of scale was a factor) of having one army commander controlling his own and another field army.

The Enemy Gets a Vote

George Pickett, of Pickett's Charge fame, was allegedly asked why Robert E. Lee had lost the Battle of Gettysburg. According to his widow Sally, Pickett answered, "I think the Union army had something to do with it." If one could adapt this question and move it forward in time and eastward geographically, asking the elder Moltke why he won in 1870 and the younger Moltke why he failed in 1914, the answer would be the same: the French army had something to do with it.

For all his acknowledged brilliance and iron nerve, plus the superb military instrument he had at hand in 1870, the elder Moltke was also fortunate in having an incompetent enemy. The performance of the French army at every level beyond that of the individual soldier could be described as abysmal. Poor performance was exacerbated by a series of awful decisions by Napoleon III and his principal commanders, which allowed Moltke to trap the French imperial armies in the twin sieges of Metz and Sedan. Although the improvised armies of the new republic caused some difficulties and thereby protracted the war, throughout the conflict, the Prussians were simply superior to their French opponents.

The younger Moltke had no such advantage. The French army of 1914, for all its defects, performed immeasurably better than its Second Empire antecedent. Despite his rather ponderous appearance, Joffre proved to be a dynamic commander who was not afraid to intervene personally with subordinate commanders, relieving those who did not measure up.[218] Once the initial French offensive in Alsace failed, Joffre kept his wits about him and shifted the focus of French operations from the right to the left. Using the excellent French road, rail, and communications systems, and maintaining close control over his forces, Joffre was consistently able to frustrate German efforts to envelop French forces. Joffre was also able to incorporate British forces into his operations, although the Allies were still a long way from developing effective cooperation.[219] Although tactical clumsiness, marked by poor coordination between infantry and artillery, often resulted in unnecessarily heavy casualties, the French army of 1914 proved to be a far more dangerous opponent than that faced by the elder Moltke in 1870.

Just as the French (and British) got a vote in the west, the Russians got a vote in the east. The Russians' ability to mount an offensive so quickly gave the *OHL* cause for concern. That concern was increased when the defeat at Gumbinnen was combined with Prittwitz's apparent loss of control of the situation. This prompted Moltke to replace Prittwitz and Waldersee with Hindenburg and Ludendorff, but also to dispatch the Guards Reserve Corps and XI Corps to the eastern front.[220] Given the slim margins the German army was operating with, this represented a potentially serious diminution of forces.

More critical to the *OHL* from a strategic point of view was the outcome of the border battles between the Russians and the Austro-Hungarians in Galicia. After a great deal of back-and-forth marked by heavy casualties, the outcome of the 1914 campaign ended with Conrad's stricken armies forced all the way back to the Carpathians. In addition, the fortress of Przemyśl and its large garrison was under siege. To add insult to injury, three invasions of Serbia ended with three stinging defeats for the Austro-Hungarians. By the end of 1914, the *OHL*, now led by Erich von Falkenhayn, had to seriously consider the prospect of devoting considerable resources to the support of Germany's closest ally. This is discussed in the next chapter.

Concluding Remarks

By the end of 1914, the Germans faced precisely what their long-term planning had attempted to avoid since Schlieffen's first days as chief of the General Staff and the elder Moltke's warnings in his final speeches and writings. The army faced a prolonged war on two fronts against substantially superior enemies, the much-feared "parallel" battlefield where mobile warfare could not be conducted, and the long-feared consequences of trying to protect Prussia's and Germany's fragile social and political structure against both foreign enemies and domestic challenges. "People's war" had finally returned on an even vaster and more dangerous scale than had been the case during the final months of the Franco-Prussian War.

The German army now had to deal with the demands of conducting a prolonged war against a coalition of opponents with a significant advantage in the resources needed to conduct modern war. On the western front, the German army needed to devise new methods to break the positional deadlock that now prevailed. The story of how the German army approached this problem is the subject of later chapters. Strategically, the German High Command, now confronted with the prospect of conducting a multifront coalition war, had to establish priorities among the competing fronts. That is the focus of the next chapter.

CHAPTER EIGHT

ADJUSTING TO THE DEMANDS OF PROLONGED WAR

With the prospect of a rapid victory entirely gone by November 1914, Germany's leadership had to address the complex questions of conducting prolonged, multifront warfare, which up to that point had been largely neglected. The new mode of warfare required major adjustments in nearly every sector of the armed forces and society. Germany required a new approach to strategy and coalition warfare. The army had to conscript vast numbers of men and equip them with a variety of old and new weapons. As it multiplied its units and corps of officers and noncommissioned officers to organize and lead the masses, the army also had to develop new doctrinal approaches to the battlefields, especially in the west. All this ensured that industrial and financial mobilization became critical elements of protracted war. The nation needed to find new allies and, even more importantly, prevent its enemies from finding new partners. Above all, the nation and, in effect, the army had to develop and execute national and military strategies appropriate to the new circumstances. The nation's failed performance in most of these areas gradually destroyed the old Prussian military system and the Hohenzollern Empire. The first task in preparing the army to deal with this new situation was to expand it in terms of manpower, organization, and equipment.

Expanding the Army

As the scope and duration of the war outstripped all prewar expectations, the army found itself seriously short of all kinds of units, equipment, weapons, munitions, and trained manpower. In August 1914 the army undertook its first expansion by creating six new reserve corps to accommodate some of the volunteers who had offered their services.[1] These included many working-class men but also thousands of relatively well-educated but previously untrained young men from the middle class.[2] The new units, which were deficient in training, capable officers, equipment of all kinds, and artillery, were ready by 10 October. Chief of the General Staff Erich von Falkenhayn sent one corps to the eastern front, one to Fifth Army, and four to Flanders. The latter four suffered devastating losses as overaged officers and untrained enlisted men fell easy victim to the enemy in the battle known to history as Langemarck.[3]

This was but the first step in expanding the army. The second took place in the winter of 1914, as the army organized the eighty-one battalions remaining in Germany into nine reserve divisions (five new reserve corps). These units contained many experienced officers and enlisted men who had recovered from wounds. Learning from Langemarck, the army also sent a substantial number of officers and noncommissioned officers from front-line regiments to give these units a solid core. Each of these reserve divisions had two field artillery regiments, more than their counterparts from earlier in 1914 had enjoyed.[4]

The third increase in divisions came about in early 1915, the product of a reorganization of existing formations. Based on a plan developed by War Ministry official Colonel Ernst von Wrisberg and accepted by Falkenhayn in February 1915, each division gave up an infantry regiment and corresponding support units. In return, the units would receive replacements and additional machine guns. Over the course of 1915, the Wrisberg plan enabled the formation of nineteen new divisions. The War Ministry accomplished near miracles in finding the necessary equipment, ranging from airplanes to communications equipment. By 1 January 1916, the army had 161 infantry divisions: 78 regular army, 54 reserve, 20 *Landwehr*, and 9 other specialized types.[5]

One of the impacts of the Wrisberg plan was that the army changed the structure of its infantry divisions and artillery units to accommodate tactical changes and provide cadres for the 1915 expansion. Infantry divisions dropped their square structure (two brigades of two regiments) for a triangular structure based on three regiments. A brigade headquarters was dropped as well. Firepower within the divisions increased as the number of machine guns and mortars grew; this compensated for the reduction in rifle strength. The resulting availability of experienced personnel allowed the number of divisions to expand. At the same time, artillery batteries adopted a four-tube organization, thereby freeing large numbers of pieces for the creation of 300 additional artillery batteries. Substantial variations among divisions existed until the full implementation of these changes, well into 1916.[6]

Mobilizing Economic and Industrial Resources

The German Empire's lack of a modern governmental mechanism for managing the myriad issues involved in industrial warfare meant that the army had to expand its range of responsibilities beyond all prewar planning. The problems associated with social and industrial mobilization threatened to deprive the army of necessary weapons and munitions, while efforts to manage them threatened the traditional political control of conservative elements and the privileged positions of Germany's industrialists. The British blockade exacerbated shortages of all kinds, particularly food, which by mid-1916 was in critically short supply. Historians have examined the army's efforts to master the problems of industrial mobilization, and their main point in this discussion is the impact on the army's ability to wage this new kind of war.[7]

The Prussian Siege Law of 1851, designed to deal with the Revolution of 1848, gave the king of Prussia and his army extensive powers to deal with emergencies of all kinds. Article 68 of the German Constitution extended that law to the empire, although many legal questions remained.[8] The army's corps commanders thereby acquired vast powers in their peacetime administrative areas. Upon the corps' deployment out of their areas, the "deputy" commanding generals assumed those powers. The law thus gave elderly generals coming out of retirement authority in numerous issues ranging from censorship to labor negotiations and police functions.[9]

The system was almost entirely unsuited to accomplish the tasks it assumed under the Siege Law and the requirements of the war. The corps areas bore little relationship to the empire's normal civilian jurisdictions. The deputy corps commanders thus assumed control over areas that were otherwise unlinked, and in fifteen cases their jurisdictional lines crossed the boundaries of different states within the empire. The deputy commanders were responsible only to the emperor, even though they worked daily with a variety of civilian authorities. The war minister, who assumed responsibility for vast nationwide programs involving armaments, manpower, the raising of new units, and so forth, could not always enforce his wishes on the deputy commanding generals.[10]

The British blockade soon produced serious shortages in German agriculture and industry. Cessation of imports from Russia was a comparatively minor problem, but it only made matters worse. By late 1914, shortages of some consumer items became apparent, and by 1916, Germany was short of food. By 1918, serious malnutrition threatened the health of millions of Germans and caused hundreds of thousands of premature deaths. Nevertheless, despite strong appeals from various corners, the military administration did not play a fundamental role in controlling and rationing food supplies throughout the war.[11] This was not the case when it came to raw materials, industrial production, and the mobilization of labor. On 13 August 1914 Falkenhayn, who was still war minister, created a new office in the War Ministry, the Raw Materials Section (*Rohstoff-Abteilung*), to work with industry to manage that aspect of economic mobilization.[12]

Munitions and Weapons

Although a recent author has denied that the Germans ever suffered from a serious shortage of munitions, there is ample proof to the contrary through much of the war.[13] The army had about 1,000 rounds available for its field guns and light howitzers in 1914, but it clearly underestimated what would be required. Even as late as November 1912, Moltke had accepted a War Ministry suggestion that 1,200 rounds per tube might suffice.[14] These quantities soon proved entirely inadequate.

Local reports of munitions shortages appeared as early as August and September 1914, primarily on the western front, but in the east as well by November.[15] The general nature of the problem was evident in an 11 October 1914 directive from the High Command to the field commanders warning of a shortage of artillery ammunition and instructing the commanders to use strict fire discipline, limiting the length of barrages and the kinds of targets engaged.[16] By October, the artillery had expended nearly all its reserve stocks of munitions and was living primarily off new production. Strenuous battlefield efforts to recover unused munitions and ammunition of all kinds yielded limited results.[17] Shortages of munitions were by no means limited to the German army, and by May 1915, investigations into shortages and demands for increased production occupied journalists and politicians across Europe.[18]

The war minister, reacting to the initiatives of Walther Rathenau, quickly established a new office, the War Material Section (*Kriegsrohstoffabteilung*, or *KRA*), to deal with the problems of mobilizing the nation's industrial resources. The *KRA* soon established a series of private corporations to manage various industrial sectors, basically granting control of production to the prewar cartels and captains of industry. Eventually, the nation had about 200 of these semipublic corporations, which used public and private capital and governmental authority to allocate raw materials and meet production goals. Numerous expedients, including changes in alloys and manufacturing methods, provided relief in 1915 until large expansions in production capabilities could be implemented.[19]

Falkenhayn, first as war minister and later as chief of the General Staff, acted energetically to induce German industries to produce more artillery munitions. Monthly ammunition production of all kinds increased to 400 percent of prewar levels by December 1914 and to 1,300 percent by October 1915.[20] By the end of 1915, production of artillery rounds had increased to nearly 3 million per month, and annual consumption stood at only about 73 percent of production.[21] As the scale of fighting increased, and as armies on both sides created more divisions, munitions requirements continued to grow. The battles around Verdun and along the Somme in 1916 resulted in a new sense of urgency by the end of Falkenhayn's tenure as chief of the General Staff.[22] The successor to Falkenhayn's policy in this regard, the Hindenburg program, is discussed in the next chapter. In the meantime, as the German army expanded in terms of men and materiel in order to meet the demands of the new situation, the German political and military leadership struggled to find a way forward.

War Aims and National Strategy

The failure to attain a rapid victory raised the separate but interdependent issues of war aims and priorities of efforts. The demands of coalition warfare, particularly those raised by Austria-Hungary, underscored the fundamental problems of defining Germany's goals, adjusting military campaigns to objectives and capabilities, and finding a realistic way to strive for victory or accommodation.[23]

Unfortunately, the German Empire's structure was ill suited for the demands of strategy. This deficit was even more obvious under the pressures of war than it had been during peace, given the multitude of concrete problems related to diplomacy, economic and social mobilization, military campaigning, and coalition warfare that suddenly became real with the outbreak of hostilities. The fragmented political structure of the empire, the weakness of the emperor, and the vicious competition that frequently divided military, naval, and civilian leaders combined to produce what seem, in retrospect, to have been shortsighted and even irrational solutions.

German prewar planning reflected the strengths and shortcomings inherent in the empire's military and political structure, as well as the highly problematic state of its civil-military relations. Only the kaiser, unassisted by any semblance of a national security advisory body, possessed the authority to direct and coordinate national policy and strategy. No institution existed for coordinating military and political plans at the highest national level, a problem compounded by the fact that dozens of individuals and agencies had direct access to the emperor. The result was a constant struggle within the government to gain influence with Wilhelm II and control over national strategy. No agency of the Reichstag, the Prussian legislature, or any other civilian body had the slightest degree of oversight. The emperor's descent into the status of a passive observer robbed the system of its only integrating institution. The Prussian General Staff, which had no authority over the imperial German navy and very limited power within the Prussian army, was the only organization capable of even limited coalition planning.[24]

At the risk of excessive simplification, one can reasonably argue that two broad groups struggled to establish German objectives in the war. One group, consisting primarily of the Foreign Office, eventually became willing to accept a relatively modest peace with security guarantees and German economic domination of central Europe, but few if any territorial acquisitions. The other group, dominated by some military leaders, Pan-Germans, and rabid nationalists, demanded substantial territorial annexations and other measures to ensure German domination of the continent and to secure German economic interests throughout the world. No major element of the government was willing to accept a peace based on the status quo ante. The government successfully prevented any public discussion of war aims until the autumn of 1916, when the *OHL* lifted the ban on such discussions in an effort to build support for the war.[25]

As a practical matter, the General Staff eventually became the dominant institution in shaping German foreign policy, military strategy, and, to a large extent, domestic mobilization for war. Falkenhayn, who was chief of the General Staff from September 1914 until August 1916, struggled to consolidate his authority and coordinate policy and military strategy, but he could neither satisfy the radical annexationists nor gain sufficient power to impose his views on a consistent basis. His nominal successor, Paul von Hindenburg, was the towering figure in Germany following the Battle of Tannenberg. Hindenburg, however, was largely a front man for Erich Ludendorff, his quartermaster general. Ludendorff, unfortunately, was intent on achieving victory at any price, and he clung to vast annexation schemes to the bitter end. Hans von Seeckt, for example, regarded the *OHL*'s advance into Lithuania in August 1915 as nothing more than a "private war" conducted by Ludendorff on behalf of expansionist-minded organizations in Germany.[26] Germany's military strategy thus came to reflect both the bitter internal conflict within the German government and the fundamental contradiction of striving for both peace and victory, the latter consisting of conditions that virtually precluded the former.

The General Staff and Strategic Adjustments, 1915–1916

The First World War placed unanticipated demands on the Prussian General Staff, straining its personnel establishment to the utmost and altering its traditional role in the command system. Upon mobilization, the *Grosser Generalstab* (the central General Staff in Berlin), supplemented by numerous other individuals, became both the command element of the field army and the core of the *Grosse Hauptquartier* (Great Headquarters) of the emperor. In theory, the Great Headquarters' membership included, in addition to the emperor and the chief of the General Staff, the chief of the admiralty; the imperial chancellor; the state secretary of the Foreign Office; the war minister; the chiefs of the Naval, Military, and Civil Cabinets; military plenipotentiaries of three of the larger federal states; heads of various civilian agencies; and diplomats of various allied and neutral states.[27] The entire entourage, which required eleven railroad trains for movement, was about as cumbersome and disjointed as a headquarters could be.[28] As the war continued into 1915, many of the civilian heads of agencies returned to Berlin, while the *OHL* moved from place to place as circumstances required. It did not return to Berlin until the end of the war. The attendant separation of civilian offices from the primary agency responsible for conducting the war became an enduring problem. Here, as elsewhere, Emperor Wilhelm II utterly failed to perform his prescribed constitutional functions or to delegate them in an effective manner.

As the war progressed and the army expanded, the *OHL* underwent numerous organizational changes. The General Staff's peacetime organization gave way to a very different wartime structure. The prewar General Staff had six sections: Central for administration; First and Third for intelligence and foreign armies; Second for mobilization; Fourth for staff rides and supervision of the War Academy; and Fifth for military history.[29] This organization was clearly unsuited for executing a war, since it lacked sections for operations, supplies, munitions, and numerous other functions necessary for a field army. Most such tasks fell under the War Ministry in peacetime.

In its mobilized form, the General Staff had four major sections. The Central Section organized staff work, correspondence, personnel matters, and so forth. The Operations Section worked on all matters concerning campaigns, orders, and the like. A third section, Intelligence, managed efforts under that rubric. The Political Section, eventually redesignated the Military-Political Section, monitored the military policies of enemy and neutral states. The Secret Intelligence Service, originally created as Section IIIb under the prewar organization, eventually became an independent section. Numerous other offices, headed by senior generals responsible for functional or branch matters, were available to advise the chief and the general quartermaster. The *Generalintendant* was responsible for provisions, while separate chiefs were responsible for railways, munitions, medical services, telegraph communications, and mail. Various other positions arose as the army changed during the war, and by 1918, the General Staff had thirteen main sections. Some of these included emerging branches of the service, such as aviation and engineers.[30]

As the previous discussions have shown, the personalities and abilities of key individuals had important impacts on the preparation and execution of war plans, as well as on the conduct of war on a daily basis. In this regard, Falkenhayn was no exception. His military background differed substantially from that of most of his fellow General Staff officers, to the point that some improperly considered him an unschooled outsider. A graduate of the War Academy (1890), he spent seven years (June 1896–June 1903) in China as a military instructor, possibly in an effort to avoid the consequences of excessive debt. Following his return to Prussia, he served in General Staff positions and commanded a regiment, which was his highest unit command. Although he spent a number of years in General Staff assignments with the units, his limited time on the central General Staff in Berlin meant that he had little direct exposure to Schlieffen's teachings. As a result, some regarded this relatively obscure and junior one-star general as unworthy of succeeding Moltke. The emperor promoted him to Generalleutnant when he became chief of the General Staff, passing over about thirty senior one-star generals. This problem was exacerbated when Wilhelm promoted Falkenhayn to General der Infanterie in early 1915 to give him a rank more commensurate with his position. Though intelligent, Falkenhayn was an anti-intellectual, boasting that his education rested on experience rather than theory. As war minister, he had relatively limited official knowledge about the campaign but realized that he would have to exercise much stricter control over field commanders than had Moltke.[31]

Although there is some truth in Holger Herwig's assertion that the German government did not reevaluate its strategy after the failure to achieve a rapid victory in 1914, Falkenhayn did adjust his military strategy to the new circumstances.[32] He adopted what his biographer has called a strategy of calculations based on goals that were militarily attainable.[33] Although he reluctantly supported Hindenburg's demand for a major offensive in Poland and at one point even considered moving the OHL to the eastern front to direct the effort, he ultimately decided to use newly raised corps in the west in the disastrous battle around Ypres. The result was a lost opportunity in the east and a bloody repulse at Ypres. Following these failures to achieve decisive results on both fronts, Falkenhayn recognized that the situation required a new strategic approach. He clearly understood, at least by the middle of November 1914, that Germany could not obtain peace by defeating all the Allied countries. Falkenhayn came to believe that a great victory in the west was no longer attainable and that the old methods of mobile warfare would not work, owing to the strength of modern defenses and German inferiority.[34] He wished to contain the human and other costs of the struggle and could not accept the idea that the war had its own dynamic that would compel German leaders to pursue victory at any price. Falkenhayn recognized that the population could not endure the burdens of war forever and that eventually a peaceful solution would have to be found. He hoped to win by holding out until a peace could be arranged, at least with France and Russia.[35] He informed Tirpitz and Bethmann-Hollweg of his views and proposed a new strategy of making peace with Russia while the navy used a submarine blockade to defeat England, which he regarded as the primary enemy. Falkenhayn was willing to renounce territorial annexations on the continent in pursuit of this strategy.[36]

The rest of the German government rejected Falkenhayn's approach, even though many agreed with his fundamental assumption that peace with Russia was essential. Bethmann-Hollweg continued to hope for territorial acquisition in both east and west and considered control of Belgium essential. Most military leaders believed the army would have to inflict additional serious defeats on the Russians prior to reaching a settlement.[37]

The eastern commanders retained their faith in a complete military victory and demanded a massive effort against the Russians. Ironically,

Falkenhayn himself was responsible for creating a power base that constituted his principal opposition. As noted previously, Falkenhayn had considered moving the *OHL* to the eastern front in the autumn of 1914. Events on the western front, however, commanded his attention. Once a second army headquarters was established on the eastern front, a local coordinating mechanism was needed. Thus, on 1 November 1914 all German forces in the east were subordinated by royal order to a new headquarters, *Oberbefehlshaber Ost* (shortened to *Ober Ost*). Hindenburg, the senior German field commander in the east, became its commander, with Ludendorff as chief of staff.[38]

The establishment of the *Ober Ost*, though a concession to operational realities that demanded the formation of a higher headquarters, also created a rather anomalous situation. Technically, the kaiser was head of the *OHL*. The chief of the General Staff issued orders in the emperor's name, but in fact he was acting largely on his own authority, even though many crucial decisions were presented to Wilhelm II for formal approval. During the course of 1915 the *Ober Ost* grew and acquired more field armies and army groups, four in all by the autumn of 1915.[39] In theory, the *Ober Ost* remained subordinate to the *OHL*, meaning that Falkenhayn, a rather junior general officer, was giving orders to a field marshal. Wilhelm II remedied this with a couple of quick promotions for Falkenhayn, but this provided only partial mitigation.

For its part, the *Ober Ost* attempted to act autonomously while Hindenburg and Ludendorff waged a lengthy campaign to unseat Falkenhayn. The *Ober Ost* often refused requests from the *OHL* to give up forces for employment elsewhere. For example, it refused Falkenhayn's request for four divisions to reinforce Mackensen's Eleventh Army in its advance into Galicia. Later, Falkenhayn had to pry 26th Infantry Division from the *Ober Ost*'s clutches for the invasion of Serbia. Falkenhayn tried to limit the *Ober Ost*'s authority in the autumn of 1915, but the crisis created by the Brusilov offensive in the summer of 1916 forced him to restore its full authority on that front.[40]

The conflicting views of Falkenhayn and the *Ober Ost* reflected more than a clash of personalities. Falkenhayn had concluded that the days of traditional campaigns of movement culminating in decisive battles were over on the western front, but he was not willing to risk defeat there by sending too much of the army to the east. Hindenburg and Ludendorff retained their belief that the traditional reliance on a war of movement would eventually produce a decisive military campaign against Russia, assuming that Germany committed enough forces in such an effort. In January 1915 Hindenburg and Ludendorff began a relentless campaign to force the kaiser to dismiss Falkenhayn, who nevertheless retained the confidence of the emperor. For his part, Falkenhayn sought to break up the duumvirate by shifting Ludendorff to the newly created *Süd* Army as chief of staff. Hindenburg's threat to resign over the matter, a challenge to the king almost unprecedented in Prussian history, was successful in thwarting Falkenhayn but turned out to be counterproductive, in that it incurred Wilhelm II's ire. The kaiser called Hindenburg "the new Wallenstein," a reference to the able but unscrupulous commander from the Thirty Years' War. The fact that Wilhelm II's only response was this dark reference displayed his true impotence. The resolution of the matter of the *Süd* Army was, however, by no means the end of the campaign against Falkenhayn.[41]

A recent historian has characterized the conflict as one between two views of warfare: traditional mobile campaigns on the one hand, and Falkenhayn's "strategy of attrition" on the other.[42] More deeply, these differences reflected the differing circumstances of the two fronts. Falkenhayn believed that mobile warfare in the traditional manner was no longer possible on the western front, but he was not opposed in principle to traditional campaigns in other circumstances. Indeed, he later conducted such a campaign in Romania. Mackensen's invasion of Serbia was also based on a plan that aimed to encircle the Serbian forces in a mobile campaign. The Serbian campaign was successful, but the envisioned annihilation of the Serbian armies never came off.[43] Likewise, despite Hindenburg and Ludendorff's demand for mobile warfare in the east, their initial emphasis on the western front was to find more efficient ways of conducting the positional warfare that had gripped the trenches since early 1915. The real issue was strategic preference based on the very different circumstances in the two theaters.

As a practical matter, the consequences of these differences are less easily demonstrated than the differences themselves. The *Ober Ost* remained committed to the idea of attaining victory through large-scale encirclements. The first attempt, launched in February 1915, aimed at destroying Russian Tenth Army. Although hopes for a decisive success were high, results were another matter, as the attack took place under brutal winter conditions. To be sure, Russian Tenth Army was severely mauled, and the Germans took more than 90,000 prisoners while encircling the Russians' XX Corps. Although it gained some territory, the German advance came up short because of a counterattack by the newly raised Russian Twelfth Army.[44]

Mackensen and Seeckt adopted the opposite approach in the Gorlice-Tarnow operation and the subsequent advance to recapture Lemberg. A combination of carefully planned but brief artillery barrages and infantry advances, followed by operational pauses, yielded no great encirclements but produced large territorial advances and enormous numbers of Russian casualties. Over the course of May 1915 alone, Mackensen's forces inflicted more than 400,000 casualties on the Russian Southwest Front, including 170,000 prisoners.[45]

The conflict over the different approaches came to a head in the summer of 1915, after the recapture of Lemberg. The *Ober Ost*, with Ludendorff as its leading proponent, wanted to execute a potentially gigantic pincer attack, aimed at a deep encirclement of the Russian forces in Poland. Falkenhayn, following a proposal put forth by Seeckt and supported by Mackensen, sought a much more conservative approach. That plan, governed by logistical and topographic considerations, called for a much more shallow encirclement. The offensive, launched on 13 July 1915, succeeded in driving the Russians out of Poland.[46] But the Russian field forces, despite suffering heavy losses, were able to evade encirclement.

The *Ober Ost* assumed that a decisive military victory in the east could eventually lead to another one in the west. Falkenhayn assumed that at some point, after suffering enough casualties, at least one of the Western Allies would be willing to accept moderate peace terms. He continued to hope that Russia could be detached from the Western Allies, but he was no more confident of a victory in the east than in the west. Given the determination of French and British leaders and their continued superiority over Germany in the total calculation of military power, efforts to reach either a diplomatic solution or a military victory were beyond Germany's reach. That did not become obvious to Germany's leaders, however, until the Allied offensives of 1918.

Despite his reservations about what could be achieved in the east and his concern for maintaining the stability of the front in the west, Falkenhayn partially relented and sent important reinforcements to the east, where the Germans won a substantial if indecisive victory in the spring of 1915 at Gorlice and recaptured the fortress of Przemyśl. He made this decision in part to mollify the Hindenburg-Ludendorff team but more because of Austria-Hungary's precarious situation.[47] Adolf Wild von Hohenborn became war minister as part of the kaiser's efforts to placate

Hindenburg and Ludendorff while keeping Falkenhayn as chief of the General Staff.[48]

To achieve these important but ultimately indecisive successes in the east and the Balkans, Falkenhayn had reluctantly accepted the necessity of fighting a defensive war on the western front. This, however, offered no solution to what he regarded as the essential problem: the hated English. In January 1915 the navy informed the High Command that it could not prevail in a great battle of capital ships and proposed instead a campaign of unrestricted submarine warfare against England. Falkenhayn resisted this until late December, when he joined the radicals in demanding that the chancellor approve such an effort.[49] From that point on, Bethmann-Hollweg and Falkenhayn were bitter opponents on many strategic questions. The chancellor became one of the leaders of the group seeking to drive Falkenhayn out of office.

Developments in High-Level Command and Control

The command problems that arose in the west in August and September 1914 revealed the difficulties in subordinating one field army commander to another. By 10 October, the western front had ten army-level commands reporting directly to the *OHL*, which also had overall responsibility for the entire ground war. Falkenhayn struggled with the difficulty of obtaining forces from the individual field armies to create reserves for rapid use in critical areas. On 25 November 1914 he therefore established a new command level, the army group, to command multiple field armies along specified sections of the front. As Falkenhayn himself admitted, this did not entirely solve the problem of parochialism. The army had not prepared its commanders to lead at this level, and they continued to focus on local matters at the expense of a broader perspective. They were usually just as unwilling to give up forces as the army commanders had been. Nevertheless, the army group proved indispensable in commanding the field armies and became a permanent feature of the command structure on both fronts.[50]

As mentioned in chapter 7, the High Command had great difficulty establishing the physical capability to exercise command over the field armies during the mobile campaign in August and September 1914. Neither Schlieffen nor Moltke had devised a satisfactory method of commanding even the western-front armies, a failure for which Moltke took the brunt of the postwar blame and for which he was indeed largely responsible.[51] Although he had been chief of the General Staff for more than seven years by August 1914, Moltke had failed to prepare the army to make effective use of emerging radio technology or aviation in maintaining contact with the field armies.

The *OHL* was in command of Eighth Army and other forces in East Prussia in 1914, but it could exercise only the most general control there. Moltke properly concentrated his personal efforts on the western campaign and moved the headquarters and its luxurious trains to Koblenz on 16 August.[52] The *OHL* moved again on 29 August to Luxembourg City, where the General Staff had to work in a school without any lighting.[53] These moves, especially the latter, created problems in maintaining proper communications with Eighth Army and actually produced only marginal improvements in commanding the right-wing armies as they moved through Belgium. Over the course of the war, the headquarters moved to various locations in the west and east, ending the war in Spa, Belgium.[54]

Positional warfare on the western front between 1915 and 1918 led to new problems for the General Staff and its relations to field commanders and their staffs. Gradually, the General Staff became more involved in the details of battles, sometimes down to battery and battalion level, in part because static battles, both large and small, took the place of mobile campaigns, and in part because the long series of crises in 1916 and 1917 demanded constant attention. As the fronts stabilized, the field armies improved their communications infrastructures, allowing much closer supervision of tactical activities than had been foreseen before the war. As early as 1916, commanders were complaining of Falkenhayn's involvement in details, and by the summer of that year, he had become totally absorbed in local affairs. As one highly respected officer described the situation in early 1916: "Positional warfare turned into a strict centralization of details."[55] This was a complete reversal of the traditional Prussian emphasis on subordinate freedom and initiative, especially as practiced and taught by the elder Moltke, but it had some precedent in Schlieffen's vision of the modern supreme commander sketched in his postretirement writings.[56]

Falkenhayn had to alter his approach when dealing with the demands of a multifront war. On 7 May 1915 Falkenhayn and most of the *OHL*'s personnel moved to Pless, near the Austrian border, in order to monitor the progress of Mackensen's Gorlice-Tarnow offensive. To handle matters on the western front, one of the *OHL*'s most able staffers, deputy operations officer Fritz von Lossberg, was left behind at headquarters in Mézières with seven other officers. Initially, Lossberg and his colleagues received reports and kept Falkenhayn up to date.[57] No changes could be made without Falkenhayn's permission. Commanders of army groups and armies soon complained about this, and Pless was not nearly as well equipped as Mézières to handle rapid communications. Confronted with this reality, Falkenhayn soon reversed himself. Thus, while the OHL was located at Pless, army group and army commanders had a bit more latitude in making tactical decisions.[58]

Perhaps because of communications issues and the anomalous situation with Hindenburg, relations between the OHL and upper echelons on other fronts were much looser. Falkenhayn rarely interfered with the Ober Ost's operations, issuing only vaguely worded general directives. Mackensen's campaigns in Galicia and Poland were conducted with a light touch. Although constant communication was maintained between Mackensen's headquarters and the OHL's eastern headquarters at Pless, control was light. Only once, near the end of May 1915, did Falkenhayn's emissary Gerhard Tappen visit Mackensen's headquarters at Jaroslau, where he was briefed by Mackensen's chief of staff Hans von Seeckt on the progress of operations and the next steps that had already been planned.[59] Likewise, Mackensen had carte blanche in Serbia, even when weather difficulties at the start of the campaign caused fretting at the OHL.[60]

German Strategy in 1916: Verdun and Submarine Warfare

The High Command faced a fundamental dilemma in devising a German strategy in 1916. Efforts to create a massive breakthrough on the western front produced many proposals but little in the way of real prospects.[61] The army, Falkenhayn correctly judged, was simply not strong enough to break through the Allied lines in France and thus had no hope of winning the war in a classic campaign based on traditional mobile warfare. Instead, both he and his Austrian counterpart recognized by early 1916 that a total victory was unattainable.[62] Nor could Germany find an answer to the gradually increasing Allied superiority in the positional warfare of the western front, which was gradually turning into the infamous and ultimately disastrous "battle of material"—a term that did not come into wide use until the British offensive on the Somme in July. Under the prevailing circumstances, the army could win in the west neither by attacking nor by defending.[63] Moreover, the war in the east continued to be a serious drain on German resources as the power of Austria-Hungary gradually slipped away.

In considering the emerging military realities early in 1916, one is tempted to agree with Holger Afflerbach that the Central Powers' one hope was to avoid American entry into the war and to hold out while expressing a willingness to compromise and make peace. Falkenhayn might have been willing to accept at least part of this effort with regard to France and Russia, but Bethmann-Hollweg clung to his desire for annexations, or at least to his refusal to renounce them.[64] Stubborn intransigence, however, was not the unique property of the Germans. Given the Allies' unwillingness to forgo their own war aims and abandon their secret commitments to one another, condemnation of Bethmann-Hollweg has validity, primarily in the realm of his extreme views and lack of realism rather than in the failure to attain results that were otherwise achievable.

Falkenhayn's solution to Germany's strategic problem was, on the one hand, to conduct unrestricted submarine warfare in the hope of defeating England and, on the other, to inflict such casualties on the French army that the nation's will to resist would be broken. His views on German strategy for 1916 survive in scattered documents and records of conversations with various civilian and military leaders.[65] In a mixture of cold calculation and self-delusion, Falkenhayn concluded that England was the main enemy, but that the British Expeditionary Forces' defensive positions in Flanders were too strong for a direct assault. He regarded France as England's "best sword" but believed it had been weakened almost to the breaking point. He proposed to bleed the weakened French army to death, primarily by massed artillery at Verdun, an exposed point from which the French could not retreat. Falkenhayn also hoped to lure the British into making a major attack in Flanders to relieve the pressure on Verdun and then to inflict heavy losses on them by exploiting the well-recognized advantages of the defender in trench warfare. This, he hoped, might even produce favorable enough conditions that a counterattack could create a serious breakthrough in the Allied trench lines. He thus launched the assault on Verdun, intending to use local artillery support to lure the French into a killing zone as they defended a target of both military and psychological value.[66]

The campaign at Verdun, then, had a rational and limited set of goals. Primarily, it was intended to force France out of the alliance with England, but eventually, the goal was to convince England to give up the struggle. Contrary to Falkenhayn's later argument, the Verdun plan did not assume unrestricted submarine warfare, although it did place substantial faith in the army's ability to use defensive fighting to inflict losses on the British.[67] The Verdun effort was thus one of the few campaigns of the First World War that was intended to achieve limited political objectives rather than result in the total defeat of the enemy. Here, as during much of the war, there is little reason to believe that either side was prepared for a comprehensive compromise to obtain peace.[68]

The Allies also planned major offensive efforts in 1916. At the Chantilly conference in December 1915, Allied representatives agreed on a series of coordinated offensives on the western, eastern, and Balkan fronts. Although the Germans struck first, these plans eventually produced the Brusilov offensive in June and the Anglo-French attack along the Somme in July.[69]

The German strategy against France and England in 1916 had a number of important shortcomings.[70] Falkenhayn proceeded with planning for the attack on Verdun as the struggle to renew unrestricted submarine warfare continued. Bethmann-Hollweg succeeded in resisting the General Staff's demands for unrestricted submarine warfare even as the battles around Verdun raged. As events soon demonstrated, Falkenhayn underestimated the powers of resistance of the French army and nation. Tactical circumstances allowed the French to impose serious attrition on the German forces as well. This in turn led local commanders to demand more and more forces. He equally underestimated the strength of Russia and failed to consider the ongoing drain on Germany's resources in the east. The British offensive to relieve pressure on Verdun, delivered on the Somme in July and lasting for months, led to far greater German losses than had been expected. The anticipated opportunity for a decisive counterstroke never materialized; indeed, merely holding out proved to be a serious challenge, worsened by the policy that ground was to be held at all costs.

Verdun has long served as a symbol of futility and the waste of human life, not to mention the idiocy of generalship in the First World War, and this seems reasonable from the vantage point of hindsight. In the short run, the battle seriously undermined Falkenhayn's position in the army, as did the British army's Somme offensive, designed to relieve pressure on the French. The Somme has long been seen as an example of stupidity and insensitivity to the loss of life, in this case engineered by Douglas Haig. Although now generally recognized as a great defeat for the British, at the time, the Somme battles caused so many German casualties that they seemed to represent another German failure. They, too, undermined Falkenhayn's position. By the end of August 1916, Falkenhayn's political and military strategies were in a state of total and costly collapse. The defeat inflicted on the Austrians by the Brusilov offensive in June 1916 only made matters worse.[71]

Falkenhayn's powerful enemies had long awaited an opportunity to prevail upon the kaiser to replace him, but they had always been thwarted by Wilhelm's substantial personal loyalty to him. Bethmann-Hollweg had wanted to see Hindenburg replace Falkenhayn as early as December 1914, and he may have hoped that Hindenburg would assist in attaining a moderate peace settlement. Important political leaders from the other German states, eventually including the king of Bavaria, joined the plotters by the end of June 1916.

Romania's decision to join the Allies in late August 1916 sealed Falkenhayn's fate. The kaiser, previously loyal to Falkenhayn despite the frequent attacks of Bethmann-Hollweg, Hindenburg, and Ludendorff, lost his nerve at the news of Romania's declaration of war on Austria-Hungary (27 August 1916). He dropped his long-standing support for Falkenhayn, possibly in a crass attempt to find a scapegoat. The chiefs of the Civil and Military Cabinets assembled Bethmann-Hollweg, Hindenburg, and Ludendorff at the Pless castle on 28 August to ratify the decision to elevate Hindenburg to the position of chief of the General Staff.[72] Ludendorff, always the driving force on this team, became the first general quartermaster and the real architect of the High Command's subsequent policies and decisions.[73] Colonel Max Bauer, though lesser known, was another extremely important member of the new team, particularly in the areas of industrial production and domestic political issues.[74]

Falkenhayn's tenure at the *OHL*, his conflicts with the *Ober Ost*, and his ouster over the issue of Romania were intertwined with two thorny issues: coalition warfare and unified command. These, along with the matter of expanding the war, are now examined in some depth.

Coalition Warfare

German-Austrian problems related to coalition warfare began long before the outbreak of war in 1914. In several crucial areas the German approach failed to meet the challenges of coalition warfare: prewar planning and preparation, accommodating allies' goals and special needs, and executing plans and adapting to wartime circumstances.[75] By 1914, prewar foundations for coalition warfare were extraordinarily weak. In planning and conducting its own army's operations, the Prusso-German General Staff system was excellent; transferring that excellence to coalition warfare was a different matter.

Strategic relationships with Germany's primary ally, Austria-Hungary, depended substantially on the policies and personalities of the chiefs of staff. The elder Moltke, chief of the General Staff from the empire's inception until 1888, normally took pains to inform the Austro-Hungarian chief of staff, Field Marshal Friedrich Baron von Beck-Rzikowsky, of the broad outlines of his plans. Moltke's desire for closer cooperation with Austria-Hungary was evident in 1882 when he agreed to an Austrian proposal to supplement the Dual Alliance with a military convention.[76] Bismarck objected and the German military gave in, although Moltke commented to Beck that his military planning was not dependent on the Foreign Office.[77]

Count Alfred von Waldersee, who succeeded Moltke in 1888, continued to work closely with his Austrian counterpart, providing him with many details of German mobilization and campaign plans in the east.[78] In 1889 the German General Staff went far beyond Bismarck's restrictions and assured the Austrians that their mobilization would be the signal for German entry into a war involving Austria-Hungary.[79] All this was possible, of course, because the Germans still intended to make their major effort in the east, in accordance with Austrian interests, and because the moderate objectives of both powers did not consistently threaten the status quo.[80]

Cooperation in planning gradually decreased and eventually ceased almost altogether after Count Alfred von Schlieffen replaced Waldersee as chief of the General Staff in July 1891.[81] Schlieffen's earliest plans were consistent with the assumptions of the Austrians, who welcomed the Germans' continued emphasis on the eastern front. Schlieffen, however, had little faith in coalitions in general and even less in his Austro-Hungarian partner in particular.[82] From 1896 to 1909 contact between the two General Staffs steadily shrank until it was limited to the perfunctory exchange of holiday greetings. Thus the two allies went their separate ways in preparing for war against their respective potential enemies, while the strategic situation became more critical and the crises associated with an increasingly aggressive German foreign policy followed.[83] On at least one occasion Schlieffen gave in to the complaints of the Austro-Hungarian chief of staff, but this was the exception that proved the rule.[84]

The elevation of the younger Moltke to chief seemed to presage an improvement in relations with the Austrians. Given the state of such relations during Schlileffen's tenure, this was a rather low bar to get over. Nonetheless, Moltke did not divulge much information about German plans.[85] It is probable, as Gerhard Ritter has argued, that as late as 1908, the Austrians had no idea as to the nature of the deployment plan or campaign concepts.[86] During the Bosnian crisis of 1908–1909 the chief of the Austrian General Staff, Count Franz Conrad von Hötzendorf, finally raised the question of what would actually happen in the event of a war with Russia. In a series of letters between January and April 1909, Moltke and Conrad outlined their general intentions, but as Norman Stone has pointed out, diplomats in both countries did not take these contacts seriously.[87] Austria-Hungary's foreign minister, Count Alois Aehrenthal, declined Conrad's proposal for closer cooperation with Germany and a military convention. However, Aehrenthal did approve a written exchange of ideas on broad strategic issues.[88]

This exchange of letters foreshadowed the nature of the coalition war that erupted a few years later. Conrad, ever eager to justify his schemes, saw in these letters a firm German commitment to support his plans for a war against Russia.[89] Moltke's marginalia on Conrad's first letters show that he wanted to manipulate his ally into an offensive, even though he knew it would be only a temporary distraction for the Russians. Moltke's intention to retain complete flexibility in the event of war is clearly indicated by the fact that Eighth Army's chief of staff was not aware of the 1909 agreements and that the General Staff's directive to him did not call for an immediate offensive in direct support of the Austrians.[90] The last prewar meeting between Conrad and Moltke, held on 12 May 1914, did nothing to overcome the intentionally vague and even dishonest nature of the military planning on both sides.[91]

The bill came due in August 1914. Each army essentially reneged on its prewar promises for what both felt were valid and pressing reasons.[92] The German army in the east remained on the defensive, while the Austrians sent a substantial portion of their army to the Serbian front and then made matters worse by reversing the original orders, thus ensuring that part of their forces would spend the critical early weeks of the war in transit rather than in combat. On 18 August German Eighth Army informed Conrad that it would not conduct the southerly attack the Austrians had been counting on.[93] The experience permanently embittered Conrad against his German allies, who in turn showed no great respect for the Austro-Hungarian army.[94] This bitterness spilled over into the diplomatic corps of both states, as Austrian diplomats joined in the criticism of Germany's military strategy.[95] In retrospect, it is clear that the prewar discussions established a basis for failure and recrimination rather than success and cooperation.

As 1914 progressed, German war aims aggressively expanded in scope, and those of Austria contracted. The first American offer of mediation fell on deaf ears in Berlin, while the Austrians (and less so the Hungarians) began to wonder if they were fighting primarily for German control of Belgium rather than for survival against Russia and Serbia.[96] Conflict in war aims thus replaced prewar plans as the basis for unsatisfactory cooperation. Over the next several years, Austria-Hungary and Germany disagreed over the postwar settlement of the Polish issue, the question of territorial concessions to Italy, a possible settlement with Serbia, and various minor issues. These disputes sometimes merely poisoned the atmosphere, but in some cases, such as the unannounced Austrian attack on Montenegro, they substantially complicated both diplomatic and military efforts. It was scant consolation that German and Austrian troops never came to the point of firing on each other in anger, as did Austrian and Bulgarian forces in Albania.[97]

Policy conflicts were sometimes magnified by the personal tastes and idiosyncrasies of leaders. The most notable example was the often stormy relationship between Conrad and Falkenhayn. Conrad could be described as a man who was more comfortable with the nineteenth century. He preferred personal meetings, which he followed up with lengthy memoranda penned in the florid nineteenth-century style. These memoranda often proposed ideas that were precisely the opposite of what had been agreed to at the meeting. Much like the younger Moltke, Conrad spent the vast majority of his time at his headquarters (*Armeeoberkommando*, or *AOK*), located at Teschen, near the German border.[98]

Falkenhayn, almost a decade younger than Conrad and a much more active person, spent a considerable amount of time traveling. He had to divide his attention among the *OHL* on the western front, then located at Mézières; Berlin; the *OHL*'s eastern-front headquarters at Pless (about an hour's drive from Teschen); and the *Ober Ost*'s headquarters at Allenstein. For Falkenhayn, personal meetings consumed far too much time. To compensate, he relied on the telephone—the best communications technology available at the time. Conrad, in contrast, was never comfortable with the device. In terms of written communications, Falkenhayn was the precise opposite of Conrad, favoring the clipped, curt Prussian style.[99]

Relations between the two men got off to a bad start. In late October 1914 Falkenhayn invited Conrad to Berlin for a meeting, ostensibly to discuss the fall campaign on the eastern front. Conrad refused to come, instead sending his aide, Lieutenant Colonel Rudolf Kundmann, to represent him. Falkenhayn was understandably irritated by what could only be described as a snub. Both men displayed a finely honed sense of sarcasm, but they were very different physically. When they did meet, it was usually Falkenhayn who took the high-speed automobile ride from Pless to Teschen. When he arrived—coated in dust, goggles over his cap, and smoking a cigar—Falkenhayn towered over the shorter, immaculately dressed Conrad, who seemed almost delicate.[100]

Conrad found other ways to dismay his allies. Psychologically, his most consistent trait was obsession. In 1914 Serbia was the obsession of the moment. In 1915 Conrad's principal obsession was his longtime mistress Gina von Reininghaus, the wife of Austrian hotel magnate Hans von Reininghaus. In January 1915 she visited him in Teschen. Conrad, a widower, wanted to marry Gina, and she publicly asked for a divorce. The matter of satisfying religious, political, and social protocols took up increasing amounts of Conrad's time, as indicated by his correspondence with the head of Francis Joseph's Military Chancery, Baron Arthur von Bolfras.[101] Ultimately, Conrad got his way; he married Gina on 19 October 1915, and the happy couple set up housekeeping in Teschen. Taking their cue from Conrad's example, a number of officers brought their wives and mistresses to the AOK. This outraged German officers, including military attaché Karl von Kaganeck, and it conveyed the impression of a lack of seriousness on the part of the Austrians.[102]

As the war expanded between 1915 and 1917, the two allies found themselves with widely divergent strategic viewpoints. At times, they were not even at war with the same powers. In 1915 Conrad's fixations moved on to a new target: Italy. Falkenhayn had sent forces to Galicia to mount the Gorlice offensive in the hope that success would deter Italy from joining the Allies. He also suggested that Austria-Hungary cede some border territories to Italy, ideas that Conrad understandably (and sarcastically) rejected out of hand. The victories in Galicia, however, came too late, as Italy signed the Pact of London on 26 April 1915 and declared war on Austria-Hungary a month later. Once Italy declared war, Conrad became consumed with punishing Italy and might have been willing to make peace with Russia and even Serbia to gain a free hand to deal with the Italians. He was also prepared to sacrifice Germany's Turkish ally in the process. For his part, Falkenhayn declined to declare war on Italy, as a way of stymieing Conrad's obsessions.[103]

Likewise, the two governments could not agree on goals and plans for the Serbian front. Once Falkenhayn made it clear that Serbia would be the next target, Conrad's obsessive tendencies came to the fore once again. Falkenhayn and Conrad agreed on the conquest of Serbia, and both recognized the need for Bulgarian participation.[104] Once Mackensen's forces had defeated the Serbian army and driven it out of Serbia, Conrad, frantic for a success that would redound solely to Austria-Hungary, wanted to mount operations against Montenegro and Albania. In addition, he wanted an offensive against the Anglo-French bridgehead at Salonika, ostensibly to punish the Entente Powers for their breach of Greek neutrality.[105] The Germans, especially Falkenhayn, wanted none of the latter. The matter was finally settled with regard to Serbia, but Montenegro and Albania were another matter. In December 1915 Conrad withdrew General der Infanterie Hermann Kövess von Kövessháza's Austro-Hungarian Third Army from Mackensen's control, against German wishes and without even informing them. Kövess's forces were then sent into Montenegro and Albania. This move completed the break between Falkenhayn and Conrad. By the end of 1915, the two men were not on speaking terms, and their representatives were lying to each other.[106] Returning the favor for Germany's failure to declare war on Italy in 1915, Austria-Hungary refused to declare war on the United States in 1917. By that time, of course, the differences in war aims had become so great that the new Austrian emperor Karl had declared that a German victory would be the ruin of Austria-Hungary.[107] Likewise, Ludendorff could not obtain any significant Austrian participation in his 1918 offensive in the west, in part because Karl feared that such an effort would damage possible peace negotiations with the Allies.[108] Considering the many fundamental differences in war aims and national strategy, it is hardly surprising that military cooperation remained as fragmentary as it did, even in the face of increasingly serious threats to both nations. After the Bolshevik Revolution, Germany and Austria-Hungary had fewer common enemies but even fewer common interests.

As the Germans increasingly dominated the coalition through sheer weight of economic and military power, relations worsened for a variety of reasons. Many Austrians resented the sacrifices they were making in the service of an ally that seemed more of a hegemon than a partner. The Germans' *Mitteleuropa* scheme, most notoriously (if secretly) suggested in

Bethmann-Hollweg's now-infamous "September memorandum," seemed almost as great a threat to the monarchy's sovereignty as did the aspirations of its internal enemies. Eventually, the German alliance came to be the main prop of the dual monarchy's German and Magyar ruling groups against their subject nationalities, who by 1916 could not be fed without German assistance. German domination of the Austro-Hungarian economy had started long before the war, but the imbalance had become so obvious by 1916 that Austrians sometimes described themselves as beggars.[109] Austro-Hungarian subservience culminated in Emperor Karl's famous journey to Spa on 12 May 1918. There, the Germans forced the emperor to agree to all the old *Mitteleuropa* schemes for German economic domination and even a military protocol that imposed German standards on Austro-Hungarian military organization and planning.[110]

The true extent of Austria's decline is apparent when one remembers that by May 1918, most of Austria-Hungary's military objectives had been attained. Serbia was occupied, and the feared partisan uprising urged by the exiled Serbian government had fizzled badly; the Romanians had been vanquished. Austrian and German troops controlled all of Poland and much of western Russia, and the Italian threat was under control. Yet at this high point of its apparent security in the east and south, the Hapsburg Empire was in fact close to complete collapse and was almost entirely dependent on the power of Germany. This had a deleterious effect on the German army as well, as Germany had to supply the majority of the 1 million soldiers needed to garrison the territories gained from the Treaty of Brest Litovsk.[111] Any thought of preserving trust and maintaining a sense of balance had long vanished from the alliance, which had ceased to exist as a treaty between sovereign states. Only military defeat and the final dissolution of the monarchy remained as possibilities to end complete German domination. Triumphant in the east, the alliance could not function to any significant degree in the final titanic struggle in the west. Ironically, one of the final meaningful military acts by Austria-Hungary was its refusal to support its "ally" in the final offensives on the western front in the spring of 1918.

At lower levels, the Dual Alliance powers established real military cooperation only in dire emergencies. From the first days of the conflict, problems ranged from the Germans' failure to inform the Austrians of events on the Marne to the simple refusal to work together on strategic or even operational plans.[112] This kind of behavior continued after Falkenhayn replaced Moltke.[113] In January 1915 Falkenhayn agreed to shore up the Austro-Hungarian position in the Carpathians by sending German forces in the form of the *Süd* Army, under Alexander von Linsingen. The *Süd* Army was part of Conrad's first abortive Carpathian offensive.[114] In April 1915 Mackensen's Eleventh Army incorporated Austro-Hungarian VI Corps as part of its order of battle. This produced good results in the Gorlice-Tarnow offensive. Mackensen's authority also extended to elements of Austro-Hungarian Third and Fourth Armies. Later, for the advance into Poland, Mackensen and Seeckt had operational control over Austro-Hungarian First and Fourth Armies. For the invasion of Serbia in the fall of 1915, Mackensen had an eponymous army group consisting of German Eleventh (now under Gallwitz), Austro-Hungarian Third, and Bulgarian First Armies.[115]

Conversely, the Germans allowed some integration of units after the 1916 Brusilov offensive. Some German noncommissioned officers were assigned to Austro-Hungarian units, and some German battalions served in Austro-Hungarian divisions. At the corps level, German divisions frequently served under Austrian command to shore up important sections of the front. Indeed, by 1916, some Hapsburg field armies had nearly as many German as Austro-Hungarian soldiers. Some sympathetic officers, such as Seeckt, blamed problems with the Austro-Hungarian army on its leaders, not its soldiers.[116] These arrangements were mere expedients, however, and reflected both Austro-Hungarian weakness and the Germans' mistrust of their ally. No substitute for a genuinely cooperative effort, these makeshift arrangements could not overcome the chaotic conditions at higher levels of the eastern front.

Germany's relations with its two other major allies, the Ottoman Empire and Bulgaria, were intertwined and double edged. For Germany, gaining Turkey as an ally had its advantages and disadvantages. Adding Turkey to the Central Powers expanded the war in a way that would allow Germany to attack Britain, at least indirectly, while also creating another front against the Russians. This would be in accordance with Falkenhayn's view that Britain was the main enemy. For its part, the Turkish government was eager to reverse the pattern of decline over the past half century.[117] The nature of the alliance, however, mandated that German help to Turkey would be indirect at best. The German navy cooperated well on a limited basis with the Turkish navy. The battle cruiser *Goeben* and light cruiser *Breslau*, commanded by Admiral Wilhelm Souchon, evaded the French and the British and arrived in Constantinople on 10 August 1914.[118] Officially "sold" to the Turkish navy, the two ships opened active hostilities between Russia and Turkey by bombarding Russian Black Sea ports two days after Russia's declaration of war. Thus, they played an important role in naval affairs on the Black Sea, while also embarrassing the British.[119]

German military cooperation with Turkey dated to before the war. In 1913 Germany had sent a military mission to the Porte. Despite tensions between the military mission and the German diplomatic corps in Constantinople, good relations were built between the two military establishments. The German military mission had a number of very capable officers to assist the Turkish army. With the mission's help, the Turkish army fought off the British in the Dardanelles campaign and inflicted a humiliating defeat on the British-Indian force in Mesopotamia, destroying most of it at the siege of Kut-el-Amara. Although the Turkish assault on the Suez Canal was a bloody failure, British and Commonwealth forces were tied up in the Middle East. Later on, the Turks sent seven divisions to Bulgaria to assist their allies there. The Turks did not support German efforts to use Pan-Islamic movements to undermine the Allied position in the Middle East and Asia, but this was not a serious problem. Only in 1917, as the strains of war became more severe, did fundamental problems emerge.[120]

Turkey's joining the Central Powers in 1914 constituted a success, but the country was isolated. Resolution of this situation demanded that Bulgaria be added to the alliance and that Serbia be overrun. For its part, Bulgaria was anxious to square accounts with Serbia and regain territory lost in the Second Balkan War. Fortunately for the Germans, Mackensen's victories in Galicia and Poland made a powerful impression on the Bulgarian court. It now looked like Germany was winning the war, and Tsar Ferdinand and his prime minister, Vasil Radoslavov, saw their opportunity. Over the summer of 1915, Bulgaria moved steadily closer to the Central Powers. The convention was signed on 6 September 1915 at Pless. It is interesting to note that the signatories were Falkenhayn, Conrad, and Bulgarian plenipotentiary Lieutenant Colonel Petur Ganchev.[121]

Practical relations with Bulgaria got off on a good foot, as the Bulgarians demanded that the 1915 invasion of Serbia be led by Mackensen. The old hussar, for his part, cultivated good relationships with the Bulgarians, notably Ferdinand.[122] In the event, the Bulgarian army performed reasonably well. Bulgarian First Army was late off the mark and did not advance at the pace desired by Mackensen and Seeckt, a problem exacerbated by communications difficulties. Bulgarian Second Army made short work of

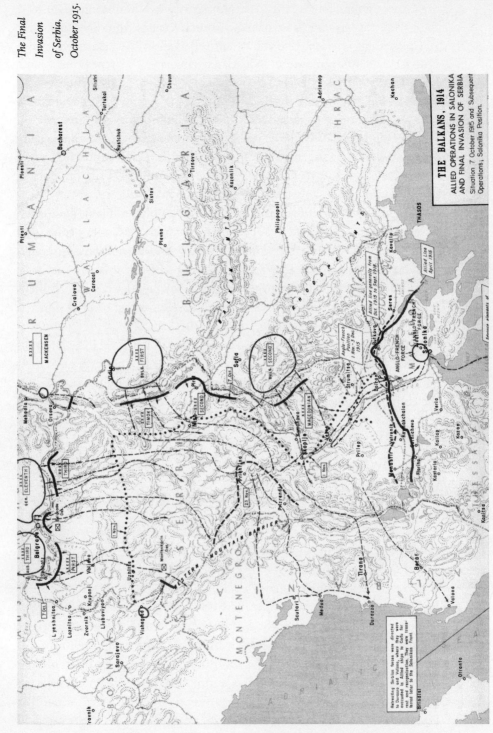

THE BALKANS, 1914

ALLIED OPERATIONS IN SALONIKA
AND FINAL INVASION OF SERBIA

Situation 7 October 1915 and Subsequent
Operations; Salonika Position.

the minor Serbian forces facing it in Macedonia and then stoutly defended the Vardar River Valley against Anglo-French thrusts from Salonika.[123]

Once Serbia was occupied and its territory was divided between Austria-Hungary and Bulgaria, further Bulgarian participation became problematic. Overrunning Serbia met all of Bulgaria's objectives. Thus, the Bulgarians, who were still recovering from the strains of the Balkan Wars and needed to incorporate the gains just made, were unwilling to commit to further offensive operations. As one unidentified Bulgarian general officer reportedly stated, "For us Bulgarians the war is over. We have all we want."[124]

The Bulgarians, aside from holding the Macedonian front, once again had to commit forces to operations when Romania entered the war. Mackensen, commanding Bulgarian Third Army, was able to bring the Romanian advance in Dobrudja to a halt. Commanding a force that contained units from every member of the Central Powers, he eventually launched a successful counteroffensive and, combined with a brilliant thrust conducted by German Ninth Army (commanded by the now deposed Falkenhayn), overran Romania. Mackensen entered Bucharest on 6 December 1916.[125]

Ultimately, however, Bulgaria was weighed down by the same problems that beset Austria-Hungary and Turkey. Although Bulgaria had gained Macedonia and part of Dobrudja, it lacked the ability to sustain a large and well-equipped force over an extended period of time. Attacked by the Entente forces based at Salonika, the Bulgarians, bereft of German support, fought bravely but ultimately collapsed.

Unified Command

Tied in with the conduct of coalition warfare was the issue of combined command. The idea of establishing a combined command in the east in case of war had been discussed by the Austrians and Germans in 1893 and 1895, but without results.[126] Conrad, reversing his prewar position, suggested the establishment of a unified command under his control; he even proposed that such a commander should direct the entire war effort of both countries. Early Austrian defeats and the emergence of Hindenburg's colossal figure quickly made that impossible.[127] Naturally, Wilhelm II would not hear of subordinating large German forces to Austrian control. In November 1914 some Austrian leaders renewed the proposal for a unified command in the east under Austrian archduke Friedrich, with Ludendorff as the chief of staff and Hindenburg and

Conrad commanding their respective national forces. Conrad himself was apparently the key figure in defeating this idea.[128]

A workable system was created for the Gorlice-Tarnow offensive. Mackensen was directly subordinate to the *OHL*, thus keeping him out of the clutches of the *Ober Ost*. This also allowed Falkenhayn to exert some control over affairs on the eastern front. The *AOK* could issue directives to Mackensen, but only with the *OHL*'s concurrence, which rankled the Austro-Hungarians. Mackensen, however, assured the Austro-Hungarians that their prestige would not be damaged. In addition, August von Cramon, the very able German representative at the *AOK*, received guarantees that any reports from Mackensen's headquarters would be sent to the *AOK* as well.[129]

This system served the Central Powers well in the 1915 campaigns in Galicia and later in Poland. As noted previously, Mackensen's authority was extended to the adjoining Austro-Hungarian Fourth and Third (and later Second) Armies. Mackensen ruffled some Austrian feathers with a rather tactless message to Vienna after the recapture of Przemyśl, but when units of the Austro-Hungarian Second Army were able to enter Lemberg, he became quite popular in Vienna. Mackensen's high standing with the Austro-Hungarians was confirmed by a tumultuous visit to Vienna in September 1915, which concluded with a small dinner party and a private audience with Francis Joseph.[130] The fall of Lemberg also resulted in Mackensen's promotion to Generalfeldmarschall, while Seeckt was elevated to Generalmajor. This mirrored the promotions received by Hindenburg and Ludendorff after Tannenberg. Seeckt speculated to his wife that he and Mackensen were being shaped by Falkenhayn into a counterweight (*Gegenspiel*) against Hindenburg and Ludendorff.[131]

The arrangement outlined above was used again for the invasion of Serbia in 1915. In the negotiations involving Germany, Austria-Hungary, and Bulgaria, Conrad wanted the predominantly German forces to be commanded by an Austro-Hungarian general. The Bulgarian representative insisted on a German commander. This turned out to be Mackensen (again, with Seeckt as chief of staff), who was specifically named as commander of the invasion in the military convention signed on 6 September 1915.[132]

As the German representative at Austrian headquarters later complained, rather than creating an effective command structure, the two nations relied on individual agreements and expressions of "brotherly alliance solidarity," as if these could win the war.[133] Russia's Brusilov offensive (June–July 1916), which crushed a major portion of the Austro-

Hungarian forces at the southern end of the eastern front, created such an emergency that something had to be done. By this time, creation of a unified command under a German (Hindenburg) had become intertwined with the ongoing efforts to replace Falkenhayn as chief of the General Staff. Weeks passed as this struggle prevented any united German approach.[134] Wilhelm II very reluctantly agreed to divide the front, with Hindenburg taking command of all forces in the north and Archduke Charles taking command in the south.[135] This temporary measure lasted from 28 July until 16 September, when the much-needed combined command more or less came into existence at about the same time as Falkenhayn's dismissal.

When Hindenburg and Ludendorff took over the *OHL* on 2 September 1916, they moved swiftly to create a combined command (*Oberste Kriegsleitung*) in the east. Under the proposal, which the Austrians, Turks, and Bulgarians quickly agreed to, the German emperor commanded all military forces through directives issued by the German High Command. A secret clause, not revealed to the secondary allies, provided that if the Austrian High Command did not approve of a measure, Wilhelm II would not issue the necessary directives without first obtaining the approval of Francis Joseph.[136] Even the German representative at Austrian headquarters considered that the unified command had finally become a reality. This new arrangement worked well in the Romanian campaign, but it did not last long.[137]

Francis Joseph, whose approval was the cornerstone of the combined-command agreement, died on 21 November 1916, and his successor, Karl, moved quickly to dismantle the *Oberste Kriegsleitung*. Karl took personal control over all Austro-Hungarian forces and restored the previous arrangement, whereby the armies cooperated through agreements between their General Staffs. From Karl's perspective, this was a necessary step to assert both his equality with Wilhelm II and Austrian sovereignty, as well as an expression of military considerations. Karl soon dismissed Conrad, who by that time had been forced by the iron law of necessity to accept the reality of German domination of the war.[138]

The events of 1917 produced a substantial measure of victory in both Italy and on the eastern front. To improve the Austrian position on the Italian front, German Fourteenth Army, with two German and two Austro-Hungarian corps, was installed as an attack force under Otto von Below. This force, using new tactics described in the next chapter, shattered the Italian armies on the Isonzo, driving them back seventy miles to the Piave River. This victory ended the Italian threat for the immediate future, but it was not decisive. In the east, the weakened state of the Austro-Hungarian forces and the near collapse of the Russian army and state under the combined blows of the German army and the Russian Revolution produced the two results Germany had long desired: military and political domination of the Dual Alliance and a substantial measure of victory in the eastern war.[139] The latter eventually led to a final desperate effort in the theater that most German leaders had always considered decisive, but it ironically caused more discord and may have hastened the final collapse of both alliance partners.

In considering the question of combined command, one should not be too critical of the German performance. The Allied powers likewise failed to develop a real combined planning or command system until very late in the war. Even after Marshal Ferdinand Foch became supreme commander in 1918, General John J. Pershing considered many of Foch's orders to be little more than suggestions.[140] Thus, it would be fair to say that neither side was very adept at planning and executing combined efforts, except in the direst emergencies.

The problems encountered in creating a unified command structure also reflected the brutal fact that the vast majority of high-ranking German officers had little if any aptitude for conducting coalition warfare. Hindenburg and Ludendorff set the pattern early, with a series of incidents in the autumn of 1914 that strained relations with the Austro-Hungarians. Ludendorff then made a series of statements critical of the Austro-Hungarians, either publicly or privately in letters to Moltke. Other senior German commanders such as Max von Gallwitz were not as intemperate as Ludendorff, but they too demonstrated an almost complete inability to work with allies.[141]

Only two German commanders proved adept at the intricacies of coalition warfare. Colmar *Freiherr* von der Goltz, who headed the German military mission to Turkey, and his officers proved most effective in raising the military proficiency of the Turkish army. The story of the partnership between Otto Liman von Sanders and Mustafa Kemal at Gallipoli is well known. Less well known but equally important, effective collaboration between Goltz and his Turkish counterpart Khalil Pasha played an important part in the major Turkish victory at Kut. Goltz's death from typhus on 16 April 1916 was a serious blow to the Central Powers.[142]

The other German commander who excelled at coalition warfare was August von Mackensen. His ability as a commander was matched by his diplomatic tact, and Mackensen worked successfully with his Austro-Hungarian, Bulgarian, and Turkish counterparts. Despite the occasional slip, such as the unfortunate announcement of Przemyśl's capture, Mackensen was sufficiently attentive to Austro-Hungarian and Bulgarian sensitivities that he was a highly esteemed figure in both Vienna and Sofia.[143] Men such as Goltz and Mackensen, however, were very much the exceptions.

From the standpoint of coalition warfare, 1915 was probably the best year for the Central Powers. Even so, underneath the patina of success, weaknesses in devising and executing strategy had become manifest by the end of the year. The lack of a unified authority within the German Empire produced confusion and inconsistency in defining war aims and precluded a consistent strategy to achieve them. The long war magnified the utter failure of Wilhelm II to offer direction, which only he could provide under the empire's structure. Even in the military realm, no unified command authority had emerged, and the army was divided into several competing fiefdoms. Worse, the lack of a single coalition High Command in the east seriously hampered cooperation and planning. This often left matters at the mercy of coalition leaders, and the fraught relationship between Falkenhayn and Conrad has already been discussed. Finally, little if any common ground could be found on the question of war aims, let alone the means to achieve them. The underlying strategic problems of the Central Powers found expression in the irony that, by the beginning of 1916, the chiefs of the General Staffs of both Germany and Austria-Hungary had come to the conclusion that total victory was no longer possible.[144]

Fighting a Prolonged War

While the upper echelons of the German army struggled to meet the demands of fighting a multifront war as the dominant member of a coalition, the army as a whole faced other problems. These included maintaining order and discipline, especially in the face of high casualties; ensuring a steady supply of replacements, particularly junior officers; and making the best possible use of existing weapons while also developing new technologies.

Machine Guns

The battles of 1914 had demonstrated a need for both lighter machine guns and more of them. Falkenhayn energetically and successfully pushed for improvements in both the quantity and quality of German machine guns. The army designated its prewar gun, the Model 08, as a heavy machine gun and developed a new version (Light MG 08/15) that was better suited for use in infantry companies. By the time of Falkenhayn's dismissal, the number of machine guns in the field had tripled since August 1914.[145] The Germans captured and used thousands of French and British machine guns, even as German production increased. In the summer of 1915 these captured weapons made up about one-quarter of all the machine guns on the western front. On the eastern front, lightly armed cavalry divisions increased their firepower by using captured Russian machine guns.[146]

The *OHL* moved aggressively to expand the number of machine guns available. Total production grew from about 7,200 in 1915 to 104,000 in 1917. Hindenburg's main emphasis was to make machine guns an integral part of infantry units, although machine gun companies, deployed across the front as the situation dictated, remained a substantial element of the army's tactical firepower. The number of such companies grew from about 325 in 1914 to 2,500 in 1918, while their complement of guns doubled. By 1918, every infantry company had at least six machine guns. A respected authority estimated that the infantry's strength in machine guns increased by a factor of eighteen from 1914 to the end of the war.[147]

Aviation and Antiaircraft Weapons

The German army and the German aircraft industry performed impressive feats of numerical expansion, mission broadening, and technological progress over the course of the war, but these enhancements were not sufficient to meet the demands of German strategy and circumstances on the western front. The variety of missions foreseen in the 1913 doctrinal manual found expression in an air force that became increasingly capable of dropping bombs, conducting aerial combat, providing close air support and interdiction, directing artillery fire, conducting deep and close reconnaissance, and transmitting orders and information.[148] The problems that emerged in 1914—lack of aircraft, erratic measures for controlling them, and failure to use intelligence gathered by aviators—gradually found solutions.[149]

Although German aircraft strength grew substantially during the war, the air force and the aviation industry could not match Allied numerical superiority over the long run. Small-state particularism continued to prevent full efficiency in the allocation of material and labor, even into

1917. The Germans developed the first machine gun synchronized to fire through a propeller and the first all-metal airplane in late 1915. Engine production remained the chief weakness in terms of both quality and quantity, but overall, German aircraft design and capabilities were somewhat superior to those of the Allies. Advances in design and materials became barriers to production efficiency, however, as the race to maintain a technological edge produced rapid obsolescence. The Germans produced more than 200 types of aircraft as new methods and designs rapidly rendered old models obsolete.

The Hindenburg program established a production goal of 1,000 new planes per month, while production itself remained under an independent office. This lofty goal could not be consistently achieved. In the spring of 1918 the German air force, anticipating American participation, planned another massive expansion called the "America Program." This unrealistic proposal, which aimed to increase the monthly production of aircraft to 2,000, had little impact on the final year of fighting.[150] At the end of the war, Germany had about 2,500 first-line aircraft, while the Allies had nearly 6,500. Ultimately, in the first air war, numbers triumphed over quality.[151]

The creation of a unified command of air units in March 1915 gave the chief of field aviation (*Feldflugchef*) authority over all aviation offices, including production. A royal cabinet order of 10 August 1916 elevated this position to the equivalent of a corps commander with the title Commanding General of Air Forces (abbreviated *Kogenluft*), with his own General Staff officer. The *Kogenluft* reported directly to the chief of the General Staff and was responsible for all aviation units, antiaircraft efforts, and the weather service, both in Germany and at the fronts.[152] Specialized units for aerial combat, bombing, and so forth emerged as the embryonic structures of 1914–1915 gave way to the functional organizations that later became standard in twentieth-century military aviation. Command arrangements were a mixture of centralized and decentralized structures, with the field armies, corps, and divisions sharing tactical control of available air units. The air force's main task gradually became an independent combat branch (*Kampftruppe*) alongside the traditional branches.[153]

Historians have generally concluded that airpower did not play a major role in the outcome of the First World War.[154] This may be true, particularly in view of the failure of what later became known as strategic bombing. The Germans' first effort to mount a bombing campaign was against

Serbia before the invasion in 1915. That operation, plagued by a lack of appropriate aircraft, small bombs, and defective bomb fuses, failed. Later, the German campaigns to bomb London using zeppelins and then large bombers—the *Gotha* and R plane (*Rieseflugzeug* [giant airplane])—certainly produced no decisive results.[155] Nevertheless, historians should not allow the postwar fascination with Douhet's theories of aerial bombardment of cities and factories obscure the very real contributions tactical airpower made to ground combat in the last three years of the war. Beginning at least with the British offensives in the spring of 1917 (around Arras), close air support became an increasingly important part of the war on the western front.[156]

For the most part, tactical aviation was not much of an asset to the German army for most of the war, although artillery fire direction was an exception. Results of aerial reconnaissance were spotty at best in both east and west in the early critical days of August and September 1914. This was due in part to shortcomings in organization and communications rather than in the aviators. After the initial campaigns, the effectiveness of aerial reconnaissance varied according to the theater. The absence of serious Russian air opposition allowed Mackesnsen's artillerists to build up a precise picture of the Russian defenses at Gorlice-Tarnow. Pairing an air unit with each corps commander's artillery component contributed to the devastating effectiveness of the opening bombardment. Heavy artillery ammunition was in short supply after a month of campaigning, so for the attack on Przemyśl, Mackensen ordered that the fall of every shot from a heavy gun be observed.[157] For the advance on Lemberg, German aerial reconnaissance ranged up to forty miles behind the front, keeping Mackensen and Seeckt well apprised of the movements of Russian reserves. By June 1915, the German army in the east regarded aircraft as indispensable for reconnaissance, especially given the impotence of the German cavalry.[158] Likewise, in the opening stages of the Serbian campaign in 1915, aerial reconnaissance gave Mackensen's forces a critical edge. German soldiers in Serbia became so reliant on aerial reconnaissance that when bad weather grounded aircraft, Eleventh Army commander Max von Gallwitz had to remind his soldiers that they were responsible for conducting reconnaissance.[159]

The western front was an entirely different matter. At Verdun, the Germans attempted to attain local air superiority to protect their artillery-spotting aircraft. Had this effort worked, it would have been very useful. They called the defensive cordon around their observers the *Luftsperre*, a name adapted from the *Sperrfeuer* of the artillery, meaning fire to block an enemy advance or movement through a selected zone.[160] The French soon won air superiority, and by 1 April 1916 they enjoyed a distinct advantage in artillery fire support around Verdun. This ultimately doomed the Germans' entire enterprise.[161]

The German air force continued its essentially defensive approach through many of the Somme battles. The Germans blunted the Allied aerial offensive on the Somme just as they halted Haig's grand attacks on the ground—inflicting and suffering great losses.[162] By this time, some of the early aerial combatants had taken their place among military history's legendary heroes, but they had little long-term impact on the grinding aerial war of attrition, the results of which depended as much on production as on combat. As a result, German sources are replete with complaints of the great difficulties imposed on ground units by Allied close air support, regardless of how costly this may have seemed to British air commanders and historians.[163] The late arrival of the new German fighter airplane—the Albatross D1, with twin machine guns—opened a new era, but only on a limited scale.[164]

By 1918, the story was a familiar one. The Germans, reacting in part to British methods used in the Cambrai battle, had developed an effective system of managing close air support.[165] The Germans massed more than 730 aircraft of all types (out of a total strength of 2,600 aircraft of all types and ages) for the opening offensive. They attained local surprise and temporary air superiority along the Michael front. Allied air forces quickly recovered, however, and soon exercised a dominating presence in the remaining German attacks and the subsequent counteroffensives that eventually brought the war to an end.[166]

An important if secondary part of the air war was antiaircraft artillery, which for much of the rest of the century was known as flak, from the abbreviation of the German term for antiaircraft cannon: *Flug-Abwehr Kanon*.[167] The Prussian army's antiaircraft experience began in 1870 when it tried to bring down balloons attempting to escape the siege of Paris. It failed, but the story resumed in 1906 when the Artillery Proving Commission directed new studies of the problems of engaging French balloons. German industry quickly produced 50mm, 65mm, and 75mm prototypes mounted on various vehicles. In 1910 Moltke extended these efforts to defense against airships, with considerable success. As the threat posed by airplanes became more apparent in the Italian campaign in Libya and the Balkan War of 1912, the army developed better systems. By 1914, the

Germans had the best antiaircraft programs in Europe, although these remained largely theoretical in nature.[168]

At the beginning of the war the army had a mere 18 such guns, but it had more than 2,550 by the time of the armistice. Along the way, the Germans attempted to adapt captured French, Belgian, and Russian field guns for antiaircraft use and then developed their own guns of 77mm and 88mm caliber. The reorganization of German aviation on 8 October 1916 placed antiaircraft units under the new commander of the air force, replacing the Inspectorate for Flak originally established in 1915. Shortly thereafter, each field army acquired a staff officer, with the honors of a regimental commander, to supervise antiaircraft matters and to coordinate all flak units, which then became separate from divisions and artillery regiments. The army eventually organized its antiaircraft defenses in zones rather than in lines parallel to the front.[169] All observers agreed that by 1917, the coordination of machine guns and antiaircraft guns had made close air support a very dangerous mission. Overall, the Germans claimed (no doubt with considerable exaggeration) that they downed nearly 1,600 enemy aircraft between 1916 and 1918.[170]

Tanks

The German army failed to develop an effective armored force during the First World War, a shortcoming widely regarded as one of its greatest failures.[171] In 1913 the Rifle Examination Commission rejected a suggestion for the development of tracked armored vehicles because it saw no need for such vehicles, given the type of warfare the army expected.[172] This lack of foresight, though understandable, carried over into the period of trench warfare. Although the army experimented with wheeled armored vehicles in 1914 and 1915, serious development began only after the British launched history's first tank attack on 15 September 1916 at Cambrai.[173] Ludendorff, who had arrived at the *OHL* only two weeks previously, was not impressed by the Cambrai attack, which ended with a highly successful German counterattack. He remained skeptical even after the German army began to create its own small tank units supplied with captured British vehicles. He thought the initial British advance succeeded only because it had struck a particularly weak portion of the German line, and he concluded that early German antitank measures were sufficient. The best weapons against tanks, he wrote after the war, were "nerves, discipline and bravery." He later attributed the German failure to produce large numbers of tanks to a lack of resources. Shifting production to tanks would have sacrificed other critical weapons and diverted critical manpower resources. He clearly doubted the utility of tanks unless they could be employed in masses.[174]

Nevertheless, the Germans developed competent designs for tanks and took the first steps toward creating a doctrine for their use. The army's first manual for tanks, written in January 1918, envisioned the new weapon as an auxiliary tool to assist the infantry in breaking into enemy positions. A few tanks accompanied storm companies in the 1918 offensive, where they were employed in the rear section of the first assault wave, behind the infantry of the lead platoons.[175] Germany produced about two dozen of its own basic model, the A7V, by the end of 1917. At war's end, the army had an additional 100 of these and nearly 600 of the LKI, a much lighter model.[176] Nevertheless, they played no significant role in the last months of fighting. Postwar writers as diverse as Hans Ritter, a vociferous critic of the *OHL* on this issue, and Hermann von Kuhl agreed that more could and should have been done in tank development.[177]

Placing the German tank issue in the overall context of the war is no easy matter. The Germans lacked sufficient quantities of aircraft, motor transport, submarines, and a wide range of other finished products and raw materials, not to mention labor. Ludendorff argued that trading any of these for more tanks would not have been productive within the strategic context, given the view that the Germans had to win the war in 1918 or not at all. A few hundred tanks might have been decisive in the early stages of the 1918 offensive, but large numbers would not have been available until 1919, by which time Allied tank superiority would have been entirely overwhelming. As Holger Herwig has noted, by the time the *OHL* recognized its mistake, it was too late.[178] A timely appreciation of the potential of tanks would have provided yet another reason for the *OHL* to drop its extravagant war aims and end the war, just as it might have provided a reason to postpone the 1918 offensive and wait for the tanks to arrive in 1919. By that time, Allied economic warfare might have ended the fighting in any case, regardless of American strength.

Artillery

Static warfare and the resulting trench lines created a variety of new challenges for the artillerymen of the First World War, and the Germans were no exception. As a result of observing the Russo-Japanese War, the Germans had partially foreseen that shrapnel rounds would be of limited use against field fortifications and had adopted the "common" round to bridge the gap between high explosives and shrapnel. This was only marginally successful. Both the field gun 96 n.A. and the light howitzer 98/09 proved inadequate against the trenches and bunkers that dominated positional warfare by the end of 1914.

The German field artillery eventually modified its basic models to produce a new generation of field pieces more suited to trench combat. These were the field gun 16, the light field howitzer 16, and the light Krupp howitzer. Since the calibers remained constant, the main advantage of the new artillery pieces was a substantially increased range.[179] Even so, German artillery gradually lost its prewar superiority as the French and British produced comparable guns in larger numbers with much greater mobility. Indeed, the use of motorized transport gave the Allies most of their superiority in 1918.[180]

The German artillery underwent a substantial expansion and rearmament during the war. The field artillery expanded from about 6,300 tubes in 1914 to 11,000 by 1916. Nearly 800 batteries had the modified pieces described above, while another 1,200 retained the prewar models.[181] The heavy artillery expanded even more, from about 575 howitzers in 1914 to 6,800 early in 1918. In addition, the army produced more than 50,000 mortars during the war.[182] Overall production of artillery of all kinds increased from about 100 pieces per month in 1914 to nearly 2,000 by early 1918. Total German heavy artillery strength peaked in February 1917 at about 7,130. This included about 1,000 captured guns, mostly Russian. Losses in 1918 reduced the total to about 5,000 by the armistice. By that time, shortages of men and horses had become an even more important limitation.[183]

Gas Warfare

On 14 January 1915 two trains proceeded from Berlin to Wahn, on the western front, carrying contents labeled, in an eerie forerunner of Auschwitz, "disinfection material." Two companies of combat engineers then began training for the first important use of poison gas in the war.[184] Although the Prussian army had entered the war entirely unprepared for chemical warfare, Germany's chemical industry, the best in the world, was well suited to develop such weapons. The War Ministry began such an effort in October 1914, fearing, correctly, that the French were doing so as well.[185] Following an early unsuccessful effort to use tear gas in January 1915, the army was ready to conduct an experimental attack three months later.[186]

Although Falkenhayn and others at the High Command had legal and moral reservations about using poison gas, the exigencies of war soon provided them with reasons to rationalize its use. On 22 April 1915 the first large-scale gas attack, using chlorine, began, with the cover name "Disinfection." Although the French had been warned by deserters, their resistance quickly collapsed. The attack's success, though considerable, was purely local, since the Germans made no effort to exploit a breakthrough. These first chlorine gas clouds, dispersed by thousands of small containers, were largely dependent on the wind and thus lacked flexibility.[187] Despite the primitive means of dispersion, gas had proved its potential and became an increasingly dangerous and flexible weapon.[188]

Contrary to many later accounts, poison gas was a very effective weapon by the final year of the war. Both sides used it in nearly every major battle on the western front that year, where gas-related deaths (perhaps 91,000 in total for the war) were only part of the story. A recent review of the evidence convincingly argues that gas served a variety of purposes beyond killing enemy soldiers, from rendering trenches unusable (mustard gas) to killing horses. The real impacts were in reducing soldiers' effectiveness and in producing heavy if non-fatal casualties.[189] For a variety of reasons, developments after the war concealed gas's tactical potential in positional warfare, even as it became a key element in the visions of the prophets of airpower.

Relationship between Front and Rear

The relationship between the front units and higher headquarters varied considerably in the German army over the course of the war. Outside the western front, the more mobile nature of the war demanded the movement of higher headquarters. This was especially true during the 1915 campaigns against Russia and Serbia. During the latter campaign, for example, Mackensen's army group headquarters had to relocate three times in six weeks. Given the relatively poor state of communications at the OHL's eastern headquarters at Pless, control over higher field commanders was exercised with a very light touch. Perhaps the most important paper communication to the OHL was the memorandum written by Seeckt that outlined the idea of a summer offensive into Poland.[190]

All three *OHLs* spent the vast majority of their time on the western front.[191] Located in places that were well serviced by every means of modern communication, the *OHL* was well situated to exercise tight control over the field armies and army groups in the west. As noted earlier, commanders of army groups and armies were soon complaining about the *OHL*'s constant intrusion into their areas of responsibility.[192] This oversight included considerable amounts of administrative trivia, including reports and correspondence of all sorts. The "paper war" on the western front eventually became a serious problem for both the *OHL* and the field units. However, much of this correspondence was essential to keep the General Staff apprised of circumstances at the front and within the army. The General Staff aggressively sought reports on lessons learned from the field and used these to prepare and disseminate numerous adjustments to all kinds of doctrinal publications, technical manuals, procedures, and the like throughout the war, but especially after Ludendorff arrived at the High Command. Between February and March 1918, for example, the High Command sent 22,000 pounds of official publications to the field, about 160,000 cartons.[193] Even Ludendorff, one of the chief instigators of both valuable and questionable paperwork, occasionally complained about the "flood of paper" that burdened the units. In 1917 a single foot artillery battery reported that in a six-week period it received the following correspondence: 1,044 numbered orders and letters, 160 monthly reports, and a daily total of 10 to 12 tactical orders and 60 to 80 routine orders.[194]

The related problem of the relationship between headquarters and the front units eventually became a serious issue on the western front.[195] Trench warfare threatened army cohesion because it created a gap, at least in perception, between the men in the trenches and the headquarters and support units whose duties kept them in rear areas, far beyond the danger of the front lines.[196] The problem had two aspects: the question of whether higher headquarters were aware of the army's real circumstances and its fighting potential, and the state of morale and discipline in the front-line units (discussed separately below).

Falkenhayn certainly made numerous trips to the front units and showed an indifference to personal danger, but the problems that began during his tenure worsened by the time Hindenburg and Ludendorff took over at the *OHL*.[197] Ludendorff made strenuous attempts to encourage General Staff officers at all levels to maintain close contact with their front-line units. An order of 22 April 1917 recognized that General Staff officers were not going to the front to see the combat zones for themselves and maintaining close personal contact with the units and their commanders. "During battle," he instructed his subordinates, "the General Staff officer belongs beside his commander; in the periods of preparation he belongs at the front as much as and as often as possible." He closed with the admonition that he expected business to be conducted this way in the future and that the chiefs of staff at the army groups and field armies would see to it.[198] Throughout the war, the General Staff continued its practice of rotating General Staff officers between field units and staff positions, although this frequently proved impossible under the pressures of continuing combat and shortages of trained staff officers.[199] After the war, when the alleged problem of *Frontfremdheit* (literally, being a stranger to the front) became a serious point of criticism, senior officers insisted that no such problem had ever existed. One argued that, in his experience, commanders and General Staff officers had visited their front-line units several times a week.[200] Nevertheless, Ludendorff clearly recognized that "frequently the higher staffs appear to have too little personal contact with the units."[201] Wilhelm Groener, writing after the war, conceded that the divisions had lost contact with higher commanders and that this problem extended all the way to the emperor. He placed ultimate responsibility on the nature of positional warfare.[202]

Discipline and Morale

There is no doubt that the German army's discipline suffered over the course of the war, but the extent to which this affected the war's outcome is unclear. The war at first obscured but then quickly accentuated the fundamental divide between social classes in the army. After the war, critics alleged that the privileged officer class had abused or at least alienated much of the army's enlisted force and that the resulting *Offizierhass* (hatred of officers) had been a major factor in eroding the army's fighting power.[203] There is no doubt that a combination of war weariness, Allied military superiority, personal resentments of various kinds, and disappointment over the failure of the 1918 offensive had seriously reduced the army's morale by mid-1918. It is likewise certain that the army's legendary discipline declined during the war and reached crisis proportions by the beginning of armistice discussions in October 1918. Beyond that, much is still in dispute.

Although German officers died in larger proportions than did enlisted men, the fact that they maintained their prewar social superiority and privileges was an important part of the army's morale and discipline problems.[204] Officers enjoyed better living quarters (except in the most forward positions), superior rations, and enhanced opportunities to receive decorations than did enlisted soldiers.[205] The shortages of food that afflicted the civilian population extended to the front by 1918. Front-line soldiers complained that rations were unsatisfactory in both quantity and quality and that the distribution system gave officers many advantages.[206] Looting of captured Allied magazines was a serious problem during the 1918 offensive.[207]

The influx of new officers into both regular units and the new divisions formed during the war may have made these problems worse. Lacking the socialization and experience of their prewar counterparts, many new officers could not deal with the problems of their soldiers.[208] By spring 1915, the shortage of experienced officers and the inadequacy of their replacements had become obvious to senior leaders.[209] This issue is revisited in a later section of this chapter.

Corruption of the army's system for awarding medals for bravery during combat both cheapened the honor of those who deserved recognition and created another gap between officers and enlisted men. Excessive and undeserved promotions and awards for senior officers had long been a hallmark of Wilhelm II's reign. Helmuth von Moltke, for example, commented in 1909 that whereas his uncle had needed a victorious campaign to win the Schwarz-Adler award, epigones such as himself required only three days of maneuvers.[210] The first large-scale distribution of wartime medals began during the Verdun campaign and continued for the remainder of the war. For example, the army passed out more than 3 million Iron Crosses, including some to civilians in Germany. This well-intentioned effort to build solidarity merely created widespread contempt on the part of front-line soldiers for those in the rear who had not earned combat awards. As the Austrian representative at the OHL noted, many officers joked sarcastically that only suicide would prevent one from receiving the Iron Cross Second Class.[211]

Enlisted men especially resented officers who received undeserved awards or who recommended awards for unworthy persons, such as their personal aides who had never seen combat. The nearly universal awarding of the Iron Cross to rear-area staff officers was particularly offensive.[212] Others blamed officers for allegedly sending enlisted men to their deaths so that commanders could win medals for their battlefield successes.[213] Regardless of the possible exaggerated nature of such accusations, the army never remedied the abuses in the awarding of decorations. Enlisted men properly felt that the army rewarded too many officers and not enough of those in the ranks.[214]

Military Justice

Throughout the war the Prussian army's disciplinary procedures were anything but harsh, and they did little to deter unauthorized absences or even desertion to Allied lines. Germany's military legal code, established in 1872 and amended by the controversial reforms of Chancellor Chlodwig Hohenlone-Schillingsfürst in 1897, accorded accused soldiers many of the rights and procedures of civil law.[215] Death sentences played no significant role in German military justice either before or during the war, and even the punishment for desertion was relatively mild.[216] The German army executed fewer than 50 soldiers during the First World War for all causes, including about 40 for offenses associated with disobedience to orders, desertion, mutiny, or assault on a superior.[217] The British and French armies, by contrast, together executed 3 officers and 347 enlisted men.[218] During the course of the war, leniency was, in effect, built into the military justice system in part because it could not adjust to the demands of massive and lengthy combat. One scholar has identified four main characteristics of the military justice system that produced leniency even in serious cases: (1) the system was slow to begin proceedings, (2) many judges had no front-line experience and were sympathetic to the accused, (3) the complicated rules offered defendants ample room for maneuver, and (4) the punishments themselves were lenient.[219] The army's historical office later concluded that in July 1918 the High Command demanded that units enforce the death penalty in appropriate cases to deter other serious breaches of discipline.[220] By 1918, there were serious disciplinary problems as tens of thousands of soldiers took various routes to avoid the front lines.[221] Many of them, including former prisoners returning from Russia, were in no mood to return to battle in the western trenches.[222] About 10 percent of the men transferred from the eastern to the western front in 1918 deserted.[223] By late summer and into the autumn, such problems multiplied as the hope of ending the war in the great offensive of 1918 faded. Even so, desertion never became a serious threat to the army's total numbers. Christoph Jahr's calculations clearly show that only a small percentage of the army's 13.5 million soldiers deserted over the course of the war.[224] Even minorities such as the Alsatians, over whom the army kept an especially watchful eye, did not desert in disproportionate numbers until late in the war.[225] In August the General Staff issued an order warning of the necessity to tighten discipline and even impose the death penalty for cowardice in the face of the enemy. An order in July had instructed officers to use their weapons if necessary when men refused to participate in attacks.[226] Thousands of soldiers, perhaps hundreds of thousands, had created chaos in parts of the army's rear areas by autumn.[227] Some critics blamed this on the lax enforcement of discipline and the routine imposition of lenient punishments, but the declining circumstances of the army and its prospects for victory were obviously the real culprits.[228] One important aspect of dealing with these problems was the vast change in the nature of the officer corps between August 1914 and the end of the battles at Verdun and on the Somme in 1916.

Replacing the Junior Officer Corps

The German army, like the armies of France and England, suffered devastating officer casualties in the opening weeks of combat in August 1914. As early as September, Colmar von der Goltz, then governor of Belgium, warned the Military Cabinet that some of his battalions had only two officers. Noncommissioned officers had taken the place of fallen officers, but Goltz's request to commission some of them fell on deaf ears at the Military Cabinet.[229] The Prussian army, according to Volkmann, entered the war with about 22,000 active and 29,000 reserve officers. New commissions granted between August 1914 and mid-November 1915 totaled about 7,500 and 52,500, respectively. Of these newly commissioned men, about 5,600 and 7,560, respectively, had been killed by the middle of November 1915, with many more wounded. By late June 1915, for example, the Kaiser Alexander Guards Regiment had suffered 100 percent turnover in its officer corps.[230] General Hans von Zwehl, using archival material now lost, calculated that about 40 percent of the regular officer corps of 1914 had been killed by the armistice and that about one-quarter of the newly commissioned regular officers had met the same fate.[231] Volkmann also estimated that the army had a total of 45,000 regular and 226,000 reserve officers during the war. Ludendorff's statement that 80 to 90 percent of the prewar officers had become casualties by 1918 may not have been much of an exaggeration.[232] Constantin von Altrock estimated that at least 90,000 officers from all the German contingents were wounded during the war.[233] Many of them, of course, returned to duty at the front, but many others did not.

By 1916, the old officer corps was no longer serving in the army's company-level units, with only rare exceptions. Regular officers had filled vacancies in the staffs and other higher positions in the old and newly created regiments, divisions, and so forth. By 1917, even many battalion command positions were held by reserve officers, an unthinkable proposition in peacetime.[234] The old Prussian officer corps had nearly ceased to exist at the levels at which officers directly commanded soldiers in training and combat.[235] Commanders and high staff officers noted the critical shortage of regular officers and the consequent weakening of the army.[236] The General Staff, responsible for conducting the war, had little influence over the army's personnel matters, which continued to rest with the ultraconservative, not to say reactionary, Military Cabinet. That institution was unwilling to make any fundamental changes in the commissioning process that might undermine the aristocratic and "old Prussian" nature of the officer corps. The changes the Military Cabinet and the emperor did authorize merely reinforced the army's traditional social policies. As one author has demonstrated, the army made numerous changes in the selection and training of potential officers and noncommissioned officers to serve as substitute officers, but it did little if anything to broaden the social base of the junior officer corps until the emergency situations of 1918.[237] The army's 5 December 1916 decision to transfer many cavalry officers to the infantry provided the latter branch with a small number of new officers, as had a previous decision to abolish superfluous positions in the dirigible program.[238]

This crisis, though more severe than anyone had foreseen, was not entirely unexpected. Realizing that the army would soon be short of officers, war minister Falkenhayn and the chief of the Military Cabinet initiated a series of changes to personnel policies in August 1914. The army offered to reinstate officers it had previously dismissed (either by military courts or courts of honor) for minor legal or social infractions, leaving individual decisions to the newly appointed substitute corps commanders in Germany.[239] New applicants for commissions were to be judged by the traditional standards of "worthiness" and social background. In September Wilhelm II made minor changes to speed the process for granting reserve commissions to enlisted men who had distinguished themselves in combat and whose social backgrounds were suitable for regular officers in peacetime. This, in effect, raised the standards for granting commissions to enlisted men. The regimental-based officer election principle remained in force for the granting of regular commissions.[240] A subsequent order of the Military Cabinet in December also stressed the consideration of social background in any personnel actions.[241] In fact, the army promoted very few enlisted men to the officer corps during the war, perhaps as few as 150 altogether.[242]

Other measures followed, but most had the effect of ensuring that the army's traditional basis of officer selection and promotion (social class and seniority, as well as ability) would endure after the temporary interruption of the war. The Prussian officer corps, much like the American army during the Vietnam era, was not willing to abandon the principles of its officer personnel system for such a minor event as war. On 1 September 1914 the Military Cabinet promoted all officer candidates to lieutenant and ordered a combing-out of staffs for officers to be sent to units at the front. The emperor and the Military Cabinet assured all officers that temporary assignments would not compromise the seniority lists and that special assignments were only a wartime measure. The War Ministry authorized the deputy corps commanders to use up to five civilians to replace adjutants who had gone to deployed units. Finally, as foreseen prior to the war, the army created the special rank of sergeant-lieutenant (*Feldwebelleutnant*) to give capable enlisted men the responsibilities of junior officers without granting them commissions.[243]

Training the army's new lieutenants was a great challenge under the conditions of continual combat and expansion in the number of units. The destruction of the archives makes an evaluation of the commission and training processes difficult. New active-duty officers spent three months in a replacement unit, three months in a front unit, and three months in the officer candidate course at Döberitz. If they passed the examination, they returned to their field units for various periods and then received commissions if their commanders and unit officers approved. A separate course for reserve officer candidates provided similar training for those not eligible for or not seeking regular commissions.[244]

Concluding Remarks

Once the initial war plans and campaigns miscarried in 1914, both sides had to reconsider their strategy. For the *Kaiserreich*, this was particularly difficult, as there was no overarching power that could successfully integrate the various elements of the German military and government. Wilhelm II, already self-limited by his prewar promise not to involve himself in military matters, could give only passive support to Falkenhayn. This meant that the direction of the German war effort throughout 1915 and 1916 was marked by a constant struggle between the two principal centers of power: the *OHL* and the *Ober Ost*. Although Falkenhayn prevailed in 1915, Hindenburg and Ludendorff, as well as their supporters in the civilian government, waged a relentless campaign against him. The kaiser's impotence was revealed by his reaction to Hindenburg's highhanded resignation threat in January 1915, which was nothing more than the utterance of imprecations. Frankly, it is difficult to imagine Wilhelm I standing for Hindenburg's behavior or, for that matter, Hindenburg even contemplating such an action.

Falkenhayn's conduct of the war was a mixture of shrewd insight and false assumptions. His judgment that Britain was the true center of gravity of the alliance was correct. The decisions to mount operations in Galicia and against Serbia were as necessary as they were astute. Falkenhayn correctly judged that the parlous condition of Austria-Hungary required an attack with major forces in Galicia, although some of his closest associates such as Wild and Tappen were skeptical.[245] Likewise, Turkey's isolated condition necessitated that Bulgaria be added to the Central Powers and that Serbia be overrun if a secure land route was to be established. Given the successes won on the eastern front and in Serbia, plus the Turkish victories over the British at Gallipoli and Kut and the failed Anglo-French offensives on the western front, 1915 marked the high point of success for the Central Powers.

Despite these successes, Falkenhayn's position as head of the *OHL* rested on shaky foundations. His direction of German strategy was hindered by the fact that he was operating with slim resources. There were instances when Falkenhayn argued with the *Ober Ost* or with Conrad over the disposition of small, lightly armed units such as individual cavalry divisions, reserve divisions, brigades, or even *Landwehr* organizations.[246] The unremitting campaign of the *Ober Ost*, abetted by many in the government, including Chancellor Bethmann-Hollweg, left Falkenhayn with no room for error, a circumstance that came true in August 1916. Also, the victories won were important, but none was of decisive importance. The major advances on the eastern front eliminated the prospect of a Russian invasion of Austria-Hungary and permanently neutralized any threat to East Prussia. The impact on the Russians, however, was transitory in nature. Although the great retreat led to the replacement of Russian commander in chief Grand Duke Nikolai by Tsar Nicholas II, and although the Russian army suffered immense losses of men and equipment, the army was not eliminated. It would recover, and far more quickly than expected by either the Germans or the Austro-Hungarians.[247]

The victory over Serbia was likewise indecisive. Mackensen could truthfully report that he had completed the mission assigned to him at Allenstein on 16 September 1915: the Serbian army had been defeated, and a land route to Turkey had been opened.[248] The remnants of the Serbian army and the government, however, had escaped to the Adriatic coast. By June 1916, the Army of the Orient at Salonika was bolstered by the arrival of six refitted Serbian divisions. This force, though quiescent for a long time, was a beacon for Serbian nationalists in occupied Serbia.[249]

The victories in 1915 also revealed underlying strains in the Central Powers over postwar goals. The disagreements between Austria-Hungary and Bulgaria over occupied Serbia and between Austria-Hungary and Germany over the Balkans were noted earlier. In the case of the latter, Conrad's actions after Serbia's occupation proved to be the final straw in the complete breakdown in relations between him and Falkenhayn. Disagreements between the dual monarchy and the *Kaiserreich* also cropped up with regard to Poland, beginning with dissension over the manner in which the Central Powers entered Warsaw. After that, matters went from bad to worse as German and Austro-Hungarian military and diplomatic authorities disagreed over the status of Poland after the war, while the Poles had their own ideas.[250]

Falkenhayn's idea that Britain was the main enemy was a shrewd insight, but he lacked the means of carrying the fight to the British, especially after he concluded that the British position in Flanders could not be assaulted. The High Seas Fleet had its one moment of tactical and technical splendor at Jutland, but then it retired to strategic irrelevance. The naval fight against Britain would have to be carried out using the distinctly unsatisfactory method of submarines and the rules of prize warfare against merchant shipping. The chief of the Admiralty Staff, Admiral Henning von Holtzendorff, wanted to mount an operation against the Baltic Islands in late 1915, but Falkenhayn would have none of it.[251] Opposing the British was also the principal reason for bringing Ottoman Turkey into the Central Powers. Although the performance of the Turkish army was a pleasant surprise, using it to carry the fight to the British was the second-best option for Falkenhayn.

Having run through his options and cleared the decks, Falkenheyn came up with the rather peculiar idea that the best way to fight Britain was by mounting an operation against France. His underlying assumptions were optimistic to the point of delusional. Falkenhayn believed he could fight a controlled battle of attrition in which the French suffered the vast majority of the casualties. In addition, Falkenhayn apparently believed the British would stand idle while this took place.[252]

Falkenhayn's assumptions were proved invalid even before the attack began, and he had to accede to the demands of Crown Prince Wilhelm and his chief of staff, Konstantin Schmidt von Knobelsdorf, for a larger assault force. Although Falkenhayn was right in assuming that the French would react strongly to an attack on Verdun, he clearly underestimated the depth of French resistance and its effectiveness. Joffre and General Phillippe Petain were able to employ French artillery to devastating effect, while also devising an excellent supply system.[253] Although the Somme offensive got off to a bad start, it also inflicted heavy casualties on the Germans, magnified by the policy of holding every inch of ground. The combination of failure at Verdun and heavy losses on the Somme under-mined Falkenhayn's position at the *OHL*. Romania's entry into the war proved to be the proverbial straw that broke the camel's back with regard to Falkenhayn's position.

While changes were occurring at the top of the German army, they were happening at the lower end as well. The pace of losses was hav-ing a profound effect on the German army in a number of ways. The Queen Elisabeth Guards Regiment, like the Kaiser Alexander Regiment, had suffered 100 percent turnover in officers. By August 1915, seven of the Elisabeth Regiment's companies were commanded by non-noble offi-cers. Several of them had reserve commissions, an almost unimaginable circumstance in the prewar army. The bloodletting of Verdun and the Somme simply completed the process begun by the onset of war: destruc-tion of the prewar army.[254]

By the end of 1916, Germany was in a perilous situation. Although Ro-mania had been brought to heel by the operational and tactical brilliance of Mackensen and Falkenhayn, the western front was another matter. The line opposite the BEF had been stabilized as both sides fell into mutual exhaustion, but Verdun was an unmitigated failure. Although Jutland was arguably a tactical success, it was a strategic failure, and the British block-ade continued to strangle the Germany economy. As 1916 turned into 1917, the operative word for Germany was "new." The war would have to be fought by a new army with new tactics and under a new *OHL*, with Germany's most popular hero at the helm.

Austro-Hungarian emperor Francis Joseph (right). Next to him is Archduke Franz Ferdinand, the heir to the throne before his ill-fated visit to Sarajevo on 28 June 1914. (National Archives)

Coalition warfare: Mackensen visiting an Austro-Hungarian unit. (Bain Collection, Library of Congress)

Enver Pasha, leader of the Young Turk movement and commander of Ottoman Turkey's armies. The former Turkish military attaché to Germany, Enver was fluent in German. (Bain Collection, Library of Congress)

Conrad von Hötzendorf, pondering war and perhaps his impending marriage. (National Archives)

Austrian archduke Friedrich, nominal commander of the Austro-Hungarian army and Conrad von Hötzendorf's boss. (National Archives)

CHAPTER NINE

THE THIRD *OHL* STRATEGIC AND

TACTICAL CHANGE, 1917–1918

The events of 1916 created a major crisis for Germany. Jutland, although tactically satisfying for the High Seas Fleet, failed to alter the strategic circumstances of the naval war. The combination of the failure at Verdun, the heavy losses on the Somme, and the crisis on the eastern front created by the Brusilov offensive and Romania's opportunistic entry into the war led to the deposing of Falkenhayn as head of the Second *OHL*, as detailed in the previous chapter. A number of people both in the government and at the court pressed Wilhelm II to turn to the most popular duo in Germany: Hindenburg and Ludendorff.

Hindenburg and Ludendorff, 1916–1918

In the area of strategy, the advent of the Third *OHL*, as the Hindenburg-Ludendorff team became known, had a number of fateful consequences.[1] Deeply committed to total military victory, the new team rejected all efforts to limit war aims and military efforts designed to reach a negotiated peace.[2] Instead, the new *OHL* became much more aggressive in political affairs and soon achieved nearly total military domination of the conflict in an effort to see the war through to victory at any cost. The arrival of Hindenburg, who was already a mythical figure, produced a renewed faith in Germany's prospects for victory in both the army and the civilian population. Hopes ran extraordinarily high that the victor of Tannenberg could achieve an even larger military success, regardless of the weakness of the foundations for such hopes. So great was the respect for Hindenburg that some argued that if worse came to worst, an unsatisfactory peace would be more acceptable under Hindenburg than under Falkenhayn.[3] Even the army's enlisted men had great confidence in Hindenburg and Ludendorff at the outset of their time in the *OHL*.[4]

Ludendorff was the central figure in the new *OHL*. His dominant will and powerful but limited intellect found their full expression, and he soon became the most important individual on the German side in the war. As Gerhard Ritter noted, Hindenburg's signature on documents authored or shaped by Ludendorff was "no more than a mere matter of form."[5] By 1917, Ludendorff no longer required the chief of staff's signature on anything but the most important documents. Decisions normally rested with Ludendorff.

The duo "reoriented German strategy, diplomacy, and domestic policy."[6] They also reinvigorated the war effort on land by accelerating changes in tactics, both offensive and defensive, and by intensifying the army's training and drive for efficiency. In the fall of 1916 they convinced the emperor to replace war minister Adolf Wild von Hohenborn with Hermann von Stein, who faithfully implemented most of their programs in the domestic and armaments arenas. In January 1917 they succeeded in bludgeoning Bethmann-Hollweg into accepting unrestricted submarine warfare. To support all this, they pushed the government into adopting the "Hindenburg program," a rash and ultimately counterproductive effort to mobilize the nation's entire material resources in a ruthless expansion of the production of munitions and weapons. To gin up public support, the duumvirate employed a major propaganda campaign aimed at the German civilian population. Hindenburg and Ludendorff thus committed the nation to military triumph at any price and sought a victory that conquest alone could produce. The policies put in place to achieve that conquest are now examined in turn.

Unrestricted Submarine Warfare

The most controversial of Ludendorff's decisions was the turn to unrestricted submarine warfare, a dismal tale that has been related many times. One study called it the "worst decision of the war."[7] The German navy began the war without any comprehensive study of the effects of a commerce war on England, but it soon began to look into the matter.[8] Although a new epoch in naval warfare began on 22 September 1914, when a German U-boat sank three English cruisers off the Dutch coast, the first discussions of a submarine blockade against England in September and October 1914 came to nothing because of a crippling shortage of U-boats.[9] In August 1914 the German navy had twenty-four submarines (actually submersibles), a number that rose to twenty-nine by year's end. They sank a mere three commercial vessels by the end of December. Germany adopted unrestricted submarine warfare in February 1915, with poor results. By the end of August, the twenty-seven available submarines had managed to sink only twenty-one England-bound ships, one of which was the *Lusitania*. The kaiser, influenced by Bethmann-Hollweg and moderate naval leaders who feared that President Woodrow Wilson's protests would lead to American entry into the war, ordered a cessation of the campaign on 18 September 1915.[10] Falkenhayn, originally opposed to unrestricted submarine warfare, reconsidered his position around Christmas 1915. Bethmann-Hollweg successfully resisted this, however, and Wilhelm agreed. Admiral Tirpitz resigned in March 1916, when the kaiser again declined to approve a resumption of unrestricted submarine warfare, and the Verdun campaign began without it.[11]

When Hindenburg and Ludendorff took over the *OHL* in September, they sensibly opposed the immediate adoption of unrestricted submarine warfare because, under the circumstances, Germany could not afford to add new enemies, particularly the United States. They decided to wait at least until the end of the campaign in Romania.[12] Legal questions played little if any role in discussions of submarine warfare, but it should be noted that moral and legal rectitude did not reside entirely on the Allied side, considering the nature of the British blockade of Germany.[13] As summer gave way to autumn, Tirpitz's successor, Admiral Henning von Holtzendorff, renewed the push for naval expansion and a submarine campaign. Radical nationalists, Pan-Germans, and other extremists soon joined in demanding all-out attacks on commercial targets.[14] The successful offensive against Romania in December 1916 removed the *OHL*'s last reservations, and on 8 December Hindenburg joined the navalists in demanding the removal of all restrictions on Germany's submarines.[15]

Regardless of whether one accepts the argument that this decision made American entry into the war and ultimate German defeat inevitable, it was certainly a fateful decision. The irony was that Ludendorff, who had long been demanding massive efforts on the eastern front, pushed for a measure that added a very powerful enemy but provided no immediate assistance against Russia. Bethmann-Hollweg, who still had the emperor's confidence, finally gave in on 9 January 1917, probably in the belief that this was the last chance to win the war. He was also no doubt discouraged by the failure of his latest proposals for negotiations.[16] These failed because of both the nature of his demands (which were moderate in comparison with prior and later goals) and the Allies' outright refusal to consider anything short of surrender.[17] His reward was a renewed effort by Hindenburg to convince the emperor to dismiss him. Germany's reward was war with the United States.[18]

This fateful decision seems especially foolish in light of the unimpressive results expected and the even more meager results achieved. Holt-zendorff hoped that the renewed unrestricted campaign would sink about 600,000 tons of Allied shipping per month. By late 1916, cruiser-type attacks were sinking about 350,000 to 400,000 tons a month, leaving an anticipated gain of a mere 200,000 tons as the booty for provoking American intervention. Based on this, the navalists hoped to induce the British to conclude a peace.[19] The campaign rarely achieved its monthly goal, and by September, sinkings were fewer than in late 1916. The Allies defeated the U-boats by a combination of convoys, mine warfare, aerial patrolling, expanded food production in England, increased ship construction, and rationing.[20] The German navy's hope for success had rested in large part on the anticipated psychological reaction in both Britain and neutral countries, but this, too, proved ephemeral.[21]

The irony was that the collapse of the tsarist regime a month after the Germans announced their decision created the long-sought opportunity to end the war in the east on favorable terms. Ludendorff had long seen such an eventuality as an opportunity to both expand war aims in the east and shift the bulk of the army for the war's decisive battle in the west. By mid-1917, then, the German position might have been quite favorable, with Russia out of the war, the United States remaining neutral, and Germany able to attack the Western Allies with all available forces.[22] In this context, the decision for unrestricted submarine warfare was both premature and foolish.

To others, the decision to adopt unrestricted submarine warfare is evidence of the triumph of technical military matters over political considerations, with catastrophic results—allegedly a predominant characteristic of German strategy in general. Actually, the decision followed logically from the political and military circumstances as they were known at the time. Ludendorff could not have predicted the imminent collapse of the tsar's government. He did recognize, however, on the basis of very concrete evidence, that the "war of material" in the west could not go on forever and that the army had insufficient means to strike a decisive blow against England and France. From the days of the elder Moltke through Schlieffen, the younger Moltke, and even Falkenhayn, German military leaders assumed that the nation could not win a long war on two fronts. Both the results of the English blockade and the emergence of positional warfare across the western front reinforced the view that Allied material superiority would eventually prevail unless a decisive blow could be struck. In discussing the decision for unrestricted submarine warfare, historians should consider the impact of the Somme fighting and the Allies' emerging ability to dictate the nature of the so-called material battle on the western front. The decision for unrestricted submarine warfare was, therefore, a fateful and ill-considered gamble, but not necessarily a completely baseless or irrational act of narrow military chauvinism.[23] The decision did not ignore political considerations; rather, it rested on a wide range of political, economic, and military factors, including war aims and possible annexations. That the navy, the chancellor, and the chief of the General Staff were entirely wrong in their estimates of the campaign's success and impact is another question.

Russia's Collapse and the Treaty of Brest Litovsk

The culmination of the Brusilov offensive and the defeat of the Romanian army in late 1916 brought the eastern front back to a condition of stasis. The imperial Russian army had made its last effort. By early 1917, the entire tsarist regime was in a state of near collapse. Even as early as January 1917 there were instances of soldiers refusing to attack.[24] The prospect of full revolution became real on 8 March 1917, when a women's protest over shortages of bread and coal in Petrograd resulted in Russian Guards Corps infantrymen refusing orders to fire on them. The disorder quickly spread and overwhelmed the spent tsarist government. Within a week, the Romanov dynasty, which had ruled Russia for three centuries, was no more.[25]

The position of the provisional government, headed by Alexander Kerensky, was that it would continue the war, at least defensively. In an ill-conceived effort to restore discipline to the army, in June 1917 Kerensky ordered an offensive against the part of the front held by the Austro-Hungarians. The attack enjoyed initial success, but it was fleeting. Within days, the attack had broken down completely under the weight of desertions and German counterattacks. The line of the Central Powers advanced some sixty miles.[26]

The final actions on the eastern front took place at the northern end of the front. On 1 September 1917 German forces seized Riga, after unveiling new tactics (discussed later in this chapter). The last action occurred in October 1917, when the German army and navy executed the most successful amphibious operation of the war. A navy armada of 300 ships, including 10 battleships wrested from the High Seas Fleet, and XXIII Reserve Corps' 24,000 men (in reality, a heavily reinforced 42nd Infantry

Division), sailed from Libau on 11 October 1917. Arriving off the island of Ösel the next morning, the Germans landed and seized the three Baltic islands of Ösel, Moon, and Dagö.[27]

The sudden fall of the tsarist regime gave the *OHL* an opportunity to finally wind up matters on the eastern front. To facilitate the prospect of a separate peace, the German government arranged the passage of noted revolutionary Vladimir Lenin from Switzerland to Petrograd. Lenin, who had publicly stated the desire to take Russia out of the war, immediately tried to undermine the provisional government. By the autumn of 1917, the provisional government, weakened by the terrible economy and self-inflicted wounds, was teetering. On the night of 6–7 November 1917 Lenin and his Bolsheviks gave it a final shove, overthrowing the government and seizing power.

Once in power, Lenin immediately sought to extricate Russia from the war. What followed was a negotiation between Leon Trotsky and *Ober Ost* chief of staff Max Hoffmann that can only be described as bizarre. After Trotsky walked out, saying that Russia would follow a policy of "no peace, no war," the *OHL* ordered the resumption of offensive operations. On 3 March 1918 Lenin ordered Trotsky to agree to Germany's terms. The Treaty of Brest Litovsk was followed by the Treaty of Bucharest in May 1918, which officially took Romania out of the war.

The two treaties satisfied all the desires of the annexationists in Germany, including Ludendorff. Germany gained vast new territories in what had been Russia's Baltic provinces. Ideally, the treaties were designed to provide the Central Powers with all the food and raw material needed to continue the war and meet Germany's domestic needs. In reality, the treaties were signed too late to make a difference. Disagreements between Germany and Austria-Hungary over Poland, as well as violations of the economic clauses, only furthered the unraveling of the alliance. Finally, the territorial gains required large commitments of manpower, 250,000 Austro-Hungarian and 500,000 German soldiers, to garrison them.[28] The "easterners" had achieved their victory.

The Hindenburg Program

Hindenburg's first major act upon replacing Falkenhayn was to launch a new effort to increase war production drastically. He succeeded in pushing through a number of internal changes to streamline industrial production and labor management. A new office, the *Allgemeine Kriegsamt* (Supreme

War Office) under Wilhelm Groener, supervised nearly the entire effort to mobilize the nation's industrial resources. Though technically an element of the War Ministry, Groener's empire worked directly for the *OHL*.[29] The Hindenburg-Ludendorff team also proposed, and the Reichstag passed (on 5 December 1916), the Auxiliary Service Law to mobilize the nation's manpower. Hindenburg saw these measures, conceived by Colonel Max Bauer and Ludendorff, as an effort to restructure German society for "total war." The programs envisioned compulsory work for men under age sixty who were not employed in the armed services, extension of service obligations to age sixty, a vast increase in the mobilization of women, curtailment of nonessential work, exploitation of foreign labor, and a restructuring of labor-management relationships and industrial pricing.[30]

Overall, the Hindenburg program and related measures were counterproductive failures. They were also unnecessary. Vast increases in the production of rifles, machine guns, and artillery were largely achieved before the Hindenburg program could accomplish anything. The program failed to rationalize or efficiently control production costs, profits, or wages. It was essentially a surrender to industrial interests rather than a forced rationalization of the war effort. Personnel displacement caused serious manpower problems both in the army and in the factories. Even the Reichsarchiv concluded that the program did not significantly increase the production of what was really needed and could be effectively used, given the lack of critical raw materials and shortage of transport capacity at the front.[31]

Propaganda

German efforts to use censorship and propaganda to control the war's image at home began in October 1914 and intensified as the war progressed. The deputy commanding generals supervised the censorship programs in their districts, while various government officials, both civilian and military, held frequent press conferences in Berlin to publicize the official news accounts of the war. In practice, the war minister's inability to control the deputy commanding generals meant that the government did not achieve uniform standards in controlling local press commentaries on the war.[32] The primary concern here was the effort to use propaganda to maintain the army's fighting spirit, a challenge that became acute as the war effort faltered under the dual pressures of Verdun and the British offensive on the Somme.[33]

Hindenburg and Ludendorff dealt with problems of morale and discipline by launching a campaign to increase soldiers' motivation, the infamous program of "patriotic instruction" (*vaterländischer Unterricht*). In a memorandum of 29 July 1917 Ludendorff recognized that a number of the field armies had already created organizations to instill patriotism in the enlisted men and stated his intention to create a unified organization for all such activity. The memorandum defined five essential areas of instruction: (1) causes of the war, (2) the scale of German successes and confidence in victory, (3) the necessity and significance of leadership and the need for authority and subordination, (4) the necessity of enduring economic and other hardships, and (5) an understanding that Germany's enemies would attempt to use peace negotiations to rob Germany of the fruits of victory.[34] Another office, the Military Bureau of the Foreign Office, took charge of foreign propaganda and collected reports to be made available within Germany.[35]

Over the next seventeen months, the program expanded widely as the *OHL*, the War Ministry, and various commands established the specific nature of "patriotic instruction" and its subjects.[36] An order of the acting commander of XIX Corps on 15 December 1917 was probably representative. The commanding general distinguished among young recruits, veterans, and wounded soldiers. Instruction for the first group would use tales of heroism to create enthusiasm for fatherland, freedom, comradeship, loyalty, obedience, and courage. Instruction for older enlisted men would stress the army's understanding of their difficult financial circumstances and the social circumstances of the war. Instruction for wounded soldiers would take note of their need for recovery. Specific themes for all three groups were as one might expect: German culture and the value of its diversity; responsibility for the war; Germany's past victories and future prospects; acceptance of economic hardships; valuing the qualities of Germany's land, geography, and people; and satisfaction with constitutional and legal issues. Significantly, only the subject of war aims was banned.[37]

One would expect the resulting massive campaign to be one-sided and its "instruction" nationalistic, but it went to extremes that remind one of the crass nature of modern governmental propaganda. Its content ranged from silliness (warning German women against having sex with Allied prisoners) to moral self-righteousness (based on alleged Allied atrocities). Along the way, it waved the flag of the Pan-German annexationists, despite the official prohibition against such subjects.[38]

By all accounts, the program accomplished little. The soldiers responded with indifference at best, while many in the Reichstag denounced the entire effort. Volkmann and Groener, no social democrats, both later wrote that the program in general and the Pan-German propaganda woven into it were futile at best and counterproductive at worst. Some commanders simply refused to participate on the scale Ludendorff demanded.[39] This does not mean that the army's morale collapsed because of the futility of patriotic instruction. On the contrary, the army's morale and fighting spirit remained high until the combination of increasingly difficult physical circumstances and failure of the 1918 offensive caused a broad collapse in the summer of 1918.

Hindenburg and Ludendorff devoted a great deal of effort to implementing policies to shape Germany's society, economy, and political order. All this, however, was of a piece. The principal problem for the new *OHL* was the same one that had flummoxed the Second *OHL*—namely, how to halt the battle of material, restore mobility to the battlefield, and achieve that elusive victory on the western front. This goal became even more imperative once the failure of unrestricted submarine warfare ensured that the United States would commit large numbers of men in the near future.

The Shortcomings Revealed in 1914

After the German offensive ebbed on the Marne, and as the so-called race to the sea failed to produce new flanks to be exploited in the mobile battles anticipated in the prewar doctrines of both sides, the tools of siege warfare gradually replaced fire and movement as the primary means of combat in the western theater. Ironically, in view of subsequent developments, the French and British were the first to question the tactical assumptions of 1914, whereas the Germans tended to attribute the failure of their opening offensive to prewar armaments policies and the shortcomings of the man who had borne the responsibility for its execution. Even after the war, many knowledgeable officers maintained that senior commanders, not tactics, were the culprits in 1914.[40]

The simple fact was that despite devoting a great deal of time and effort to preparing for war, the army had fallen short in several critical respects. These included the effectiveness of the army reserve component, especially in terms of individual soldiers; poor training for reserve officers; haphazard tactical performance; and a failure to coordinate the actions of infantry and artillery.

Training Deficiencies

One of the problems in preparing the German army for war in 1914 was that it, like most of its friends and enemies, was a cadre army dependent on reservists, particularly reserve officers, for much of its tactical performance. In 1914, for example, a typical full-strength regular unit had only a few more active soldiers (54 percent) than newly assigned reservists (46 percent). Reserve units had active officers in all ranks above captain, but these made up only about 1 percent of the unit's total strength.[41] The units that went to war were thus quite different from those that participated in peacetime training. The massive influx of reservists into mobilizing units may have robbed many battalions of any finesse and in some cases may have reduced tactics to massed headlong attacks.[42]

The prewar training cycle itself made unit-level training difficult. After the autumn maneuvers, and after the departure of soldiers completing their second year of active duty and any temporarily activated reservists, the training challenges of the company commander became critical. The need to repair equipment, maintain buildings, and train draftees in the most basic military skills left the commander with no unit to train in company-level tactics. This situation persisted well into the next year, and even then, companies and battalions trained with just over half their wartime strength. This made realistic practice in tactical formations difficult, particularly in the areas of maintaining distances within skirmish lines and accustoming junior officers to the difficulties of controlling their units.[43] Otto von Moser's 1914 handbook warned of the danger of conducting training with platoons and companies at peacetime strength because, once these units deployed in combat with their full complements of soldiers, they tended to be too tightly bunched together.[44]

More serious were the training shortcomings of the reservists. Although every reservist was obligated to undergo two training sessions of up to eight weeks each year, and every *Landwehr* soldier up to fourteen days of training, as a practical matter, financial issues curtailed training in the majority of cases. This fact, usually overlooked by historians, meant that most reserve soldiers, in either the reserve units or the *Landwehr*, actually had only about half the training the formal programs required.[45] Men who were not called to military duty went into the *Ersatz* reserve, to be used as replacements in wartime. But only a fraction of these men, perhaps as few as 3 percent, had been to the units for training or field exercises.[46]

Most command positions—indeed, virtually all ranks above captain—

were reserved for officers of the active army, but reserve officers dominated numerically at the lower levels, particularly in the reserve and *Landwehr* units. As a result, reserve officers were more important in the battles of 1914 than most writers recognize, and from 1915 on, they were the real combat leaders.

Numerous military writers had warned before the war that reserve officers were not sufficiently trained to lead their units in wartime. It may be, as one noted historian has argued, that reserve officers were more likely to "go by the book" than were their better-trained and more experienced active counterparts, exhibiting more enthusiasm than coordination, but this is by no means a satisfactory general explanation. A contemporary officer named Bärensprung, writing in 1913, warned that reserve officers did not know what was in "the book" and thus did not know how to make tactical decisions and give good orders.[47] The "book," consisting of all the army's manuals on infantry and combined-arms tactics, did not call for dense formations in every case. Nevertheless, Dennis Showalter is correct in the substance of his argument that reserve officers tended to follow established norms rather than think flexibly and develop tactical forms based on their local situation, which was the essential requirement of the 1906 infantry regulations.[48] Indeed, Bärensprung argued that lack of initiative was the key shortcoming of reserve officers.[49]

Here, it should be noted that some historians critical of the army's social exclusivity have argued that reserve officers had sufficient qualifications and that the war proved they were just as good as the active officers of the prewar army.[50] Neither argument stands up to examination. Reserve officers had only a fraction of the active officers' experience in commanding units, they had much less opportunity to study on their own and participate in the official and unofficial war games that were a staple of the army's training, and they had very differentiated experiences in their time as one-year volunteers. While it is true that differences in tactical proficiency between experienced active and reserve officers had diminished by 1918, the near absence of prewar officers at the company level makes any meaningful comparison almost impossible. Equally important, by 1918, all the units and their officers on the western front were so accustomed to trench warfare that a return to mobile warfare required emergency measures to train them to follow the new regulations of mobile warfare. It is worth noting that when units were transferred from the western front for operations in the east or Serbia in 1915, they took extensive hikes to prepare them for mobile warfare.[51]

Efforts to find other sources of reserve officers also proved unavailing. The War Ministry's attempt to train one-year volunteers as combat leaders in July 1914 was quickly overcome by events.[52] Those who had spent years on active duty before moving into reserve positions had difficulty maintaining currency in tactics, and although they were more experienced, they might be even less prepared than one-year volunteers just leaving active duty.[53] Regular units also complained about the difficulties in training reserve officers, the requirements of which could be difficult to meet.[54] In fact, it seems that some units all too willingly excused their reserve officers from annual field maneuvers, a practice that may have eased the units' tasks in the short run but harmed both the reserve officers and the army in the long term.[55] By 1914, many voices in the Prussian army were warning that reserve officers, though hopefully better than those of other nations, were not fully prepared to take their places beside their active counterparts—an especially important issue because even the open literature recognized that the majority of infantry officer positions would be occupied by reservists.[56] The highly respected General Otto von Moser warned in the fourth edition (1914) of his prewar handbook that many active and reserve officers made serious mistakes in tactics.[57] The experience of 1914 showed that these concerns were quite justified.

Excessive Haste in Infantry Attacks

Excessive haste in training may have been the foundation of the army's fundamental weaknesses going into the war. But the prewar criticism and the early war experience related to unrealistic views of combat primarily involved the tendency to practice tactical deployments and movements too rapidly. Connected with this was the refusal by many commanders to consider protracted, methodical attacks on prepared positions. Nearly twenty years prior to 1914, Schlichting had warned against excessive haste in simulating combat in training of all kinds. He was by no means the first to issue such a caution.[58] The experiences of 1870–1871 had shown the dangers of sending units against enemy positions without proper preparations ranging from sufficient reconnaissance to adequate artillery support. The much-maligned infantry regulations of 1906 recognized that training tended to proceed much more quickly than real battles. Article 253 of the regulations specifically warned against unrealistic haste in peacetime practice. This was difficult to execute in practice, as commanders pushed their units to move and attack quickly. The resulting hasty course of the action created "peace tactics" that did not correspond to reality. To deal with this, the regulations instructed umpires to work to slow down attacks to attain realism.[59]

Numerous authors—some in accord with Schlieffen and the army establishment, as well as some mavericks—warned in subsequent years that the army had not heeded these words of caution. Hugo von Freytag-Loringhoven and Konstantin Hierl were among those who repeated the warnings after Schlichting's influential writings gave the issue substantial prominence.[60] The semiofficial weekly *Militär-Wochenblatt* contained a number of articles on the "hunting attack," one conducted with the haste of hunting rather than with the caution and reduced speed appropriate to real combat.[61] Other articles recalled the elder Moltke's warnings against excessive haste or called for more energetic action by umpires to prevent commanders and units from attaining false victories by rapid acts of bravado.[62]

The results of early combat in 1914 were mixed. Some units moved immediately to attack without proper reconnaissance and artillery support, while others exercised much caution. The Prussian emphasis on rapid judgment and speedy execution of decisions encouraged haste, as did the battlefield situation. Delay, after all, frequently assisted the defender more than the attacker, particularly where large units were involved in critical efforts to turn enemy flanks or gain valuable terrain before its defenders could strengthen their positions.

Combined-Arms Action

This led to a related issue, also much discussed in the prewar literature on training and combat: combined-arms warfare. Long before 1914, numerous doctrinal publications and private writings emphasized the need to bring all available weapons to bear in combat.[63] Nevertheless, it is clear that commanders frequently did not wait or make the effort to achieve ideal or even minimal combined-arms effects before sending their infantrymen into the jaws of the defender's firepower, a shortcoming by no means limited to the Germans.[64] Prewar warnings on this point went unheeded.[65] Given the limitations of communications tools in 1914, the conflict between the requirement for speed in mobile warfare and the need to synchronize infantry and artillery was a serious issue for all armies.[66] The army's prewar literature recognized this problem, but no solution was at hand until late in the war.[67] Attacking forces everywhere were unable to overcome the disadvantages they faced, a challenge surmounted only later in the war with improved infantry tactics and combined-arms cooperation.

Overall, it is reasonable to conclude that although the official regulations foresaw most of the problems inherent in conducting offensive combat, too many commanders failed to train their officers and units in how to implement those official recommendations.[68] One prewar officer warned that regiments massed their infantry in areas that the regulations set forth as appropriate for platoons. Here again, the problems of peacetime training with understrength units created distortions that found their revenge on the battlefields of 1914.[69] This was due in part to the principle of decentralization in training, whereby the twenty-five corps commanders could create their own priorities and systems, and individual commanders could maintain outdated and erroneous practices throughout their tenures, which in some cases lasted eight years or more.[70]

In conclusion, it is difficult to disagree with the postwar views of those officers and contemporary historians who posited that although the regulations were strong in many respects, training and practice did not always follow them.[71] Overall, the experience of the Germans in the period 1900–1914 is another illustration that doctrine is only as valuable as its implementation, no matter how solid its content. Once the deficiencies in the army's doctrine and practice had been exposed by the test of combat in 1914, the army had to correct them, while also fighting a war on at least three fronts.[72]

The Challenges of *Stellungskrieg*

The tactical challenges of what the Germans called *Stellungskrieg* (positional warfare) on the western front led to two immediate problems. The most pressing was making the transition to preparing extensive defensive works and relying on defensive rather than offensive tactics as the primary means of conducting warfare. The other, then only dimly emerging, was the problem of attacking in trench warfare. Most authors agree that the Germans quickly adapted to the need to construct effective field fortifications and trench systems, but in the long run, this was only a partial solution to the first problem and was of no relevance to the second.

As the trench lines became more continuous and the stalemate along the western front became more rigid, both sides sought to fight primarily by intensifying their prewar tactical methods. This meant, in the defense, reliance on stronger field fortifications supplemented by increased reliance on machine guns and continuing emphasis on defending and retaining every foot of the front line. On the offense, both armies began to stress artillery preparation to create gaps that could be exploited by what were still relatively dense lines of riflemen. Thus, by the end of 1914, circumstances had forced battalions and even companies to abandon the so-called parade-ground tactics of the prewar era and to adopt the spirit of the infantry regulations of 1906, intensifying their efforts to achieve close tactical coordination with the artillery.[73] As early as March 1915, a War Ministry memorandum conceded the failure of prewar tactical methods under the circumstances of the ongoing war.[74] It should also be noted that the development of new equipment tailored to the requirements of attacking trench lines was already under way by the end of 1914.[75] The problem, then and later, was that movement had disappeared from tactics, and the traditional balance between fire and movement had been lost.[76]

Defensive Strategy in the West

Several factors combined to place defensive warfare at the center of the German army's concerns on the western front. In November 1914 Falkenhayn, who had replaced the younger Moltke as chief of the General Staff and thus as the head of *OHL*, decided to send reinforcements to the eastern front. The greater opportunities for successful offensive operations and the dire necessity of rescuing the Austro-Hungarian army from its disastrous defeats in Galicia dominated Germany's short-term concerns. In any case, additional major offensives on the western front were unlikely to succeed because of the army's heavy losses during the opening campaign, the severe shortage of artillery munitions, and the seemingly impossible task of attaining decisive results without lengthy and detailed preparations. For the most part, the German army remained on the defensive on the western front from the fall of 1914 until the Verdun offensive of 1916, and it did not mount a major offensive until March 1918.

Two major long-term factors gradually reshaped the army's approach to positional warfare in the west until December 1917. Most important from the strategic point of view was the effort to find defensive methods that could cope with the increasingly dangerous Allied offensives at a cost the army could bear in a lengthy war. Defending became increasingly diffi-

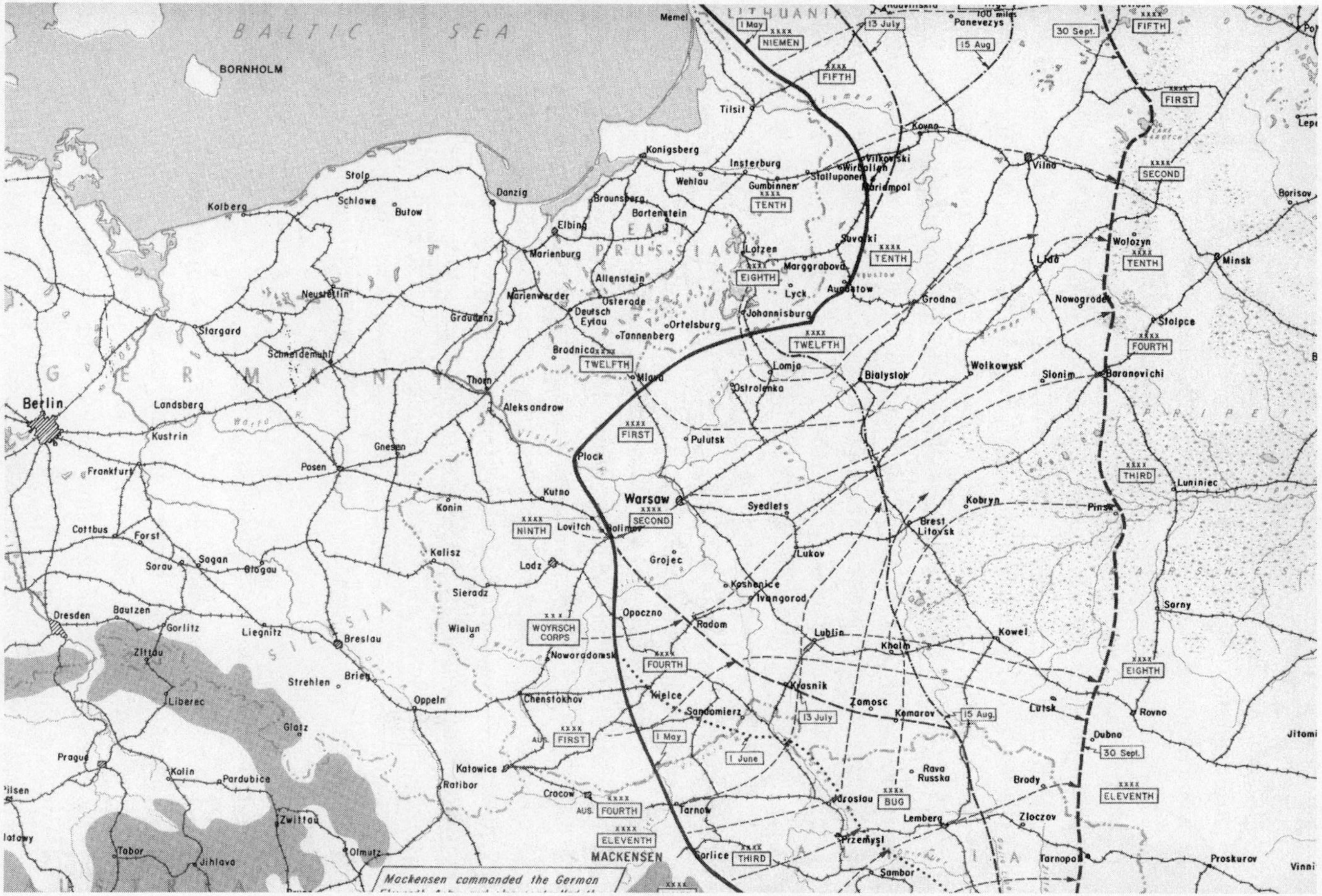

Gorlice-Tarnow Offensive.

cult and costly as the enemy's superiority in artillery and aviation became more pronounced. By 1916, in fact, no system of field fortifications could protect the Germans from the enormous barrages mounted by the British and French, although the full extent of that problem was only dimly apparent in early 1915. The German army thus faced the dual problem of preventing Allied breakthroughs and avoiding levels of attrition that would gradually destroy its powers of resistance.

In a related but separate development, the army sought new methods of attacking in positional warfare, which were necessary both to recover defensive positions lost to Allied offensives and to build the foundation for effective offensive action when the strategic situation allowed it. Experimentation by small units eventually produced a series of innovations that offered a partial solution to the problems of tactical stalemate. These were termed, with questionable validity, "infiltration tactics." Since tactical developments required adaptation to the changing nature of warfare on the western front between 1915 and 1918, that theater became a place of fairly constant, if gradual, change.

Falkenhayn, who still hoped to achieve a decisive victory in the west, at first adhered to the traditional Prussian concept of holding ground at all costs. In memoranda to the western field armies in January 1915, he insisted on defending the front line of trenches and recovering them if necessary. He was subsequently severely criticized by subordinate commanders and historians for his stubborn inflexibility. Conversely, even in January 1915 he advocated defense in depth, calling on the armies to create second lines of trenches and even authorizing units to retreat to those trenches for protection against enemy artillery fire. In this, he was at least a year out in front of the tactical changes for which others later gained fame. Thus, while it is true that he demanded a static defense along the front positions, his views were realistic, in that he allowed the units to move within the forward positions as the situation required.[77]

Tactical Developments Elsewhere

While the Germans adopted a defensive posture on the western front, major offensive operations were conducted on the eastern front and in Serbia in 1915.[78] Combat on both fronts was conducted using standard infantry tactics. The most important development was the Germans' ability to combine the capabilities of aerial reconnaissance, artillery, and infantry. For the Gorlice attack, aerial reconnaissance allowed Mackensen's artillery officers to pinpoint targets for the opening four-hour bombardment. The infantry assault was timed to begin in the final moments of the barrage, so that the infantry would reach the enemy trenches just as the barrage was lifting.[79] Against the Russians, this formula proved devastatingly effective in the 1915 campaigns. The same system was employed with success against Serbia, although bad weather and poor observation occasionally resulted in German artillery rounds falling short, into their own infantry positions.[80] In both cases the Germans were aided by the weakness of the enemy's artillery response. The German forces also employed practices that were contrary to those used on the western front. While the War Ministry was emphasizing night combat operations, for example, German forces in Russia and Serbia sought to maximize the advantages of daylight.[81] Thus, the experiences gained on other fronts offered little help to the OHL as it attempted to solve the problem of deadlock on the western front.

Defense in Depth

By the middle of 1915, the Germans had begun to debate the correctness of their doctrinal requirement that the front line be held under all circumstances.[82] It should be noted that at some locations the Germans had already begun to prepare a second line of strongpoints behind the front line, in a manner, according to some, suggested by Schlieffen in 1905.[83] The British assault on the German lines at Neuve Chapelle on 10 March 1915 was a case in point. At Neuve Chapelle, German Seventh Army's forces had deployed in considerable depth, in accordance with Falkenhayn's very broad directives. The front lines were weak, but about 1,000 yards behind them was a line of concrete machine gun nests. A local backup force stood ready behind the machine guns. The main reserve force was about 4,000 yards behind the front line. The British quickly overcame the front line but could make no headway beyond it, a failure perhaps equally attributable to the German defense and a bungling British command system.[84] The German reserves restored most of the lost ground in a rapid counterattack.[85] Not too much should be made of this single battle, as other German units managed to repulse Allied attacks whether they had fully adopted Falkenhayn's system or not.[86] A preliminary manual published by the High Command in February 1915 required the stubborn defense of every foot of land and warned that defense in depth did not mean a weakening of the forward positions. Accordingly, it called for deployment of reserves in the front line if it became seriously threatened.[87] Over the next few months, the entire German front began to correspond to Falkenhayn's vision of a static but deep defense, relying on a double system of combat trenches connected with communications trenches and numerous machine gun nests for firepower.

In October 1915 the General Staff issued a new version of the February manual with the title "Instructions for Positional Warfare." This document called for at least two defensive positions (preferably three) sufficiently separated so that the enemy would have to undertake two attacks. Each position was to have at least two lines, and each line of trenches was to be separate so that enemy artillery could not attack them simultaneously. The first line was the main line of resistance, to be held or taken back.[88]

Here, it must be noted that the origins of the revised German tactics are in dispute. G. C. Wynne, one of the authors of the official British history of the war, argued that these relatively minor changes were copied from a French document captured early in 1915.[89] Though widely accepted, this view is incorrect. The original impetus came from German Third Army, which had already partially adopted these changes; the French document merely provided a corroborating argument.[90] The French document, moreover, contained only the sketchiest outline of a defensive system. It was less detailed than Falkenhayn's instructions of January, and its provisions were primitive compared with both the preliminary manual (February 1915) and the system being implemented by several German field armies, in particular Seventh Army at Neuve Chapelle.[91] The captured order may have had some influence at the High Command, as Wynne suggests, but only after April 1915.[92] Even then, its influence would have been indirect and delayed, since the German army had already started to move toward defense in depth and had already gone far beyond the French order.

At about the same time, a higher-level debate began on essentially the same subject. A group of General Staff officers at the *OHL*, led by Bauer, argued for a general thinning of the front lines to protect the infantry against the increasingly effective Allied artillery fire. Little remains of the actual views held by these officers in mid-1915. Wynne concluded that they went so far as to propose methods that would invite enemy breakthroughs on a small scale to set up flanking machine gun fire and vigorous local counterattacks. This extreme view, if it really existed, found no favor with senior officers at the *OHL*, then or later.

Opposed to this group was an officer later associated with tactical flexibility, Colonel Fritz von Lossberg, head of the Operations Section of that portion of the General Staff–*OHL* that had not moved to the eastern front.[93] Lossberg accepted the principle of defense in depth but insisted on the necessity of the prewar doctrine of holding the front line at whatever cost. Accordingly, in August the *OHL* ordered German Second Army to issue a doctrinal pamphlet on defensive positions emphasizing both the necessity and the limits of flexibility. The publication noted that the enemy might penetrate the front line and that deep positions must be available to halt further advances. Lossberg, who later remarked that his subordinates at the Operations Section lacked experience at the front, thus maintained Falkenhayn's position of limited flexibility within the context of holding or recovering the front line. Some divisions resisted even this slight modification to prewar doctrine, and the *OHL* felt compelled to send General Eberhard von Claer to supervise implementation of the army-level regulation.[94]

Some commanders, in contrast, readily accepted the need for more flexibility and even began to link defense with a revival of offensive tactics. In May 1916 General Hermann von Stein, commander of XIV Reserve Corps and later war minister, issued a pamphlet covering the defense of his area of the front. He ordered a reduction in the number of defenders in the front line, with the main line of resistance to be in the second line of trenches, where the bulk of the machine guns were placed. The enemy's penetrations were to be defeated by flanking counterthrusts.[95]

The German reactions to British and French attacks in September 1915 marked another step in the evolution of German defensive methods and the emergence of Lossberg as the army's chief expert on conducting defensive battles. Following some initial losses, German Third Army proposed a significant retreat under enemy pressure. Falkenhayn, who had returned to discuss matters with the kaiser, appointed Lossberg chief of the General Staff of that field army. From that time until the end of the war, Lossberg served as a sort of fireman for the western front, moving from one field army to another as the Allies mounted major offensives at various points along the lengthy front from Verdun to the English Channel.[96] According to Wynne, Third Army halted the Allied offensive primarily because of the defensive system Lossberg quickly established. This is no doubt an exaggeration, since Third Army had long since adopted a deep defensive system along the lines previously established by Falkenhayn and the High Command. The system had a well-positioned line of

PERONNE AND VICINITY, 1916
BATTLE OF THE SOMME
Situation 1 July 1916 and Allied Gains
through 19 November 1916

outposts on a ridge crest, a front line on the reverse slope, a rear position on the forward slope of the next ridge (giving good fields of fire and observation of the first ridge's reverse slope, down which the attackers had to advance), and a second strong position on the reverse slope of the second ridge. The total depth was about 8,000 yards, placing the final positions beyond the range of most Allied artillery.[97] The enemy offensive ended at this second main position, on the reverse slope of the second ridgeline.

The Reichsarchiv historians concluded that, although the two German armies attempted to adhere to the prewar principle of holding the most forward position, both actually relied on a second position beyond the range of enemy artillery fire. The success also demonstrated the potential effectiveness of immediate local counterattacks as the enemy force lost some of its cohesion when taking portions of the front line, where a garrison of one man for each two to three yards of front had proved sufficient. Both armies successfully used enfilading fire to engage the flanks of those portions of the enemy forces that advanced beyond the front line.[98] Lossberg no doubt vigorously executed the defensive efforts of Third Army, but he did not create the dispositions on which they were based.

Defense along the Somme

In October 1915 the General Staff circulated a new manual called "Principles for Positional Warfare," outlining a new defensive doctrine. The brief document (twenty large pages) laid out general principles for the defense. Every stretch of front had to have at least two positions located far enough apart so that assaulting them both would require two separate attacks. Each position had to have at least two defensive lines, which were required to have sufficient distance between them so that enemy artillery could not attack both simultaneously. The manual designated the first line of the first position as the "main line of resistance" (*Hauptkampflinie*), which was to be held or taken back if lost. The publication emphasized the construction of protective positions sufficient to withstand artillery attacks and located so that the defenders could quickly occupy the firing line. Positions were to emphasize flanking fire by machine guns and barriers with gaps to facilitate counterattacks. Finally, the manual emphasized cooperation between the defender's infantry and artillery, and it demanded close communications with higher headquarters.[99]

As the Battle of Verdun progressed, Falkenhayn recognized the need to create field manuals to incorporate lessons learned and techniques for using new weapons. In cooperation with the War Ministry, he issued a series of new manuals under the title "Regulations for Positional Warfare for all Arms." The initial titles included "Mine Warfare," "Illumination Methods," "Construction of Positions," and "Means of Close Combat." This series was in its infancy when the British attack in the Somme sector began.[100]

The next major test of the deepened German defensive system was the famous Battle of the Somme, perhaps the Germans' most wrenching battlefield experience next to Verdun and Langemarck. The sacrifices of the British and, to a lesser degree, the French have dominated the historiography of the Somme battle, which became a symbol of futility, poverty of leadership, and stubborn squandering of human life in an act of enormous stupidity.[101] It was a traumatic experience for the Germans as well, for the same battle marked a new phase in combat on the western front—the emergence of the infamous "battle of materiel," in which the great weight of Allied firepower and resources was matched against the primarily human resources of the German army. The experience also produced the famous German defensive manual of 1917, one of two fundamental reorientations in German combat methods during the war.[102]

The weight of the primarily British attack on the Somme fell on German Second Army, commanded by General Fritz von Below, with Lossberg arriving as chief of the General Staff just as the ground assault began on 1 July 1916. Lossberg's predecessor had proposed a local retreat as the British infantry approached, but Falkenhayn would not hear of it and dispatched his defensive specialist to oversee that part of the front.[103]

Second Army had prepared a static but deep defense according to principles that had been generally accepted if not ideally implemented across the entire western front. The defense consisted of three positions to provide immediate tactical defense and local support and reserves for the front units. The first position apparently consisted of three lines of trenches 150 to 200 yards apart. The second position, located beyond the range of the bulk of the British artillery as deployed on 1 July, was also strong, while the third, about 3,000 yards behind the second, was still under construction. The German plan was to use a combination of determined resistance along the first line of trenches and local counterattacks in an effort to defend the first position, where about half the available infantry awaited the assault. The first position was on a forward slope to increase its field of fire, with the hope that the entrenchments and bunkers could withstand the anticipated Allied artillery barrage. The defenders knew a major assault was coming, although Falkenhayn thought the main effort would be against neighboring Sixth Army.[104]

The British attack, aimed at a major breakthrough, opened on 23 June 1916 with an enormous artillery barrage. Over the next seven days the British artillery, densely concentrated and greatly superior to that of German Second Army, fired between 1 million and 1.5 million rounds at the German positions. On 1 July dense waves of British infantrymen, disdaining more sophisticated fire and movement tactics and expecting the total destruction of the German trenches, moved forward.[105] Their expectations were largely correct as far as the German trenches were concerned but fatally incorrect about the nature of the remaining resistance.

By 1 July, the weight of the British bombardment had almost completely annihilated the entire first German position. Telephone links to rear headquarters quickly fell victim, even though they had been dug into the ground. Trench lines, bunkers, and wire entanglements disappeared over the course of the weeklong shelling.[106] The entire front line became a mass of craters as all but the deepest living quarters succumbed to the British artillery. The few survivors of the forward garrison, joined by those who emerged from the deep dugouts, took up defensive positions in the craters, from which they inflicted massive losses on the advancing enemy. Around 60,000 British soldiers fell on that infamous day, making it a lasting symbol of military failure. That development has frequently obscured other important aspects of the Somme battles.

The first of these overlooked aspects is the lengthy duration of the campaign and the enormity of the resulting struggle, which seemed to be a defeat for both sides in the long run. Despite their initial losses, the British and French continued their attacks along the Somme for months, with pauses for regrouping and preparations. Lossberg initially demanded that the forward commanders maintain every foot of ground and forbade any retreats, even while work on rear positions continued.[107] The British responded with continued massive artillery bombardments and the insertion of additional infantry divisions. British aerial observers directed artillery fire onto successive German positions with deadly effectiveness, so that by 1 August, many rear lines and even the communications trenches had disappeared in the mass of craters.[108] This actually turned into a sort of advantage for the defenders, however, as isolated groups of soldiers with their machine guns could not be identified visually. Nevertheless, unit after unit fell victim to the relentless British artillery fire.[109] The Germans gave ground grudgingly and inflicted great losses. The British never managed to achieve a serious breakthrough, partly due to the determination of the defenders, but also partly due to their own shortcomings.

The second major development during the course of the epic struggle along the Somme was the changed nature of the German defensive system and its accompanying tactics. The Germans began to occupy the forward craters with very light garrisons and to rely on local counterattacks, called counterthrusts (*Gegenstösse*), controlled by subordinate commanders to recover lost ground. If these failed or if the front-line units were unable to mount them, higher commanders prepared full-scale counterattacks (*Gegenangriffe*). Lossberg began to change the emphasis from holding ground to containing the enemy advance and inflicting losses while reducing German casualties. Many divisions caught in this to-and-fro combat across the moonscape of the battlefield lost up to 90 percent of their infantry strength by the time they were relieved.[110] Front soldiers had to live in the shell holes, where the most basic necessities were lacking, opening an entirely new chapter in the war.[111] Great problems emerged as the infantrymen found themselves plagued by thirst, made worse by their salty rations, and they were unable to acquire regular hot meals. The individual soldier's single flask of water hardly sufficed, and basic standards of hygiene lapsed. One division commander recommended, apparently with some success, the distribution of "hard spirits" as part of the infantryman's provisions.[112] The first cracks in the army's discipline, which later turned into a serious problem, began to show along the Somme by September.[113]

By the end of August, it was clear to the Germans that the English would not achieve a major breakthrough, but that hardly signified an end to the fighting. Sir Douglas Haig shifted his focus from German Second Army's front to First Army, in the Cambrai area, where heavy assaults continued into October. There the Germans experienced the same basic results: initial Allied successes against front lines annihilated by artillery fire, bitter back-and-forth fighting around rear positions, costly counterthrusts to restore critical positions, and eventual stalemate—all achieved at a terrible cost in men and material. Although precise figures are difficult to determine, when the final count was in, the bill was staggering indeed. The Somme battles can be seen as the end of the prewar army. The Germans suffered about 465,000 casualties (dead and seriously wounded) in the battles, many fewer than the British (420,000) and French (200,000) combined, but many more than their overstretched resources could comfortably bear.[114] After the Somme, as historians have remarked, the German army no longer had large numbers of prewar officers, noncommissioned officers, and soldiers in its infantry units. The army had truly become a militia army, commanded at battalion level and higher by the regular officers of the old Prussian army, but actually populated by citizens in arms who were relatively poorly trained and lacked many of the best qualities of the prewar force.[115] Such battles could not recur indefinitely.

By September 1916, the High Command recognized the necessity of making fundamental changes in defensive fighting and began to collect reports and recommendations from divisional and higher headquarters that had participated in the battle.[116] Although the specifics of the new concepts for defensive fighting varied, surviving accounts are remarkably consistent in their broad outlines and basic considerations. Perhaps the most important point was that the defending units had to assign fewer soldiers to the very vulnerable front-line positions. As the *OHL*'s own study concluded, "The more strength that was placed in the first line, the greater were the losses." Nor should large numbers of soldiers take shelter in the deep platoon-sized bunkers that had been constructed along the front lines of trenches, even though they provided good protection from artillery. If their occupants did not get out of these bunkers between the end of the barrage and the arrival of the enemy infantry, as was frequently the case, they became death traps or collection points for prisoners. Instead, most agreed, the main body of the defending infantry should be in the second and third defensive positions, far enough to the rear to be protected from the enemy's preparatory artillery fire and the initial infantry assault.[117]

Equally important, most observers recognized that the units had to become more proficient in conducting counterattacks to regain important positions lost to enemy infantry. Gallwitz was brutally direct: "The infantry is not sufficiently trained for the attack."[118] This in turn required a major change in the nature of command in infantry tactics. Responsibility for ordering and conducting counterthrusts (immediate local counterattacks by the front units) rested with local commanders, usually at battalion level, using small units. The use of large units almost always produced high losses and failure. At this point, the concepts of offense and defense, separated by the realities of positional warfare and by German military strategy since early 1915, began to converge in a rebirth of the old Prussian theory of mobile warfare, although this return to traditional basics was only dimly recognized at the time.[119] Many observers were critical of the command practices that had developed over nearly two years of positional warfare and admonished commanders to move closer to the forward lines, where they could directly intervene in tactical developments.

Finally, the army began to reexamine its use of artillery based on the Somme experience. Gallwitz and others identified shortcomings in artillery as one of the primary problems that emerged during the Allied offensive. The infantry division commanders, even at this stage of the war, had insufficiently coordinated their measures with the supporting artillery. The latter, in turn, had relied too much on the use of gas to disrupt the enemy's artillery rather than trying to destroy it. Both Gallwitz and the *OHL* stressed utilizing aerial observation in directing fire (a strength of Allied artillery) as an imperative. Furthermore, the High Command's report concluded, the heavy artillery should conduct the counterbattery battle, while the field artillery should concentrate on blocking the advance of enemy infantry. The continuing shortage of artillery munitions remained in evidence. In short, although the German defense had prevented a major Allied victory in the Somme battles, its manpower and other resources would not allow a repetition of this outcome, which many regarded as a failure because of the losses incurred.[120]

New Principles of Defensive Combat

Generalfeldmarschall Paul von Hindenburg replaced Falkenhayn as chief of the General Staff at the end of August 1916, but the real force behind the High Command until the end of the war was First *Generalquartiermeister* Erich Ludendorff. Neither Ludendorff's failed strategies nor his sinister reputation as a rabid anti-Semite and prophet of the Radical Right parties during the Weimar Republic should obscure the fact that he brought a fresh spirit of innovation and flexibility in both organization and tactics. He led the way in implementing a solution to the cruel dilemma that had arisen on the Somme and elsewhere—that is, a defense that succeeds in the short run is bound to destroy the army's combat capability in the long run.[121]

Ludendorff has rightly received credit for many of the changes in offensive and defensive tactics, but it is useful to remember that the two most famous regulations, dealing with principles of defense and offense in positional warfare, were part of a larger ongoing effort.[122] As previously noted, Falkenhayn instituted a comprehensive review of the army's basic combat and related regulations beginning in April 1916. That project had started to bear fruit by the time Ludendorff arrived at the High Command.

Ludendorff vigorously pushed the process of doctrinal reform, with the goals of updating individual manuals and integrating the results into general sets of instructions for defense and offense. The new series of specialized manuals, completed by 1 January 1917, covered the construction of positions, employment of artillery spotters, mortars, and the infantry's communication with aviators and balloons; they also included a revision of Falkenhayn's "Means of Close Combat."[123]

A team led initially by Bavarian Generalleutnant von Hoehn and Colonel Max Bauer (probably the key figure) prepared various drafts of comprehensive new regulations. Hoehn, Bauer, and *OHL* staff officer Captain Geyer had access to the full range of field reports, including those by Gallwitz, Crown Prince Rupprecht, and Lossberg, on which to base their new manual.[124] It officially appeared on 1 December 1916 under the title "Principles for the Conduct of the Defensive Battle."[125] Part of this effort to improve the army's defense was the requirement that every corps and division that had participated in the Somme battles submit a report on its experiences.[126] The new regulations were intended primarily for the western front. The High Command was willing to accept the relatively minor price of some inconsistencies between practices in the east and those in the west, since the defensive problems of the latter were much more critical.[127]

Ludendorff's subsequent account wrongly claimed that the manual replaced a static defense that was lacking depth and burdened by excessive garrisons, a criticism of the previous system that was only partly true.[128] Nevertheless, the manual is rightly seen as a fundamental change in procedure if not an entirely new approach to defense. The manual's most important innovation, from which all else flowed, was the emphasis on inflicting the maximum number of enemy casualties while preserving friendly forces to the greatest extent possible, a recognition that manpower relationships were more important than terrain.[129] Accordingly, the defender was to substitute weapons for humans, mobility for standing fast, and lower-level flexibility for the rigid defense of lines.[130] Although various editions of the manual changed slightly over the course of 1917 and 1918, the basic principles remained the same.[131]

The Reichsarchiv historians, reflecting the judgment of senior participants after the war, concluded that the most important points of the new regulations and its defensive system were (1) maintaining the initiative even while on the defensive; (2) substituting machines (e.g., machine guns, artillery) for soldiers; (3) employing a mobile defense, using terrain to create conditions as unfavorable to the attacker as possible; and (4) utilizing depth in defending.[132] A supplemental General Staff instruction to the field in 1917 summarized the new system simply: "This offensive conduct of the defense, with a multi-sided surprise of the enemy, and the greatest possible preservation of our own human material with the greatest possible attrition (*Verblütung*) of the enemy is the main mission of the defensive battle in the West."[133] To achieve this reduction of losses, the January 1917 directive authorized extensive local withdrawals if the preexisting positions were especially exposed to enemy firepower.[134]

The earliest edition established three defensive zones: forward, main battle, and rear battle. Each was to be prepared with multiple lines and positions in great depth, with at least 3,000 yards from the front of the main battle zone to the front of the rear zone. Each zone was to have numerous strongpoints to produce flanking fire against groups of the enemy that managed to advance into them. All editions stressed granting flexibility to junior commanders in conducting their local engagements, although no zone was to be surrendered voluntarily.[135] This flexibility gave division and even battalion commanders great latitude in moving their units from position to position and in choosing the time and place to use local counterthrusts to annihilate or eject the attacker.

Counterattacks

The manual stressed the use of two kinds of counterattacks to repel the enemy where appropriate, but not necessarily in all cases. The first, a local action, was to be used at the discretion of division or lower commanders when circumstances were such that they could carry it out with their own units. This counterstroke (*Gegenstoss*) required rapid action and little systematic preparation (reconnaissance, artillery, engineers, and so forth). The second action—a larger effort termed a counterattack (*Gegenangriff*)—was to be used when additional large units had to be brought into the battle. This required extensive preparation and had to be planned very carefully, because the assumption in this case was that the attacker had consolidated his position and was on the defense. Hence the roles were reversed, and the counterattack would be a potentially costly attack in its own right. The solution, appearing only in the last edition of the manual, was to move the counterattacking forces, called *Engreif* divisions, closer to the front where possible.[136] This reduced the time available to the original attacker to prepare a defense of the captured sector. This kind of revision indicates the continuing role of Generalleutnant Hoehn, who was behind much of the effort to reallocate the reserve divisions.[137]

These innovations involved a major change in the Prussian army's old system of command. The division commander, located near the battle zone, replaced the corps commander as the primary leader of the defensive battle. The corps commander's primary role was to provide support of various kinds.[138] Some of the details of that support, particularly the artillery, remained unresolved and controversial.[139]

Although Ludendorff had initiated a training program to improve individual marksmanship throughout the western army, the regulations shifted the emphasis from individual action with rifles and grenades to machine guns as the basis for close combat. The relatively few machine guns in the forward line were to be used in a mobile manner. Ironically, the German army was gradually returning to its traditional offensive way of fighting, even as it remained mired in defensive combat in positional warfare.

The first proposals for such revisions, as well as the first edition of the manual, received a cool reception in portions of the western army, including Lossberg, who continued to resist what he regarded as excessive flexibility and surrendering of terrain.[140] There seems to be no doubt that Ludendorff, in an unusual move that reflected his respect for Lossberg, gave the latter's point of view a fair hearing and even circulated copies of Lossberg's own proposals with drafts of the new regulations. Nevertheless, Ludendorff finally decided in favor of the Bauer-Geyer approach, the so-called elastic defense.[141] "Elastic," of course, referred to snapping back as well as bending under pressure.[142] Many officers enthusiastically accepted the new approach, and the army began the process of learning how to implement it.[143] Even Lossberg, who implemented defensive measures in his various subsequent assignments, successfully reconciled his views with those of the new regulations, effectively compromising between his concerns about holding important positions and the manual's stress on mobility within combat zones.[144]

The various editions of the regulations addressed other questions related to a more cost-effective defense. From the outset of his tenure at the High Command, Ludendorff stressed increasing and improving artillery support for the infantry, and the new regulations contained numerous provisions for better cooperation between the two main branches. In addition, the new system emphasized using the air force for a range of missions, from artillery spotting to attacking enemy artillery and other important targets.[145]

Training the Army in the New Tactics

To spread these new defensive concepts throughout the army as quickly as possible, Ludendorff ordered the establishment of a number of schools. General Otto von Moser, later a harsh critic of the army's conduct of the war, established the first such school at Solesmes in January 1917. The school had a complete infantry division to test and teach the doctrine. The first class taught eight officers above the rank of regimental commander, while subsequent iterations at Sedan and Valenciennes taught younger staff officers and commanders who had not attended the peacetime War Academy. Eventually, the course at Solesmes had about 100 students per session, including German officers from the eastern and western theaters as well as guests from Austria-Hungary, Bulgaria, and Turkey. Observers of the *OHL*, including Captain Geyer, attended, and two were permanently stationed there to incorporate lessons learned into the various editions and amendments to the defensive manuals under preparation and modification. The training division established a combat test ground near the school to conduct exercises examining new concepts of defensive positions and the use of mortars, gas, aviation, communications, and so forth.[146] Nine special artillery schools conducted training in Colonel Georg Bruchmüller's artillery methods.[147]

A few records of the General Staff describe the most famous courses taught at Sedan in 1917, offering glimpses into their content and methods. The seventh iteration, taught between 11 and 18 May 1917, covered the following general subjects by day: (1) main principles for the conduct of the defensive battle, including French artillery methods and the construction of field positions; (2) construction of positions during the battle, such as command posts and antitank schemes; (3) infantry and artillery tactics in defense; (4) construction of rear positions, including the use of infantry and machine guns in these positions; (5) infantry and artillery aerial observation, including the use of gas munitions by artillery; (6) mortars and grenade launchers, which involved a trip to visit the Rohr Battalion; (7) intelligence; and (8) demonstrations of various activities by a storm company.

Experts who lectured at and taught these courses, which included both classroom instruction and field trips, included a company commander from the Rohr Battalion, commanders of various weapons schools, a fly-ing squadron commander, and an artillery expert. The surviving list of students shows officers ranging in rank from captain to three-star general and coming from all kinds and levels of unit assignments. The surviving records, limited to the eighteenth iteration of the course taught in September 1917, reveal only slight variations in subjects and days.[148]

Intensified General Staff Oversight

In supervising the implementation of these new defensive measures, Ludendorff intensified the General Staff's involvement in the details of tactical planning and execution, a long-term trend that eventually became a serious source of disgruntlement among the front-line units and their staffs, however necessary it may have been in some cases.[149] The General Staff demanded that all field armies submit maps of their defensive systems. These had to contain, among other items of information, unit boundaries, locations of all positions, artillery deployments, communications networks, and resupply plans. The field armies also had to estimate their requirements for divisions, artillery support, aircraft, and so forth, as well as plans for their employment. This was, to say the least, a great burden for staffs at all levels, but it offered some insurance against casual neglect of the new system.[150]

By early October 1916, field commanders and their General Staff officers were complaining bitterly about the burdens of dealing with the High Command's constant inquiries, instructions, and demands for written reports. A new pejorative term, *Generalstabswirtschaft* (General Staff husbandry), arose to describe the emergence of the General Staff's parallel systems of gathering information, demanding reports, and issuing orders outside the regular command channels.[151]

Of course, there were many variations in practice and results throughout the long German defensive line on the western front. Although the German defense was not entirely successful everywhere, the new defensive tactics staved off any serious breakthroughs and inflicted massive losses on the Allied forces. The French and British launched bloody attacks around Arras and along the Aisne in April, at the Chemin des Dames in May, at Messines Ridge in June, at the Third Battle of Ypres in July, near Verdun in August, and at Passchendaele and Cambrai in November. The results were meager in most places, despite massive artillery preparations and an increasing number of tanks.

Testing the New German Defense

Arras–Vimy Ridge

The first test of the Germans' new defensive methods came in a British offensive in the Arras–Vimy Ridge sector in April 1917. Following a very lengthy bombardment and a short period of relative calm, British and Canadian infantry assaulted German Sixth Army on 9 April, closely following a brief but intense bombardment. The attacks, which achieved complete tactical surprise, quickly overran major portions of the German front positions and resulted in an initial penetration of four miles along a nine-mile front. The British thus captured Vimy Ridge and inflicted a major tactical defeat on Sixth Army, commanded by the elderly General Falkenhausen.[152]

Ludendorff dispatched Lossberg to assume the duties of Sixth Army's chief of the General Staff, giving him plenipotentiary powers (*Vollmacht*) to take whatever steps were necessary. Lossberg, who arrived on 14 April, quickly implemented an elastic defense along the lines preferred by Ludendorff and abandoned his own insistence on a static (but deep) defense. By 23 April, his efforts had begun to prevail. The offensive faltered, and the British suffered heavy losses as the combination of flexibility in defense and local counterattacks overcame British artillery superiority.[153] The British stubbornly continued their assaults until 3 May. From the German perspective, the crisis had passed.[154] Nevertheless, many Germans, then and later, considered the action a "serious defeat."[155] It was certainly costly.[156]

The *OHL* sent officers to investigate the causes of Sixth Army's defeat and summoned others from the front-line units to Kreuznach for interviews. Even Ludendorff may have been temporarily concerned that his new defensive system would not work in practice.[157] The investigation concluded that numerous problems had contributed to the poor performance but that the system was basically sound. Falkenhausen's Sixth Army, for various reasons, had not effectively implemented the new defensive scheme.[158] Its positions were improperly prepared and lacked depth, while the reserves were too far to the rear for effective counterattacks.[159] Sixth Army's artillery, substantially overmatched, was largely ineffective, partly due to poor coordination with the overall defensive scheme. Sixth Army, expecting the enemy to fire a lengthy, heavy barrage immediately prior to the infantry assault, was entirely surprised and poorly prepared when the British infantry attacked after less than thirty minutes of artillery fire. Finally, and most worrisome in the long run, the defeat was attributable to the nearly inescapable power of enemy artillery fire, which was twice as heavy as that in the Somme offensive in the summer of 1916.[160] Ludendorff, in a rare move, convinced the Military Cabinet to relieve Falkenhausen, who became the new governor-general of Belgium, even though Lossberg strongly opposed the punitive action.[161] Falkenhausen's successor, Otto von Below, who came from the eastern front, was quite willing to follow Lossberg's suggestions—a common-sense attitude, given the latter's high standing with Ludendorff. Lossberg himself apparently came to see the advantages of the elastic defense and adapted his own methods accordingly.[162]

The Nivelle Offensive

The British attack had actually been a large diversionary effort to draw German forces away from the long-planned French attack known to the Allies and to most historians as the (ill-fated) Nivelle offensive.[163] General Robert Nivelle, commander in chief of the French army, had prepared a very large offensive to be conducted in the area of the front between Reims and St. Quentin. He massed 4,800 pieces of artillery (about twice as many as the Germans had in that area), a thousand aircraft, and fifty-two divisions for the assault. Nivelle promised a decisive victory, a deep advance, and at least 200,000 German prisoners.[164] He confidently planned to use the weight of his artillery to crush the defenders in the front positions and assumed that a subsequent rolling barrage advancing at the rate of 1,000 yards per hour would lead the infantry to an easy occupation of the territory in the German rear. The infantrymen supposedly would not need their watches, as the precisely calculated and shifting barrage would determine the nature and speed of the advance.[165] Nivelle's staff had planned everything in advance, thus depriving commanders at division level and above of nearly all tactical flexibility.[166] The First World War had a way of dashing the hopes of most optimists, especially the foolish ones, and Nivelle was no exception.[167]

The initial impetus of Nivelle's opening assault lasted only a few days, although the offensive eventually took some ground and by that measure did not totally fail. Its primary consequence was the French army mutinies of 1917. Due to numerous indiscretions at the highest levels of the French army and to effective tactical reconnaissance, the Germans had ample warning of the impending attack.[168] The army group of the German crown prince prepared by reinforcing the threatened Seventh and Third Armies, arranging defensive positions according to the new system, improving artillery preparations, and positioning reserves effectively. Bavarian General Boehn, who arrived shortly before the offensive began, took command of Seventh Army, which had been equally thorough in preparing its sector.[169] The terrain, moreover, was in many areas conducive to defending rather than attacking.[170]

Nivelle's offensive began on 16 April after an artillery preparation of nearly ten days. The advancing French infantry found the German forward positions transformed into the usual land of craters, but it also encountered determined and well-prepared defenders scattered throughout the pock-marked land. In most places the attack came to a halt within the first position. After the initial attack, there was virtually no chance of a rapid victory.[171] Nevertheless, the French army persisted with dogged determination while the soldiers on both sides sacrificed themselves in the usual manner and to the customary degree until June, long after Petain had replaced the disgraced Nivelle. The final reckoning included 163,000 German casualties and between 250,000 and 300,000 French losses. The French mutinies began in earnest on 20 May, rendering the offensive a nearly complete and counterproductive failure.[172]

Messines Ridge and the Flanders Offensive

By June 1917, Sir Douglas Haig was ready for another offensive, this one in the Ypres-Passchendaele area of Flanders. Although this can be seen as an effort to relieve the hard-pressed French, its main purpose was to create a strategic breakthrough, seize the German submarine bases along the coast, and inflict a decisive blow on the Germans. Haig hoped to decide the war before the Americans, whom he disliked, could arrive in force.[173] The opening blow was the famous destruction of the main German positions on Messines Ridge by an enormous underground detonation. Nearly a year of mining efforts had placed about 600 tons of explosives at key locations beneath the German positions. The resulting series of nineteen major explosions produced shock waves detectable in London and utter devastation of the unsuspecting defenders. Following the detonation on 7 June, British forces easily occupied the Messines Ridge area and rounded up the dazed survivors as the rear German units rushed to recover from one of the most unpleasant and spectacular surprises of the war.

The rest of the British offensive in Flanders followed an all too familiar pattern of successive costly attacks that lasted until mid-November. For this study's purposes, the main innovations involved the tactics of both sides. The British, chastened by their experiences, realized that penetrations into the Germans' deep positions would result in failure under the pressure of German counterattacks against their forward infantry. Accordingly, British units employed very heavy bombardments to destroy the forward German positions, followed up by limited infantry advances to occupy only the front areas. The British units then reverted to the tactical defense to meet the German counterattacks in consolidated and effective positions of their own.[174] Whereas the Germans incorporated offensive tactics into their defensive strategy on the western front, the British integrated defensive tactics into their strategic offensives. Although John Keegan exaggerated in concluding that, by the end of the Passchendaele attack, the two sides' tactics "resemble[d] each other exactly," he had a point, in that both used defensive attrition as the basis for conducting the war on the western front.[175]

As the battles in Flanders raged, the Germans discovered that local counterattacks would not prevail in the expected manner against the British tactics of limited advances. Lossberg, whom Ludendorff had sent to the threatened Fourth Army as part of the typical rotation of General Staff chiefs, briefly experimented with stronger front-line garrisons to halt the initial British infantry assault. This soon proved costly and futile in the face of British artillery, and the Germans reverted to their proven elastic defense, although by October, it was much less effective.[176] A new form of bloody stalemate had emerged.

Cambrai

The last of the British offensives of 1917 was the surprise attack at Cambrai, undertaken on 20 November against a small section of the Hindenburg Line in the area around Cambrai–St. Quentin–La Fere. After a relatively brief artillery barrage and a large aerial attack on the German positions, British Third Army, with substantial surprise, advanced with a supporting force of 360 tanks. The attackers broke through the front positions easily and quickly, but they had no larger concept of exploiting what was a minor victory. While this may have been a harbinger of future warfare, equally important for the First World War was the successful counterattack delivered by units of German Second Army using the "infiltration" tactics that were beginning to restore mobility to the tactical attack.[177] The Germans had been developing these tactics since 1915, and by the end of 1917, their efforts had begun to bear fruit, although the real impact would not be apparent until the following March.

New Offensive Tactics

At this point, it is necessary to return to the other problem of positional warfare: attacking under conditions that clearly favor the defender. The basic idea of using new formations, weapons, and tactics for assaulting trench lines preceded the formation of those units that eventually became the famous *Sturmabteilungen*, or storm (assault) battalions. At first, enterprising units tried to use light artillery, metal shields, and grenades to overcome the defender's trench lines. The available artillery pieces were too heavy, and the metal shields were not very effective. However, the German army's variety of grenades developed since the Russo-Japanese War showed promise. Enterprising combat engineer officers, especially Captain Walter Beumelberg of 30th *Pionier* (Combat Engineer) Battalion, were the main innovators in the fall of 1914 in battles in the Argonne region.[178] In this regard, the history of the earliest assault unit equipment supports those who see the process of change as being primarily the product of tactical units. However, officers at the German High Command, especially Colonel Max Bauer, were interested in new tactical forms and equipment. Bauer, in fact, ordered the creation of three special experimental units to test new items such as trench mortars, flamethrowers, and light assault cannons to accompany the infantry to forward positions.[179] Thus, even at the earliest stages, the impetus for reform came as much from the highest levels of the German army as from the lowest.

In fact, it was the *OHL* that first formalized the concept of special assault units. On 2 March 1915 it ordered VIII Corps to establish a *Sturmabteilung*. The High Command chose to use 18th *Pionier* Battalion to establish a special assault unit at the firing range located at Wahn. The experimental unit consisted of two pioneer companies equipped with metal shields and one artillery section equipped with twenty light guns (37mm). In this respect, the first real initiatives in offensive tactics in trench warfare came from the artillery. The experimental unit at Wahn quickly identified the four critical tasks of breaking through trench lines: (1) advancing from one's own lines up to the enemy position, (2) clearing obstacles, (3) breaking into the enemy's position and fighting its garrison, and (4) further advances against rear lines in and beyond the trenches.[180]

Such specialized units found their basic concepts in the prewar regulations on fortress warfare, which called for the formation of special assault columns (*Sturm-Kolonnen*) to attack permanent fortifications.[181] The prewar term "assault column" remained with the special units well into their development during the First World War. An active officer, Major Calsow from the combat engineers, was the first commander of such a unit. His detachment had 21 officers and about 630 enlisted men.[182] Its initial employments were disasters, and the unit was virtually destroyed between 15 and 18 June 1915.[183] Calsow blamed this on the failure to employ his unit according to regulations. In particular, the new mobile field gun proved to be of little value.[184]

The War Ministry assigned the remnants of Calsow's unit to Army Detachment Gaede and selected a new commander from the Guards Rifle Battalion. Bauer claimed that he made this selection personally.[185] The commander was the famous Captain Willi Rohr, who gave his name to that detachment and to the history of tactical change in the First World War. General Hans Gaede selected Rohr because he was an infantryman (rather than an engineer) with combat experience, and he gave Rohr full scope to train his new unit accordingly. Gaede, whose units were almost entirely *Landwehr* formations, was glad to have the assistance of a unit with handpicked young men.[186] Rohr's tactical concepts emphasized the offensive use of machine guns and hand grenades and close cooperation between infantry and artillery.[187] Another officer, *Landwehr* Major Hermann Reddemann, a flamethrower specialist, developed the idea of abandoning long skirmish lines and substituted deeply echeloned small units (*Trupps*, or squads) for the attack. He also created the term *Stosstrupp*. By December 1915, Rohr's battalion had developed a course to broaden the army detachment's skills in these new methods. After many months of training and deployment in companies and smaller units, the new *Sturmabteilung* went into action as an entire unit on 22 December 1915 and was quite successful.[188]

During this long period, Rohr's unit developed its methods more fully, participated substantially in combat, and saw its principles spread to other parts of the German army. Rohr defined his unit's mission as leading infantry platoons and companies, rolling up enemy trenches, and taking whatever strongpoints were in the area. The infantry, according to his ideas, would follow in long columns through the gaps in the wire prepared by the storm troops. The infantry units would then finish clearing the enemy positions and strengthen them against enemy counterattacks.[189] Rohr's unit officially became a battalion, Storm Battalion 5, on 1 April 1916.[190]

In the meantime, the Rohr Battalion found itself enmeshed in the Verdun fighting, with mixed results. Beginning on 3 February 1916, the battalion participated in a number of actions undertaken by 6th Infantry Division. The two regiments to which the battalion's elements were attached made no progress and suffered substantial losses. Both regiments' reports were highly critical of the battalion's assault elements, with one remarking that the Rohr Battalion seemed to be unaccustomed to such difficult combat. The assault units, moreover, had no clear idea of how they should be employed. Another regimental report blamed the failure on a lack of reconnaissance and preparation, while acknowledging that the assault units accomplished as much as possible under the circumstances. Rohr attributed the problems to a lack of proper coordination and little understanding of the real task of his battalion's soldiers. Clearly, the infantry units lacked confidence in the Rohr Battalion.[191]

Two initiatives to clarify the relationship between the Rohr Battalion's *Sturmtrupps* (squad-sized elements) and the regular infantry soon followed. In cooperation with Captain Rohr, Fifth Army produced a report (17 March 1916) to the High Command on the proper use of these specialized units. This report recommended for the first time that the battalion should have both combat and training missions.[192] The Rohr Battalion itself soon produced guidelines for the use of its elements in support of regular infantry.

The Rohr Battalions's report, which is the earliest evidence of systematic thought on the tactics of the assault units, appeared on 27 May 1916. The document apparently no longer exists, but Helmuth Gruss's book and a few other sources give broad outlines of its main features. The Rohr Battalion was to deploy its *Sturmtrupps* of engineers, attached to regular infantry units, in "especially difficult places of attack."[193] These *Sturmtrupps* were to lead infantry platoons in "opening the breaking-in position," in "rolling up the trenches," and in "taking any block houses" encountered. The objective, therefore, was not to bypass enemy positions but to destroy them so that the infantry units could advance without suffering excessive losses.

Rohr's guidelines warned against using lines of riflemen in assaults on fortified positions. Instead, small columns of the assault units should advance against preselected positions deemed vulnerable to attack. The *Sturmtrupps* should closely follow the artillery barrage in order to surprise the enemy, and infantry units (squads, half platoons, or entire platoons) should follow immediately behind. Other infantry and labor units were to form a third wave to completely clean out and consolidate the objective. The instructions emphasized the proper use of machine guns for fire support while the *Sturmtrupps* advanced, flamethrowers for clearing trenches, and light field guns and mortars for artillery support.[194]

The Rohr Battalion's role as a training unit for regular infantry units began quite by chance during the Verdun battles. During one pause in the fighting, the German crown prince asked Rohr why the German infantry had not been more effective in attacking trenches. Rohr replied that the reason was insufficient training in the use of hand grenades. Soldiers had discarded many thousands of grenades on a nearby battleground because they had no faith in them. The crown prince assigned the Rohr Battalion the task of training the divisions in his command (Fifth Army) how to use grenades and how to use combined arms in trench fighting. This led to the creation of a specialized training institution at Doncourt.[195]

Chief of the General Staff Falkenhayn kept the army informed of the evolving tactics of the assault battalions. A surviving unit report with a compilation of lessons learned prepared by the General Staff and an overall after-action report from April 1916 described the organization and basic tactics of these early storm battalions. According to a report by III Reserve Corps, the General Staff study supplied the following information: The typical storm battalion attacked with a breadth of about 400 yards, with three companies in the first line and one in reserve. Each company had two platoons in its first line, with a third following closely to clear the trenches overrun by the first two. Each platoon, in turn, normally had two "assault columns," each consisting of four combat engineers and three squads of infantry. The remaining squads followed closely, carrying spades and picks to construct defensive positions. Behind each company came another unit of engineers (nine men) with rapidly emplaced wire barriers to create hasty defensive positions at the objective.[196]

Falkenhayn recognized the potential of the Rohr concept and on 15 May 1916 ordered all field armies and army detachments to send officers and noncommissioned officers to school to study storm battalion methods for two weeks. Upon returning to their units, these officers were to supervise the formation of storm detachments throughout their commands, until every division had sufficient trained personnel to form the kernels of such units. Falkenhayn's order stipulated that these personnel had to come from men already assigned to the various units, since there was no intention of establishing these units on a regular basis with official tables of organization and equipment.[197] This was a potentially serious problem because many commanders were reluctant to give up capable soldiers for these essentially ad hoc units, regardless of their overall value.[198] Nevertheless, those who criticized Falkenhayn for his indifference to revitalizing German tactics, the most prominent of which was General Wetzell, were clearly in error. Most of the basic programs to use storm units to test war experience, improve small-scale offensive skills, and provide training to other units began and found vigorous support during Falkenhayn's tenure, sometimes against considerable resistance from front-line units and commanders. In this area, the army group commanded by Crown Prince Rupprecht of Bavaria had already acted. On 11 February 1916 it ordered each of its field armies to create a storm battalion, both for teaching tactics to infantry units and for use in combat.

A number of authors have created the false impression that tactical change was driven primarily by enthusiastic reformers at lower levels of the army. In fact, many field units refused to cooperate with efforts to expand the storm units and refused to use them properly. This attitude went back to the days of the Calsow detachment, whose initial failures were at least partly due to improper use by the units whose attacks it was supporting.[199] Gruss's study has a number of concrete examples of the front units' resistance to the order to establish their own storm battalions, primarily because of manpower shortages, but also because of the failure to recognize their tactical value.[200] Some commanders actually tried to eliminate their newly established storm battalions because they had to fill their ranks from other units. As of 1916, the storm battalions lacked their own independent authorizations for personnel. Even Crown Prince Rupprecht's army group vacillated between filling the units with personnel and taking them away, eventually re-forming the battalions.[201]

At higher command levels, some field armies enthusiastically embraced the new concepts. In February 1916, as previously noted, Crown Prince Rupprecht of Bavaria ordered each of his army group's field armies to create a storm battalion with a special establishment of machine guns, light infantry field guns, mortars, and flamethrowers. In this area, as in so many others, the influence of Hermann von Kuhl was evident.[202]

During the course of 1916 the OHL and the Prussian War Ministry issued a number of directives that had an important impact on the storm units themselves and on the tactical training of the broader army. In June 1916 the High Command withdrew two Jäger (light infantry) battalions from the front for training in assault unit tactics. The response within the battalions was favorable, as Rohr's concepts seemed to offer the prospect of success.[203] In July 1916 the War Ministry converted four *Jäger* battalions to storm battalions, instructed the general in charge of the Engineer and Pioneer Corps to assign pioneer officers to the units, and repeated the General Staff's previous requirement that young soldiers be assigned to these units.[204] By that time, the General Staff had established the strength of a storm unit as follows: a commander and a small staff, four assault companies, a machine gun company, an infantry cannon battery, a small trench mortar detachment, a flamethrower squad, and various items of equipment, including spades, carbines, and radios.[205] In August the War Ministry converted three additional *Jäger* battalions to storm battalions. In December the War Ministry began the process of giving the storm units a regular designation by establishing Storm Battalion 1 in First Army. The German term *etasiert* meant that a unit had become a regular rather than an ad hoc unit.[206]

The Romanian campaign showed the potential of Rohr's approach. The deposed Falkenhayn, now commanding Ninth Army, employed units such as the Württemberg Mountain Battalion in terrain that was well suited to its capabilities. The German units, using combined-arms tactics and rapid maneuver, quickly reversed a dangerous situation and sent the Romanian forces in the Transylvanian Alps into a headlong retreat. Meanwhile, Mackensen's force in Dobrudja, drawn from every member of the Central Powers, relied on a combination of standard infantry tactics and carefully timed artillery bombardments to defeat the Romanian and Russian forces south of the Danube. His forces ultimately severed the Constanta-Cernavoda rail line, effectively isolating Romania from further Russian assistance.[207] As pointed out by Michael Barrett, by 1916 standards, the Romanians were "neophytes" at conducting modern combat operations, and the Central Powers made sure that the learning curve was too steep for the Romanians to achieve tactical parity.[208]

The few assault battalions in existence had little impact on the course or the outcome of the battles around Verdun or on the Somme River. Nevertheless, the contribution their tactics might make if applied on a wider scale was starting to be recognized by the time Hindenburg and Ludendorff arrived at the High Command in late August 1916. Also by that time, Storm Battalion 5 (Rohr) had begun to offer courses to personnel from all the western field armies. By then, Wilhelm II had visited the Rohr training course and had become an advocate of the new methods.[209] The transition from Falkenhayn to Ludendorff, coupled with the dual crisis in the east (the Brusilov offensive and Romania's entry into the war), caused a delay in the full implementation of Falkenhayn's plans for expansion of the storm units. Ludendorff soon visited part of the Rohr Battalion at the headquarters of the German crown prince and, after a short delay, ordered a rapid expansion of the number of storm battalions. Within a few days, the War Ministry was pressing for information on the speed of the new units' formation and their real strength.[210]

On 4 December 1916 the War Ministry gave the storm battalions a regular establishment of men and material, thus ending their dependence on regular units for replacements.[211] Shortly thereafter, as more storm battalions became functional, the Prussian War Ministry ordered all units of the army's replacement battalions to send officers and noncommissioned officers to the field army's training courses.[212] The Bavarian War Ministry followed suit for its replacement units in January 1917.[213] Ludendorff pushed this program forward with great energy and substantial results.[214] He also ordered the German armies in the east to send officers and men to be trained by the Rohr Battalion.[215] By that time, various reports had recorded successful small-scale attacks by storm units.[216] Some units, however, continued to be suspicious and were won over only gradually as pressure from the High Command and successful local attacks changed attitudes.[217]

In October 1916 Ludendorff ordered all field armies and equivalent commands (only army groups on the eastern front) to create teaching units to universalize training fundamentals and the experiences of storm battalions.[218] By March 1917, the army had ten storm battalions on the western front, usually with numerical designations corresponding to their parent field armies. The Rohr Battalion, although the first in existence, thus became Storm Battalion 5.[219] At the beginning of 1918 the army had sixteen assault battalions, numbered 1 through 12 and 14 through 17, and two assault companies.[220] Eastern-front units followed suit on a lesser scale, but with great enthusiasm in some cases. In fact, the training capacity of the western front could not accommodate the eastern High Command's requests for places in the training courses.[221]

The Rohr Battalion was not the only unit conducting extensive training by December 1916. First Army's storm battalion began teaching a similar course, to which each division had to send nine officers and thirty-six noncommissioned officers. First Army had developed a double function for its assault unit, called the "assault-training section," and this later became a common characteristic of assault units. The assault unit's dual functions were to prepare assault squads (*Sturmtrupps*) for combat and to serve as an instructional unit for the regular infantry formations. The training program (lasting six days) for this unit consisted of more than thirty basic tasks for assault unit training and a number of others for cooperation with infantry and artillery units. Many of these were basic infantry skills, while others were directly related to the unit's role as a leading assault element.[222] These subjects included assaulting trenches, overcoming barriers, using grenades, engaging in combat in fields of craters, counterattacking to recover lost positions, using enemy weapons, and employing flamethrowers and light machine guns. In November 1916 the High Command decreed that the primary mission of the storm battalions was to train other units; actual employment in combat was to be the exception.[223]

Throughout 1917 storm unit attacks were purely local affairs with very limited objectives. Ludendorff's strategic approach to the war called for the German army to remain on the defensive on the western front in 1917 while it recovered from the heavy fighting on both fronts in 1916.[224] This consideration, when combined with the increasingly heavy Allied artillery bombardments and the German army's inability to sustain excessive losses in defensive fighting, led Ludendorff to turn his energies to the development of improved defensive tactics in 1917, discussed previously. Nevertheless, it should be remembered that as assault unit tactics became more widespread, they improved the army's capacity to conduct vigorous counterattacks as part of the evolving concepts of defense in depth and, later, elastic defense.[225] The larger challenge was to incorporate them into an offensive strategy, but that was of no practical value as long as the German army remained on the defensive on the western front.

Preparing for an Offensive in the West

In the fall of 1917, as Ludendorff turned his attention to the possibility of a great offensive in the west in 1918, he realized that the army was trained and prepared only for defense and limited tactical attacks. Preparing the army for offensive action in the west entailed a wide range of activities, only a few of which are considered here. The tactical changes adopted in the more flexible and offensively oriented manuals for defense might be applicable to offensive measures in trench warfare, as were the tactics developed by the storm battalions. A larger problem was that the German army in the west was very different from the prewar army, which had been steeped in offensive theory and trained to conduct mobile warfare. The officer corps of 1914 had been decimated, as had the corps of noncommissioned officers and the highly trained enlisted men. The army in the east could make some divisions available, but although they were more accustomed to the traditional ways of conducting mobile offensive warfare, they were entirely unaccustomed to the much more lethal and constraining conditions of the western front. There were, moreover, serious questions about the availability of horses, supplies of various kinds, and virtually everything else a decisive strategic offensive would require. Despite these daunting problems, Hindenburg and Ludendorff realized that they had to win the war in 1918 or lose it to their enemies the following year.[226] As a result, in the fall of 1917 the German army began to prepare for its last great offensive, set to begin in the spring of 1918.

New Manuals and Regulations, 1916–1918

The *OHL* produced a number of new manuals between late 1916 and early 1918 to provide the doctrinal basis for training leaders, individual soldiers, and units in the new offensive tactics and in carrying out large-scale offensives when the strategic situation allowed.

Training Regulations for Company Commanders

One of the first new manuals to be produced was the 1916 edition of the training regulations for company commanders. This manual reflected the decentralization of tactics that eventually became the hallmark of German combat methods over the last two years of the war. The regulations established the squad commander, the *Gruppen-Führer*, as the person responsible for executing the breakthrough attack in positional warfare. Battalion or higher-level commanders had held that responsibility in the prewar regulations. Although the 1916 regulations recognized the traditional distinction between mobile and positional warfare, the emphasis was on the latter. The manual set forth the basic concepts of applying storm unit principles to the line infantry company.[227]

The company commanders' regulations stressed the same principles as Rohr's 1916 manual; indeed, the two were remarkably similar in many respects. The storm units, advancing in small columns, were to follow immediately behind the artillery barrage and conduct surprise attacks. The remainder of the company was to follow closely in squads, half platoons, or platoons. The company should advance in three waves, with the first penetrating as rapidly as possible to the established objective, while the second and third waves, also deployed in small units, cleared the remainder of the enemy position. The company commander was to use machine guns, flamethrowers, and light field guns to support his attack. The *Stosstrupps* would be drawn from the ranks of each company, at least three from each.[228] Contemporary manuals frequently used the terms *Sturmtrupps* and *Stosstrupps* interchangeably. As a rule of thumb, the former referred to small units of the storm battalions, and the latter to small units of regular infantry trained in the new assault tactics. Not every portion of every infantry company functioned as part of these assault units.

The regulations, however, did not place the entire burden of the assault on the elite units of *Stosstrupps*, even though they wore insignia reflecting their special status. The manual stressed: "In any case, however, the training of the *Stosstrupps* must not so influence the energy of the units that they believe that the *Stosstrupps* do everything." Only the most ruthless drive to advance on the part of every man of the attacking infantry, in conjunction with the *Stosstrupps*, would produce victory, according to the regulations.[229]

Two important distinctions, frequently overlooked by historians, prevailed in German tactical doctrine throughout the new offensive procedures and at all levels. The first distinction was between positional warfare and mobile warfare. Storm unit tactics applied primarily to positional warfare, with its detailed planning and precisely defined objectives; they became less relevant under the conditions of mobile warfare. It should also be noted that in positional warfare, the purpose of attacks conducted as part of a large offensive was to allow the German army to escape the shackles of the trenches. The second important distinction was that the more traditional form of the infantry attack, the line of skirmishers, did not disappear entirely, either in positional warfare or in mobile warfare.[230]

The September 1918 edition of the company commanders' regulations reflected the practices that had proved effective in the 1916 version and incorporated a few changes developed in the interim. For the most part, however, the two were nearly identical.[231] The 1918 version specified that companies should have their own *Stosstrupps*, but it also urged commanders to train as many junior leaders and soldiers as possible for action according to storm unit tactics. *Stosstrupps* could either precede the regular infantrymen or follow them, according to circumstances.

The 1918 regulations formalized a common concept that had developed over time—the reinforced assault team, called a *Sturmblock* or *Sturmklotz*. Such a unit was a temporary amalgamation of men and equipment into a stronger assault group. It had its regular *Sturmtrupp* leader and six to eight soldiers, but it also contained three infantry squads to bring up ammunition and to provide flank security, a squad of combat engineers to destroy obstacles and underground shelters, one or two light machine gun squads, and various kinds of additional equipment.[232]

Based on its organization, as well as numerous references in the text, the manual largely limited *Stosstrupp* tactics to positional warfare. In this form of combat, the squad leaders were "those who conduct the infantry engagement."[233] In conditions of mobile warfare, in contrast, the platoon *"should serve as the unit for the conduct of battle for as long as possible"* (emphasis in original).[234] When conditions of mobile warfare returned, the company's *Stosstrupps* would be dissolved and the soldiers returned to their platoons. There, the men of the *Stosstrupps* would assist attacks against enemy centers of resistance encountered by their permanent units.[235] The company commander should thus deploy his platoons one behind another, not side by side, to give depth to the attack. The regulations further recognized that in mobile warfare, thin skirmish lines with intervals of five or six paces might be appropriate, especially in the second wave of the attacking company.[236] Both versions of the company commanders' regulations thus sought to restore mobile combat to both the offensive and defensive forms of war at the company and platoon levels.[237]

The 1918 company commanders' manual explained that the burden of combat remained with the regular infantry, even when special *Stosstrupps* were formed for positional warfare. The manual marked a return to the old principles of the German infantry: "In no case may even the training of special *Stosstrupps* so affect the energy of the units that they believe the *Stosstrupps* do everything. Only a ruthless drive forward by every single man of the attacking infantry in conjunction with the *Stosstrupps* creates victory. This old experience must remain in the minds of the soldiers and be the common knowledge of everyone."[238]

New Infantry Training Regulations

After the crises on the Somme subsided in late 1916, Ludendorff turned his attention to the broader issues of training the infantry, which nearly everyone agreed had declined during two years of trench warfare. On

13 November 1916 he instructed Third Army Headquarters to prepare "a short, simple and experience-based training regulation for the infantry."[239] General Fritz von Below, Third Army commander, thus became the primary author of the overall infantry training manual. Though largely forgotten today, Below was a well-known and highly respected officer in his time. The young reformers on the General Staff—Geyer, Bauer, and Harbou—were apparently not directly involved to a great extent.[240]

The new manual was ready in January 1917 and was titled "Training Regulation for the Infantry in War." Because individual training had suffered as new recruits replaced most of the trained infantry soldiers of 1914, the new regulations emphasized a variety of basic skills in close combat, requiring all soldiers to become skilled in precise shooting and in the use of hand grenades, machine guns, and trench mortars. Unlike prewar infantry regulations, it omitted nearly all drill and parade-ground formations while concentrating on those skills vital for combat, both offensive and defensive.

The manual maintained the German differentiation between mobile and positional warfare and carefully distinguished between the traditional methods of the two forms of combat.[241] The regulations continued the old concept of the firing line as the basic tactical formation for mobile warfare. Even in this case, however, the process of decentralizing responsibilities and command was evident in the provision that the platoon was the basic unit for combat and was to be maintained as a single tactical unit for as long as possible.[242] The regulations warned that there could be no universal tactical formation for the platoon. Only when the platoon could not move as a unit would squads, half squads, or individual riflemen move in combat independently. The regulations also stressed, as did nearly all German tactical manuals during the war, the use of machine guns.

The 1917 infantry training manual devoted considerable space to the attack in positional warfare.[243] There, the new concepts of storm units came to the fore. Even in positional warfare, however, the regulations stipulated that circumstances at jumping-off positions, terrain, and the presence of barriers would determine whether the attack used small columns, *Trupps*, or thin firing lines. Usually, it stated, the *Sturmtrupps*, composed of the most capable men in the company, would attack in the first wave. It proposed that the attack be conducted in the form of "waves" of units: *Sturmtrupps* within the infantry of the first wave, supporting units, groups advancing to entrench and construct positions, communications specialists, and supply units.[244] The section on *Sturmtrupps* emphasized light mortars, flamethrowers, and the new mobile "infantry guns."

The manual contained the usual broad concepts for using elements of the storm battalions in positional warfare. It made the army-level storm battalions responsible for training the regular infantry and for providing direct combat support. In the latter case, the *Sturmtrupps* would be attached to the regular infantry, but not in company-sized units. Various parts of the regulations recognized the storm battalions' roles as trainers for regular units.[245]

A revised version of the infantry training regulations became available in January 1918. This version, along with the broader regulations on the attack in positional warfare, was one of the most important foundations of the final German offensives that year. It, too, retained the fundamental distinction between positional and mobile warfare. It established thin firing lines with intervals of five to six paces between riflemen as one of the formations in which the units had to be trained for mobile warfare.[246]

Over the course of 1917 the General Staff supervised the preparation of a series of new manuals (fifteen in all) on positional warfare. These regulations, of varying length, covered signals, communications, construction of positions, aviation, and artillery. Other regulations followed in 1918; some were updates of 1917 editions, and some were entirely new. The most important two were "Defense in Positional Warfare" and "Attack in Positional Warfare." The latter was important because it served as a capstone manual to prepare the army for the 1918 offensive.[247]

The January 1918 infantry training manual treated the new tactics in positional warfare in two ways. First, it stipulated that all officers and enlisted men should be trained in *Stosstrupp* tactics. The units, primarily companies, should form temporary ad hoc storm units consisting of especially capable men as individual circumstances required.[248] When not needed for a particular *Stosstrupp* action, these individuals remained in their normal positions in their platoons and companies. In combat, the storm units could precede or follow the regular infantry.

Second, the 1918 manual dealt with the use of storm battalions. Their task was to support the infantry by deploying *Stosstrupps* in the first wave, strengthened by several infantry squads. Elements of the storm battalions were not to be sent into combat without these attached infantrymen. The local commander of the attack acted as the overall commander of these ad hoc platoons of soldiers created from the storm battalions and the line infantry units. Use of *Trupps* from the storm battalion was restricted to attacks prepared long in advance because the field army headquarters had to approve their deployment; in addition, they were to be used only after they had been given sufficient time to practice as a unit for the local circumstances.[249]

In practice, German tactical formations in 1918 showed substantial variation. The infantry training regulations demanded this flexibility, which the army had traditionally attempted to develop in its units. Accordingly, the regulations gave subordinate commanders substantial freedom to use their units as the terrain and the situation demanded. In general, however, the distance between individual soldiers was doubled from the one yard in the prewar regulations to two yards. The company line consisted of two companies, each deployed on a breadth of about 120 yards, but in two lines of half a platoon each. The third platoon followed by at least 200 yards, in a very wide line of riflemen. If special storm troops were used, they would be deployed in the first line of the forward half platoon. Most machine gun support would be attached to these forward half platoons. Under the new infantry training regulations, German infantry tactics were, in short, a mixture of the storm unit tactics needed to break through enemy defensive lines and the wider formations more suitable for the other types of combat that would be undertaken when the breakthrough had been achieved and more traditional mobile warfare had been restored.[250]

Nevertheless, the main problem in 1918 was finding a way to break through the enemy's prepared defensive lines, regardless of all other considerations. Therefore, perhaps the best starting point in considering the assault unit tactics of 1918 is to realize that the storm units' objective was to destroy centers of resistance, not to bypass them. For that reason, the term "infiltration tactics" is quite inappropriate, and historians should stop using it. Infiltration is a method of movement through enemy lines without combat, whereas the storm troops' purpose was to seek out and destroy main centers of enemy resistance.[251]

"The Attack in Positional Warfare"

This brings the discussion to the best known of the 1918 regulations, "The Attack in Positional Warfare."[252] That manual, as its name implies, had a very limited scope and purpose, since it was intended to establish general principles of attacking only in trench warfare. It focused on two types of limited attacks, which were clearly laid out in the opening remarks: "The

Regulation concerns the attack in positional warfare with a limited objective and the major attack that leads out of positional warfare to a breakthrough."[253] The attack with limited objectives had the goal of improving one's tactical position, drawing enemy forces away from the main sector, deceiving the enemy, or gathering intelligence. The regulations went on to say that the offensive battle (*Angriffsschlacht*) seeks the tactical break-in and, ultimately, the resulting operative breakthrough. The *Angriffsschlacht* thus expands to the breakthrough battle, "which seeks to achieve the transition to the war of movement (*Bewegungskrieg*)."[254] The provisions did not apply to warfare beyond the enemy's defensive positions once mobile warfare had resumed. An amendment to the regulations, dated 1 February 1918, stated in no uncertain terms: "The great breakthrough battle requires liberation of commanders and troops from the practices and patterns of thought of positional warfare. The tools and tactics have changed in details. Nevertheless, the great military principles which formed the basis of our military training in peace, and to which we owe all the great successes of the war, remain the same. They are to be revived wherever they have been forgotten."[255]

The subject of "The Attack in Positional Warfare" was thus exactly what its name stated and nothing more. In the context of 1918, it was designed to promulgate a common method for achieving a breakthrough in trench warfare. It was not a universally applicable revision of all German infantry doctrine. Its assumptions and provisions were limited to trench warfare and were irrelevant to the opposite form, mobile war. Historians and others should also remember that it was merely one of fifteen volumes of regulations for positional warfare.[256] This volume was intended to enable the German army to make the transition to mobile warfare but was considered irrelevant beyond that. The many historians who have tried to analyze the methods of 1918 without making this important distinction—that storm unit tactics and the related regulations were applicable only to positional warfare—have failed to understand the true nature of German doctrine. The Germans always regarded positional warfare as an aberration, as the opposite of real war. The purpose of "The Attack in Positional Warfare" was to end trench warfare, not to extend its principles beyond the trenches or to continue it for the remainder of the war. If successful, these methods would have become irrelevant, as they were in the Second World War. Thus, historians who have written about the great revolution in German infantry tactics with reference to "The Attack in Positional Warfare" based their discussions on the wrong manual. It was the infantry training manual, not the narrower manual on positional war, that dominated tactical thought during the Weimar period.

In the section on general principles, the regulations stressed strict control, careful and detailed instructions for the coordination of all arms, and the establishment of clear goals. The next sentence, in contrast, emphasized that the attack offered the opportunity for free activity and responsibility in action all the way down to the individual soldier. The manual's opening section also stressed maintaining close contact among all arms and all commanders from the front to the rear, from the rear to the front, and to the sides. If accomplished, this would secure an offensive advance according to plan and would prevent surprises, especially on the flanks. Finally, every attack must have a center of gravity, that is, a main effort focused on the primary objective.[257]

The manual then considered the various branches of the army and the role of each in the attack. It was not a new way of fighting in any sense beyond a few simple procedures unique to combined-arms combat in positional (trench) warfare. It addressed battle primarily at the division level and referred readers to the infantry training regulations of 1918 for details about the infantry attack.[258]

The opening section of the manual argued that the first task, breaking into the enemy position, was relatively easy. This was a clear recognition of the power of artillery against even the most fully prepared positions. The challenge was to maintain the attack beyond the first positions and to prevent the defender from recovering. Speed was essential. Artillery and infantry firepower was more important than masses of soldiers, according to the manual, just as excessive strength only made matters of command and resupply more difficult. "Everything depends on rapid and independent action by all arms acting within the overall framework, as well as upon the ability to bring up artillery and munitions." Surprising the enemy was therefore "of decisive importance." Tactical flanking of entire positions was to be attempted in the breakthrough battle.[259]

The regulations then presented a lengthy discussion of general preparations for the breakthrough battle. Of course, sufficient artillery and munitions were the first issue, but the discussion also stressed that the leading divisions should attack and advance deeply as long as their strength allowed. Divisions should attack on a width of up to two miles, but not less than one. The manual then presented a lengthy list of preparations that had to precede such a breakthrough battle.[260]

The next subject was command, where, in the traditional Prussian approach, tactics and command were completely interwoven. The division conducted attacks, even limited ones, because it alone had the requisite resources and means to ensure the unified control of actions in combat, especially arranging and directing artillery fire and combined-arms actions. In large-scale attacks the division was the unit of combat. Attack orders had to contain many details dealing with time and space, "since all arms in the entire sector had to work closely together to the minute."[261] The closer the breakthrough came to achieving the objective of mobile warfare, the more forward the higher commander had to go, often on horseback.[262] This might seem obvious, but it was the kind of action that had frequently been lacking in the years of positional warfare.

The regulations devoted considerable space to the roles of the various main branches in the breakthrough battle, but substantially more to artillery than to infantry. This point is usually not fully appreciated by those who wish to see primarily a revolution in infantry tactics in the German offensives of 1918. In considering the artillery, the regulations stressed integration of all weapons and types of munitions in close coordination with the infantry, and it put forth a number of basic principles for using artillery to support the close assault. Major provisions included warnings that premature bombardments would eliminate the possibility of surprise and that enemy resistance would survive in the craters. The regulations designated enemy command posts, rear railway facilities, unit assembly areas, and ammunition depots as additional major targets.[263] The regulations struggled with the question of the rolling barrage, stating, on the one hand, that it required precise regulation in the attack order, but cautioning, on the other hand, that the pace of the infantry advance must not be slowed because of the speed of the barrage.[264] The regulations recognized that artillery support would be particularly difficult in breakthrough attacks where the artillery would have to move forward to support the infantry advance. Despite these difficulties, the regulations cautioned that "the infantry may not be without strong artillery support for even a moment."[265]

The manual's consideration of the infantry attack stressed the use of artillery and skillful action to reduce casualties. The combat power of the infantry, it stated, "rests not only in the number of riflemen and grenade throwers, but equally in firepower."[266] When considering the infantry, the manual first argued that success depends not on numbers but on the individual infantryman's combat power, the care given to preparations, the skill of the commanders and the units, and the rapidity and decisiveness of the measures taken. A few paragraphs later, after warning against the use of inflexible schema, the manual stated that the infantry should attack using the forms laid out in the training manual (discussed above). It said that although goals and conditions usually demanded the use of storm units, these units should be formed with infantrymen trained and reinforced for this purpose. Next the manual stated very clearly that "the decision, whether to use waves of riflemen in line or waves of *Stosstrupps*, or a mixture of the two, must be decided on a case by case basis."[267] The regulations nevertheless stressed that the final assault depended on the proper use of artillery and machine guns in providing supporting fire-power to allow the infantry assault to succeed.

In discussing the course of the attack, the regulations required that when battle groups or storm units became mixed up, they should rejoin their loosely formed lines of riflemen as quickly as possible, as stated in the infantry training regulations, so that they would be available to serve as reserves and for flank protection, patrols, and forward or sideward advances and to guard against surprises.[268] In a remarkable section, the manual warned that looting of enemy bunkers and depots by soldiers in search of food were more likely to weaken the attacker than were enemy firepower or exhaustion.[269]

The theoretical basis of the 1918 offensives was both sets of regula-tions, but ultimately, "The Attack in Positional Warfare" depended on the training regulations for the infantry for its basic tactical forms below the regimental level. There was, therefore, no single manual for the 1918 of-fensive. Rather, there was only a single concept, that of fighting through the trenches so that mobile war could resume. The resulting concept can be found in several manuals.[270]

The manual also devoted a relatively lengthy section to the use of air-power in the offensive, a point frequently overlooked in the literature. Consistent with much of the manual's concern with surprise, its treat-ment of the German air force emphasized the danger of compromising an upcoming offensive through excessive preparatory activity. Once the battle had been joined, the manual called for aircraft to give close support and to attack enemy airfields, railroad stations, rolling stock, and head-quarters. It also stressed spotting support for friendly artillery fire and attacks on enemy artillery.[271]

Overview of Offensive Infantry Tactics in 1918

Only at the risk of some oversimplification can one devise a general description of the storm unit tactics used in 1918. An assault company might consist of 80 to 100 men deployed in three successive groups, or waves, since depth was more necessary than breadth for this kind of unit. A company typically had three platoons, each consisting of three or four squads and an assault squad. The first platoon (wave) had a combination of grenade throwers, riflemen, and machine gunners. The second wave was smaller, designed in part to protect the first wave in case of a local counterattack. Both waves had the task of penetrating as rapidly as possible through successive enemy positions to the greatest possible depth. Disregarding developments to their flanks and rear, these waves were to continue forward to the final objective—usually the enemy's forward artillery position. Their commanders had full freedom of action in deciding how to achieve this. The third wave came after most of the fighting was over to consolidate and fortify positions that had been taken. The timing of the first attack had to be carefully coordinated with the artillery and other fire support, since the best hope for success was for the assault elements to close on the enemy's defensive positions before their occupants had recovered from the artillery fire.[272] All this, of course, pushed basic combat decisions downward to the platoon and squad levels, where great independence of action was critical once the assault had begun.[273] In some cases the storm companies did not lead the infantry assault but instead followed in a second wave to attack particularly difficult objectives.[274] Where storm companies were not available, units formed their own storm squads to deploy in the first line of infantry, as described above. Commanders had the option of using loose skirmish lines or columns of individual soldiers, depending on circumstances. In difficult cases, all kinds of specialized weapons were attached to assaulting regiments, and these were attached to lower-level assault elements as required. These included light cannons, mortars, flamethrowers, and engineers with demolitions.[275]

In conditions of open or mobile warfare, German units returned to a variation of their prewar tactics. Units moved to combat in columns of squads or in single file with intervals of one to two yards between soldiers. The latter formation offered gaps through which machine gunners could deliver fire support. Commanders, especially platoon leaders, chose their own formations according to local circumstances. Final assaults had the option of using traditional skirmish lines to gain fire superiority. Actual entry into enemy trench lines could be accomplished by either squads acting individually or skirmish lines.[276]

New Artillery Methods

The German army stood on the defensive (with the exception of Verdun) in the west, but in the east and in Serbia it more often employed artillery in offensive actions. Two factors governed artillery employment in these cases: complete German air dominance and the relatively limited supply of artillery munitions available.

German control of the air allowed for extensive aerial photography of enemy defenses both before and during operations. Orders from the army and later army group level called for the rapid development of aerial reconnaissance photos and the widest possible dissemination of reports.[277] The effectiveness of the artillery preparation, planned by Ziethen, for the Gorlice operation has already been discussed. Later on, during the siege of Przemyśl, Mackensen's headquarters ordered that every round from heavy artillery pieces be observed. This allowed the old hussar to make the most of his very limited stock of heavy munitions.[278]

The Germans adopted a somewhat more conventional approach with regard to Serbia. German and Austro-Hungarian guns used registration fire after moving into their firing positions. Once again, observation, aided by aerial reconnaissance, proved critical in the success of the opening bombardment (planned in this case by Richard von Berendt) prior to the river crossings. The assaults against the Serbian positions, like those in Galicia and Poland, depended on precise timing between the lifting of the artillery bombardment and the start of infantry assaults.[279]

The most important commonalities of the two attacks involved caliber and duration. The use of heavy artillery in sufficient quantity was regarded as critical to the success of both attacks. Particularly desirable were the very large caliber howitzers that were capable of high-angle fire. Perhaps the most notable hit in the Serbian campaign occurred when a Krupp 420mm howitzer (popularly known as a "Big Bertha") literally removed the top of the Anatema Hills. The other important aspect of the German artillery bombardment in this attack was its relatively brief duration. Following periods of harassing fire, the preassault artillery barrages lasted about four hours, with the last hour before the infantry assault being the most intense. Once the campaigns were under way, the preparatory bombardments were shortened considerably, sometimes to less than an hour. This conserved artillery ammunition and minimized wear and tear on the tubes.[280]

The revised offensive doctrine of the German army, though known primarily for its new infantry tactics, was equally dependent on fire support from the various kinds of artillery. Several aspects of the artillery preparation and procedures for the 1918 offensives stand out. New artillery methods that eliminated the need for careful registration at the front enhanced effectiveness and concealed much of the branch's preparations for a major offensive. By 1918, the German artillery had begun to focus on temporarily disrupting the enemy infantry and artillery rather than trying to destroy targets completely. The army attempted to create mobile infantry guns that could be transported across the battlefields and through the craters to provide close artillery support as the attack advanced beyond the range of the original artillery positions. Finally, the army took important steps to ensure closer cooperation between infantry and artillery than had been achieved in its previous offensives.[281]

The German army successfully massed a substantial amount of artillery to support the first of the 1918 offensives (the "Michael" attack), but the most important innovations were in methods. In numbers, the Germans were still markedly inferior to the Allies.[282] For the Michael offensive, the army had around 2,700 pieces of artillery available to support the three attacking field armies. The real strength of the artillery was the maturation of a number of procedural changes that had been in development since 1915 and were known by the names of their creators: Pulkowski and Bruchmüller.

The first of these innovations was the so-called Pulkowski method of fire direction. Developed by a captain of the foot artillery, this procedure required determining the unique characteristics of each piece of artillery and ammunition batch and coordinating this information with variations in weather to establish the precise azimuth and deflection for hitting known targets. These data could be developed behind the front, using maps to plot accurate fire from the location of any piece of artillery. Previous fire direction procedures required lengthy trial-and-error adjustments based on visual observation of the points of impact. Undertaken on a large scale, this traditional preparatory phase eliminated all hope for secrecy and deception. Pulkowski's procedures, the forerunner of modern artillery methods, allowed individual crews, using data from test ranges and a touch of trigonometry, to fire accurately on the basis of maps and calibration data on each tube. The French had developed similar procedures at an earlier stage of the war, but the Germans were unaware of this.[283] The March 1918 offensive was the first time the German army relied exclusively on this method of fire direction, although it had been under development, especially on the eastern front, for some time.[284]

Another important innovation was the detailed method of coordinating artillery and infantry associated with Colonel Georg Bruchmüller, nicknamed *Durchbruchmüller* for his use of artillery in positional warfare.[285] His system stressed relatively short preparatory bombardments designed to create gaps in wire barriers, force the enemy to take cover, disrupt and reduce enemy artillery support, and inflict casualties among rear installations. To achieve his primary objective of supporting the infantry assault, Bruchmüller's system relied on centralized and detailed control of artillery, elaborate combined-arms coordination through the use of detailed fire plans as part of the infantry scheme of attack, surprise, and a rapidly moving creeping barrage (*Feuerwalz*) to assist the infantry's advance through the depth of the enemy's position.[286] Bruchmüller himself regarded surprise as the key to linking artillery preparations to effective infantry attacks.[287]

The Bruchmüller method of creating the rolling barrage differed slightly from that of the British and French. Essentially, it consisted of a moving line of artillery fire advancing at regular intervals through the enemy positions, with the infantry following about 200 yards behind.[288] In their spring 1918 offensive, the Germans' rolling barrages advanced in phases, about 200 to 400 yards at a time. The goal was to neutralize enemy artillery temporarily and disrupt the enemy defense, rather than to annihilate the entire defensive system.[289] Bruchmüller's system thus stressed relatively brief barrages of great intensity, both to suppress enemy resistance and to preserve the element of surprise, which had always been lost owing to the lengthy bombardments common to previous offensives on both sides.[290] The goal was to force the enemy infantry to take cover, in the hope that the German infantry could then overrun the defenders' positions without suffering unbearable losses.[291] Ludendorff, who had great respect for Bruchmüller, ordered all units to adopt his system of artillery support in planning for the 1918 offensives.[292]

A surviving artillery order for 28th Infantry Division from 15 March 1918 provides a useful illustration of the detailed and mechanistic nature of the Bruchmüller system.[293] The artillery preparation had seven preliminary stages, with the *Feuerwalz* constituting an eighth. The first stage, 120 minutes in length, consisted of general barrages against enemy artillery, telephone centers, and other rear installations. The second stage, 10 minutes long, consisted of fire on enemy second-line positions, especially against known mortar locations, and enemy artillery. The third stage, also 10 minutes long, consisted of gas and shrapnel attacks on the second position. The fourth stage, also of 10 minutes' duration, emphasized observation of results and assumed that some enemy soldiers would expect the infantry attack and occupy exposed positions. The fifth stage, lasting 70 minutes, consisted of heavy fire on all kinds of targets from the front-line positions back to the enemy artillery. The sixth stage lasted 75 minutes and consisted of fire, including mortars, against many close targets and particular areas identified individually in the order. The seventh stage was the first 5 minutes of the rolling barrage, behind which the assaulting infantry closely advanced. The eighth stage was the execution of a detailed fire plan for the rolling barrage, calculated to coordinate the infantry attack with the forward movement of the artillery fire. At the breakthrough point, each battery was to concentrate its fire on a front of about 100 yards.[294]

Bruchmüller's system was not perfect, and many senior infantry and artillery officers did not agree with either his centralized command system or what they regarded as the excessively rapid rate of the rolling barrage's advance.[295] Other western-front commanders objected to devoting a large proportion of the effort to counterbattery fire, to Bruchmüller's demand that the artillery be as far forward as possible, and even to the use of nonpersistent gas against the enemy's advanced infantry positions. The resulting debate over which headquarters, divisional or corps, should control artillery support was an old one. Corps control, according to many, had not worked well at Verdun, but artillery officers resisted subordination to division commanders.[296] The matter had been decided in favor of division control by the beginning of 1918, but the High Command's imposition of centralization at corps headquarters reversed this decision.[297] Hindenburg and Ludendorff, in the meantime, had created a new position, the General of the Artillery, to unify foot and field artillery in large concentrations of brigades for coordinated efforts for individual situations.[298]

A final innovation that attempted to make artillery support immediately available to the advancing infantry was the infantry gun, literally the "accompanying gun." This concept began as an experiment of the Rohr Battalion in 1916, although by then the French had devised a similar solution to providing mobile artillery support. After moderately successful attempts to adapt captured Russian 75mm guns to the task, the army finally turned to Krupp for a new weapon, the Infantry Gun 18. By the end of 1917, the army had fielded at least fifty batteries for attachment directly to infantry units. The enduring problem was that while the crew could drag this gun forward briefly, at least two horses were required to do so over extended distances or rough ground. This proved impractical under combat conditions in deep defensive zones. Supplying ammunition was an equally difficult task. Overall, the experiment was a failure, but this was not evident until well after the 1918 offensive had begun.[299]

In the end, the artillery procedures for the 1918 offensive were a compromise between competing schools of artillery theory, on the one hand, and the infantry's need for substantial artillery support against enemy positions, on the other. Seizing on Bruchmüller's emphasis on surprise (which was also a basic tenet of the infantry regulations), many argued for artillery bombardments of only an hour or so before the main infantry attack. After careful consideration and consultation with many of the General Staff officers in the field, Ludendorff compromised and decided that artillery bombardments would last several hours. He reasoned that surprise, though essential, was not enough, and no attack could succeed without considerable artillery preparation.[300]

Dress Rehearsals: Riga and Caporetto

The Germans had the luxury of testing their revamped infantry and artillery tactics in two operations in late 1917. On 1 September 1917 General Oskar von Hutier's Eighth Army launched an attack against Russian General Vladimir Klemboski's Northern Front, positioned along the Dvina River covering Riga. Using an artillery barrage planned by Bruchmüller, Hutier's forces attacked on a narrow front. The German forces, spearheaded by LI Corps and using the new infantry tactics, quickly broke through the Russian defenses. By mid-September, Riga was in German hands.[301]

One month later the Germans staged another rehearsal for the employment of the new tactics. To bolster the severely strained Austro-Hungarian forces on the Italian front, the *OHL* installed General Otto von Below's Fourteenth Army, comprising two German and two Austro-Hungarian corps, on a narrow sector of the Isonzo River front. Launched on 24 October 1917, the attack, originally envisioned as a limited endeavor, produced results beyond all expectations. Below's Fourteenth Army completely routed its opponents, driving the Italian forces back some seventy miles to the Piave River. The territorial gain was accompanied by an enormous haul of prisoners and booty.[302]

The questions in 1918 were basically the same as they had been in 1914. In tactics, could the infantry break through enemy lines? In strategy, could the army use its traditional means of mobile warfare and decisive battle? Reforms instituted in 1916 and 1917 showed some promise in answering these questions. The experiences of Riga and Caporetto confirmed that mobility could be restored, at least in Russia and Italy. The western front, however, was not Russia or Italy. It would provide the ultimate test for the revamped German army.

CHAPTER TEN

THE FINAL TEST, 1918

Although the German army had been on the strategic defensive on the western front from the end of the Verdun offensive through the end of 1917, hopes of attaining a decisive victory through offensive action against the British and French had never entirely expired. Both Fritz von Lossberg and Konrad Krafft von Dellmensingen claimed they had suggested various major offensive actions in the west as early as March 1915. Neither thought attacks against the French positions and fortresses south of the Meuse all the way to Switzerland had any prospect of major success, which reduced the possibilities to an offensive against the British sector north of the Somme. Both men proposed to separate the French and British forces and push the latter back to the channel coast, where they would either stand and be destroyed or disembark and leave the French to fight alone along the entire western front.[1]

Falkenhayn, though favorably inclined to seek a decision on the western front, reluctantly rejected both proposals. In the spring of 1915 the exigencies of the two-front war required that all forces beyond those absolutely necessary for defense on the western front be sent to the east, as discussed earlier in this study (see chapter 8). Falkenhayn's opponents Hindenburg and Ludendorff incessantly demanded that Germany seek a decisive victory in the east. Falkenhayn, who thought such a victory impossible because of the vast spaces and logistical problems in Russia, nevertheless recognized the critical need to prevent the collapse of the Austro-Hungarian army. As a result, although he regarded England as the primary enemy, Falkenhayn sent limited reinforcements to the east, where events bore out his assessment that the Russians, though less dangerous than the French and the British, could survive even major German offensives.[2] So throughout 1915 the German army remained on the defensive in the west while the nation struggled to mobilize greater resources to support the war effort. The one German offensive in the west, at Verdun in 1916, along with the Battle of the Somme, produced mainly heavy casualties, one of which was Falkenhayn's position as head of the *OHL*.

Despite their previous pronouncements, Hindenburg and Ludendorff soon discovered the complexities, realities, and limitations of a multifront war. They too remained on the strategic defensive in the west for the remainder of 1916 and all of 1917, while the ever-increasing firepower of the Western Allies drained Germany's human and material resources. As we have seen, it took all of Ludendorff's energies and the experiences of many costly battles to create new defensive systems that could withstand the hammer blows of Allied artillery. As the army's system of deep defenses and counterattacks became more effective, and as offensive skills gradually improved over the course of numerous local counterattacks, voices urged the High Command to drop its almost exclusively defensive strategy, pejoratively labeled "the system of the pure defensive battle." The strongest advocate may have been Max von Gallwitz, who in April 1917 pressed the army to become more offensively oriented because the defense was too costly and had robbed the army of its moral strength.[3] The best Ludendorff could do, although he certainly agreed in principle, was to endorse limited local attacks, since the overall situation precluded major offensive action.[4] Even after the defeat of the Nivelle offensive and the first reports of mutinies in the French armies, the *OHL* declined to approve even major counterattacks against the weakened French forces.[5]

Considerations of a Major Offensive in the West

Despite the multitude of problems facing the Germans on the western front in 1917, events seemed to offer some prospects for ending hostilities in the east and seeking a decisive victory against the Allies. Ludendorff discussed sending substantial forces from the eastern front to the west with the *Ober Ost*'s chief of the General Staff during a meeting at Kreuznach on 17 April 1917. He recognized that an offensive in the west would be much more difficult than those in the east, and nothing much came of these conversations, particularly as the fighting in the east continued during the rule of the Kerensky government.[6]

About six months later, a number of senior military and civilian leaders attended a cabinet meeting to report on the overall strategic situation to the new chancellor, Prince Max of Baden. Although the conference did not address a western offensive in any detail, the army leaders discussed bringing divisions back from Russia and improving the replacement system. Ludendorff assured the attendees that the crisis in the west had passed and that the army could hold out against the Allies until more units were available. From that time on, the *OHL* entertained specific proposals on the nature of a great offensive in the spring of 1918.[7]

Reasons for the 1918 Offensive

Although historians have been critical of the decision to launch the costly and ultimately failed offensive of 1918, the decision reflected a thoughtful and logical assessment of Germany's strategic situation.[8] The failure of unrestricted submarine warfare dashed one of the High Command's most cherished if politically reckless hopes. It may have been Major Georg Wetzell, chief of the *OHL*'s Operations Section, who first raised the possibility that the submarine campaign would not produce victory and that a major offensive on one of the fronts would be necessary. By the summer of 1917, Ludendorff was also coming around to the view that the submarine war would not bring England to its knees and that the eventual collapse of Russia would enable the Central Powers to reach a more conventional military decision.[9] The impending arrival of the Americans lent a sense of urgency; this was first recognized in Wetzell's memorandum of 23 October 1917, but it was endorsed by others who participated in the deliberations.[10]

Ludendorff probably never seriously considered a negotiated settlement that would compromise his expansionist war aims, but there is little evidence that the Allies were interested in anything less than a total victory.[11] The irony was that American entry into the war, which made a decision in early 1918 imperative, also reduced or even eliminated the British and French need for a compromise peace.[12] Certainly, the French, the British, and even the Americans had made demands that seemed impossible to meet, especially with regard to Alsace-Lorraine and Belgium. Signs of political unrest, from the Reichstag's Peace Resolution of 19 July 1917 to vocal parliamentary opposition to the war minister, added to the sense of urgency, as did a general sense of war-weariness.[13] The deteriorating economic and social circumstances within Germany also constituted a compelling reason to end the war as quickly as possible and on the most favorable terms.

The German army, like almost all its counterparts, had an ingrained bias in favor of strategic offensives, in this case, for two reasons: the defensive offered only a continuation of the disastrous casualties produced by warding off the Allied offensives of 1917, and the offensive seemed likely to give the Germans the initiative and bring an end to the miseries of trench warfare. Only a decisive offensive could prevent the war from dragging on until defeat became inevitable. Another year of defensive combat threatened to undermine the army's willingness to continue the struggle.[14] Continuing the war indecisively was an especially unacceptable proposition, regardless of the risks, because Germany's allies were in a precarious situation that could not continue indefinitely. Many German military leaders, moreover, were convinced that standing on the defensive would not produce fewer losses than would a successful offensive.[15] As some historians have suggested, the ultimate rationale for an offensive in 1918 was that it offered some hope for victory, whereas a continuation of the war offered only certain defeat in the long run.[16]

On 23 October 1917 Wetzell presented a memorandum discussing alternatives for 1918 and proposing a decisive offensive in the west. Wetzell's memorandum stressed that victory on the western front remained, as always, the key to the entire situation and that the Germans must deliver an annihilating blow to the English before the Americans arrived in force. By that time, Ludendorff's attitude had changed dramatically, as just a few weeks earlier he had still been speaking of winning merely by holding out against the ongoing but weakening Allied offensives.[17] Although he thought events on the Italian front would have to run their course first, Ludendorff, in essence, endorsed the concept of a great western offensive in 1918.[18] Most recognize that the Wetzell memorandum contained the basic idea that came to fruition in March 1918.[19] The memorandum was, however, only a beginning, for there was no agreement within the High Command or among the army group commanders on where or against whom the offensive should be directed.

On 9 November a new memorandum from Wetzell to Ludendorff proposed making the major effort against the French in the Argonne-Verdun area. Wetzell argued that no decisive results could be expected against the British because of the swampy terrain in most of their sector of the front and the abundance of reserves available to counter such an attack. He hoped to destroy at least eleven French divisions and deal the French a massive blow from which they could not recover. In a manner reminiscent of the despised Falkenhayn, Wetzell concluded that the fall of Verdun would have enormous psychological consequences for friend and foe, to the point of having a decisive impact on the outcome of the war. At the very least, he argued, it would disrupt all Allied offensives.[20] This memorandum also contained an unusual note of doubt, asking whether it were reasonable to expect this offensive to succeed when all previous efforts—French, German, and British—had failed.[21]

The Conference at Mons, November 1917

In an effort to clarify where and against whom the offensive should be undertaken, Ludendorff convened a meeting of key commanders and their chiefs at Mons, the headquarters of Army Group Crown Prince Rupprecht of Bavaria, on 11 November 1917. Present were Ludendorff, Rupprecht, the chiefs of staff of Army Groups German Crown Prince (Kuhl) and Crown Prince of Bavaria (General Count Schulenburg), Wetzell, Colonel Max Bauer, and one or two minor figures.[22] Schulenburg, supported by Wetzell, argued for an attack on the French around Verdun, while Kuhl argued for an attack in Flanders against the British (to be code-named St. George). Rupprecht had already proposed the latter alternative to Ludendorff, who found it unacceptable because weather would delay any action until April or even May. Nor did he look favorably on the Verdun-Argonne area; he feared the British would support the French with a renewal of the Somme offensive of 1917, which Ludendorff wished to avoid at all costs. Actually, Ludendorff may have simply used the conference to allow the army groups to have their say before presenting his own solution. Bauer proposed an attack primarily against the British in the area around St. Quentin, south of the area suggested by Rupprecht and Schulenburg.[23]

Ludendorff closed the conference by rendering his decision, preserved in a memorandum that survived the First World War but not the Second. It stated in part:

> The situation in Russia and Italy will presumably enable us to deliver a single blow in the Western theater in the new year. The strength of the opposing sides will be approximately equal. About thirty-five divisions and 1,000 heavy guns can be made available for an offensive. These forces will suffice for *one* offensive; a second large offensive, perhaps to tie down enemy forces, will not be possible. Our overall situation demands an attack as soon as possible, perhaps at the end of February or the beginning of March, before the Americans can throw large forces onto the scale. We must strike the English.[24]

The memorandum then concluded that the attack should be in the St. Quentin area and drive to the northeast to roll up the entire British position in France. Although the memorandum clearly shows the general direction of Ludendorff's thought, it turned out to be a poor prognostication of the future. The Germans in fact prepared many more divisions than the thirty-five envisioned at the Mons conference, as well as a greater number of artillery pieces. They also attempted more than a single attack and began in a different location. Still, the memorandum clearly shows Ludendorff's willingness to gamble everything on a single blow. However, not too much should be made of this, because thorough preparations and developments in other theaters increased the forces available. Since the resources, especially artillery, could support only one offensive at a time, a choice was essential.

Ongoing Discussions of Alternatives

The discussion did not end with Ludendorff's memorandum on the Mons conference. Feeling (correctly, as it turned out) that it had won half the argument, Crown Prince Rupprecht's headquarters renewed its studies and arguments on the best place to attack the British, considering weather, terrain, and enemy forces. His headquarters, probably under Kuhl's influence, commented as early as 20 November that the attack must take place where there was the greatest opportunity for a breakthrough. This was probably the first time specific planning addressed the very difficult issue of whether strategic or tactical considerations should be given the greatest weight in planning and executing the offensive. The army group sent a series of memoranda to the *OHL* between 15 and 21 December 1917, continuing to argue for the northern attack. Kuhl, the actual author of these documents, repeated his argument that the main consideration was to attain a breakthrough, since that was the only way to avoid another "battle of materiel" like that on the Somme in 1916. The memorandum of 21 December reexamined the situation in light of both Russia's withdrawal from the war and the recent battlefield developments around Cambrai.

One problem was that the area for the attack around Cambrai–St. Quentin (by then, code-named "Michael") had become less favorable between the Mons conference (11 November) and late December. On the one hand, British forces there had improved their defensive positions and increased their local reserves. On the other hand, the successful counterattack against the British assault around Cambrai (30 November 1917) had raised hopes of tactical success. There, German counterattacks, using the new offensive tactics described in the previous chapter, threw back a British assault after recovering from the shock of the first major use of tanks.[25] This action might have warned the British of changes in the Germans' tactical doctrine, but this lesson apparently went unnoticed.[26]

Wetzell and his ally, Crown Prince Wilhelm of Germany, did not give up after Ludendorff's decision to strike the English. His memorandum, written the day after the conference, reiterated the proposal to attack the French in the Argonne-Verdun region. Another memorandum, prepared on 12 December, repeated the request for a major offensive there, on the grounds that it would be more decisive than an assault on the British. But because Ludendorff had already indicated his decision to launch the offensive against the British rather than the French, Wetzell's memorandum discussed that case as well. He argued that a single major offensive against the French would suffice, whereas the English were so strong that the Germans would be unable to achieve a breakthrough in a single attack. He therefore proposed that if the Germans chose to attack the English, the army should launch numerous successive attacks and shift forces from one to another. He wanted the Michael offensive to be the first one, with the goal of drawing forces away from Flanders; this would be followed by a second major attack there, allowing two weeks for the Germans to reposition their forces. The Flanders attack, he suggested, might rupture the British army and roll it up from the north.[27] Wetzell was not alone in questioning Ludendorff's initial decision. The army group of the German crown prince also argued against the decision to attack the British. Wetzell found support for his plan to conduct multiple individual attacks as part of the overall offensive. Lossberg also proposed a series of attacks leading to a final great breakthrough, but he did not argue in favor of any one particular area for the final assault.[28]

Wetzell persisted even further. In a 25 December memorandum he again proposed that the major attack take place against the French around Verdun. He warned that the British were expecting a major attack, that their section of the front was more strongly held, and that they had more reserves available. He suggested using the British expectation of an attack to deceive the Allies and thus make the major effort in the Verdun area more effective.[29]

By 27 December, Ludendorff had heard enough. He summoned the General Staff chiefs of the three army groups to Kreuznach to discuss the alternative targets for the planned offensive.[30] Although he had definitely decided to attack the British army, Ludendorff wanted to plan for several alternatives. He gave the chiefs a written directive, for their eyes only, informing them that the offensive would begin in March 1918.[31] He ordered Rupprecht's army group to prepare three offensives against the British: St. George, which had two alternatives—one in the area of Armentieres (St. George I) and one in the area around Ypres (St. George II); and Mars in the area around Arras.[32] Ludendorff also ordered the German crown prince's army group to prepare a local withdrawal in the Argonne region and a counterattack in Champagne. He ordered the army group of Duke Albrecht to prepare an attack near Strassburg. He also ordered the army groups of Albrecht and the German crown prince to plan but not actively prepare for an offensive west and south of Verdun. All this planning and preparation was to be finished by 10 March 1918.[33] Some of these plans, of course, would be used as diversions or supplementary attacks, but no definite priorities were established at this time, although the army groups were informed that the double attack around Verdun would be a diversion to tie down French forces.[34]

Ludendorff visited the front between 18 and 21 January to examine the local prospects for a successful breakthrough attack. He announced his final decision in a meeting with Kuhl and Schulenburg, the chiefs of staff of the army groups involved.[35] The Flanders offensive, St. George, was too dependent on the weather, which might delay it until May. The Mars attack, around Arras, offered too few prospects for a breakthrough because of tactical difficulties. Ludendorff thus chose Michael, the attack around St. Quentin, with some adjustments extending it to the north.[36]

Ludendorff later explained that the most important issue was creating a breakthrough in a timely manner (in March). He justified his decision with this now infamous statement: "Tactics took priority over pure strategy. Without a tactical success, [strategy] could not be pursued. A strategy which did not consider this would be fore-ordained to failure. The Entente's attacks of the first three years of the war give numerous examples of this."[37] After the war, Kuhl wrote that the St. George attack was seen as an alternative in case Michael failed, but this was a later development; Ludendorff had decided it was impossible to launch Georgette (discussed later) in a timely manner or with any confidence of a breakthrough.[38] It also seems clear that Ludendorff preferred to attack the British because he considered them a less dangerous opponent in open warfare than the French.[39]

Lack of Consensus and Clarity

By this time, three basic considerations had become paramount in planning for the 1918 offensive: (1) the available strength would suffice for one major attack but not for a second, and not even for a major diversion to precede the first; (2) the attack must be made before American intervention became too great; and (3) the attack must be directed against the

British. There was broad consensus among the General Staff in the field units and at the High Command on the first two points but not the third. Ludendorff had made that decision with the support of some but against the opposition of others.[40]

Nevertheless, one should remember that Wetzell and Ludendorff hedged their bets on a single offensive by planning for other efforts. This signified a lack of resolution and unanimity in the High Command, and it is clear that the field commanders had differing views of Ludendorff's intentions. This set the stage for second-guessing after the war, if not for inappropriate action in the spring of 1918. Writing in 1922, Ludendorff claimed that the High Command had planned ahead of time for "many successive attacks following one another at irregular intervals before they would lead to an operation."[41]

This was not the understanding at the time, at least in many quarters. Rupprecht believed the St. George attack would take place only if Michael failed, a view held by Gallwitz as well.[42] Kuhl, perhaps the most involved of the field chiefs and the most respected of the senior General Staff officers overall, also believed the army would execute St. George only if Michael failed.[43] Implementing St. George would thus be a sign of failure, not of success. Krafft von Dellmensingen, writing after the war, blamed the failure of the 1918 offensive on Wetzell's success in obtaining approval for several attacks in succession, which he thought divided the army's resources and, as a result, meant that none of the blows was strong enough.[44] This was part of the related criticism that Ludendorff, with more than one offensive in the back of his mind, did not give Michael all the divisions and supporting artillery available.[45]

Command Arrangements

During his meeting with Kuhl and Schulenburg on 21 January, Ludendorff announced his intention to realign the army groups and assigned specific responsibilities to those involved in the forthcoming offensive. He created a new field army, the Seventeenth, under Otto von Below and assigned it to Rupprecht's army group. He assigned Eighteenth Army to the German crown prince and gave this army group an important role in the Michael offensive. He also created a new army group, named Gallwitz, to take over the German crown prince's sector around Verdun.[46] The result was that two army groups were responsible for conducting the Michael offensive, with neither having any authority over the other.

Ludendorff justified this arrangement with reference to his experience in Poland in 1914, but the influence of domestic political concerns and dynastic politics is apparent. German Crown Prince Wilhelm had played no great role in the war up to that point and could not take credit for any glamorous victories. Ludendorff may have divided control over the offensive, which be hoped would produce a war-winning victory, to avoid the Bavarian crown prince receiving all the credit while the future king of Prussia and German emperor remained in the background. A number of contemporary observers believed this was the case, and the official history felt obliged to issue a denial. Ludendorff's own memoirs unconvincingly defended the decision on the grounds that experience had shown it was better to have more than one army group involved in preparing and executing a large offensive.[47]

Following receipt of the emperor's approval on 23 January 1918, the High Command sent out official orders for reorganizing the western front and preparing for the offensive. The original offensive concept thus consisted of Michael, divided into Michael I (Rupprecht's Seventeenth Army, northeast of Baupaume), Michael II (Rupprecht's Second Army), and Michael III (Wilhelm's Eighteenth Army, on both sides of St. Quentin), along with two supporting attacks—Mars (Rupprecht's Seventeenth Army on both sides of the Scarpe) and Archangel (Wilhelm's Seventh Army south of the Oise).[48] The following text treats all these together and refers to them simply as Michael, to avoid excessive detail. Ludendorff's order reflects a note of hesitation, if not a lack of confidence, for he also ordered Rupprecht's army group to continue to work on the St. George offensive (in Flanders) and to have it ready by the beginning of April.[49]

Kuhl and Rupprecht lacked confidence in Ludendorff's plans for executing the offensive. Even as preparations began, they continued to object to the command arrangements, to the local objectives and directions of the planned advances, and to the lack of a good plan to protect the right flank of the Michael assault.[50] They were particularly concerned that the series of blows, as advocated by Wetzell, had no chance of success.

Ludendorff's Military Goals

Ludendorff had two broad goals for the 1918 offensive, although one of these should be considered a means rather than an end in itself. In the initial stages—that is, during the breakthrough battle—the offensive's primary purpose was the one laid out in "The Attack in Positional Warfare": a resumption of mobile warfare following a successful breakthrough of the British positions. Everything depended on a successful breakthrough and a successful mobile campaign, which was the only kind of war the Germans felt capable of winning. The German army hoped to defeat the British in mobile warfare beyond the trench lines, separate them from the French, and roll up their positions, forcing them against the coast.[51]

There was clear agreement on this point among most writers at the time, even though the proposition has earned the scorn of many historians since then. As one of the field army commands wrote during the early planning stages of Michael: "The tactical breakthrough can never be a goal in and of itself. It is much more a means to bring into use the strongest form of the offense, the flanking attack. A successful breakthrough gives the command freedom to conduct operations, which in positional war exists only within narrow boundaries, and offers the means to force the transformation to mobile warfare."[52] Mobile warfare, in turn, would lead to the ultimate goal: a great victory that enabled Germany to dictate the terms of peace to the Allies.[53] The Michael order of 10 March 1918 presented no overarching strategic goal; rather, it stressed the immediate goal of creating a breakthrough and freeing the army from positional warfare so that it would then be able to advance. The official history explained this relatively narrow focus by referring to Ludendorff's acceptance of Moltke's famous argument that "no plan of campaign extends with any certainty beyond the first encounter with the enemy's main force."[54] In a sense, the army repeated the performance of 1914, in that no single document simply and clearly laid out the means and concepts of the strategy on which the campaign was based. This overall concept existed in the mind of Ludendorff (and presumably Hindenburg), but not in great detail anywhere else.[55]

In any case, with this concept in mind, the staffs of the army groups and field armies made preparations at their respective levels, while the bulk of the army worked feverishly to bring its capabilities up to the tactical demands of the anticipated breakthrough and the resulting mobile war. Historians have criticized Ludendorff for prioritizing tactics over strategy in planning the 1918 offensive, arguing that he understood tactics but not strategy or "operations." A later section of this chapter considers this dubious proposition in detail. On the eastern front, Ludendorff had established a solid record of preparing and executing sweeping operations to exploit breakthroughs and achieve limited strategic goals. The Michael offensive had a major strategic goal: the destruction of the British army and the end of Britain's effective participation in the ground war. This required movements after the breakthrough, which was the sine qua non of the entire campaign. Only later, as the General Staff and the army groups looked for a point where a significant breakthrough seemed possible, did tactical considerations come to the fore. The plan for Michael had a solid strategic foundation only if a breakthrough succeeded. The execution of the series of offensives was another matter.[56]

Preparing the Army for the Offensive

Preparing the German army to implement these new and old ideas in a large-scale offensive with sufficient skill, strength, and endurance to produce a decisive victory was no easy task. Leaving aside the questions of strategy and the choice of locations, the army in late 1917 was utterly unprepared for any major attack in the west. It lacked manpower, equipment and supplies of various kinds, horses (for mobility once a breakthrough was achieved), and, perhaps above all, a core of leaders and soldiers trained for mobile warfare. A new generation of noncommissioned officers and junior officers had entered the army without undergoing traditional training in the Prusso-German way of mobile warfare. Most of the regimental officers of 1914 were either dead or disabled, and their replacements, for the most part, knew only positional warfare, with its emphasis on defense and limited local attacks. Only in exceptional cases were prewar officers still serving at battalion level and lower.[57] Divisions coming from the eastern front had to be acclimated to a different kind of war on the western front, and many of these divisions were politically suspect. Indeed, the war's destabilizing impact on German society had begun to erode the capabilities and cohesion of the officer corps and the enlisted force. The German army, including the junior officer corps, had to be reinforced, reequipped, retrained, redeployed, and reinvigorated before any major offensive was possible, quite aside from all the questions related to strategy and tactics.[58]

Transfers

The army took a number of measures to mass its available manpower for the great task ahead of it. On 1 April 1918 the army had just over 4 million men in the west and about 1.5 million in the east, the Balkans, and Turkey.[59] Although precise numbers are in dispute, it now seems certain that the German army transferred at least thirty-three divisions, of varying quality and strength, from the eastern front to the western front in preparation for the 1918 offensive.[60] Kuhl's postwar study stated that forty divisions were transferred from the east to the west through the middle of March, while the official history reported that thirty-three had been transferred as of the day the offensive began, 21 March 1918.[61] More recently, using intelligence reports on a French study continued by the American Expeditionary Force, one historian supports the Kuhl figure, although he states that forty-four divisions were moved between December and March.[62]

Nor is there agreement on the total number of divisions available in the west when the offensive began. The official history cited 200 as the total divisional strength in the west on 21 March, while Kuhl's corresponding number was 192. The official number seems more reliable. In any case, about 15 percent of the divisions participating in the western offensive were transferred from the eastern front during the period of planning and preparation for the 1918 offensive.[63] The final differences are small, since the official history gave the German army only four fewer divisions by May 1918 (200 versus Kuhl's 204).[64] The western field armies thus undertook the offensive predominantly with their own resources, but that is not the real issue.

The larger question concerns the strength remaining in Russia, about forty divisions, and whether Ludendorff could have drawn on them for even more strength to support what he knew was the final effort to win the war. The annexationist war aims pursued by Ludendorff, as well as the unrest in Russia as the Bolshevik regime attempted to consolidate its power, required an ongoing German presence. Germany hoped to exploit this territory, especially the Ukraine, so some divisions had to remain there. Numbers, however, do not give a full picture of the extent to which the army massed its last reserves for the 1918 offensive.

The *OHL* combed out the eastern divisions for nearly all available resources that would be of use in the forthcoming western campaign. Beginning in October 1917, the War Ministry transferred from the east to the west almost all the younger soldiers (those under thirty-five years of age) who were physically capable and otherwise qualified for the extremely rigorous and dangerous combat conditions in France.[65] The eastern units also sent their best equipment and many thousands of horses to the west. Kuhl argued, convincingly in the eyes of most, that little remained in the east or in the Balkans that could have been of use in the 1918 offensive.

The High Command planned at one point to send 140,000 to 150,000 recruits from the class of 1899 to the recruit depots in the east and receive in exchange an equal number of physically qualified men between twenty-five and thirty years of age. As it turned out, it could find only 107,000 to send, and dispatching even this number proved impossible. Almost 20 percent of the combat-capable soldiers in the east were from Alsace-Lorraine, and the army considered them too unreliable to use on the western front. About half of the total strength in the eastern units was considered unreliable for various reasons, and those men were being watched over by the remaining half. Many of the reliable soldiers were too old for duty on the western front. The result was that about 30,000 to 40,000 young men from the class of 1899 were sent to the western recruit depots for training and maturation before being assigned to divisions at the front.[66] Overall, as the official history concluded, very little remained in the east that might have been useful on the western front, even for the construction of rear defensive lines.[67] An additional problem was that soldiers arriving from the east, even in November 1917, had notoriously poor discipline and showed little respect for officers.[68]

The overall German manpower situation in March 1918 was on the verge of a fatal crisis, awaiting only a single additional campaign, offensive or defensive, to usher in an irreversible decline. Even so, the official history tried to paint a rosy picture.[69] Many divisions had been filled up with men from the *Landsturm*, some of whom were older than forty. The recruit class of 1917, born in 1898, had been exhausted, and the class born in 1899 was already in training programs. The class of 1918, born in 1900, could not be drafted until the late autumn. Even if it had been available, this class of recruits had only about 250,000 men, while the normal monthly wastage was about 150,000. The army was thus short about 354,000 men even before the offensive began.[70] This situation could only worsen once the offensive started, and this proved to be the case. As the Americans started to arrive at alarming rates, up to 200,000 per month, German strength was on an irreversible downward spiral. Training in the units and skill in leadership had to compensate for manpower weaknesses.

Structure

By this phase of the war, the old distinctions among the divisions (active, reserve, *Landwehr*, and *Ersatz*) had disappeared, except for the names.[71]

Instead, the army divided its infantry divisions into two broad categories in preparing for the offensive: positional (*Stellungsdivisionen*) and mobile.[72] All infantry divisions had the basic triangular infantry structure (three infantry regiments), but the mobile divisions had full or nearly full complements of horses and wagons to enable them to conduct open warfare in the traditional manner. The positional divisions had very little mobility and were of much less value in both offensive combat and a war of movement. Even this distinction eroded once the offensive began, however, as the field armies and corps had to use their positional divisions in the same manner as the mobile units, to the extent possible.

The army designated 44 divisions as "mobile" for the 1918 offensive, while the other 196 divisions, including about 160 on the western front, were considered positional divisions. These mobile divisions, which would both participate in the attack and conduct mobile operations to crush the Allied forces, had nearly full complements of horses, extra machine gun units, attached aviation sections, vehicles for munitions and supplies of all kinds, and mobile bakeries, kitchens, and medical facilities. Their infantry battalions had their full authorized strength of 850 soldiers, not including their machine gun companies (one each).[73] They also underwent a comprehensive training program, described below.

The positional divisions were not equivalent with regard to their initial equipment, but they were broadly similar in terms of mobility. About 26 of these divisions received nearly full complements of men and equipment and were trained to participate in the opening attacks on Allied defensive positions. Their utility could decrease, however, if the battlefields became fluid. Thus, about 70 divisions were at least marginally equipped and manned for the offensive.[74] All other divisions on the western front, about 130 in all, were suitable only for defense and very limited local offensive action. The formal distinction between mobile and positional divisions fell by the wayside by the end of the Michael offensive, as the demands of the war forced commanders to use whatever divisions were available at any given point or time.[75]

Training

The *OHL* recognized the need to retrain virtually the entire army in a variety of skills prior to the offensive. These needs fell into several categories: (1) training officers and men in the new breakthrough tactics; (2) training officers and men, as well as units at several levels, for a return to mobile warfare, in which the western army had very little experience at battalion level and above; and (3) training the eastern divisions in the new tactics and for the very different combat conditions of the western front. Some of this training had been in progress since 1917, primarily in defensive fighting and, at the small-unit level, in assault unit tactics since 1916. The demands placed on junior leaders by the new manuals for offensive tactics in positional warfare and for the very different requirements at all levels in mobile warfare made this training essential.[76]

The army thus established training programs of several types to prepare the divisions, especially the mobile divisions, for the 1918 offensive. Junior officers in the mobile divisions and in many of the positional divisions that would be participating in the initial assault attended training courses at Sedan and Valenciennes, beginning in September 1917. These courses eventually became more comprehensive and were extended to four weeks.[77] Officers from the eastern units in particular were in need of additional training to prepare them for the difficult conditions in the west. The general inspector of the Field Artillery Gunnery School reported that the young eastern-front officers knew nothing of the new regulations and not much about the old ones, either.[78]

In addition to these courses for leaders, the field armies used their rear-area training areas to prepare entire mobile divisions for the upcoming offensive. The High Command ordered each field army to prepare such a course, initially set to last three weeks.[79] Eventually, a typical course consisted of about six weeks of training in mobile warfare arranged in sequence, moving from individual soldier skills to company, battalion, regimental, and even brigade levels. This training concentrated on loose lines of skirmishers, use of mobile guns and mortars in support of open-field attacks, and assaults on trench lines. The training sequence culminated in brigade-level movements and combat exercises, as well as lengthy marches to contact. Overall, the training program incorporated the two new tactical elements—reliance on lower-level units as combat elements and use of extended skirmish lines—within the older framework of large-unit maneuver. At the end, a brigade of three regiments, supported by the division's supporting elements, was expected to conduct an advance leading to a successful meeting engagement in the open field. Ludendorff kept in touch with the training program to some degree, at least. For example, in February he warned the divisions to make better preparations for using their gas capabilities.[80]

The units coming from the eastern and Balkan fronts required a training program tailored to their peculiar and acute needs.[81] In November 1917 the *OHL* endorsed a formal training program developed by Fourth Army and produced a miniature regulation (twenty-six pages) for use in training all the divisions coming to the western front. The regulation cautioned officers that combat in the west was much more demanding than in the east. Units would have to make adjustments to avoid heavy losses and failure, and they were warned not to underestimate the British and French artillery or to overestimate their own.[82] Ludendorff's guidelines stressed preparations for mobile warfare and exercises by divisions as a whole. The directive stressed "exercises in combined arms, the division in the advance, and the attack across open areas and at great distances to revive the deeply-rooted fresh offensive spirit of the German soldier."[83] Ironically, at the middle levels of command (regimental and battalion), the eastern units were better prepared for mobile warfare than were some western units.[84]

The main doctrinal materials used in the training program reflected the effort to return these divisions to the prewar emphasis on offensive warfare, as modified by the practical experiences of the war in the west. These materials were the *Sammelheft* for positional warfare, the training regulations for the infantry (1918), *Anleitung für Kompanieführer* (discussed above), the pamphlet *Der Sturmangriff* (1917), and the training regulations for the field artillery. The guidelines provided a lengthy list of individual combat skills that had to be mastered by soldiers from the eastern units and an even more comprehensive list of skills to be acquired at the battalion level. In addition to comprehensive training programs at every unit level, the guidelines urged eastern and western units to exchange the following officers for several weeks of duty with the other: division commanders, General Staff officers and other officers on the division staffs, infantry brigade staffs, artillery commanders, and officers from regiments (infantry and artillery) and from combat engineers, mortars, and communications sections.[85]

The storm battalions participated in the army's training program by conducting a series of intensive courses between January and May 1918. Numerous divisions withdrew from the front lines for a four-week training program beginning in December 1917. The courses emphasized the offensive mobile warfare the army hoped to conduct after breaking through the Allied defensive lines. By the end of February, at least thirty-one divisions had undergone such a training course and were ready for employment in the upcoming offensive.[86]

Weapons and Mobility

The army had sufficient weapons in the spring of 1918 to support the planned offensive. More than enough artillery and munitions were available, subject to the limitations of what could be deployed in trained and reasonably mobile units. Likewise, substantially more machine guns and rifles were on hand than were required. The increases in machine gun production had allowed the army to equip nearly every infantry battalion with twelve heavy machine guns, while each company had five light machine guns and two mortars directly under its control.[87] The central difficulty was bringing these weapons and munitions to the front and then forward to the advancing battlefront—a question of tactical mobility and transport.[88]

The German army's transport system in 1918, just as in 1914 and 1941, was largely dependent on horses for tactical mobility and for logistical and fire support. Insufficient horses and a shortage of fodder had been problems even in the opening campaign of 1914, and they only became worse over the course of the war. The mere expansion of the army, not to mention the loss of horses, meant that it had actually become less mobile between 1914 and the end of 1917. While the army had increased in size by roughly 140 percent, the number of horses had increased by only 80 percent. Losses were staggering—an average of 16,000 per month in 1916—and the army struggled in vain to replace them. The army lost another 215,000 horses the following year, with about 90 percent of these losses being attributable to illness and exhaustion rather than combat. The prewar regulations on provisions called for twelve to twenty-six pounds of "hard" fodder per day, but by 1918, the army could provide each horse with only about half of that. Trucks could not make up for the shortage of transport, even though the army's totals had risen from about 5,000 trucks in 1914 to 35,500 in 1918. The German army in the west had about 23,000 trucks, only one-quarter of the number available to the Allies.[89] The entire country, including the army, was critically short of fuel and rubber for tires, and iron wheels were no substitute. As a result, the army's transport system would not have allowed the 130 positional divisions or the eastern divisions to be turned into "mobile" divisions, regardless of any other considerations. A successful offensive would only have made the situation worse. It is small wonder that many high commanders regarded the shortage of capable horses as the most serious concern at the outset of the 1918 offensive.[90]

Doubtful Commanders, Hopeful Soldiers

The army's highest leaders, disregarding the enigmatic and frequently irrelevant figure of the emperor, were aware that the challenges facing Germany in the spring of 1918 were enormous. Ludendorff allegedly told Wilhelm II that the forthcoming offensive was "the most enormous military task that had ever been given to an army."[91] Although numerous confident statements emerged in the early months of 1918, many high-ranking officers had their personal doubts about the prospects of the planned offensive.[92] Both Rupprecht and Wilhelm, as well as their respective chiefs Kuhl and Schulenburg, recorded their private doubts that the army could achieve a decisive victory.[93] Wilhelm II, with his usual lack of judgment, allegedly acknowledged the difficulties of the offensive but found comfort in Ludendorff's assurances that the Germans could prevail even if a great breakthrough did not result.[94] Wilhelm Groener regarded the offensive as doomed from the outset.[95] Ludendorff's own inner feelings are difficult to judge. His confidence seems to have reassured Chancellor Prince Max of Baden, even though Ludendorff acknowledged that failure would result in the ruination of Germany.[96] Yet just a few days later, Ludendorff expressed his own private doubts to Groener, who was on his way to take over a corps in the Ukraine.[97] Apparently, officers coming from the eastern front were more confident than those who were more familiar with the circumstances in France.[98] Most observers agree, however, that the army as a whole, especially the field units, acquired a new spirit of optimism and had substantial confidence in what many hoped would be the final great campaign of the war.

Michael

The story of the German offensive in 1918 has been told many times.[99] Here, only a brief overview is possible. At the risk of oversimplification, the High Command plan called for two army groups to begin the offensive on 21 March using the code names Michael, Mars, and Archangel. Michael involved an effort to cut off the Cambrai salient with converging attacks by two of Rupprecht's armies (Seventeenth and Second), while farther south, Wilhelm's Eighteenth Army attacked on both sides of St. Quentin. The Mars attack by Seventeenth Army (in Wilhelm's army group) was a simultaneous advance south of the Scarpe River. In the other connected attack, Archangel, Wilhelm's Seventh Army was to attack south of the Oise River, but not immediately. His forces were to advance along the Somme River to the area around Arras and continue to the Crozat Canal, where they were to protect the German offensive's left flank against French counterattacks. The plan was to cut off the Cambrai salient and destroy the British forces, drive a wedge between the French and British armies, and win the war with a mobile campaign against the separated enemies. The main effort was that of Rupprecht's forces north of the Somme. The long-studied St. George attack, against the British and Belgians farther north in Flanders, was not part of the opening offensive.[100]

The German forces in France were by no means superior overall to those of the Allies, although the involved armies had local superiority at the outset. Gerhard Ritter, then a junior officer in one of the mobile divisions, drew a sober picture of the weaknesses already apparent in what should have been one of the army's best units.[101] The German army deployed a total of 192 divisions, many of them understrength, against 178 Allied divisions. Three American divisions were at the front but not in the areas of the opening assaults. The Allies enjoyed significant superiority in aircraft (4,500 to 3,670), artillery (18,500 to 14,000), tanks (800 to 10), and trucks (100,000 to 23,000). Seventeenth Army deployed about 19 divisions, including 2 of the positional variety; Second Army 18, including 3 positional; and Eighteenth Army had 24 divisions, including 3 positional ones. Including the forces ready for Mars, a total of 76 divisions were ready to begin the offensive on 21 March 1918.[102]

The British had ample reason to expect a major attack, but they were not yet well prepared in the area opposite the two German army groups. They were in the process of adopting a defensive system similar to the one the Germans had developed in 1917, but the effort had only partially succeeded by the day the attack began.[103] The British divisions were in a state of transformation, as they had just reduced the number of infantry battalions from thirteen to ten. On the plus side for the British, the terrain was suitable for the defense, as the ground had been churned up in previous battles and the area had been devastated by the German withdrawal to the Siegfried Line the previous year.[104] Deserters had warned of an impending attack as early as 2 March, and captured aviators and infantry soldiers taken on 18–19 March had confirmed that the attack would follow on 20 or 21 March.[105]

On 21 March 1918, at 5:05 a.m., the German offensive began with a five-hour artillery barrage of about 6,000 artillery pieces and 3,000 mortars.[106] The fog of war literally obscured the battlefield, and the thick mist

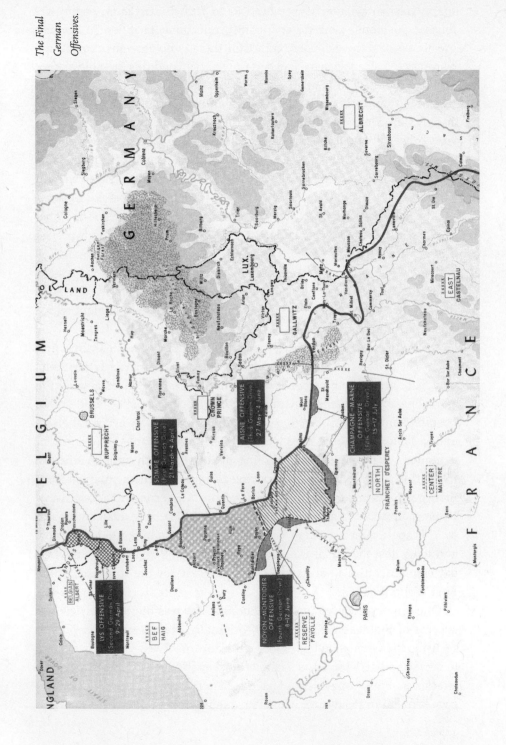

The Final
German
Offensives.

created great confusion as the German infantry moved to the attack at 9:40. German aviation soon moved in to launch attacks on enemy defensive positions, artillery, and communications facilities.[107] The fog greatly assisted the defenders, although there is no agreement on its decisiveness.[108] The Germans had certainly anticipated this kind of weather problem, but they were unable to deal with it effectively.[109] German units moved to the wrong places and had difficulty observing enemy positions and signaling to the artillery for fire adjustment. The artillery, deprived of visual observation, had to use Pulkowski's procedures and the preplanned shifting of fires in accordance with the rolling barrage's schedule.[110] The preplanned fires sometimes inflicted casualties on Germans who were in the targeted areas, but the artillery more often advanced too quickly, leaving the German infantry to deal with surviving defensive positions alone. The first assault waves neutralized some British positions and bypassed others, which then had to be engaged by following echelons, sometimes with great losses. In spite of these problems, the attack achieved substantial results on the first day. On a frontage of about fifty miles, the Germans had advanced an average of two miles, a fantastic accomplishment on the western front.

Nevertheless, in most places the Germans failed to achieve their first day's objective, which was to penetrate into the enemy's artillery zone, usually behind the third position and thus about five miles beyond the front lines.[111] Seventeenth Army, for example, overran the first British position along most of its front but made little headway against the second, a failure that kept the British artillery in the battle.[112] The British defended capably, even though some historians, such as John Keegan, have criticized them harshly. Surviving machine gunners emerged from their positions and inflicted heavy losses on the German attackers. Local British counterattacks stopped the German advance at several points, and by afternoon, Allied aviation had begun to provide effective air support and to contest the initial German air superiority.[113] In any case, the first day can be seen as a substantial German victory by the standards of the First World War.

One important development on the first day was the relatively greater success of Eighteenth Army, which originally had the defensive goal of securing the German left flank along the Somme River–Crozat Canal line to serve as a barrier to French counterattacks.[114] Since Eighteenth Army's attack was highly successful, Ludendorff reinforced it substantially and gave it free rein to advance where the enemy was weakest. This changed the emphasis of the attack, shifting the German *Schwerpunkt* (main effort) to the far southern flank of the Michael attack. This seemed reasonable in a purely tactical context, since Ludendorff was reinforcing success and widening the attempted breakthrough, but it bore little if any positive relationship to the overall framework of the offensive.[115]

On the second and third days of the offensive, 22–23 March, the Germans seemed to achieve a major victory. The advance continued along most of the front, but more so in the center and south than in the north. By 23 March, the crown prince's Eighteenth Army had apparently achieved a significant breakthrough, advancing far beyond the Somme-Crozat line, nearly forty miles at one point, and opening a very wide gap in the Allied line. On the northern flank, the Germans had not broken through the British third position by 23 March, but they had penetrated to a depth of around four miles. In the center and south, however, the penetration had reached twelve miles, and a return to mobile warfare in the desired manner seemed possible, even though the British forces in the Cambrai salient had not been annihilated.[116] German artillery support decreased substantially as the infantry advanced, since the guns simply could not move forward quickly enough to keep the front line in range.

On 23 March Ludendorff, in a meeting with the army group chiefs and in the presence of the emperor, definitely shifted the weight of the attack to the south, thus decisively altering the concept of the 10 March order. He redirected Second Army's attack to the south and allowed Eighteenth Army to begin a major assault against the French before the British had been decisively defeated.[117] Seventeenth, Sixth, and Fourth Armies were instructed to throw the English into the sea. The new goal was to attack vigorously on both sides of the Somme River. This, in effect, split the German offensive into three divergent thrusts to the west, southwest, and northwest. The entire Michael offensive had thus reached a crossroads. Given the apparent success on both sides of the Somme, Ludendorff had to decide whether the army had sufficient strength to attack in three directions simultaneously. To retain the original concept of massing all available strength for a single decisive stroke while defending elsewhere, Ludendorff would have to halt the most successful attack, thus giving the enemy opposite Eighteenth Army an opportunity to recover. Instead, he ordered the diverging advances to continue. This decision gave rise to Kuhl's well-known question: "But what else should have been done?" For the moment, the results seemed to justify the decision to continue the attack based on these very visible successes.[118]

Both sides overestimated the scope of these initial German successes. The British, alarmed by the Germans' progress on their front, considered withdrawing to the channel ports, lest they be disastrously defeated before French assistance arrived.[119] A great crisis had obviously arisen on the Allied side, and on 24 March Ludendorff announced in an official press release that the opening battle had been won.[120] The statement gave many details about the advances of the individual field armies and boasted of the 30,000 prisoners and 600 guns captured.[121] The ever-impetuous kaiser began an extremely premature public celebration. He awarded Hindenburg the Iron Cross with Golden Rays, an award that had last been given to Marshal Blücher, as Herwig points out, "for ridding Prussia of Napoleon."[122] By 25 March, in fact, the fundamental weaknesses of the German war machine came into play as exhausted units had to remain at the front and logistical support of the forward units began to weaken.[123]

The Allies reacted to their initial defeats by taking a variety of measures to restore the front and ensure a cooperative effort. The most important of these was the creation of a limited unified supreme command on 26 March under Marshal Foch, who quickly dispatched twenty French divisions to assist the British and restore confidence in Allied solidarity.[124] This solution was a limited one, in that the united command extended only to French and British forces, and even for them, it merely authorized the commander "to coordinate the action" of the Allied armies.[125] Still, it was an important step. On 9 April the governments agreed to expand Foch's authority and to appoint him commander in chief of the Allied armies in France.[126]

Actually, the German offensive had already lost much of its momentum. By 26 March, the British and French resistance, though costly and unable to hold ground, had inflicted very heavy losses on the German infantry units. Of the thirty-seven divisions at the front of the advance on 26 March, for example, eight had already been withdrawn for rest and then reinserted. They had to be sent back into the front line because the divisions that replaced them were already in need of rest—after only five days of attacking and advancing. Only twenty-two mobile divisions had yet to be employed on the entire Michael-Mars-Archangel front. Officer casualties had already outstripped the available "commander reserve." Losses in horses were so severe that all available mounts had to be taken out of headquarters and dispatched to the logistical or artillery units. The muddy ground frequently forced the artillery to use double teams of horses, ten per gun, to move forward.[127] Communications were very slow, and orders took hours to cross the cratered and otherwise devastated area through which the Germans had to advance. As a result, attacks ordered to begin at dawn did not start until midday in many cases.[128]

By 26 March, the Allied air forces had gained air superiority and were beginning to inflict severe losses on the Germans. As a result, German aerial reconnaissance and artillery spotting became very difficult. Morale among the soldiers also began to falter under the pressure of Allied aviation. Indeed, by 28 March, the units estimated that Allied airpower was responsible for about half their casualties; even if exaggerated, this indicated the problems encountered when the German air force lost its temporary superiority.[129]

Despite all this, on 26 March Ludendorff renewed his decision to continue the attack. Army Group Rupprecht continued its assault, as did Army Group Wilhelm to the south of the Somme. Ludendorff established far-reaching goals: for Sixth Army, Boulogne; for Eighteenth Army, Compiegne. Within the next twenty-four hours, however, Allied resistance stiffened and halted the German advance at most points. Losses on both sides were high, about 75,000 for the British and 90,000 for the Germans. Fresh Allied divisions mounted powerful local counterattacks, and the German reserves were nearly exhausted.

On 28 March the general failure to achieve decisive results became clear even to Ludendorff. Wetzell proposed to conclude Michael and regroup the forces for the St. George offensive, but Ludendorff declined. By this time, the Mars attack had also failed, and all hopes rested on Eighteenth Army. But little progress was made there, for Allied defenses along that section of the front proved the equal of the new German tactical methods, at least when conducted without extensive preparations.[130] The new tactics were heavily dependent on very lengthy and detailed preparations of all kinds. When time or resources were lacking for these preparations, mere "assault unit" tactics were not sufficient, as experience repeatedly demonstrated.

On 30 March the bill for failure had surpassed even Ludendorff's ability to ignore or juggle the figures. The German armies made no progress on that date, and by the following day, Ludendorff recognized that the army could no longer mount major attacks. He accepted a pause while the divisions and corps improved their communications and logistical situation, but he still hoped the southern attack would be able to continue.[131] All these hopes were in vain, however, and on 5 April the *OHL* ordered an end to the Michael offensive, except where local circumstances required attacks to improve defensive positions. Along this section of the front, the circumstances of 1917 returned.[132]

Georgette

As the Michael attack lost momentum, Ludendorff turned his attention, possibly at Wetzell's insistence, toward an attack against the British in Flanders. Originally known as St. George, this plan, long the favorite of Rupprecht and Kuhl, had undergone a reduction in size and a concomitant change in name. The smaller version, called Georgette, was larger than the extremely scaled-down version first discussed under that code name, but it was much reduced from the earliest concept. The official history used the name Georgette, although many German documents and later accounts still called it St. George or referred to the resulting combat as the Battle of Armentieres.[133] On 1 April Ludendorff decided to launch Georgette on the eighth of that month.[134]

The plan called for an attack by two of Rupprecht's armies against the British and Portuguese sector of the front near Armentieres. Sixth Army was to attack from Armentieres on the La Bassee Canal to the northwest, toward Hazebrouck, a key rail junction about fifteen miles beyond the front line, and Cassel, a town about twenty-five miles from the start line. Fourth Army, starting a day later due to delays in artillery deployment, was to advance generally to the west and southwest from Messines (north of Armentieres) to strike the British rear and flank. The real object of this attack was unclear, and it bore no resemblance to the original St. George proposal, which involved a sweeping attack against the entire British-Belgian position in Flanders. The most that could be hoped for under these reduced circumstances was taking some relatively unimportant high terrain around Kemmel Ridge or inflicting a local (if costly) defeat on the British forces on both sides of Armentieres.[135] Army Group Rupprecht's attack order stated that if Georgette achieved great success, the army group would immediately send all available forces there to exploit the victory. Earlier proposals had aimed at pushing the entire British army in Flanders back to the coast, but this far-reaching goal seemed to be secondary in the actual Georgette preparation and planning.

Army Group Rupprecht had a total of twenty-nine divisions available for the attack, only nineteen of which were mobile or attack divisions, and not all of which were fresh. The available artillery and air support was far weaker than had been the case for Michael, and few of the careful preparations of the former were completed by 9 April.[136] One innovation was the effort to use fifteen tanks (organized in three sections of five each), using some captured Allied vehicles, to attack bypassed enemy centers of resistance.[137]

The British army knew the attack was coming, but its position was not a strong one along much of the threatened area. Divisional fronts averaged 7,500 yards, far too large for even fully capable units of this size. Many of the British divisions had suffered serious losses in the Michael attack, although others were fresh. Worse, in an effort to pull the Portuguese corps out of the line before the Germans struck, the British had temporarily doubled the frontage of one of the two Portuguese divisions. As a result, an important sector was thinly held by troops that, according to Cruttwell, "were undoubtedly the worst of any nation in the West, and had always been regarded as practically worthless."[138]

The British defenses, though deep and laid out in three positions in most areas, were aboveground due to the high water levels in the low-lying areas along much of the front. The Germans could thus easily observe and engage these breastwork-type positions, a problem previously faced by German defenders in this area in 1916 and 1917. Remarkably, Rupprecht and Kuhl seemed to be reasonably confident of a substantial victory.[139] They had wanted to undertake a version of this offensive since November 1917, and their chance had come at last, though under much less favorable circumstances than originally assumed.

Like Michael, the German attack made substantial progress on the first day (9 April), but once again, neither as much progress as planned nor as seemed necessary.[140] The Portuguese division broke and ran, losing some soldiers to fire from their British allies, who thought they were advancing Germans. The German tanks, only two sections of which were actually available, quickly became mired in the mud and contributed absolutely nothing. Sixth Army advanced to a depth of about five miles and captured around 6,000 prisoners and 100 guns. Nevertheless, the first day's goals were not achieved, and by the night of 9 April, Sixth Army had to hope it would receive assistance from Fourth Army's attack, scheduled for the following morning.

In the rain and fog of first light on 10 April, Fourth Army launched its infantry assault, a mere three divisions on a front of about seven miles. The attack made little progress against stiff resistance. The Germans took about 1,300 prisoners but could not achieve a real breakthrough. The battle continued for the next several days in much the same manner. The

Germans achieved several local successes—for example, on the tenth they seized Armentieres and captured 3,000 prisoners—but their accounts paint a picture of failure and frustration. Even a local breakthrough by 16th Division near Merville, in which a British brigade staff and two batteries were captured, offered only limited hope for a decisive victory. Nevertheless, the threat seemed serious enough to alarm the British Supreme Command. Haig's headquarters gave preliminary orders for the evacuation of Calais and for massive flooding west of Dunkirk. On 11 April Haig issued his famous "backs to the wall order," which in retrospect seems to be a reflection of panic rather than a commendable act of heroic leadership.

The Germans, for their part, recognized from the outset that the battle was not going as well as their situation required. This was, of course, a consistent theme in 1918. No offensive achieved what was necessary for the strategy to succeed. Optimism and faulty estimates of the situation nearly always led to unrealistic expectations that were beyond the capabilities of the units or that failed to consider effective enemy countermeasures. Foch, the Allied supreme commander, regarded the entire attack as a diversion and consistently declined to replace worn-out British divisions with French forces, which he hoped to use only in important counterattacks. As usual, his strategic judgment proved sound, even if it made those who had to accept it uncomfortable.[141] His resolve weakened only twice. On 12 April he agreed to send two infantry and three cavalry divisions to reinforce the British, and by 19 April, he established two new French field armies of nine infantry and three cavalry divisions under Haig's command. These were used, however, according to his concepts, rather than as piecemeal replacements all along the line.[142]

The course of the battle made Ludendorff just as nervous as Haig. He sent numerous General Staff officers to the front-line corps and divisions to monitor the situation and thus gained knowledge of developments sooner than did the personnel of the army and army group headquarters. He then frequently issued orders and admonitions directly to the front units, violating the hallowed authority and responsibility of his highest field leaders. This was nothing new, of course, as complaints about Ludendorff's and his staff's involvement (or interference) in tactical matters were long-standing. Nevertheless, the intensity and frequency of this kind of intervention increased to new levels during the Georgette offensive.[143]

From 16 to 29 April the battle raged relentlessly as the Germans continued to press forward against increasingly effective Allied defenses and local counterattacks. On 19 April Rupprecht requested that the *OHL* abandon the attack and go over to the defense, since further attacks would require strong artillery and detailed preparations if they were to have any hope of success.[144] Nevertheless, Ludendorff persisted, demanding ever greater efforts and ruthless exertion of will. Still, the battlefields in the Flanders lowlands retained their ability to impose a sense of reality on the armies that attacked across them. The last major German attack ended in complete failure on 29 April, when the Georgette effort was effectively over except for some sporadic local actions in May. The second offensive of 1918 thus failed to achieve important results beyond worsening the already precarious German strategic situation, although that fact was still beyond Ludendorff's grasp. German losses were about 86,000; those of the Allies were about 100,000, including 30,000 prisoners.[145] Attrition, unfortunately, was precisely the outcome that the entire effort of 1918 had been designed to avoid.

The causes of the failure were many, but two points stand out. First, the offensive was a failure primarily in its strategic context. To the Germans in 1918, "winning" or "succeeding" meant a decisive breakthrough that restored mobile warfare and led to a strategic victory and a favorable peace within a relatively short time. Prospects of the latter decreased monthly with the arrival of the Americans. Thus, no amount of tactical virtuosity could compensate for failing to achieve the strategic goal. Second, the new German system of the infantry attack was proving to be less productive in tactics than hoped for (or than some historians have portrayed).

The real causes of failure, therefore, were merely manifestations of the same fundamental weaknesses and institutional shortcomings that had always been present in the German army. German losses could not be replaced, and the infantry units gradually lost their power for sustained attack, just as they had lost their defensive strength in 1917. Artillery support again failed to achieve close coordination with the infantry's advance; worse, neither it nor its munitions could be brought forward in sufficient quantity. Lack of battlefield mobility remained a central problem beyond the enemy's first lines.[146]

In a related problem, the new infantry tactics, here as elsewhere, were only as effective as the infantry's artillery support. German theory never accepted the French view that artillery conquers and the infantry occupies, but the latter view was closer to reality in these circumstances. Equally important, the new German methods of attack failed when either time or resources for detailed preparations were lacking or when, after a local success against front-line positions, subsequent attacks had to be improvised.[147] Defense remained the stronger form of warfare, particularly if the defender were capable of effective counterattacks. It is also clear that the German supply system and the soldiers' morale were beginning to falter under the pressure of sustained combat. The German official history tried to cover this up with the seemingly innocuous statement that "provisioning created no difficulties, since this could be covered for the most part from the conquered area."[148] Other accounts made it clear that even at this stage of the war, hungry German soldiers frequently stopped to loot the well-stocked British field positions and depots, which was a potentially serious problem.[149]

For its part, the *OHL* concluded that its new offensive tactics had proved themselves again in Georgette. The artillery preparation had been effective against the English artillery, but once again, the rolling barrage had not been entirely satisfactory.[150] The *OHL* indicated that future rolling barrages should be slower, with four to five minutes allowed for each 100 yards of advance. The issue of linking the rolling barrage with the infantry advance "remained an unresolved problem," in the words of the official history's summary of the High Command's conclusions. In a meaningful commentary on the army's ability to use the new tactical methods, the High Command admonished the infantry not to rely on the artillery alone to overcome enemy resistance, but to use its own primary weapon—the machine gun. Better training in machine guns was necessary, despite the emphasis placed on this aspect of training and rearming the army in the winter of 1917–1918. The High Command also recommended rear attacks on Allied tanks with mortars, machine guns, and hand grenades.[151] A lengthy General Staff notice to the field on 17 April made numerous points about the strengths and weaknesses of the offensive tactics to date.[152]

Following the failure and termination of Georgette, the *OHL* had to decide on a course of action commensurate with the strategic situation, its objectives, and the available resources, or it could decide to abandon the entire project and revert to the defensive. Ludendorff faced the same unavoidable problem he had confronted from the earliest planning for the Michael offensive: the American army continued to arrive, irrevocably turning the force ratios against Germany in the long run. If the German army could not win a military victory soon, defeat would follow. Whether a negotiated peace was possible at this point, given hardened objectives and increased determination in France and Britain, is doubtful, but Ludendorff stubbornly refused to give up his annexationist policies and to conclude a peace on the best terms obtainable from the Allies. He answered the unanswerable logic of the increasingly unfavorable imbalance of strength by reverting to an old principle of the Prussian way of war: the strength of human will and its ability to overcome superior numbers.[153] The High Command, which by May 1918 was particularly sensitive to the worsening domestic political situation, may have desired another series of attacks to combat defeatism and unrest within Germany.[154] So Ludendorff persevered in what was, in retrospect, a hopeless or nearly hopeless situation. It should be noted that the *OHL* felt compelled to hide the real results from the public and the Reichstag, pretending it had planned successive offensives from the outset.[155]

The basic strategic design of the 1918 campaign would have called for a renewed attack against the British, a step that was never far from Ludendorff's mind. But the High Command thought the balance of forces along the Michael-Georgette sections of the front was too unfavorable to offer any immediate prospects of an important success. The dual pressure of securing a strategic victory without suffering crippling losses thus forced Ludendorff to attack a relatively weak sector of the front, not merely, as is often maintained, because of the conflict between tactics and strategy but also because such a strategic design was not capable of execution in the circumstances after Michael-Georgette.

The High Command had to find a vulnerable sector that it could attack productively with the twenty-five to thirty divisions available.[156] It found such a place in the French position in the Champagne, generally on the line between La Fere and Reims, along the Aisne River. Ludendorff hoped to use an offensive there to draw Allied forces away from Flanders and thus enable an eventual renewal of the attack there, code-named Hagen.[157] Ludendorff apparently never recognized that the entire scheme was bankrupt from the outset, since the weakened German forces could not concentrate sufficient forces to attain a meaningful superiority on either sector, let alone mount two offensives simultaneously. He later justified the decision on the usual grounds that remaining on the defensive would be just as costly as launching the new attack.[158] Ludendorff decided that this offensive could not succeed unless he could convince the Allied forces there to thin out in support of other areas.

Blücher and Gneisenau

To prepare the way for Hagen, the *OHL* devised two sets of attacks in an effort to pull French and perhaps English reserves away from the Flanders front. The first, usually known as Blücher, would strike French Sixth Army along the Chemin des Dames and the area to the southeast around Reims.[159] The second effort, known as Gneisenau, would be a smaller and later supporting attack farther to the north, near Noyon. The Blücher attack was the product of Army Group Wilhelm and Wetzell, and Ludendorff accepted it because he saw no prospect of a renewed attack in the Michael sector.[160]

The Blücher attack, launched by German Seventh Army (Army Group Wilhelm), aimed at a deep penetration through French Sixth Army's front and was one of the most carefully prepared of the 1918 offensives. Bruchmüller again supervised what was probably the most effective German artillery bombardment on the western front. The German artillery massed an average of 144 guns per mile of front (5,263 along the thirty-four miles of the line), a denser concentration than that available for Michael or Georgette, though on a smaller scale. Although the terrain, pockmarked by previous battles and positions, favored the defender, the French garrison was relatively weak and particularly vulnerable because its commander had disproportionately concentrated it in the forward positions. The Germans hoped to achieve success through a combination of close cooperation between infantry and artillery and the achievement of tactical surprise. They frequently subordinated their infantry tactics to the pace and nature of the rolling barrage, the responsibility for which was given to division commanders to some extent.[161] Most of the attacking divisions, though relatively refreshed from the earlier battles, were seriously understrength in their infantry battalions.[162]

German First and Seventh Armies began Blücher in the predawn hours of 27 May with the normal Bruchmüller-Pulkowski artillery bombardment, followed by the infantry assault at dawn. The attack, assisted by almost total surprise, achieved extraordinary success at most points, though initially it was hindered as much by the confusing intervention of the High Command as by French resistance. Like the British in the early days of Michael, the French had failed to prepare an effective defense in depth, with similar results.[163] The German successes created "consternation" at French headquarters, which had expected an attack farther north.[164] Foch kept his nerve despite a wide and deep penetration of the French lines over the next five days. He correctly recognized this as a diversionary effort that was less threatening than it appeared.[165] The German High Command, astonished by its own success, expanded the offense and extended its goals beyond the limited and indefinite original objectives. By 30 May, German soldiers had advanced along a twelve-mile front and had taken 42,000 prisoners and more than 400 pieces of artillery. This marked their first return to the Marne River since their original retreat forty-five months previously, and they were within thirty-five miles of Paris.[166]

The unexpected magnitude of the initial success both deceived the attackers about the true nature of the overall situation and presented its own problems. Ludendorff had to decide whether he should retain the available forces for the future major attack in the north (Hagen) or commit them in Blücher. He chose to send much of the small force available to exploit the initial success along the Chemin des Dames.[167] Even this effort to find a local victory, however, soon proved illusory.

The increasingly skillful French resistance soon took its toll, and over the next twenty-four hours the overall German inferiority (thirty German against thirty-three Allied divisions) gradually emerged as the decisive factor. By 2 June, the attack had obviously lost its momentum, despite Ludendorff's dispatch of reinforcements. Wetzell, always on the brink between insightful creativity and mad self-delusion, may have thought the lagging attack was actually a serious threat to Paris. On 4 June the field armies reduced their efforts to well-prepared local attacks as the period of mobile warfare quickly came to an end and the normal positional warfare of the western front returned.[168] The effective action of the US Marines at Belleau Wood on 4 June was not decisive, but it symbolized the futility of the entire German effort of 1918.[169] By 4 June, even Petain realized that the crisis, always more apparent than real in the strategic sense, was over.[170] The German High Command finally recognized this reality and officially ended the offensive on 14 June, nearly two weeks after its failure had become clear to all.

As even the official history recognized, the Blücher offensive was a counterproductive failure in nearly every possible respect. The forces available were insufficient to achieve any strategic success or even to attract large enemy reserves, and the reinforcements came too late because the *OHL* still regarded Blücher as a diversion at least until 1 June. German reinforcements came partly from Flanders, where their transfer weakened rather than strengthened the overall strategic design. Worse, the French decision to send reinforcements did not weaken their position in Flanders because the fresh divisions came from other areas of the front. The Blücher offensive thus accomplished the opposite of its original intent. The exchange of casualties, though favorable to the Germans, was not enough to have any long-term positive impact on the overall German position in the west.[171]

The related Gneisenau offensive between Montdidier and Noyon, initiated on 9 June, was much smaller in scale (about eighteen divisions on both sides). Once again, the Germans had to use positional divisions that were largely unsuited for attacks in trench warfare and even less prepared for mobile combat. The offensive ended only three days later as French resistance stiffened and reinforcements began a series of local counterattacks against the exposed Germans. The French were not surprised, and they were able to rely on their second line of defensive positions to contain the original attack. This allowed them to overcome the serious overall weaknesses in the construction of their defensive positions. Once again, the Allies' ability to use a superior transportation system (railroads and motor vehicles) allowed them to deploy forces much more effectively and rapidly than the Germans.[172]

By the end of Gneisenau, the German manpower situation had become sufficiently critical, especially in the infantry, that the War Ministry proposed dissolving the storm battalions and sending their men to the regular units. Ludendorff had already queried the field armies about this proposal, originally put forth by First Army. All but two of the other field armies opposed the idea, and Ludendorff apparently supported them. On 22 August the War Ministry disbanded one storm battalion (17th) and reduced seven others by one company each. The remaining storm battalions survived intact through the withdrawal from France after the armistice.[173]

Ludendorff refused to recognize that the Blücher-Gneisenau attacks had been failures, but he conceded they had not pulled significant forces away from the Flanders front.[174] A situation report prepared by the High Command on 2 June concluded that neither the French nor the British were capable of offensive action and that "the Entente has suffered one of its most serious defeats, which has created for us new foundations for further success."[175] Even after the subsequent meager results of Gneisenau, the High Command clung to the hope that renewed attacks south of Flanders would draw away sufficient forces to enable a renewed and decisive attack against the British on the old Michael sector of the front.

Marneschutz

The High Command evaluated two possibilities for a diversionary offensive—one by Third Army in Champagne, and another by First and

Seventh Armies along the Marne, roughly between Château-Thierry and Reims. It selected the latter because such an offensive could be commenced more quickly and offered better prospects for surprise.[176] Ludendorff subsequently explained his decision to launch this offensive, code-named Marneschutz, on the grounds that the Germans would be attacking at a point where the enemy was weak and from which he could transfer forces to Flanders in an offensive set to begin two weeks after this one ended. He added that the Marneschutz attack would divert enemy forces from Flanders. His forces had no other option, he argued after the war, than to continue the series of offensives in order to convince the Allies to conclude peace.[177] Throughout the planning for Marneschutz, Ludendorff and the High Command believed the decision would ultimately come against the British, against whom the Hagen attack would be conducted by Army Group Rupprecht.[178] The dubiousness of this entire project is perhaps best indicated by the contemporaneous doubts expressed in Rupprecht's headquarters that Hagen could produce a decisive victory.[179]

At the same time, the High Command conducted studies and solicited opinions on what should be done if both Marneschutz and Hagen failed to force a favorable decision.[180] In this, of course, Ludendorff and his helpers overlooked the fundamental assumption on which the entire series of offensives had been based: if Michael and the related attacks failed, the war would be lost. Indeed, desperation in the face of the long-term situation and the arrival of the Americans was the single most compelling reason to expend the last reserves of the army's strength. So unrealistic was the view at the High Command that on 22 June 1918 Ludendorff proposed subsequent attacks in the directions of Armentieres and Paris should the Marneschutz and Hagen offensives fail. Similarly, Marneschutz and Hagen were necessary only because Blücher and Gneisenau had failed, and they, in turn, had been necessary only because Michael and Georgette had failed. Ludendorff and others realized, if one reads between the lines, that the series of offensives had to continue in order to maintain the initiative. Once the Allies gained the initiative, the power and agility of their offensives would soon break the resistance of the weakened German forces.

The *OHL* retained a substantial measure of confidence in the army's ability to conduct further offensives, regardless of the growing problem of maintaining the strength of the front-line units. Choosing to focus on the early successes of previous attacks, the High Command concluded that the new offensive methods had "fully proven themselves." Its directives stressed ruthless exploitation of local victories until strong resistance forced a return to more cautious procedures. Ludendorff rejected all suggestions that the units lacked sufficient strength for these attacks. When warned that widespread influenza outbreaks had reduced the units' combat strength, Ludendorff replied, "the units must become accustomed to dealing with reduced combat strength. I do not recognize influenza."[181] It should be noted that a number of officers, including the chief of the General Staff of Army Group Wilhelm, lacked confidence in the Marneschutz concept. Schulenburg and others feared that the weak German forces would only become more vulnerable to a French flanking counterattack.[182]

The degree to which Ludendorff and at least some of his advisers lost touch with reality can be seen in discussions of the alternatives should the anticipated Hagen attack (Flanders) fail. Wetzell proposed a return to his old idea of transferring forces to Italy for a decisive offensive there, which Ludendorff quickly dismissed. Wetzell then suggested an attack toward Paris in the middle of September. Ludendorff revised this to a renewal of the attack around Reims (which had not yet been attempted) and toward Amiens. Even the army groups, usually anxious to promote offensives in their own sectors, argued against the feasibility of such attacks if Marneschutz and Hagen failed. All these speculations may have revealed the intellectual gaps between the *OHL* and the army groups and exposed the unrealistic assumptions of the former, but as the official history noted, any further development of these concepts was "reduced to nothing by the events of the following weeks."[183]

These "events" began shortly after midnight on 15 July as Army Group Wilhelm opened the Marneschutz attack with a massive artillery barrage on the sixty-mile front along the Marne and southeast of Reims. The objective was simply to cut off the French forces in the Reims salient and drive as deeply as possible into the French position. To do this, the Germans had massed about 6,400 pieces of artillery, 2,200 mortars, and 900 aircraft to support the forty-seven divisions available for the assault. Some of these divisions were fresh, but many were either mobile divisions that had not recovered from the earlier battles or positional divisions, with all their inherent weaknesses.[184] Third Army divided its storm battalions into small units and assigned them to the assault regiments in an effort to deal with the strongest parts of the French defenses.[185] After nearly five hours of artillery fire, the forward infantry divisions commenced their assault at 4:50 a.m.[186] The "diversionary" attack, on which all else depended, thus began. By 17 July, French counterattacks had become a threat to the exposed Germans in their advanced and unfortified positions.

Within two days, the Marneschutz attack proved to be a complete fiasco. By this time, the French had learned they needed to defend their second lines of positions rather than their first, and they were prepared to launch effective local counterattacks.[187] For the first time, the new German offensive tactics met their match along the main line of enemy resistance. The French had good prior knowledge of the impending attack, and the effectiveness of their new tactical system was enhanced by executing planned withdrawals to strong rear positions largely untouched by German artillery.[188] French artillery fire was especially effective, and Allied airpower proved devastating in attacking German bridges across the Marne and the forces trying to use them.[189] French reinforcements quickly arrived and deprived the attackers of any vestiges of their narrow numerical superiority.[190] The German artillery's failure to pave the way for the infantry led to bitter postwar recriminations against Bruchmüller and his alleged inflexibility.[191]

The French Counterattack at Villers-Cotterets

On 17 July Ludendorff recognized the complete failure of this, the last offensive of the imperial German army. A few minor efforts to cut off the city of Reims continued, but by the seventeenth the initiative had passed to the French, although the consequences would be postponed for another twenty-four hours. The collapse of the Marneschutz attack also entailed the cancellation of Hagen, since British forces in Flanders remained as strong as ever, while the Germans had actually become weaker. Nothing remained to the German army in the west beyond a return to the kind of defensive battles that had been so costly in 1917. Kuhl must have understated the attitude in the High Command when he concluded, "the disappointment was great." Nevertheless, that was not the worst of the situation, in view of the events of the following day.[192]

On 18 July one of Ludendorff's most cherished illusions, that the French were incapable of major offensive action, fell victim to reality. A sudden French attack from the forest around Villers-Cotterets caught Crown Prince Wilhelm's forward divisions entirely by surprise. Deployed in exposed and improvised defensive positions, the German defenders quickly fell victim to a massive combined-arms attack of artillery, infantry, tanks, and more than 1,000 Allied aircraft. This, the Second Battle of the Marne, can rightly be seen as the turning point of the 1918 campaign in France. In true Clausewitzian fashion, the German offensive reached its culminating point short of victory and quickly fell victim to the "flashing sword of retribution" wielded by the predominantly French counteroffensive.[193]

The Final Defensive Effort

From that point on, the Allies retained the initiative and delivered a number of punishing blows to the German army.[194] These Allied offensives, particularly those of the British, successfully used both the traditional approach of massed artillery assaults and what one historian has termed "mechanical warfare," relying on tanks in large numbers. The emperor's forces suffered another major defeat on 8 August 1918, which became a "black day" for the German army. A few days later, even Ludendorff recognized that the army was "more or less *kaput.*" On 29 September he informed the civilian government and demanded an immediate ceasefire.[195]

Even so, the German army still had considerable defensive fight left in it and inflicted substantial losses in tanks, men, and aircraft on the relentless attackers. The Germans continued to show considerable skill in covering local retreats, constructing new defensive positions, and even halting local Allied assaults, but they could not recover from the losses incurred in their own offensives of 1918.[196] Its ultimate defeat was no longer in doubt, yet the German army inflicted more than 300,000 casualties on the British alone between August and November 1918.[197] Nevertheless, the German army remained in a permanent state of emergency that ended only with the armistice. The offensive was over and the war was lost, despite twenty years of subsequent denial in Germany.

The defeat of the German army on the western front meant more than just the loss of the war. With German supports removed, the other Central Powers, hollowed out by years of war and economic, social, and political conflict, collapsed under the weight of Allied military offensives. Ottoman Turkey, Bulgaria, and finally Austria-Hungary succumbed over the summer and fall of 1918. Only Bulgaria's government would emerge relatively intact.

The defeats of 1918 brought down the German political order. This was aided in part by President Woodrow Wilson's demand that Germany "be rid of its military masters" before requests for an armistice would be honored. Clearly, this meant first the fall of both Hindenburg and Ludendorff. Various schemes to preserve the Hohenzollern dynasty proved unworkable. Under the threat of being tried as a war criminal, and now a figure of scorn in Germany, Wilhelm II, on the blunt advice of Hindenburg and others, abdicated and crossed the Dutch frontier at Eysden on 10 November 1918. With Ludendorff now gone and a republic declared, a delegation headed by Reichstag deputy Matthias Erzberger went to Foch's headquarters at Compiegne to sign the armistice.[198] Those who had entered, fought, and lost the war were off the hook. The embryonic republican government was left holding the proverbial bag for both the armistice and the soon to be dictated peace treaty. Like the Romanov and Hapsburg dynasties, the Hohenzollern dynasty had been consigned to the dustbin of history.

Evaluation of the Failure of 1918

The usual verdict on the German offensive of 1918 is that the tactical methods were good and solved the problems of the breakthrough battle, but the offensive failed because the Germans simply lacked the necessary strength or because Ludendorff's strategy was irresolute and faulty.[199] Ludendorff's decision to launch other offensives after the failure of Michael, rather than using his remaining strength to continue the effort there or go on the defensive, found its critics. An evaluation of the events of 1918 is neither easy nor simple even today, in view of the difficulties the Germans faced and the ingrained views that have taken hold over the last eighty years. The 1918 offensive was clearly a defeat for the Germans. It failed to win the war, and the losses consequent to the four months of attacks greatly weakened the army's ability to resist the Allied counteroffensives. Some have argued that on this basis alone the Germans should have stood on the defensive throughout 1918.[200] But many writers have reached the opposite conclusion—that the decision to seek a decisive victory was correct and that continuing the war beyond 1918 could only have led to defeat in the long run.[201]

Contrary to what most historians have written, the German tactics of 1918 were not particularly successful after the initial shock of their use on 21 March 1918. The first great successes against the British were due in large part to the fact that the British were in the process of adapting a version of the German defensive methods but had not yet completed the transition.[202] Like the Red Army in 1941, the British army was caught in its weakest moment, just as the old system was giving way to the new, but before the new methods could be fully understood or implemented.

British Fifth Army was particularly vulnerable in March 1918. It was overextended in frontage, substantially outnumbered, and poorly prepared for the new defensive measures. Nor had the 1918 reorganization of the British infantry division been entirely successful.[203]

Others have argued that the British and especially the French acted quickly to devise answers to the new German tactics. In discussing Champagne (July 1918), General Konrad Krafft von Dellmensingen concluded that the German assault tactics had outlived their usefulness. Another German author, writing in 1927, concluded that the tactics failed because they were too slow and could not meet the strategic demand for speed in breakthroughs and exploitation. They frequently failed, that writer pointed out, not in the enemy fortified areas but beyond them, where the powers of the defense again became superior.[204] Others have argued that the Germans did not always use their new tactics, citing reports of traditional advances in lines.[205] One should remember, however, that the assault group tactics were designed only for long-prepared methodical attacks against mature trench systems. German doctrine called for more rapid and traditional attacks once the conditions of mobile warfare had returned. Most German units almost certainly used the assault unit tactics where appropriate, but using them in mobile warfare would have caused a unilateral halt for detailed planning.

This leads to another explanation for the failure of 1918: the tactics could provide a breakthrough but not a "breakout" to open warfare. Some attribute this to the fact that reserves (if available) could be moved by rail to blunt an offensive more rapidly than the attacker could fight through local defenders. In this view, Allied reserves doomed the 1918 offensive. Others have argued that the weakened state of the German cavalry meant that the breakthrough in Fifth Army's sector could not be rapidly exploited, and this was the cause of the Allied recovery.[206] Certainly the Germans had great difficulty moving their artillery, munitions, and reinforcements forward to maintain the momentum of their breakthrough, even during Michael. As had been the case throughout 1917 and 1918, the army's weaknesses in transportation limited its tactical mobility and the ability to exploit success.[207]

Still controversial is the impact of the supply situation on the German offensive. Supplies of many items, including food and ammunition, were inadequate, and the army had great difficulty moving what was available to the forward units. A related problem was that German units frequently stopped to loot captured positions rather than continue their advances in the rapid manner required by the situation, the regulations, and their orders for the offensive. The consequences of this are still in dispute. Some historians cite this looting as a key reason for failure in 1918, while others regard it as a minor problem.[208] By April, Allied air forces were increasingly effective in attacking German supply and transport units and in providing direct combat support to ground units. Likewise, as air superiority passed to the Allies, the Allied artillery become increasingly effective.[209]

Given the strategic situation and the German army's manpower situation, the tactics of 1918 were particularly lacking in strategic prospects. Despite everything written about the unbearable losses caused by the old, allegedly linear tactics of 1914, the offensive tactics did not reduce German casualties to an acceptable level. On the contrary, the German offensive quickly consumed the instrument that conducted it. One calculation estimated that 10,000 Germans died on the first day of Michael. Total casualties, including prisoners, on the first day may have been as high as 40,000 Germans and 38,000 British. Among those killed on 21 March was Ludendorff's stepson, a pilot. Between 21 March and the end of June 1918, the German army in the west suffered nearly 800,000 casualties, with more than 100,000 killed. These losses, of course, fell most heavily on the infantry regiments and other close combat units, such as the storm battalions. By 26 March, many of these units had lost half their infantry soldiers. Numerous other losses could not be prevented or made good. For example, by 24 March, one-third of the artillery assigned to the opening offensive (Michael) had been destroyed or was broken down. The three main assault armies committed a total of fifty-seven divisions to Michael. Of these, forty-one suffered heavy losses between 21 March and 9 April.[210] Attrition remained a serious problem on quiet sectors of the front. Crown Prince Rupprecht's army group, for example, lost 1,000 men per day in June, even though it did not participate in major combat that month.[211]

The real bill for this lavish expenditure of manpower came in mid to late summer 1918. The army was forced to disband twenty-nine divisions as Allied counterattacks pressed the weakened German forces.[212] Some of the storm battalions lost companies, and two were disbanded entirely.[213] In spite of extensive measures to comb out soldiers from rear-echelon units, the strength of the front-line divisions could not be maintained. By July, many had only around 600 men in their battalions. Total German army strength declined from about 5.1 million in March to 4.2 million in July, of which only 3.6 million were on the western front. When the Allied counterblows eventually began, the German army had already exhausted its last reserves.[214] Total German casualties in the two offensives aimed primarily at the British, Michael and Georgette, may have been as great as those of the defenders, and perhaps more.[215]

Numerous historians have condemned Ludendorff for his alleged statement that he did not want to hear the word "operation" and that punching a hole in the Allied line was the main thing.[216] The essence of this argument is that Ludendorff did not understand strategy, or even operations, and that he subordinated strategy to the demands of tactics, thus depriving his offensive of any overall strategic plan. A number of Ludendorff's critics among the officer corps wrote similar criticisms after the war.[217] There is a definite element of truth in the argument that the plan placed a tactical breakthrough, and thus the location of an attack, above strategic considerations, which fit the offensive into an overall plan. Even some divisional orders reflected this emphasis.[218] To further this indictment, one respected historian commented that this reversed Clausewitz and the traditional military emphasis of strategy over tactics.[219]

Ludendorff was not alone in reaching this conclusion, nor was it as illogical as it might seem. As early as 15 December 1917, a memorandum by General Hermann von Kuhl, a respected officer, argued that the essential point was to make a breakthrough, which was possible only where surprise could be attained and where the enemy was weakest. As a later German officer wrote, this was all the more remarkable because Kuhl's army group, that of Crown Prince Rupprecht, was well known for its perceptive strategic thought.[220] Ludendorff himself, writing after the war, explained his position:

> I was speaking out against the dominant point of view, which can be traced back to Count Schlieffen. Just as in the case of free operations of mobile warfare the tactical victory crowns the strategy, so the opposite was the case in positional warfare. One could emerge from positional warfare into operations, that is to create freedom of movement on the other side of the enemy position, only through a successful tactical attack—through a breakthrough. If this tactical attack lay in the strategically available direction, that would have been the best. If that were not possible, then other attack fronts had to be selected, which also led to operations. Naturally an attack against a section that precluded operations was out of the question.[221]

There are really two issues in this dispute. The first is whether Ludendorff was correct in emphasizing tactical considerations, the nature and place of the breakthrough battle, over strategic concerns, which reflected the campaign's military and political goals. The second issue is the presence or absence of a clear goal for the 1918 offensive. Numerous contemporaries and later historians have criticized Ludendorff and the 1918 offensive for lacking a strategic plan.[222]

Two generations of historians have castigated various generals of the First World War for pursuing grand strategic schemes that led to nothing beyond a huge loss of life and few if any territorial gains. In most cases prior to 1918, these offensives failed because their opening event, a breakthrough battle, failed or because the attacking units could not exploit a tactical victory. Most of these offensives had very clear strategic goals that, if attained, would have had major or even decisive results in the war. It is strange that historians should criticize British, French, and other generals for trying to achieve strategic goals and plans that had no prospect of victory because they could not defeat the enemy's forward defenses, and at the same time criticize Ludendorff for stating that until a breakthrough could be achieved, nothing of strategic value could be attained.

Others have argued that Ludendorff's statements on the relations between strategy and tactics indicate that he understood only tactics and not operations, the so-called operational level, or strategy. Dennis Showalter has written that Ludendorff never rose above the level of an infantry colonel in this regard partly because of his belief that "victory in the field would generate strategic success" if the resources were available.[223] Part of the problem may be related to a lack of understanding of what the Germans meant by "operations." In Prusso-German theory, operations meant, very simply, the movement of large forces to the battlefield or large-scale movements leading directly to the beginning of a battle. An attack, regardless of its scale, was a matter of tactics, of battle. An operation was an act of strategy, relating the purpose and outcome of the battle to the goal of the war or campaign. When Ludendorff said he did not want to speak of "operations," he simply meant that it was useless to plan great movements because they could begin only after a successful battle—in this case, a breakthrough battle, including what others now call the breakout. Thus, it was no accident that the first day of Michael was the "attack day," and the second was the "operations day."[224] Ludendorff's comments written during and after the war clearly show that by an "operation" he meant large-scale movements in a war of movement (*Bewegungskrieg*). Such operations were impossible, by definition, in *Stellungskrieg* (positional warfare). Only after the battle, in this view, could movement of large units (operation) begin. As he pointed out in his memoirs of the war, "Without a tactical victory, strategy could not be pursued. A strategy that does not consider a tactical victory is preordained to fail. The Entente attacks of the first three years of the war give sufficient examples of that." Ludendorff was simply recognizing the fundamental truth that wars are won not by great schemes of maneuver but by attaining battlefield success. Before we judge him too harshly, we should remember that few if any armies have won wars by losing battles, and the World War I graveyards in France and Belgium are filled with men who died while failing to carry out some general's grand scheme of maneuver that was founded on a false hope of tactical victory.

This raises the question of Ludendorff's plan for the campaign of 1918. Here, the critics are on firmer ground. Most historians agree with Crown Prince Rupprecht of Bavaria, who wrote in his memoirs that one cannot find any real statement of intent in the various directives issued by the *OHL* for the 1918 offensive.[225] It is clear that the Michael attack had the objective of separating the British Expeditionary Force from the French, pushing it toward the English Channel, and destroying it, thus forcing the British out of the war.[226] This goal was as clear as the goals of most of the failed Allied offensives throughout the war. The goals of neither could be achieved without a preceding tactical breakthrough. Without that, great offensives consisted of nothing but grand designs on maps in headquarters far to the rear and dead bodies in front of the enemy's lines of defenses.

Marshal Joseph Joffre, commander of the French armies in 1914. (National Archives)

Albert I, king of Belgium. He was perhaps the most heroic and sympathetic national leader in the war. (National Archives)

Commander of the Russian armies in 1914–1915, Grand Duke Nikolai Nikolaevich (six feet, six inches tall), towering over his cousin, Tsar Nicholas II. (National Archives)

Voivode Radomir Putnik, commander of the Serbian armies. His armies thwarted three Austro-Hungarian invasions in 1914, but they were defeated by Mackensen's invasion in 1915. Sick with influenza, Putnik led his armies in an epic retreat to the Adriatic coast. He was blamed for the defeat and was dismissed by the government after the evacuation to Corfu. Putnik never saw Serbia again, dying in Nice, France, in 1917. (Bain Collection, Library of Congress)

General Luigi Cadorna. Commander of the Italian armies, Cadorna proved inept in both tactics and operations. He was dismissed after the disastrous defeat at Caporetto. (Bain Collection, Library of Congress)

Romanian infantry. Once in the war, Romania's army discovered that it was poorly prepared to engage in modern warfare against the better-equipped and better-led Central Powers. (Bain Collection, Library of Congress)

Queen Marie of Romania. English born, she was a zealous advocate of Romania joining the Allies. (Bain Collection, Library of Congress)

King Ferdinand of Romania. His opportunistic entry into the war quickly blew up in his face, as Romania was overrun by the Central Powers. (Bain Collection, Library of Congress)

Marshal Phillippe Petain. The hero of Verdun, he became commander of the French army after the disastrous tenure of Robert Nivelle. (National Archives)

Marshal Ferdinand Foch. A prolific writer in the prewar period, in 1918 he proved to be an effective coordinator of the Allied forces. (National Archives)

General John J. Pershing, commander of the American Expeditionary Force. (Bain Collection, Library of Congress)

The reality of war. A French sniper using a modified rifle and optics system, circa 1915. (National Archives)

Field Marshal Sir Douglas Haig and General John J. Pershing, 1918. (Bain Collection, Library of Congress)

British commanders of World War I. (National Archives)

CONCLUSIONS

Although their roots can be traced as far back as Frederick the Great or even the Great Elector, the main elements of the Prussian way of war developed gradually over the nineteenth century. Its main tenets grew out of the reaction to the political, social, and military changes that engulfed Europe between 1789 and 1914. Prussian military reformers sought to adjust the state's military institutions to the new demands of warfare, while the state's political and social elites sought to limit the modernizing and liberalizing forces unleashed by the French Revolution and Napoleon. In the area of institutional reform, Scharnhorst remains the primary figure, while Clausewitz, his pupil, became the leading theorist of the Prussian way of war. The tensions between those who would modernize Prussia's institutions and those who would preserve their elitist core endured to the end of the Hohenzollern monarchy and its army. Because its foundations were anchored as securely in politics and society as in the realm of military affairs, an understanding of its nature must consider a wide range of institutional developments and ideology.

The Prussian army's two most important purposes were preservation of the old Prussian monarchical state and preparation for traditional land warfare in Europe. The former largely determined the army's social structure and political ideology, while the latter both inspired and limited its way of fighting battles and waging campaigns. Though fervently nationalistic in some respects, the Prussian army remained primarily loyal to the king and the state of Prussia rather than to the German Empire right up to 1914. When officers took their oaths to Prussia, they were pledging fealty to the illiberal social and political system embodied in the Prussian Constitution of 1850 and the traditional rights of the Hohenzollern monarchy. This monarchical state, in turn, rested on social and class distinctions founded in Europe's feudal past and only grudgingly reformed under the pressures of modernization in the nineteenth century. The army's ethos rested on this feudal base, even as it had to adapt to the demands of the state's increasingly industrialized and urbanized structure. As indicated in this study, no effort to understand the army's officer corps, its educational system, its unit structure, or its tactics can avoid considering this issue.

In preparing for land warfare in Europe, primarily against France and later against Russia, the Prussian way of war found a more narrowly military expression. For a variety of factors, the army's horizon was confined to ground campaigns. Most of its leaders and intellectuals accepted this and regarded the navy—correctly, as it turned out—as primarily a rival in the struggle for limited financial support. The military tenets of the Prussian system can thus be found in its view of land warfare rather than in the concept of war as a single national effort engulfing all the state's potential tools to attain its strategy. Most of these tenets remained unchanged between the time of the elder Moltke and 1914, despite disagreements over tactics and the nature of campaigns.

Within the military realm, one of the most prominent characteristics of the Prussian approach was its emphasis on using battles of annihilation to achieve military victory, regardless of the political circumstances that gave rise to war. Equally important, the army stressed mobile warfare as the only desirable form of fighting. Mobile warfare's opposite, positional warfare, was an aberration to be avoided or terminated. The army thus taught its officers to conduct rapid operations and to seek military victory in short wars. Campaigns were conducted largely independent of political considerations, which came into play only before war, in establishing its purposes, and after the fighting, as political leaders determined the details of the peace settlement. Annihilation meant destroying the enemy's armed forces in the limited Clausewitzian sense and did not necessarily extend to the enemy state.

These approaches naturally led to an emphasis on theater-level campaigns and effective tactical capability. Taken to the extreme, however, they were counterproductive to effective grand strategy. The efforts to achieve competence in operations (the use of large-scale movements to create favorable circumstances for decisive battle) and to prepare the army to fight encounter battles produced the army's greatest strengths and weaknesses. Army planners made little effort to coordinate military strategy with the nation's other military and nonmilitary resources in a single integrated national strategy. Instead, the army sought to maximize its effectiveness in those areas over which it had control: preparing the officer corps and the army for the kind of war it wished to wage.

In the sphere of conducting battles, the army established a number of fundamental principles and demanded that innovations be consistent with these principles, except in the most pressing of circumstances. Army doctrine and training stressed independent judgment to facilitate rapid action. It eschewed rigid tactical systems in theory, though in practice, this was difficult to reconcile with the hoary Prussian traditions of tactics dating to Frederick the Great and beyond. The army stressed offensive action at all levels of unit command and encouraged its commanders to solve tactical problems through aggressive action, even if this meant heavy local losses. It stressed the role of the infantry as the decisive arm, even as it gradually replaced shock action with firepower. It tried to preserve a role for traditional cavalry action, even as modernized weaponry from machine guns to artillery made that branch increasingly obsolete. Positional warfare never became an acceptable form of warfare because it was contrary to these and other cherished principles of the army's way of fighting.

The Prussian system had many strengths and developed many approaches that rightly found their imitators elsewhere. The Prussian army of 1914, along with the other contingents incorporated into the wartime German army, was at least as capable as any other large military force, friend or foe. The old army unintentionally laid a solid base for the rapid expansion and adaptation in methods and equipment that became essential after the opening battles in the west in 1914. Its principle that any army that could attack effectively could also defend proved to be correct. Respected or even feared before the war because of its offensive potential, the army became the most effective defending military force of the First World War, in part, ironically, because of its ability to restore movement and offensive action to the battlefield in 1917.

The Prussian system of creating and preparing reserve forces has seldom been equaled, even in modern times. The Prussian army was, above all, a cadre force. It could not conduct large-scale warfare without a massive mobilization of its reservists, both as individual fillers in active units and as corps deployed alongside the active army. In large part because of its unshakable determination to link officer commissions to social class, the regular army was incapable of staffing its fighting formations as prolonged fighting produced heavy casualties and as expansion created new formations. As a result, by 1917, the old officer corps, built on social exclusivity and "quality" over quantity, had nearly ceased to exist at the company level. Prussian and other German reserve units performed remarkably well in 1914, even without a prolonged period of intensive training between mobilization and deployment. In the active units, reservists fought alongside their active-duty comrades in the east and the west, both as individuals and as units. After casualties removed the active officer corps from direct combat, the reserve officer corps continued the war for years. In a sense, the reserve officer system was thus the most important instrument of the entire Prussian military system. As the war progressed, however, shortcomings among the reserve officer corps became a source of grave internal weakness.

The Prussian army's system was extraordinarily effective in combat throughout the war. It adapted rapidly and effectively as the conditions of combat changed. A recent and very careful review of casualty statistics concludes that "in all battle periods, the Germans inflicted more casualties than they suffered, and in all battle periods (with the exception of the 1918 German offensives), the French and British each suffered more casualties than they inflicted."[1] Of course, effectiveness in individual engagements or large battles does not automatically produce success in campaigns, victory in war, or even sufficiency in combat itself. Though more effective than its opponents in combat, the Prusso-German army did not possess sufficient superiority to overcome the other shortcomings of the German war effort.

The Prussian system effectively integrated the important subsystems of military activity into an effective if imperfect instrument that functioned within its intellectual framework. These subsystems included officer development, individual and unit training, doctrinal literature, the concept of campaigns leading to major battles, rapid mobilization and deployment, and, above all, fighting spirit. These foundations enabled the army to blunt the offensives of its enemies in 1914, rescue Austria-Hungary, adapt to the increasingly destructive nature of warfare on the western front, and vanquish its major opponent in the east. These strengths, however, were not sufficient to produce victory or to stave off eventual defeat and collapse.

The army's failure to achieve victory in the First World War revealed many shortcomings in its way of warfare. The most obvious of these sprang from the structure of Prussia and the German Empire. The constitution of the German Empire tacitly assumed that the positions of emperor and chancellor would be filled by supremely competent and capable individuals.[2] This circumstance obtained for almost the first two decades of the empire. Once Wilhelm I and Bismarck left the stage, however, monarchy became a luxury the Germans could not afford. Wilhelm II failed to be the central institution needed to prepare the nation prior to the outbreak of a conflict. Although intelligent, the kaiser lacked the intellect, discipline, and temperament needed to perform his duties, and his military advisers knew it. Wilhelm II confirmed their doubts and recognized his own failure in this regard when he promised not to interfere in day-to-day military matters. This continued into the war, with the result that Germany lacked an effective military or governmental agency to coordinate national efforts. The kaiser lacked the clout of his grandfather and proved unable to bring obstreperous commanders to heel. Hence, Wilhelm II had no choice but to endure Hindenburg's high-handed threat to resign in January 1915.[3]

The kaiser's failure to provide an institutional coordinating mechanism ensured that top levels of the German leadership would create the toxic environment of a war of all against all. Falkenhayn actively sought to undermine the position of the deteriorating Moltke. Once installed as second head of the *OHL*, Falkenhayn was at the center of a vortex of internecine warfare against the *Ober Ost*, elements of the court, the civilian government, and the navy. Once the Hindenburg-Ludendorff team seized power, the army demanded and got total control and consistently pursued its agenda in diplomacy, economic and social policy, resource distribution, alliance politics and planning, and home-front morale. Although the coordinating mechanism was now in place, the amount of control gained by the army put it in charge of activities related to the economy, society, and politics—areas in which the army as an institution lacked even minimal competence. The army thus revealed that it was unable to manage the war effectively and was unwilling to seek institutions that could.

The army's view that war is warfare proved to be a disastrous manifestation of its narrow approach to both subjects. The War Academy and the General Staff produced generations of trained experts in tactics and operations but failed to educate the army's intellectual leaders to coordinate warfare with statecraft and mobilization of the entire nation for total war. The result was a vacuum in grand strategy. The army was satisfied with its sovereignty in land warfare, and most of its leaders were equally accepting of its isolation in the broader arenas of preparation.

The prewar lack of unity in the military hierarchy found its revenge both in the army's preparations for war and in its conduct of the war from the outset. Although the German Empire's military strategy depended entirely on a rapid victory in France and Belgium in 1914, the army and navy made no effort to act jointly to hinder the British or to provide naval support for the land campaign. Neither service was particularly interested in such cooperation, and no higher agency, other than the emperor, had the authority to act to ensure cooperation. The navy probably could not have prevented or diverted the British landing, but its overall contributions could not have been more negative.[4] With rare exceptions, such as the amphibious operation against the Baltic islands in October 1917, the navy and the army failed to render even minimal mutual support.

The disruptive effects of the lack of unity in the army's hierarchy are even more obvious. Because the *OHL* had to focus on the land war on the western front, it could exercise only limited supervision over events in the east. The attempt to create and pursue a consistent strategy in the land war produced endless controversies over the relative weight of effort devoted to the two major theaters. Bitter personal rivalries exacerbated the problem. In 1914 the *OHL* had great difficulty coordinating the acts of field army commanders and eventually lost any semblance of control. This failure was the result of at least four factors: (1) Moltke and his loose system of command, (2) the lack of army group headquarters, (3) the failure of communications systems, and (4) the excessive independence of local commanders.

The war revealed a number of potential shortcomings in the Prussian system of officer education and training. The elder Moltke's methods of designing campaigns and his emphasis on subordinate initiative were more appropriate to the conditions of 1866 and 1870, when the Prussian army fought under very different circumstances. Numerical superiority, advantages in weapons technology, and superior individual and unit capabilities allowed the elder Moltke to overcome the mistakes of his subordinates and turn their potentially excessive independence to his advantage. In addition, the elder Moltke was fortunate in his enemies. The plethora of errors committed by the Austrians in 1866 and the French in 1870 proved to be of great assistance to him.[5] In 1914 his nephew's army had a margin of error that was insufficient to overcome the mistakes, insubordination, and stubbornness of his commanders, not to mention a much-improved French opponent.[6] The fundamental officer attributes of independent action, initiative, and local innovation improved the prospects for victory in tactics, but they proved disruptive in terms of executing theater strategy, especially against a competent enemy.

The army had recognized these potential problems in its prewar training and education, but it never resolved the tension between independent action and the need to remain within the overall framework of the campaign plan. This problem was not confined to the field army commanders, several of whom were not graduates of the War Academy or members of the General Staff. On the contrary, strong-willed chiefs of staff of the field armies frequently encouraged their commanders to act rashly and contrary to the overall campaign intent. Here, the social structure of the high officer corps added its negative effects, as princes sought glory for their states or their family names. Soon, of course, the iron law of the trenches reduced the scope of such failures, but by then, the opportunities available in 1914, such as they were, had disappeared.

The traditional approach to warfare eroded decisively in 1915 and 1916, at least on the western front. "Operations" in the Prussian sense became impossible as large-scale movement and maneuver became impossible. The spirit of the offensive yielded to the need to stay alive. As survivors of the prewar officer corps moved from tactical units to higher positions or the invalid lists, reserve and new officers took their place. The army became good at defending trenches and, later, deeply echeloned zones, but at the cost of suffering great casualties and losing its skills in mobile warfare. When tactical mobility began to return to the trenches in both offense and defense, the army had to substantially retrain both its officers and its enlisted force. Combined-arms actions became the norm, as close coordination of infantry, artillery, and engineer functions reached levels unimagined before 1914. This new cooperation, however, reflected a forced abandonment of the old system because it could restore neither the encounter battle as the model for tactics nor mobile campaigning as the method of theater strategy.

The new infantry training regulations and the manuals for attacking in trench warfare marked a partial return to the principles of mobile, offensive combat. They attempted to restore the principle of junior initiative and lowered the focal point of tactical action from the battalion or company level to that of platoons and squads. Tactical decision making devolved downward to lieutenants, sergeants, and even lower enlisted men. Nevertheless, the inescapable facts of trenches and firepower reduced tactical systems to planning and executing breakthroughs, with all the lengthy preparations necessary for success in those circumstances. The plans for the 1918 offensive hoped to build on tactical success in breakthroughs to achieve a large-scale return to mobile warfare across large areas of the western front.

The realities of the western front dictated otherwise. The substantial tactical breakthroughs in early 1918, attributable to both German capabilities and Allied shortcomings, led to brief interludes of advance and then a return to costly positional warfare rather than to extended mobile operations. The intellectual framework for a return to traditional warfare was in place in 1918, but the army's limitations and the nature of the enemy frustrated all efforts to make it a reality. The army's determination to return to massive offensives to achieve a decisive victory proved to be its final undoing, as the shattering casualties and failures sapped its physical and mental strength. As in 1914, the force ratios and terrain of the western front served as effective antidotes to the traditional Prussian system, as did the growing capabilities of the enemy's forces.

The Germans rightly regarded the campaigns in the east and in the Balkans as quite different matters. The extended fronts, smaller force-space ratios, and very different qualities of the army's opponents validated the argument that mobile warfare was still possible, but only to a limited degree. Methods that produced tactical victories in the east would be suicidal in the west, as the eastern officers who moved to the western front soon realized, and as the army's training efforts had to recognize. Ultimately, it was the relentless process of attrition and domestic collapse that produced victory against Russia, while the decisive victories against minor opponents merely increased the strain on the primary theater.

The coalition war in the east revealed other weaknesses in the Prussian approach to war, though the faults were hardly on the German side alone. Conrad's ill-conceived and poorly executed offensives in the Carpathians only reduced an already damaged army to near ashes.[7] A combined German-Austrian strategy proved as elusive as efforts to create an effective centralized command structure. In moments of supreme crisis, the Austrians and Germans could temporarily resolve their differences in goals and methods, but ultimately, Hindenburg and Ludendorff found cooperation with Conrad and his successor as difficult as Falkenhayn had.[8] Matters were made worse by the fact that the German army had very few high-ranking officers with an aptitude for coalition warfare. Tactical and even operational virtuosity in the east could overcome many difficulties, but years of attrition ultimately made the victory a pyrrhic one.

The army's social underpinnings proved to be nearly as durable as those of other armies, but its deep interpenetration with monarchical and ultraconservative elites became a major source of weakness as circumstances deteriorated in 1918. Drawn from narrow social circles and imbued with radical nationalist outlooks, the officer corps lost much of its credibility with enlisted men and with the mass of the population by the fall of 1918. Normal resentment within the ranks grew into deep distrust as the army's circumstances and prospects for victory declined after the failure of the 1918 offensives. The misery of the trenches, with their deprivations and sense of social injustice, rose to the level of what one historian labeled the "military strike" of 1918. Concerned about the welfare of their families in Germany and disillusioned with their leaders, a very large number of enlisted men could no longer be relied on to continue the apparently hopeless struggle in the face of Allied offensives. The army was surely a beaten force in the autumn of 1918, as even its most conservative commanders realized, although this was not yet apparent on maps of the western front.

The army's refusal to draw on wider social circles for junior officer replacements maintained its social homogeneity but undermined its relationship with a people at war. Such policies may have deprived the army of quality junior leaders, although it should be noted that many platoon-level leaders were noncommissioned officers and men holding the rank of sergeant-lieutenant. Unsatisfactory officer replacements became a scapegoat of the old officer corps, but there is no doubt that restricting commissions to those who met prewar social standards widened the gap between officers and enlisted men.

Many former officers argued after the war that the Prussian army of 1914 was the most magnificent army of all time. That may have been the case, but its foundations and its capabilities were simply not sufficient to meet its leaders' extravagant expectations, and it was ultimately no match for an impressive array of military forces fielded by more modern societies and governments. The Prussian way of war had its time and place, but both were gone by the end of 1914. Efforts to preserve or resurrect important elements of that way of war produced another magnificent fighting force by 1940, but solutions to the enduring problems of faulty policy, deficient strategy, and, above all, the iron laws of industrialized warfare were still missing. What had been added was a genocidal ideology far deadlier than the spirit of 1914.

NOTES

ABBREVIATIONS
BA/MA undesarchiv/Militärchiv, Freiberg, Germany
BH/KA Bayerisches Hauptstaatsarchiv-Kriegsarchiv, Munich, Germany
ÖSA/KA Österreichischer Staatsarchiv-Kriegsarchiv, Vienna, Austria

PREFACE

1. An older example of this is Hajo Holborn, "The Prusso-German School: Moltke and the Rise of the General Staff," in *Makers of Modern Strategy: From Machiavelli to the Nuclear Age*, ed. Peter Paret (Princeton, NJ: Princeton University Press, 1986), 281–295. Holborn's essay appeared in the first edition of this work, published in 1943. A more recent notable example is Robert M. Citino, *The German Way of War: From the Thirty Years' War to the Third Reich* (Lawrence: University Press of Kansas, 2005).

2. The US Army, for example, adopted Prussian-style uniforms and headgear in the 1870s.

3. The US Army's admiration of all things German in the 1970s and 1980s is a good example of this. For a cautionary note on this phenomenon, see Daniel J. Hughes, "Abuses of German Military History," *Military Review* 66, 12 (December 1986): 66–76.

4. The corpus of literature on this subject is immense and cannot be examined here. For an interesting collection of articles covering both world wars, see Williamson Murray, *German Military Effectiveness* (Baltimore: Nautical and Aviation Publishing, 1992). On the persistence of traditional German operational and tactical thinking into the nuclear age, see Gerhard P. Gross, *The Myth and Reality of German Warfare: Operational Thinking from Moltke the Elder to Heusinger*, ed. David T. Zabecki (Lexington: University Press of Kentucky, 2016), 300–301.

5. Although one the authors of this study (DJH) is retired, the other (RLD) is currently a professor of national security affairs at the US Marine Corps Command and Staff College in Quantico, Virginia. Thus, the following disclaimer is issued: the material in this volume represents solely the views of the authors and does not reflect the views of the Department of Defense, Department of the Navy, or US Marine Corps.

6. Although this volume includes a detailed discussion of war planning and the mobilization plans produced by the General Staff, we do not intend to rehash the controversies initiated by Terence Zuber's revisionist work *Inventing the Schlieffen Plan: German War Planning 1871–1914* (Oxford: Oxford University Press, 2002).

7. The literature on each of the topics mentioned in this paragraph is vast and will be addressed in the appropriate sections of subsequent chapters.

8. The Prussian General Staff and the German General Staff produced official

histories of the Austro-Prussian and Franco-Prussian Wars, respectively. Geoffrey Wawro has authored two excellent works on these conflicts: *The Austro-Prussian War: Austria's War with Prussia and Italy in 1866* (Cambridge: Cambridge University Press, 1996) and *The Franco-Prussian War: The German Conquest of France in 1870–1871* (Cambridge: Cambridge University Press, 2003). Older but still useful is Michael Howard, *The Franco-Prussian War*, reprint ed. (London: Routledge, 1988). An excellent one-volume treatment of the era is Dennis Showalter, *The Wars of German Unification* (London: Arnold, 2004).

9. To complete the table of ranks, a *General der Infanterie* (as well as *Kavallerie*, *Artillerie*, or *Pioniere*) is the equivalent of a three-star American rank, while a *Generaloberst* is the equivalent of a four-star rank. There is no American equivalent of a *Generalfeldmarschall*. The American rank General of the Armies, essentially a five-star rank, has been held by only a few individuals and is more of an honorific than an actual rank.

CHAPTER ONE. THE MID-NINETEENTH-CENTURY FOUNDATIONS

1. For an account of the parade, see Eckart von Naso, *Moltke. Mensch und Feldherr* (Berlin: Wolfgang Krüger Verlag, 1937), 438–439.

2. Many of these conventions had their origins in 1848 and 1849, following the final disposition of the revolutionaries of 1848. See Manfred Messerschmidt, "Die politische Geschichte der preussisch-deutschen Armee," in *Deutsche Militärgeschichte*, ed. Militärgeschichtliches Forschungsamt, 6 vols. (Munich: Bernard & Graefe, 1964–1979), 3:9–25; Georg Hoffmann, *Preussen und die Norddeutsche Heeresgleichschaltung nach der achtundvierziger Revolution* (Munich: C. H. Beck'sche Verlagsbuchhandlung, 1945). See also Klaus-Dieter Kaiser, "Die Eingliederung der ehemals selbständigen Norddeutschen Truppenkörper in die preussischen Armee in den Jahren nach 1866" (Ph.D. diss., Free University of Berlin, 1972); Rolf Wilhelm, *Das Verhältnis der süddeutschen Staaten zum Norddeutschen Bund 1867–1870* (Husum: Matthiesen Verlag, 1978). Copies of many of the conventions can be found in the German military archives, BA/MA, PH 2/268.

3. The best introduction in English remains Gordon A. Craig's *The Politics of the Prussian Army 1640–1945* (New York: Oxford University Press, 1956), 1–32. An important recent contribution in the military realm is Robert M. Citino, *The German Way of War: From the Thirty Years' War to the Third Reich* (Lawrence: University Press of Kansas, 2005).

4. *Freiherr* Karl vom und zum Stein (1757–1831) and *Freiherr* (later Prince) Karl August von Hardenberg (1750–1822) led the reform of the Prussian state after 1806. For a brief overview, see Koppel Pinson, *Modern Germany: Its History and Civilization*, 2nd ed. (New York: Macmillan, 1966), 33–39; David Blackbourne, *The Long Nineteenth Century: A History of Germany, 1780–1918* (New York: Oxford University Press, 1998), 70–94. On the Prussian reform movement, see Walter R. Simon, *The Failure of the Prussian Reform Movement, 1807–1819* (Ithaca, NY: Cornell University Press, 1955); Peter Paret, *Yorck and the Era of Prussian Reform, 1807–1815* (Princeton, NJ: Princeton University Press, 1966); Peter Paret, *Clause-*

witz and the State (Oxford: Oxford University Press, 1976). The relevant sections of Craig's *Politics of the Prussian Army* are also useful.

5. Heinrich Otto Meisner, *Der Kriegsminister* (Berlin: Hermann Reinshagen Verlag, 1940), remains the most detailed treatment. Craig, *Politics of the Prussian Army*, 37–75 has a comprehensive survey that has withstood the test of time.

6. Meisner, *Der Kriegsminister*, 12.

7. Messerschmidt, "Die politische Geschichte," 298–299, points out that the 1808 order specifically excluded officials of the War Ministry from exercising authority over the commanding generals in wartime and that the cabinet order of 1787, which reserved overall wartime command for the king, remained in force. Meisner, *Der Kriegsminister*, 11–12, has some other details.

8. Karl Kraus, "Der preussische Generalstab und der Geist der Reformzeit," *Wehrwissenschaftliche Rundschau* 7, 4 (1957): 209–210.

9. Rudolf Schmidt-Bückeburg, *Das Militär-Kabinett der preussischen Könige und deutscher Kaiser. Seine geschichtliche Entwicklung und staatsrechtliche Stellung 1787–1918* (Berlin: E. S. Mittler, 1932), remains the only scholarly study of this institution. Meisner, *Der Kriegsminister*, includes many discussions of the relationship between the Military Cabinet and the War Ministry. Both volumes are based on archival sources now lost.

10. Schmidt-Bückeburg, *Das Militär-Kabinett*, 2.

11. Ibid., 37; Meisner, *Der Kriegsminister*, 19.

12. Schmidt-Bückeburg, *Das Militär-Kabinett*, 58.

13. Messerschmidt, "Die politische Geschichte," 294.

14. Gerhard Ritter, *The Sword and Scepter: The Problem of Militarism in Germany*, trans. Heinz Norden, 4 vols. (Coral Gables, FL: University of Miami Press, 1964–1973), 2:123–124.

15. Friedrich Christian Stahl, "Preussische Armee und Reichsheer 1871–1914," in *Zur Problematik Preussen und das Reich*, ed. Oswald Hauser (Köln: Bölau Verlag, 1984), 205; Schmidt-Bückeburg, *Das Militär-Kabinett*, 222.

16. Messerschmidt, "Die politische Geschichte," 294; Schmidt-Bückeburg, *Das Militär-Kabinett*, 87.

17. Baron Fritz Adolf Marschall von Bieberstein, *Verantwortlichkeit und Gegenzeichnung* (Berlin: Verlag von Franz Vahlen, 1911), 158. This order was not made public until 17 March 1909.

18. Lamar Cecil, *Wilhelm II*, 2 vols. (Chapel Hill: University of North Carolina Press, 1989–1996), 2:270–271.

19. Anonymous, *Das alte Heer, von einem Stabsoffizier* (Charlottenburg: Verlag der Weltbühne, 1920), 19–20.

20. G. von Gleich, *Die alte Armee und ihre Verirrungen*, 2nd ed. (Leipzig: K. F. Koehler, 1919), 82.

21. Friedrich Karl von Preussen, *Prince Friedrich Karl von Preussen. Denkwürdigkeiten*, ed. Wolfgang Foerster, 2 vols. (Stuttgart: Deutsche Verlags-Anstalt, 1910), 2:129.

22. Franz von Lenski, *Lern- und Lehrjahre in Front und Generalstab* (Berlin: Verlag Bernard & Graefe, 1939), 98. See also Hans von Zwehl, *Generalstabsdienst im*

Frieden und in Kriege (Berlin: E. S. Mittler, 1923), 14. The younger Moltke unsuccessfully opposed the ill-fated appointment of General von Prittwitz and Gaffron to the command of Eighth Army, which was entrusted with the defense of East Prussia in case of war. See Otto von Moser, *Die obersten Gewalten im Weltkrieg. Das Werk der Staatsmänner, Heerführer, Parlaments- Press- und Volksführer bei der Entente und bei den Mittelmächten* (Stuttgart: Chr. Belser, 1931), 165.

23. Count Alfred von Waldersee, *General-Feldmarschall Alfred Graf von Waldersee in seinem militärischen Wirken*, 2 vols. (Berlin: Verlag R. Eisenschmidt, 1929), 2:29.

24. Count Bogdan von Hutten-Czapski, *Sechzig Jahre Politik und Gesellschaft*, 2 vols. (Berlin: E. S. Mittler, 1936), 1:179–181. Although self-serving, Hutten-Czapski's account seems plausible.

25. Ibid., 162.

26. Stahl, "Preussische Armee," 205–206.

27. Ernst R. Huber, *Deutsche Verfassungsgeschichte seit 1789*, 4 vols. (Stuttgart: Kohlhammer, 1957–1969), 4:531, lists some of the deputies' terms for this "anti-constitutional alien body."

28. Bieberstein, *Verantwortlichkeit*, 574.

29. See the comments of Hans von Below, "Lebenserinnerungen," *Nachlass Beseler*, BA/MA, N 30/46.

30. Walter Görlitz, *History of the German General Staff 1657–1945*, trans. Brian Battershaw (New York: Frederick A. Praeger, 1953), 11–20. Still useful for the earliest history is Paul Bronsart von Schellendorff, *The Duties of the General Staff*, 4th ed., trans. British General Staff (London: HMSO, 1905), 10–17. There is no scholarly history of the Prussian General Staff. Wiegand Schmidt-Richberg, *Die Generalstäbe in Deutschland 1871–1945. Aufgaben in der Armee und Stellung im Staate* (Stuttgart: Deutsche Verlags-Anstalt, 1961), is useful but hardly definitive. The older essay "Generalstab," in J. D. Hittle, *The Military Staff: Its History and Development*, 3rd ed. (Harrisburg, PA: Stackpole, 1961), is largely obsolete. A relatively useful work aimed at a more popular audience is Trevor N. Dupuy, *A Genius for War: The German Army and General Staff, 1807–1945* (New York: Prentice-Hall, 1977).

31. Kraus, "Der preussische Generalstab," 203–204.

32. Ibid., 203.

33. Paul Bronsart von Schellendorff, *Der Dienst des Generalstabs*, 2 vols. (Berlin: E. S. Mittler, 1875–1876), 1:20.

34. Baron Ottomar von der Osten-Sacken und bei Rhein, *Preussens Heer von seinen Anfang bis zur Gegenwart*, 3 vols. (Berlin: E. S. Mittler, 1914), 2:232.

35. Görlitz, *History of the German General Staff*, 30–40.

36. Max Jähns, *Feldmarschall Moltke* (Berlin: Ernst Hofmann, 1900), 265–267. Schmidt-Richberg, *Die Generalstäbe*, 18, points out that officers performing these two kinds of assignments formed a single entity within the army. Arden Bucholz, *Moltke, Schlieffen and Prussian War Planning* (New York: Berg, 1991), frequently treats them as separate entities. This may obscure the fact that they formed a unitary group consisting of the same men—the General Staff officer corps—with their own uniform markings, selection process, military education, and, most im-

portant, career pattern (*Generalstab Laufbahn*). Count Helmuth von Moltke and his nephew were two of the relatively few exceptions.

37. This is not meant to imply that the basic procedures changed in the revitalized West German army after 1955. The army of the Federal Republic is beyond the scope of this study.

38. Helmut Otto, *Schlieffen und der Generalstab* (East Berlin: Deutscher Militärverlag, 1966), 15. This volume, despite its Marxist ideological slant, remains useful. See also Osten-Sacken, *Preussens Heer*, 2:234, on the numbers.

39. Chiefs Müffling (1821–1829) and Krauseneck (1829–1848) willingly accepted this subordinate position. See Messerschmidt, "Die politische Geschichte," 310–311; Hanns Martin Elster, *Kriegsminister, General-Feldmarschall, Ministerpräsident Graf Albrecht von Roon. Sein Leben und Wirken* (Berlin: Verlag Karl Siegismund, 1938), 99–100.

40. Osten-Sacken, *Preussens Heer*, 2:344–345.

41. The best of the enormous literature on Helmuth von Moltke is available primarily in German. Eberhard Kessel, *Moltke* (Stuttgart: K. F. Koehler Verlag, 1957), is the best biography. Arden Bucholz, *Moltke and the German Wars* (New York: Palgrave, 2001), though short, is the best in English. William O'Connor Morris, *Moltke: A Biographical and Critical Study* (1893; reprint, New York: Haskell House, 1971), retains some value for private matters. On Moltke's importance as a commander and theoretician, see the introduction to *Moltke on the Art of War: Selected Writings*, ed. Daniel J. Hughes (Novato, CA: Presidio Press, 1993), 1–19. See also Dennis Showalter, *The Wars of German Unification* (London: Arnold, 2004), 67–70. Of fundamental importance are the articles by Hajo Holborn, "Moltke and Schlieffen: The Prussian-German School," in *Makers of Modern Strategy: Military Thought from Machiavelli to Hitler*, ed. Edward Mead Earl (Princeton, NJ: Princeton University Press, 1943), 172–205; and Gunther Rothenberg, "Moltke, Schlieffen and the Doctrine of Strategic Envelopment," in *Makers of Modern Strategy: From Machiavelli to the Nuclear Age*, ed. Peter Paret (Princeton, NJ: Princeton University Press, 1986), 296–325.

42. Kessel, *Moltke*, 245–246, 278. Bucholz, *Moltke, Schlieffen and Prussian War Planning*, 39–43, has a useful introduction to Moltke's new emphasis on railroads.

43. Jähns, *Feldmarschall Moltke*, 276–277; Kessel, *Moltke*, 230–231. The precise numbers vary slightly, depending on the source and the way certain calculations are made.

44. Bucholz, *Moltke, Schlieffen and Prussian War Planning*, 226–227, summarizes the growth and the related literature.

45. Simon, *Failure of Prussian Reform*, 145–170, is a useful introduction to this complex subject. Older but still useful is William O. Shanahan, *Prussian Military Reforms 1786–1813* (New York: Columbia University Press, 1945). Ritter, *Sword and Scepter*, 1:93–119, is a broader overview.

46. Ritter, *Sword and Scepter*, 1:168–169.

47. Simon, *Failure of Prussian Reform*, 181–183.

48. Ritter, *Sword and Scepter*, 1:100–102; Messerschmidt, "Die politische Geschichte," 64, 70.

49. Simon, *Failure of Prussian Reform*, 184–185.

50. Messerschmidt, "Die politische Geschichte," 2; Wilhelm Dorow, *Job von Witzleben* (Leipzig: Verlag von Bernhard Tauchnitz, 1842), 103–104, 113. Witzleben served as chief of the Military Cabinet from 1816 to 1834. He later supported the two-year service commitment, while most of his fellow officers considered three years the minimum acceptable time for recruits to serve with active units.

51. The first statement was made in 1861 by well-known liberal Benedikt Waldeck. See Reinhard Höhn, *Die Armee als Erziehungsschule der Nation. Das Ende einer Idee* (Bad Harzburg: Verlag für Wissenschaft, Wirtschaft und Technik, 1963), 98. Höhn's *Verfassungskampf und Heereseid. Der Kampf des Bürgertums um das Heer (1815–1850)* (Leipzig: Hirzel, 1938), is another rich source on the debate over the *Landwehr*.

52. Osten-Sacken, *Preussens Heer*, 2:216, 262–263; Messerschmidt, "Die politische Geschichte," 71, 80.

53. Eduard von Fransecky, *Denkwürdigkeiten des preussischen Generals der Infanterie Eduard von Fransecky*, ed. Walter von Bremen (Berlin: Boll & Pickardt, 1913), 147, includes the comments of an especially capable officer. Messerschmidt, "Die politische Geschichte," 100, points out that the annual excess of officer applicants (about 1,000) over the yearly requirements (about 600) did not alleviate the problem of training deficiencies.

54. Ritter, *Sword and Scepter*, 1:102–103.

55. For details, see Messerschmidt, "Die politische Geschichte," 82–83; Osten-Sacken, *Preussens Heer*, 2:220–222, 313. Messerschmidt's overall evaluation of the *Landwehr* is more favorable (83).

56. Michael Howard, "William I and the Reform of the Prussian Army," in *Studies in War and Peace* (New York: Viking Press, 1970), 73.

57. Osten-Sacken, *Preussens Heer*, 3:9–14. See also Messerschmidt, "Die politische Geschichte," 23–24.

58. Osten-Sacken, *Preussens Heer*, 3:338, 357.

59. Ritter, *Sword and Scepter*, 1:102. Messerschmidt, "Die politische Geschichte," 98, agrees on this point. Hermann Rahne, *Die Mobilmachung. Militärische Mobilmachungsplanung und -Technik in Preussen und im deutschen Reich von Mitte des 19. Jahrhunderts bis zum Zweiten Weltkrieg* (East Berlin: Militärverlag der deutschen demokratischen Republik, 1983), 15–18, discusses the many shortcomings of both active and reserve forces in those years.

60. Wilhelm has not found his modern scholarly biographer in either German or English. The best is still Erick Marcks, *Kaiser Wilhelm I*, 3rd ed. (Leipzig: Verlag von Duncker und Humboldt, 1899), a classic example of Wilhelmine academic writing on the monarchy.

61. Craig, *Politics of the Prussian Army*, 141, provides a good introduction to the future king's involvement in the reforms of 1860. See also Showalter, *Wars of German Unification*, 75–79.

62. Marcks, *Kaiser Wilhelm I*, 165; Craig, *Politics of the Prussian Army*, 139.

63. The title of the memorandum in German is "Bemerkungen und Entwürfe zur vaterländische Heeresverfassung." It is available in Wilhelm I, *Militärische*

Schriften weiland Kaiser Wilhelms des Grossen Majestät, ed. Prussia Kriegsminis-terium, 2 vols. (Berlin: E. S. Mittler, 1897), 2:344–378. Another slightly different version is in Count Albrecht von Roon, *Denkwürdigkeiten aus dem Leben des Gen-eralfeldmarschalls Kriegsministers Grafen von Roon*, ed. Count Waldemar von Roon, 3 vols. (Breslau: Verlag von Eduard Trewendt, 1897), 2:521–572. The former is the original text.

64. Messerschmidt, "Die politische Geschichte," 27–28; Craig, *Politics of the Prussian Army*, 98–99.

65. Wilhelm I, *Militärische Schriften*, 2:349–350.

66. Kessel, *Moltke*, 339; Ritter, *Sword and Scepter*, 1:184. On Roon, see Elster, *Kriegsminister, General-Feldmarschall, Ministerpräsident Graf Albrecht von Roon*; Reinhard Hübner, *Albrecht von Roon. Preussens Heer im Kampf um das Reich* (Hamburg: Hanseatische Verlagsanstalt, 1933); Roon, *Denkwürdigkeiten*. There is no good biography of Roon in English. The new chief of the General Staff, Helmuth von Moltke, had little if anything to do with the reform measures and their implementation.

67. Messerschmidt, "Die politische Geschichte," 183. Craig, *Politics of the Prussian Army*, 144–150, has a good summary of the Roon reform bill and the struggle over it.

68. Kurt Jany, *Geschichte der königliche preussische Armee*, 4 vols. (Berlin: Verlag von Karl Siegismund, 1933), 3:229; Osten-Sacken, *Preussens Heer*, 3:31–32; Wolf-gang Foerster, ed., *Prinz Friedrich Karl von Preussen. Denkwürdigkeiten aus seinem Leben*, 2 vols. (Stuttgart: Deutsche Verlags-Anstalt, 1910), 1:222, 3:31–32; Messer-schmidt, "Die politische Geschichte," 183–184.

69. On the impact of these changes, see Michael Geyer, *Deutsche Rüstung-spolitik 1860–1980* (Baden-Baden: Suhrkampf, 1984), 37, 65; Messerschmidt, "Die politische Geschichte," 183.

70. Messerschmidt, "Die politische Geschichte," 27–28; Gordon Craig, "Por-trait of a Political General: Edwin von Manteuffel and the Constitutional Conflict in Prussia," in *War, Politics, and Diplomacy: Selected Essays* (1951; reprint, New York: Praeger, 1966), 97–99; Jonathan Steinberg, *Bismarck: A Life* (Oxford: Ox-ford University Press, 2011), 159. See also Ritter, *Sword and Scepter*, 1:127.

71. Geyer, *Deutsche Rüstungspolitik*, 25, makes the internal political argument, as did many historians of the former German Democratic Republic. Representa-tive of this interpretation is Rahne, *Mobilmachung*, 30.

72. Wilhelm Deist, ed., *Militär und Innenpolitik im Weltkrieg 1914–1918*, 2 vols. (Düsseldorf: Droste Verlag, 1970), 1:xxiv. See also Wolfram Wette, *Militarismus in Deutschland: Geschichte einer kriegerischen Kultur* (Frankfurt: Fischer Taschenbuch Verlag, 2011), 50.

73. Friedrich Wilhelm IV's statement of 1 July 1849 is printed in Carl Her-mann, *Deutsche Militärgeschichte. Eine Einführung*, 3rd ed. (Frankfurt: Bernard & Graefe, 1979), 198–199. On Bismarck's comment, see Prince Otto von Bis-marck-Schönhausen, *Die gesammelten Werke*, 19 vols. (Berlin: Verlag für Politik und Wirtschaft, 1924–1932), 9:489.

74. Prinz Krafft zu Hohenlohe-Ingelfingen, *Aus meinem Leben*, 4 vols. (Berlin:

E. S. Mittler, 1907), 1:4, comments on the unmilitary appearance of Friedrich Wilhelm IV. Deist, *Militär und Innenpolitik*, 1:xv, points out that Wilhelm II did not always inspire full respect for the person of the monarch. For post-1918 statements of continued admiration for the kaiser from two very different officers, see Baron Hugo von Freytag-Loringhoven, *Menschen und Dinge wie ich sie in meinem Leben sah* (Berlin: E. S. Mittler, 1923), 68–69, 168–169, and Friedrich von Bernhardi, *Denkwürdigkeiten aus meinem Leben* (Berlin: E. S. Mittler, 1927), 175. Writing much later, a young prewar officer wrote fondly of his pride that the old army had been monarchical and Prussian, marked by unconditional obedience (*Kadavergehorsam*) to the monarch. See "Erinnerungen," *Nachlass* Ludwig von der Leyen, BA/MA, N 154/1, 15.

75. Fransecky, *Denkwürdigkeiten*, 21–23.

76. This and the following section are based on Daniel J. Hughes, *The King's Finest: A Social and Bureaucratic Profile of Prussia's General Officers, 1871–1914* (New York: Praeger, 1987), 60–62, unless otherwise noted.

77. Bucholz, *Moltke, Schlieffen and Prussian War Planning*, 27, argues that the Prussian army of 1808 "was characterized by its emphasis on education," a feature that he claims continued into the Moltke period. Even as a characterization of the General Staff and the War Academy, this is surely an exaggeration.

78. Even an official commission concluded in 1882 that many officer candidates from the division schools were almost totally uneducated. See Wilhelm I, *Militärische Schriften*, 1:61. See also the comments of Heinrich von Brandt, ed., *Aus dem Leben des Generals der Infanterie z. D. Dr. Heinrich von Brandt*, 3 vols. (Berlin: E. S. Mittler, 1868), 2:12–19, and, more generally, Messerschmidt, "Die politische Geschichte," 92–98.

79. The 1808 order is available in Bernard Poten, *Geschichte des Militär- Erziehungs- und Bildungswesens*, 4 vols. (Osnabrück: Biblio Verlag, 1982), 4:143–145.

80. Ibid., 205–216; Karl Demeter, *Das deutsche Offizierkorps in Gesellschaft und Staat 1650–1945*, 4th rev. ed. (Frankfurt: Bernard & Graefe, 1965), 82–83.

81. Bernard Schwertfeger, *Die grossen Erzieher des deutschen Heeres. Aus der Geschichte der Kriegsakademie* (Potsdam: Rütter & Loening Verlag, 1936), 31, discusses the abolition of the division schools. Eduard von Peucker (1791–1876), ennobled in 1816, was quite unusual among high generals in the old Prussian army. The son of a merchant, he received his education in both the cadet corps and a *Gymnasium*. A career artillery officer, he became a general of infantry upon receiving his third star. He served as general inspector of training and education from 1854 until his retirement in 1872 and was a close associate of Hermann von Boyen. See Kurt von Priesdorff, ed., *Soldatisches Führertum*, 10 vols. (Hamburg: Hanseatische Verlagsanstalt, 1936–1942), 6:146–152.

82. The *Primareifezeugnis* was a certificate confirming a student's eligibility to begin the highest level of an approved nine-year secondary school. It was the equivalent of an American high school diploma but without a certification of eligibility to attend a university. See Holger Herwig, *The German Naval Officer Corps: A Social and Political History, 1890–1918* (Oxford: Clarendon Press, 1973), 41.

83. On Peucker's efforts and the opposition within the army, see Otto von Hoffmann, *Lebenserinnerungen des Königlichen preussischen Generalleutnants Otto von Hoffmans*, ed. Col. V. Hoffmann (Oldenburg: Schulzsche Hof-Buchhandlung & Hof-Buckdruckerei, 1907), 93. On the Roon proposal, see Steven E. Clemente, "Mit Gott! Für König und Kaiser" (Ph.D. diss., University of Oklahoma, 1989), 34–36, 78–79.

84. Clemente, "Mit Gott!" 84–85. The navy, by contrast, attracted a larger proportion of officer candidates with the *Abitur*—about 90 percent. See Manfred Messerschmidt, "The Military Elites in Germany since 1870: Comparisons and Contrasts with the French Officer Corps," in *The Military and Politics in Society in France and Germany in the Twentieth Century*, ed. Klaus-Jürgen Müller (Oxford: Berg, 1995), 57.

85. Clemente, "Mit Gott!" 82.

86. Ibid., 5–6. See also Jürgen Herrguth, *Deutsche Offiziere an öffentlichen Hochschulen* (Munich: Bernard & Graefe, 1979), 21.

87. Messerschmidt, "Military Elites," 55.

88. See the comparison with the British army in Martin Samuels, *Command or Control? Command, Training and Tactics in the British and German Armies, 1888–1918* (London: Frank Cass, 1995), 80.

89. Quoted in Höhn, *Die Armee als Erziehungsschule der Nation*, 103.

90. Descriptions are available in Demeter, *Das deutsche Offizierkorps*; Martin Kitchen, *The German Officer Corps, 1890–1918* (Oxford: Clarendon Press, 1968); Hughes, *King's Finest*.

91. Some officers insisted that there were no differences between officer candidates and ordinary soldiers, except that the former were absolved from cleaning and such chores. See Kurt von Bülow, *Preussischer Militarismus zur Zeit Wilhelms II. Aus meiner Dienstzeit* (Schweidnitz: Hugo Reisse, 1930), 21. However, officer candidates were expected to be better than the other soldiers in the performance of their duties.

92. As a practical matter, corps commanders rarely interfered in this process, one of the most important functions of the entire regimental system. The 1861 regulation governing the officer replacement process can be found in Manfred Messerschmidt and Ursula Gersdorff, eds., *Offiziere in Bild von Dokumenten aus drei Jahrhunderten* (Stuttgart: Deutsche Verlags-Anstalt, 1964), 182–187.

93. Rudolf Absolon, *Die Wehrmacht im dritten Reich*, 6 vols. (Boppard: Harald Boldt Verlag, 1969–1995), 3:291.

94. Clemente, "Mit Gott!" 139, argues that the period of duty prior to attendance at the war schools decreased substantially by 1891. Most evidence indicates, however, that six months remained the norm in practice as well as under the regulation's formal requirements. See Osten-Sacken, *Preussens Heer*, 3:55; Friedrich von der Boeck, *Deutschland. Das Heer*, 3rd ed. (Berlin: Verlagsbuchhandlung Alfred Schal, 1902), 129; Günter W. Hein, *Das kleine Buch vom deutschen Heere* (Leipzig: Verlag von Lipsius & Tischer, 1901), 96.

95. Exceptions of various types were available, as circumstances warranted. The famous Hugo *Freiherr* von Freytag-Loringhoven was allowed to take the offi-

cer examination before he went to the war school at Anklam because of his prior service in the Russian army. See his *Menschen und Dinge*, 31.

96. Von der Schulenburg-Tressow was typical of the exceptions that proved the rule. A friend of Wilhelm II from his student days in Heidelberg, Schulenberg-Tressow received a commission after only nine months with his regiment. See his "Erlebnisse," *Nachlass* v. d. Schulenburg-Tressow, BA/MA, N 58/1, 3.

97. Two books on the cadet corps are Jürgen Zabel, *Das preussische Kadettenkorps. Militärische Jugenderziehung als Herrschaftsmittel im preussischen Militärsystem* (Frankfurt: Haag & Herchen, 1978), and the much more sympathetic and, on most issues, more balanced John Moncure, *Forging the King's Sword: Military Education between Tradition and Modernization: The Case of the Royal Prussian Cadet Corps, 1871–1918* (New York: Peter Lang, 1993). Also very laudatory is Jörg Muth, *Command Culture: Officer Education in the US Army and the German Armed Forces, 1901–1940, and the Consequences for World War II* (Denton: University of North Texas Press, 2011), 85–112.

98. Demeter, *Das deutsche Offizierkorps*, 13.

99. Hughes, *King's Finest*, 15.

100. Ibid., 12, 126–127.

101. Bucholz, *Moltke, Schlieffen and Prussian War Planning*, 3, stresses this point. Of course, the figures for any given point in time are a mere snapshot, since officers routinely moved among unit command positions, the *Truppengeneralstab*, and the *Grosser Generalstab*.

102. While any officer was *hoffähig*, civil servants had to hold a rank equivalent to colonel (*Rat*, second class) to have this privilege. See Hartmut John, *Das Reserveoffizierkorps im Deutschen Kaiserreich 1890–1914* (Frankfurt: Campus Verlag, 1981), 205. In Bavaria an officer gained such status upon promotion to major. See Wiegand Schmidt-Richberg, "Die Regierungszeit Wilhelms II," in Militärgeschichtliches Forschungsamt, *Deutsche Militärgeschichte*, 3: 87; Hermann Rumschöttel, *Das bayerische Offizierkorps 1860–1914* (Berlin: Duncker & Humboldt, 1973), 209–210.

103. Demeter, *Das deutsche Offizierkorps*, 58. The destruction of the Prussian army's personnel records in the Second World War probably precludes a more precise or broader determination than Demeter's, which was based on material in the archives, although he was unable to use modern quantitative methods.

104. Hughes, *King's Finest*, 42–49. There were some important differences within the old Prussian categories. Bourgeois generals were less likely to have landed and military fathers and much more likely to have fathers who served in the upper levels of the bureaucracy. About 12 percent of the bourgeois generals were sons of businessmen, while less than 4 percent of the noble generals could be so classified.

105. Lysbeth Walker Muncy, *The Junker in the Prussian Administration under William II, 1888–1914* (Providence, RI: Brown University Press, 1944), assumes a landed connection, as does Hanna Schissler, "Die Junker, zur Sozialgeschichte und historischen Bedeutung der agrarischen Elite in Preussen," in *Preussen im Rückblick*, ed. Hans-Jürgen Puhle and Hans-Ulrich Wehler (Göttingen: Vanden-

hoeck & Rupprecht, 1989), 89–123. Representative of the broader interpretation, which indiscriminately treats all nobles as Junkers, is Ulrich Trumpener's "Junkers and Others: The Rise of Commoners in the Prussian Army, 1871–1918," *Canadian Journal of History* 14 (April 1979): 29–47.

106. Hughes, *King's Finest*, 41–47, examines the question in some detail.

107. For details, see ibid., 42, 47–48.

108. Ibid., 69–74, examines the financial aspects of a military career.

109. Gerhard Bry, *Wages in Germany 1871–1945* (Princeton, NJ: Princeton University Press, 1960), 51.

110. In 1914 an active infantry battalion had an authorized strength of twenty officers and received another six or so from its reserve officer corps. See Count Edgar von Matuschka, "Organsationsgeschichte des Heeres 1890–1918," in Militärgeschichtliches Forschungsamt, *Deutsche Militärgeschichte*, 3:160.

111. For the earlier period, see Osten-Sacken, *Preussens Heer*, 2:159; Alfred Vagts, *A History of Militarism, Civilian and Military*, rev. ed. (New York: Free Press, 1959), 179; Messerschmidt, "Die politische Geschichte," 102–103.

112. Heine, *Das kleine Buch vom deutschen Heere*, 83–84, lists the kinds of expenses incurred by one-year volunteers. John, *Reserveoffizierkorps*, 56–57, estimates the total at about 2,000 marks for infantry and 3,000 for cavalry and field artillery. Heiger Ostertag, *Bildung, Ausbildung, und Erziehung des Offizierkorps im deutschen Kaiserreich 1871 bis 1918* (Frankfurt: Peter Lang, 1990), 287–288, cites similar figures. According to Fritz Nagel, *Fritz: The World War I Memoirs of a German Lieutenant*, ed. Richard A. Baumgartner (Huntingdon, WV: Der Angriff Publications, 1981), 9–10, his year cost his father 7,500 marks, a relatively high total. Some regiments were more expensive than others because of the high cost of living in a large city or because of their extravagant lifestyles.

113. For details, see John, *Reserveoffizierkorps*, 58.

114. Ibid., 255–256.

115. Ibid., 57–58.

116. For 1914, Osten-Sacken, *Preussens Heer*, cites the figure of 14,000 one-year volunteers. Anonymous, "Die militärische Vorbildung unserer Offiziere des Beurlaubtenstandes," *Militär-Wochenblatt* 7 (1914): col. 123, gives the figure as 14,000 to 15,000, which is close to that of Rahne, *Mobilmachung*, 116, citing official figures from the Reichsarchiv. Rahne's number for 1898 is 9,000, which is lower than that of Osten-Sacken. Erich Ludendorff, *Mein militärischer Werdegang* (Munich: Ludendorffs Verlag, 1935), 151, said there were about 7,000 one-year volunteers in 1875.

117. Anonymous, "Die Uebungen des Beurlaubtenstands," *Militär-Wochenblatt* 93 (1905).

118. Some men apparently had enough leisure time to continue their university studies if their garrisons were well located. See John, *Reserveoffizierkorps*, 60, 126–127; Count Hermann von Wartensleben-Carow, *Hermann Graf von Wartensleben-Carow. Ein Lebensbild 1826–1921*, ed. Countess Elisabeth von Wartensleben (Berlin: E. S. Mittler, 1923), 4–5; Max van den Bergh, *Das deutsche Heer vor dem Weltkriege* (Berlin: Sanssouci Verlag, 1934), 80. Others were brutally and some-

times financially exploited by noncommissioned officers. See John, *Reserveoffizierkorps*, 129ff.

119. John, *Reserveoffizierkorps*, 148. About 10 percent were sent to the reserves without eligibility to serve as noncommissioned officers.

120. On the 1909 decision, see ibid., 259–260. On the general commissioning process, see ibid., 239–242. The widely repeated argument of Eckart Kehr and Han-Ulrich Wehler, that the active regiments chose the reserve officers, is incorrect. See Reinhard Stumpff, *Die Wehrmacht-Elite. Rang und Herkunftsstruktur der deutschen Generale und Admirale 1933–1945* (Boppard: Harald Boldt, 1982), 205–206, n. 40.

121. Dilthey, *Militär-Dienst Unterricht für Freiwillige* (Berlin: E. S. Mittler, 1887), 6.

122. See Deist, *Militär und Innenpolitik*, 1:xxiii and the literature cited therein.

123. John, *Reserveoffizierkorps*, 264–266, has a substantial analysis based on a very comprehensive listing from 1906. Ostertag, *Bildung, Ausbildung, und Erziehung*, 289, has similar data.

124. Ritter, *Sword and Scepter*, 2:103–104. John, *Reserveoffizierkorps*, 243–244, cites the example of the son of the Bavarian military plenipotentiary in Berlin, who was denied a reserve commission for not obeying uniform regulations. He also explains how these dismissals were disguised in the official announcements (ibid., 505).

125. Ritter, *Sword and Scepter*, 2:102, gives examples. John, *Reserveoffizierkorps*, 305, cites the case of von Armin-Üsedom, leader of the Conservative Party in the Reichstag, who, upon reaching the age of seventy, preferred to be known as first lieutenant of the *Landwehr* (retired) rather than *wirklicher geheimer Rat*, a very prestigious honor in the bureaucracy.

126. Messerschmidt, "Die politische Geschichte," 277–278; John, *Reserveoffizierkorps*, 52–53.

127. On the alleged militarization of the middle classes, see Messerschmidt, "Die politische Geschichte," 277–278; Ritter, *Sword and Scepter*, 2:101–102. Dilthey's popular handbook *Militär-Dienst Unterricht*, 5, argued that this was a positive development.

128. For a representation of Wilhelm I's views, see Ernst Werner, ed., *Kaiser Wilhelms des Ersten. Briefe, Reden und Schriften*, 2 vols. (Berlin: E. S. Mittler, 1906), 2:19–20. Examples of kissing the royal hand can be found in Count Robert von Zedlitz-Trützschler, *Zwölf Jahre am deutschen Kaiserhof: Aufzeichnungen* (Stuttgart: Deutsche Verlags Anstalt, 1924), 84, and Gunther Martin, "Gruppenschicksal und Herkunftsschicksal. Zur Sozialgeschichte der preussischen Generalität 1812–1918" (Ph.D. diss., Saarbrücken, 1970), 82. Mackensen was one of the most successful field army commanders in the east during the First World War.

129. Most notable are Samuel Huntington and those who based certain concepts of professionalism and civilian control of the military on the fanciful notion of the nonpolitical Prussian officer corps.

130. The German word *Erziehung*, frequently rendered as "education," con-

notes values and a proper upbringing rather than the simple impartation of technical knowledge or general education.

131. Hans von Beseler, *Vom Soldatenberuf* (Berlin: E. S. Mittler, 1904), 19.

132. Helmuth von Moltke, *Essays, Speeches, and Memoirs of Count Helmuth von Moltke*, trans. Charles Fling McClumpha, C. Barter, and Mary Herms, 2 vols. (New York: Harper & Brothers, 1893), 2:107; H. von Löbell, "Der Offizier als Erzieher des Volkes," *Beiheft zur Militär-Wochenblatt* (1888): col. 75. Similar comments can be found in Hermann von Chappuis, *Bei Hofe und im Felde. Lebenserinnerungen* (Frankfurt: Carl Jügels Verlag, 1902), 19–20; Paul von Hindenburg, *Aus meinem Leben* (Leipzig: Verlag von G. Hirzel, 1920), 65; and Mathilde Freifrau von Gregory (an officer's wife), *Dreissig Jahre preussische Soldatenfrau* (Munich: Rudolf M. Rohrer Verlag, ca. 1931), 77.

133. Höhn, *Die Armee als Erziehungsschule der Nation*, 33. Osten-Sacken, *Preussens Heer*, 2:251–253, a semiofficial source, openly explains the origins and functions of the concept.

134. Thomas Rohkrämer, *Der Militarismus der "kleinen Leute." Die Kriegervereine in Deutschland 1871–1914* (Munich: R. Oldenbourg, 1990), 68–69, 204; Moncure, *Forging the King's Sword*, 128–129. Ludendorff's comments in *Mein militärischer Werdegang*, 7, 24, are the source for some of this. Ulrich von Hassel, *Erinnerungen aus meinem Leben 1848–1918* (Stuttgart: Belsersche Verlags-Buchhandlung, 1919), 133, notes that Christianity was not popular during the *Kulturkampf*. Colmar *Freiherr* von der Goltz, *Denkwürdigkeiten*, ed. Friechrich Freiherr von der Goltz and Wolfgang Foerster (Berlin: E. S. Mittler, 1929), 24–25, argues, contrary to Moncure, that religion was a serious issue in the cadet corps.

135. Erich Brandenburg, ed., *Briefe Kaiser Wilhelm des Ersten* (Berlin: Insel Verlag, 1911), 23, and Werner, *Kaiser Wilhelms des Ersten*, 1:423–424, 2:141–142, 159, 408–410, contain ample evidence of the old emperor's beliefs. Similar views can be found in Goltz, *Denkwürdigkeiten*, 47; Freytag-Loringhoven, *Menschen und Dinge*, 10–11; Thilo Krieg, *Hermann von Tresckow. General der Infanterie und General-Adjutant Kaiser Wilhelms I* (Berlin: E. S. Mittler, 1911), 12; Karl Friedrich von Steinmetz, *General-Feldmarschall von Steinmetz. Aus den Familienpapieren dargestellt*, ed. Hans von Krosigk (Berlin: E. S. Mittler, 1900), 10–11; Dorow, *Job von Witzleben*, 101; Count Alfred von Waldersee, *Denkwürdigkeiten des Generalfeldmarschalls Alfred Grafen von Waldersee*, ed. H. O. Meisner, 3 vols. (Berlin: Deutsche Verlags-Anstalt, 1925), 1:13; Roon, *Denkwürdigkeiten*, 3:41–43.

136. BA/MA, PH 1/28, 115–116, has two of his typically excessive orations.

137. *Nachlass* v. Waldersee, BA/MA, N 182/11, has such a schedule.

138. Osten-Sacken, *Preussens Heer*, 2:347.

139. Von Rabenau, *Die deutsche Land- und Seemacht und die Berufspflichten des Offiziers* (Berlin: E. S. Mittler, 1914), 35; Höhn, *Die Armee als Erziehungsschule der Nation*, 181. See also Hans Pommer, *Zwanzig Jahre im Reichslande* (Frankfurt: Neuer Frankfurter Verlag, 1914), 44.

140. Höhn, *Die Armee als Erziehungsschule der Nation*, 186–188, 220–280. The official view is faithfully and succinctly stated in Löbell, "Der Offizier," 70–84.

141. Lenski, *Lern- und Lehrjahre*, 12–13.

142. Krieg, *Hermann von Tresckow*, 48.

143. Prussia Statistical Bureau, *Statistisches Handbuch für den preussischen Staat* (Berlin: Verlag des Koenigliches Statischen Bureaus, 1888), 294–395; Klaus Epstein, *Matthias Erzberger and the Dilemma of German Democracy* (Princeton, NJ: Princeton University Press, 1959), 69. On Catholics in the bureaucracy, see Lysbeth Walker Muncy, "The Prussian Landräte in the Last Years of the Monarchy: A Case Study of Pomerania and the Rhineland in 1890–1918," *Central European History* 6, 4 (December 1973): 326.

144. Friedrich von Schulte, "Adel im deutschen Offizier- und Beamtenstand," *Deutsche Revue* 21 (April–June 1896): 186, gives a much lower estimate and said that many were highly placed and well-connected nobles.

145. Hughes, *King's Finest*, 33.

146. General Eugen von Wülffen was a good example. He and his mother were Catholics, but they were the only ones in the family since at least 1669. His sister and two brothers were Evangelical. His father, grandfather, and great-grandfather had all been officers.

147. Demeter, *Das deutsche Offizierkorps*, 213; Werner, *Kaiser Wilhelms des Ersten*, 1:330.

148. For some examples, see Ekkehard-Teja Wilke, *Political Decadence in Imperial Germany: Personnel-Political Aspects of the German Government Crisis, 1894–1897* (Urbana: University of Illinois Press, 1976), 87.

149. Representative examples can be found in Friedrich von Boetticher, "Der Lehrmeister des neuzeitlichen Krieges," in *Von Scharnhorst zu Schlieffen 1806–1906. Hundert Jahre preussisch-deutscher Generalstab* (Berlin: E. S. Mittler, 1933), 252; "Lebenserinnerungen," *Nachlass* von Beseler, BA/MA, N 30/46; Beseler to wife, 16 October 1884, ibid., N 30/52; Waldersee, *Denkwürdigkeiten*, 1:248.

150. Werner T. Angress, "Prussia's Army and the Jewish Reserve Officer Controversy before World War I," *Leo Baeck Institute Year Book* 17 (1972): 21, concludes that about sixty Jews may have received commissions during the Franco-Prussian War. Most of them must have been baptized. Alexander von Kluck recalled that his company had a single Jewish officer during the war and that the others treated him with great reserve. See Alexander von Kluck, *Wanderjahre-Krieg-Gestalten* (Berlin: Verlag R. Eisenschmidt, 1929), 13.

151. The case is cited, from documents now lost, in Priesdorff, *Soldatisches Führertum*, 10:161.

152. Angress, "Prussia's Army," 32–33. Kitchen, *German Officer Corps*, 46, concludes, without reference to evidence, that there were no Jewish reserve officers by 1909.

153. See, for example, Warren B. Morris Jr., *The Road to Olmütz: The Career of Joseph Maria von Radowitz* (New York: Revisionist Press, 1976), 60; Albrecht von Stosch, *Denkwürdigkeiten des Generals und Admirals Albrecht von Stosch*, ed. Ulrich von Stosch (Stuttgart: Deutsche Verlags-Anstalt, 1904), 39; van den Bergh, *Das deutsche Heer*, 23. Even Waldersee's anti-Semitism was based on grounds of religion, culture, and politics rather than the racial views of the more extreme anti-Semites. See Waldersee, *Denkwürdigkeiten*, 2:39, 159.

154. Hughes, *King's Finest*, 37–38, 164, provides details about and sources for the background of these two men.

155. Louis von Scharfenort, *Die königlich preussische Kriegsakademie* (Berlin: E. S. Mittler, 1910), 178, cites the case of Siegfried Hirsch, teacher of history at the War Academy and professor at the University of Berlin. Hassel, *Erinnerungen*, 104, cites the case of a Jew teaching at the War Academy until 1870, when he was dismissed because the new director, General von Ollech, decided that such a person had nothing of value to teach Prussian officers.

156. Hughes, *King's Finest*, 95–102, discusses the financial issues of marriage and the practice of trading money for social standing. Adolf Wild von Hohenborn, later war minister, had a Jewish wife of American origins.

157. Lamar Cecil, "Jew and Junker in Imperial Berlin," *Leo Baeck Institute Yearbook* 20 (1975): 49. Other examples can be found in *Nachlass* Keitel, BA/MA, N 54/2, 75, 143; *Nachlass* v. Below, ibid., N 87/38, 181.

158. Terence Cole, "Kaiser versus Chancellor: The Crisis of Bülow's Chancellorship," in *Society and Politics in Wilhelmine Germany*, ed. Richard J. Evans (London: Croon Helm, 1978), 42.

159. Osten-Sacken, *Preussens Heer*, 2:24, 263–264; Absolon, *Die Wehrmacht im Dritten Reich*, 2:3–4.

160. Absolon, *Die Wehrmacht im Dritten Reich*, 2:236–238, 241–251; Osten-Sacken, *Preussens Heer*, 2:291–292. Hans Driftmann, *Grundzüge des militärischen Erziehungs- und Bildungswesens in der Zeit 1871–1939* (Regensburg: Walhalla & Praetoria Verlag, 1979), 98, also has useful information. The fundamental regulation was Prussia, Kriegsministerium, *Verordnungen über die Ehrengerichte der Offiziere (Ehr. V.) vom 2. 5. 1874* (Berlin: Reichsdruckerei, 1910).

161. Zwehl, *Generalstabsdienst*, 21.

162. Steinberg, *Bismarck*, 267.

163. The subject of war planning is covered in chapters 5 and 6.

164. Dennis Showalter, *Instrument of War: The German Army 1914–1918* (New York: Osprey Publishing, 2016), 42–43; David R. Stone, *The Russian Army in the Great War: The Eastern Front, 1914–1917* (Lawrence: University Press of Kansas, 2015), 215; Yuri N. Danilov, *Russland im Weltkriege 1914–1915* (Jena: Frommannsche Buchhandlung, 1925), 364. Owing to a smaller population and a lower birthrate, the French army eventually resorted to using large numbers of colonial troops. Douglas Porch, "The French Army in the First World War," in *Military Effectiveness*, vol. 1, *The First World War*, ed. Allan R. Millett and Williamson Murray (Boston: Allen & Unwin, 1988), 198–199.

165. The background of Wilhelm I, which dated back to the Napoleonic Wars, has already been noted. Friedrich III, whose reign was tragically cut short by throat cancer, had a distinguished career of military service, commanding armies in both the Austro-Prussian and Franco-Prussian Wars.

166. Cecil, *Wilhelm II*, 2:211. For vignettes indicative of Wilhelm II's behavior at headquarters, see Walter Görlitz, ed., *The Kaiser and His Court: The Diaries, Note Books and Letters of Admiral Georg Alexander von Müller, Chief of the Naval Cabinet 1914–1918*, trans. Mervyn Savill (New York: Harcourt, Brace & World, 1961), 81–82.

1. Carl von Clausewitz, *On War* [1832], ed. and trans. Michael Howard and Peter Paret (Princeton, NJ: Princeton University Press, 1976), is the standard English version to which all citations refer unless otherwise noted. This is based on the authoritative German edition: Carl von Clausewitz, *Vom Kriege*, ed. Werner Hahlweg, 19th ed. (Bonn: Ferdinand Dümmlers Verlag, 1980).

2. A useful introduction to Frederick's wars and thought is R. R. Palmer, "Frederick, Guibert, Bülow," in *Makers of Modern Strategy from Machiavelli to the Nuclear Age*, ed. Peter Paret (Princeton, NJ: Princeton University Press, 1986), 91–105. The best modern treatment of the king's wars is Dennis Showalter, *The Wars of Frederick the Great* (London: Longman, 1996).

3. Palmer, "Frederick, Guibert, Bülow," 114–119, discusses Bülow.

4. On Scharnhorst, see Charles White, *The Enlightened Soldier: Scharnhorst and the Militärische Gesellschaft in Berlin, 1801–1805* (New York: Praeger, 1989).

5. This study does not consider the writings of Wilhelm von Willisen, who, though important in his own day, was much less significant in the longer-term development of Prussian theory. On Willisen's middle position between Clausewitz and Jomini on various issues, see Volker Mollin, *Auf dem Wege zur "Materialschlacht": Vorgeschichte u. Funktionen d. Artillerie-Industrie-Komplexes im Deutschen Kaiserreich* (Pfaffenweiler: Centaurus Verlag, 1986), 102ff.

6. The German title was *Der Geist des neueren Kriegssystems*; it appeared in an English version in 1806. In addition to Palmer, "Frederick, Guibert, Bülow," see Azar Gat, *The Origins of Military Thought: From the Enlightenment to Clausewitz* (Oxford: Clarendon Press, 1989), 79–94. Peter Paret, *Clausewitz and the State* (Oxford: Oxford University Press, 1976), 91–94, has an important perspective.

7. Gat, *Origins of Military Thought*, 79–80. Gat's succinct treatment of Enlightenment military theory is the best available.

8. Ibid., 87. Paret, *Clausewitz and the State*, 93, argues that Bülow's reaction to criticism was tolerant.

9. Michael Howard, "Jomini and the Classical Tradition," in *The Theory and Practice of War: Essays Presented to Captain B. H. Liddell Hart*, ed. Michael Howard (New York: Praeger, 1966), 8; Julius von Verdy du Vernois, *Strategie*, 3 vols. (Berlin: E. S. Mittler, 1902–1904), 3:148.

10. Peter Paret, "Clausewitz," in Paret, *Makers of Modern Strategy* (1986), 190. See also Rudolf von Caemmerer, *The Development of Strategical Science during the 19th Century*, trans. Karl von Donat (London: Hugh Rees, 1905), 9; Donald Stoker, *Clausewitz: His Life and Work* (New York: Oxford University Press, 2014), 34–35.

11. See, for example, Sigfried Mette, *Vom Geist deutscher Feldherren. Genie und Technik 1800–1918* (Zurich: Scientia, 1938), 15. Bülow was not mentioned in the collection of essays edited by Wolfgang von Groote and Klaus-Jürgen Müller, *Napoleon I. und das Militärwesen seiner Zeit* (Freiberg: Rombach, 1968).

12. Gat, *Origins of Military Thought*, 89.

13. White, *Enlightened Soldier*, is excellent. Rudolf Stadelmann, *Scharnhorst, Schicksal und geistige Welt* (Wiesbaden: Limers Verlag, 1952), is still important,

as are the relevant sections of Paret's *Clausewitz and the State*. Max Lehmann, *Scharnhorst*, 2 vols. (Leipzig: Verlag von S. Hirzel, 1886–1887), is still the basic biography.

14. On Lloyd's influence on Scharnhorst, see White, *Enlightened Soldier*, 10–12.

15. Gat, *Origins of Military Thought*, 166–167, comments on the "decisive" influence of Scharnhorst's views on Clausewitz. Many other examples could be adduced beyond those enumerated by Gat. Paret, *Clausewitz and the State*, 56–77, devotes an insightful chapter to Scharnhorst.

16. Clausewitz was born on 1 July, not 1 June, the date erroneously used in most studies, a mistake that endured for more than 150 years. He was thus eleven, not twelve, when he entered the army. See Klaus Hilbert, "Ergänzung zum Lebensbild des Generals Carl von Clausewitz," *Militärgeschichte* 20, 2 (1981): 208–213, who uncovered this error.

17. The best brief introduction is Michael Howard, *Clausewitz* (Oxford: Oxford University Press, 1983). The most profound treatment in English is Paret, *Clausewitz and the State*. Roger Parkinson, *Clausewitz: A Biography* (New York: Stein & Day, 1971), is useful as a biography but contributes little to an understanding of the larger issues. Better in this regard is Stoker, *Clausewitz*, 83–85.

18. Ulrich Marwedel, *Carl von Clausewitz. Persönlichkeit und Wirkungsgeschichte seines Werkes bis 1918* (Boppard: Harald Boldt Verlag, 1978), 36–45, has an excellent discussion of this issue. Years later, some nationalist historians, such as Heinrich von Treitschke, still held this against Clausewitz.

19. Jehuda Wallach, *Kriegstheorien. Ihre Entwicklung im 19. und 20. Jahrhundert* (Frankfurt: Bernard & Graefe, 1972), 32–34, attributes the delayed publication of Clausewitz's major writings to distrust at the Prussian court. Other evidence indicates that Clausewitz preferred it that way. On the matter of the unfinished state of *On War*, see John Tetsuro Sumida, *Decoding Clausewitz: A New Approach to On War* (Lawrence: University Press of Kansas, 2008), 4.

20. For introductions to this vast literature, see the introductory comments to the German and English versions cited above; Marwedel, *Clausewitz*; Paret, *Clausewitz and the State*. Gat, *Origins of Military Thought*, 255–263, has challenged many of Paret's interpretations, especially the nearly universal assumption that few chapters of the work were finished at the time of the author's death. Gat's argument, though compelling, is marred by its strident tone and has had little influence on the literature.

21. Christopher Bassford, *Clausewitz in English: The Reception of Clausewitz in Britain and America 1815–1945* (New York: Oxford University Press, 1994).

22. John Shy, "Jomini," in Paret, *Makers of Modern Strategy* (1986), 177. For statements by serving officers that Clausewitz's work was a sort of military bible, see Prince Bernhard von Bülow (quoting *Freiherr* von Löe), *Denkwürdigkeiten*, 4 vols. (Berlin: Ullstein, 1931), 4:254; Egon *Freiherr* von Gayl, *General von Schlichting und sein Lebenswerk* (Berlin: Verlag von Georg Stilke, 1913), 264–265.

23. Peter Paret, "Clausewitz and the Nineteenth Century," in Howard, *Theory and Practice of War*, 23–24; Paret, "Clausewitz," 211.

24. Wilhelm Rüstow, *Die Feldherrnkunst des neunzehnten Jahrhunderts. Zum*

Selbststudium und für den Unterricht an höheren Militärschulen, 2nd ed. (Zurich: Druck & Verlag von Friedrich Schulthess, 1867), 536. Marwedel, *Clausewitz,* 117, cites the 1857 edition to the same effect. This author's (DJH) twenty years of experience with "professional military education" in the United States confirms that few officers have the interest or the diligence to read more than a tiny fraction of *On War* or any other serious work of theory or history. In this respect, the average Prussian officer might not have been very different from his twentieth-century American counterparts.

25. Marwedel, *Clausewitz,* 53, 113, cites, among others, the Brockaus und Meyer Lexicons of 1845–1850.

26. Marwedel, *Clausewitz,* 114.

27. Karl Pönitz (not von Pönitz, as usually cited), *Militärische Briefe eines Verstorbenen an seine noch Lebenden Freunde historischen, wissenschaftlichen und humoristischen Inhalts,* 3 vols. (Adorf: Verlagsbureau, 1841–1845). The "deceased" is Clausewitz. Another author's reply to this work, Anonymous, *Militärische Briefe eines Lebenden an seinen Freund Clausewitz in Olymp.* (Leipzig: Verlag Otto Wigant, 1846), has been wrongly attributed to Pönitz. It may have been written by the Prussian General Staff officer Karl Bade. Numerous libraries and bibliographies have accepted this wrong attribution. Note that unlike Pönitz, this author claimed to have known Clausewitz personally. See Friedrich Doepner, "Karl Eduard Pönitz 1795–1858," *Zeitschrift für Heereskunde* 52, 340 (November–December 1988): 140–143, and "Ergänzung zu: Karl Eduard Pönitz," *Zeitschrift für Heereskunde* 53, 341 (January–February 1989): 25. I (DJH) am indebted to John Tashjean for this information.

28. Friedrich Karl, *Denkwürdigkeiten aus seinem Leben,* ed. Wolfgang Foerster, 2 vols. (Stuttgart: Deutsche Verlags-Anstalt, 1910), 1:371, printing an 1856 essay. Paret, "Clausewitz and the Nineteenth Century," 23–24, argues for the rapid growth of familiarity with Clausewitz among military thinkers both in Germany and abroad, despite much confusion over *On War*'s content.

29. For example, Caemmerer, *Development of Strategical Science,* 82; Wilhelm von Blume, "Selbsttätigkeit der Führer im Kriege," *Beiheft zum Militär-Wochenblatt* 10 (1896): 528; Julius von Verdy du Vernois, *Studien über den Krieg,* 3 vols. (Berlin: E. S. Mittler, 1892–1902), 3:6.

30. Hahlweg's introduction to *Vom Kriege,* 56–57, points out that German officers ignored or misunderstood many of Clausewitz's points but that he certainly had some impact. Gunther Rothenberg, "Moltke, Schlieffen and the Doctrine of Strategic Envelopment," in Paret, *Makers of Modern Strategy,* 297–298, also raises doubts.

31. Paret, "Clausewitz," 212–213; Michael Howard, "The Influence of Clausewitz," in *On War,* 33–35; Marwedel, *Clausewitz,* 213–214.

32. Herbert Rosinski, *The German Army* (London: Hogarth Press, 1940), 125–126; Gerhard Ritter, *The Sword and the Scepter: The Problem of Militarism in Germany,* trans. Heinz Norden, 4 vols. (Coral Gables, FL: University of Miami Press, 1964–1973), 1:55.

33. Marwedel, *Clausewitz,* 121, 173–174, 202, lists some of these critics, as does

Hahlweg's introduction to *Vom Kriege*, 60–62. Sigismund von Schlichting, a very important General Staff officer and writer around the turn of the century, was certainly influenced by Clausewitz and is a good illustration that criticism is actually a demonstration of Clausewitz's continuing influence. See Gayl, *General von Schlichting*, 269–270. The same may be said of the important theorist Wilhelm von Scherff. See Joachim Hoffmann, "Die Kriegslehre des Generals von Schlichting," *Militärgeschichtliche Mitteilungen* 1 (1969): 28. Antulio J. Echavarria II, "Borrowing from the Master: Uses of Clausewitz in German Military Literature before the Great War," *War in History* 3, 3 (1996): 274–292, makes the broader point and summarizes some of the "neo-Clausewitzian" literature of late Wilhelmine Germany. For a spirited if inelegantly written defense of Clausewitz's continuing relevance, see Bart Schuurman, "Clausewitz and the 'New Wars' Scholarship," *Parameters* 40, 1 (March 2010): 89–100.

34. A few of Moltke's theoretical writings are now available in Daniel J. Hughes, ed., *Moltke on the Art of War: Selected Writings* (Novato, CA: Presidio, 1994). Numerous other selections of Moltke's writings on campaigns and his correspondence during the Franco-Prussian War are also available in English translation.

35. See the comments by Paret, *Clausewitz and the State*, 314–315, 339 n. 12.

36. See Walter Schering, *Carl von Clausewitz. Geist und Tat, Das Vermächtnis des Soldaten und Denkers* (Stuttgart: Alfred Kroner Verlag, 1941), xxvi.

37. Gat, *Origins of Military Thought*, 232–234, has a discussion of the debate. See also Paret's introduction to *On War*, 15.

38. As Gat has pointed out, Romanticism taught German thinkers that war was not subject to the rules of the natural sciences. See Azar Gat, *The Development of Military Thought: The Nineteenth Century* (Oxford: Clarendon Press, 1992), 2, 46–48. See also Richard Blaschke, *Carl von Clausewitz* (Berlin: Junker & Dünnhaupt, 1934), 13, 256ff; Walter Schering, *Die Kriegsphilosophie von Clausewitz* (Hamburg: Hanseatische Verlagsanstalt, 1935), 105ff.

39. Schering, *Die Kriegsphilosophie von Clausewitz*, 108, 122; Blaschke, *Clausewitz*, 13. It should be pointed out that Schering argued that Clausewitz was not a mere follower of Kant and that he deserves his own place in the intellectual history of Germany.

40. Hew Strachan, *European Armies and the Conduct of War* (London: Allen & Unwin, 1983), 91–92.

41. See Paret, *Clausewitz and the State*, 156–157. Clausewitz wrote an essay titled "On Art and Theory of Art" before he wrote *On War*. See Gat, *Origins of Military Thought*, 176–177. Gerhard Östreich's assertion that Clausewitz was from the school of Neostoicism has not taken root. See his *Neostoicism and the Early Modern State*, ed. Brigitta Östreich and H. G. Koenigsberger (London: Cambridge University Press, 1982), 88.

42. *On War*, 75. The English translation slightly changes the emphasis in the original. It states: "To secure that object we must render the enemy powerless." The German actually reads: "To achieve this goal with certainty . . . " (*Um diesen Zweck sicher to erreichen*). See *Vom Kriege*, 192.

43. *On War*, 77. A very useful and unique index to *On War* is Jon Tetsuro

Sumida, "A Concordance of Selected Subjects in Carl von Clausewitz's *On War*," *Journal of Military History* 78, 1 (January 2014): 271–331.

44. *On War*, 81.

45. Ibid., 91. These reasons were the improbability of victory and the unacceptable cost of continuing the struggle. On this point, see ibid., 92, 94.

46. For a corrective, see Edward J. Villacres and Christopher Bassford, "Reclaiming the Clausewitzian Trinity," *Parameters* 25 (Autumn 1995): 9–19.

47. *On War*, 89.

48. Ibid., 580. The relevant chapter, "Absolute War and Real War" (book 8, chapter 2), begins the sustained discussion that continues throughout the remainder of the book. Numerous other references to these limits can be found in books 1 and 2.

49. Ibid., 585.

50. Ibid., 87, 605. The German word *Politik* can mean either "politics" or "policy." Since Clausewitz almost always used it in the sense of a state's foreign policy, this study uses the term "policy" throughout. Likewise, "political" should be understood in this sense.

51. On Scharnhorst and this issue, see Sigfrid Mette, *Vom Geist deutscher Feldherren*, 54.

52. The usual citation from Moltke is his essay on strategy, written in 1871, now available in Hughes, *Moltke on the Art of War*, 44–47. Wilhelm Balck, *Taktik*, 6 vols. (Berlin: R. Eisenschmidt, 1908–1912), 1:1; *Prinz* Krafft zu Hohenlohe-Ingelfingen, *Letters on Strategy*, 2 vols. (London: Kegan Paul, Trench, Trübner, 1898), 1:103; Reinhold Wagner, *Grundlagen der Kriegstheorie* (Berlin: E. S. Mittler, 1912), 313; Colmar *Freiherr* von der Goltz, *Krieg- und Heerführung* (Berlin: R. von Decker's Verlag, 1901), 11, 23; and Friedrich von Bernhardi, *On War of Today*, trans. Karl von Donat, 2 vols. (New York: Dodd, Mead, 1914), 2:182, quote Clausewitz directly. Numerous other examples could be adduced. See Reyher's letter to Friedrich Karl in the latter's *Denkwürdigkeiten aus seinem Leben*, 2:373.

53. Kriegsministerium, *D.V.E. Nr. 53, Grundzüge der höhere Truppenführung vom 1 Januar 1910* (Berlin: Reichsdruckerei, 1910), 7.

54. *On War*, 606, 681, 687.

55. Ibid., 87.

56. Ibid., 606. The Howard-Paret translation renders *Einzelheiten* (details) as "operational details," which changes the meaning. The translation renders at least forty German terms or phrases into the collective catch-all "operations" or "operational," in some cases to the harm of the text's felicity to the German, especially when read by modern Western officers. For Clausewitz and all subsequent German theory, the term "operation" had a much more specific and limited meaning than it has in modern American and NATO usage. This subject is revisited later in this chapter.

57. An exception would be John Keegan, *A History of Warfare* (New York: Alfred A. Knopf, 1993), 21–22, who states that Clausewitz argued that the "nature" of war "was to serve only itself." For more solid analyses, see Paret, *Clausewitz and the State*, 369; Wallach, *Kriegstheorien*, 44. Wallach also cites Clausewitz's letter of

22 December 1827 to a General Staff officer, apparently unaware that these views were stated even more concisely in *On War*. See "Zwei Briefe des General von Clausewitz, Gedanken zur Abwehr," *Militärwisenschaftliche Rundschau*, special issue, March 1937. Peter Paret published "Two Letters on Strategy" with a clarifying commentary in 1984, included in his *Understanding War: Essays on Clausewitz and the History of Military Power* (Princeton, NJ: Princeton University Press, 1992), 123–129.

58. See the postwar observations of General Otto von Moser, *Die oberste Gewalten im Weltkrieg* (Stuttgart: Chr. Belser, 1931), 7–12.

59. Hughes, *Moltke on the Art of War*, 44–45. This essay should be regarded as a continuation of Moltke's bitter dispute with Bismarck over the conduct of the war against France. See Stig Förster, "Optionen der Kriegführung im Zeitalter des Volkskrieges-zu Helmuth von Moltkes militärisch-politischen Überlegungen nach den Erfahrungen der Einigungskriege," in *Militärische Verantwortung in Staat und Gesellschaft. 175 Jahre Generalstabsausbildung in Deutschland*, ed. Detlef Bald (Koblenz: Bernard & Graefe, 1986), 92.

60. Hughes, *Moltke on the Art of War*, 36. Gerhard Ritter disputed the authenticity of part of this essay, but its overall tenor seems entirely consistent with Moltke's point of view and, more importantly, with the army's widespread belief regarding the domination of military strategy over policy during war.

61. Scherff quoted in Wallach, *Kriegstheorien*, 85. Scherff repeated this argument in his widely read *Die Lehre vom Kriege auf der Grundlage seiner neuzeitlichen Erscheinungsformen. Ein Versuch* (Berlin: E. S. Mittler, 1897), 28. Marwedel, *Clausewitz*, 147–149, cites several other influential writers in the same vein.

62. Friedrich von Bernhardi, writing in 1920, still insisted that diplomacy had a role only in preparing for war and in exploiting victories according to the instructions given by civilian authorities. See his *The War of the Future in Light of the Lessons of the World War*, trans. F. A. Holt (London: Hutchinson, 1920), 196–197. Many others, of course, accepted Clausewitz's views on the total dominance of policy over military strategy.

63. *On War*, 608. See Friedrich Deoepner, "Hat Graf Brühl Clausewitz verfälscht?" *Europäische Wehrkunde* 32, 5 (May 1983): 245–247.

64. Wallach, *Kriegstheorien*, 41–42.

65. Nor was Moltke's legacy the only factor. The nature of the monarchy, of the army and the officer corps, and of Prussia's entire history made for a troubled civil-military relationship.

66. Verdy du Vernois, *Strategie*, 59–61.

67. Ritter, *Sword and Scepter*, 1:220–221; Rudolf Stadelmann, *Moltke und der Staat* (Krefeld: Scherpe Verlag, 1950), 205–213; Marwedel, *Clausewitz*, 153–154; Otto Pflanze, *Bismarck and the Development of Germany*, 3 vols. (Princeton, NJ: Princeton University Press, 1961–1990), 1:474–475. Albrecht von Boguslawski's opposing view, properly cited in Marwedel, *Clausewitz*, 153, was an exception. For an excellent review of this issue, see Stig Förster, "The Prussian Triangle of Leadership in the Face of Peoples' War: A Reassessment of the Conflict between Bismarck and Moltke, 1870–71," in *On the Road to Total War: The American Civil*

War and the German Wars of Unification 1870–71, ed. Stig Förster and Jörg Nagler (Cambridge: Cambridge University Press, 1997), 115–140.

68. *On War*, 111–112.

69. Baron Antoine Jomini, *The Art of War*, reprint ed. (Westport, CT: Greenwood Press, 1971), 91. An excellent introduction to Jomini is Shy, "Jomini," 143–185.

70. Gerhard P. Gross, *The Myth and Reality of German Warfare: Operational Thinking from Moltke the Elder to Heusinger*, ed. David T. Zabecki (Lexington: University Press of Kentucky, 2016), 43; Ritter, *Sword and the Scepter*, 2:239; Dennis Showalter, *Instrument of War: The German Army 1914–1918* (New York: Osprey, Publishing, 2016), 18. This kind of compartmentalized approach to civil-military relations has been favored by generations of American military officers. This comment is based on our combined experience in American professional military education extending over four decades.

71. Clausewitz used the term *Wissenschaft*, which in German means any disciplined body of knowledge, not merely science in the sense implied by the English term. Jomini, of course, also concluded that war is an art, but his essentially mathematical and potentially rigid system places him more in the tradition of eighteenth-century writers than in that of Clausewitz. Indeed, he termed *On War* a "learned labyrinth." See Raymond Aaron, *Clausewitz: Philosopher of War*, trans. Christine Booker and Norman Stone (Englewood Cliffs, NJ: Prentice-Hall, 1985), 173. See also Sumida, *Decoding Clausewitz*, 143–144. Anyone interested in Jomini must now consider the interpretation of Gat, *Origins of Military Thought*, 106–135.

72. See Walter Schering, "Clausewitz' Lehre von Zweck und Mittel," *Wissen und Wehr* 7, (1936): 606–631, who may have been the first to identify the connection between Clausewitz and the theory of art. Gat, *Origins of Military Thought*, 176–177, relates Clausewitz's ideas on art to those of the great philosopher Immanuel Kant. Clausewitz's essay on art and the theory of art probably had little direct influence, since it was not widely available until the twentieth century.

73. On Enlightenment science, see Gat, *Origins of Military Thought*, 28–29, 139. The analysis of Paret, *Clausewitz and the State*, 164, is slightly different, but he agrees that Clausewitz considered science to be primarily analysis and art to be "the force of synthesis."

74. *On War*, 148–149.

75. Ibid., 148; Hughes, *Moltke on the Art of War*, 124; Verdy du Vernois, *Studien über den Krieg*, 2:109, 136. The classic 1933 German manual began with this statement: "The conduct of war is an art, a free creative activity based on a scientific foundation." See Germany, Chef der Heeresleitung, *Truppenführung*, 2 vols. (Berlin: E. S. Mittler, 1933), 1:1.

76. Max Jähns, "Die Kriegskunst als Kunst," in *Militärgeschichtliche Aufsätze*, ed. H. Schottelius and Ursula von Gersdorff (Osnabrück: Biblio Verlag, 1970), 3–4.

77. Compare Gat, *Origins of Military Thought*, 178.

78. *On War*, 141, 168, 578. The first part of this discussion in *On War* is headed: "Theory should be study, not doctrine [*Lehre*]."

79. Ibid., 132.

80. Ibid., 517.

81. Ibid., 141.

82. Paret, "Clausewitz," 193.

83. Both the private works of individuals and official publications used the term *Lehre* to describe, respectively, personal theories and official doctrine. In neither case does the modern term "doctrine" fit very well. No American officer would describe his views as "doctrine," which assumes a formal institutional approval reserved for official publications. Clausewitz usually used the term *positive Lehre* when warning against binding regulations as opposed to the more general concepts he proposed. This distinction is not always clear in the Howard-Paret translation.

84. John I. Alger, *The Quest for Victory: The History of the Principles of War* (Westport, CT: Greenwood Press, 1982), remains the basic source on this subject. The idea of principles of war goes back to the Enlightenment and to Jomini. Fuller was certainly in that tradition. See Azar Gat, *Fascist and Liberal Visions of War: Fuller, Liddell Hart, Douhet and Other Modernists* (Oxford: Clarendon Press, 1998), 23–25. On Fuller, Jomini, and Liddell Hart as proponents of the "scientific" view of war, see Jay Luvaas, "Clausewitz, Fuller and Liddell Hart," *Journal of Strategic Studies* 9, 2/3 (June–September 1986): 197–212. Richard M. Swain, "The Hedgehog and the Fox: Jomini, Clausewitz, and History," *Naval War College Review* (Spring 1990): 98–109, is also useful.

85. German officers sometimes concluded that the regulations merely provided a few essential points or clues (*Anhaltspunkten*). See Hugo Baron von Freytag-Loringhoven, *Betrachtungen über den russisch-japanischen Krieg*, 2 vols. (Berlin: E. S. Mittler, 1913), 1:116; Anonymous [C. von K.], "Zusammenwirken von Infanterie und Artillerie," *Militär-Wochenblatt* 56 (1914): cols. 1210–1211. On individual study beyond the regulations, see Blume, "Selbsttätigkeit der Führer im Kriege," 528; Wilhelm Balck, *Development of Tactics—World War*, trans. Harry Bell (Fort Leavenworth, KS: General Service Schools Press, 1922), 7. The reader should be aware that this is not the same as the more widely cited *Development of Tactics during the World War* by the same author.

86. On this point, see Colonel Hellmuth Volkmann, *Befehlstechnik, Winke und Anregungen für ihre Anwendung im Rahmen der Division und des verstärkten Regiments* (Berlin: E. S. Mittler, 1936), 5. Friedrich *Freiherr* von Falkenhausen, *Ausbildung für den Krieg*, 2 vols. (Berlin: E. S. Mittler, 1902), 1:295, warned that Prussian regulations could not be taken literally and required a genuine understanding of their subjects.

87. Even the manuals themselves sometimes stated that they were not rules, and on occasion they instructed officers to be prepared to disregard what they were reading. See Prussia, Generalinspektion des Militär-Erziehungs und Bildungswesen, *Leitfaden für den Unterricht in der Taktik auf den Königlichen Kriegsschulen*, 17th ed. (Berlin: E. S. Mittler, 1912), 2 (copy in BA/MA, PH D 11/37). See also Anonymous, "Die Heranbildung von Unterführern auf dem Exercirplatz," *Beiheft zum Militär-Wochenblatt*, (1884): 230; Balck, *Taktik*, 1:15. Balck's standard textbooks appeared in several editions.

88. Balck, *Taktik*, 1:175–176.

89. *On War*, 186. As Gat has pointed out, Clausewitz's emphasis on moral factors long antedated *On War* and was the essence of the broad change in the intellectual paradigm from the Enlightenment to Romanticism. See Gat, *Origins of Military Thought*, 182–183.

90. See 1869 *Instructions for Large Unit Commanders* in Hughes, *Moltke on the Art of War*, 172. See also Moltke's *Militärische Werke*, 17 vols. (Berlin: E. S. Mittler, 1892–1918), 4(3):126.

91. This was reiterated in the last prewar *Instructions for Large Unit Commanders*, 7. See also Friedrich *Freiherr* von Falkenhausen, *Kriegführung und Wissenschaft* (Berlin: E. S. Mittler, 1913), 8; Oskar von Lettow-Vorbeck, *Der Feldzug in Böhmen 1866*, 2nd ed. (Berlin: E. S. Mittler, 1910), 5; August Keim, "Kriegslehre und Kriegführung," *Beiheft zum Militär-Wochenblatt* (1889): 4, 15–16.

92. Friedrich von Bernhardi, "Die Artillerie beim Infanterieangriff, Eine Entgegnung," *Militär-Wochenblatt* 84 (1912): col. 1929 (a commentary on Rohne's criticism of Bernhardi's books). General Rohne was one of the army's premier experts on artillery in the pre-1914 period.

93. Even lower-ranking officers expressed this confidence in moral factors. See Lieutenant Mueller, "Über Gefechtsverluste," *Vierteljahrshefte für Truppenführung und Heereskunde* 2 (1905): 429–430; Colonel Wolf von Lindenau, "Was lehrt uns der Burenkrieg für unseren Infanterieangriff?" *Beiheft zum Militär-Wochenblatt* (1902): 159.

94. Jehuda Wallach, *The Dogma of the Battle of Annihilation: The Theories of Clausewitz and Schlieffen and Their Impact on the German Conduct of Two World Wars* (1967; reprint, Westport CT: Greenwood Press, 1986), 75, argues that moral factors played a small part in Schlieffen's writings. Helmut Otto, *Schlieffen und der Generalstab* (East Berlin: Deutscher Militärverlag, 1966), 146, argues the contrary more convincingly.

95. Friedrich Immanuel, *Handbuch der Taktik*, 2 vols. (Berlin: E. S. Mittler, 1910), 2:42–43. Immanuel was an author of substantial international reputation just prior to 1914.

96. Friedrich von Bernhardi, "Ueber Angriffsweise Kriegführung," *Beiheft zum Militär-Wochenblatt* 4 (1905): 138. Balck, *Taktik*, 1:93, also warned against excessive emphasis on moral factors, which he saw as a weakness in the French approach to combat.

97. Paret, introduction to *On War*, 11, provides a succinct summary of what Clausewitz meant by genius. He scattered his views on genius throughout the book.

98. *On War*, 100–112, 136. Paret, *Clausewitz and the State*, 160–161, discusses the roots of Clausewitz's views on personality and genius. On the divergence from Scharnhorst, see ibid., 166; Gat, *Origins of Military Thought*, 179.

99. *On War*, 101. An inherent "fog of war" as a specific and independent concept does not exist in *On War*. See Eugenia C. Kiesling, "*On War*: Without the Fog," *Military Review* 63, 5 (September–October 2001): 85–87.

100. *On War*, 102.

101. Ibid., 108.

102. Ibid., 140.

103. Ibid., 119.

104. Ibid., 120, 121.

105. Schering, *Clausewitz. Geist und Tat*, xxxi–xxxii.

106. *On War*, 112, 147–148.

107. Ibid., 119. See also Carl von Clausewitz, *Historical and Political Writings*, ed. and trans. Peter Paret and Daniel Moran (Princeton, NJ: Princeton University Press, 1992), 165–166.

108. *On War*, 101–103, 106–108.

109. Ibid., 105–108. Clausewitz occasionally made this point in his historical writings. See Blaschke, *Clausewitz*, 238.

110. On Scharnhorst's formulation, see Karl Linnebach, "Charakter und Begabung des Feldherrn im Lichte der Kriegsdenker von Scharnhorst bis zur Gegenwart," *Wissen und Wehr* 10 (1938): 697–698.

111. Generalinspektion des Militär-Erziehungs-und Bildungswesens, *Leitfaden für den Unterricht in der Taktik auf dem Königlichen Kriegsschulen* (Berlin: E. S. Mittler, 1912), 125; General Paul von Holleben, "Wissenschaftliche Grundlage für den Offizier," *Jahrbücher für die deutsche Armee und Marine* (1902), 462; Immanuel, *Handbuch der Taktik*, 1:31.

112. Kart Litzmann, "Die Macht der Persönlichkeit im Kriege," *Militär-Wochenblatt* 129 (1905): cols. 2945–2946. See Hugo Baron von Freytag-Loringhoven, *The Power of Personality in War*, trans. Oliver Spaulding (Harrisburg, PA: Military Service Publishing Company, 1955), 144, 154; Freytag-Loringhoven, *Betrachtungen über den russisch-japanischen Krieg*, 1:116.

113. On Schlichting's views, see Mette, *Vom Geist deutscher Feldherren*, 168. On Blume, see his "Selbstthätigkeit der Führer im Kriege," 523. For others, see Anonymous [C. von K.], "Die Taktik im Gesamtgebiet der Kriegführung," *Militär-Wochenblatt* 53 (1914): cols. 1137–1141; Anonyomous [B], "Über Verantwortlichkeit im Kriege," *Militär-Wochenblatt* 30 (1913): cols. 3817–3818.

114. John Moncure, *Forging the King's Sword: Military Education between Tradition and Modernization: The Case of the Royal Prussian Cadet Corps 1871–1918* (New York: Peter Lang, 1993), 186–187, has a useful summary of the expanded definition of "character." However, he seems to understate the term's goal of exclusivity based on social class and occupation rather than individual personal characteristics.

115. See Marwedel, *Clausewitz*, 165–166, for a discussion of this issue.

116. Manfred Messerschmidt, "Die politische Geschichte der preussisch-deutschen Armee," in *Deutsche Militärgeschichte*, ed. Militärgeschichtliches Forschungsamt, 6 vols. (Munich: Bernard & Graefe, 1964–1979), 3:69. See also Martin Kitchen, *The German Officer Corps 1890–1918* (Oxford: Clarendon Press, 1968), 30.

117. Hermann Vogt, *Das Buch vom deutschen Heer* (Bielefeld: Velhagen & Klasing, 1886), 23; Karl Demeter, *Das deutsche Offizierkorps in Gesellschaft und Staat 1650–1945*, 4th rev. ed. (Frankfurt: Bernard & Graefe, 1965), 270, citing a Military Cabinet document of 24 March 1909.

118. A recent review of the German performance in this period, considering both the domestic and foreign contexts of Prussian-German strategy, is Holger H. Herwig, "Strategic Uncertainties of a Nation-State: Prussia-Germany, 1871–1918," in *The Making of Strategy: Rulers, States and War*, ed. Williamson Murray, MacGregor Knox, and Alvin Bernstein (Cambridge: Cambridge University Press, 1994), 242–277. But compare Herwig's harsher views in "From Tirpitz to Schlieffen Plan: Some Observations on German Military Planning," *Journal of Strategic Studies* 9, 1 (March 1988): 53–63, and his "The Dynamics of Necessity: German Military Policy during the First World War," in *Military Effectiveness*, ed. Allan R. Millett and Williamson Murray, 3 vols. (Boston: Allen & Unwin, 1988), 1:80–115. One of the harshest critics, but not unrepresentative, is Martin Kitchen, "The Traditions of German Strategic Thought," *International History Review* 1, 2 (April 1979): 163–190. For a more balanced perspective, see Dennis Showalter, "Total War for Limited Objectives," in *Grand Strategies in War and Peace*, ed. Paul Kennedy (New Haven, CT: Yale University Press, 1991), 105–123.

119. Gat, *Origins of Military Thought*, 40–42.

120. *On War*, 128, 132, 177. Clausewitz devoted an entire book (177–275) to strategy and interlaced many additional comments throughout *On War*. German theory frequently distinguished between minor combat, called an engagement (*Gefecht*), and a battle (*Schlacht*), which was a collection of engagements, the difference being one of scale. Clausewitz used these terms in a somewhat undifferentiated manner, and the Howard-Paret translation added other inconsistencies. Broadly speaking, however, these terms retained their distinctive meaning throughout the period of this study. These terms found their way into some US Army doctrinal manuals in the 1980s, as Clausewitz came back into fashion.

121. Ibid., 194.

122. Ibid., 263–270.

123. Author's translation from *Vom Kriege*, 345. A slightly different version appears in *On War*, 177. I (DJH) dropped the Howard-Paret reference to "operational side" because no such words appear in the German.

124. *On War*, 177.

125. Ibid., 128, 263, 363, 386.

126. Ibid., 96–98, 227–228.

127. Ibid., 386. Clausewitz also wrote (97): "Every important victory—that is, the destruction of the opposing forces—reacts on all other possibilities. Like liquid, they will settle at a new level."

128. Ibid., 386, where Clausewitz writes: "we think it is useful to emphasize that all strategic planning rests on tactical success alone, and that—whether the solution is arrived at in battle or not—this is in all cases the actual fundamental basis for the decision."

129. Ibid., 386, 227–228 (emphasis in original).

130. See Immanuel, *Handbuch der Taktik*, 1:111; Anonymous, *Die Truppenführung* (Berlin: R. Eisenschmidt, 1914) 16; Hohenlohe-Ingelfingen, *Letters on Strategy*, 1:40, for an earlier statement.

131. On Moltke, see Heinz-Ludger Borgert, "Grundzüge der Landkriegführung

von Schlieffen bis Guderian," in *Deutsche Militärgeschichte*, ed. Militärgeschtliches Forschungsamt, 6 vols. (Munich: Bernard & Graefe, 1964–1979), 6:385–388. See also Hans Hitz, "Taktik und Strategie," *Wehrwissenschaftliche Rundschau* 6, 11 (1956): 611–628; Colmar *Freiherr* von der Goltz, *The Nation in Arms*, trans. Philip Ashworth (London: W. H. Allen, 1906), 304–305, 331–332. Balck's views are in his widely read *Taktik*, 1:7–8, and his *Development of Tactics—World War*, 260–261. Kuhl's views are in his "Bemerkungen des Generals v. Kuhl zum vorstehenden Aufsatz" [by Hans Delbrück], *Militär-Wochenblatt* 101, 11 (1925): col. 363. Delbrück's original article is "Strategie und Taktik in der Offensive von 1918," *Militär-Wochenblatt* 101, 11 (1925): cols. 361–363.

132. Hughes, *Moltke on the Art of War*, 43–47. This discussion can also be found in a slightly different and later essay in ibid., 124–125. Moltke repeated Clausewitz's admonition that "the entire strategic advance is entirely based on tactical success" (68). In defending his views on the primacy of tactics in the Franco-Prussian War, Moltke pointed out that "there will be few cases where a tactical victory does not fit into the strategic plan. Success of arms will always be thankfully accepted and fully utilized" (152–153).

133. Some, perhaps more modern, views were virtually forgotten after Moltke's writings became influential. For example, in an anonymous 1858 pamphlet, Prince Friedrich Karl wrote: "What is strategy other than the art of attaining the goals of policy through the employment of the available forces?" See Friedrich Karl, *Denkwürdigkeiten*, 1:180–181.

134. On Schlichting and this issue, see Daniel J. Hughes, "Schlichting, Schlieffen and the Prussian Theory of War in 1914," *Journal of Military History* 59, 2 (April 1995): 257–278, and the literature cited therein. See also Antulio J. Echevarria II, *After Clausewitz: German Military Thinkers before the Great War* (Lawrence: University Press of Kansas, 2000), 38–42.

135. Sigismund von Schlichting, *Taktische und strategische Grundsätze der Gegenwart*, 3 vols. (Berlin: E. S. Mittler, 1898–1899), 2:91. It is noteworthy that E. S. Mittler, a semiofficial publishing house with an extremely close relationship to the army and the General Staff, published Schlichting's most important work and that the General Staff incorporated it into the curriculum of the War Academy, despite its harsh criticism of Clausewitz on some points.

136. Verdy du Vernois, *Studien über den Krieg*, 3:30–33.

137. Ibid., 44: "Strategy is equally a part of the theory (*Lehre*) of war, and a part of the conduct of war itself, and, to be sure, that part that includes consideration of all operational periods in relationship to scientific evaluations and the preparation and execution of war." Verdy du Vernois (1832–1910) was a close associate of Moltke. He became war minister and a distinguished military writer. See Kurt von Priesdorff, ed., *Soldatisches Führertum*, 10 vols. (Hamburg: Hanseatische Verlagsanstalt, 1936–1942), vol. 10, no. 3358.

138. Balck, *Taktik*, 1:6, wrote, quoting Delbrück: "Strategy is the theory (*Lehre*) of the employment of the means of war for attaining the goal of war; tactics is the art of commanding units (*Truppenführung*) up to and in combat."

139. An examination of almost any modern work on military theory or official

doctrine will illustrate the complete dominance of this tripartite layering of the "levels of war."

140. On Bülow's use of the term, see Rüstow, *Die Feldherrnkunst des neuenzehnten Jahrhunderts*, 188. There are many discussions of strategy and tactics in the pre-1914 literature, but virtually none imposes operations as a third category or uses levels at all. See Balck, *Taktik*, 1:1–6; Schlichting, *Taktische und strategische Grundsätze*, 2:14, 146, 149, 3:133; Anonymous, *Die Truppenführung*, 7–8. Verdy du Vernois, *Studien über den Krieg*, 3:2, concludes that all operational concepts "belong to the elements of strategy." He was typical in titling this section of his study "General Strategic (Operative) Concepts." Balck, *Taktik*, 3:16, also wrote of an "operative (strategic) unit." In the pre-1939 period, this interpretation generally continued intact. Hermann Foertsch, *Kriegskunst heute und morgen* (Berlin: Verlag Wilhelm Andermann, 1939), 30–31, wrote: "Usually the concepts 'operation,' 'operational decisions,' and so forth are used as subordinate concepts of strategy. Precisely speaking, one terms as operations the movements of the forces which lead to a battle." As Goltz, *Krieg- und Heerführung*, 123, pointed out, merely waiting for the enemy to attack, even at the theater level, is not an operation. Both distinctions—that "operations" are not an independent category of thought and that the divisions between tactics and strategy are concept based (spheres or areas of very different types of activity) rather than hierarchy based—reflect the German belief that these differences are matters of substance rather than quantity or hierarchies of the same activity.

141. As Schlichting pointed out, a mere battle, even if conducted by several field armies, is not an operation. See his *Taktische und strategische Grundsätze*, 2:131. See also Schlichting's harshest critic, Wilhelm von Scherff, *Der Schlachtenangriff* (Berlin: Verlag von R. Eisenschmidt, 1898), 7–8. This has been the source of much misunderstanding of Ludendorff's concepts and statements he made in 1918. See also Gross, *Myth and Reality of German Warfare*, 53–55.

142. *Allgemeine Militär Encyclopedia*, 2nd ed. (1873), 6:329.

143. Bernard Poten, ed., *Handwörterbuch der gesamten Militärwissenschaften*, 9 vols. (Bielefeld: Velhagen & Klasing, 1877–1880), 7:259.

144. Schlichting, *Taktische und strategische Grundsätze*, 2:89; Balck, *Taktik*, 5:3; Konstantin Hierl, "Die Bedeutung der kriegsgeschichtlichen Studium der Napoleonischen Epoche," *Beiheft zum Militär-Wochenblatt* 4 (1902): 208.

145. *D.V.E. Nr. 53: Grundzüge der höheren Truppenführung vom 1 Januar 1910*, 7–44.

146. *On War* has actual German usages at 183, 342, 344, 365, and 558. Of course, I (DJH) may have overlooked some instances when comparing the texts. The German concept most like the broad English word "operation" is *Unternehmung* (literally, "undertaking"), which appears about thirty times. The translation is thus consistent with modern English-language dual usage (sometimes broad in scope, sometimes referring to the intermediate level of war) but entirely inconsistent with the very specific and limited use in *Vom Kriege* and other German literature.

147. Aron, *Clausewitz*, 96.

148. *On War*, 75, 95–99.

149. Ibid., 90: "The fighting forces must be *destroyed*: that is, they must be *put in such a condition that they can no longer carry on the fight*. Whenever we use the phrase 'destruction of the enemy's forces,' this alone is what we mean." This, of course, has both physical and psychological dimensions.

150. Ibid., 90, 99. See the insightful comments of Wallach, *Kriegstheorien*, 46–47.

151. Goltz, *Krieg- und Heerführung*, 8.

152. Wallach, *Dogma of the Battle of Annihilation*, is the strongest in this line of interpretation. Perceptive analysis can also be found in Echevarria, *After Clausewitz*, 189–190.

153. *On War*, 99, 625. See also Paret, *Clausewitz and the State*, 333, who correctly notes that in his historical studies, Clausewitz spent little space relating the details of battles. Hitz, "Taktik und Strategie," 612, covers the indecisiveness of maneuvering, while Max Jähns, *Feldmarschall Moltke* (Berlin: Ernst Hoffman, 1900), 577, notes the clash with Archduke Charles.

154. Liddell Hart was perhaps Clausewitz's leading critic on this point, although John Keegan took on that mantle late in his life. See the acerbic article by Christopher Bassford, "John Keegan and the Grand Tradition of Trashing Clausewitz: A Polemic," *War and Society* 1, 3 (November 1994): 317–336.

155. Gat, *Origins of Military Thought*, 213–223, argues that Clausewitz's 1827 note indicates this and that Clausewitz's entire theory was thrown into crisis late in his life when he realized that annihilation could not be a universal law. Sumida, *Decoding Clausewitz*, 187, unpersuasively suggests a connection between real war and guerrilla warfare.

156. Arden Bucholz, *Hans Delbrück and the German Military Establishment: War Images in Conflict* (Iowa City: University of Iowa Press, 1985), 26–44. Compare Gordon Craig, "Delbrück: The Military Historian," in Paret, *Makers of Modern Strategy*, 340–344. See also Robert Foley, *German Strategy and the Path to Verdun: Erich von Falkenhayn and the Development of Attrition, 1870–1916* (Cambridge: Cambridge University Press, 2005), 38–55.

157. Marwedel, *Clausewitz*, 158–160, is representative. Wallach, *Dogma of the Battle of Annihilation*, blames this primarily on Schlieffen and his disciples. The intermediate position is in Echevarria, *After Clausewitz*, 183–188.

158. Förster, "Optionen der Kriegführung," 104, n. 17, criticizes Wallach for not considering Moltke's contribution to the consensus on annihilation. This has some validity, but as Förster himself argued, Moltke's views were not always constant or extreme.

159. Ibid., 88–89.

160. Gross, *Myth and Reality of German Warfare*, 47–49; Förster, "Optionen der Kriegführung," 90–91. Förster's interpretation relies heavily on Stadelmann, *Moltke und der Staat*.

161. Hughes, *Moltke on the Art of War*, 175; *D.V.E. Nr. 53: Grundzüge der höheren Truppenführung*, 12, 15. Balck, *Taktik*, 1:5–6, made this point and cited the American Civil War as one of those rare cases in which destruction of the enemy state would be necessary.

162. Dennis Showalter, "German Grand Strategy: A Contradiction in Terms?"

Militärgeschichtliche Mitteilungen 48, 2 (1990): 81, argues this case effectively. Wallach, *Dogma of the Battle of Annihilation*, equates and thus confuses the two matters. For representative Prussian views, see Balck, *Taktik*, 5:3; Goltz, *Nation in Arms*, 306; Goltz, *Krieg- und Heerführung*, 14.

163. Paret, introduction to *On War*, 21, provides the early views of Clausewitz, which suggest that Gat is incorrect in arguing that Clausewitz's views of limited war were developed late in life.

164. A point recognized by Wallach, *Kriegstheorien*, 17, 47.

165. This is, of course, a main issue in the argument over German strategy and doctrine leading up to Schlieffen and the First World War and is considered later.

166. Books 1–5 of *On War* concern, respectively, the nature of war, its theory, strategy, combat, and military forces. Book 6 is on defense, and book 7 discusses offense. The final book covers war plans.

167. *On War*, 357. Sumida, *Decoding Clausewitz*, 164–165, notes that in book 6 Clausewitz suggested that the defense could be aided by guerrilla warfare. See also *On War*, 483.

168. *On War*, 358.

169. Ibid., 370. He discussed this further in chapter 37, "Defense of a Theater of Operations." See ibid., 484–485.

170. Wallach, *Kriegstheorien*, 57.

171. *On War*, 358.

172. See the brief introduction to this enduring question in *Vom Kriege*, 1215–1216, n. 206.

173. Jack Snyder, *The Ideology of the Offensive: Military Decision Making and the Disasters of 1914* (Ithaca, NY: Cornell University Press, 1984), remains the basis of this view of prewar theory.

174. *On War*, 495–496.

175. Ibid., 524. Recent research has demonstrated the critical importance of the counteroffensive in German thought, planning, and war-gaming, even in the days of Schlieffen and the younger Moltke.

176. Ibid., 545–547. From Clausewitz and Moltke onward, German theory made much of the moral advantages of the attacker, as did the French, especially after 1871.

177. Ibid., 548–549.

178. Ibid., 566.

179. Ibid., 571–572.

180. See Daniel J. Hughes, "Schwerpunkt (Center of Gravity)," in *International Military and Defense Encyclopedia*, ed. Trevor N. Dupuy et al., 6 vols. (New York: Brassey's, 1993), 3:2362–2364. The following section is based on this article. See also Antulio J. Echervarria, *Clausewitz's Center of Gravity: Changing Our Warfighting Doctrine—Again!* (Carlisle, PA: US Army Strategic Studies Institute, 2002).

181. The German titles of book 4's chapters 9, 10, and 11, for example, are *Hauptschlacht*, the potentially climactic battle between the main forces in a theater. The English version uses the simpler word "battle" in both the title and the text, thus shifting the focus from the main effort to battle in a generic sense. See

On War, 248–262, and compare *Vom Kriege*, 453–473. Subsequent German theory often used the *Hauptschlacht* concept in discussing decisive battles. See Immanuel, *Handbuch der Taktik*, 1:1; Balck, *Taktik*, 5:3–6.

182. In the German sense, one designates one's own center of gravity, focusing the main effort on a particular aspect of a campaign or battle. In the reversed American usage, the Jominian approach to Clausewitz, the center of gravity becomes a key enemy weakness to be identified and attacked. Some modern writers equate nearly all significant targets with centers of gravity, to the point that a midsized country might have dozens or hundreds. This entirely reverses Clausewitz's concept of concentrating effort and makes an absurdity of the basic idea, since in Newtonian physics (leaving aside quantum mechanics), an object, by definition, can have only one center of gravity.

183. Baron Hugo von Freytag-Loringhoven, *Die Heerführung Napoleons und Moltkes. Eine vergleichende Studie* (Berlin: E. S. Mittler, 1897), 121; Goltz, *Krieg- und Heerführung*, 26–29. Other, less-known authors also considered the question. See Lieutenant Vogel, "Der Angriff und die Krisis in der Schlacht," *Militär-Wochenblatt* 18 (1908): col. 387, who repeated Clausewitz's basic position.

184. Falkenhausen, *Kriegführung und Wissenschaft*, 37, expressed this confidence. Despite his earlier statements about problems of a diminishing offensive, even Goltz appeared to doubt that most defenders would be able to mount a serious counterstroke. See his *Krieg- und Heerführung*, 44–45.

185. *On War*, 195, 204.

186. Ibid., 546–547, 630.

187. Goltz, *Nation in Arms*, 147.

188. *On War*, 75–76, 260.

189. Ibid., 117. The German version in on p. 258 of Hahlweg's standard German edition of *Vom Kriege*. *Nachrichten* can also refer to communications within one's own army.

190. *On War*, 117, 122.

191. Eberhard Kessel, *Moltke* (Stuttgart: K. F. Koehler, 1957), 480. There is no modern biography in English. The best introduction is Arden Bucholz, *Moltke and the German Wars, 1864–1871* (New York: Palgrave, 2001). Jähns, *Feldmarschall Moltke*, retains its value. Franz Herre, *Moltke. Der Mann und sein Jahrhundert* (Stuttgart: Deutsche Verlags-Anstalt, 1984), adds nothing to Kessel. Numerous older biographies are now largely obsolete.

192. Kessel, *Moltke*, 47.

193. Stadelmann, *Moltke und der Staat*, 353–357.

194. Bucholz, *Moltke and the German Wars*, has the best summary of Moltke's background, career, and personality.

195. Rothenberg, "Moltke, Schlieffen, and the Doctrine of Strategic Envelopment," 237; David Chandler, *Atlas of Military Strategy* (New York: Free Press, 1980), 198.

196. Stig Förster, "Facing 'People's War': Moltke the Elder and Germany's Military Options after 1871," *Journal of Strategic Studies* 2 (June 1987): 209, 218. Note the similar comments by Wallach, *Kriegstheorien*, 86.

197. L. C. F. Turner, "The Significance of the Schlieffen Plan," in *The War Plans of the Great Powers, 1880–1914*, ed. Paul Kennedy (London: Allen & Unwin, 1979), 200.

198. For overviews of Moltke's views, see Hughes, *Moltke on the Art of War*, 1–19. The articles by Hajo Holborn, "The Prusso-German School: Moltke and the Rise of the General Staff," and Rothenberg's "Moltke, Schlieffen, and the Doctrine of Strategic Envelopment," in Paret, *Makers of Modern Strategy*, 281–295 and 296–325, respectively, are essential to understanding Moltke and his importance.

199. For a useful introduction, see Stig Förster, "Facing 'People's War': Moltke the Elder and Germany's Military Options after 1871," *Journal of Strategic Studies* 10, 2 (June 1987): 209–230.

200. Ibid., 213–217.

201. Stig Förster, "Der deutsche Generalstab und die Illusion des kurzen Krieges 1871–1914. Metakritik eines Mythos," *Militärgeschichtliche Mitteilungen* 54 (1995): 72, n. 36, points out that by 1827, the ubiquitous *Meyers Lexicon* used the distinction.

202. Förster, "Facing 'People's War,'" 213–222. See also Foley, *German Strategy and the Path to Verdun*, 17–20.

203. Förster, "Facing 'People's War,'" 220–221. See Karl-Ernst Jeismann, *Das Problem des Präventivkriegs im europäischer Staatensystem mit besonderem Blick auf die Bismarckzeit* (Freiburg: Verlag Karl Alber, 1957). Moltke and other military leaders were hardly alone in considering preventive war both before and after German unification. Bismarck eventually turned decisively against such a concept.

204. The speech is most readily available in Moltke, *Gesammelte Schriften und Denkwürdigkeiten*, 8 vols. (Berlin: E. S. Mittler, 1892–1918), 7:137–140.

205. Compare Förster, "Facing 'People's War,'" 224, and the more skeptical view of Foley, *German Strategy and the Path to Verdun*, 24.

206. Dennis Showalter, "From Deterrence to Doomsday Machine: The German Way of War, 1890–1914," *Journal of Military History* 64, 3 (July 2000): 681, 695; Showalter, "German Grand Strategy," 65–102. See also Echevarria, *After Clausewitz*, 201.

207. For an excellent summary, see Foley, *German Strategy and the Path to Verdun*, 25–34.

208. Hughes, *Moltke on the Art of War*, 47–73, arranges representative views in chronological order. See also Kessel, *Moltke*, 517–518. It was perhaps characteristic of later German thought that General Walther Reinhardt cited the same passages to show that Moltke's thought had moved in the opposite direction between 1866 and 1882. See Walther Reinhardt, *Wehrkraft und Wehrwille. Aus seinem Nachlass mit einer Lebensbeschreibung*, ed. Ernst Reinhardt (Berlin: E. S. Mittler, 1932), 151–153.

209. Hughes, *Moltke on the Art of War*, 56. The passage was written between 1882 and 1886.

210. Ibid., 202.

211. Ibid., 208.

212. Ibid., 216.

213. Ibid., 98–113. The use of railroads became one of the hallmarks of Moltke's campaigns. Dennis Showalter's *Railroads and Rifles: Technology and the Unification of Germany* (1975; reprint, Hamden, CT: Archon, 1986), is the classic account.

214. Representative samples may be found in Moltke, *Militärische Werke*, vol. 2, pt. 2. Hughes, *Moltke on the Art of War*, contains several such discussions.

215. Wilhelm Meier-Dörnberg, "Moltke und die taktisch-operative Ausbildung im preussisch-deutsche Heer," in *Generalfeldmarschall von Moltke. Beduetung und Wirkung*, ed. Roland G. Förster (Munich: R. Oldenbourg, 1991), 39–43.

216. Hughes, *Moltke on the Art of War*, 259.

217. Ibid., 47, 92, 125, 129, 152–153.

218. The classic account is Gordon Craig, *The Battle of Königgrätz: Prussia's Victory over Austria, 1866* (Westport, CT: Greenwood Press, 1975). The study by Geoffrey Wawro, *The Austro-Prussian War: Austria's War with Prussia and Italy in 1866* (Cambridge: Cambridge University Press, 1996), is an important supplement. Bucholz, *Moltke and the German Wars*, 103–138, has the best summary.

219. Moltke had no great fear of this, given his faith in the firepower of the defense and his confidence in the tactical competence of a Prussian corps, which, he said, could not be defeated in a single day. Thus, Moltke, like Schlieffen, actually built his offensive planning on the defensive capabilities of the Prussian army.

220. The standard account in English remains Michael Howard, *The Franco-Prussian War: The German Invasion of France, 1870–1871* (New York: Collier Books, 1969). Geoffrey Wawro, *The Franco-Prussian War: The German Conquest of France in 1870–1871* (Cambridge: Cambridge University Press, 2003), is an important contribution. See also Bucholz, *Moltke and the German Wars*.

221. See Hughes, "Schlieffen, Schlichting, and the Prussian Theory of War."

222. Examples can be found in the three most important doctrinal manuals of the postwar German armed forces: *Führung und Gefecht, Truppenführung*, and *Operative Lufkriegführung*.

223. For Moltke's rationale and a brief explanation, see Hughes, *Moltke on the Art of War*, 11–12, 53–56, 175, 188–189, 262–264.

224. Ibid., 184–187, 228–235, gives Moltke's thoughts on directives and orders.

225. See ibid., 230–231, 245–250, for examples of directives that the Prussian General Staff thought representative and instructional.

226. Prussia, Army, Grosser Generalstab, *Geschichte der deutsch-französische Krieg 1870–71*, 5 vols. (Berlin: E. S. Mittler, 1874–1881), 1:155. The same principle, much older perhaps, was at the root of so-called *Auftragstaktik*, a much-misunderstood and poorly translated term that became a slogan in the US Army in the 1980s. On this issue, see Daniel J. Hughes, "Abuses of German Military History," *Military Review* 66, 12 (December 1986): 66–76; Hughes, "Auftragstaktik," in *International Military and Defense Encyclopedia*, 1:328–333.

227. Hughes, *Moltke on the Art of War*, 78–79, 82, 84, 87.

228. Hubert von Boehn, *Generalstabsgeschäfte. Ein Handbuch für Offiziere aller Waffen* (Potsdam: Verlag von Eduard Döring, 1862), 278–279, discusses the need for short orders. On Reyher's influence, see Hohenlohe-Ingelfingen, *Letters on Strategy*, 1:133. On the difference between directives and orders, see Goltz, *Na-*

tion in Arms, 117–118. Schlichting's influential writing also pointed out the need for flexibility in the form of orders. See his *Taktsiche und strategische Grundsätze*, 3:232. Bucholz, *Moltke and the German Wars*, 58, errs when he attributes the formal five-paragraph field order to Moltke.

229. Kriegsministerium, *D.V.E. Nr. 130. Exerzier-Reglement Für die Infanterie* (Berlin: E. S. Mittler, 1906), 85; *D.V.E. Nr. 267. Felddienst-Ordnung* (Berlin: E. S. Mittler, 1908), 19–21. See also *Leitfaden für den Unterricht in der Taktik auf den Königlichen Kriegsschulen*, 97; Anonymous, *Die Befehlstechnik bei der höheren Kommando-behörden* (Oldenburg: Druck & Verlag des Deutschen Offizierblatts, 1907), 3–4. Private theories on brief orders and their suggested content can be found in Goltz, *Nation in Arms*, 117–118; Schlichting, *Taktische und strategische Grundsätze*, 3:232; Goltz, *Krieg- und Heerführung*, 248–249; Boehn, *Generalstabsgeschäfte*, 278–279; Franz Karl Endres, "Wie bestrebe sich Napoleon, wie Moltke die Einheitlichkeit der Heerführung zu gewährleisten," *Jahrbücher für die deutsche Armee und Marine* (1910): 42–54, 162–178; Jacob Meckel, *Allgemeine Lehre von der Truppenführung im Kriege*, 3rd ed. (Berlin: E. S. Mittler, 1890), 3–4.

230. Any glance at modern doctrine for ground warfare will illustrate the point.

231. Bucholz, *Moltke and the German Wars*, 58ff, wrongly attributes this to Moltke. For a corrective, see Carl-Gero von Ilsemann, "Das operative Denken des Älteren Moltke," in *Operatives Denken und Handeln in deutschen Streitkräften im 19. und 20. Jahrhundert*, ed. Militärgeschichtliches Forschungsamt (Bonn: E. S. Mittler, 1988), 23. See also the detailed discussion in Hughes, "Auftragstaktik."

232. Goltz, *Nation in Arms*, 285–287. Borgert, "Grundzüge der Landkriegführung," 407, discusses the controversy.

233. Heinrich Friedjung, *Der Kampf um die Vorherrschaft in Deutschland*, 2 vols. (Stuttgart: Cotta, 1901–1902); J. F. C. Fuller, *A Military History of the Western World* (New York: Minerva Press, 1936), 3:134. Note also the comments by Brian Holden Reid, *J. F. C. Fuller: Military Thinker* (New York: St. Martin's Press, 1987), 109.

234. Jähns, *Feldmarschall Moltke*, 417. See also the remarks of Holborn, "Prusso-German School," 281.

235. Jähns, *Feldmarschall Moltke*, 415–416. The original is in Moltke, *Militärische Werke*, 2(2):279–286.

236. *D.V.E. Nr. 53: Grundzüge der höheren Truppenführung*, 32.

237. It is both interesting and somewhat amusing to note that at the *Führungsakademie*, the German *Bundeswehr*'s version of the *Kriegsakademie*, the Howard-Paret translation of *On War* is read; it is considered much more readable than the original German.

CHAPTER THREE. INSTITUTIONAL DEVELOPMENTS, 1871–1914

1. Older histories, especially those of contemporaries, stressed the continuing independence of these forces, especially those of Bavaria. Recent scholarship has stressed the contingents' integration into a single German army. See Friedrich Christian Stahl, "Preussische Armee und Reichsheer," in *Zur Problematik Preussen und das Reich*, ed. Oswald Hauser (Köln: Böhlau Verlag, 1984), 181–245. The

army was a single entity in doctrine, budgetary matters, and force structure, but many individual differences remained, particularly in personnel matters.

2. See the comments of the influential Bavarian officer Hermann Mertz von Quirheim, *Der Führerwille in Entstehung und Durchführung, erläutert an den Vorgängen in den Reichslanden August–September 1914* (Oldenbourg: Gerhard Stalling, 1932), 20–27. On Prussian-Bavarian tensions under the pressure of war, see Dieter Storz, "'This Trench Warfare Is Horrible!' The Battles in Lorraine and the Vosges in the Summer of 1914," in *The Schlieffen Plan: International Perspectives on the German Strategy for World War I*, ed. Hans Ehlert, Michael Epkenhans, and Gerhard P. Gross, trans. David T. Zabecki (Lexington: University Press of Kentucky, 2014), 172–173.

3. Ottomar Baron von Osten-Sacken und bei Rhein, *Preussens Heer von seinen Anfängen bis zur Gegenwart*, 3 vols. (Berlin: E. S. Mittler, 1914), 3:275–281. In the absence of Bismarck, who was ill, Count Moltke used his influence to get the bill, the *Reichs-Militärgesetz*, through the parliament.

4. Ibid., 281. By 1873, the actual active strength of the army had fallen to about 357,000. The new law maintained the 1 percent goal of the constitution, or 401,659 men for the years 1875–1881.

5. Ibid., 290–291. An additional 2,172 officers, some holding only honorary commissions, were not assigned to units. These included paymasters, doctors, and the like, who were not considered officers.

6. Ludwig *Freiherr* Rüdt von Collenberg, "Das deutsche Heer von 1867 bis 1918," in *Deutsche Heeresgeschichte*, ed. Karl Linnebach (Hamburg: Hanseatische Verlagsanstalt, 1935), 348.

7. Hermann Rahne, *Mobilmachung. Militärische Mobilmachung, Planung und Technik in Preussen und im deutschen Reich von Mitte des 19. Jahrhunderts bis zum Weltkrieg* (East Berlin: Militärverlag der deutschen demokratischen Republik, 1983), 78. There were also replacement (*Ersatz*) formations, but these had direct links to units on active duty.

8. Generally, though not universally, the General Staff wanted more units of all types and more soldiers than the War Ministry was willing to propose to the kaiser or the Reichstag.

9. Holger H. Herwig, *"Luxury" Fleet: The Imperial German Navy 1888–1918*, reprint ed. (London: Ashfield Press, 1987), 75–76. For infighting within the navy over the allocation of resources in terms of ships, tactics, and control, see Patrick J. Kelly, "Strategy, Tactics and Turf Wars: Tirpitz and the Oberkommando der Marine, 1892–1895," *Journal of Military History* 66, 4 (October 2002): 1033–1060.

10. The most dominant force in this new interpretation, if somewhat extreme, is Stig Förster, *Der doppelte Militarismus. Die deutsche Heeresrüstungspolitik zwischen Status-Quo-Sicherung und Aggression, 1890–1913* (Stuttgart: Franz Steiner Verlag, 1985). See also Thomas Röhkramer, "Heroes and Would-be Heroes: Veterans' and Reservists' Associations in Imperial Germany," in *Anticipating Total War: The German and American Experience, 1871–1914*, ed. Michael F. Boemeke, Roger Chickering, and Stig Förster (Cambridge: Cambridge University Press, 1999), 204–211.

11. General Staff (Prussia), *Taschenbuch des Generalstabsoffizieres. (Geheim)* (Berlin: E. S. Mittler, 1914), 14; General (ret.) Ernst von Wrisberg, "Organisation der Armee," in *Ehrendenkmal der Deutschen Armee und Marine 1871–1918*, ed. General Ernst von Eisenhart-Rothe (Berlin: Deutscher National-Verlag, 1928), 40. Friedrich Immanuel, *Handbuch der Taktik*, 2 vols. (Berlin: E. S. Mittler, 1910), 1:16, gives slightly different figures for manpower, horses, and wagons. An organizational sketch can be found in Reichsarchiv (Germany), *Der Weltkrieg 1914–1918* (Berlin: E. S. Mittler, 1925–1942), 1:686.

12. General Staff, *Taschenbuch des Generalstabsoffiziers*, 14.

13. Reichsarchiv, *Der Weltkrieg 1914–1918*, 1:687. The artillery regiment was equipped with twelve 77mm field cannons.

14. Prior to the disruptions of 1915–1918, a corps retained its subordinate elements for lengthy periods, fostering cohesion and combat effectiveness. It moved and fought as a single entity and was the basic German unit for "operations." See the striking characterization in Dennis E. Showalter, *Tannenberg: Clash of Empires* (Hamden, CT: Archon Books, 1991), 118. Before the war, some influential writers attempted to add a third division to the corps to avoid having to take regiments from one of the divisions to form a corps reserve. These efforts failed. See Wilhelm Balck, *Taktik*, 6 vols. (Berlin: R. Eisenschmidt, 1908–1912), 3:27–29, 34. Rudolf von Caemmerer, *The Development of Strategical Science during the 19th Century*, trans. Karl von Donat (London: Hugh Rees, 1905), 161–162, also supported this change. The elder Moltke wished at one point to abolish the corps and have the field armies supervise divisions directly in order to simplify the system of transmitting orders, but this also came to nothing. See Eberhard Kessel, *Moltke* (Stuttgart: K. F. Koehler, 1957), 287, 518–519. Schlichting, ironically, regarded the corps as essential to Moltke's system of command and concluded that the experiences of 1870 showed the necessity of corps to avoid the direct transmission of orders from field armies to divisions. See Sigismund von Schlichting, *Taktische und strategiche Grundsätze der Gegenwart*, 3 vols. (Berlin: E. S. Mittler, 1898–1899), 2:96–97.

15. See the comparison in Immanuel, *Handbuch der Taktik*, 2:193. Colmar *Freiherr* von der Goltz, *The Nation in Arms*, trans. Philip Ashworth (London: W. H. Allen, 1906), 39–40, has a more comprehensive list of the corps support services.

16. General Staff, *Taschenbuch der Generalstabsoffiziers*, 12.

17. Theodor Jochim, *Die Operationen und rückwärtigen Verbindungen der deutschen 1. Armee in der Marneschlacht 1914* (Berlin: E. S. Mittler, 1933), 1–3. See also Balck, *Taktik*, 3:19.

18. General Staff, *Taschenbuch des Generalstabsoffiziers*, 12; Osten-Sacken, *Preussens Heer*, 3:294.

19. General Staff, *Taschenbuch des Generalstabsoffiziers*, 16. Hermann Cron, *Geschichte des deutschen Heeres im Weltkriege 1914–1918* (Berlin: Militärverlag Karl Siegismund, 1937), 95, gives a larger total than the General Staff handbook.

20. General Staff (Prussia), *Anhaltspunkte für den Generalstabsdienst. (Nur für Dienstgebrauch)* (Berlin: Reichsdruckerei, 1914), 24–33, copy in BA/MA, PH D 200/38.

21. See his essay "Thoughts on Command," in *Moltke on the Art of War: Selected Writings*, ed. Daniel J. Hughes (Novato, CA: Presidio, 1993), 76. For an opposing point of view from an American perspective, see Gary W. Gallagher, ed., *Fighting for the Confederacy: The Personal Recollections of General Edward Porter Alexander* (Chapel Hill: University of North Carolina Press, 1989), 236. For an interesting comparative perspective, see Richard L. DiNardo, "Southern by the Grace of God but Prussian by Common Sense: James Longstreet and the Exercise of Command in the U.S. Civil War," *Journal of Military History* 66, 4 (October 2002): 1011–1032.

22. Rahne, *Mobilmachung*, 37.

23. Wilhelm Groener, *Lebenserinnerungen. Jugend, Generalstab, Weltkrieg*, ed. Frriedrich *Freiherr* Hiller von Gaertringen (Göttingen: Vandenhoeck & Rupprecht, 1957), 62, cites the case of the XIII Corps commander in 1888–1890.

24. Karl von Bülow, Bemerkungen des Kommandierenden Generals III Armeekorps zu den Herbstübungen 1903–1911, BA/MA, PH D 9/18, demonstrates the impact of a strong personality on training throughout the corps over a long period. On the origins of the position, see Manfred Messerschmidt, "Die politische Geschichte der preussisch-deutschen Armee," in *Deutsche Militärgeschichte*, ed. Militärgeschichtliches Forschungsamt (Munich: Bernard & Graefe, 1962–1976), 1:303–307; Osten-Sacken, *Preussens Heer*, 2:212. On Haeseler, see Ernst Buchfinck, "Feldmarschall Graf von Haeseler 19. 1. 1838–26. 10. 1919," *Wissen und Wehr* 1 (1936): 3–9. Hans von Seeckt, *Aus meinem Leben 1866–1917*, ed. Friedrich von Rabenau (Leipzig: Hase & Kohler, 1938), 39, mentions Haeseler and Lentze, as does Max van den Bergh, *Das deutsche Heer vor dem Weltkriege* (Berlin: Sanssouci Verlag, 1934), 38–39. On the limited ability of even the elder Moltke and Schlieffen to influence such appointments, see Franz von Lenski, *Lern- und Lehrjahre in Front und Generalstab* (Berlin: Bernard & Graefe, 1939), 202. On the 1850 siege law, see Wilhelm Deist, *Militär und Innenpolitik im Weltkriege 1914–1918*, 2 vols. (Düsseldorf: Droste Verlag, 1970), 1:xl.

25. The famous Julius von Bose forced a prince of Mecklenburg out of the army following the latter's performance in annual maneuvers. See August Keim, *Erlebtes und Erstrebtes. Lebenserinnerungen* (Hannover: Ernst Letsch Verlag, 1925), 31. Corps commanders could cause the promotion or removal of subordinates, even their General Staff officers. See the cases of Otto von Manteuffel in Kurt von Priesdorff, ed., *Soldatisches Führertum*, 10 vols. (Hamburg: Hanseatische Verlagsanstalt, 1936–1942), 8:269, and of Otto von Hoffmann, *Lebenserinnerungen des königlich preussischen Generalleutnants Otto von Hoffmann*, ed. Colonel von Hoffmann (Oldenburg: Schulzsche Hof-Buchhandlung & Hof-Buchdruckerei, 1907), 55.

26. Cron, *Geschichte des deutschen Heeres*, 92.

27. The opening paragraph of the General Staff officers' handbook set forth an idealistic view of the responsibilities and ethos of officers on that career path. See *Anhaltspunkte für den Generalstabsdienst*, 5–7.

28. There is no scholarly study of the General Staff for the period 1815–1919. Though hagiographical in many respects, the book by Walter Görlitz, *History of the German General Staff 1657–1945*, trans. Brian Battershaw (New York: Praeger,

1953), retains its utility. The German edition has numerous passages that were omitted from the English translation. Arden Bucholz, *Moltke, Schlieffen and Prussian War Planning* (New York: Berg, 1991), is an important contribution.

29. A very few men gained admission as a result of superior duty as adjutants, as teachers in schools, or as officers in units. See Hans von Zwehl, *Generalstabsdienst in Frieden und im Kriege* (Berlin: E. S. Mittler, 1923), 7.

30. Kessel, *Moltke*, 232.

31. About 14 percent of the officers promoted to flag rank during the imperial period had been General Staff officers. An additional 15 percent had seen limited duty with the General Staff but either withdrew or were dismissed at no great cost to their careers. See Daniel J. Hughes, *The King's Finest: A Social and Bureaucratic Profile of Prussia's General Officers, 1871–1914* (Westport, CT: Praeger, 1987), 84.

32. Although some historians have described a German system of "dual command," no such concept or term ever existed. Although General Staff officers in the units had special powers in directing operations, they were not co-commanders.

33. Walter Bronsart von Schellendorff, *Der Dienst des Generalstabes*, 4th ed. (Berlin: E. S. Mittler, 1905), 3.

34. August von Janson, *Der Dienst des Generalstabes im Frieden*, 2nd ed. (Berlin: E. S. Mittler, 1901), 1–2.

35. German Great General Staff, *Der deutsch-französische Krieg 1870–71* (Berlin: E. S. Mittler & Sohn, 1874), 2:692; Paul Bronsart von Schellendorf, *Geheimes Kriegstagebuch 1870–1871*, ed. Peter Rassow (Bonn: Athenäun Verlag, 1954), 71.

36. Emperor Friedrich III, *Das Kriegstagebuch von 1870/71*, ed. Heinrich Otto Meissner (Berlin: Verlag von K. S. Koehler, 1926), 6; Kessel, *Moltke*, 547; DiNardo, "Southern by the Grace of God," 1018.

37. Reichsarchiv, *Der Weltkrieg 1914–1918*, 1:675–678; Dennis Showalter, *Instrument of War: The German Army 1914–18* (New York: Osprey Publishing, 2016), 46–47. A judicious assessment of Rupprecht's conduct in the war is Holger Afflerbach, "Kronprinz Rupprecht von Bayern im Ersten Weltkrieg," *Militärgeschichtliche Zeitschrift* 75 (2016): 21–54.

38. Basil H. Liddell Hart, *History of the First World War*, reprint ed. (London: Cassell, 1970), 170. See also John Wheeler-Bennett, *Wooden Titan: Hindenburg in Twenty Years of German History 1914–1934* (New York: William Morrow, 1936), 17; John Lee, *The Warlords: Hindenburg and Ludendorff* (London: Weidenfeld & Nicholson, 2005), 54.

39. Peter Broucek, ed., *Ein österreichischer General gegen Hitler. Feldmarschallleutnant Alfred Jansa: Erinnerungen* (Vienna: Böhlau Verlag, 2011), 297; Seeckt, *Aus meinem Leben 1866–1917*, 116; Richard L. DiNardo, "Modern Soldier in a Busby: August von Mackensen, 1914–1916," in *Arms and the Man: Military History Essays in Honor of Dennis Showalter*, ed. Michael S. Neiberg (Boston: Brill, 2011), 157.

40. Gerhard Tappen to Wolfgang Foerster, 22 October 1935, *Nachlass* Gerhard Tappen, BA/MA, N 56/5; Richard L. DiNardo, *Invasion: The Conquest of Serbia, 1915* (Santa Barbara, CA: Praeger, 2015), 42.

41. Chief of General Staff, III Korps, "Bestimmungen für die Aufnahmeprüfung zur Kriegsakademie, 1906," 12 March 1906, BA/MA, PH 3/31.

42. Numerous handbooks were available to prepare for the examinations. See Hermann Vogt, *Das Buch vom deutschen Heer* (Bielefeld: Velhagen & Klasing, 1886), for details of the examination system. See also Franz von Lenski, *Aus den Leutnantsjahren eines alten Generalstabsoffiziers: Erinnerungen an den Rhein und die Reichshauptstadt aus den 80er und 90 Jahren des 19. Jahrhunderts* (Berlin: Bath, 1922), 134; Bernard Schwertfeger, *Die grossen Erzieher des deutschen Heeres. Aus der Geschichte der Kriegsakademie* (Potsdam: Rütten & Loening Verlag, 1936), 66.

43. Chief of General Staff, III Korps, "Bestimmungen für die Aufnahmeprüfung zur Kriegsakademie, 1907," and a similar document from XVII Korps, *Nachlass* Karl Friedrichs, BA/MA, N94/27.

44. Groener, *Lebenserinnerungen*, 46; Hermann von Stein, *Erlebnisse und Betrachtungen aus der Zeit des Weltkrieges* (Leipzig: K. F. Koehler, 1919), 32; *Nachlass* von der Schulenburg-Tressow, BA/MA, N 58/1, 16. See also the comments of Max von der Leyen, "Erinnerungen," 52, *Nachlass* von der Leyen, BA/MA, N 54/1, and Count Bogdan von Hutten-Czapski, *Sechzig Jahre Politik und Gesellschaft*, 2 vols. (Berlin: E. S. Mittler, 1936), 1:65. These discrepancies in opportunities existed throughout the nineteenth century. See Julius von Hartmann, *Lebenserinnerungen, Briefe und Aufsätze*, 2 vols. (Berlin: Verlag von Gebrüder Paetel, 1882), 1:132, discussing his examination experience in 1838.

45. Hughes, *King's Finest*, 85–91, examines the evidence on this point.

46. Bucholz, *Moltke, Schlieffen and Prussian War Planning*, 133–134. Emil Obermann, no friend of the old army, argued that social bias lost all significance in the General Staff. See his *Soldaten, Bürger, Militaristen. Militär und Demokratie in Deutschland* (Stuttgart: J. G. Cotta'sche Buchhandlung Nachfolger, [ca. 1955]), 92, and, in a similar vein, Friedrich von Boetticher, *Schlieffen* (Göttingen: Musterschmidt Verlag, 1957), 80. For contrary conclusions, see Martin Kitchen, *The German Officer Corps 1890–1918* (Oxford: Clarendon Press, 1968), 24; Heiger Ostertag, *Bildung, Ausbildung, und Erziehung des Offizierkorps im deutschen Kaiserreich 1871 bis 1918* (Frankfurt: Peter Lang, 1990) 214–215; Hughes, *King's Finest*, 124–142.

47. Ostertag, *Bildung, Ausbildung, und Erziehung*, 163.

48. For a list of 227 officers who graduated from the War Academy but did not join the General Staff, see BA/MA, PH 3/7. Some became colonels and generals.

49. Bucholz, *Moltke, Schlieffen and Prussian War Planning*, 185–186, 236–237; Ostertag, *Bildung, Ausbildung, und Erziehung*, 161.

50. Bernhard Poten, *Geschichte des Militär-Erziehungs- und Bildungswesens in den Landen deutscher Zunge*, 4 vols. (Berlin: A. Hofmann, 1889–1897), 4:264, 305.

51. On dropping earlier historical periods, see Bucholz, *Moltke, Schlieffen and Prussian War Planning*, 236–237.

52. Poten, *Geschichte des Militär-Erziehungs- und Bildungswesens*, 4:306. See also Steven E. Clemente, "Mit Gott! Für König und Kaiser" (Ph.D. diss., University of Oklahoma, 1989), 339–340.

53. See Antulio J. Echevarria II, *After Clausewitz: German Military Thinkers before the Great War* (Lawrence: University Press of Kansas, 2000), 183–186. This assertion is based on my (DJH) twenty-five years of experience in the educational systems of the army and air force. Note that US General Tommy Franks got philosopher Bertrand Russell's name wrong (calling him "Bertram") when bragging about his personal efforts to study statecraft and diplomacy. See Tommy Franks, *American Soldier* (New York: HarperCollins, 2004), 203. In this respect, retired officers such as David Zabecki and Antulio Echevarria II, both respected German military historians, and Robert Doughty, an expert on the French army, are exceptions, although there are some others. Instead of undertaking the laborious and time-consuming task of writing scholarly works, many retired senior officers serve as commentators for various television networks to discuss military issues when they arise.

54. Clemente, "Mit Gott! Für König und Kaiser," 321–322.

55. Bucholz, *Moltke, Schlieffen and Prussian War Planning,* 91–92; Hermann von Kuhl, *Der Deutsche Generalstab in Vorbereitung und Durchführung des Weltkrieges* (Berlin: E. S. Mittler, 1920), 135–136.

56. See Kessel, *Moltke,* 103.

57. This section is based on Bucholz, *Moltke, Schlieffen and Prussian War Planning,* unless otherwise noted.

58. At least two subsequent generals did this: Franz Wandel in 1891 and Ernst von Zastrow 1890. See Priesdorff, unpublished ms. to continue *Soldatisches Führertum,* in BA/MA. DJH used these materials in the archive in 1976, at which time they were not in the catalog.

59. Kriegsministerium (Prussia), *D.V.E. No. 40. Bestimmungen über Generalstabsreisen, 14 April 1908* (Berlin: E. S. Mittler, 1908); Bucholz, *Moltke, Schlieffen and Prussian War Planning,* 251–254, describes the administrative staff rides.

60. Helmut Schnitter, *Militärwesen und Militärpublizistik. Die militärische Zeitschriften Publizistik in der Geschichte des bürgerliche Militärwesens in Deutschland* (East Berlin: Deutsche Militärverlag, 1967), 75–122, has a Marxist but still useful introduction to the army's professional literature.

61. Ibid., 108.

62. Michael Salewski, "Zur preussischen Militärgeschichtsschreibung im 19. Jahrhundert," in *Militärgeschichte in Deutschland und Oesterreich vom 18. Jahrhundert bis in die Gegenwart,* ed. Othmar Hackel (Bonn: E. S. Mittler, 1985), 47–64. See also Keim, *Erlebtes und Erstrebtes,* 41–42; Hans L. Borgert, *Grundzüge der Landkriegführung von Schlieffen bis Guderian* (Munich: Bernard & Graefe, 1979), 430–431.

63. Eric Dorn Brose, *The Kaiser's Army: The Politics of Military Technology in Germany during the Machine Age, 1870–1918* (Oxford: Oxford University Press, 2001), 102–103, relies on Schnitter.

64. Hugo Baron von Freytag-Loringhoven, *Menschen und Dinge wie ich sie in meinem Leben sah* (Berlin: E. S. Mittler, 1923), 125–126. For extensive examples of these debates, see Echevarria, *After Clausewitz.*

65. Heinrich Rohne, "Bemerkungen zu dem Aufsatz 'Gegentiefen, Entfernungen, Visieranwendung,'" *Militär-Wochenblatt* 141 (1908): cols. 3267–3273;

Generalmajor Reisner Freiherr von Lichtenstern, "Zur Feuergeschwindigkeit," *Militär-Wochenblatt* 67 (1908): cols. 1649–1654.

66. Schnitter, *Militärwesen und Militärpublizistik*, 46–122, with a complete list at 193–216. See also Bucholz, *Moltke, Schlieffen and Prussian War Planning*, 24, and, more critical, Hermann Müller-Brandenburg, *Von Schlieffen bis Ludendorff* (Leipzig: Ernst Oldenburg Verlag, 1925), 13–14.

67. This section is based on Paul Schneider, *Die Organisation des Heeres* (Berlin: E. S. Mittler, 1931), 71–86, except as otherwise noted.

68. Kriegsministerium, *D.V.E. Nr. 130. Exerzier-Reglement für die Infanterie, 29 Mai 1906* (Berlin: E. S. Mittler, 1906), 1–2.

69. See Dieter Storz, *Kriegsbild und Rüstung vor 1914. Europäische Landstreitkräfte vor dem Ersten Weltkrieg* (Herford: E. S. Mittler, 1992), 107; Generalmajor von Bartenwerffer, "Die Manöver," in Eisenhart-Rothe, *Ehrendenkmal*, 212–218. Many considered the brigade-level maneuvers a waste of time.

70. Kessel, *Moltke*, 278. The last edition of the manual was Prussia, War Ministry, *D.V.E. 270. Bestimmungen für die grösseren Truppenübungen—Manöver Ordnung* (Berlin: E. S. Mittler, 1914).

71. Annika Mombauer, *Helmuth von Moltke and the Origins of the First World War* (Cambridge: Cambridge University Press, 2001), 58–59, has a representative and balanced account.

72. See Holger Herwig, "The Dynamics of Necessity: German Military Policy during the First World War," in *Military Effectiveness*, ed. Allan R. Millett and Williamson Murray, 3 vols. (Boston: Allen & Unwin, 1988), 1:107; Bucholz, *Moltke, Schlieffen and Prussian War Planning*, 266. Even officers were critical. See Friedrich von Bernhardi, *Denkwürdigkeiten aus meinem Leben* (Berlin: E. S. Mittler, 1927), 212; Freytag-Loringhoven, *Menschen und Dinge*, 105–106; Hans von Beseler, letter of 26 September 1901, *Nachlass* Beseler, BA/MA, N 30/58; Anonymous, *Das alte Heer, von einem Stabsoffizier* (Charlottenburg: Verlag der Weltbühne, 1920), 60–65; Baron Paul von Schoenaich, *Mein Damaskus. Erlebnisse und Bekenntnisse* (Berlin-Hessenwinkel: Verlag der Neuen Gesellschaft, 1926), 82–84; Colmar *Freiherr* von der Goltz, *Denkwürdigkeiten*, ed. Friedrich *Freiherr* v. d. Goltz and Wolfgang Foerster (Berlin: E. S. Mittler, 1929), 62 (1903 letter); Prince of Saxe-Meiningen to Schlichting, 11 November 1903, *Nachlass* Schlichting, BA/MA, N 313/3.

73. Bernd-Felix Schulte, *Die deutsche Armee. Zwischen Beharren und Verändern* (Düsseldorff: Droste Verlag, 1977), cites Repington's articles in the *Times* and those of some other journalists. For a balanced view, see Hubert C. Johnson, *Breakthrough: Tactics, Technology and the Search for Victory on the Western Front in World War I* (Novato, CA: Presidio, 1994), 200–201; Storz, *Kriegsbild und Rüstung vor 1914*, 62–63, 111, 195; Brose, *Kaiser's Army*, 156–157.

74. Storz, *Kriegsbild und Rüstung vor 1914*, 108, citing archival sources. See also Rudolf von Janson, "Das militärische Ausbildungsjahr der Infanterie," *Beiheft zum Militär-Wochenblatt* (1901): 140; Groener, *Lebenserinnerungen*, 120–121. On the 1830 order, see Rudolf Absolon, *Die Wehrmacht im Dritten Reich*, 6 vols. (Boppard: Harald Boldt Verlag, 1969–1995), 2:9.

75. See the comments of Thomas Rohkrämer, *Der Militarismus der "kleinen*

Leute." *Die Kriegervereine in Deutschland 1871–1914* (Munich: R. Oldenbourg, 1990), 167. See also Bucholz, *Moltke, Schlieffen and Prussian War Planning*, 245–249; Bartenwerffer, "Die Manöver," 217.

76. Moltke took charge of the 1905 maneuvers and prevented Wilhelm II from taking an active part. See Moltke's letter to his wife, 16 September 1905, in Helmuth von Moltke [the younger], *Erinnerungen, Briefe, Dokumente 1877–1916*, ed. Eliza von Moltke (Stuttgart: Der Kommende Tag Verlag, 1922), 341.

77. Moltke wrote to his wife on 29 January 1905 that he could not tolerate such phony games. See ibid., 308. For favorable reactions to his ability to contain Wilhelm's successes, see Bernhardi, *Denkwürdigkeiten*, 126, 215, 272; Kuhl, *Der deutsche Generalstab*, 49. On the 1890 incident, see Count Alfred von Waldersee, *Denkwürdigkeiten des Generalfeldmarschalls Alfred Grafen von Waldersee*, ed. H. O. Meisner, 2 vols. (Berlin: Deutsche Verlags-Anstalt, 1925), 2:145, 153; Norman Rich, *Friedrich von Holstein: Politics and Diplomacy in the Era of Bismarck and Wilhelm II*, 2 vols. (Cambridge: Cambridge University Press, 1965), 1:354–357; Eduard von Liebert, *Aus Einem bewegten Leben* (Munich: J. F. Lehmanns Verlag, 1925), 138–139.

78. Boetticher, *Schlieffen*, 50–51.

79. Stein, *Erlebnisse und Betrachtungen*, 34.

80. Hermann von Staabs, *Aufmarsch nach zwei Fronten. Auf Grund der Operationspläne von 1871–1914* (Berlin: E. S. Mittler, 1925), 32–33.

81. For a more negative evaluation, see Bucholz, *Moltke, Schlieffen and Prussian War Planning*, 242–243.

82. Moltke to War Minister, No. 37181, "Grösser Truppenübungen," 14 March 1912, BA/MA, PH 3, 8 (also in PH 3/650); War Minister to General Staff, "Manöver 1913," 17 December 1912, BA/MA, PH 3/650, 30–31; Anonymous, "Grössere Truppenübungen im Jahre 1913," *Militär-Wochenblatt* 27 (1913): col. 599.

83. Anonymous, "Die Herbstübungen der preussischen Armeekorps [including] XIII (k.W.) Armeekorps," *Militär-Wochenblatt* 76 (1914): cols. 1663–1664.

84. General Staff, VI Abteilung, Report to Chiefs of General Staff, 25 June 1912, BA/MA, PH 3/642, 8–12.

85. General Inspection of the Cavalry to General Staff, 1 November 1912, BA/MA, PH 3/642, 273–275; General Staff, VI Abteilung, Report to Chiefs of General Staff, 25 June 1912. See also Captain Anders, "Zur Kriegsmässigkeit unserer Uebungen," *Militär-Wochenblatt* 148 (1911): cols. 3408–3409; Hermann Mueller-Brandenburg, *Von der Marne zur Marne* (Berlin: Verlag für Sozialwissenschaft, 1919), 6–7.

86. Anonymous, "Das Kaisermanöver 1913 in Schlesien," *Militär-Wochenblatt* 137 (1913): col. 3085.

87. See General Staff, VI Abteilung, Report on the 1911 Kaiser Maneuvers, 25 June 1912, BA/MA, PH 3/642, 15. Borgert, "Landkriegführung von Schlieffen bis Guderian," 489–491, has a summary of lessons learned in Moltke's reforms of the kaiser maneuvers. Storz, *Kriegsbild und Rüstung vor 1914*, 112, 172–173, 191–194, has many examples.

88. Anonymous, "Das Kaisermanöver 1913 in Schlesien," col. 3099.

89. Wilhelm II to army inspections, corps, and other army elements, 12 March 1914, BA/MA, PH 3/650, 153–157. The file also contains preliminary drafts.

90. *Nachlass* Schwertfeger, BA/MA, N 1015/44, has copies of these instructions, dated 1909 and 1911, respectively.

91. Report of Bavarian General Staff, No. 3004, "Betr. Divisions-Übungen 1913," 22 November 1913, BA/MA, PH 3/650, 64–73.

92. Lenski, *Lern- und Lehrjahre*, 91–92.

93. Janson, "Gedanken über Ausbildung und Truppenübungen," col. 231; Storz, *Kriegsbild und Rüstung vor 1914*, 105–107, 175–176.

94. This citation, in one form or another, found its way into much of the literature. Here the citation is from van den Bergh, *Das deutsche Heer*, 152–153.

95. Some exceptions were independent battalions, designated *Jäger* or *Schützen* and designed as light infantry, with superior skills in skirmishing and firing. See *So war die alte Armee*, ed. Ernst von Eisenhart-Rothe and Franz Schauwecker (Berlin: Frundsberg Verlag, 1935), 19.

96. Hughes, *King's Finest*, 77.

97. See the criticism of Anonymous, *Das alte Heer, von einem Stabsoffizier* (Charlottenburg: Verlag der Weltbühne, 1920), 29–30.

98. Hughes, *King's Finest*, 87.

99. From the 1850s on, such distinguished personalities as chief of the General Staff Reyher (against this view) and Prince Friedrich Karl (in favor or it) debated the continuing relevance of such bravado. See Wolfgang Foerster, ed., *Prinz Friedrich Karl von Preussen. Denkwürdigkeiten aus seinem Leben* (Stuttgart: Deutsche Verlags-Anstalt, 1910), 1:110–111.

100. Dennis Showalter, "Prussian Cavalry 1806–1871: The Search for Roles," *Militärgeschichtliche Mitteilungen* 14, 1 (1976): 7–22, is the best summary of German cavalry issues in this period. See also Eric-Günter Blau, *Die operative Verwendung der deutschen Kavallerie im Weltkrieg 1914–1918*, vol. 1, *Friedensvorbereitung* (Munich: C. H. Beck'sche Verlagsbuchhandlung, 1934).

101. Kessel, *Moltke*, 248.

102. David R. Dorondo, *Riders of the Apocalypse: German Cavalry and Machine Warfare, 1870–1945* (Annapolis, MD: Naval Institute Press, 2012), 17–18.

103. Hughes, *Moltke on the Art of War*, 208–210. It should be noted that Moltke also repeated the old adage: "Prussian cavalry never awaits an imminent attack, but on the contrary goes forth to meet it, even when outnumbered."

104. Showalter, "Prussian Cavalry," 7, 15; Dorondo, *Riders of the Apocalypse*, 19–26.

105. Deines quoted in Lenski, *Lern- und Lehrjahre*, 168.

106. Osten-Sacken, *Preussens Heer*, 3:349–350, discusses these changes. Also useful is Eugen von Frauenholz, *Das Gesicht der Schlacht. Taktik und Technik in der deutschen Kriegsgeschichte* (Stuttgart: Union Deutscher Verlagsgesellschaft, 1937), 159–160. Major General Karl von Schmidt was a hero of the war against France, and his valor earned him a government grant of 10,000 talers. As a young officer, he wrote several controversial works on cavalry training and enjoyed a wide international reputation in his day. See Priesdorff, *Soldatsiches Führertum*, 8:377–382.

Freiherr Karl von Willisen (1819–1886), a General Staff officer, also worked on the first postwar revision. See Priesdorff, *Soldatisches Führertum*, 9:172–175.

107. Osten-Sacken, *Preussens Heer*, 3:351, 364. Colonel-General Count Gottlieb von Haeseler was one of the most famous Prussian generals between 1871 and 1914, mentioned previously for his fame as a corps commander. The others who worked on the regulations were General of Cavalry Gebhard von Krosigk (1835–1904), who later held one of the highest cavalry positions (head of the first cavalry inspection), and General of Cavalry Heinrich von Rosenberg (1833–1900). On Haeseler and Kleist, see Bogislav von Kleist, ed., *Die Generale der königlich preussischen Armee von 1840–1890*, 3 vols., 2nd ed. (Leipzig: Zuckschwerde & Möschke, 1894–1895), nos. 1563 and 1728, respectively; Priesdorff, *Soldatisches Führertum*, 9:66–70.

108. Frauenholz, *Das Gesicht der Schlacht*, 160.

109. Blau, *Die operative Verwendung der deutschen Kavallerie*, 4–5.

110. See Frauenholz, *Das Gesicht der Schlacht*, 160–161; M. von Poseck, "Die Kavallerie," in Eisenhart-Rothe, *Ehrendenkmal*, 115–118; Count Edgar von Matuschka, "Organisationsgeschichte des Heeres 1890–1918," in *Deutsche Militärgeschichte*, 3:170; and the harsh view of General Liebmann, "Die deutschen Gefechtsvorschriften von 1914 in der Feuerprobe des Krieges," *Militärwissenschaftliche Rundschau* 2 (1937): 475–476.

111. Balck, *Taktik*, 5:14, 15, 19–20.

112. Goltz, *Nation in Arms*, 320–321; Immanuel, *Handbuch der Taktik*, 1:263, 252.

113. Jacob Meckel, *Allgemeine Lehre von der Truppenführung im Kriege*, 3rd ed. (Berlin: E. S. Mittler, 1890), 47–51. Count Alfred von Waldersee wanted to reduce the cavalry and shift resources to infantry and artillery, but he did not hold the position of chief of the General Staff long enough to have any effect. See Kitchen, *German Officer Corps*, 72; Waldersee, *Denkwürdigkeiten*, 2:2–3.

114. Friedrich von Bernhardi, "Der Kampf der drei Waffen und die Organisation der Kavallerie," *Militär-Wochenblatt* 69 (1910): col. 1616. Bernhardi was correct in believing that these views, among others in his books, made him unpopular in influential circles in the army. See Anonymous, *Das alte Heer*, 30.

115. Captain Stockhausen, "Die Verwendung grösser Kavalleriemassen in selbständigen Unternehmungen gegen Flanke und Rücken der feindlichen Armee," *Militär-Wochenblatt* 57 (1908): cols 1331–1335, 58 (1908): cols. 1351–1354. His long articles were directed against previous writings in the Munich-based *Kavalleristischen Monatshefte* calling for changes in the branch.

116. Generalinspektion des Militär-Erziehungs und Bildungswesens, *Leitfaden für den Unterricht in der Taktik auf den Königlichen Kriegsschulen*, 17th ed. (Berlin: E. S. Mittler, 1912), 131.

117. Storz, *Kriegsbild und Rüstung vor 1914*, 277; Showalter, *Tannenberg*, 118–119; Dorondo, *Riders of the Apocalypse*, 60–61.

118. Showalter, *Tannenberg*, 151–152. Certainly this proved to be the case with Russian cavalry, which had a longer and stronger tradition of dismounted combat. See ibid., 147–148.

119. Schlichting, *Taktische und strategische Grundsätze*, 2:147–148, 160–161.

120. Stockhausen, "Die Verwendung grössere Kavallerie-massen," col. 1332, made this point. A semiofficial handbook for preparing for the War Academy examinations contained instructions and a diagram on this. See Anonymous, *Die Befehlstechnik bei den höheren Kommandobehörden* (Oldenburg: Gerhard Stalling, Druck & Verlag des Deutschen Offizierblattes, 1907), 70–71. See also Colonel Karl von Pelet-Narbonne, "Die Aufklärungseskadron," *Militär-Wochenblatt* 79 (1908): cols. 1859–1861.

121. *Leitfaden fur den Unterricht in der Taktik auf den Königlichen Kriegsschulen*, 37. See the after-action report of Bülow, *Bemerkungen des Kommandierendes Generals III Armeekorps* (1911), BA/MA, PH D 9/18, 78.

122. Blau, *Die operative Verwendung des deutschen Kavallerie*, 7–11.

123. Anonymous, "Die Kaisermanöver 1913 in Schlesien," *Militär-Wochenblatt* 137 (1913): col. 3099.

124. Storz, *Kriegsbild und Rüstung vor 1914*, 278. On prewar foreign impressions of the German cavalry, see David G. Hermann, *The Arming of Europe and the Making of the First World War* (Princeton, NJ: Princeton University Press, 1996), 88–89.

125. Bernhardi, "Der Kampf der drei Waffen," cols. 1646–1647; Storz, *Kriegsbild und Rüstung vor 1914*, 272, 277–278.

126. Prior to 1890 the army had three cavalry divisions. Wilhelm II abolished the non-Guards divisions and established two cavalry inspectors reporting directly to him. See Stahl, "Preussische Armee und Reichsheer 1871–1914," 224.

127. Matuschka, "Organisationsgeschichte des Heeres," 167–168.

128. General Inspektion der Kavallerie, No. 2517, to General Staff, subject: Wünschen für grösser Kavallerie-Uebungen, 30 September 1913, BA/MA, PH 3/650, 55–59.

129. Blau, *Die operative Verwendung der deutschen Kavallerie*, 8.

130. See ibid. for many examples of private and public controversies over this issue.

131. Osten-Sacken, *Preussens Heer*, 3:377. Osten-Sacken's account, though published by the official press (E. S. Mittler), was seen as a criticism of the existing organization.

132. General Inspektion der Kavallerie, No. 2517, to General Staff. See also Poseck, "Die Kavallerie," in Eisenhart-Rothe, *Ehrendenkmal*, 119–120, for the 1909–1913 exercises. For Bernhardi's debate with General von der Boeck, see his "Der Kampf der drei Waffen," col. 1681.

133. Schlichting, *Taktische und strategische Grundsätze*, 2:184. An informative summary can be found in Dermot Bradley, *Generaloberst Heinz Guderian und die Enstehungsgeschichte des modernen Blitzkrieges* (Osnabrück: Biblio Verlag, 1978), 55–60.

134. For an assessment (perhaps too critical) of General Max Edler von der Planitz's role, see Storz, *Kriegsbild und Rüstung vor 1914*, 270–271; Priesdorff, *Soldatisches Führertum*, 8:440–444.

135. Cron, *Geschichte des deutschen Heeres*, 93. Because of these shortcomings,

these cavalry units were not called corps, nor were their commanders considered "commanding generals"; that prestigious title was reserved for corps commanders.

136. Ibid., 136.

137. The criticism began with Hans Ritter, *Kritik des Weltkrieges. Das Erbe Moltkes und Schlieffens im grossen Kriege*, 2nd rev. ed. (Leipzig: K. F. Koehler, 1921). Recent additions include Ostertag, *Bildung, Ausbildung, und Erziehung*; Schulte, *Die deutsche Armee*. See also Volker Mollin, *Auf dem Wege zur "Materialschlacht." Vorgeschichte u. Funktionen d. Artillerie-Industrie-Komplexes im Dt. Kaiserreich* (Pfaffenweiler: Centaurus Verlag, 1986); Storz, *Kriegsbild und Rüstung vor 1914.* Dennis Showalter, "Prussia, Technology and War: Artillery from 1815–1914," in *Men, Machines and War*, ed. Ronald Haycock and Keith Neilson (Waterloo, ON: Wilfrid Laurier University Press, 1988), 113–152, is a valuable summary.

138. Showalter, "Prussia, Technology and War," 118–119; Dennis Showalter, *Railroads and Rifles: Soldiers, Technology and the Unification of Germany* (Hamden, CT: Archon Books, 1975), 143.

139. Showalter, "Prussia, Technology and War," 118–119. Mollin, *Auf dem Wege zur "Materialschlacht,"* has a good introduction to technical and organizational issues for the period 1850–1866.

140. Showalter, "Prussia, Technology and War," 124–126, summarizes the results.

141. Max Köhler, *Der Aufstieg der Artillerie bis zum Grossen Kriege* (Munich: Hugo Meiler, 1938), 106–108.

142. Ibid., 108–109; Mollin, *Auf dem Wege zur "Materialschlacht,"* 166–167. Some of the technological aspects are covered in Ulrich Wergenroth, "Industry and Warfare in Prussia," in *On the Road to Total War: The American Civil War and the German Wars of Unification 1870–71* ed. Stig Förster and and Jörg Nagler (Cambridge: Cambridge University Press, 1997), 250–266.

143. Köhler, *Der Aufstieg der Artillerie*, 111–112.

144. Showalter, "Prussia, Technology and War," 126–127.

145. Köhler, *Der Aufstieg der Artillerie*, 114. See also Geoffrey Wawro, *The Franco-Prussian War: The German Conquest of France in 1870–1871* (New York: Cambridge University Press, 2003), 59.

146. Osten-Sacken, *Preussens Heer*, 3:353–354; Showalter, "Prussia, Technology and War," 130.

147. Lieutenant Colonel Marx, "Die Feldartillerie," in Eisenhart-Rothe, *Ehrendenkmal*, 123, discusses the old organization.

148. Osten-Sachen, *Preussens Heer*, 3:288–289, has a factual overview. The foot artillery initially consisted of two foot artillery inspections, which served as supervising headquarters, and four brigades. The foot artillery remained small, with only twenty-six batteries under the army appropriations law of 1874. Köhler, *Der Aufstieg der Artillerie*, 117–121, discusses the decision.

149. Showalter, "Prussia, Technology and War," 136, makes this point, which much of the contemporary literature neglected in the hope of avoiding sensitive

subjects. H. Müller, *Die Entwicklung der Feldartillerie von 1870 bis 1892* (Berlin: E. S. Mittler, 1892), 245–246, summarizes Hindersin's memorandum.

150. Marx, "Die Feldartillerie," 123, cites the memorandum, now lost. Hindersin, the son of a bourgeois pastor, joined the army as an enlisted man in 1823, won a commission, attended the General War School, and became a General Staff officer in 1846. In 1864 he arranged the decisive artillery bombardment against the Danish positions at Düppel and was granted a patent of nobility as a result (18 July 1864). When he was promoted to full general, it was as a general of infantry, surely a sign of the relative standing of the two branches. See Priesdorff, *Soldatisches Führertum*, 6:461–465. Hindersin died suddenly in January 1872.

151. Lieutenant General Hermann Müller, one of the most respected authorities on German artillery, argued that most high officers were in favor of the split. See his *Die Entwicklung der Feldartillerie*, 3 vols. (Berlin: E. S. Mittler, 1892–1894), 2:241, 250. Krafft Hohenlohe-Ingelfingen, the army's highest-placed artilleryman, was opposed. See Marx, "Die Feldartillerie," 124. Friedrich von Boetticher, "Der Lehrmeister des neuzeitlichen Krieges," in *Von Scharnhorst zu Schlieffen 1806–1906. Hundert Jahre preussisch-deutscher Generalstab*, ed. Friedrich von Cochenhausen (Berlin: E. S. Mittler, 1933), argues that many foot artillery officers were also in favor; he notes that Schlieffen was opposed.

152. Storz, *Kriegsbild und Rüstung vor 1914*, 40, presents the standard interpretation. Osten-Sacken, *Preussens Heer*, 3:356, cannot avoid some of the same criticisms. Lenski, *Lern- und Lehrjahre*, 133–134, is likewise critical, as is Müller, *Die Entwicklung der Feldartillerie*, 2:310–311. Podbielski, a career cavalry officer and General Staff officer, had become extraordinarily influential based on his activities as *Generalquartiermeister* and in the War Ministry. He received the enormous sum of 100,00 talers in 1872 as recognition for his work as *Generalquartiermeister* in the army headquarters. See Priesdorff, *Soldatisches Führertum*, 7:397–400.

153. These regulations are summarized in Count Edgar von Matuschka and Wolfgang Petter, "Organisationsgeschichte der Streitkräfte," in *Deutsche Militärgeschichte*, 2(2):353–354; Frauenholz, *Das Gesicht der Schlacht*, 161–162; and Mollin, *Auf dem Wege zur "Materialschlacht*," 173–175. Osten-Sacken, *Preussens Heer*, 3:355–356, comments on Podbielski's successors. General Julius von Voigts-Rhetz, the more important, rose through the guards artillery, became a General Staff officer and a prominent figure in the campaigns of 1866 and 1870–1871, and served in important positions in the War Ministry. See Priesdorff, *Soldatisches Führertum*, 8:322. The branch normally established ad hoc commissions to revise the regulations.

154. Matuschka and Petter, "Organisationsgeschichte der Streitkräfte," 354.

155. Osten-Sacken, *Preussens Heer*, 3:355, mentions these, particularly Captain Leo and Majors von Boguslawski and von Schell.

156. Köhler, *Der Aufstieg der Artillerie*, 121–122.

157. Storz, *Kriegsbsild und Rüstung vor 1914*, 182, discusses the new regulation.

158. Anonymous ["K"], "Die neuen Deckblätter zum Exerzier-Reglement für die Feldartillerie," *Militär-Wochenblatt* 113 (1912): col. 2568; Anonymous, "Der

Neuabdruck des Exerzier-Reglements für die Feldartillerie," *Militär-Wochenblatt* 53 (1914): col. 1144.

159. Osten-Sacken, *Preussens Heer*, 3:356–358, summarizes them.

160. Köhler, *Der Aufstieg der Artillerie*, 124.

161. Mollin, *Auf dem Wege zur "Materialschlacht,"* 184–185.

162. Ibid., 190.

163. Köhler, *Der Aufstieg der Artillerie*, 129–130.

164. Mollin, *Auf dem Wege zur "Materialschlacht,"* 190.

165. Storz, *Kriegsbild und Rüstung vor 1914*, 155.

166. Lt. General Ziethen, "Die Fussartillerie," in Eisenhart-Rothe, *Ehrendenkmal*, 148; Marx, "Die Feldartillerie," 125; Storz, *Kriegsbild und Rüstung vor 1914*, 40, 182–183.

167. Köhler, *Der Aufstieg der Artillerie*, 145.

168. The foot artillery, for example, more readily embraced indirect firing than did the field artillery, and by 1912 it had begun to use aerial observers, its own officers, for artillery adjustment. See Ziethen, "Die Fussartillerie," 150; Hans Linnenkohl, *Vom Einzelschuss zur Feuerwalze. Der Wettlauf zwischen Technik und Taktik in Ersten Weltkrieg* (Munich: Bernard & Graefe, 1990), 147–148.

169. Frauenholz, *Das Gesicht der Schlacht*, 162–163. The earlier regulations of 1896 and 1900 were not truly tactical manuals. For a contrary interpretation of these, see ibid.

170. Anonymous ["Sch"], "Exerzier-Reglemente für die Fussartillerie," *Militär-Wochenblatt* 155 (1908): col. 3613.

171. Matuschka, "Organisationsgeschichte des Heeres," 175–176, makes the point.

172. Ziethen, "Die Fussartillerie," 138–140, is a remarkably candid assessment. The regimental commander's only remaining link to his units was that he retained control over officer replacements.

173. Showalter, "Prussia, Technology and War," 130–133; Matuschka, "Organisationsgeschichte des Heeres," 173. See also Herbert Jäger, *German Artillery of World War One* (Ramsbury, UK: Crowood Press, 2001), 14–17.

174. Jäger, *German Artillery of World War One*, 1–17.

175. Köhler, *Der Aufstieg der Artillerie*, 133.

176. Ibid., 134.

177. Showalter, "Prussia, Technology and War," 141–143. Hermann, *Arming of Europe*, 18–19, recounts efforts of a number of armies to copy the French 75. This French innovation and its substantial but temporary superiority over the C96 is the basis for much of Schulte's one-sided attack on the prewar German artillery.

178. Storz, *Kriegsbild und Rüstung vor 1914*, 69–70; Marx, "Die Feldartillerie," 130; Jäger, *German Artillery of World War One*, 17; Matuschka, "Organisationsgeschichte des Heeres," 173. For a contrary view, see Schulte, *Die deutsche Armee*, 126–148, 381–393. See also Köhler, *Der Aufstieg der Artillerie*, 136–139, which provides a useful picture of a battery on maneuvers.

179. Linnenkohl, *Vom Einzelschuss zur Feuerwalze*, 88; Brose, *Kaiser's Army*, 149.

180. Storz, *Kriegsbild und Rüstung vor 1914*, 152, 182–186; Ernst von Wrisberg, *Wehr und Waffen 1914–1918* (Leipzig: Verlag von K. F. Koehler, 1921), 10.

181. Hew Strachan, *The First World War*, vol. 1, *To Arms* (Oxford: Oxford University Press, 2001), 999–1001.

182. Wilhelm Müller-Loebnitz, *Von Schlieffen bis Ludendorff* (Leipzig: Ernst Oldenburg Verlag, 1925), 7–9, discusses this.

183. Matuschka, "Organisationsgeschichte des Heeres," 176–178. Useful tables of data on various German artillery pieces in 1914 are in Jäger, *German Artillery of World War One*, 33–34.

184. Liebmann, "Die deutschen Gefechtsvorschriften," 468.

185. Linnenkohl, *Vom Einzelschuss zur Feuerwalze*, 144–145.

186. Köhler, *Der Aufstieg der Artillerie*, 131–138.

187. Lueerssen, "Feldartillerie im Zusammenwirken mit Infanterie 1870/71 und Heute," *Militär-Wochenblatt* 141 (1910): cols. 3273–3277.

188. Bavarian Major Friedrich Reuss, "Flieger und Artillerie," *Militär-Wochenblatt* 29 (1914): cols. 593–594; Storz, *Kriegsbild und Rüstung vor 1914*, 180–181; Generalmajor (ret.) Johann Richter (ennobled in 1913), "Wandlungen der Anschauungen über Verwendung der Feldartillerie," *Militär-Wochenblatt* 62 (1912): col. 1411. See Priesdorff, *Soldatisches Führertum*, 10:102. Köhler, *Der Aufstieg der Artillerie*, stresses the weaknesses of communications with units in covered positions.

189. Linnenkohl, *Vom Einzelschuss zur Feuerwalze*, 145–146, 150.

190. Showalter, "Prussia, Technology and War," 127–128.

191. On this development, see Mollin, *Auf dem Wege zur "Materialschlacht,"* 201–202.

192. Heinrich Rohne, "Die Artillerie beim Infanterieangriff," *Militär-Wochenblatt* 47 (1912): cols. 1042–1043. Rohne argued that the German artillery would be firing at unknowable targets and that the only way to use infantry and artillery together was a common effort to achieve fire superiority for the former. Richter, "Wandlungen der Anschauungen über Verwendung der Feldartillerie," col. 1407, joined Rohne on this point, as did Immanuel, *Handbuch der Taktik*, 1:395.

193. Storz, *Kriegsbild und Rüstung von 1914*, 208–209, cites authoritative French regulations and theorists.

194. Inspektion der Feldartillerie, I, Nr. 170/ii I, "Bemerkungen über die Schiessausbildung im Jahre 1910," 18 January 1911, *Nachlass* Karl Friedrichs, BA/MA, N 94/35.

195. Anonymous, "Die Artillerie beim Infanterieangriff," *Militär-Wochenblatt* 100 (1912): cols. 2271–2273; Captain Brückner, "Die Rolle der gepanzerten Schnellfeuerartillerie beim Angriff und in der Verteidigung," *Militär-Wochenblatt* 124 (1906): col. 2858; C. Koerner, "Gedanken über Artillerieverwendung," *Militär-Wochenblatt* 96 (1913): col. 2159. Friedrich *Freiherr* von Falkenhausen, *Kriegführung und Wissenschaft* (Berlin: E. S. Mittler, 1913), 32, also spoke out in favor of the artillery duel.

196. The direct exchange between Rohne and Bernhardi can be found in Rohne, "Die Artillerie beim Infanterieangriff," and in Friedrich von Bernhardi, "Die Ar-

tillerie beim Infanterieangriff," *Militär-Wochenblatt* 83 (1912): cols. 1895–1901, 84 (1912): cols. 1924–1929. Liebmann, "Die deutschen Gefechtsvorschriften," 467, cites the somewhat inconsistent guidelines of the artillery regulations.

197. *Loebell's Jahresberichte* 26 (1899): 340–341, explains the implementation of this measure and its efforts to utilize the maximum amount of artillery at the earliest possible moment. For background, see Heinrich Rohne, "Die Entwicklung der modernen Feldartillerie," *Vierteljahrshefte für Truppenführung und Heereskunde* 1 (1904): 481–531. Some were opposed to this practice, arguing that it reduced the artillery's emphasis on its firing skills. See Lenski, *Lern- und Lehrjahre*, 75–76; Köhler, *Der Aufstieg der Artillerie*, 136.

198. *Freiherr* Friedrich von Falkenhausen, "Angriff und Verteidigung," *Vierteljahrshefte für Truppenführung und Heereskunde* 4 (1906): 395.

199. Anonymous, "Feld- und Fussartillerie in ihrer gemeinsamen Schlachten-tätigkeit," *Militär-Wochenblatt* 42 (1909): col. 968; Anonymous ["BcK"], "Wie lösen Infanterie und Artillerie gemeinsam einen Gefechtsauftrag?" *Militär-Wochenblatt* 153 (1910): col. 3574. Bernhardi, "Die Artillerie beim Infanterieangriff," col. 1926, doubted that the infantry commanders could do this in a timely manner; instead, he wanted the local artillery commanders to get themselves into position to make their own judgments.

200. Heinrich Rohne, "Nochmals: Die Artillerie beim Infanterieangriff," *Militär-Wochenblatt* 94 (1912): col. 2156.

201. Anonymous, "Die neuen Deckblätter zum Exerzier-Reglement für die Feldartillerie," *Militär-Wochenblatt* 113 (1912): cols. 2569–2570; Generalmajor (ret.) Richter, "Aenderungen des Exerzier-Reglements für die Feldartillerie," *Militär-Wochenblatt* 102 (1912): col. 2320. Richter remarked that only those very familiar with the material would recognize that the changes were substantive, but he insisted they were. The key words *allgemeine Grundsätze* (general principles), describing the nature of the infantry commander's instructions to his artillery commander, were changed to *bestimmte Gefechtsaufträge* (definite battle tasks). Prior to these revisions, German procedures allowed greater freedom to artillery commanders than did the French. See Major Zwenger, "Die taktische Verwendung der deutschen im Vergleich zu derjenigen der französischen Feldartillerie," *Militär-Wochenblatt* (1904): cols. 2784–2785, although Zwenger was apparently trying to minimize the differences.

202. On the older criticism, see Ritter, *Kritik des Weltkrieges*, esp. 29–30; G. von Gleich, *Die alte Armee und ihre Verirrungen*, 2nd ed. (Leipzig: Verlag von K. F. Koehler, 1919), 21ff; Max Bauer, *Der Grosse Krieg in Feld und Heimat. Erinnerungen und Betrachtungen* (Tübingen: Osiander'sche Buchhandlung, 1921), 70. Karl Jüstrow, *Feldherr und Kriegstechnik* (Oldenburg: Gerhard Stalling, 1933), esp. 61–114, is still an important source. More recently, see Martin Kitchen, "Traditions of German Strategic Thought," *International History Review* 1, 2 (April 1979): 167–168 (on Clausewitz's legacy); Herwig, "Dynamics of Necessity," 84–75, and the sources cited therein. Brose, *Kaiser's Army*, has a balanced account. John Keegan, *The First World War* (New York: Alfred A. Knopf, 1999), 257–258, extends the criticism to all the armies of 1914. Lothar Burchardt, "Operatives Denken und Planen von Schlief-

fen bis zur begin des Ersten Weltkrieges," in *Operatives Denken und Handeln in deutschen Streitkräften im 19. und 20. Jahrhundert*, ed. Militärgeschichtliches Forschungsamt (Bonn: E. S. Mittler, 1988), 58, echoes the Ritter-Jüstrow stereotype.

203. Storz, *Kriegsbild und Rüstung vor 1914*, 3–5, 14–15; Hermann, *Arming of Europe*, 67–68. On Einem, see also David Stevenson, *Armaments and the Coming of War: Europe 1904–1914* (Oxford: Clarendon Press, 1996), 103–104.

204. Bucholz, *Moltke, Schlieffen and Prussian War Planning*, 179–184.

205. Storz, *Kriegsbild und Rüstung vor 1914*, 202–205; Immanuel, *Handbuch der Taktik*, 1:50, 222–225; Fritz Thiele, *Zur Geschichte der Nachrichtentruppe: 1899–1924* (Berlin: Preuss, 1925), 35; Otto Mueller (Major A. D.), "Kampfmittel und Taktik der deutschen Infanterie im Weltkriege," in *Deutsche Infanterie. Das Ehrenmal der vordersten Front*, ed. Ernst von Eisenhart-Rothe, Erich von Tschischwitz, and Walther Beckmann (Zeulenroda: Verlag Bernhard Sporn, 1939), 208; Linnenkohl, *Vom Einzelschuss zur Feuerwalze*, 160–162, 188; Matuschka, "Organisationsgeschichte des Heeres," 252–254.

206. Matuschka, "Organisationsgeschiche des Heeres," 199–200.

207. The section was titled "Militärischtechnische Umschau," with each issue covering a single subject or a variety of topics.

208. Generalmajor (ret.) Schott, "Geschichtlicher Überblick über die Entwicklung unserer Truppe," in *Zur Geschichte der Nachrichten-Truppe 1899–1924*, ed. First Lieutenant Thiele (Berlin: F. S. Preuss, 1925), 55; Lt. Randewig, "Organisatorische Entwicklung der Nachrichtentruppe im Weltkriege," ibid., 97.

209. An excellent if old introduction is Paul W. Evans, "Strategic Signal Communications—A Study of Signal Communication as Applied to Large Field Forces, Based on the Operations of the German Signal Corps during the March on Paris in 1914," *Signal Corps Bulletin* 82 (January–February 1935): 24–58.

210. Schott, "Geschichtlicher Überblick über die Entwicklung unserer Truppe," 38–39; Bucholz, *Moltke, Schlieffen and Prussian War Planning*, 240–241.

211. General Staff, 6th Section, No. 386 [Report on Kaiser Maneuvers of 1909–1911], 25 June 1912, BA/MA, PH 3/63.

212. Randewig, "Organisatorische Entwicklung der Nachrichtentruppe," 98–99; *Leitfaden für den Unterricht in der Taktik auf den Königlichen Kriegsschulen*, 92.

213. Lieutenant Colonel Thiele, "Führung und Nachrichtenverbindungen," *Jahrbuch für Wehrpolitik und Wehrwissenschaften* (1939): 69. See also Daniel R. Headrick, *The Invisible Weapon: Telecommunications and International Politics 1851–1945* (New York: Oxford University Press, 1991), 155–156.

214. On the doctrinal questions, see Lieutenant General Schniewindt, "Signal Communications between the Headquarters Staffs during the Warfare of Movement in 1914," *Signal Corps Bulletin* 74 (September–October 1933):1, 15; Evans, "Strategic Signal Communication," 38. The Schniewindt article first appeared in *Wissen und Wehr* in 1929.

215. See, above all, Dennis Showalter, "From Deterrence to Doomsday Machine: The German Way of War 1890–1914," *Journal of Military History* 64, 3 (July 2000): 700–701; Storz, *Kriegsbsild und Rüstung vor 1914*, 352–353; Holger Afflerbach, *Falkenhayn. Politisches Denken und Handeln im Kaiserreich* (Munich: R. Oldenbourg,

1994), 62–63. See also Anonymous, "Kraftfahrprotzen," *Militär-Wochenblatt* 46 (1913): cols: 1049–1051; Grosser Generalstab, Abteilung T, report titled "Kraftwagen," October 1909, BA/MA, PH 3/215; Sussdorf, "Das Feldkraftfahrwesen," in *Der grosse Krieg 1914–1918*, ed. Max Schwarte, 10 vols. (Leipzig: Johann Ambrosius Barth, 1921), 8:342. The new manual was titled *Kraftfahrtruppen im Felde*. See Anonymous, "Kraftfahrtruppen im Felde," *Militär-Wochenblatt* 87 (1913): col. 1996.

216. Reichsluftministerium (Germany), *Die Militärluftfahrt bis zum Beginn des Weltkrieges 1914* (Berlin: E. S. Mittler, 1941), 3–5. Surviving documents from the early period may be found in the *Anlageband* (Berlin: E. S. Mittler, 1941).

217. Reichsluftministerium, *Die Militärluftfahrt bis 1914*, 25.

218. Echevarria, *After Clausewitz*, 166–167.

219. Hermann, *Arming of Europe*, 75–76, has a useful summary of the early days of the dirigible.

220. The complicated story of the army's efforts to stimulate the private aircraft industry and to acquire pilots (which it wanted to have before it bought any airplanes), as well as the attendant bureaucratic conflict between the War Ministry and the General Staff, can best be followed in John H. Morrow Jr., *Building German Air Power, 1909–1914* (Knoxville: University of Tennessee Press, 1976), 6–33.

221. Hermann, *Arming of Europe*, 16–17, 138–139. See also Reichsluftfahrtministerium, *Das Militärluftfahrt bis 1914*, 90–132.

222. Morrow, *Building German Air Power*, 17.

223. Ibid.; Hermann, *Arming of Europe*, 77–78.

224. Hermann, *Arming of Europe*, 139–140, cites the reports of the German military attaché in Paris.

225. Generalstab, 2nd Section, Abteilung T, untitled report on technical developments, October 1909, sections in BA/MA, PH 3/215.

226. Ibid.; Chef des Generalstabes der Armee, "Die weitere Entwickelung der Militärluftfahrt in Frankreich," 20 April 1912 (signed by Moltke) and November 1912; "Das Luftfahrwesen in den französischen Armee-Manövern 1912," January 1913 and 4 December 1913, all in BA/MA, PH 8I/493.

227. Chef des Generalstabes der Armee, "Die Luftaufklärung in der englischen Armeeübung 1913," December 1913, BA/MA, PH 8I/493. Examples of collections of press clippings may be found in BA/MA, PH 3/222. The original file designation was Gr[osser] Generalstab, 2nd Abt. T(L).

228. Moltke to War Ministry, 26 September 1912, subject: Aufstellung von Fliegerformationen, in Eric Ludendorff, *Urkunden der Obersten Heeresleitung über ihre Tätigkeit 1916/18*, 3rd rev. ed. (Berlin: E. S. Mittler, 1922), 33.

229. Morrow, *Building German Air Power*, 52. The total aviation acquisition budget rose from about 3.2 million marks in 1909 to 52.5 million in 1914. Airplane procurement totaled about 36,000 marks in 1909 and 26 million in 1914.

230. Morrow, *Building German Air Power*, 61–62, 70–71.

231. The best summary of the two armies' conclusions from the 1910 and 1911 maneuvers is Hermann, *Arming of Europe*, 143–145. For Ludendorff's memorandum, see James S. Corum and Richard R. Muller, *The Luftwaffe's Way of War: German Air Force Doctrine 1911–1945* (Baltimore: Nautical and Aviation Publish-

ing Company of America, 1998), 34–36. See also Echevarria, *After Clausewitz*, 169.

232. Echevarria, *After Clausewitz*, 168, has an excellent summary of the contemporary literature. The first German aviation manual is translated and published in Corum and Muller, *Luftwaffe's Way of War*, 37–44.

233. Hans Beseler, "Krieg und modernes Verkehrswesen," *Preusssiche Jahrbücher* 151 (February 1913): 402–403; Major Stockhausen, "Über des Herabwerfen von Sprengkörpern aus Luftschiffen und Flugzeugen," *Militär-Wochenblatt* 155 (1902): cols. 3589–3591.

234. Grosser Generalstab, T-L, 11-2/7 Nr. 16 [1911], "Der Fliegeraufklärung im Kaisermanöver 1911, ihr Wert und Einfluss auf die Führung im Vergleich zur Kavallerieaufklärung," BA/MA, PH 3/219, 1, 5, 10, 26–27.

235. *Leitfaden für den Unterricht in der Taktik auf den Königlichen Kriegsschulen*, 110–112.

236. Beseler, "Krieg und modernes Verkehrswesen," 392, 401.

237. See, for example, Captain G. Schmidt, "Die Entwicklung des Flugwesens in dem Jahrfrist 1908 bis 1912 und ihre militärische Bedeutung," *Militär-Wochenblatt* 34 (1913): col. 764. Beseler, "Krieg und modernes Verkehrswesen," 402, argued for the utility of aircraft in assisting communications, but this proved a serious shortcoming in August and September 1914.

238. Linnenkohl, *Vom Einzelschuss zur Feuerwalze*, 266.

239. Moltke to War Ministry, 3 December 1912, subject: "Flieger bei der Artillerie," in Ludendorff, *Urkunden*, 36–37.

240. Wentscher, "Artilleriekampf mit Fliegerbeobachtung" in *Das Ehrenbuch der deutschen Feldartillerie*, ed. Albert Benary (Berlin: Verlag Tradition Wilhelm Kolk, ca. 1930), 97–100. On the early use of aerial photography, see Moltke's memorandum "Denkschrift über den Wert die Verwendungsgebiete der Photographie," 12 January 1911, in Ludendorff, *Urkunden*, 44–45, and Linnenkohl, *Vom Einzelschuss zur Feuerwalze*, 266.

241. Morrow, *Building German Air Power*, 86–87.

242. Ibid., 14–15.

243. Moltke to General-Inspektion des Militär-Verkehrswesens, subject: "Flugzeugwesen," 9 March 1910, in Ludendorff, *Urkunden*, 25.

244. Moltke to War Ministry, "Beschaffung von Luftschiffen," 2 March 1911, in Ludendorff, *Urkunden*, 24–25.

245. Morrow, *Building German Air Power*, 14–15, 25, 116–117, has details.

246. Moltke to War Ministry, 26 September 1912 and 14 January 1913, in Ludendorff, *Urkunden*, 29, 37–39.

247. Reichsarchiv, *Der Weltkrieg 1914–1918*, 1:127, notes the lack of aircraft immediately available to the High Command.

248. Morrow, *Building German Air Power*, 86–87; John H. Morrow Jr., *The Great War in the Air: Military Aviation from 1909 to 1921* (Washington, DC: Smithsonian Institution Press, 1993), 57. Echevarria, *After Clausewitz*, 170–173, provides useful analyses of comparative developments in France, Russia, and the United States.

249. Cron, *Geschichte des deutschen Heeres*, 202–203; General of Cavalry Ernst

von Hoeppner, *Germany's War in the Air: The Development and Operations of German Military Aviation in the World War*, reprint ed. (Nashville, TN: Battery Press, 1994), 24.

250. Major Stockahusen, "Flak," in Benary, *Das Ehrenbuch der deutschen Feldartillerie*, 906.

251. Lieutenant Colonel Fritsch (commander, 5th Pioneer Battalion), "Wird man im Kriege auf Luftschiffe und Flugzeuge von unten Schiessen?" *Militär-Wochenblatt* 141 (1913): cols. 3193–3197.

252. Echevarria, *After Clausewitz*, 170, cites the manual and other literature. A translation is now available in Corum and Muller, *Luftwaffe's Way of War*.

253. For an introduction to this underresearched area, see Michael Epkenhans, "Military-Industrial Relations in Imperial Germany, 1870–1914," *War in History* 10, 1 (January 2003): 1–16.

254. Lothar Burchardt, *Friedenswirtschaft und Kriegsvorsorge. Deutschlands wirt-schaftliche Rüstungsbestrebungen vor 1914* (Boppard: Harald Boldt Verlag, 1962), 14.

255. On the overall constitutional-institutional shortcomings and their impact on economic preparations, see Burchardt, *Friedenswirtschaft und Kriegsvorsorge*, 7, 243–245; Stig Förster, "Der deutsche Generalstab und die Illusion des kurzen Krieges 1871–1914. Metakritik eines Mythos," *Militärgeschichtliche Mitteilungen* 54 (1995): 91–93, who also stresses the short-war expectations.

256. Burchardt and Ritter provide examples of the General Staff's efforts to make institutional preparations. See Ritter, *Kritik des Weltkrieges*, 74; Burchardt, *Friedenswirtschaft und Kriegsvorsorge*, 219ff. See also Wiegand Schmidt-Richberg, "Generalstäbe in Deutschland," in *Beiträge zur Militär-und Kriegsgeschichte*, ed. Militärgeschichtliches Forschungsamt, 6 vols. (Stuttgart: Deutsche Verlags-Anstalt, 1962), 3:32, who stresses the limits of the General Staff's authority.

257. Burchardt, *Friedenswirtschft und Kriegsvorsorge*, 74–75, discusses the War Ministry's practical problems. Afflerbach, *Falkenhayn*, 172–173, blames the war minister's reliance on a short war for the failure to stockpile raw materials in 1914. On the reluctance of civilian ministries to get involved in economic preparations, see Burchardt, *Friedenswirtschaft und Kriegsvorsorge*, 57–78; Count Peter Kielmansegg, *Deutschland und der Erste Weltkrieg*, 2nd ed. (Stuttgart: Klett-Cotta, 1980), 162.

258. Frederic Trautmann, trans. and ed., *A Prussian Observes the American Civil War: The Military Studies of Justus Scheibert* (Columbia: University of Missouri Press, 2001), 122. It is worth noting at this point that the elder Moltke never made any comment deriding the Union and Confederate armies as "armed mobs." See Friedrich von Boetticher to Truman Smith, 4 February 1957, *Nachlass* Friedrich von Boetticher, BA/MA, N 323/175.

259. This summary is based on Burchardt, *Friedenwirtschaft und Kriegsvorsorge*, 25, 52–74, 158–159, 195, 202–202. A 1911 War Ministry report may be found in Reichsarchiv, *Kriegsrüstung und Kriegswirtschaft. Anlage Band*, 226–239. For General Staff efforts to stockpile goods and prepare railway plans in advance, see Gerhard Tappen, *Bis zur Marne 1914. Beiträge zur Beurteilung der Kriegführung bis zum*

Abschluss der Marne-Schacht (Oldenburg: Gerhard Stalling, 1920), 4; Burchardt, *Friedenwirtschaft und Kriegsvorsorge*, 25. But note the doubts raised by Förster, "Der deutsche Generalstab und die Illusion des kurzen Krieges," 92–93.

260. This summary is from Strachan, *First World War*, 1:1018–1020; Burchardt, *Friedenswirtschaft und Kriegsvorsorge*, 93–95.

261. Strachan, *First World War*, 1:834–837; Burchardt, *Friedenswirtschaft und Kriegsvorsorge*, 6–8, 43–44.

262. Showalter, *Instrument of War*, 29.

263. David R. Stone, *The Russian Army in the Great War: The Eastern Front, 1914–1917* (Lawrence: University Press of Kansas, 2015), 71.

CHAPTER FOUR. GERMAN THEORY AND DOCTRINE TO 1914

1. See Jehuda L. Wallach, *The Dogma of the Battle of Annihilation: The Theories of Clausewitz and Schlieffen and Their Impact on the German Conduct of Two World Wars* (1967; reprint, Westport, CT: Greenwood Press, 1986), who blames Schlieffen for much of what happened in both world wars. The classic defense of Schlieffen is contained in the writings of Wilhelm Groener, *Das Testament des Grafen Schlieffen. Operative Studien über den Weltkrieg* (Berlin: E. S. Mittler, 1927), and *Der Feldherr wider Willen. Operative Studien über den Weltkrieg*, 2nd ed. (Berlin: E. S. Mittler, 1931). Also fundamental is Wolfgang Foerster, *Graf Schlieffen und der Weltkrieg*, 2nd ed. (Berlin: E. S. Mittler, 1925), and *Aus der Gedankenwerkstatt des Deutschen Generalstabes* (Berlin: E. S. Mittler, 1931).

2. James J. Schneider, *The Structure of Strategic Revolution: Total War and the Roots of the Soviet Warfare State* (Novato, CA: Presidio, 1994), 169–174. The following sections on Schlieffen and Schlichting draw heavily on Daniel J. Hughes, "Schlichting, Schlieffen, and the Prussian Theory of War in 1914," *Journal of Military History* 59, 2 (April 1995): 257–277.

3. The sweeping influence of Schlichting's views, even in the days of Schlieffen, can be seen in the most comprehensive contemporary guide to German theory. See Wilhelm Balck, *Taktik*, 6 vols. (Berlin: R. Eisenschmidt, 1908–1912), esp. 5:172–177. The debate over Schlichting's ideas did not end with the First World War. See Sigfrid Mette, *Vom Geist deutscher Feldherren. Genie und Technik 1800–1918* (Zurich: Scientia, 1938).

4. On Schlichting, see Joachim Hoffmann, "Die Kriegslehre des Generals von Schlichting," *Militärgeschichtliche Mitteilungen* 1 (1969): 5–35; Werner Gembruch, "General von Schlichting," *Wehrwissenschaftliche Rundschau* 10, 4 (1960): 188–196. Schlichting's main theoretical work was *Taktische und strategische Grundsätze der Gegenwart*, 3 vols. (Berlin: E. S. Mittler, 1898–1899). He first became prominent as a writer through his article "Über das Infanteriegefecht," *Beiheft zum Militär-Wochenblatt* 1 (1879): cols. 37–68. Rudolf von Caemmerer, *The Development of Strategical Science in the 19th Century*, trans. Karl Donat (London: Hugh Rees, 1905), is a good introduction. Schlichting's papers have been lost, but there is a good summary in the valuable biography by Egon *Freiherr* von Gayl, *General von Schlichting und sein Lebenswirk* (Berlin: Verlag von Georg Stilke, 1913). Donald Cranz, "Understanding Change: Sigismund von Schlichting and

the Operational Level of War" (unpublished paper, School of Advanced Military Studies, Fort Leavenworth, KS, 1990), has a useful introduction and a translation of a small part of Schlichting's *Taktische und strategische Grundsätze*. On Schlichting's influence on Russian and Soviet thought, see A. A. Svechin, "Evolution of Strategic Theories," trans Harold S. Oreinstein (unpublished paper, Soviet Army Studies Office, Fort Leavenworth, KS, ca. 1988). I (DJH) am indebted to Professor James Schneider of the School of Advanced Military Studies at Fort Leavenworth for providing this and other insights. His *Structure of Strategic Revolution* is a valuable contribution to the discussion.

5. The German nobility considered age of title to be more important than formal rank. The oldest clans (*Uradel*) held a higher position than those clans (*Briefadel*) whose claims to nobility were based on more recent patents from royalty conferring noble status. German genealogies then and now continue to draw this distinction.

6. On the role of the cadet schools in the production of officers for the Prussian and later German armies, see the interesting but flawed study by Jörg Muth, *Command and Culture: Officer Education in the U.S. Army and the German Armed Forces 1901–1940* (Denton: University of North Texas Press, 2011), 85–112.

7. See Schlieffen's comments in a letter to his future wife, 22 July 1866, in Count Alfred von Schlieffen, *Generalfeldmarschall Graf Alfred Schlieffen. Briefe*, ed. Eberhard Kessel (Göttingen: Vandenhoeck & Ruprecht, 1958), 194.

8. Friedrich von Boetticher, *Schlieffen* (Göttingen: Musterschmidt Verlag, 1957), 13.

9. *Nachlass* Schlieffen, BA/MA, N 121/35, has Moltke's evaluations of 1869, 1872, 1873, 1874, and 1875.

10. See Freytag-Loringoven's introduction to Generalfeldmarschall Graf Alfred von Schlieffen, *Gesammelte Schriften* (Berlin: E. S. Mittler, 1913), 1:xvi.

11. For some interesting examples drawn from personal observation, see Franz von Lenski, *Lern- und Lehrjahre in Front und Generalstab* (Berlin: Bernard & Graefe, 1939), 178ff.

12. Gerhard Ritter, *Sword and Scepter: The Problem of Militarism in Germany*, vol. 2, *The European Powers and the Wilhelminian Empire, 1890–1918*, trans. Heinz Norden, 2nd ed. (Coral Gables, FL: University of Miami Press, 1970), 106–107, 193–194. See also Arden Bucholz, *Moltke, Schlifefen and Prussian War Planning* (New York: Berg, 1991), 30–31.

13. Wolfgang Foerster, "Einige Bemerkungen zu Gerhard Ritters Buch 'Der Schlieffenplan,'" *Wehrwissenschaftliche Rundschau* 7, 1 (1957): 41. Foerster was one of Schlieffen's greatest champions in the interwar years.

14. See, for example, the memoirs of August von Mackensen, *Mackensen: Briefe und Aufzeichnungen des Generalfeldmarschalls aus Krieg und Frieden*, ed. Wolfgang Foerster (Leipzig: Bibliographisches Institut, 1938), 19–20. For summaries of the types of opponents Schlieffen encountered, see Gunther Rothenberg, "Moltke, Schlieffen and the Doctrine of Strategic Envelopment," in *Makers of Modern Strategy from Machiavelli to the Nuclear Age*, ed. Peter Paret (Princeton, NJ: Princeton University Press, 1986), 315; Hughes, "Schlichting, Schlieffen, and the Prussian

Theory of War." Azar Gat's *The Development of Military Thought: The Nineteenth Century* (Oxford: Clarendon Press, 1992), 94–104, has an interesting section on Schlieffen and his opponents.

15. This was quite the opposite of Clausewitz's views on the role of history in theory and education. See Carl von Clausewitz, *On War* [1832], trans. Michael Howard and Peter Paret (Princeton, NJ: Princeton University Press, 1976), 170–171.

16. Many of Schlieffen's most important works are now available in English. See *Alfred von Schlieffen's Military Writings*, ed. and trans. Robert T. Foley (London: Frank Cass, 2003).

17. For Schlieffen's comment that "war is only a means of policy," see "Der Feldherr," in *Gesammelte Schriften*, 1:4.

18. Either type of battle could occur during a war of movement. If the entire war took on the characteristics of siege warfare or static battles along trench lines, the result would be the dreaded positional warfare, which everyone wanted to avoid.

19. Boetticher, *Schlieffen*, 31–32. Schlieffen apparently did not specifically develop this concept in any of his theoretical writings, but the basic principle underlay his entire planning process. He thus limited Moltke's view that strategy was a system of expedients, although he was not nearly as one-sided as many historians have portrayed him.

20. See Helmut Otto, *Schlieffen und der Generalstab* (East Berlin: Deutscher Militärverlag, 1966), 123.

21. Mette, *Vom Geist deutscher Feldherren*, 277; Otto, *Schlieffen und der Generalstab*, 124. For Schlieffen's own comments, see his *Gesammelte Schriften*, 1:259–266.

22. Schlieffen, "Der Feldherr," 8–9; Schlieffen, "Cannae," in *Gesammelte Schriften*, 1:127.

23. Emanuel von Kiliani, "Die Operationslehre des Grafen Schlieffen und ihre deutschen Gegner," *Wehrkunde* 10 (1961): 75; Gerhard P. Gross, *The Myth and Reality of German Warfare: Operational Thinking from Moltke the Elder to Heusinger*, ed. David T. Zabecki (Lexington: University Press of Kentucky, 2016), 71.

24. For a summary of these criticisms and an extension of them that blames Schlieffen for nearly everything that went wrong in both world wars, see the carefully argued but extreme views in Wallach, *Dogma of the Battle of Annihilation*. See also Arden Bucholz, *Hans Delbrück and the German Military Establishment: War Images in Conflict* (Iowa City: University of Iowa Press, 1985); Jack Snyder, *The Ideology of the Offensive: Military Decision Making and the Disasters of 1914* (Ithaca, NY: Cornell University Press, 1984), 133–156. A popular example is Barbara Tuchman, *The Guns of August* (New York: Macmillan, 1962), 26.

25. Thus we conclude that Wallach goes too far when he argues that Schlieffen excluded all consideration of breakthrough battles; see his *Dogma of the Battle of Annihilation*, 45. See Schlieffen's concluding remarks at the 1905 General Staff war games, 23 December 1905, National Archives and Records Administration microfilm series (no number). Note the comments of Ferdinand von Senger und

Etterlin, "Cannae, Schlieffen and die Abwehr," *Wehrwissenschaftliche Rundschau* 13, 1–2 (January–February 1963): 11, 32, 40; Colonel (ret.) Mantey, "Umfassung, Umgehung und Durchbruch. Eine Schlieffen Studie," *Wissen und Wehr* 10 (1931): 583.

26. This emphasis on flanking attacks was the hallmark of Schlieffen's theoretical writings and his influential campaign concept. It was also the basis for his famous extended essay "Cannae"; on this point, see *Gesammelte Schriften*, 1:148. Historians have criticized him for this one-sided approach to combat. See especially Helmut Otto, "Entstehung und Wesen der Blitzkriegsstrategie des deutschen Imperialismus vor dem ersten Weltkrieg" *Zeitschrift für Militärgeschichte* 6 (1957): 407. At the opposite pole, Rothenberg, "Moltke, Schlieffen and the Doctrine of Strategic Envelopment," 323, argues that the successful operations in the east in 1914 showed that the concept was sound.

27. On this point, see Mantey, "Umfassung, Umgehung und Durchbruch," 570.

28. See, for example, Colmar *Freiherr* von der Goltz, *Krieg- und Heerführung* (Berlin: R. von Decker's Verlag, 1901), 120; Hugo Baron von Freytag-Loringhoven, "Die Umfassung," in *Betrachtungen über den russisch-japanischen Krieg*, 2 vols. (Berlin: E. S. Mittler, 1913), 2:86–92; Balck, *Taktik*, 1:308. This had been Moltke's view as well; see *Moltkes Militärische Werke*, 17 vols. (Berlin: E. S. Mittler, 1892–1918), 4(3): 210. The 1906 infantry regulations, paragraph 392, stated, "the combination of the frontal and flank attack furnishes the best assurance of success."

29. General-Inspektion des Militär-Erziehungs und Bildungswesens (Prussia), *Leitfaden für den Unterricht in der Taktik auf den königlichen Kriegsschulen*, 17th ed. (Berlin: E. S. Mittler, 1912), 139ff.

30. "Über die Aussichten des taktischen und operativen Durchbruchs," unpublished paper, *Nachlass* Schlieffen, BA/MA, N 43/108.

31. Mantey, "Umfassung, Umgehung, und Durchbruch," 584. A balanced assessment of Schlieffen's views of the defense can be found in Senger und Etterlin, "Cannae, Schlieffen und die Abwehr," 26–43.

32. Foley, *Schlieffen's Military Writings*, 148–149. I (DJH) slightly changed Foley's translation. The German is at Count Alfred von Schlieffen, *Dienstschriften des Chefs des Generalstabes der Armee Generalfeldmarschalls Graf von Schlieffen*, ed. General Staff, 2 vols. (Berlin: E. S. Mittler, 1937–1938), 2:174.

33. Schlieffen, "Der Krieg in der Gegenwart," in *Gesammelte Schriften*, 1:15–16.

34. On this point, see Rothenberg, "Moltke, Schlieffen and the Doctrine of Strategic Envelopment," 313–314. E. G. Blau, "Der ältere Moltke und Schlieffen," *Wissen und Wehr* 1 (1934): 833–834, also argues that Schlieffen, convinced that his plan must be rigidly followed, was determined to prevent a repeat of the performances of Moltke's subordinates during the wars of unification.

35. Schlieffen, *Dienstschriften*, 2:50.

36. For his criticism of Moltke's use of directives, see Schlieffen to Hahnke, 13 July 1910, in Schlieffen, *Briefe*, 310. By the time of his retirement, he harshly criticized Moltke's subordinate commanders, to whom the master's methods were "entirely foreign." See Schlieffen, *Gesammelte Schriften*, 1:125.

37. Blau, "Der ältere Moltke und Schlieffen," 833–834, makes this point. Moltke had superiority of numbers, an advantage that would not be repeated in Germany's circumstances after the turn of the century.

38. See *Drill Regulations for the Infantry, German Army, 1906*, trans. Francis J. Behr (Washington, DC: Government Printing Office, 1907), 9, 65–66, 68–69. See also Balck, *Taktik*, 1:94–95, 347, and Baron Hugo von Freytag-Loringhoven, *The Power of Personality in War*, trans. Colonel Oliver L. Spaulding (Harrisburg, PA: Military Service Publishing Company, 1955), 34–35, for examples of how this was interpreted. See also Walter Elze, *Das deutsche Heer vor 1914* (Osnabrück: Biblio Verlag, 1968), 8. The Prussian army's field service regulations (*Felddienst Ordnung*), translated by the British General Staff in 1908, also admonished officers to act with initiative and independence. Many other examples could be cited from the pre-1914 literature of the Prussian army.

39. On this principle, which remained unchanged until late in the Second World War, see Daniel J. Hughes, "Abuses of German Military History," *Military Review* 66, 12 (December 1986): 66–76; Daniel J. Hughes, "Auftragstaktik," in *International Military and Defense Encyclopedia*, ed. Trevor N. Dupuy et al., 6 vols. (New York: Brassey's, 1993), 1:328–333. See also Robert M. Citino, *The German Way of War: From the Thirty Years' War to the Third Reich* (Lawrence: University Press of Kansas, 2005), 152–153, 308–310.

40. On Scharnhorst's perceived place in this, see Sigismund von Schlichting, *Moltkes Vermächtnis* (Munich: Verlag der Allgemeinen Zeitung, 1901), 15.

41. The account of Hermann von Kuhl, *Der deutsche Generalstab in Vorbereitung und Durchführung des Weltkrieges* (Berlin: E. S. Mittler, 1920), 145–147, effectively addresses this issue, despite the author's obviously partisan position.

42. Wallach, *Dogma of the Battle of Annihilation*, 209–211, who accepts the existence of such a "school," traces this view to 1915; however, Wallach clearly recognizes that not everyone agreed with Schlieffen. On the lack of consensus on many points in 1914, see Hans Ritter, *Kritik des Weltkrieges. Das Erbe Moltkes und Schlieffens in grossen Kriege*, 2nd rev. ed. (Leipzig: K. F. Koehler, 1921), 25ff.

43. On Schlieffen's doubts that he had convinced everyone, see the comments of his close associate Hugo Baron von Freytag-Loringhoven, *Menschen und Dinge wie ich sie in meinem Leben sah* (Berlin: E. S. Mittler, 1923), 138.

44. This section draws heavily on Hughes, "Schlichting, Schlieffen, and the Prussian Theory of War," 257–278.

45. Kurt von Priesdorff, ed., *Soldatisches Führertum*, 10 vols. (Hamburg: Hanseatisches Verlagsanstalt, 1936–1942), 8:446–447, has details of Schlichting's career. The only biography is Gayl, *Schlichting*.

46. The common belief that all General Staff officers had to pass through the War Academy has no foundation in fact. Throughout the nineteenth century, especially capable or fortunate officers entered the General Staff in a probationary status without having attended the three-year course at the War Academy.

47. Priesdorff, *Soldatisches Führertum*, 8:448. Waldersee's term as chief of the General Staff (1888–1891) apparently did not affect Schlichting's career. In fact, some had thought that Schlichting would succeed Moltke.

48. Gayl, *Schlichting*, 13–14.

49. John T. Nelson II, "Where Do We Go from Here? Considerations for the Formal Adoption of *Auftragstaktik* by the U.S. Army" (unpublished paper, School of Advanced Military Studies, Fort Leavenworth, KS, 1988), has a useful introduction to the regulations' place in the development of modern tactics. The 1888 regulations terminated the formal parade ground tactical formations that had been enshrined in the infantry regulations since 1847. These tactics had proved unsuitable in 1866 and even more so in 1870–1871. A series of amendments between 1873 and 1876 had failed to ameliorate the regulations' most serious shortcomings. The 1888 manual freed tactics from all parade ground formations and gave lower commanders the authority to use whatever tactical formations they thought appropriate. The ensuing debate over forms lasted until 1914.

50. For representative examples, see Colmar *Freiherr* von der Goltz, *The Nation in Arms: A Treatise on Modern Military Systems and the Conduct of War*, trans. Philip Ashworth (London: Hugh Rees, 1906), 145–146, 159, 266–267, 303–304; Friedrich von Bernhardi, "Über Millionenheere," *Deutsche Revue* 37 (February 1912): 208–209. See also Wallach, *Dogma of the Battle of Annihilation*. Stig Förster, "Die deutsche Generalstab und die Illusion des kurzen Krieges, 1871–1914. Metakritik eines Mythos," *Militärgeschichtliche Mitteilungen* 54 (1995): 86, blames Gerhard Ritter for establishing the false view of the universal expectation of short war.

51. Kriegsministerium (Prussia), *D.V.E. Nr. 53. Grundzüge der höheren* Truppenführung (Berlin: Reichsdruckerei, 1910), 16.

52. The substance of this lengthy debate can be followed in several of the articles in Wolfgang von Groote and Klaus-Jürgen Müller, eds., *Napoleon I und das Militärwesen seiner Zeit* (Freiburg: Rombach, 1968). See also Gross, *Myth and Reality of German Warfare*, 61.

53. Schlichting, *Taktische und strategische Grundsätze*.

54. See Goltz, *Krieg- und Heerführung*, 14–15, 23; Goltz, *Nation in Arms*, 306. Friedrich von Cochenhausen, "Kampfertum gegen Übermacht," in *Wehrgedanken. Eine Sammlung wehrpolitischer Aufsätze*, ed. Friedrich von Cochenhausen (Hamburg: Hanseatische Verlagsanstalt, 1933), 10, has Schlieffen's views. Mette, *Vom Geist deutscher Feldherren*, 52–53, examines Scharnhorst's views, which were a subject of dispute at the time of Mette's writing.

55. Sigismund von Schlichting, *Moltke und Benedek. Eine Studie über Truppenführung zu den 'Taktische und strategischen Grundsätze der Gegenwart'* (Berlin: E. S. Mittler, 1900), 14; Schlichting, *Moltkes Vermächtnis*, 30. See also Gayl, *Schlichting*, 275–276; Hoffmann, "Die Kriegslehre des Generals von Schlichting," 25–26.

56. Moltke's views are available in Daniel J. Hughes, ed. and trans., *Moltke on the Art of War: Selected Writings* (Novato, CA: Presidio, 1993), 11–12, 175–176, 188–189, 219, 262–264.

57. Schlichting, *Taktische und strategische Grundsätze*, 2:90–91. This did not signify rejection of Clausewitz's broader views on the nature of war. Schlichting's writings contained numerous references to the continuing relevance of many of Clausewitz's arguments. Indeed, his books and articles, like those of many other late-century Prussian authors, indicate the wrongness of the widely

held view of modern historians that Clausewitz had little if any influence on German theory.

58. Prusso-German theory used the term *Festungskrieg* (fortress warfare) to designate positional warfare until the First World War, with some exceptions. After 1918, *Stellungskrieg* came into universal use. Likewise, writers before 1914 frequently used the term *Feldkrieg* to designate a war of movement.

59. See the explanation by Robert Foley, *German Strategy and the Path to Verdun: Erich von Falkenhayn and the Development of Attrition, 1870–1916* (Cambridge: Cambridge University Press, 2005), 66.

60. Schlichting, *Taktische und strategische Grundstäze*, 2:16, 111–112, 3:171; Schlichting, *Moltke und Benedek*, 132–133. See also Gayl, *Schlichting*, 77, 322–323.

61. Schlichting, *Taktische und strategische Grundsätze*, 2:111; Gayl, *Schlichting*, 322–323, 349–350. See also Mette, *Vom Geist deutscher Feldherren*, 181–188.

62. Gayl, *Schlichting*, 322–326; Mette, *Vom Geist deutscher Feldherren*, 187–188; Friedrich von Bernhardi, *On War of Today*, trans. Karl von Donat, 2 vols. (New York: Dodd, Mead, 1914), 2:161ff.

63. Schlichting, *Taktische und strategische Grundsätze*, 3:45.

64. Gayl, *Schlichting*, 441–442, quoting a letter by Schlichting from 1908–1909; 354–355, quoting an unpublished essay critical of Schlieffen's views on the subject. See also Citino, *German Way of War*, 152.

65. Albert von Boguslawski (1834–1905) authored numerous books and articles between 1869 and 1904. The most important were *Die Entwicklung der Taktik von 1793 bis zur Gegenwart* (Berlin: Luckhardt, 1869), *Betrachtungen über Heerwesen und Kriegführung* (Berlin: R. Eisenschmidt, 1897), and *Strategische Erörterungen, betreffend die vom General v. Schlichting vertretenen Grundsätze* (Berlin: R. Eisenschmidt, 1901). On his career, see Hermann Kunz, "Zum 70. Geburtstag des Generalleutnants z. D. v. Boguslawski," *Militär-Wochenblatt* 157 (1904): cols. 3719–3725. Boguslawski had not attended the War Academy and was not a General Staff officer.

66. See, for example, Boguslawski, *Strategische Erörterung*, 4–6, 74–75.

67. Ibid., 76, 81, 108, 149.

68. Boguslawski, *Betrachtungen über Heerwesen und Kriegführung*, 103. On tactical questions, Boguslawski saw himself as a precursor of Schlichting and took a middle ground between the latter and his main opponent, Wilhelm von Scherff, who advocated strict rules and procedures for infantry tactics. See Ernst Buchfinck, "General Albert von Boguslawski. Ein Gedenkblatt zu seinen 100. Geburtstag: 24-12 1834–1934," *Wissen und Wehr* 12 (1934): 816–824, esp. 819. Caemmerer, *Development of Strategical Science*, 241–243, to some degree minimizes the differences between Schlichting and Boguslawski.

69. Goltz, *Krieg- und Heerführung*, 80–84. See also Hoffmann, "Die Kriegslehre des Generals von Schlichting," 23–24. Goltz's most famous book, *The Nation in Arms*, first published in 1883, went through several editions in various languages prior to the First World War.

70. Goltz, *Krieg- und Heerführung*. A translation is available as *The Conduct of War: A Short Treatise on Its Most Important Branches and Guiding Rules*, trans.

Major G. F. Leverson (London: Kegan Paul, 1908). Dennis Showalter's "Goltz and Bernhardi: The Institutionalization of Originality in the Imperial German Army," *Defense Analysis* 3, 4 (1987): 305–318, is a useful introduction to Goltz.

71. Goltz, *Conduct of War*, 125.

72. Ibid., 135–144.

73. Hugo *Freiherr* von Freytag-Loringhoven, one of Schlieffen's most devoted disciples and perhaps the most prolific uniformed historian in the two decades before 1914, returned to this theme in many of his publications. See especially his *Die Heerführung Napoleons und Moltkes. Eine vergleichende Studie* (Berlin: E. S. Mittler, 1897) and *Die Heerführung Napoleons in ihrer Bedeutung für unsere Zeit* (Berlin: E. S. Mittler, 1910). Friedrich von Bernhardi expressed his views very generally in *On War of Today*, 1:14–29, 2:308, and more pointedly in his article "Über angriffsweise Kriegführung," *Beiheft zum Militärwochenblatt* 4 (1905): 125–151. On Bernhardi, see Showalter, "Goltz and Bernhardi."

74. J. F. C. Fuller, *A Military History of the Western World*, 3 vols. (New York: Funk & Wagnalls, 1954–1956), 3:134, states: "Moltke brought his armies to the starting point and then abdicated his command and unleashed them."

75. Wilhelm von Scherff, *Die Lehre von Krieg auf der Grundlage seiner neutzeitlichen Erscheinungsformen* (Berlin: E. S. Mittler, 1897); Wilhelm von Scherff, *Von der Kriegführung*, 2nd ed. (Berlin: E. S. Mittler, 1883).

76. Schlichting, *Taktische und strategische Grundsätze*, 2:93, 3:223–228. This had been Moltke's view, which he expressed most forcefully in his 1869 *Instructions for Large Unit Commanders*. This document, a manual for senior commanders, received very limited distribution prior to 1900.

77. Schlichting, *Taktische und strategische Grundsätze*, 3:59, 222–223.

78. Freytag-Loringhoven, *Die Heerführung Napoleons und Moltkes*, 51–52. One of the best overviews of Napoleonic warfare reached essentially the same conclusion about the relationship between Napoleon and his subordinate commanders. See Peter Paret, "Napoleon and the Revolution in War," in *Makers of Modern Strategy*, 137. The vast controversy over this interpretation of Napoleonic methods is beyond the scope of this work. On this issue, see the perceptive views of Martin Van Creveld, *Command in War* (Cambridge, MA: Harvard University Press, 1985), 96–98.

79. Boguslaswki warned against allowing the term to become a mere slogan and cautioned that subordinate independence would be limited in practice. See his "Grundsatz, Schlagwort und Phantasie," *Militär-Wochenblatt* 73 (1903): cols. 1779–1785, 74 (1903): cols. 1810–1816. Goltz, *Nation in Arms*, 160, warned that commanders ran the risk of losing control of events. On the question of subordinate initiative, see the carefully considered remarks of Rothenberg, "Moltke, Schlieffen and the Doctrine of Strategic Envelopment," 300–301.

80. This has been a major theme of the US Army's professional literature for some time. For a cautionary note about the possible lack of broad perspective and misuse of German terms, see Hughes, "Abuses of German Military History," 66–76.

81. At the highest level, the fundamental regulation was *Principles for Large*

Unit Commanders (1910), a version of Moltke's 1869 *Instructions for Large Unit Commanders*. The infantry drill regulations and the field service regulations are available in English translations.

82. Prussian and German training literature sometimes cautioned officers that regulations alone would not suffice. The prewar Prussian army had a rich literature, possibly unmatched in relative quantity by any of its contemporaries. By way of comparison, one author suggested that fewer than 10 percent of British officers had ever read a book on military subjects. See Dennis Winter, *Haig's Command: A Reassessment* (New York: Viking, 1991), 134.

83. See Goltz, *Krieg- und Heerführung*, 22. See also the comments of Hermann Foertsch, "Training and Development of German General Staff Officers," vol. 8 of *The German General Staff*, ed. Historical Division, European Command, manuscript P-031b (1948), 34.

84. On the term's origins, see Azar Gat, *The Origins of Military Thought: From the Enlightenment to Clausewitz* (Oxford: Clarendon Press, 1989), 40–41. For a typical Prussian definition at the turn of the century, see Goltz, *Krieg- und Heerführung*, 22.

85. Günther Blumentritt, *Strategie und Taktik. Ein Beitrag zur Geschichte des Wehrwesens vom Altertum bis zur Gegenwart* (Konstanz: Akademische Verlagsgesellschaft Athenaion, 1960), 113–114.

86. Ottomar *Freiherr* von der Osten-Sacken und bei Rhein, *Preussens Heer von seinen Anfängen bis zur Gegenwart*, 3 vols. (Berlin: E. S. Mittler, 1914), 2:375–376. Eugen von Frauenholz, *Das Gesicht der Schlacht. Taktik und Technik in der deutschen Kriegesgeschichte* (Stuttgart: Union Deutscher Verlagsgesellschaft, 1937), 152–153.

87. On the cabinet orders of 1853 and 1854 and their ultimate failure to increase flexibility at the lowest levels, see Dennis Showalter, *Railroads and Rifles: Soldiers, Technology and the Unification of Germany* (Hamden, CT: Archon Press, 1986), 102–103. In addition to the sources cited therein, the interested reader should consult Kriegsministerium (Prussia), ed., *Militärische Schriften weiland Kaiser Wilhelms des Grossen Majestät* (Berlin: E. S. Mittler, 1897), 2:197ff.

88. Freytag-Loringhoven, *Menschen und Dinge*, 48–50; Gayl, *Schlichting*, 88–89.

89. Hoffmann, "Die Kriegslehre des Generals von Schlichting," 29; Gayl, *Schlichting*, 88–89, quoting Schlichting's 1897 brochure "Über das ganze Dienstjahre 1885–1886." See also Antulio J. Echevarria II, *After Clausewitz: German Military Thinkers before the Great War* (Lawrence: University Press of Kansas, 2000), 38–40, 96.

90. See, for example, J. Scheibert, ed., *Illustrirtes Deutsches Militär-Lexikon* (Berlin: Verlag von W. Pauli's, 1897), 46.

91. Echevarria, *After Clausewitz*, 36–37, 95, gives a remarkably clear presentation of the views of Boguslawski and Scherff.

92. Dieter Storz, *Kriegsbild und Rüstung vor 1914. Europäische Landstreitkräfte vor dem Ersten Weltkrieg* (Herford: E. S. Mittler, 1992), 31–32. See also Balck, *Taktik*, 1:178–179, quoting Scherff, *Einheitsangriff oder Individualisierter Angriff* (1902).

93. See Buchfinck, "General Albert von Boguslawski," 818, commenting on the views of another leading officer, Jacob Meckel.

94. Kriegsministerium (Prussia), *Exerzier-Reglement für die Infanterie* (Berlin: E. S. Mittler, 1888). Eric Dorn Brose, *The Kaiser's Army: The Politics of Military Technology in Germany during the Machine Age, 1870–1918* (Oxford: Oxford University Press, 2001), 58, and Echevarria, *After Clausewitz,* have excellent discussions of Schlichting's views and role in producing the new regulations. See also Wilhelm Groener, *Lebenserinnerungen, Jugend, Generalstab, Weltkrieg,* ed. Friedrich *Freiherr* Hiller von Gaertringen (Göttingen: Vandenhoeck & Rupprecht, 1957), 61–62; Hoffmann, "Die Kriegslehre des Generals von Schlichting," 14; Gayl, *Schlichting,* 120–123; Storz, *Kriegsbild und Rüstung,* 28–31; Martin Samuels, *Command or Control? Command, Training and Tactics in the British and German Armies 1888–1918* (London: Frank Cass, 1995), 71–73.

95. For a differing view of the 1888 regulations, see Bernd-Felix Schulte, *Die deutsche Armee 1900–1914. Zwischen Beharren und Verändern* (Düsseldorff: Droste, 1977).

96. *Loebell's Jahresberichte* 15 (1888): 307.

97. *Exerzier-Reglement für die Infanterie* (1888), 93, 96–97, 117, 127–128.

98. See Moltke's "Instructions for Large Unit Commanders," in Hughes, *Moltke on the Art of War,* 171–224.

99. *Exerzier-Reglement für die Infanterie* (1888), 108–109, 125–133. Note the comments of Wilhelm Blume, "Selbstthätigkeit der Führer im Kriege," *Beiheft zum Militär-Wochenblatt* 10 (1896): col. 497.

100. Brose, *Kaiser's Army,* 59–62, has many details. See also Storz, *Kriegsbild und Rüstung,* 167. Groener, *Lebenserinnerungen,* 62, has an example of a corps commander resisting the new tactics. Echevarria, *After Clausewitz,* 41–42, has a comprehensive survey of the continuing controversy. See also Hoffmann, "Die Kriegslehre des Generals von Schlichting," 27.

101. Buchfinck, "General Albert von Boguslawski," 819; Gayl, *Schlichting,* 122–123; Schulte, *Die deutsche Armee,* 166–168. Fritz Hoenig, *Inquiries into the Tactics of the Future,* trans. Carl Reichmann (London: W. H. Allen, 1898), 266–270, has a useful account.

102. Generalleutnant Emil von Lessel, *Böhmen, Frankreich, China 1866–1901. Erinnerungen eines preussischen Offiziers,* ed. Walter Hubatsch (Cologne: G. Grote'sche Verlagsbuchhandlung, 1981), 137–138, 146–147. See also Storz, *Kriegsbild und Rüstung,* 167; Freytag-Loringhoven, *Menschen und Dinge,* 80.

103. Freytag-Loringhoven, *Menschen und Dinge,* 48; August Keim, "Die gegenwärtige Stand der Gefechtslehre," *Beiheft zum Militärwochenblatt* (1890): 16.

104. Brose, *Kaiser's Army,* 61.

105. Hanns Möller, *Fritz von Below. General der Infanterie* (Berlin: Bernard & Graefe, 1939), 19; Freytag-Loringhoven, *Menschen und Dinge,* 123; Storz, *Kriegsbild und Rüstung,* 167–168.

106. Storz, *Kriegsbild und Rüstung,* 168–169, relying on Bavarian archival sources; Ludwig Freiherr von Gebsattel, *Generalfeldmarschall Karl von Bülow* (Munich: J. F. Lehmans Verlag, 1929), 33–34.

107. Storz, *Kriegsbild und Rüstung,* 169.

108. Kriegsministerium (Prussia), *Exerzier-Reglement für die Infanterie* (Berlin:

E. S. Mittler, 1906). This account uses the 1909 edition with amendments (*Deck-blätter*) 1–78, BA/MA, PH 3/130. The manual, without subsequent amendments, is available in English as *Drill Regulations for the Infantry, German Army*, trans. Francis J. Behr (Washington, DC: Government Printing Office, 1907). See also Friedrich *Freiherr* von Falkenhausen, "Exerzieren und Fechten," *Vierteljahrshefte für Truppenführung und Heereskunde* 4 (1907): 479.

109. *Exerzier-Reglement für die Infanterie* (1906), 102, para. 351.

110. Ibid., 1, para. 3.

111. A very clear example of applied tactics based on the 1906 manual can be found in Otto von Moser, *Ausbildung und Führung des Bataillons, des Regiments und der Brigade*, 4th ed. (Berlin: E. S. Mittler, 1914), 4, 76.

112. Daniel J. Hughes, "Tactics and Command in the Prusso/German Army 1870–1914" (paper presented at the annual conference of the Society for Military History, 1999), 1–11. See also Echevarria, *After Clausewitz*, 123–124; Brose, *Kaiser's Army*, 153. Echevarria sees more of Scherff's continuing influence than we do.

113. *Exerzier-Reglement für die Infanterie* (1906), 47, para. 142. The English translation erroneously gives the standard interval as one yard.

114. Ibid., 52–59, para. 166–170, 188.

115. Ibid., 52, para. 166.

116. Ibid., 1, 50, 51, paras. 2, 158, 162.

117. Kriegsministerium (Prussia), *D.V.E. Nr. 267. Felddienstordnung* (Berlin: E. S. Mittler, 1908), 20–21, sets forth the basic procedures, as did *Leitfaden für Kriegs-schulen*, 126.

118. This went back to Reyher and Moltke. See *Prinz* Krafft zu Hohenlohe-Ingelfingen, *Letters on Strategy*, 2 vols. (London: Kegan Paul, Trench, Trübner, 1898), 1:133. See also General Staff (Prussia), *Anhaltspunkte für den Generalstabsdi-ent* (1914), 41. The infantry regulations made the same point. Goltz, *Nation in Arms*, 117–118, has a summary.

119. See Echevarria, *After Clausewitz*, 126–127, and the literature cited therein.

120. Ernst Buchfinck, "Feldmarschall Graf von Haeseler 19. 1. 1836–26. 10. 1919," *Wissen und Wehr* 1 (1936): 6.

121. Bernhardi, *On War of Today*, 2:92.

122. See the summary by Heinz-Ludger Borchert, "Landkriegführung von Schlieffen bis Guderian," in *Deutsche Militärgeschichte*, ed. Militärgeschichtliches Forschungsamt, 6 vols. (Munich: Bernard & Graefe, 1964–1979), 6:431.

123. Buchfinck, "Feldmarschall Graf von Haeseler," 6–7.

124. Konstantin Hierl, "Gefechtsausdehnungen," *Vierteljahrshefte für Trup-penführung und Heerskunde* 2 (1908): 290–298; Falkenhausen, "Exerzieren und Fechten," 464–472; Frauenholz, *Gesicht der Schlacht*, 157–158.

125. Falkenhausen, "Exerzieren und Fechten," 483. His major publications were *Ausbildung für den Krieg*, 2 vols. (Berlin: E. S. Mittler, 1902, 1904); *Kriegführung und Wissenschaft* (Berlin: E. S. Mittler, 1913); and *Flankenbewegung und Massenheer. Der Gedanke von Leuthen in Anwendung auf die Gegenwart* (Berlin: E. S. Mittler, 1911).

126. Gayl, *Schlichting*, 122. Freytag-Loringhoven's *Das Exerzier-Reglement für*

die Infanterie vom 29. Mai 1906, kriegsgeschichtlich erläutert (Berlin: E. S. Mittler, 1907), was generally favorable. Freytag-Loringhoven was, of course, a supporter of Schlieffen on the larger issues of war. See also Anonymous [K. v. W.], "Zur Gefechtsgliederung der Infanterie," *Militär-Wochenblatt* 75 (1909): col. 1723.

127. Heiger Ostertag, *Bildung, Ausbildung, und Erziehung des Offizierkorps im deutschen Kaiserreich 1871 bis 1918* (Frankfurt: Peter Lang, 1990), 197, lambastes the manual for excessive romanticism in its depiction of the heroic attacking leader. Curt Liebmann, "Die deutschen Gefechtsvorschriften vor 1914 in der Feuerprobe des Krieges," *Militärwissenschaftliche Rundschau* 2 (1937): 470, is harshly critical. Schulte, *Die deutsche Armee*, condemns the regulations' tactical forms. Hans Linnenkohl, *Vom Einzelschuss zur Feuerwalze. Der Wettlauf zwischen Technik und Taktik in Ersten Weltkrieg* (Munich: Bernard & Graefe, 1990), 39–40, is moderately critical. Storz, *Kriegsbild und Rüstung*, 170, rejects Schulte's accusations and reaches a moderate conclusion, as do Brose, *Kaiser's Army*, and Echevarria, *After Clausewitz*. Samuels, *Command or Control?* 76–77, has a balanced view that is difficult to characterize. Hans L. Borgert, *Grundzüge der Landkriegführung von Schlieffen bis Guderian* (Munich: Bernard & Graefe, 1979), 431, argues that the manual was no improvement over that of 1888. Falkenhausen, "Exerzieren und Fechten," 464, praised the regulations for ending years of uncertainty.

128. The last prewar manual for tactics at the war schools made this explicit, repeating Moltke's earlier phrases.

129. A representative exposition of criticism of the "cult of the offensive" is Stephen van Evera, "The Cult of the Offensive and the Origins of the First World War," in *Military Strategy and the Origins of the First World War*, ed. Steven E. Miller (Princeton, NJ: Princeton University Press, 1985), 58–107.

130. David Stevenson, *Cataclysm: The First World War as Political Tragedy* (New York: Basic Books, 2004), 8.

131. John Maurer, *The Outbreak of the World War: Strategic Planning, Crisis Decision Making and Deterrence Failure* (Westport, CT: Praeger, 1995), 3–8, aptly summarizes the evidence on this point. See the analysis in David G. Hermann, *The Arming of Europe and the Making of the First World War* (Princeton, NJ: Princeton University Press, 1996), 28–29. See also Stig Förster, "Dreams and Nightmares: German Military Leadership and the Images of Future Warfare, 1871–1914," in *Anticipating Total War: The German and American Experiences 1871–1914*, ed. Manfred Boemke, Roger Chickering, and Stig Förster (Cambridge: Cambridge University Press, 1999), 343–376; Holger H. Herwig, "Germany and the 'Short-War' Illusion: Toward a New Interpretation?" *Journal of Military History* 66, 3 (July 2002): 681–694.

132. Holger Herwig, severely critical of Schlieffen and others for the short-war dogma, cites numerous important officers in the General Staff and elsewhere who doubted that a rapid victory was possible. See his *The First World War: Germany and Austria-Hungary 1914–1918*, 2nd ed. (London: Arnold Bloomsbury, 2014), 49–51. See also Förster, "Der deutsche Generalstab und die Illusion des kurzen Krieges," 66, 86–88.

133. Foley, *German Strategy and the Path to Verdun*, 59–63.

134. On the widespread recognition of the inevitability of great losses, see Storz, *Kriegsbild und Rüstung*, 332–333; Dennis Showalter, *Tannenberg: Clash of Empires* (Hamden, CT: Archon Books, 1991), 33–34; Michael Howard, "Men against Fire: Doctrine in 1914," in Paret, *Makers of Modern Strategy*, 510–511, 521. On the recognition that the heavy losses of 1870–1871 would be repeated, see Hugo Baron von Freytag-Loringhoven, *Grundbedingungen kriegerischen Erfolgen. Beiträge zur Psychologie des Krieges im 19. und 20. Jahrhundert* (Berlin: E. S. Mittler, 1914), 123–124; Captain Loeffler, "Taktische Fragen," *Vierteljahrshefte für Truppenführung und Heereskunde* 1 (1904): 407; Captain Warneberg, "Die Nerven im Gefecht und das Exerzier-Reglement fur die Infanterie," *Militär-Wochenblatt* 84 (1908): col. 1972; Lt. Mueller, "Über Gefechtsverluste," *Vierteljahrshefte fuer Truppenfuehrung und Heereskunde* 2 (1905): 429–451. On the expectation of high officer losses, see Balck, *Taktik*, 1:165.

135. On the broad grounds for the nearly universal belief among European armies that offensive action was both necessary and possible, see Hermann, *Arming of Europe*, 22; Showalter, *Tannenberg*, 121–122.

136. Hughes, "Auftragstaktik," 1:328–333.

137. Moser, *Ausbildung und Führung des Bataillons, des Regiments und der Brigade*, 188.

138. Moltke, *Militärische Werke*, 4(3):87. See also the comments of Balck, *Taktik*, 1:14–15. Hohenlohe-Ingelfingen made essentially the same argument in his *Letters on Strategy*, 1:70.

139. *Exerzier-Reglement für die Infanterie* (1906), 90–91, para. 304.

140. As early as 1894, the Prussian army's field service regulation had incorporated Moltke's statement that delay was worse than a mistake. See Wilhelm von Blume, "Selbsttätigkeit der Führer im Krieg," *Beiheft zum Militär-Wochenblatt* 10 (1896): cols. 494–504. By 1906, many of the army's tactical manuals included versions of this exhortation for leaders to take initiative and responsibility.

141. Moltke, *Militärische Werke*, 4(3):87.

142. Schlichting, *Taktische und strategische Grundsätze*, 3:59; Balck, *Taktik*, 1:346–347; Bernhardi, *On War of Today*, 1:330; Max Jähns, *Feldmarschall Moltke* (Berlin: Ernst Hofmann, 1900), 583–584.

143. Representative examples can be found in Goltz, *Krieg- und Heerführung*, 230–231; Lt. Vogt, "Der Angriff und die Krisis in der Schlacht," *Militär-Wochenblatt* 18 (1908): cols. 387–392; Balck, *Taktik*, 1:176; Anonymous, "Die Heranbildung von Unterführern auf dem Exerzierplatz," *Beiheft zum Militärwochenblatt* (1884): 229; and Blume "Selbsttätigkeit der Führer im Kriege," cols. 498–499.

144. Goltz, *Nation in Arms*, 143–144. This sentiment persisted beyond the experiences of 1914. See Theodor Jochim, *Die Vorbereitung des deutschen Heeres für die grosse Schlacht in Frankreich im Frühjahr 1918*, vol. 1, *Grundsätze für die Führung* (Berlin: E. S. Mittler, 1927), 23.

145. Hugo *Freiherr* von Freytag-Loringhoven, "Studien über Clausewitz: Der Krieg is das Gebiet der Gefahr," *Vierteljahrshefte für Truppenführung und Heereskunde* 1 (1904): 159–160; Albert von Boguslawski, "Grundsatz, Schlagwort und

Phantasie," *Militär-Wochenblatt* 73 (1903): col. 1783; Wilhelm Balck, "Gefechtsausgaben bei Infanteriebesichtigungen," *Militär-Wochenblatt* 24 (1913): cols. 540–541.

146. Note the comments of Ritter, *Kritik des Weltkrieges*, 11.

147. *Leitfaden für die Kriegsschulen*, 22; Goltz, *Krieg- und Heerführung*, 113–115; Balck, *Taktik*, 1:144–145, 5:221; Friedrich von Bernhardi, "Die Elemente des modernen Krieges," *Beiheft zum Militär-Wochenblatt* (1898): 437; Friedrich von Bernhardi, "Über angriffsweise Kriegführung," *Beiheft zur Militär-Wochenblatt* 4 (1905): col. 130; Gayl, *Schlichting*, 87; Caemmerer, *Development of Strategical Science*, 174; Keim, "Die gegenwärtige Stand der Gefechtslehre," 9.

148. Wolf, "Moderne Frontausdehnungen," *Militär-Wochenblatt* 151 (1906): cols. 3567–3568, used the Boer's defensive lines as examples.

149. Brose, *Kaiser's Army*, 87–90, has an excellent account.

150. See the semiofficial Anonymous, *Die Truppenführung* (Berlin: R. Eisenschmidt, 1914), 9–10; Lt. Vogel, "Der Angriff und die Krisis in der Schlacht," *Militär-Wochenblatt* 18 (1908): col. 391; Balck, *Taktik*, 1:309; Goltz, *Krieg- und Heerführung*, 120; Freytag-Loringhoven, "Die Umfassung," 2:86–92.

151. *Leitfaden für Kriegsschulen*, 143–144; Jacob Meckel, *Allgemeine Lehre von der Truppenführung im Kriege*, 3rd ed. (Berlin: E. S. Mittler, 1890), 221; Bernhardi, "Über angriffsweise Kriegführung," cols. 131–133; Keim, "Die gegenwärtige Stand der Gefechtslehre," 14; Hierl, "Gefechtsausdehnungen," 302–304. Similar cautions can be found in the orthodox writings of Goltz and Bernhardi.

152. Meckel, *Truppenführung im Kriege*, 222–223; Balck, *Taktik*, 1:308.

153. Lt. Krafft, "Der Kriegsschulleitfaden für Taktik, ein taktischer Handbuch," *Militär-Wochenblatt* 2 (1911): col. 41. See also *Leitfaden für Kriegsschulen*, 140.

154. Goltz, *Krieg- und Heerführung*, 231; Balck, *Taktik*, 5:243; *Loebell's Jahresberichte* 26 (1899), 298; Lt. Ludwig, "Der Sturm im Festungskriege," *Vierteljahrshefte für Truppenführung und Heereskunde* 2 (1905): 19–28; Freytag-Loringhoven, "Der Durchbruch," in *Betrachtungen über den russisch-japanischen Kriege*, 2:70–85; and, looking backward, Friedrich von Bernhardi, *The War of the Future in Light of the Lessons of the World War*, trans. F. A. Holt (London: Hutchinson, 1920), 72–76.

155. See Moser, *Ausbildung und Führung des Bataillons, des Regiments und der Brigade*, 76ff, for a particularly clear example.

156. Goltz, *Nation in Arms*, 360–362.

157. Moser, *Ausbildung und Führung des Bataillons, des Regiments und der Brigade*, 217–218; Generalmajor Richter, "Übungen zur Förderung des Zusammenwirkens zwischen Infanterie und Artillerie," *Militär-Wochenblatt* 42 (1910): cols. 1016–1017.

158. *Exerzier-Reglement für die Infanterie* (1906), 96.

159. Goltz, *Krieg- und Heerführung*, 111.

160. Meckel, *Allgemeine Lehre von der Truppenführung im Kriege*, 9.

161. Balck, *Taktik*, 1:13.

162. Hermann, *Arming of Europe*, 24–25, rightly states that most theorists recognized the need for effective combined-arms cooperation.

163. General Staff, 6th Section, [Report on 1910–1911 kaiser maneuvers], 25 June 1912, BA/MA, PH 3/642, 43.

164. Borgert, "Landkriegführung von Schlieffen bis Guderian," 481–482, cited several examples. Freytag-Loringhoven, *Menschen und Dinge*, 123, made the same point. Both authors realized that more could have been done.

165. Anonymous, "Neues auf dem preussischen Etat 1914," *Militär-Wochenblatt* 160 (1913): col. 3645.

166. *Leitfaden für Kriegsschulen*, 137. See also Kriegsministerium (Prussia), *D.V.E. 230: Feldbefestigungs-Vorschrift* (1906), 4. See also Richter, "Übungen zur Förderung des Zusammenwirkens zwischen Infanterie und Artillerie," cols. 1011–1012.

167. The editor, Janson, made this point in "Lose Gedanken über Übungen mit gemischten Waffen," *Militär-Wochenblatt* 62 (1908): cols. 1425–1429. See also Anonymous [C. v. K.], "Zusammenwirken von Infanterie und Artillerie," *Militär-Wochenblatt* 99, 1 (1914): cols. 1210–1214; Captain Wilhelmi, "Die schwere Artillerie in Felddienst- und Manöver-Ordnung," *Militär-Wochenblatt* 93, 1 (1908): col. 1527; and, earlier, Rudolf von Caemmerer, "Zur Frage der Infanterietaktik," *Militär-Wochenblatt* 9 (1903): cols. 271–272.

168. Anonymous [v. W.], "Der geschlossene Angriff," *Militär-Wochenblatt* 59 (1910): col. 1410, is illustrative of the common assumptions about the use of heavy artillery in coordination with the infantry.

169. *Exerzier-Reglement für die Infanterie* (1906), 98.

170. Hermann, *Arming of Europe*, 24–25, makes this point.

171. Ernst Kabisch, "Angriffsaussichten in der modernen Schlacht," *Militär-Wochenblatt* 104 (1913): cols. 2327–2331.

172. Anonymous [W. v. H.], "Die Wechselbeziehung und das Zusammenwirken der Infanterie und Artillerie," *Militär-Wochenblatt* 93, 1 (1908): col. 1633.

173. Lenski, *Lern- und Lehrjahre*, 323.

174. Freytag-Loringhoven, *Menschen und Dinge*, 124.

175. See Liebmann, "Die deutschen Gefechtsvorschriften," 469–470.

176. *Exerzier-Reglement für die Infanterie* (1906), paras. 253, 326, 333–336, 443, 446, 455–463. Other paragraphs stressed local initiative, use of entrenching tools, brevity of orders, and fire superiority.

177. Balck, *Taktik*, 1:307. See also David R. Dorondo, *Riders of the Apocalypse: German Cavalry and Machine Warfare, 1870–1945* (Annapolis, MD: Naval Institute Press, 2012), 47–49.

178. Borgert, "Landkriegführung von Schlieffen bis Guderian," 480–482, has a critical but reasonably balanced conclusion to this effect.

179. This went back to the 1888 infantry regulations, which called for precisely this kind of attack when necessary. See *Exerzier-Reglement für die Infanterie* (1888), 102–105.

180. Major Walter von Hülsen, "Zahl und Raum im Kampfe der vorderen Linien," *Militär-Wochenblatt* 155 (1906): col. 3592. See also Captain Warneberg, "Die Nerven im Gefecht und das Exerzier-Reglement für die Infanterie," *Militär-Wochenblatt* 84 (1908): col. 1972.

181. Rohne, "Zur Beurteilung der Wirkung beim gefechtsmässigen Abteilungs-schiessen," *Militär-Wochenblatt* 2 (1913): col. 27. Balck argued in *Taktik*

(1908) that German marksmanship was superior. Note the perceptive comments in Showalter, *Tannenberg*, 120–123.

182. Anonymous, "Frontalangriff und infanteristisch Feuerüberlegenheit," *Militär-Wochenblatt* 76 (1906): cols. 1602–1606.

183. *Exerzier-Reglement für die Infanterie* (1906), 78–79.

184. Walter von Hülsen, "Feuerüberlegenheit," *Militär-Wochenblatt* 29 (1909): cols. 639–645; "Die Schützenformen im Angriff," *Militär-Wochenblatt* 124 (1910): cols. 2883–2887, 125 (1910): cols. 2905–2909, 126 (1910): cols. 2927–2931, 127 (1910): cols. 2493–2551, 128 (1910): cols. 2975–2979; "Noch einmal, kampfkräftige Schützenlinie," *Militär-Wochenblatt* 56 (1910): cols. 1251–1254.

185. *Exerzier-Reglement für die Infanterie* (1906), 78–79.

186. Anonymous, "Dichte und dünne Schützenlinie," *Militär-Wochenblatt* 40 (1910): cols. 965–968; Generalmajor von der Esch, "Frontausdehnung und Tiefengliederung," *Militär-Wochenblatt* 53 (1909): cols. 1213–1219; Ardenne, "Langsames Feuer dichter Schützenlinien?" *Militär-Wochenblatt* 65 (1909): cols. 1481–1482.

187. Compare Samuels, *Command or Control?* 160–161, with Holger Herwig, "The Dynamics of Necessity," in *Military Effectiveness*, vol. 1, *The First World War*, ed. Allan R. Millett and Williamson Murray (Boston: Allen & Unwin, 1988), 95. Herwig's argument that the regulations called for holding every inch and to reconquer it if lost is not a fair statement of the manual's provisions or their overall context.

188. *Exerzier-Reglement für die Infanterie* (1906), paras. 367–411.

189. Gross, *Myth and Reality of German Warfare*, 59–60. In the German army both during the imperial era and in the interwar period, a publication signed by a general officer was considered an invitation to enter into a lively debate. Rank was no shield against criticism. In the American armed forces, an article signed by a general officer often has the effect of stifling debate.

CHAPTER FIVE. THE SCHLIEFFEN ERA: STRATEGIC PLANNING, 1890–1905

1. Wilhelm Groener, speech on the situation, 19–20 May 1919, BA/MA, PH 367, 1–2.

2. For a preliminary examination of the phenomenon of losers writing history, see Richard L. DiNardo, "The Falsest of Truisms: Who Writes History?" *World History Connected* 12, 1 (February 2015), http://worldhistoryconnected.press.illinois.edu/12.1/forum_dinardo.html.

3. Hermann von Kuhl, *Der deutsche Generalstab in Vorbereitung und Durchführung des Weltkrieges* (Berlin: E. S. Mittler, 1920). Wilhelm Groener's two books fall into this category: *Das Testament des Grafen Schlieffen. Operative Studien über den Weltkrieg* (Berlin: E. S. Mittler, 1927); and *Der Feldherr Wider Willen. Operative Studien über den Weltkrieg*, 2nd ed. (Berlin: E. S. Mittler, 1931). Similar in view but more solid in substance are the works of Wolfgang Foerster: *Graf Schlieffen und der Weltkrieg*, 2nd ed. (Berlin: E. S. Mittler, 1925); and *Aus der Gedankenwerkstatt des deutschen Generalstabes* (Berlin: E. S. Mittler, 1931). Hans Ritter, *Kritik des Welt-*

krieges: Das Erbe Moltkes und Schlieffens im grossen Kriege, 2nd rev. ed. (Leipzig: K. F. Koehler, 1921), harshly criticizes many aspects of the prewar army but lavishes praise on Schlieffen's concepts.

4. Terence Zuber, *Inventing the Schlieffen Plan: German War Planning 1871–1914* (Oxford: Oxford University Press, 2002), 1–51; Hans Ehlert, Michael Epkenhans, and Gerhard P. Gross, eds., *Der Schlieffenplan: Analysen und Dokumente* (Paderborn: Ferdinand Schöningh, 2006). The English version of the latter is *The Schlieffen Plan: International Perspectives on the German Strategy for World War I*, trans. David T. Zabecki (Lexington: University Press of Kentucky, 2014).

5. The phrase comes from Emanuel von Kiliani, "Die Operationslehre des Grafen Schlieffen und ihre deutschen Gegner," *Wehrkunde* 10 (1961): 71–76, 133–138.

6. Gerhard Ritter, *The Schlieffen Plan: Critique of a Myth*, trans. Andrew Wilson and Eva Wilson (London: Oswald Wolf Publishers, 1958).

7. Azar Gat, *The Development of Military Thought: The Nineteenth Century* (Oxford: Clarendon Press, 1992), 95–101, reviews part of the historiography. Holger Herwig, *The First World War: Germany and Austria-Hungary 1914–1918*, 2nd ed. (London: Arnold Bloomsbury, 2014), 87, is representative in his argument that the plan was "a high risk operation born of hubris and bordering on recklessness." Jehuda Wallach, *The Dogma of the Battle of Annihilation: The Theories of Clausewitz and Schlieffen and Their Impact on the German Conduct of Two World Wars* (1967; reprint, Westport, CT: Greenwood Press, 1986), linked Schlieffen's influence to much of what went wrong in both world wars, from Ludendorff to Hitler. His *Kriegstheorien. Ihre Entwicklung im 19. und 20. Jahrhundert* (Frankfurt: Bernard & Graefe, 1972), continued the criticism. The most convincing argument for the plan's logistical shortcomings is Martin Van Creveld, *Supplying War: Logistics from Wallenstein to Patton* (Cambridge: Cambridge University Press, 1977), 109–141. The representative East German view can be found in Helmut Otto, *Schlieffen und der Generalstab* (East Berlin: Deutscher Militärverlag, 1966), 188.

8. See especially Dennis Showalter, "Total War for Limited Objectives: An interpretation of German Grand Strategy," in *Grand Strategies in War and Peace*, ed. Paul Kennedy (New Haven, CT: Yale University Press, 1991), 105–123, and the older book by Herbert Rosinski, *The German Army* (London: Hogarth Press, 1939). Gordon Craig concluded, curiously, that although the plan ignored political considerations and alternative solutions, it would have attained an overwhelming initial success if carried out with an energetic and stubborn commander. See his *The Politics of the Prussian Army 1640–1945* (New York: Oxford University Press, 1956), 277–283.

9. Jack Snyder, *The Ideology of the Offensive: Military Decision Making and the Disasters of 1914* (Ithaca, NY: Cornell University Press, 1984).

10. Herwig, *First World War*, 4. For information on Dieckmann's life and career, see Gerhard P. Gross, "There Was a Schlieffen Plan: New Sources on the History of German Military Planning," in Ehlert et al., *Schlieffen Plan*, 126. In a conversation with one of us (RLD), Dr. Bernard Chiari explained that the East German government sat on this material for nearly half a century because the

communist regime never figured out how to deal with the Great War as a historical event from an ideological perspective.

11. See the articles by Zuber cited in the bibliography and, in more detail, his *Inventing the Schlieffen Plan*.

12. Zuber, *Inventing the Schlieffen Plan*, 6–8, 21, 291–292, cites a letter from Hermann Mertz von Quirheim, chief of the Army Historical Section, to Wilhelm Groener, 11 October 1919, as the first mention of the plan and thus the beginning of the legend. Zuber notes that Hugo von Freytag-Loringhoven, a close associate of Schlieffen, stressed the latter's ideas as a continuation of the elder Moltke's concepts and does not cite the 1905 memorandum.

13. See the articles by Terence Holmes, Robert Foley, and Terence Zuber listed in the bibliography. The best update of this controversy and an essential collection of documents can be found in Ehlert et al., *Der Schlieffenplan*, 1–16. That volume also includes a rejoinder by Zuber, which stemmed in part from a conference hosted by the Militärgeschichtliches Forschungsamt (MGFA). In 2013 the MGFA was reorganized and renamed the Zentrum für Militärgeschichte und Sozialwissenschaft der Bundeswehr (ZMSB). Zuber declined to give permission to include his response in the English translation, published in 2014.

14. The best summary is still Gerhard Ritter, *The Sword and the Scepter: The Problem of Militarism in Germany*, vol. 2, *The European Powers and the Wilhelminian Empire, 1890–1914*, trans. Heinz Norden, 2nd ed. (Coral Gables, FL: University of Miami Press, 1970), 196–199. Moltke's deployment plans are available in Ferdinand von Schmerfeld, ed., *Die deutschen Aufmarschpläne 1871–1890* (Berlin: E. S. Mittler, 1929). See also Ritter, *Schlieffen Plan*, 19–20; Jehudah Wallach, "Feldmarschall von Schlieffens Interpretation der Kriegslehre Moltkes [der Ältere]," in *Generalfeldmarschall von Moltke. Bedeutung und Wirkung*, ed. Roland G. Foerster (Munich: R. Oldenbourg, 1991), 53.

15. E. G. Blau, "Der ältere Moltke und Schlieffen," *Wissen und Wehr* 1 (1934): 829, errs in arguing that the two approaches were basically the same. On other points, however, Blau's analysis is shrewd and convincing.

16. See Moltke's essay written after the Franco-Prussian War, "Plan of Operations," in *Moltke on the Art of War: Selected Writings*, ed. Daniel J. Hughes (Novato, CA: Presidio, 1993), 91–92. Similar concepts can be found in the same source at 45–46, 69–71. See also Hermann von Staabs, *Aufmarsch nach zwei Fronten. Auf Grund der Operationspläne von 1871–1914* (Berlin: E. S. Mittler, 1925), 11.

17. Schmerfeld, *Die deutschen Aufmarschpläne*, 20–42, has a summary of Moltke's approach and reprints the deployment concept papers at 121–164.

18. Zuber, *Inventing the Schlieffen Plan*, 114–125, makes the argument that each of these amounted to a western deployment similar to the extreme concepts later developed by Schlieffen.

19. On Waldersee's plans, see Eberhard Kessel, "Die Tätigkeit des Grafen Waldersee als Generalquartiermeister und Chef des Generalstabes der Armee," *Die Welt als Geschichte* 14, 2 (1954): 81–121; Arden Bucholz, *Moltke, Schlieffen and Prussian War Planning* (New York: Berg, 1991), 103–104, 124, which relies on

Kessel's article supplemented with Mohs's edition of Waldersee's military works. Waldersee contemplated changes, to be sure, but he remained within the general framework established by Count Moltke.

20. For a review of the newly discovered material and Zuber's thesis, see Gross, "There Was a Schlieffen Plan," 85–136.

21. Ritter, *Schlieffen Plan*, 22–23. Neither Foerster nor Dieckmann make reference to this memorandum, which Ritter used in 1943, before the destruction of the army archives. See also Zuber, *Inventing the Schlieffen Plan*, 142.

22. Although the exact date can no longer be determined, Schlieffen soon came to the conclusion that repulsing the anticipated French offensive and following up with a counteroffensive would not produce a decision. A defeated French army could withdraw behind its fortifications, where the Germans would face the same challenge that had been the basis of Moltke's decision not to seek a rapid decision in the west. See Friedrich von Boetticher, "Der Lehrmeister des neuzeitlichen Krieges," in *Von Scharnhorst zu Schlieffen 1806–1906. Hundert Jahre preussisch-deutscher Generalstab*, ed. Friedrich von Cochenhausen (Berlin: E. S. Mittler, 1933), 259–260.

23. Wilhelm Dieckmann, "Der Schlieffenplan," 61–62 (all citations refer to the Bundesarchiv/Militärchiv folder's page numbers rather than the page numbers in the original typescript).

24. Zuber, *Inventing the Schlieffen Plan*, 135–136, summarizes this information from archival sources. Ritter, *Schlieffen Plan*, 33, which cites the August memorandum only from Foerster's *Gedankenwerkstatt*, concludes that Schlieffen expected a French offensive. Dieckmann, who had the memorandum for his research, is probably correct in his argument that Schlieffen did not expect a French attack at the outset of a war.

25. Dieckmann, "Der Schlieffenplan," 9–10, 65–66; Ritter, *Schlieffen Plan*, 24–25. Ritter also argues that Schlieffen's interest in destroying the enemy's army was another departure from Moltke, a point discussed later. Zuber, *Inventing the Schlieffen Plan*, 142, creates the impression that Schlieffen wrote a second memorandum in December 1892. The Dieckmann manuscript has no evidence of this.

26. Ehlert et al., *Schlieffen Plan*, 339–344, describes the surviving deployment documents, which are very fragmentary.

27. Dieckmann, "Der Schlieffenplan," 65–70. Boetticher, "Der Lehrmeister des neuzeitlichen Krieges," 263, has a diagram. Ritter, *Schlieffen Plan*, 38, refers to the deployment plan briefly but rests his discussion on a subsequent memorandum dated July 1894. The older plan of Moltke would have sent eleven corps to the western front, while Schlieffen's 1893–1894 deployment increased this to sixteen, with four active corps and a number of reserve divisions moving to the eastern front. This deployment would have sent forty-eight divisions to the west and fifteen to the east.

28. Dieckmann, "Der Schlieffenplan," 69, quoting the memorandum. Ritter gives no source for his discussion of the contents of this memorandum.

29. Ibid., 63–65.

30. Ibid., 100–101. In 1895 Schlieffen also told the war minister that the Germans would have to remain on the defensive as long as they could not deploy more rapidly than the French.

31. Ehlert et al., *Schlieffen Plan*, provides no documentation on this point. Both Dieckmann and Boetticher explain the intent of the 1893–1894 deployment plan on the basis of the memorandum of July 1894, and neither discusses the intervening deployment plan of 1894–1895 (which would have taken effect on 1 April 1894). Since both had access to the General Staff archives, it is reasonable to assume that the deployment plan of 1894–1895 did not differ substantially from that of the previous year. The eastern-front deployments, which are known, reinforce this conclusion. Zuber fails to explain that his analysis of the 1893–1894 deployment plan is based on a memorandum written months after the plan was completed.

32. Dieckmann, "Der Schlieffenplan," 78, 94, 101. The planned strength for 1896–1897 stood at fifty infantry and six cavalry divisions.

33. Ibid., 95. See also Zuber, *Inventing the Schlieffen Plan*, 149–150.

34. None of the authors who had access to the documents prior to 1945 mentioned any major changes in these years. The evidence, therefore, is indirect, but it can be accepted unless further research indicates otherwise. The documents in Ehlert et al., *Schlieffen Plan*, shed no light on deployment areas.

35. Ehlert et al., *Schlieffen Plan*, 349–352.

36. The French substantially strengthened these fortifications beginning in 1895.

37. Köpke (1845–1918), a son of the director of the *Ritterakademie* in Brandenburg, was a veteran of 1866 and 1870–1871 and a graduate of the War Academy. He alternated between duties on the central General Staff, unit command positions (company, battalion, regiment, brigade, division), and General Staff officer in the units (*Truppengeneralstab*). He served as *Oberquartiermeister* for two years (April 1895 to June 1897) and then commanded a brigade and a division. He retired in 1901 as a Generalleutnant. See Kurt von Priesdorff, *Soldatsches Führertum*, 10 vols. (Hamburg: Hanseatische Verlagsanstalt, 1936–1942), 10:60–62. He was also known for his efforts to improve the foot artillery, even though he had always been an infantry officer.

38. Dieckmann, "Der Schlieffenplan," 105–106.

39. Zuber argues that the first concept of marching into Belgium is found in the *Aufmarsch* plan of 1899–1900. He apparently overlooked this part of the Dieckmann manuscript. See Zuber, "Der Mythos vom Schlieffenplan," in Ehlert et al., *Der Schlieffenplan*, 76–77.

40. The following discussion of the memorandum, unless otherwise noted, is based on Dieckmann, "Der Schlieffenplan," 114–119.

41. Ehlert et al., *Schlieffen Plan*, 354–359.

42. Dieckmann, "Der Schlieffenplan," 118–124.

43. The Dieckmann manuscript gives the eastern figure as twenty divisions. The surviving deployment plan in Ehlert et al., *Schlieffen Plan*, 359, has eight corps (sixteen divisions) in the east.

44. Again, the numbers in Ehlert et al., *Schlieffen Plan*, 356–359, are slightly different from those of Dieckmann.

45. Dieckmann, "Der Schlieffenplan," 158.

46. See Stig Förster, *Der doppelte Militärismus: Die deutsche Heeresrüstungspolitik zwischen Status-Quo-Sicherung und Aggression 1890–1913* (Stuttgart: Franz Steiner Verlag, 1985), 97–108, 114–115.

47. Dieckmann, "Der Schlieffenplan," 170. On French plans in 1898–1904, see Zuber, *Inventing the Schlieffen Plan*, 159–160.

48. Dieckmann, "Der Schlieffenplan," 171.

49. Ibid., 172–173. At that time, Italy was a member of the Triple Alliance. Plans from late in Moltke's tenure through Schlieffen's term as chief of the General Staff had vague references to Italy. Upon mobilization, Italy would supposedly send a force of five corps (ten divisions) to the Rhine to bolster the German left. How seriously this could be taken is a matter of conjecture, especially given the almost glacial pace of Italian mobilization in 1915, when speed was of the utmost importance. Richard L. DiNardo, *Germany and the Axis Powers: From Coalition to Collapse* (Lawrence: University Press of Kansas, 2005), 8; John Gooch, "Italy during the First World War," in *Military Effectiveness*, vol. 1, *The First World War*, ed. Allan R. Millett and Willimason Murray (Boston: Allen & Unwin, 1988), 166.

50. Dieckmann, "Der Schlieffenplan," 173–174.

51. The 1898 memorandum abandoned the idea of the previous year that Third and Fourth Armies should attack the line of French forts between Toul and Verdun.

52. Dieckmann, "Der Schlieffenplan," 169, 176–177. Boetticher, "Der Lehrmeister des neuzeitlichen Krieges," 266, has a diagram superimposed on a map of the western front.

53. Dieckmann, "Der Schlieffenplan," 177. Boetticher, "Der Lehrmeister des neuzeitlichen Krieges," 265–266, who had an enormous influence on the standard versions of Schlieffen's evolving thought, ignores this deployment plan entirely. He discusses only the one-front case and suggests in his diagram (266) that the right-wing advance was much farther north than was actually the case. Boettticher, of course, was trying to reinforce the pro-Schlieffen legend.

54. Ehlert et al., *Der Schlieffenplan*, 400, reprints Boetticher's sketch. The sketch was not included in the English translation.

55. Dieckmann, "Der Schlieffenplan," 157–158; Boetticher, "Der Lehrmeister des neuzeitlichen Krieges," 265–267.

56. Ehlert et al., *Schlieffen Plan*, 368–369.

57. It is conceivable that Boetticher used this, the second plan for 1899–1900, but his deployed strength for the individual armies is not consistent with the October deployment concept.

58. Dieckmann, "Der Schlieffenplan," 180.

59. Ibid., 185.

60. Ibid., 199–201.

61. Hans Hartwig von Beseler (born 1850, ennobled in 1904) was an engineer officer and a career General Staffer. His exalted position was indicated by both

his position on the General Staff and his command of an infantry regiment and an infantry division. As chief of the Engineer and Pioneer Corps (1905–1910), he was a general of infantry. Some expected him to succeed Schlieffen as chief of the General Staff. He retired in 1911. See Zuber, *Inventing the Schlieffen Plan*, 163–164.

62. Ehlert et al., *Schlieffen Plan*, 377–383. The Dieckmann text (199) states that the Schlieffen memorandum discussed above provides the basis for an evaluation (*Beurteilung*) of case II's western deployment, but it does not argue that the memorandum was actually the basis of the deployment plan. On the contrary, the memorandum assumed that this deployment would already be in effect.

63. Dieckmann, "Der Schlieffenplan," 195.

64. Ibid., 194–198, has many details.

65. Two field armies with five or six active corps were to deploy on the southern frontiers of the provinces of West and East Prussia behind the line Thorn-Strassburg-Lautenburg-Rudzanny. Two other field armies with nine active corps were to deploy on the eastern frontier of East Prussia behind the line Arys-Orlowen-Darkehmen-Stallupönen-Pilkallen-Schmolleningken. See Dieckmann, "Der Schlieffenplan," 199. Ehlert et al., *Schlieffen Plan*, 383, varies slightly from Dieckmann's account.

66. The original Dieckmann text (199) stated that the 1899 memorandum was an evaluation (*Beurteilung*) of the western deployment for case II. He later struck this out and inserted the word *Bearbeitung* to support the argument that the memorandum was used to prepare the deployment plan. The documents in Ehlert et al., *Schlieffen Plan*, are silent on the western forces for case II.

67. Dieckmann, "Der Schlieffenplan," 203ff.

68. Ehlert et al., *Schlieffen Plan*, 385.

69. Count Alfred von Schlieffen, *Dienstschriften des Chefs des Generalstabes der Armee Generalfeldmarschalls Graf von Schlieffen*, ed. General Staff, 2 vols. (Berlin: E. S. Mittler, 1937–1938), 2:177. This very important point is not clear from the Foley translation, which reproduces only Schlieffen's closing remarks. See *Alfred von Schlieffen's Military Writings*, ed. and trans. Robert T. Foley (London: Frank Cass, 2003), 51–60. Zuber, *Inventing the Schlieffen Plan*, 171–172, has a more precise account of this portion of the staff ride.

70. Dieckmann, "Der Schlieffenplan," 204–205.

71. Ehlert et al., *Schlieffen Plan*, 384–390; Dieckmann, "Der Schlieffenplan," 206.

72. Dieckmann, "Der Schlieffenplan," 206.

73. The text in Ehlert et al., *Schlieffen Plan*, is based only on maps for each case. Dieckmann apparently had more information available.

74. Dieckmann, "Der Schlieffenplan," 210.

75. Ibid., 207–209. Dieckmann relied on unspecified documents beyond the deployment plan, possibly on a 1902 Schlieffen memorandum.

76. Boetticher, "Der Lehrmeister des neuzeitlichen Krieges," 264; Dieckmann, "Der Schlieffenplan," 207–208.

77. Dieckmann, "Der Schlieffenplan," 207–210. According to Dieckmann (210–211), the assumption that the French would invade Belgium and Luxem-

bourg might have been based on ongoing discussions of an Anglo-German alliance, but this lacks a documentary base.

78. Boetticher, it should be noted, cites the study as evidence that Schlieffen exhausted all alternatives to the massive movement through Belgium and Luxembourg. Zuber, *Inventing the Schlieffen Plan*, 177–181, has a full account based on archival material.

79. Dieckmann, "Der Schlieffenplan," 211–212. The very sketchy information, based on maps alone, in Ehlert et al., *Schlieffen Plan*, 391–392, provides little assistance.

80. Dieckmann, "Der Schlieffenplan," 212–213.

81. Ibid.

82. Ehlert et al., *Schlieffen Plan*, 403.

83. Dieckmann, "Der Schlieffenplan," 216–217.

84. Ibid., 215–216. It should also be noted that many of Schlieffen's staff rides had only a limited relationship to the annual deployment plans.

85. Zuber, *Inventing the Schlieffen Plan*, 189–190, discusses the question without arriving at a firm conclusion.

86. Ehlert et al., *Schlieffen Plan*, 411–413; Eugen Zoellner, *Schlieffens Vermächtnis* (Berlin: E. S. Mittler, 1938), 43–44.

87. Ritter, *Schlieffen Plan*, 42.

88. Gross, "There Was a Schlieffen Plan," 109.

89. Zoellner, *Schlieffens Vermächtnis*, 43.

90. According to Zoellner's sketch (ibid., 44), part of the French left wing was surrounded southeast of Namur in a limited double envelopment, even though the overall result on the German right was indecisive.

91. Ritter, *Schlieffen Plan*, 44–45, based on Zoellner, concludes that the staff ride was the basis for a radically new deployment in 1905.

92. Ritter, *Schlieffen Plan*, 45.

93. Ehlert et al., *Schlieffen Plan*, 416–423.

94. Boetticher, "Der Lehrmeister des neuzeitlichen Krieges," 267, included a sketch. Zoellner, *Schlieffens Vermächtnis*, 48, gave slightly different figures—fifty-two active and eighteen reserve divisions—and suggested a deployment of the right wing extending north to Wesel. Zoellner at this point was attempting to demonstrate similarities between the 1905–1906 mobilization plan and one variant of Schlieffen's tripartite last General Staff ride—a dubious proposition, as will be seen below.

95. Some of these are preserved in General Staff of the Army, ed., *Dienstschriften des Chefs des Generalstabes der Armee Generalfeldmarschalls Graf von Schlieffen*, 2 vols. (Berlin: E. S. Mittler, 1937–1938). Volume 1 has the tactical-strategic problems of 1891–1905, while volume 2 has the General Staff rides conducted in the east during those years. Some are now available in translation in Foley, *Schlieffen's Military Writings*. The western General Staff rides are available only in fragments, scattered throughout the Schlieffen literature. Zuber, *Inventing the Schlieffen Plan*, has pointed analyses of a number of these rides, based in part on new archival discoveries.

96. Ritter, *Schlieffen Plan*, 33, notes the lack of a direct connection with the war plan itself. For the methods of Schlieffen's General Staff rides, see Boetticher, "Der Lehrmeister des neuzeitlichen Krieges," 295–296. On the winter exercises, see Zoellner, *Schlieffens Vermächtnis*, 45–46. The kaiser participated from 1899 until 1904, with some of the same negative impacts displayed in the annual kaiser maneuvers. The winter exercises retained the name *Schlieffen-Aufgaben*, even after 1905.

97. Perhaps the harshest criticism of Schlieffen's use of these exercises to prove his concepts was made by General Hermann von François, *Marneschlacht und Tannenberg. Betrachtungen zur Deutschen Kriegführung der ersten sechs Kriegswochen* (Berlin: August Scherl, 1920), 125–126.

98. See the memoirs of Martin Chales de Bealieu, BA/MA, N 187/3, 154. See the confirming analyses in Robert Foley, "The Schlieffen Plan," in Ehlert et al., *Schlieffen Plan*, 72–73, and Gross, "There Was a Schlieffen Plan," 100–101.

99. Foley, "Schlieffen Plan," 72.

100. Zoellner, *Schlieffens Vermächtnis*, 20–25. In 1894 the climactic battle occurred near Tannenberg. In 1898 Prittwitz's solution was to withdraw behind the Vistula (as he originally proposed in 1914), while Hindenburg, then chief of the General Staff of a corps, proposed an aggressive offensive solution. On the 1894 staff ride, see Schlieffen, *Dienstschriften*, 2:2–50; Foley, *Schlieffen's Military Writings*, 13–24, provides a translation of Schlieffen's closing remarks. See also Zuber, *Inventing the Schlieffen Plan*, 147–150.

101. Schlieffen, *Dienstschriften*, 2:52–104; Zuber, *Inventing the Schlieffen Plan*, 153–156.

102. Zoellner, *Schlieffens Vermächtnis*, 41–42.

103. Terence Zuber, "The Schlieffen Plan Reconsidered," *War in History* 6, 3 (1999): 281–282. Zoellner, *Schlieffens Vermächtnis*, 33–34, and Dieckmann, "Der Schlieffenplan," 204–205, discuss these staff rides. In 1901 the subsequent eastern staff ride reflected the transfer of these forces from the western to the eastern front. See Schlieffen, *Dienstschriften*, 2:177–178. The victory against France occurred on the twenty-third day of mobilization.

104. Count Helmuth von Moltke, *Erinnerungen, Briefe, Dokumente 1877–1916*, ed. Eliza von Moltke (Stuttgart: Der Kommende Tag Verlag, 1922), 292, gives June as the month of the "General Staff Ride West" but mentions only one of the two that are now known to have taken place. Moltke had been reassigned to the General Staff on 1 January 1904. It was on 18 June, during this staff ride, that Moltke noted the great differences between Schlieffen's views and his own.

105. This account is based on Schlieffen's closing remarks, "Übersicht der Operationen der 1. Grossen Generalstabsreise 1904 mit Anlagen," n.d., BA/MA, PH 3/659; and Zuber, "Schlieffen Plan Reconsidered," 285–288. Zoellner, *Schlieffens Vermächtnis*, 30, 42–44, discusses this staff ride, but only as prefiguring the 1905 memorandum. His account is extremely unreliable.

106. BA/MA, PH 3/661; Zuber, "Schlieffen Plan Reconsidered," 289–291.

107. Zoellner, *Schlieffens Vermächtnis*, 30, 42–44, may contain important distortions of these staff rides. He mentions only the first ride, describing the French

defeat between Strassburg and Metz, and fails to discuss the futility of the German right wing advancing through Belgium and Holland. In stressing the victory in Lorraine, Zoellner fails to mention the opposite and more catastrophic results of the second staff ride of 1904.

108. Ritter, *Schlieffen Plan*, 45. Ritter's argument is more plausible if one assumes that Schlieffen was already dogmatically committed to an extreme version of the great swing through Belgium as an end in itself. But as new evidence shows, and as Dieckmann's sketchy account suggests, this was not the case. Ritter's own conclusion, that the famous plan had its origins in the staff ride of 1904, also contradicts such an assumption.

109. Zoellner, *Schlieffens Vermächtnis*, 30. Zoellner, no defender of the younger Moltke and an advocate of Schlieffen's brilliance, blamed the failure of 1914 on poor execution rather than a fundamentally faulty plan.

110. Boetticher, "Der Lehrmeister des neuzeitlichen Krieges," 310. Gross, "There Was a Schlieffen Plan," 101–102, discusses this staff ride.

111. Boetticher, "Der Lehrmeister des neuzeitlichen Krieges," 311.

112. Gross, "There Was a Schlieffen Plan," 102. Ehlert et al., *Schlieffen Plan*, also includes printed copies of the exercise maps.

113. Ritter, *Schlieffen Plan*, 46. Zoellner, *Schlieffens Vermächtnis*, 48, used similar words. Zoellner faithfully described the three scenarios, but Ritter concentrated on the third, possibly because he wanted to view the staff ride exclusively to support his account of the origins of the 1905 memorandum. Zuber, *Inventing the Schlieffen Plan*, 203–206, 291–293, discusses the issue but seems unaware of Boetticher's account, cited above. Both Boetticher (1933) and Zoellner (1938) relied on archival sources. Zoellner does not cite Boetticher in his bibliography.

114. Zoellner, *Schlieffens Vermächtnis*, 50.

115. See Foerster's letter to Boetticher, 7 September 1932, BA/MA, N 323/150. Foerster conceded that in two cases in the staff ride Schlieffen acted entirely differently from the concepts in his great memorandum and entirely in accord with Moltke's later actions on many General Staff rides, which Foerster and the entire military literature had previously understood as the precise opposite of Schlieffen's staff rides and his 1905 memorandum. Foerster also conceded that the solution in case I (a major French attack in Lorraine) was a complete justification of Moltke's decision to strengthen the left wing in Lorraine.

116. Foerster to Boetticher, 7 September 1932. Foerster also criticized Hermann von Kuhl, who led the French party, for his postwar criticism of Moltke for doing precisely what Schlieffen had done in the staff ride.

117. The concluding discussion, titled "Kriegsspiel November/Dezember 1905. Schlussbesprechung (Secret), Berlin December 23, 1905," with a covering note indicating that it had been sent to the chiefs of the General Staffs of the army corps, is in BA/MA, PH 3/46. It is also available in the National Archives and Records Administration, Schlieffen Papers, roll 3, frame 32. A translation with an informative introduction is now available in Robert T. Foley, ed. and trans., "Schlieffen's Last Kriegsspiel," *War Studies Journal* 3 (1998): 117–133, 4 (1998): 97–115. It is also available in Foley, *Schlieffen's Military Writings*, 119–129. An earlier commentary

attracted little attention. See Ulrich Liss, "Graf Schlieffen's letztes Kriegsspiel," *Wehrwissenschaftliche Rundschau* 15, 3 (1965): 162–166. Bucholz, *Moltke, Schlieffen and Prussian War Planning*, 203–206, discusses the war game. Zuber's *Inventing the Schlieffen Plan*, 206–212, has maps and a pointed discussion.

118. Foley, "Schlieffen's Last Kriegsspiel," 113. Liss, "Graf Schlieffen's letztes Kriegsspiel," erred when he said that the final decision in the west was reached before the arrival of strong forces from East Prussia.

119. Foley, "Schlieffen's Last Kriegsspiel," 113–114.

120. Ibid., 99.

121. Ibid., 106.

122. Ibid., 129.

123. Ibid., 132.

124. Ibid. This section is on page 13 of the German original. I (DJH) changed the translation slightly.

125. Ibid., 132–133. The citations are from pages 14–15 of the original, and again, I (DJH) made slight alterations in the translation.

126. Ritter, *Schlieffen Plan*, 131–134, gives the background of the surviving documents. Zuber's views are in *Inventing the Schlieffen Plan*, 45–46. See also Foley, *Schlieffen's Military Writings*, 163–177. Much more information is now available on the origins, purposes, and fate of the memorandum, which itself has become the source of a new controversy. The best analyses are in Ehlert et al., *Schlieffen Plan*. As of this writing, there is no comparable overview in English, although the journal *War in History* has published the basic articles. Readers should consult this volume's bibliography for the works of Terence Zuber, Terence Holmes, Annika Mombauer, and Robert Foley.

127. See Zuber, *Inventing the Schlieffen Plan*, 32–33.

128. Friedrich von Boetticher, *Schlieffen* (Göttingen: Musterschmidt Verlag, 1957), 68, argued that Schlieffen's memorandum and his discussions with Holstein, approved by Bülow and the kaiser, foresaw the 1906–1907 deployment plan, but he does not claim that Schlieffen actually prepared the deployment based on the memorandum. Schlieffen retired on 1 January 1906, four months before the 1906–1907 deployment plan was finalized, and it is known that Moltke and those around him did not discuss these matters with Schlieffen after his retirement. Moltke in any case continued the usual practice of preparing an alternative eastern deployment until 1913. It is therefore unlikely that the 1905 memorandum was the basis of the 1906–1907 deployment plan and, given Moltke's reservations (discussed later), the likelihood of that decreased every year between 1906 and 1914. Boetticher was almost exclusively concerned with establishing the wisdom of the 1905 memorandum and discounted the alternatives prepared by Schlieffen in almost every year prior to his retirement.

129. The mobilization directive for Eighth Army in East Prussia for the 1914–1915 mobilization year can be found in Walter Elze, *Tannenberg. Das deutsche Heer von 1914, seine Grundzüge und deren Auswirkung im Sieg an der Ostfront* (Breslau: Ferdinand Hirt, 1928), 185–197. See also the documents in Ehlert et al., *Schlieffen Plan*.

130. Schlieffen's supporters, from Groener on, saw this planned advance west of Paris as proof of the bold genius of his plan, the abandonment of which doomed the enterprise to failure. Historians have used the advance to the west and south of Paris as proof of Schlieffen's single-minded folly.

131. Ritter, *Schlieffen Plan*, 140.

132. Ibid.

133. Among the many authors who have cited the memorandum, few have recognized this fundamental point. An exception is Gross, "There Was a Schlieffen Plan," 156–157. See also the articles by Terence Holmes listed in the bibliography.

134. Ritter, *Schlieffen Plan*, 147.

135. Map 5A is available in the Schlieffen microfilms and, much more clearly, in *Nachlass* Schlieffen, BA/MA, N 43/141.

136. Map 5 clearly shows the right wing's main turn to the south, east of Maubeuge, toward Hirson, even more distant from Paris. See Ritter, *Schlieffen Plan*, 190, and the archival sources cited above.

137. Zuber, "Schlieffen Plan Reconsidered," 266, 297–300.

138. Groener, *Das Testament des Grafen Schlieffen*, 196–197. Reichsarchiv, *Der Weltkrieg 1914 bis 1918*, 14 vols. (Berlin: E. S. Mittler, 1925–1944), 1:55, while joining those who regarded this as a sort of operational plan, also admitted that it was a program to expand the army. Ritter's defense of his view—that is, if the memorandum had been a program rather than a plan, it would not have been kept secret—is without merit. General Staff documents dealing with such matters were routinely kept from public scrutiny. Ritter, *Sword and Scepter*, 2:215–216.

139. Ritter's maps are thus not reproductions of the originals, as the text claims, but a new rendering on different maps, done in this case by the Wehrwissenschaftliche Abteilung of the Ministry of Defense. This explanation appears in the German edition but not in the English one.

140. The *Nachlass* in Freiburg has twelve maps; the microfilm has only eleven. The difference is the *Nachlass* map labeled 2A by the Bundesarchiv, titled "Advance to the French Frontier (22nd Day)." Unlike maps 1–5, this one does not have the printed or handwritten General Staff label.

141. Zuber, "Schlieffen Plan Reconsidered," 297–298, mentions this issue without developing it in detail.

142. One, labeled "Map 10," has the title "Anticipated French Deployment," with the date 1911 entered in pencil. The other, labeled "Map 12" by the archives, has the title "Fortress Map West. Deployment Study 1906. Count Schlieffen's Working Copy."

143. Foerster, "Hat es seine Schlieffen-Legende gegeben?" 2, note, in *Nachlass* Boetticher, BA/MA, N 121/34.

144. Schlieffen wrote that the forward attacking corps would "try, as in siege warfare, to come to grips with the enemy from position to position, day and night, advancing, digging in, advancing [again], digging in again, etc., using every means of modern science to dislodge the enemy behind its cover. The attack must never be allowed to come to a standstill as happened in the war in the Far East." See Ritter, *Schlieffen Plan*, 144.

145. The Reichsarchiv, one of the chief supporters of the pro-Schlieffen legend, admitted as much in volume 1 of its *Der Weltkrieg* series, when it stated that the completed *Aufmarsch* I for 1905 was the basis for the memorandum and that the real deployment plan for 1905 sent three active corps to the eastern front, along with seven *Landwehr* brigades and two cavalry divisions. In attempting to reconcile the memorandum's inclusion of more forces than were actually available, the Reichsarchiv argued that the memorandum was also a program for the expansion of the army and its mobilization. See Reichsarchiv, *Der Weltkrieg*, 1:55, text and n. 1.

146. General Staff des Feldheeres, Kriegsgeschichtliche Abteilung 1, No. 418, 29 March 1919, to General Gerhard Tappen, in *Nachlass* Tappen, BA/MA, N 56/2, 23.

147. See the thorough discussion in Gross, "There Was a Schlieffen Plan," 125–127.

148. President of the Reichsarchiv Hans Haeften, Nr. 9637B, to General Tappen, 21 July 1924, *Nachlass* Tappen, BA/MA, N 56/3, 272. This letter was a reply to Tappen's comments on the draft of volume 1 of the *Weltkrieg* series, which considered the early plans and campaign up to the end of August 1914. Haeften rejected Tappen's argument that such a unified order was unnecessary.

149. Mueller-Loebnitz to Tappen, 23 December 1920, in *Nachlass* Tappen, BA/MA, N 56/2, 139–140.

150. Boetticher, *Schlieffen*, 61.

CHAPTER SIX. GERMAN STRATEGIC PLANNING, 1906–1914

1. Schulenburg-Tressow, "Erlebnisse," *Nachlass* von der Schulenburg-Tressow, BA/MA, N 50/1, 18.

2. General Karl von Bülow, who commanded Second Army in 1914, seemed to be a candidate for chief when Schlieffen appointed him *Oberquartiermeister* in 1901, but his view of offensive warfare proved unacceptable to Schlieffen, and he returned to the field units. See Wilhelm Groener, *Lebenserinnerungen. Jugend, Generalstab, Weltkrieg*, ed. Friedrich *Freiherr* Hiller von Gaertringen (Göttingen: Vandenhoeck & Rupprecht, 1957), 90; Franz von Lenski, *Lern- und Lehrjahre in Front und Generalstab* (Berlin: Bernard & Graefe, 1939), 146. Bülow's uncritical biographer tried to blame the Military Cabinet for his failure to succeed Schlieffen, but this seems unlikely or, at best, an additional indication of Schlieffen's eventual lack of confidence in Bülow. The Military Cabinet, after all, placed Bülow in one of the most important positions in the army. See General Ludwig *Freiherr* von Gebsattel, *Generalfeldmarschall Karl von Bülow* (Munich: J. F. Lehmanns Verlag, 1929), 27–30.

3. Hugo Rochs, *Schlieffen* (Berlin: Vossische Buchhandlung, 1926), 87, records the relationship between Schlieffen and Goltz. Others in General Staff circles were also opposed to Goltz, who seemed to be something of a radical. See *Nachlass* Otto von Below, BA/MA, N 87/43, 512. On Goltz, see Dennis Showalter, "Goltz and Bernhardi: The Institutionalization of Originality in the Imperial German Army," *Defense Analysis* 3, 4 (1987): 305–318. The only biography is the brief study by Hermann Teske, *Colmar Freiherr von der Goltz. Ein Kämpfer für den*

militärischen Fortschritt (Göttingen: Musterschmidt, 1957). Goltz's memoirs are among the most interesting of his period; see *Denkwürdigkeiten*, ed. Friedrich *Freiherr* von der Goltz and Wolfgang Foerster (Berlin: E. S. Mittler, 1929). His books *The Nation in Arms* and *The Conduct of War*, cited frequently in earlier chapters, were important in their time.

4. He was also the author of the Beseler memorandum, cited in the Dieckmann manuscript; see chapter 5.

5. See Hans von Beseler, "Lebenserinnerungen," n.p., *Nachlass* Hans von Beseler, BA/MA, N 30/46. Beseler blamed General Hans von Plessen, one of Wilhelm's closest associates. See also Anonymous, *Das alte Heer, von einem Stabsoffizier* (Charlottenburg: Verlag der Weltbühne, 1920), 63–64, 88. Beseler apparently had substantial support within the General Staff. See *Nachlass* von Below, BA/MA, N 87/41, 410. Beseler later gained some notoriety for commanding the siege of Antwerp. Beseler also had a controversial tenure as the governor general of Poland after 1915. For details, see Jesse Kauffman, *Elusive Alliance: The German Occupation of Poland in World War I* (Cambridge, MA: Harvard University Press, 2015).

6. Friedrich von Boetticher, *Schlieffen* (Göttingen: Musterschmidt Verlag, 1957), 71–72, discusses the case of Paul von Hindenburg, who allegedly told Schlieffen he preferred to remain a corps commander. Arden Bucholz, *Moltke, Schlieffen and Prussian War Planning* (New York: Berg, 1991), 215–216, mentions these and other candidates, several of whom died prematurely. The most authoritative source on Moltke is now Annika Mombauer, *Helmuth von Moltke and the Origins of the First World War* (Cambridge: Cambridge University Press, 2001). See also Helmuth von Moltke, *Erinnerungen, Briefe, Dokumente, 1877–1916*, ed. Eliza von Moltke (Stuttgart: Der Kommende Tag Verlag, 1922).

7. *Nachlass* Martin Chales de Beaulieu, BA/MA, N 187/3, 157. See also Boetticher, *Schlieffen*, 72. Jehuda L. Wallach, *The Dogma of the Battle of Annihilation: The Theories of Clausewitz and Schlieffen and Their Impact on the German Conduct of Two World Wars* (1967; reprint, Westport, CT: Greenwood Press, 1986), 87, denies that Schlieffen and the army were surprised by the appointment.

8. Moltke, *Erinnerungen*, 306; Bucholz, *Moltke, Schlieffen and Prussian War Planning*, 215–216.

9. Bucholz concluded that Moltke was one of the emperor's close friends. See his *Moltke, Schlieffen and Prussian War Planning*, 216, and the literature cited therein. The definitive biography (if such a thing can exist) of the emperor concludes that although the two were friends, Moltke was not in Wilhelm's closest circles. See Lamar Cecil, *Wilhelm II*, 2 vols. (Chapel Hill: University of North Carolina Press, 1989, 1996), 2:196.

10. Groener's assertion in *Lebenserinnerungen* that Schlieffen thought Moltke unsuitable is an example of these secondhand renditions, as he never claimed to have heard Schlieffen address the subject. On Moltke as a scapegoat, see Robert T. Foley, "Preparing the German Army for the First World War: The Operational Ideas of Alfred von Schlieffen and Helmuth von Moltke the Younger," *War & Society* 22, 2 (October 2004): 2–3.

11. Friedrich von Bernhardi, *Denkwürdikeiten aus meinem Leben* (Berlin: E. S.

Mittler, 1927), 255; Karl Demeter, ed., "Politische Berichte Ludwig Freiherr von Gebsattels," *Preussische Jahrbücher* 231 (January–June 1933): 30–32; *Nachlass* Otto von Below, BA/MA, N 87/43, 512. Karl von Einem, *Erinnerungen eines Soldaten 1853–1933* (Leipzig: K. F. Koehler, 1933), 148, claimed he objected to Moltke's appointment, arguing instead for Beseler. Apparently, the chief of the Military Cabinet also wanted Beseler. See Karl von Einem's diary, 13 October 1914, *Nachlass* Karl von Einem, BA/MA, N 324/26, 124.

12. Wallach, *Dogma of the Battle of Annihilation*, 100–101. See also Hew Strachan, *The First World War*, vol. 1, *To Arms* (Oxford: Oxford University Press, 2001), 172.

13. Wallach refers to Moriz *Freiherr* von Lyncker as the chief who opposed Moltke's original appointment, but Lyncker was not chief of the Military Cabinet in 1906. Despite this, the attribution of that view to Lyncker seems valid. The chief at the time was Count Dietrich von Hülsen-Haeseler, who also opposed Moltke and did not hesitate to make this known in his usual blunt manner. See the newspaper article by Hans von Zwehl, "Vom Operationsplan des Grafen Schlieffen," *Kreuz-Zeitung*, 30 March 1921, available in *Nachlass* Peter Rassow, Bundesarchiv Koblenz, N 1128/101. Mombauer, *Moltke and Origins of the First World War*, 67–72, reviews the literature. Hülsen-Haeseler's opposition ended with his death on 14 November 1908 under bizarre circumstances. See Cecil, *Wilhelm II*, 2:138.

14. Josef *Graf* von Stürgkh, *Im deutschen Grossen Hauptquartier* (Leipzig: Paul List Verlag, 1921), 81–82, recorded the doubts of his German acquaintances. Stürgkh was the Austro-Hungarian representative in the German High Command in the first two years of the war. General Karl von Einem made a similar comment in his diary, 13 December 1914, *Nachlass* Einem, BA/MA, N 324/26, 124. This was, of course, written after the fact but before the postwar controversy emerged.

15. See the essay by Jens Heisterkampf, "Helmuth von Moltke—Ein Lebensskizze," in *Helmuth von Moltke 1848–1916. Dokumente zu seinem Leben und Wirken*, ed. Thomas Meyer, 2 vols. (Basel: Perseus Verlag, 1993), 25–41.

16. Goltz mentioned the negative evaluations in the press in a letter to his son, 9 January 1906, in *Denkwürdigkeiten*, 279. Goltz himself did not agree with the critics, arguing that Moltke was as yet a "blank page."

17. Holger Herwig, *The First World War: Germany and Austria-Hungary 1914–1918*, 2nd ed. (London: Arnold Bloomsbury, 2014), 46. The source, a memorandum written by Moltke's son, cites a letter from General von Mantey (undated). Adam Moltke wrote this memorandum in response to Walter Görlitz's book on the German General Staff (ca. 1952) and was thus far removed in time from Schlieffen's original report on his father. There is no reason to believe that Adam Moltke ever saw the document to which Mantey's letter referred. The document in question is in *Nachlass* Moltke, BA/MA, N 78/37, 2.

18. Moltke, *Erinnerungen*, 292, 296, 320. The staff ride in question took place in June 1904.

19. Ibid., 337–339.

20. Hahnke to former crown prince Wilhelm, 2 April 1922, and Hahnke to

retired general Hugo *Freiherr* von Freytag-Loringhoven, 5 May 1929, *Nachlass* von Hahnke, BA/MA, N 36/10, 70 and 7–10, respectively.

21. Mombauer, *Moltke and Origins of the First World War*, 98–99.

22. Wilhelm Groener, *Der Feldherr wider Willen. Operative Studien über den Weltkrieg*, 2nd ed. (Berlin: E. S. Mittler, 1931), xiii; Boetticher, *Schlieffen*, 89.

23. Moltke's views on how to conduct a western campaign differed greatly from the postwar accounts of these officers, but whether his views were radically different from Schlieffen's concepts is another matter, considered later. See also Foley, "Preparing the German Army for the First World War," 3–4.

24. For Hülsen-Haeseler's description of Moltke as a religious dreamer, see Count Bogdan von Hutten-Czapski, *Sechzig Jahre Politik und Gesellschaft*, 2 vols. (Berlin: E. S. Mittler, 1936), 2:410. Moltke's religious views can be sampled in his *Erinnerungen*, 244–245, 282–283. His comments on hearing Stoecker are in ibid., 101–102. His views on the harmful effects of modern science are in ibid., 45. The best summary of his health issues and the influence of Steiner is in Bucholz, *Moltke, Schlieffen and Prussian War Planning*, 218–222. The frequently overlooked commentary of his doctor is in August Hermann, "Die Erkränkung des Generalobersten Helmuth von Moltke," *Militär-Wochenblatt* 111 (1926): cols. 331–335. Hermann reported that Moltke had serious heart and circulation problems that worsened after 1912. After his death, Moltke's widow vehemently denied all this. See Moltke, *Erinnerungen*, ix–x.

25. A strident critique of Moltke can be found in the impressive article by Annika Mombauer, "A Reluctant Military Leader? Helmuth von Moltke and the July Crisis of 1914," *War in History* 6, 4 (1999): 417–446, and her subsequent book, *Moltke and Origins of the First World War.*

26. Bucholz, *Moltke, Schlieffen and Prussian War Planning*, 223.

27. Wallach, *Dogma of the Battle of Annihilation*, 99–100, cites representative examples. Ernst von Eisenhart Rothe, *Im Banne der Persönlichkeit. Aus der Lebenserinnerunen des Generals der Infanterie a. D. E. von Eisenhart Rothe* (Berlin: Verlag Oskar Franz Hübner, 1931), 46–48, cites a case of vacillation from a prewar kaiser maneuver.

28. According to Wallach, *Dogma of the Battle of Annihilation*, 87–88, the allegation of Moltke's reluctance to become chief was a lie promoted by Groener and Hahnke. Most accounts, however, agree on his initial reluctance. See Moltke's own letter of 29 January 1905 in *Erinnerungen*, 307–310. Wolfgang Foerster, *Aus der Gedankenwerkstatt des Deutschen Generalstabes* (Berlin: E. S. Mittler, 1931), who had access to sources that are no longer available, concluded that Groener's argument was too extreme but that it had a certain basis in Moltke's own writings. On the problems of using Moltke's limited remaining papers, see Jehuda L. Wallach, *Das Dogma der Vernichtungsschlacht: die Lehren von Clausewitz und Schlieffen und ihre Wirkungen in zwei Weltkriegen* (Frankfurt: Bernard & Graefe, 1967), 130, n. 4, which contains information not available in the English edition. Stig Förster also reaches a middle position in his "Der deutsche Generalstab und die Illusion der kurzen Krieges 1871–1914. Metakritik eines Mythos," *Militärgeschichtliche Mitteilungen* 54, 1 (1995): 83. The unpublished memoirs of Count Friedrich

von der Schulenburg-Tressow, written in 1920 before the publication of Moltke's memoirs and Groener's book, indicate prior knowledge of Moltke's self-doubts. See Schulenburg-Tressow, "Erlebnisse," *Nachlass* Schulenburg-Tressow, BA/MA, N 57/1, 18.

29. See the later discussion of Moltke's accomplishments.

30. His uncle was nearly seventy when the Franco-Prussian War began in 1870. Many Prussian generals were older than is now fashionable for senior officers.

31. Lenski, *Lern- und Lehrjahre*, 136, contains the praise of one of Moltke's subordinates in the Guards Corps.

32. A representative example can be found in Paul Klette, "Erlebnisse und Gedanken aus dem Weltkrieg 1914–1918," *Nachlass* Paul Klette, BA/MA, N 201/1, 2–3. Hugo *Freiherr* von Freytag-Loringhoven, though less critical, also cited Moltke's lack of preparation for his position; see his *Menschen und Dinge wie ich sie in meinem Leben sahen* (Berlin: E. S. Mittler, 1923), 135. Groener made this part of the image-shaping picture of Moltke in his *Der Feldherr wider Willen*, xiv.

33. Förster, "Der deutsche Generalstab," 84, 89, 93–95, makes a strong case that Moltke was deeply pessimistic about Germany's situation even in 1914 and regarded war as a sort of suicide. Bucholz, *Moltke, Schlieffen and Prussian War Planning*, 218–221, discusses Moltke's interest in Rudolf Steiner's theosophy, concluding that it contributed to his pessimism. This charge goes back to the most unreliable of sources on such questions, Erich Ludendorff; see his *Mein militärischer Werdegang* (Munich: Ludendorffs Verlag, 1935), 89–90. Bucholz has extended the argument, claiming a general mystical inclination among numerous German leaders in the last years before the war. The strongest denial of the harmful influence of Rudolf Steiner is in Meyer, *Helmuth von Moltke 1848–1916*, 1:14–15, 2:passim. There is a substantial amount of material on this, some dubious, in *Nachlass* Friedrich von Boetticher, BA/MA, N 323.

34. Lenski, *Lern- und Lehrjahre*, 374. This tale may have originated in Freytag-Loringhoven, *Menschen und Dinge*, 136–137.

35. Gerhard Tappen, *Bis zur Marne 1914. Beiträge zur Beurteilung der Kriegführung bis zum Abschluss der Marne-Schlacht*, 2nd ed. (Oldenburg: Gerhard Stalling, 1920), 8–9. Tappen was head of the Operations Section of the General Staff, but his account is compromised by his clear intention to defend himself and Moltke against the criticism that they had unnecessarily lost the 1914 campaign.

36. See the views of Stig Förster cited at note 33. Holger Herwig seemingly moved in this direction in his study of Germany and Austria-Hungary. In Herwig's insightful article "Imperial Germany," in *Knowing One's Enemies: Intelligence Assessment before the Two World Wars*, ed. Ernest R. May (Princeton, NJ: Princeton University Press, 1984), 87–88, 94–95, he described Moltke's increasing pessimism despite some outward signs of optimism in 1914. In his more recent *First World War*, 36–37, he cites Moltke's pessimistic memorandum of 28 July 1914.

37. Mombauer, "A Reluctant Military Leader?" The opposite interpretation, more convincing in our view, can be found in Förster, "Der deutsche Generalstab," 88–89.

38. Gerhard Ritter, *The Sword and the Scepter: The Problem of Militarism in Ger-

many, trans. Heinz Norden, 4 vols. (Coral Gables, FL: University of Miami Press, 1964–1973), 2:116–117, 219. On Moltke's pessimism, see Stig Förster, "Dreams and Nightmares: German Military Leadership and the Images of Future Warfare, 1871–1914," in *Anticipating Total War: The German and American Experiences 1871–1914*, ed. Manfred Boemke, Roger Chickering, and Stig Förster (Cambridge: Cambridge University Press, 1999), 363–364.

39. Groener's *Der Feldherr wider Willen* is a representative example. See also Hans Ritter, *Kritik des Weltkrieges. Das Erbe Moltkes and Schlieffens im grossen Kriege*, 2nd rev. ed. (Leipzig: K. F. Koehler, 1921), 83. Ritter, a General Staff officer, was probably the first writer to outline the Schlieffen Plan. His book, which first appeared in 1919, stated that Schlieffen's plan was to cut the French off from Paris, but he did not mention the concept of sending the right wing around the city. Ritter was one of the first to use the term the "Schlieffen Plan" (95). L. C. F. Turner, "The Significance of the Schlieffen Plan," in *The War Plans of the Great Powers, 1880–1914*, ed. Paul M. Kennedy (London: Allen & Unwin, 1979), 212, condemns the changes in the deployment, arguing that Moltke "effectively nullified his chances of victory." Gotthard Jäschke's impressive article "Zum Problem der Marne-Schlacht von 1914," *Historische Zeitschrift* 190 (1960): 314–316, argues that Moltke's career left him poorly prepared for his position.

40. See Herwig, *First World War*, 44. John Maurer, *The Outbreak of the First World War: Strategic Planning, Crisis Decision-Making and Deterrence Failure* (Westport, CT: Praeger, 1995), 37, has a less favorable view of Moltke's intellectual gifts, primarily because, unlike Schlieffen, Scharnhorst, the elder Moltke, and Clausewitz, he did not write about military history or theory.

41. Martin Kitchen, *The German Officer Corps, 1890–1918* (Oxford: Clarendon Press, 1968), 4, comments on Moltke's unsuitable background, relying primarily on Boetticher, *Schlieffen*, 72. See also Groener, *Lebenserinnrungen*, 91–92. Lenski, *Lern- und Lehrjahre*, 370, notes that Moltke never served in General Staff positions at the division and corps level and therefore lacked the "correct preparation" as a younger officer.

42. Bucholz, *Moltke, Schlieffen and Prussian War Planning*, 242–243, relying on Hermann von Staabs, *Aufmarsch nach zwei Fronten. Auf Grund der Operationspläne von 1871–1914* (Berlin: E. S. Mittler, 1925), 35. Staabs was actually referring only to Moltke's lack of detailed knowledge of the railway movement plan when he returned to the General Staff in 1906, not to his lack of confidence in it in 1908.

43. Foley, "Preparing the German Army for the First World War," 1–25.

44. Strachan, *First World War*, 1:178–179.

45. Terence Zuber's pioneering "The Schlieffen Plan Reconsidered," *War in History* 6, 3 (1999): 262–305, opened a new phase of the discussion, since he convincingly denies both assumptions. He expanded this discussion in *Inventing the Schlieffen Plan: German War Planning, 1871–1914* (Oxford: Oxford University Press, 2002).

46. Gunther Rothenberg, for example, argued that Moltke made such significant changes that the 1914 plan should be regarded as his, not Schlieffen's. See his "Moltke, Schlieffen and the Doctrine of Strategic Envelopment," in *Makers of*

Modern Strategy from Machiavelli to the Nuclear Age, ed. Peter Paret (Princeton, NJ: Princeton University Press, 1986), 322–323.

47. See Foley, "Preparing the German Army for the First World War."

48. Ibid., 17–18, regards this as the greatest difference between Schlieffen and the younger Moltke.

49. Ibid. Foley makes a strong case for this, relying in part on newly discovered archival sources.

50. The following account is based on Moltke's concluding remarks, "Secret. Great General Staff Ride 1906," now available in BA/MA, PH 3/663. Zuber, *Inventing the Schlieffen Plan*, 224–228, has a slightly different interpretation.

51. Moltke, "Secret. Great General Staff Ride 1906," 1–4. The Germans intended for the right wing to reach the line Rocroi-Stenay by the twentieth day of mobilization. This meant a turning movement forty-three to forty-seven miles southwest of Namur and no advance at all in the Liege area. Two armies, Fourth and Fifth, were to remain in place east of Metz to await the expected French attack. One should remember that mobilization and deployment concluded on day thirteen, so that day twenty was only a week into the campaign.

52. See Ernst Kabisch, *Streitfragen des Weltkrieges 1914–1918* (Stuttgart: Bergers Literarisches Büro & Verlagsanstalt, 1924), 18–19. Kabisch was obviously familiar with the 1906 General Staff ride, but his account is quite misleading, especially with regard to Moltke's thinking. See also Zuber, *Inventing the Schlieffen Plan*, 228.

53. Foerster, *Gedankenwerktstatt*, 38.

54. Ibid., 22–23. Schlieffen's words can also be interpreted as comparing this to a parade-ground exercise, as some historians have done, but the paraphrased quotation used the terms *Exerziermässigen* and *Bataillons-Exerzieren*, which can also refer to standard battlefield movements executed in a coordinated manner.

55. The document is "Grosse Generalstabsreise 1908," BA/MA, PH 3/664. Zuber, *Inventing the Schlieffen Plan*, 228–232, has maps and a detailed description.

56. The German player thus used Schlieffen's enveloping move, but only to create a strategic flank attack in northern France, not to envelop Paris. This was in accord with the 1905 memorandum's most extreme case—that of a French defensive strategy.

57. Zuber, *Inventing the Schlieffen Plan*, 16–18, 22.

58. For example, Moltke pointed out that the French commander had failed to bring a large part of his force, more than 200,000 men, into combat. He praised the German player for deploying all but about 13,000 into the combat areas.

59. See Foerster, *Gedankenwerkstatt*, 37–38, for examples of the sweeping criticisms of the younger Moltke's war games.

60. This section is based on Hans Ehlert, Hans, Michael Epkenhans, and Gerhard P. Gross, eds., *The Schlieffen Plan: International Perspectives on the German Strategy for World War I*, trans. David T. Zabecki (Lexington: University Press of Kentucky, 2014), 343, 424–435, unless otherwise noted.

61. This section based on ibid., 403, 426–431, unless otherwise noted.

62. This section based on ibid., 404, 432–442, unless otherwise noted.

63. This section based on ibid., 468, 467–477, unless otherwise noted.

64. Annika Mombauer, "German War Plans," in *War Planning 1914*, ed. Richard F. Hamilton and Holger H. Herwig (New York: Cambridge University Press, 2010), 63; Ehlert et al., *Schlieffen Plan*, 503. See also the discussion in the following chapter.

65. Reichsarchiv, *Der Weltkrieg, 1914 bis 1918*, 14 vols. (Berlin: E. S. Mittler, 1925–1944), 1:60–61; Groener, *Lebenserinnerungen*, 99. This has become the accepted version of how Schlieffen's plan was altered between 1906 and 1914.

66. Reichsarchiv, *Der Weltkrieg*, 1:62.

67. Gerhard Ritter, *The Schlieffen Plan: Critique of a Myth*, trans. Andrew Wilson and Eva Wilson (London: Oswald Wolf Publishers, 1958), 165–167. The memorandum is dated 1911, but Moltke probably wrote it much earlier than that. He also made marginal comments on the final draft, but these are of little significance beyond indicating his conviction that the French would probably take the offensive in Alsace-Lorraine.

68. "If, as may be expected, the French army remains on the defensive behind that front, there is no chance of quickly breaking through . . . the fortified frontier-line must be outflanked." Ritter, *Schlieffen Plan*, 165.

69. "If one wishes to engage the opponent in the open field, the fortified frontier line must be circumvented (*umgegangen werden*)." Ibid.

70. Gerhard Tappen wrote after the war that when he arrived in the General Staff's Operations Section in the fall of 1910, the plan for the coup at Liege was already in place. Moltke's memorandum mentions only that the reconnaissance was finished, not that the plan was ready. Of course, one must not assume too much from such tenuous indications. See Tappen to Mantey, 20 March 1933, *Nachlass* Tappen, BA/MA, N 56/5, 894. Robert Foley, *German Strategy and the Path to Verdun: Erich von Falkenhayn and the Development of Attrition, 1870–1916* (Cambridge: Cambridge University Press, 2005), 77–78, summarizes the changes.

71. Whether the right wing could have used more forces effectively is another question, discussed later.

72. It thus deprived the government of some flexibility, since the seizure of Liege had to be completed before the Belgian army was able to supplement the regular garrison units.

73. Förster, "Der deutsche Generalstab," 83–84; Heinz-Ludger Borchert, "Landkriegführung von Schlieffen bis Guderian," in *Deutsche Militärgeschichte*, ed. Militärgeschichtliches Forschungsamt, 6 vols. (Munich: Bernard & Graefe, 1964–1979), 6:471. The standard statement of the logistics issues in the right-wing concept is Martin Van Creveld, *Supplying War: Logistics from Wallenstein to Patton* (Cambridge: Cambridge University Press, 1977), 109–141.

74. Both Ritter, *Sword and the Scepter*, 2:266, and David Stevenson, *Cataclysm: The First World War as Political Tragedy* (New York: Basic Books, 2004), 19, deny that Moltke informed the government. However, he certainly informed Chancellor Bethmann-Hollweg of the broader intention of invading Belgium. See his memorandum to Bethmann-Hollweg, 21 December 1912, in Reichsarchiv, *Kriegsrüstung und Kriegswirtschaft. Anlage zum ersten Band* (Berlin: E. S. Mittler, 1930),

91, and Annika Mombauer, "Der Moltkeplan: Modifikation des Schlieffenplans bei gleichen Zielen?" in *Der Schlieffenplan. Analysen und Dokumente*, ed. Hans Ehlert et al. (Paderborn: Ferdinand Schöningh, 2006), 51–60.

75. Groener, *Lebenserinnerungen*, 99–101, has a summary, but the documentation is lost. Groener's account does not indicate whether he is referring to General Staff rides or war games conducted within the staff.

76. Ludendorff, *Mein militärischer Werdegang*, 94–95. See also Gerhard P. Gross, "There Was a Schlieffen Plan: New Sources on the History of German Military Planning," in Ehlert et al., *Schlieffen Plan*, 132.

77. Reichsarchiv, *Der Weltkrieg*, 1:186–187.

78. Ibid.

79. Ibid., 64–65.

80. Mombauer, "A Reluctant Military Leader?" argues that Moltke and his military colleagues aggressively pushed for war in 1914. This impressive article is an extension of the Fritz Fischer interpretation of Germany's responsibility for unleashing the First World War. The view of Moltke and of German officers in general should be balanced by Förster, "Der deutsche Generalstab," 61–95.

81. Indeed, he used almost those exact words in the so-called war council of 8 December 1912. The Fischer school interprets this as an indication of his eagerness for a preventive war in 1914, but it may have reflected fatalism rather than eagerness.

82. See Strachan, *First World War*, 1:1005–1006, on Moltke's recognition that a short war was unlikely.

83. Helmuth von Moltke, "Verhalten Deutschlands in einem Dreibundkrieg," in Walter Elze, *Tannenberg. Das deutsche Heer von 1914. Seine Grundzüge und deren Auswirkung im Sieg an der Ostfront* (Breslau: Ferdinand Hirt, 1928), 157–162. Mombauer, "A Reluctant Military Leader?" 443, errs in concluding that the document is no longer available.

84. Moltke, "Verhalten Deutschlands in einem Dreibundkrieg," 162.

85. See Stevenson, *Cataclysm*, 21.

86. Moltke to War Ministry, 28 January 1919, subject: Munitions-usw. Nachschub; 2 March 1911, subject: Förderung unserer Kampfmittel; 1 November 1912, subject: Muntionsausrüstung des Heeres, in Erich Ludendorff, *Urkunden der Obersten Heeresleitung über ihre Tätigkeit 1916/1918*, 3rd rev. ed. (Berlin: E. S. Mittler, 1922), 2–4, 5–6, 13–17. See also the archival sources cited by Förster, "Der deutsche Generalstab," 87.

87. Moltke, *Erinnerungen*, 308.

88. Lothar Burchardt, *Friedenswirtschaft und Kriegsvorsorge. Deutschlands wirtschaftliche Rüstungsbestrebungen vor 1914* (Boppard: Harald Boldt Verlag, 1962), 24–25.

89. Ibid., 25–26, discusses this intellectual dilemma facing Moltke.

90. Bucholz, *Moltke, Schlieffen and Prussian War Planning*, 224, ridicules Moltke's alleged predilection for clockwork in the kaiser maneuvers and his extreme nervousness over timely execution. His criticism would be more valid if directed at Wilhelm II.

91. Hermann von Kuhl, *Der deutsche Generalstab in Vorbereitung und Durchführung des Weltkrieges* (Berlin: E. S. Mittler, 1920), 148–149; Wolfgang Foerster, *Graf Schlieffen und der Weltkrieg*, 2nd ed. (Berlin: E. S. Mittler, 1925), 16; Lenski, *Lern- und Lehrjahre*, 370.

92. Foley, "Preparing the German Army for the First World War," makes this case convincingly.

93. Moltke had known the kaiser while in the Guards Corps and was certainly more effective in dealing with him than was Schlieffen. In 1909 the two had a disagreement over work assigned to junior General Staff officers, but this was an exception. See Moltke, *Erinnerungen*, 350–351. On his generally good relationship with Wilhelm, see Max van den Bergh, *Das deutsche Heer vor dem Weltkriege* (Berlin: Sanssouci Verlag, 1934), 197. See also see Dieter Storz, *Kriegsbild und Rüstung vor 1914. Europäisches Landstreitkräfte vor dem Ersten Weltkrieg* (Herford: E. S. Mittler, 1992), 192.

94. Even Groener, an inveterate critic of Moltke, recognized the importance of limiting the kaiser's interference in the maneuvers, although he thought Moltke may have gone too far. See Groener, *Lebenserinnerungen*, 92, and the comments of Ludendorff, *Mein militärischer Werdegang*, 42–43.

95. Eugen Zoellner, *Schlieffens Vermächtnis* (Berlin: E. S. Mittler, 1938), 10; Lothar Burchardt, "Operatives Denken und Planen von Schlieffen bis zur begin des Ersten Weltkrieges," in *Operatives Denken und Handeln in deutschen Streitkräften im 19. und 20. Jahrhundert*, ed. Militärgeschichtliches Forschungsamt (Bonn: E. S. Mittler, 1988), 64. Moltke had taken an interest in expanded training in frontal attacks as early as 1905, which earned the sharp criticism of the Schlieffen adherents. See Boetticher, *Schlieffen*, 78–79. On the larger question of modernization, see Storz, *Kriegsbild und Rüstung*, esp. 271–272. Bucholz, though generally critical of Moltke, recognizes his bureaucratic skills and his ability to deal with the difficult and impetuous emperor. But Bucholz's criticism that Moltke reduced the scope of war games played by young General Staff officers is largely unfounded, since his own source states that Moltke soon returned to the more expansive practices of Schlieffen. See Bucholz, *Moltke, Schlieffen and Prussian War Planning*, 224–225; Groener, *Lebenserinnerungen*, 93. Also note the very favorable and convincing evaluation of Moltke's training in Foley, "Preparing the German Army for the First World War."

96. Gordon H. Craig, "The Military Cohesion of the Austro-Hungarian Alliance of 1914–1918," in *War, Politics, and Diplomacy: Selected Essays*, ed. Gordon H. Craig (New York: Praeger, 1966), 48–49. A succinct summary can be found in Richard L. DiNardo and Daniel J. Hughes, "Germany and Coalition Warfare in the World Wars: A Comparative Study," *War in History* 8, 2 (2001): 166–169.

97. Burchardt, *Friedenswirtschaft und Kriegsvorsorge*, 27. Bucholz, *Moltke, Schlieffen and Prussian War Planning*, 224, also concludes that Moltke worked effectively with other government agencies.

98. Herwig, *First World War*, 51, concludes that Moltke maintained the basic tenets of the Schlieffen Plan: war against France first, rapid victory in a few weeks, and an invasion of Belgium. Bucholz, *Moltke, Schlieffen and Prussian War Planning*,

265, stresses the changes in basic concepts. Förster, "Der deutsche Generalstab," 83, says that Moltke was not the right man to prepare a radical new operational plan, although he did make important changes. Here, Förster is referring to the necessity of a rapid victory at Liege because of the decision not to invade Holland.

99. Reichsarchiv, *Der Weltkrieg*, 1:17–18, justifies Moltke's decision, based on his conviction that there could be no war against Russia alone and that the major German effort in any war would have to be against the French. The volume's other argument, that maintaining two plans was too difficult, seems baseless in view of the experience of previous years. The postwar Schlieffen school, for the most part, defended the decision. See Wilhelm Groener, *Das Testament des Grafen Schlieffen. Operative Studien über den Weltkrieg* (Berlin: E. S. Mittler, 1927), 110; Groener, *Lebenserinnerungen*, 102. See also Foerster, *Graf Schlieffen und der Weltkrieg*, 20–21; and Kabisch, *Streitfragen des Weltkrieges*, 52–53, who doubted the railway system's ability to support a major campaign in the east. Most historians agree that a rapid decision was not possible in the east. See Ritter, *Schlieffen Plan*, 21–32; Ritter, *Sword and the Scepter*, 2:202–204.

100. Compare the comments of Maurer, *Outbreak of the First World War*, 92–93. Maurer criticizes Moltke for regarding Schlieffen's plan as "Holy Writ—a re-evaluation from the God of War, with Schlieffen as his prophet."

101. Most accounts have presented the details of the mobilization in the context of the Schlieffen Plan, assuming that the army intended to execute the 1905 memorandum with Moltke's changes, discussed previously. Herwig, *First World War*, 58–62, has a clear account.

102. Zuber, *Inventing the Schlieffen Plan*, 254–255, argues that, contrary to popular belief, it was the Entente Powers, not the Germans, that had detailed war plans by 1914. One should note, however, that the French Plan XVII was a deployment plan, not a design for a particular strategic course of action. See Robert Doughty, "French Strategy in 1914: Joffre's Own," *Journal of Military History* 67, 2 (April 2003): 427–454. Sewell Tyng, *The Campaign of the Marne 1914* (New York: Longman, Green, 1935), 634, had made this point decades earlier, but with no effect.

103. Roger Chickering, *Imperial Germany and the Great War 1914–1918* (Cambridge: Cambridge University Press, 1998), 21. Holger Herwig, "Germany and the Short-War Illusion: Toward a New Interpretation," *Journal of Military History* 66, 2 (July 2002): 681–694, repeats this view in an otherwise exemplary and suggestive essay.

104. General Staff des Feldheeres, Kriegsgeschichtliche Abteilung 1, No. 418, 29 March 1919, *Nachlass* Tappen, BA/MA, N 56/2, 23; letter from President of Reichsarchiv (signed Haeften) to Tappen, Nr. 9637B, 21 July 1924, ibid., N 56/3, 272.

105. Reichsarchiv, *Der Weltkrieg*, 1:257. Instead, the Reichsarchiv cited a very general paragraph of the deployment instructions and the following statement of Tappen: "The operational goals of the High Command by the immediately forthcoming decisive battle [written on 20 August] were the simplest imaginable: The advance, as a unified undertaking, in a large-scale turning movement to the left around the pivot point Metz-Diedenhofen should lead to a great right-flank attack upon the enemy. Thereby the right wing acquired the single task of immediately

conducting a right flank attack, while the conduct of the inner armies must adjust to the attacks of the right wing."

106. Friedrich (Fritz) von Lossberg, chief of staff for XIII Army Corps, recorded that even as late as 15 August, he did not know whether his units would march to the west into France and Luxembourg or to the south into Lorraine. See Friedrich von Lossberg, *Meine Tätigkeit im Weltkriege* (Berlin: E. S. Mittler, 1939), 5.

107. See Moltke's discussion at the conclusion of the 1908 General Staff ride, in "Grosse Generalstabsreise 1908," BA/MA, PH 3/664. Tappen's comments are in his *Bis zur Marne*, 11.

108. For example, the instructions for training at the war schools made it clear that detailed plans were inappropriate because they could not extend with certainty beyond the first encounter with the main enemy forces. It went on to paraphrase Moltke's famous statement that no campaign could be planned and executed in detail in advance of actual events. See General Inspektion des Militär-Erziehungs und Bildungswesens (Prussia), *Leitfaden für den Unterricht in Taktik auf den Königlichen Kriegsschulen*, 17th ed. (Berlin: E. S. Mittler, 1912), 94.

109. Ritter, *Schlieffen Plan*, 68–69, n. 50. Ritter himself, in an almost universally overlooked passage, concluded that the younger Moltke had no operational plan beyond this memorandum (which in fact denied the possibility of a detailed plan).

110. Gotthard Jäschke, "'Schlieffenplan' und 'Marneschlacht,'" in *Militärgeschichte, Militärwissenschaft und Konfliktforschung*, ed. Dermot Bradley and Ulrich Marwedel (Osnabrück: Biblio Verlag, 1977), 196, n. 4, citing a letter from Tappen to Müller-Loebnitz, 19 November 1920.

111. According to an unpublished memorandum by Wolfgang Foerster, Schlieffen prepared no such detailed plan prior to the 1905 memorandum, the main purpose of which was to leave instructions for his successor, whose abilities he doubted. See Foerster, "Hat es eine Schlieffenplan-Legende gegeben?" in *Nachlass Gerhard Ritter*, BA/MA, N 1166/99a, 4.

112. See Hermann von Kuhl, *Der Marnefeldzug 1914* (Berlin: E. S. Mittler, 1921), 63–64, and his general discussion of the Schlieffen Plan on 15. See Kuhl's *Der Weltkrieg 1914–1918*, 2 vols. (Berlin: Vaterländischen Verlag E. A. Weller, 1930), 1:10, 34–35, for the later account.

113. Alexander von Kluck, *The March on Paris and the Battle of the Marne 1914* (London: Edward Arnold, 1920), 4.

114. Wolfgang Förster, "Hat es eine Schlieffenplan Legende gegeben?" unpublished paper, *Nachlass* Förster, BA/MA, N 121/34, 2.

115. Friedrich Immanuel, *Siegen und Niederlagen im Weltkriege. Kritische Betrachtungen* (Berlin: E. S. Mittler, 1919), 5, 9.

116. Zuber, *Inventing the Schlieffen Plan*, 259–260; Reichsarchiv, *Der Weltkrieg*, 1:73.

117. Zuber, *Inventing the Schlieffen Plan*, 262–263.

118. See the suggestive comments of Ulrich Liss, "Der Nachrichtendienst in den Grenzschlachten im Westen im August 1914," *Wehrwissenschaftliche Rundschau* 12, 3 (March 1962): 148. On 13 August the High Command had what it con-

sidered reliable information that very strong French forces, up to sixteen corps, had deployed to Lorraine. See Reichsarchiv, *Der Weltkrieg*, 1:183–184. This may have influenced the decision on where to send the *Ersatz* divisions.

119. On the availability of trains to move parts of these armies to the right flank, see Reichsarchiv, *Der Weltkrieg*, 1:64; Staabs, *Aufmarsch nach zwei Fronten*, 44.

120. The Reichsarchiv's official history, in a very brief treatment of Moltke's planning prior to 1914, concluded that he left no memoranda on his concept of operations that would explain the deployments of 1914. However true this might be, the authors overlooked the surviving war games and exercises that clearly laid out his thinking. See Reichsarchiv, *Der Weltkrieg*, 1:62–64.

121. Immediately after the onset of war in 1914, and later after his dismissal, Moltke damned Italy's behavior in the harshest terms. See Franz Baron Conrad von Hötzendorf, *Aus Meiner Dienstzeit 1906–1918*, 6th ed. (Vienna: Rikola Verlag, 1921–1925), 4:193–194; Moltke, *Erinnerungen*, 9.

122. Ritter, *Sword and the Scepter*, 2:239.

123. Dennis Showalter, *Tannenberg: Clash of Empires* (Hamden, CT: Archon Books, 1991), 154.

124. A senior army officer once explained to an audience, including myself (RLD), that simply deploying the forces in the run-up to Operation Desert Storm—a process not undertaken by the US Army on that scale since the Korean War—presented all manner of thorny problems, most notably with regard to logistics.

CHAPTER SEVEN. THE TEST OF 1914

1. A surviving placard, in this case from XVIII Army Corps, can be found in BA/MA, PH 6/I. The army had gradually shifted from individual letters to the use of placards and press announcements. See Hermann Rahne, *Mobilmachung. Militärische Mobilmachungsplanung und Technik im Preussen und im deutschen Reich von Mitte des 19. Jahrhunderts bis zum Zweiten Weltkrieg* (East Berlin: Militärverlag der deutschen demokratischen Republik, 1983), 120–121. As Rahne points out (ibid., 171), mobilization was part of the German Constitution, which made Prussian laws on mobilization valid for the entire empire.

2. The most noteworthy of the dozens of books that appeared in the first stage were Sidney B. Fay, *The Origins of the World War*, 2 vols. (New York: Macmillan, 1928, 1930); Bernadotte A. Schmitt, *The Coming of the War*, 2 vols. (New York: Charles Scribner's Sons, 1930); Luigi Albertini, *The Origins of the War of 1914*, trans. Isabella M. Massey, 3 vols. (reprint, New York: Enigma Books, 2005). Also of note was Pierre Renouvin, *The Immediate Origins of the War*, trans. Theodore C. Hume (Oxford: Oxford University Press, 1927). Many other writers made important contributions. Fay minimized Germany's responsibility, while Schmitt and Albertini stressed Germany's military and political actions as the primary culprits. Albertini's massive study had the most thorough documentary basis and the most balanced judgments.

3. Fritz Fischer, *Germany's Aims in the First World War* (New York: W. W. Norton, 1967). The original was *Griff nach der Weltmacht. Die Kriegszielpolitik des kaiserli-*

chen Deutschland 1914/18 (Düsseldorf: Droste, 1961). Fischer followed this with an even more pointed discussion of the prewar period in *Krieg der Illusionen. Die deutsche Politik von 1911 bis 1914*, 2nd ed. (Düsseldorf: Droste, 1969). His response to his critics was *World Power or Decline: The Controversy over Germany's Aims in the First World War*, trans. L. L. Farrar, Robert Kimber, and Rita Kimber (New York: W. W. Norton, 1974). The German edition was *Weltmacht oder Niedergang* (Frankfurt: Europäische Verlagsanstalt, 1965).

4. Annika Mombauer, *The Origins of the First World War: Controversies and Consensus* (London: Pearson Education, 2002), is currently the best place to begin an investigation of the war-guilt question. Though an avowed supporter of Fischer, Mombauer has produced a remarkably balanced account. The most recent scholar who is skeptical of Fischer's thesis is Alexander Watson, *Ring of Steel. Germany and Austria-Hungary in World War I: The People's War* (New York: Basic Books, 2014), 31.

5. Immanuel Geiss, "The Outbreak of the First World War and German War Aims," in *1914: The Coming of the First World War*, ed. Walter Lacqueur and George L. Mosse (New York: Harper, 1966), 75. This collection of essays is still one of the most instructive. Geiss's own works are also fundamental to the documentary base of the discussion; see Immanuel Geiss, ed., *Julikrise und Kriegsausbruch: Eine Dokumentensammlung*, 2 vols. (Hannover: Verlag für Literatur und Zeitgeschehen, 1963–1964), and *July 1914: The Outbreak of the First World War: Selected Documents* (New York: W. W. Norton, 1967).

6. A recent case for the army's role in pushing for war in 1914 is Annika Mombauer, *Helmuth von Moltke and the Origins of the First World War* (Cambridge: Cambridge University Press, 2001). The equivocal nature of even her argument is apparent in her discussion of the government's vacillation in the last days of July and the confusing welter of contradictory evidence (198–200). This should be balanced, however, by Terence Zuber's *Inventing the Schlieffen Plan: German War Planning, 1871–1914* (Oxford: Oxford University Press, 2002).

7. Hew Strachan, *The First World War*, vol. 1, *To Arms* (Oxford: Oxford University Press, 2001); David Stevenson, *Cataclysm: The First World War as Political Tragedy* (New York: Basic Books, 2004).

8. Stevenson, *Cataclysm*, 9.

9. See Strachan, *First World War*, 1:103–105, 110, 141, 151–162. Of the skeptics, the best study to date in English is Jeffrey Verhey, *The Spirit of 1914: Militarism, Myth, and Mobilization in Germany* (Cambridge: Cambridge University Press, 2000). For an overview of the opposing view, see Michael Epkenhans, "Neuere Forschungen zur Geschichte des Ersten Weltkrieges," *Archiv für Sozialgeschichte* 38 (1998): 458–487. The main scholarly monographs cited by Epkenhans are Benjamin Ziemann, *Front und Heimat. Ländliche Kriegserfahrungen im südlichen Bayern, 1914–1923* (Essen: Klartext Verlag, 1997); Christian Geinitz, *Kriegsfurcht und Kampfbereitschaft. Das Augusterlebnis in Freiburg* (Essen: Klartext Verlag, 1998); and Gerhard Hirschfeld, ed., *Kriegserfahrungen. Studien zur Sozial- und Mentalitätsgeschichte des Ersten Weltkrieges* (Essen: Klartext Verlag, 1997). For a nuanced intermediate position, see Watson, *Ring of Steel*, 73–78.

10. As previously discussed, reserve and *Landwehr* officers held the ranks of captain and below. All field-grade and higher officers were active officers or retired active officers called back to duty.

11. On the details of the mobilization process, see Holger H. Herwig, *The First World War: Germany and Austria-Hungary 1914–1918*, 2nd ed. (London: Arnold Bloomsbury, 2014), 57–59. Herwig relies on the very detailed presentation in Arden Bucholz, *Moltke, Schlieffen and Prussian War Planning* (New York: Berg, 1991), 300–302. Both overlook the critical role of the War Ministry, which was responsible for most of the details involved in implementing the plan, except for railway movements. See Hans von Zwehl, *Generalstabsdienst im Frieden und im Kriege* (Berlin: E. S. Mittler, 1923), 14–15.

12. Hermann von Staabs, *Aufmarsch nach zwei Fronten. Auf Grund der Operationspläne von 1871–1914* (Berlin: E. S. Mittler, 1925), 41–42. Gerhard Tappen, *Bis zur Marne 1914. Beiträge zur Beurtilung der Kriegführung bis zum Abschluss der Marne-Schlacht* (Oldenburg: Gerhard Stalling, 1920), points out that the deployment plan (as opposed to the mobilization plan, which sent the units by train to the frontiers) called for offensive movements in the west to begin on 18 August. Many units, particularly on the right flank, disembarked from the trains some distance from their jumping-off points and had to march to complete their mobilization and deployment. Staabs, *Aufmarsch nach zwei Fronten*, 37, has a useful railway map of the western deployment areas.

13. Still useful as an introduction to the complexities of mobilization is Erich Ludendorff, *Mein militärischer Werdegang* (Munich: Ludendorffs Verlag, 1935), 77–84. See also Dennis Showalter, *Instrument of War: The German Army 1914–1918* (New York: Osprey Publishing, 2016), 42–45.

14. Rahne, *Mobilmachung*, 114, 117, 122–123, 143; Watson, *Ring of Steel*, 73. These numbers by no means exhausted the available trained men. An additional 1.4 million men with some military training escaped the initial call to the colors. Most were no doubt accorded later opportunities.

15. Kriegsministerium, *D.V.E. 219. Mobilmachungsplan für das Deutsche Heer vom 9 Oktober 1913* (Berlin: Reichsdruckerei, 1913), 19. As noted in an earlier chapter, the active army corps were administrative as well as tactical units, and their administrative responsibilities under the Prussian Siege Law actually increased during wartime.

16. Wilhelm Groener, *Lebenserinnerungen. Jugend, Generalstab, Weltkrieg*, ed. Friedrich *Freiherr* Hiller von Gaertringen (Göttingen: Vandenhoeck & Rupprecht, 1957), 143. Groener's attitude was not cavalier, nor did he make the statement in jest. The General Staff had already included the loss of one bridge in its prewar exercises and had contingency plans ready.

17. Reichsarchiv, *Der Weltkrieg 1914 bis 1918*, 14 vols. (Berlin: E. S. Mittler, 1925–1944), 1:144–145. Staabs, *Aufmarsch nach zwei_Fronten*, 41, gives slightly different figures. For a favorable evaluation by a recent scholar who is generally critical of the army, see Mombauer, *Moltke and Origins of the First World War*, 227–228.

18. Wilhelm Deist, "Zur Institution des Militärbefehlhabers und Obermilitär-

befehlshabers im Ersten Weltkrieg," *Jahrbuch für die Geschichte Mittel-und Ost-deutschlands* 13–14 (1963): 229–230.

19. This was the result of an excessively optimistic message from the German ambassador in London, Lichnowsky, and it quickly passed.

20. Moltke feebly commented in his memoirs that this upset him very much and he never claimed to be the equal of the field marshal. See Helmuth von Moltke, *Erinnerungen, Briefe, Dokumente, 1877–1916*, ed. Eliza von Moltke (Stuttgart: Der Kommende Tag Verlag, 1922), 19–20. Herwig, *First World War*, 59, has a mainstream account. See also John H. Maurer, *The Outbreak of the First World War: Strategic Planning, Crisis Decision Making and Deterrence Failure* (Westport, CT: Praeger, 1995), 91–92.

21. Groener, *Lebenserinnerungen*, 145. Groener also wrote that he was opposed on strategic grounds. Rahne, *Mobilmachung*, cites a letter to Kuhl in which Groener admitted that the consequences could be catastrophic.

22. Staabs, *Aufmarsch nach zwei Fronten*, 55–61. See Maurice Pearton, *Diplomacy, War and Technology since 1830* (Lawrence: University Press of Kansas, 1984), 129. Maurer, *Outbreak of the First World War*, 93–94, reaches the same conclusion by comparing the circumstances with other large-scale railroad movements during the period.

23. See Martin Kitchen, *The Silent Dictatorship: The Politics of the German High Command under Hindenburg and Ludendorff, 1916–1918* (New York: Holmes & Meier, 1976), 45, and the sources cited therein. The term *OHL* apparently originated in October 1914. See Wilhelm Deist, *Militär und Innenpolitik im Weltkrieg 1914–1918*, 2 vols. (Düsseldorf: Droste Verlag, 1970), 1:lii. Hermann Cron, *Geschichte des Deutschen Heeres im Weltkriege 1914–1918* (1937; reprint, Osnabrück: Biblio Verlag, 1990), 5, has a list of members of the headquarters.

24. Lamar Cecil, *Wilhelm II*, vol. 2, *Emperor and Exile, 1900–1941* (Chapel Hill: University of North Carolina Press, 1996), 211. Holger Afflerbach, "Kaiser Wilhelm II as Supreme War Lord in the First World War," in *The Kaiser: New Research on Wilhelm II's Role in Imperial Germany*, ed. Annika Mombauer and Wilhelm Deist (Cambridge: Cambridge University Press, 2004), 195–216, summarizes the literature and offers the conclusions stated above. Typically, the position and term *Oberster Kriegsherr* had no constitutional foundation; it was a product of Prussian and German history.

25. Holger Afflerbach, "Wilhelm II as Supreme Warlord in the First World War," *War in History* 5, 4 (November 1998): 448.

26. Adolf Wild von Hohenborn, *Briefe und Aufzeichnungen des preussischen Generals als Kriegsministers und Truppenführer im Ersten Weltkrieg*, ed. Helmut Reichold (Boppard: Harald Boldt Verlag, 1986), 84.

27. Sewell Tyng, *The Campaign of the Marne 1914* (New York: Longman, Green, 1935), 36–37, has a useful introduction. Cron, *Geschichte des Deutschen Heeres*, 9–23, has more details.

28. A comprehensive summary of these changes, written by Wilhelm Nicolai after the war, can be found in BA/MA, PH 3/285.

29. Robert A. Doughty, "French Strategy in 1914: Joffre's Own," *Journal of Military History* 67, 2 (April 2003): 427–454; Robert A. Doughty, *Pyrrhic Victory: French Strategy and Operations in the Great War* (Cambridge, MA: Harvard University Press, 2005), 377–378. For an examination of Plan XVII and its relationship to French foreign policy, see Stefan Schmidt, "French Plan XVII: The Interdependence between Foreign Policy and Military Planning during the Final Years before the Outbreak of the Great War," in *The Schlieffen Plan,* ed. Hans Ehlert, Michael Epkenhans, and Gerhard P. Gross (Lexington: University Press of Kentucky, 2014), 209–246.

30. In addition to the recent work of Robert Doughty, one should consult Samuel R. Williamson Jr., "Joffre Reshapes French Strategy, 1911–1913," in *The War Plans of the Great Powers, 1888–1914,* ed. Paul Kennedy (London: Allen & Unwin, 1979), 133–154. Herwig, *First World War,* 65–68, is a succinct summary.

31. As noted in the previous chapter, the concept of the surprise attack on Liege dates to an unknown period prior to the autumn of 1910. See Tappen to Mantey, 20 March 1933, *Nachlass* Tappen, BA/MA, N 56/15, 894. Mombauer, *Moltke and Origins of the First World War,* 97–98, discusses this at length. John Keegan, *The First World War* (New York: Alfred A. Knopf, 1999), 77–78, discusses the forts around Liege.

32. Holger H. Herwig, *The Marne 1914: The Opening of World War I and the Battle that Changed the World* (New York: Random House, 2009), 114. See also Tyng, *Campaign of the Marne,* 53–59, 94. For similar conclusions, see C. R. M. F. Cruttwell's classic *A History of the Great War 1914–1918,* 2nd ed. (Chicago: Academy Publishers, 1992), 15. Those who wish to criticize Moltke have exaggerated the delay by ignoring the fact that the right wing was not in a position to move forward much earlier than it did. See Gotthard Jäschke, "'Schlieffenplan' und 'Marneschlacht,'" in *Militärgeschichte, Militärwissenschaft und Konfliktforschung,* ed. Dermot Bradley and Ulrich Marwedel (Osnabrück: Biblio Verlag, 1977), 190.

33. Hermann von Kuhl, *Der Marnefeldzug 1914* (Berlin: E. S. Mittler, 1921), 9. Tyng, *Campaign of the Marne,* 52, discusses the strength of the forts around Liege and has a full discussion of the battle. See also Count Peter Kielmansegg, *Deutschland und der Erste Weltkrieg* (Frankfurt: Akademische Verlagsgesellschaft Athenaion, 1968), 35. Reichsarchiv, *Der Weltkrieg,* 1:108–120, provides a full account. Ludendorff and General von Emmich, the nominal commander of the assault forces, received the first awards of the order of the *Pour le Merite* in the war.

34. See the analysis by Ulrich Liss, "Der Nachrichtendienst in den Grenzschlachten im Westen in August 1914," *Wehrwissenschaftliche Rundschau* 12, 3 (March 1962): 141–142, 144, 151. During the course of the campaign, however, the Germans' mounted and aerial reconnaissance was less successful on a consistent basis, as discussed later.

35. Hermann von Kuhl blamed Karl von Bülow, the Second Army commander, for the scope of this diversion. See his *Der Marnefeldzug,* 36. Wilhelm Müller-Loebnitz, *Die Führung im Marne-Feldzug 1914* (Berlin: E. S. Mittler, 1939), 16–17, convincingly argues that fewer forces would have sufficed and blames both Bülow and Moltke for this decision.

36. Between 24 and 26 August all the western field armies except Kluck's had

reported "complete" victories, "fleeing" opponents, and "decisively defeated" or "completely defeated" enemy forces. Tappen and Moltke thought the western campaign was already decided in Germany's favor by 25 August 25. See Müller-Loebnitz, *Die Führung im Marne-Feldzug*, 25; Cruttwell, *History of the Great War*, 26–27; Liss, "Der Nachrichtendienst in den Grenzschlachten," 156.

37. The Seventh Army commander was Colonel General Josias von Heeringen, the former war minister. In addition to not being of a royal house, Heeringen was junior to Crown Prince Rupprecht, having been promoted to Generaloberst on 27 January 1914.

38. Crown Prince Rupprecht of Bavaria, *In Treue Fest. Mein Kriegstagebuch*, ed. Eugen von Frauenholz, 3 vols. (Munich: Deutscher National Verlag, 1929), 3:31–34, prints much of the *Aufmarschanweisung* for Sixth Army. A specific order of 10 August formally enacted the subordination of Seventh Army. See Reichsarchiv, *Der Weltkrieg*, 1:184.

39. Rupprecht, *In Treue Fest*, 3:31–34. See also the specific comments by Hermann Mertz von Quirhiem, *Der Führerwille in Entstehung und Durchführung, erläutert an den Vorgängen beim Gemeinsamen Oberbefehl in den Reichslanden August–September 1914* (Oldenburg: Gerhard Stalling, 1932), 186–187. Mertz also prints a large portion of Sixth Army's deployment instructions. He was the General Staff operations officer of Sixth Army.

40. Mertz, *Der Führerwille*, 186–187.

41. Ibid., 30–32, prints extensive excerpts. Zuber's version, *Inventing the Schlieffen Plan*, 260–263, is based on a document in Krafft's *Nachlass* in Munich. The titles vary. It is possible that Zuber used Krafft's personal version of his estimate, while Mertz used a more formal report to the crown prince. They are clearly closely related.

42. Mertz, *Der Führerwille*, 30–31.

43. Zuber, *Inventing the Schlieffen Plan*, 263.

44. Mertz, *Der Führerwille*, 25–29, 63; Herwig, *Marne*, 91. Dieter Storz argues that while Rupprecht and Krafft were indeed seeking opportunities to go over to the offensive, they were still acting within the construct of the *OHL* directive under which they were operating. See Dieter Storz, "This Trench and Fortress Warfare Is Horrible! The Battles in Lorraine and the Vosges in the Summer of 1914," in Ehlert et al., *Schlieffen Plan*, 143–144.

45. Not surprisingly, in view of subsequent events, Rupprecht did not include Krafft's estimate among the documents attached to his war diary.

46. Mertz, *Der Führerwille*, 35, citing his contemporary notes at length.

47. Reichsarchiv, *Der Weltkrieg*, 1:183–184, 193–194. The High Command erroneously believed that as many as sixteen French corps might be massed for an attack south of Metz.

48. Rupprecht, *In Treue Fest*, 1:12, 18.

49. Mertz, *Der Führerwille*, 24–26. See also Jehuda L. Wallach, *The Dogma of the Battle of Annihilation: The Theories of Clausewitz and Schlieffen and Their Impact on the German Conduct of Two World Wars* (Westport, CT: Greenwood Press, 1986), 97. See also Storz, "This Trench and Fortress Warfare Is Horrible!" 153.

50. Reichsarchiv, *Der Weltkrieg*, 1:256, recounting conversations between Krafft von Dellmensingen and the General Staff's *Oberquartiermeister*, General Stein, and between Moltke and the crown prince. See also ibid., 210.

51. Ibid., 302.

52. On the Dommes mission, which was only generally similar to the later Hentsch visit to the right-flank armies in September, see Mertz, *Der Führerwille*, 67–72; Jürgen von Grone, "Wie es zur Marneschlacht 1914 kam," in *Helmuth von Moltke 1848–1916. Dokumente zu seinem Leben und Wirken*, ed. Thomas Meyer, 2 vols. (Basel: Perseus Verlag, 1993), 1:439–440. On Rupprecht's direct defiance, see his own account in *In Treue Fest*, 1:18–19, quotation on 19.

53. Ernst Buchfinck, "Der Meinungskampf um den Marnefeldzug," *Historische Zeitschrift* 152, 2 (1935): 291–292, endorsed this common view. More sympathetic is Storz, "This Trench and Fortress Warfare Is Horrible!" 150–153. Mertz von Quirheim, a close associate of the crown prince, denied such motives, explaining Rupprecht's actions by suggesting that other officers, encouraged by the opportunity to lead their soldiers in the attack, would have done the same thing. See Mertz, *Der Führerwille*, 75–76.

54. Reichsarchiv, *Der Weltkrieg*, 1:569–570. The Reichsarchiv apparently believed that the *Aufmarschanweisung* had instructed Sixth Army to be prepared to send forces to the right wing, though not necessarily as far as First Army. Mertz von Quirheim denied that this was in the deployment instructions, and no such statement is included in the selections printed in either his account or that of the crown prince. See also Zuber, *Inventing the Schlieffen Plan*, 269.

55. Rupprecht, *In Treue Fest*, 1:53–54; Reichsarchiv, *Der Weltkrieg*, 1:592–593. The crown prince, ever anxious to cover all his bets, tried to blame the entire counteroffensive in Lorraine on the High Command. For its part, the *OHL* sought to lay the blame at the feet of the Bavarians. See Storz, "This Trench and Fortress Warfare Is Horrible!" 168–169.

56. Rupprecht, *In Treue Fest*, 1:58, 77. The second officer was Major Max Bauer, who demanded an attack on the Nancy position south of Metz. Bauer seemed to be empowered with a *Vollmacht*, an authorization to issue orders on Moltke's authority, but as in the case of the infamous Hentsch mission, this was not completely clear. See Mertz, *Der Führerwille*, 149–151.

57. Sixth Army eventually transferred one of its *Ersatz* divisions to Fifth Army. See Reichsarchiv, *Der Weltkrieg*, 1:583–584. Later, Crown Prince Rupprecht's entire army moved to the north.

58. Ibid., 569–570.

59. Cruttwell, *History of the Great War*, 22, mentions the incident. See also Walter Görlitz, ed., *The Kaiser and His Court: The Diaries, Note Books and Letters of Admiral Georg Alexander von Müller, Chief of the Naval Cabinet 1914–1918*, trans. Mervyn Savill (New York: Harcourt, Brace & World, 1961), 28.

60. Clearly, Fourth and Fifth Armies should have remained on the defensive in order to fix the French forces as far east as Luxembourg. This would have made the turning movement shorter and more effective and might have rendered a subsequent counterattack more useful. War games and exercises had repeatedly

studied this possibility, but the crown prince of Germany, who had not participated, would not be restricted.

61. Reichsarchiv, *Der Weltkrieg*, 1:654–655. Note the bitter criticism of the Schlieffen school in Wilhelm Groener, *Das Testament des Grafen Schlieffen. Operative Studien über den Weltkrieg* (Berlin: E. S. Mittler, 1927), 17.

62. The lack of control by the German High Command was clear. Lacking clear and definite instructions, Fourth and Fifth Armies attacked in an uncoordinated, even premature manner. These episodes also allowed ample opportunity for Moltke's critics to emphasize his inability to execute the grand design. See Groener, *Das Testament des Grafen Schlieffen*, 17; Reichsarchiv, *Der Weltkrieg*, 1:654–655.

63. See John Horne and Alan Kramer, *German Atrocities, 1914: A History of Denial* (New Haven, CT: Yale University Press, 2001). Note the broader context, primarily the German colonial experience, in Isabel V. Hull, *Absolute Destruction: Military Culture and the Practices of War in Imperial Germany* (Ithaca, NY: Cornell University Press, 2005). Alexander Watson noted similar behavior by French troops in Alsace in his *Ring of Steel*, 124.

64. The General Staff had prepared a plan for attacking Namur before the war began. See Max von Gallwitz, *Meine Führertätigkeit im Weltkriege 1914/1916* (Berlin: E. S. Mittler, 1929), 4.

65. Cruttwell, *History of the Great War*, 20, and Tyng, *Campaign of the Marne*, 99–100, have summaries. The French continued to believe that only German cavalry units were moving north of the Maas. As late as 23 August, French intelligence continued to underestimate the strength of the German right wing. See Liss, "Der Nachrichtendienst in den Grenzschlachten," 276, 279.

66. First Army lost III Reserve Corps to the investment of Antwerp and part of IV Reserve Corps as a garrison at Brussels. Bülow's Second Army left a corps (VII Reserve) and one brigade of VII Corps to invest Maubeuge, which did not fall until 8 September 1914. See Tyng, *Campaign of the Marne*, 136.

67. Reichsarchiv, *Der Weltkrieg*, 1:258–259, examines the issue of command on the right flank. The kaiser's safety was not an important concern, but locating headquarters where its work could continue with minimal disturbance was. This was, however, secondary to the issue of effective communications. Coblenz, far to the rear by the standards of the day, had better communications than any comparable forward location could offer.

68. Reichsarchiv, *Der Weltkrieg*, 1:260. Of course, First Army objected to this. See Kuhl, *Der Marnefeldzug*, 27. Kielmansegg, *Deutschland und der Erste Weltkrieg*, 37, suggests that Moltke had greater confidence in Bülow than in Kluck.

69. Kuhl, *Der Marnefeldzug*, 45, 83.

70. Ludwig *Freiherr* von Gebsattel, *Generalfedmarschall Karl von Bülow* (Munich: J. F. Lehmanns Verlag, 1929), 52–55.

71. A general directive issued by Moltke on 20 August instructed First and Second Armies to attack enemy forces west of Namur in coordination with Third Army (in the Namur-Givet area) and expected the commanders to coordinate their efforts. See Reichsarchiv, *Der Weltkrieg*, 1:260–262.

72. Martin Van Creveld, *Supplying War: Logistics from Wallenstein to Patton* (Cambridge: Cambridge University Press, 1977), 128–134.

73. Ibid., 124–126, relying on Maximilian von Poseck, *The German Cavalry: 1914 in Belgium and France*, trans. Alexander C. Strecker et al. (Berlin: E. S. Mittler, 1923). Van Creveld's account seems to be more negative than its original source. See also David R. Dorondo, *Riders of the Apocalypse: German Cavalry and Modern Warfare, 1870–1945* (Annapolis, MD: Naval Institute Press, 2012), 54; Hans Martens and Ernst Zipfel, *Geschichte der Ulanen-Regiments von Schmidt (1. Pommersches) Nr. 4* (Berlin: Tradition Wilhelm Kolk, 1929), 202–203.

74. Theodor Jochim, *Die Operationen und rückwärtigen Verbindungen der deutschen 1. Armee in der Marneschlacht 1914* (Berlin: E. S. Mittler, 1933), 24–25. Poseck, *German Cavalry*, has numerous examples of the cavalry's lengthy movements and engagements. See also Dorondo, *Riders of the Apocalypse*, 53–55.

75. Hermann von Kuhl and Walter von Bergmann, *Movements and Supply of the German First Army during August and September, 1914: A Treatise* (Fort Leavenworth, KS: Command and General Staff School Press, 1929), 55.

76. Alexander von Kluck, *The March on Paris and the Battle of the Marne 1914* (London: Edward Arnold, 1920), 36–37, presents his views.

77. Tyng, *Campaign of the Marne*, 123–127, has a good summary. Herwig, *First World War*, 98, has a much harsher interpretation, concluding that Sir John French "panicked and withdrew from Mons, certain that disaster was inevitable." Cruttwell, *History of the Great War*, 21–22, concludes that Mons was indeed a significant defeat for the BEF. Kuhl blamed Bülow for the failure to turn the British flank and thus achieve a decisive victory over the French left flank. See Kuhl, *Der Marnefeldzug*, 40, 43–44, 47, 50, 76.

78. Reichsarchiv, *Der Weltkrieg*, 1:651–652, naturally blamed Moltke and Bülow for limiting Kluck's freedom of action. Strachan, *First World War*, 1:221, reaches a similar conclusion. Zuber, *Inventing the Schlieffen Plan*, 276, blames Kuhl rather than the First Army commander for failing to concentrate "his" (!) army against the British but concludes that First Army had no choice but to act as it did under the circumstances of 31 August.

79. Tyng, *Campaign of the Marne*, 139–144. Fought on the anniversary of the Battle of Crecy, Le Cateau doubled the total British losses to date, but German casualties were also substantial. Tyng judges Kluck harshly for failing to pursue energetically. Somewhat less critical is Herwig, *Marne*, 182–183.

80. Kluck, *March on Paris*, 56–57, blamed the lack of proper intelligence about the British on the fact that the main cavalry force, Marwitz's I Cavalry Corps, was under the command of Second Army rather than his First Army. Of course, he also faulted Bülow's judgment, with good reason. Bülow's biographer and apologist blamed Kluck's insistence on subordinating tactical considerations to operational movements, meaning a wider turning movement, and his lack of a sense of urgency. See Gebsattel, *Generalfeldmarschall Karl von Bülow*, 59–60.

81. All this is beyond the scope of this study. See Cruttwell, *History of the Great War*, for an introduction.

82. Tyng, *Campaign of the Marne*, 101–118, has a comprehensive and clear ac-

count of a battle that was fought with great confusion on both sides and only loosely controlled by both headquarters. The Germans proved superior in tactics but did not coordinate their actions sufficiently for a decisive victory over the stubborn French defense.

83. Ibid., 371–374, prints the directive, as does Reichsarchiv, *Der Weltkrieg*, 3:4–10, with some commentary interspersed. See also Kuhl, *Der Marnefeldzug*, 90–94.

84. Liss, "Der Nachrichtendienst in den Grenzschlachten," 158–159, argues that, at least at this point, the German High Command was not excessively optimistic about the course of events. Herwig, *Marne*, 170, strongly suggests that this was not the case.

85. Reichsarchiv, *Der Weltkrieg*, 4:3.

86. Müller-Loebnitz, *Die Führung im Marne-Feldzug*, 32–33, sees a complete abandonment of Schlieffen's concept of annihilation. Wolfgang Foerster, who is generally more balanced if steadfastly pro-Schlieffen, reaches the more moderate conclusion stated above. See his *Graf Schlieffen und der Weltkrieg*, 2nd ed. (Berlin: E. S. Mittler, 1925), 52–53.

87. This account based on Reichsarchiv, *Der Weltkrieg*, 3:4–10.

88. See chapters 5 and 6.

89. Kluck had concluded from captured orders and prisoner interrogations that the 25 August battles had dispersed the French territorial divisions on his right flank, and there was no longer any threat from that direction. See Reichsarchiv, *Der Weltkrieg*, 3:127.

90. Ibid., 126.

91. Kluck, *March on Paris*, 75–77. The paragraphs of the *OHL* directive are in Reichsarchiv, *Der Weltkrieg*, 3:4–11.

92. Reichsarchiv, *Der Weltkrieg*, 3:130, 166.

93. The Germans were in possession of an order taken from the captured chief of the General Staff of French II Corps that reinforced Kluck's belief that a southern thrust would produce a significant flanking attack. On the evening of 30 August Kluck received a message from Bülow that bolstered his belief that a great victory might be achieved by attacking the flanks and rear of what then appeared to be an enemy in full retreat. What was necessary to rescue Bülow now seemed even better—exploiting a victory to the fullest. See Reichsarchiv, *Der Weltkrieg*, 3:134, 137–139. Kuhl's thinking is evident in a memorandum of 1 September 1914. See ibid., 202–203; Kuhl, *Der Marnefeldzug*, 110.

94. Reichsarchiv, *Der Weltkrieg*, 3:126.

95. Ibid., 132–133; Jochim, *Operationen und Verbindungen der 1. Armee*, 7–8; Tyng, *Campaign of the Marne*, 162–165. Keegan's *First World War*, 106, criticizes Kluck based on the incorrect assumption that Moltke's 27 August directive ordered an advance across the Seine and west of Paris. The directive contained no such instructions. Kielmansegg, *Deutschland und der Erste Weltkrieg*, 39–40, correctly notes that the 30 August directive implied the opposite intent by converting First Army to a flank guard. Even if there had been a plan to send the mass of the right flank around Paris, that directive marked the end of any such idea, as Kielmansegg notes.

96. Reichsarchiv, *Der Weltkrieg*, 3:140. Kuhl's staff gave the message to the radio section at around 10:30 p.m. on 30 August. The operators took until 12:45 a.m. to put it in code and did not send it until 2:54 a.m.

97. Ibid., 220.

98. Tyng, *Campaign of the Marne*, 167–169; Reichsarchiv, *Der Weltkrieg*, 3:186–187.

99. Reichsarchiv, *Der Weltkrieg*, 3:237, explains this decision, which was greatly influenced by the results of aerial reconnaissance. Kuhl's own account can be found in *Der Marnefeldzug*, 121–124. He claimed that he informed the High Command but received no response.

100. Reichsarchiv, *Der Weltkrieg*, 3:243.

101. Herwig, *First World War*, 100. Herwig declines to pass judgment on the decision but rightly emphasizes First Army's diminished strength on 3 September.

102. See the comments of Foerster, *Graf Schlieffen und der Weltkrieg*, 59–60, comparing Kluck's daring move with those of Hindenburg and Ludendorff at Tannenberg: "May one criticize [Kluck] while one praises Hindenburg and Ludendorff?" This is also one of the principal themes in Robert M. Citino, *The German Way of War: From the Thirty Years' War to the Third Reich* (Lawrence: University Press of Kansas, 2005), 308–310.

103. The unit in question was IX Corps, commanded by General Quast. See Reichsarchiv, *Der Weltkrieg*, 3:235–237. Kuhl, *Der Marnefeldzug*, 114, praised Quast's action as an example of the proper use of subordinate initiative.

104. Tyng, *Campaign of the Marne*, 171–174.

105. See Reichsarchiv, *Der Weltkrieg*, 3:240–241. The risk here was not entirely different from Hindenburg's bold action at Tannenberg. Kuhl, *Der Marnefeldzug*, 110, cites a contemporary memorandum written as First Army crossed the Oise, recognizing the danger created by extending its flank to the south.

106. Kluck, *March on Paris*, 99, later complained of his lack of overall information. See also Tyng, *Campaign of the Marne*, 205.

107. Kluck, *March on Paris*, 94–96. Gotthard Jäschke, "Zum Probleme der Marne-Schlacht von 1914," *Historische Zeitschrift* 190 (1960): 330–331, is representative of the postwar criticism of Kluck's disobedience.

108. Reichsarchiv, *Der Weltkrieg*, 3:310, 4:22–23.

109. So it has been described many times. See Tyng, *Campaign of the Marne*, 204–206. Reichsarchiv, *Der Weltkrieg*, 3:307, notes the High Command's astonishment when it learned that Kluck's forces had crossed the Marne.

110. Reichsarchiv, *Der Weltkrieg*, 4:3–5, has the text.

111. The directive was therefore the official end of the great turning movement. See ibid., 128.

112. The directive did not reach First Army until about 7:00 a.m. on 6 September, twelve hours after it was sent. See Tyng, *Campaign of the Marne*, 206–207. For the overall situation as seen in Luxembourg and the field armies, see Cruttwell, *History of the Great War*, 27–29; Gebsattel, *Generalfeldmarschall Karl von Bülow*,

93–95. Gebsattel, of course, was trying to defend Bülow's actions and to blame most of the problems on Kluck.

113. The kaiser also inadvertently created confusion during a visit to Sixth Army headquarters. When asked about the transfer, he told Krafft von Dellmensingen that he knew nothing of the High Command's request for two army corps. Sixth Army attempted to use this to reverse the decision, but Tappen sent them a written order and included Seventh Army headquarters among those elements to be moved. See memorandum of Krafft von Dellmensingen in Rupprecht, *In Treue Fest*, 1:73–75, footnote.

114. Reichsarchiv, *Der Weltkrieg*, 4:130.

115. Ibid., 421.

116. Herwig, *First World War*, 101.

117. Keegan, *First World War*, 112–113. See also Tyng, *Campaign of the Marne*, 267.

118. Müller-Loebnitz, *Die Führung im Marne-Feldzug*, 58–59.

119. On the discussions and disagreements about this course of action and the resulting problems with Second Army, see Reichsarchiv, *Der Weltkrieg*, 4:84–85.

120. Ibid., 141–142, summarizes Kluck's outlook.

121. The Reichsarchiv (ibid.) was particularly critical of Moltke for leaving the armies to make their own decisions at this critical time. Poor communications were only part of the problem.

122. Jäschke, "Zum Problem der Marne-Schlacht," 337–338.

123. Ibid., 337. See also Reichsarchiv, *Der Weltkrieg*, 4:134–135.

124. The Reichsarchiv noted that this passive waiting while the army commanders conducted their battles weighed heavily on Moltke. See Reichsarchiv, *Der Weltkrieg*, 4:140. Nevertheless, Moltke was unable to devise a solution and seize control of the battle, let alone of the entire campaign.

125. See the comments of Tyng, *Campaign of the Marne*, 267. On Moltke's refusal to establish a forward command post, see Reichsarchiv, *Der Weltkrieg*, 4:129.

126. Reichsarchiv, *Der Weltkrieg*, 4:221–223, discusses the meeting, which is aptly summarized in Herwig, *First World War*, 103. See also Tyng, *Campaign of the Marne*, 322.

127. See Rupprecht, *In Treue Fest*, 1:103, diary entry of 8 September 1914.

128. *Nachlass* Tappen, BA/MA, N 56/5, 891–892, has a commentary by Tappen and Dommes for the newspaper *Deutscher Zeitung* in February 1933.

129. Tyng, *Campaign of the Marne*, 270, incorrectly states that Hentsch had been head of the Operations Section. He had been head of the Third Section, dealing primarily with France.

130. Hentsch was quite junior, considering the importance of the assignment. He had been promoted to major on 27 March 1909 and to lieutenant colonel shortly before the war. His last prewar assignment had been as chief of the Third Section (France), and he moved to the Intelligence Section upon mobilization. See Wilhelm Müller-Loebnitz, *Der Sendung des Oberstleutnants Hentsch am 8–10 September 1914. Auf Grund von Kriegsakten und persönliches Mitteilungen, bearbeitet*

(Berlin: E. S. Mittler, 1922), 13. Herwig, *Marne*, 270–277, carefully reconstructs Hentsch's tour.

131. During his first visit to Second Army on 6 September, Hentsch portrayed the overall situation in the "darkest colors." Hentsch foresaw dangers to the right flank, defeat of the Austrians, and so forth, suggesting that the war could not be won without four additional corps. He still believed in the possibility of Russian soldiers landing in Belgium and may have influenced Moltke to send the reconstituted Seventh Army there rather than to the right wing opposite Paris. See Reichsarchiv, *Der Weltkrieg*, 4:67–68, 130–131. Tappen, no ally of Hentsch on the question of the mission of 8–9 September, denied that Hentsch was excessively pessimistic. See his letter to the Reichsarchiv, 6 November 1934, *Nachlass* Tappen, BA/MA, N 56/5, 954. Bauer argued that Hentsch's intelligence reports always overestimated the enemy and that he increasingly became a pessimist (*Schwarzseher*). See Max Bauer, *Der grosse Krieg in Feld und Heimat. Erinnerungen und Betrachtungen* (Tübingen: Osiander'sche Buchhandlung, 1921), 36.

132. See Hermann von François, *Marneschlacht und Tannenberg. Betrachtungen zur Deutschen Kriegführung der ersten sechs Kriegswochen* (Berlin: August Scherl, 1920), 108–109.

133. Gerhard Tappen, in an essay written in 1934, said that Hentsch had no authority to order a retreat or a *Vollmacht* of any kind; he merely had the authority to coordinate the moves of First and Second Armies if a retreat were being conducted by the armies on their own authority. See his essay "Vor zwanzig Jahren. Generaloberst v. Moltke," *Nachlass* Tappen, BA/MA, N 56/5, 939–940. In his *Bis zur Marne*, 24–25, Tappen made much the same argument but also emphasized that during the meeting the High Command remained resolved not to order a retreat. According to the Reichsarchiv, *Der Weltkrieg*, 4:224, both Dommes and Tappen took this position during the army's official investigation in 1917.

134. Reichsarchiv, *Der Weltkrieg*, 4:226. Tappen later denied the possibility, raised by some, that Hentsch had a private conversation with Moltke before departing. See Tappen's letter to the Reichsarchiv, 6 November 1934, *Nachlass* Tappen, BA/MA, N 56/5, 956. However, the Reichsarchiv (*Der Weltkrieg*, 4:227) conceded the possibility, since the two may have been alone together for an intelligence briefing. As Müller-Loebnitz, *Die Führung im Marne-Feldzug*, 88–89, pointed out, neither Moltke nor Hentsch ever claimed they had a second, completely private conversation.

135. Reichsarchiv, *Der Weltkrieg*, 4:225, 227–228, 230. During the trip Hentsch complained bitterly to his companions that he had no written instructions.

136. Their transportation was provided by the Royal Volunteer Automobile Corps, one of the few times that organization found its way into the history books.

137. Reichsarchiv, *Der Weltkrieg*, 4:231–232, 233–234, relates the comments of Captain Hönig, who accompanied Hentsch from Luxembourg.

138. The Reichsarchiv relied primarily on the memorandum written by Hentsch on 15 September and the memories of the two captains who accompanied him. These three had a common *OHL* view of the conversations. Lieutenant Colonel Matthes, first General Staff officer of Second Army, disagreed in a mem-

orandum written immediately after Hentsch's visit and gave the more optimistic view of Bülow's statement noted earlier. Another General Staff officer with Second Army, Captain Thilo, later wrote that Bülow had described the strength of his units as "unbroken."

139. Herwig, *First World War*, 103, interprets all this to mean that Hentsch was shaken by Bülow's staff officers' suggestions that some units had been reduced to ashes (a term Hentsch made famous by using it to describe Second Army to the First Army staff). This seems unlikely on several grounds. Hentsch's own self-justifying report was the only near-contemporary source that supported this version. Another contemporary account, written by Lieutenant Colonel Matthes, indicated that Bülow did not believe his units were greatly weakened. Finally, Captain König, one of Hentsch's companions, later (1926) specifically denied that either Bülow or his staff had used this phrase.

140. Reichsarchiv, *Der Weltkrieg*, 4:233–242. On Bülow's lack of knowledge about Kluck's success on the Ourcq, see ibid., 201.

141. Ibid., 242, points out that Hentsch did not make the short trip to Fourth Army headquarters, where he could have spoken to Moltke using the very good telephone connections available there.

142. In response to Hentsch's repeated claim to have a *Vollmacht*, Second Army's staff proposed that Bülow demand a written confirmation from the High Command. The proud old general declined, remarking that if a retreat were necessary, he would assume full responsibility. See ibid., 243.

143. It was at this point that Moltke proposed a general withdrawal all along the front. The kaiser, accepting the contrary advice of Plessen, Lyncker, and Stein, declined until additional information was available. See ibid., 317–319.

144. Ibid., 243–246. Tyng, *Campaign of the Marne*, 271, 273–274, has a summary of events at Second Army headquarters.

145. Reichsarchiv, *Der Weltkrieg*, 4:255–257, discusses the automobile trip and the differing reactions of Hentsch's companions. Jochim, *Operationen und Verbindungen der 1. Armee*, 82, concluded that the apparent confusion Hentsch witnessed was normal for an army that was turning and moving so quickly, and if Hentsch had had more experience as a front officer, he would have understood this. See also Haeften, president of the Reichsarchiv, to Tappen, 23 January 1925, *Nachlass* Tappen, BA/MA, N 56/3, 310.

146. Reichsarchiv, *Der Weltkrieg*, 4:259. Nor did the Second Army staff create a written record. The Reichsarchiv thus had to use fragmentary accounts written years after the events. Some have concluded that Kluck was not at First Army headquarters during Hentsch's visit. Years later, however, the army's *Oberquartiermeister*, General Bergmann, insisted that Kluck had been present but did not wish to speak to Hentsch. Kluck, one should remember, was not a General Staff officer. See Bergmann's article "Noch einmal Marneschlacht," *Lübecker General-Anzeiger*, 12 February 1933, copy in *Nachlass* Bernhard Schwertfeger, BA/MA, N 1015/353, 32–33.

147. This discussion is based on Reichsarchiv, *Der Weltkrieg*, 4:258–266, unless otherwise noted. Kuhl was optimistic, since III and IX Corps had redeployed

and were enjoying success in striking the flank of the French offensive along the Ourcq. See ibid., 199–200.

148. Ibid., 264.

149. The word used, and ridiculed in some accounts, was *Schlacke*.

150. Kluck, *March on Paris*, 137. Hentsch was still present when Kuhl reported the decision to Kluck, so the latter could have demanded to speak with him. See Kuhl's article (a book review), "Die Schlacht an der Marne 1914," *Militär-Wochenblatt* 106, 8 (1921): col. 160.

151. Jochim, *Operationen und Verbindungen der 1. Armee*, 82–83, argues that such a radio capability was available at the time. The Reichsarchiv, *Der Weltkrieg*, 4:265, tried to gloss over this omission by stating that by then, neither Kuhl nor key persons at Second Army doubted the correctness of Hentsch's convincing arguments.

152. Kuhl, report on the Hentsch mission, verified by Colonel Bergmann, *Ober-quartiermeister* of First Army, entered at La Ferere-Milon, 10 September 1914. The document is attached to a letter, Reichsarchiv to Tappen, 23 December 192(?), in *Nachlass* Tappen, BA/MA, N 56/3, 303–309. The key sentence in Kuhl's note, probably written as an annex to the war diary, is: "He (Hentsch) maintained that this directive remains in force without regard to any other arriving communications. He has '*Vollmacht*.'" Kluck cited this memorandum in *March on Paris*, 137–138, from First Army files. By 1930, however, Kuhl argued in *Der Weltkrieg 1914–1918*, 2 vols. (Berlin: Vaterländischen Verlag E. A. Weller, 1930), 1:44–45, that Hentsch had exceeded his authority.

153. François, *Marneschlacht und Tannenberg*, 109–110.

154. Tyng, *Campaign of the Marne*, 322. See also an account of 13 July 1919 by Tappen, in High Command records now lost, attached to a letter from the Reichsarchiv to Tappen, 11 May 1920, *Nachlass* Tappen, BA/MA, N 56/2, 89.

155. See Tyng, *Campaign of the Marne*, 309–310. Such an order would have been inconsistent with what Hentsch had already approved. The crown prince may have invented this episode to burnish his own reputation.

156. Tyng, *Campaign of the Marne*, prints sections of the messages sent by First and Second Armies on the morning of 10 September 1914.

157. See Mombauer, *Moltke and Origins of the First World War*, 257–260. Mombauer's thoughtful discussion reaches a similar conclusion, though on slightly different grounds.

158. On Kuhl's possible exaggeration of his opposition to a retreat, see the correspondence between Gerhard Ritter and Hans Moeller, 11 May and 15 June 1959, *Nachlass* Gerhard Ritter, Bundesarchiv, N 1166/301.

159. Sections of Hentsch's report of 15 September 1914 were quoted in a letter from the Reichsarchiv to Tappen, 27 February 1920, *Nachlass* Tappen, BA/MA, N 56/2, 51–52. The excerpts of Moltke's comments are in the same letter. A copy of Hentsch's written report, with some portions missing, is in ibid., N 56/3, 303–308, attached to the letter Reichsarchiv Nr. 17470 to Tappen, 23 December 1924, signed by Haeften.

160. Chef der Generalstab des Feldheers, Nr. 2229, 24 May 1917, BA/MA, PH

3/60. The report, which obviously sought to end accusations against Hentsch, did not reach the conclusions given above.

161. This account is based on Reichsarchiv, *Der Weltkrieg*, 4:267–270.

162. Ibid., 448–452. Tappen, *Bis zur Marne*, 27–28, has a sympathetic account. As chief of the Operations Section, Tappen had a shared responsibility for these decisions, especially since he was with Moltke.

163. Reichsarchiv, *Der Weltkrieg*, 4:451, 456.

164. Ibid., 473–474, 483.

165. Tyng, *Campaign of the Marne*, 321–333, has the details and a harsh judgment on the Entente's cavalry. These developments can also be followed in Reichsarchiv, *Der Weltkrieg*, 4:486–507.

166. See Strachan, *First World War*, 1:260–261; Hubert C. Johnson, *Breakthrough: Tactics, Technology and the Search for Victory on the Western Front in World War I* (Novato, CA: Presidio, 1994), 48–50.

167. Colonel General Max von Prittwitz und Gaffron, usually shortened to "Prittwitz," was a General Staff officer and a graduate of the War Academy. He had participated in several prewar exercises studying how to defend East Prussia in roughly the same circumstances he faced in 1914.

168. Walter Elze, *Tannenberg; das deutsche heer von 1914, seine grundzüge und deren auswirkung im sieg an der ostfront* (Breslau: F. Hirt, 1928), 185–197, prints most of the directive. Reichsarchiv, *Der Weltkrieg*, 2:43–45, has limited excerpts. Gerhard Seyfert, *Die militärischen Beziehungen und Vereinbarungen zwischen dem deutschen und dem österreichischen Generalstab vor und bei Beginn des Weltkrieges* (Leipzig: Buckdruckerei Johannes Moltzen, 1934), 93–95, has a useful discussion. Groener, *Das Testament des Grafen Schlieffen*, 125, harshly criticizes the document.

169. Reichsarchiv, *Der Weltkrieg*, 2:45. Other comments from Dommes to chief of the General Staff of Eighth Army laid even greater stress on offensive action.

170. Ibid., 51.

171. The account of the Tannenberg campaign is based on Dennis Showalter, *Tannenberg: Clash of Empires* (Hamden, CT: Archon Books, 1991), which rendered all previous accounts obsolete. In addition to Showalter, see Reichsarchiv, *Der Weltkrieg*, 2:72–78. François stated his case in *Marneschlacht und Tannenberg*, 174–175. Ernst Kabisch, *Streitfragen des Weltkrieges 1914–1918* (Stuttgart: Bergers Literarisches Büro & Verlagsanstalt, 1924), 71, is still interesting. For the Russian perspective, see David R. Stone, *The Russian Army in the Great War: The Eastern Front, 1914–1917* (Lawrence: University Press of Kansas, 2015), 62–76; Paul Robinson, *Grand Duke Nikolai Nikolaevich: Supreme Commander of the Russian Army* (De Kalb: Northern Illinois University Press, 2014), 161–168. Still useful is Norman Stone, *The Eastern Front 1914–1917* (New York: Charles Scribner's Sons, 1975).

172. Showalter, *Tannenberg*, 172–199, examines this critical engagement with clarity and his usual wit.

173. This meant that General Georg von Waldersee, Prittwitz's *Oberquartiermeister*, also had to go. The principle of coresponsibility assured that Waldersee shared the fate of his commander. See ibid., 199.

174. The best introduction to Hindenburg is William J. Astore and Dennis

Showalter, *Hindenburg: Icon of German Militarism* (Washington, DC: Potomac Books, 2005). Hindenburg's own account is *Out of My Life by Marshal von Hindenburg*, trans. F. A. Holt, 2 vols. (New York: Harper & Brothers, 1921). The actual author of this memoir was Hermann Mertz von Quirnheim, a retired officer and head of the military archives after the war.

175. Showalter, *Tannenberg*, 199–205, discusses the appointments in a more sympathetic and realistic manner than have most historians writing since the Second World War.

176. At Hoffmann's suggestion, Eighth Army used the village of Tannenberg to name the battle, since it was the site of a major Polish victory over the Teutonic knights five centuries earlier. Russian losses are detailed in Stone, *Russian Army in the Great War*, 76.

177. Herwig's masterful account in *First World War*, 81–87, draws largely on Showalter's version but is exceptionally clear and much shorter. The most recent account of the September 1914 battles in East Prussia is Stone, *Russian Army in the Great War*, 76–80.

178. Robert Foley, *German Strategy and the Path to Verdun: Erich von Falkenhayn and the Development of Attrition, 1870–1916* (Cambridge: Cambridge University Press, 2005), 97–103.

179. Ibid., 105–108.

180. See Stig Förster, "Dreams and Nightmares: German Military Leadership and the Images of Future Warfare, 1871–1914," in *Anticipating Total War: The German and American Experiences 1871–1914*, ed. Manfred Boemke, Roger Chickering, and Stig Förster (Cambridge: Cambridge University Press, 1999), 344–345.

181. See Strachan, *First World War*, 1:1049–1050.

182. See Kielmansegg, *Deutschland und der Erste Weltkrieg*, 89. Note also the broader application of this phenomenon in Strachan, *First World War*, 1:98–99, 1007–1009.

183. Dennis Showalter, "Goltz and Bernhardi: The Institutionalization of Originality in the Imperial German Army," *Defense Analysis* 3, 4 (1987): 315.

184. Tyng, *Campaign of the Marne*, 337–338.

185. Herwig, *First World War*, 105–106. See also Herwig, *Marne*, 266–271.

186. Mombauer, *Moltke and Origins of the First World War*, 260–261. Eberhard Kessel also argued in his introduction to Schlieffen's letters that the experience of the Second World War showed that a German victory on the Marne would not have ended the war. See Eberhard Kessel, ed., *Graf Alfred Schlieffen. Briefe* (Göttingen: Vandenhoeck & Rupprecht, 1958), 14. Such a view obscures much more than it clarifies when one remembers that the French were eliminated quickly in 1940, even if not in the manner envisioned in the approach taken by Schlieffen and Moltke.

187. Groener, *Das Testament des Grafen Schlieffen*, 11. Groener oversimplified and distorted the Reichsarchiv's accounts of the campaign, which demonstrate the complexities of the plans, movements, and battles.

188. See Hans Ritter, *Kritik des Weltkrieges. Das Erbe Moltkes und Schlieffens Im Grossen Kriege*, 2nd rev. ed. (Leipzig: K. F. Koehler, 1921), 89–90.

189. Wallach, *Dogma of the Battle of Annihilation*, 97–98, 109.

190. Reichsarchiv, *Der Weltkrieg*, 1:183–184, 193–194; Liss, "Der Nachrichtendienst in den Grenzschlachten," 147.

191. Moltke's decision on 15 August to send the *Ersatz* divisions to Saarbrücken may have been an indication that he sought a decision on the left wing from the outset.

192. Reichsarchiv, *Der Weltkrieg*, 1:185.

193. Moltke's critics emphasized this as one of his most decisive departures from the Schlieffen memorandum of 1905. See Jäschke, "Zum Problem der Marne-Schlacht," 323–324; Ritter, *Kritik des Weltkrieges*, 83; Foerster, *Graf Schlieffen und der Weltkrieg*, 44–45, 53–54. This criticism may have been wrongly directed, since it is by no means certain that Schlieffen ever seriously planned a campaign based on those concepts; however, it correctly shows that Moltke violated the cardinal principle of the entire German approach to warfare: using economy of force to obtain superiority at the decisive point. Tappen's defense of the decision, in which he and Dommes took part, can be found in Tappen, *Bis zur Marne*, 14–15.

194. Strachan, *First World War*, 1:243.

195. Reichsarchiv, *Der Weltkrieg*, 4:255; Ritter, *Kritik des Weltkrieges*, 110–113. Though an iconoclast, Ritter was a prominent writer in his day. The more respected Ernst Kabisch reached the same conclusion in his *Streitfragen des Weltkrieges*, 127. Herwig, *Marne*, 277, puts the onus more on Bülow than Hentsch.

196. Ritter, *Kritik des Weltkrieges*, 111–112.

197. Walther Reinhardt, *Wehrkraft und Wehrwille. Aus seinem Nachlass mit einer Lebensbeschreibung*, ed. Ernst Reinhardt (Berlin: E. S. Mittler, 1932), 136.

198. Stevenson, *Cataclysm*, 48–49, relying in part on the older writing of Corelli Barnett, *The Swordbearers: Supreme Command in the First World War*, rev. ed. (Bloomington: Indiana University Press, 1975), 92–94, concluded that the retreat was probably unnecessary.

199. Jäschke, "Zum Problem der Marneschlacht," 319–320. The Reichsarchiv exaggerated only slightly when it concluded that Moltke's methods caused the campaign to dissolve into a series of individual battles conducted alone by each army headquarters. See Reichsarchiv, *Der Weltkrieg*, 1:657. See also Müller-Loebnitz, *Die Führung im Marne-Feldzug*, 29.

200. Mombauer, *Moltke and Origins of the First World War*, 254–255, rightly emphasizes the role of tradition. Tyng, *Campaign of the Marne*, concludes that Moltke was trying to duplicate the successful efforts of his uncle in the Franco-Prussian War. Reichsarchiv, *Der Weltkrieg*, 1:259, establishes Moltke's trust in Bülow.

201. Such was Tappen's argument, cited in Reichsarchiv, *Der Weltkrieg*, 1:187.

202. During the days prior to the Battle of Tannenberg, Moltke feared losing contact with the eastern front for even a brief time. See Reichsarchiv, *Der Weltkrieg*, 1:187. He became accustomed to using subordinate officers to deliver messages and produce personal reports. The *OHL* remained in Berlin until 17 August, when it moved to Coblenz. Moltke moved it to Luxembourg City on 20 August, into very unfavorable quarters in a deserted schoolhouse. He declined the suggestion by Wilhelm II that he establish a forward command post, an expedi-

ent adopted by many army commanders. See Jäschke, "Zum Problem der Marne Schlacht," 321.

203. Kuhl, *Der Marnefeldzug*, 28–29, comments very unfavorably on Moltke's shortcomings as compared with Joffre. Tyng, *Campaign of the Marne*, 187–188, has impressive examples of the differences. Strachan, *First World War*, 1:276, records that Joffre traveled more than 430 miles on 26 and 28 August alone. See also Robert A. Doughty, "'Papa' Joffre and the Great War," *Journal of Military History* 79, 4 (October 2015): 967.

204. Strachan, *First World War*, 1:235.

205. Buchfinck, "Der Meinungskampf um den Marnefeldzug," 292–293.

206. Kabisch, for example, though generally critical of the campaign, praised the talents of most of the leaders available on the German army's right wing in 1914. See his *Streitfragen des Weltkrieges*, 108. Tyng, *Campaign of the Marne*, also praised the ability of the key officers in the right-wing armies but pointed out that they could not overcome jealousy and distrust.

207. Crown Prince Rupprecht of Bavaria, though of a royal house, was widely respected in the army and was considered by many to be a real officer. For favorable comments by respected officers, see Hermann von Kuhl, *Der deutsche Generalstab in Vorbereitung und Durchführung des Weltkrieges* (Berlin: E. S. Mittler, 1920), 197; Josef Graf von Stürgkh, *Im deutschen Grossen Hauptquartier* (Leipzig: Paul List Verlag, 1921), 92.

208. Aside from princes, the Prussian army in 1914 had three field marshals: Colmar *Freiherr* von der Goltz, Max von Bock und Polach, and the venerable Count Gottlieb von Haeseler. The latter two were in retirement for all practical purposes. See Kriegsministerium (Prussia), *Rangliste der Königlich Preussischen Armee und des XIII (Königlich Württembergischen) Armeekorps* (Berlin: E. S. Mittler, 1914), 1225.

209. Von der Schulenburg-Tressow, chief of staff of the Guards Corps in Bülow's army, complained that he was too old for this command. See his "Erlebnisse," BA/MA, N 58/1, 78. Bülow's biographer took pains to deny the various postwar reports that Bülow had been in ill health. See Gebsattel, *Generalfeldmarschall Karl von Bülow*, 42–46. See also Herwig, *First World War*, 83; Richard L. DiNardo, "Modern Soldier in a Busby: August von Mackensen 1914–1916," in *Arms and the Man: Military History Essays in Honor of Dennis Showalter*, ed. Michael S. Neiberg (Boston: Brill, 2011), 133–135.

210. Strachan, *First World War*, 1:226–227; Doughty, *Pyrrhic Victory*, 59–60. While noting that not all these reliefs were justified, Doughty argues that they improved the command of the French army. Conrad relieved forty-four generals, including four of six army commanders. See Manfred Rauchensteiner, *Der Erste Weltkrieg und das Ende der Habsburgermonarchie 1914–1918* (Vienna: Böhlau Verlag, 2013), 244. Commanders were also relieved in the Russian army, but at a much lower rate.

211. One subordinate General Staff officer argued that German Crown Prince Wilhelm was unable to deal with his domineering and micromanaging chief of staff Schmidt von Knobelsdorff. See von der Schulenburg-Tressow, "Erlebnisse,"

BA/MA, N 58/1, 108. For a more sympathetic portrait of the crown prince, see Showalter, *Instrument of War*, 46–47.

212. Tyng, *Campaign of the Marne*, 259–260, criticizes Hausen for weakness in showing too much deference to Bülow's desires during the campaign. Buchfinck, "Der Meinungskampf um den Marnefeldzug," 292, makes a similar complaint.

213. Information based on the author's (DJH) collection of biographical information and Gebsattel, *Generalfeldmarschall Karl von Bülow*, 21–34. Despite his alleged problematic relationship with Schlieffen and his theories, Bülow had been a serious candidate to succeed him in 1906. Though not a graduate of the War Academy, Bülow had graduated from a *Gymnasium*.

214. A guards officer, Prittwitz had attended a *Gymnasium* rather than the cadet corps, was a graduate of the War Academy, and held numerous General Staff positions in addition to commanding at all appropriate levels. Like Heeringen and Bülow, Prittwitz was from a very old noble family with numerous connections to the army and the royal bureaucracy.

215. Wallach, *Dogma of the Battle of Annihilation*, 158, relying on Kabisch, *Streitfragen des Weltkrieges*, 65–66. Kabisch paints a poor picture of Prittwitz, noting that he was a very difficult man to work for, but Kabisch seems unaware of Prittwitz's role in war games that closely replicated the actual situation in 1914. Falkenhayn, the war minister, apparently opposed Moltke's efforts in early 1914 to have Prittwitz relieved from his position in East Prussia because he feared that Prittwitz would return to Berlin and become too influential with the kaiser. See Showalter, *Tannenberg*, 40.

216. Cron, *Geschichte des Deutschen Heeres*, 42–45.

217. Ibid., 62.

218. The deficiencies of the French army are outlined in Douglas Porch, "The French Army in the First World War," in *Military Effectiveness*, vol. 1, *The First World War*, ed. Allan R. Millett and Williamson Murray (Boston: Allen & Unwin, 1988), 190–228. A more positive view is presented in Doughty, "'Papa' Joffre and the Great War," 967–979. Rather than sending relieved general officers to Paris, Joffre sent them to the city of Limoges; collectively, they eventually became known as the *limogés*. Doughty, *Pyrrhic Victory*, 59.

219. Herwig, *Marne*, 313–314; Elizabeth Greenhalgh, *Victory through Coalition: Britain and France during the First World War* (Cambridge: Cambridge University Press, 2005), 40–41.

220. Herwig, *Marne*, 156; Showalter, *Tannenberg*, 294.

CHAPTER EIGHT. ADJUSTING TO THE DEMANDS OF PROLONGED WAR
1. BA/MA, PH 1/3, items 8–16, include some basic documents on the structure and manning of the new corps, especially a letter from War Minister to Acting Corps Commanders, 16 August 1914.

2. Alexander Watson, "For Kaiser and Reich: The Identity and Fate of the German Volunteers, 1914–1918," *War in History* 12, 1 (2005): 44–74, studies the volunteers in detail. The standard account in German is Karl Unruh, *Langemarck: Legende und Wirklichkeit* (Koblenz: Bernard & Graefe, 1986). See also Count Peter

Kielmansegg, *Deutschland und der Erste Weltkrieg*, 2nd ed. (Stuttgart: Klett-Cotta, 1980), 66.

3. Hans Kling, "Die Organisation der deutschen Infanterie im Weltkriege," in *Deutsche Infanterie. Das Ehrenmal der vordersten Front*, ed. Ernst von Eisenhart-Rothe et al. (Zeulenroda: Bernhard Sporn, 1939), 198; Dennis Showalter, *Instrument of War: The German Army 1914–1918* (New York: Osprey Publishing, 2016), 87–88.

4. Hermann Cron, *Geschichte des deutschen Heeres im Weltkriege 1914–1918* (Berlin: Militärverlag Karl Siegismund, 1937), 100–107, has an extensive summary of the expansion of the army's divisions during the war.

5. Ernst von Wrisberg, *Heer und Heimat 1914–1918* (Leipzig: K. F. Koehler, 1921), 20–30; Holger Afflerbach, *Falkenhayn: Politisches Denken und Handeln im Kaiserreich* (Munich: R. Oldenbourg, 1994), 286; Richard L. DiNardo, *Breakthrough: The Gorlice-Tarnow Campaign, 1915* (Santa Barbara, CA: Praeger, 2010), 33–34; Cron, *Geschichte des deutschen Heeres*, 104. The others included two marine and six replacement divisions, as well as one ad hoc emergency division.

6. Cron, *Geschichte des deutschen Heeres*, 147. Martin Samuels, *Command or Control? Command Training and Tactics in the British and German Armies, 1888–1918* (London: Frank Cass, 1995), 137, has examples of variations during the lengthy period of restructuring.

7. One of the fundamental sources is Gerald D. Feldman, *Army, Industry and Labor in Germany 1914–1918* (Princeton, NJ: Princeton University Press, 1966). The later period of the war is covered by Martin Kitchen, *The Silent Dictatorship: The Politics of the German High Command under Hindenburg and Ludendorff, 1916–1918* (New York: Holmes & Meier, 1976). Holger Herwig, *The First World War: Germany and Austria-Hungary 1914–1918*, 2nd ed. (London: Arnold Bloomsbury, 2014), has detailed treatments of the issues involved.

8. The official proclamation for Berlin and the province of Brandenburg (dated 31 July 1914) is in Wilhelm Deist, ed., *Militär und Innenpolitik im Weltkrieg 1914–1918*, 2 vols. (Düsseldorf: Droste Verlag, 1970), 1:7–8, with rich explanatory footnotes. See also ibid., xxxi–xxxii, on the law's background.

9. Kitchen, *Silent Dictatorship*, 50–52; David Stevenson, *Cataclysm: The First World War as Political Tragedy* (New York: Basic Books, 2004), 226–228.

10. Roger Chickering, *Imperial Germany and the Great War, 1914–1918* (Cambridge: Cambridge University Press, 1998), 33–34, has a useful summary.

11. On the increasing difficulties of feeding the population and the declining quantity of calories available, see Laurence V. Moyer, *Victory Must Be Ours: Germany in the Great War 1914–1918* (New York: Hippocrene Books, 1995), 122–125, 157–209, 259–260; Herwig, *First World War*, 290–294; Alexander Watson, *Ring of Steel. Germany and Austria-Hungary in World War I: The People's War* (New York: Basic Books, 2014), 330–341; Reichsarchiv, *Der Weltkrieg 1914 bis 1918*, 14 vols. (Berlin: E. S. Mittler, 1925–1944), 14:10. On early demands for military control of food supplies, see Feldman, *Army, Industry and Labor in Germany*, 99–106.

12. Feldman, *Army, Industry and Labor in Germany*, 45–47; Herwig, *First World War*, 167.

13. Niall Ferguson, *The Pity of War* (New York: Basic Books, 1999), 260; Fritz von Lossberg, *Meine Tätigkeit im Weltkriege* (Berlin: E. S. Mittler, 1939), 63; Wilhelm Groener, *Lebenserinnerungen. Jugend, Generalstab, Weltkrieg*, ed. Friedrich *Freiherr* Hiller von Gaertringen (Göttingen: Vandenhoeck & Rupprecht, 1957), 174–175; Eric Dorn Brose, *The Kaiser's Army: The Politics of Military Technology in Germany during the Machine Age, 1870–1918* (Oxford: Oxford University Press, 2001), 210–211; Afflerbach, *Falkenhayn*, 198.

14. See Moltke's memoranda to War Ministry, 1 January and 1 November 1912, in Erich Ludendorff, *Urkunden der Obersten Heeresleitung über ihre Tätigkeit 1916/18*, 3rd rev. ed. (Berlin: E. S. Mittler, 1922), 12–15. Hew Strachan, *The First World War*, vol. 1, *To Arms* (Oxford: Oxford University Press, 2001), 995–996, has many details and a good guide to the sources.

15. Theodor Jochim, *Die Operationen und rückwärtigen Verbindungen der deutschen 1. Armee in der Marneschlacht 1914* (Berlin: E. S. Mittler, 1933), 55. Crown Prince Rupprecht, *In Treue Fest. Mein Kriegstagebuch*, ed. Eugen von Frauenholz, 3 vols. (Munich: Deutscher National Verlag, 1929), records a similar comment on 8 September 1914, at the opposite end of the western front. Even the Guards Corps recorded shortages. See the memoirs of Schulenburg-Tresckow, "Erlebnisse," *Nachlass* Schulenberg-Tresckow, BA/MA, N 58/1, 95; and the comments of General Fritz von Unger, commander of 38th Reserve Infantry Brigade, in "Kriegserlebnisse 1914–1918," *Nachlass* Unger, BA/MA, N 83/4, 3. By mid-September, Unger's artillery had only a single round per gun per day. General Karl von Einem made a similar complaint in his diary on 3 November 1914, *Nachlass* Einem, BA/MA, N 324/26, 133. On the eastern front, see Kielmansegg, *Deutschland und der Erste Weltkrieg*, 61, 68. See also Lothar Burchardt, *Friedenswirtschaft und Kriegsvorsorge. Deutschlands wirtschaftliche Rüstungsbestrebungen vor 1914* (Boppard: Harald Boldt Verlag, 1962), 49.

16. Order of Chief of Staff of the Field Army, 11 October 1914, *Nachlass* Hauffer, BA/MA, N 11/2.

17. Feldman, *Army, Industry and Labor in Germany*, 53–54; Jochim, *Operationen und Verbindungen der 1. Armee*, 24.

18. Herwig, *First World War*, 165. See also Ernst von Wrisberg, *Wehr und Waffen 1914–1918* (Leipzig: Verlag von K. F. Koehler, 1921), 84. For a comprehensive examination of the issue, see Strachan, *First World War*, 1:994–1005.

19. Chickering, *Imperial Germany and the Great War*, 35–40; Strachan, *First World War*, 1:1027–1029.

20. Herwig, *First World War*, 166–167. German studies of the Russo-Japanese War may have been a factor in this failure to understand how much artillery ammunition would be needed. See Hans Ritter, *Kritik des Weltkrieges. Das Erbe Moltkes und Schlieffens im grossen Kriege*, 2nd ed. (Leipzig: K. F. Koehler, 1921), 69.

21. Strachan, *First World War*, 1:1037.

22. Kitchen, *Silent Dictatorship*, 67; Max von Gallwitz, *Erleben im Westen 1916–1918* (Berlin: E. S. Mittler, 1932), 5–6.

23. On the question of war aims, see Stevenson, *Cataclysm*; H. E. Goemans, *War and Punishment: The Causes of War Termination in the First World War*

(Princeton, NJ: Princeton University Press, 2000). See also Watson, *Ring of Steel*, 257–276.

24. Holger H. Herwig, "Admirals versus Generals: The War Aims of the Imperial German Navy, 1914–1918," *Central European History* 8, 2 (2001): 166–190; Lamar Cecil, *Wilhelm II*, vol. 2, *Emperor and Exile, 1900–1941* (Chapel Hill: University of North Carolina Press, 1996), 232–238; Holger Afflerbach, "Wilhelm II as Supreme Warlord in the First World War," in *The Kaiser: New Research on Wilhelm II's Role in Imperial Germany*, ed. Annika Mombauer and Wilhelm Deist (Cambridge: Cambridge University Press, 2004), 204–206.

25. Chickering, *Imperial Germany and the Great War*, 87; Watson, *Ring of Steel*, 257–259.

26. Seeckt to wife, 14 August 1915, *Nachlass* Seeckt, BA/MA, N 247/58.

27. The German states represented were Bavaria, Saxony, and Württemberg.

28. Reichsarchiv, *Der Weltkrieg*, 1:179. Hermann Cron, *Die Organisation des deutschen Heeres im Weltkriege* (Berlin: E. S. Mittler, 1923), 8–24, has many details.

29. Herwig, *First World War*, 57–58, has a summary.

30. Cron, *Die Organisation des deutschen Heeres*, 9–17. In their correspondence, each section used the first letter of its name (e.g., O for Operations) as an identifying symbol.

31. On his career progression, see Hans von Zwehl, *Erich von Falkenhayn, General der Infanterie* (Berlin: E. S. Mittler, 1926), 320–321. Afflerbach, *Falkenhayn*, 17–47, covers the China period. For comments on his lack of experience in operational matters, see Theodor Jochim, "Der Herbstfeldzug 1914," *Wissen und Wehr* 2 (1929): 83, 273. Falkenhayn's contempt for theoretical training is well established in Afflerbach, *Falkenhayn*, 60. On the matter of Falkenhayn's rapid promotions, see Hans von Seeckt, "Diary Notes," 24 January 1915, *Nachlass* Seeckt, BA-MA, N 247/22; Adolf Wild von Hohenborn, *Briefe und Tagebuchaufzeichnungen des preussischen General als Kriegsminister und Truppenführer im Ersten Weltkrieg*, ed. Helmut Reichold (Boppard: Harald Boldt Verlag, 1986), 53.

32. Herwig, *First World War*, 126.

33. Holger Afflerbach, "Die militärische Planung des deutschen Reiches im Ersten Weltkrieg," in *Der Erste Weltkrieg. Wirkung, Wahrnehmung, Analyse*, ed. Wolfgang Michalka (Munich: Piper, 1994), 298.

34. Gerhard Ritter, *The Sword and the Scepter: The Problem of Militarism in Germany*, trans. Heinz Norden, 4 vols. (Coral Gables, FL: University of Miami Press, 1964–1973), 3:43–44, discusses the decision. See also Robert T. Foley, *German Strategy and the Path to Verdun: Erich von Falkenhayn and the Development of Attrition, 1870–1916* (Cambridge: Cambridge University Press, 2005), 103–107.

35. Afflerbach, "Die militärische Planung des deutschen Reiches," 298; Hermann von Kuhl, *Der Weltkrieg 1914–1918*, 2 vols. (Berlin: Vaterländischen Verlag E. A. Weller, 1930), 1:509–510.

36. Afflerbach, "Die militärische Planung des deutschen Reiches," 287–288; L. L. Farrar, "The Strategy of the Central Powers 1914–1917," in *The Oxford Illustrated History of the First World War*, ed. Hew Strachan (Oxford: Oxford University Press, 1998), 30–31.

37. The view that a great victory in the east must precede any major success in the west was not confined to officers on the eastern front. See the comments of Albrecht von Thaer, *Generalstabsdienst an der Front und in der OHL. Aus Briefen und Tagebuchaufzeichnungen 1915–1919*, ed. Siegfried Kaehler (Göttingen: Vandenhoeck & Rupprecht, 1958), 23.

38. DiNardo, *Breakthrough*, 13.

39. Cron, *Die Organisation des deutschen Heeres*, 25. The army groups, named for their commanders, were Hindenburg (later Eichhorn), Prince Leopold of Bavaria, Linsingen, and Mackensen. In the autumn of 1915 the Mackensen Army Group headquarters was transferred to southern Hungary for the invasion of Serbia.

40. Falkenhayn to *Ober Ost* and *Ober Ost* to Falkenhayn, 28 May 1915, BA/MA, RH 61/1536; Richard L. DiNardo, *Invasion: The Conquest of Serbia, 1915* (Santa Barbara, CA: Praeger, 2015), 38. Afflerbach, *Falkenhayn*, 310–311, has some background, partly based on Ritter, *Sword and the Scepter*, 3:603.

41. War Diary of *Süd* Army, 1 January 1915, BA/MA, PH 5 II/322; Erich Ludendorff to Helmuth von Moltke, 9 January 1915, *Nachlass* Ludendorff, BA/MA, N 77/2; Foley, *German Strategy and the Path to Verdun*, 120–124; DiNardo, *Breakthrough*, 22. For a broader account of the intrigues against Falkenhayn, see Afflerbach, *Falkenhayn*, 218–232.

42. Foley, *German Strategy and the Path to Verdun*, 124–125.

43. Afflerbach, *Falkenhayn*, 465–468, has a summary. See also Michael B. Barrett, *Prelude to Blitzkrieg: The 1916 Austro-German Campaign in Romania* (Bloomington: Indiana University Press, 2013), 299–300. For a discussion of the plan for the Serbian campaign, see DiNardo, *Invasion*, 58. For the difficulties in actually executing an encirclement in World War I, see Richard L. DiNardo, "The Limits of Encirclement: The Invasion of Serbia, 1915," *Historian* 78, 3 (Fall 2016): 486–503.

44. General der Infanterie Karl Litzmann, *Lebenserinnerungen* (Berlin: Verlag R. Eisenschmidt, 1927), 329; Robert Kosch to wife, 11 February 1915, *Nachlass* Kosch, BA/MA, N 754/2; Otto von Below, "Winterschlacht in Masuren," *Nachlass* Below, BA/MA, N 87/58; Manfred Nebelin, *Ludendorff: Diktatur im Ersten Weltkrieg* (Munich: Siedler Verlag, 2010), 159–160; David R. Stone, *The Russian Army in the Great War: The Eastern Front 1914–1917* (Lawrence: University Press of Kansas, 2015), 134.

45. DiNardo, *Breakthrough*, 83; Falkenhayn to Conrad, 17 May 1915, BA/MA, RH 61/1536; Stone, *Russian Army in the Great War*, 176.

46. Erich Ludendorff, *Meine Kriegserinnerungen* (Berlin: E. S. Mittler, 1919), 114–117; Reichsarchiv, *Der Weltkrieg*, 8:124; DiNardo, *Breakthrough*, 107; German Eleventh Army, Estimate of the Situation as of Noon, 15 June 1915, BA/MA, RH 61/1536; Hans von Seeckt, *Aus meinem Leben 1866–1917* (Leipzig: Hase & Kohler, 1938), 153; August von Mackensen, *Mackensen. Briefe und Aufzeichnungen der General-feldmarschalls aus Krieg und Frieden*, ed. Wolfgang Foerster (Leipzig: Bibliographisches Instituts, 1938), 183–184; Hans von Plessen diary, 2 July 1915, BA/MA, RH 61/933.

47. See Foley, *German Strategy and the Path to Verdun*, 109–110; Stevenson, *Cataclysm*, 125; DiNardo, *Breakthrough*, 27–31.

48. Stevenson, *Cataclysm*, 123; Wild, *Briefe und Tagebuchaufzeichnungen*, 53.

49. Farrar, "Strategy of the Central Powers," 34–35; James Goldrick, *Before Jutland: The Naval War in Northern European Waters, August 1914–February 1915* (Annapolis, MD: Naval Institute Press, 2015), 71–73; Holger H. Herwig, *"Luxury" Fleet: The German Imperial Navy 1888–1918*, reprint ed. (London: Ashfield Press, 1987), 148–149.

50. Cron, *Die Organisation des deutschen Heeres*, 26. On the western front the army groups initially had positional names: right flank, center, and left flank. The three groups then took their names from their commanders, as did others established later. See Cron, *Geschichte des deutschen Heeres*, 43–45; Ernst von Wrisberg, "Ausbau und Ergänzung des Heeres," in *Der grosse Krieg 1914–1918*, ed. Max Schwarte, 10 vols. (Leipzig: Johann Ambrosius Barth, 1921), 8:19.

51. See the comments of Otto von Moser, *Die obersten Gewalten im Weltkrieg* (Stuttgart: Chr. Belser, 1931), 155.

52. Annika Mombauer, *Helmuth von Moltke and the Origins of the First World War* (Cambridge: Cambridge University Press, 2001), 232–233, describes the circumstances of the move.

53. Reichsarchiv, *Der Weltkrieg*, 3:190–191; Helmuth von Moltke, *Erinnerungen, Briefe, Dokumente 1877–1916*, ed. Eliza von Moltke (Stuttgart: Der Kommende Tag Verlag, 1922), 382.

54. From Luxembourg, the headquarters moved to Mézières-Charleville on 25 September 1914, then to Pless (in Silesia) on 7 May 1915.

55. Quoted in Gallwitz, *Erleben im Westen*, 160–161. See also Afflerbach, *Falkenhayn*, 437–438; Moser, *Die oberste Gewalten im Weltkrieg*, 184–185.

56. Gallwitz, *Erleben im Westen*, 130. See especially Schlieffen's 1910 article "Der Feldherr," in *Alfred von Schlieffen's Military Writings*, ed. Robert Foley (London: Frank Cass, 2003), 219–226.

57. Lossberg, *Meine Tätigkeit im Weltkriege*, 148; Afflerbach, *Falkenhayn*, 148.

58. Lossberg, *Meine Tätigkeit im Weltkriege*, 151–152.

59. Tappen diary, 30–31 May 1915, BA/MA, RH 61/986; Lossberg, *Meine Tätigkeit im Weltkriege*, 129; Seeckt, *Aus meinem Leben*, 142.

60. DiNardo, *Invasion*, 89–90.

61. Foley, *German Strategy and the Path to Verdun*, 157–163, provides a summary of these proposals.

62. Afflerbach, "Die militärische Planung des Deutschen Reiches," 295–297.

63. On Falkenhayn's dilemma, see ibid., 297–298. See also Chickering, *Imperial Germany and the First World War*, 66–67.

64. Afflerbach, "Die militärische Planung des deutschen Reiches," 299.

65. Afflerbach, *Falkenhayn*, 360–368, discusses the decision to attack at Verdun. Erich von Falkenhayn, *The German General Staff and Its Decisions, 1914–1916* (New York: Dodd, Mead, 1920), 239–250, reprints a memorandum allegedly submitted to Wilhelm II around Christmas 1915. This "Christmas memorandum" is almost certainly a postwar fabrication. See Afflerbach, *Falkenhayn*, 534–535.

66. Foley, *German Strategy and the Path to Verdun*, 181–208, convincingly portrays Falkenhayn's strategic outlook and the bases of his plans.

67. Afflerbach, *Falkenhayn*, 398.

68. Goemans, *War and Punishment*, 142–147 (on France), 186–195 (on Great Britain). Modifications in war aims for both nations centered on peripheral areas outside the main issues with Germany.

69. Stevenson, *Cataclysm*, 130–139; Elizabeth Greehalgh, *Victory through Coalition: Britain and France during the First World War* (Cambridge: Cambridge University Press, 2005), 42–46.

70. Kielmansegg, *Deutschland und der Erste Weltkrieg*, 301–304, argues that the plan for Verdun was not the barbaric lack of imagination it has so often been portrayed; instead, it was a dubious attempt to think strategically under conditions that allowed strategy little room for action.

71. Watson, *Ring of Steel*, 313; Peter Hart, *The Somme: The Darkest Hour on the Western Front* (New York: Pegasus Books, 2008), 531. See also Ritter, *Sword and the Scepter*, 3:186. For the Brusilov offensive, see John R. Schindler, "Steamrolled in Galicia: The Austro-Hungarian Army and the Brusilov Offensive, 1916," *War in History* 10, 1 (2003): 27–59. The most recent study of the Brusilov offensive is Timothy C. Dowling, *The Brusilov Offensive* (Bloomington: Indiana University Press, 2008).

72. Cecil, *Wilhelm II*, 2:236–237, discusses the kaiser's relationship with Falkenhayn and his decision to replace him with Hindenburg.

73. Ritter, *Sword and the Scepter*, 3:204–2055, is still an excellent account. Afflerbach's *Falkenhayn* is now an indispensable source. Karl Heinz Janssen, "Der Wechsel in der Obersten Heeresleitung 1916," *Vierteljahrshefte für Zeitgeschichte* 7, 4 (October 1959): 337–371, stresses the importance of Falkenhayn's civilian opponents. See also Nebelin, *Ludendorff*, 213.

74. Deist, *Militär und Innenpolitik in Weltkrieg*, 1:55–56.

75. The best introduction to the Dual Alliance's military problems is still Gerard E. Silberstein, *The Troubled Alliance: German-Austrian Relations 1914–1917* (Lexington: University of Kentucky Press, 1970). Jehuda Wallach, *Uneasy Coalition: The Entente Experience in World War I* (Westport, CT: Greenwood Press, 1993), has a useful introduction to alliance problems. See also Paul Kennedy, "Military Coalitions and Coalition Warfare over the Past Century," in *Coalition Warfare: An Uneasy Accord*, ed. Keith Neilson and Roy A. Prete (Waterloo, ON: Wilfrid Laurier University Press, 1983), 1–15; Greenhalgh, *Victory through Coalition*. This section draws extensively on Richard L. DiNardo and Daniel J. Hughes, "Germany and Coalition Warfare in the World Wars: A Comparison," *War in History* 8, 2 (April 2001): 166–190.

76. On Beck's interest in closer cooperation, see Holger Herwig, "Disjointed Allies: Coalition Warfare in Berlin and Vienna, 1914," *Journal of Military History* 34, 3 (July 1990): 269–270.

77. Nor was Bismarck's policy dependent on advice from the German army, whose leaders apparently had not been informed of the Reinsurance Treaty. See the comments of Graydon A. Tunstall Jr., *Planning for War against Russia and*

Serbia: Austro-Hungarian and German Military Strategies 1871–1914 (Boulder, CO: Social Science Monographs, 1993), 28. Bismarck supposedly leaked the details of the Reinsurance Treaty to the *Hamburg Nachrichten* in 1895, after the signing of the Franco-Russian alliance, as a way to embarrass his successors. See Jonathon Steinberg, *Bismarck: A Life* (Oxford: Oxford University Press, 2011), 460–461.

78. Gerhard Seyfert, *Die militärische Beziehungen und Vereinbarungen zwischen dem deutschen und dem österreichischen Generalstab vor und bei Beginn des Weltkrieges* (Leipzig: Buckdruckerei Johannes Moltzen, 1934), 34.

79. Ibid., 33.

80. Helmut Otto, "Zum strategisch-operativen Zusammenwirken des deutschen und österreichisch-ungarischen Generalstabes bei der Vorbereitung des ersten Weltkrieges," *Zeitschrift für Militärgeschichte* 2 (1963): 426; Seyfert, *Die militärischen Beziehungen und Vereinbarungen*, 15–17, 26–27, 33–34. See also Tunstall, *Planning for War against Russia and Serbia*, 33–34.

81. Seyfert, *Die militärischen Beziehungen und Vereinbarungen*, 36–41; Lothar Höbelt, "Schlieffen, Beck, Potiorek und das Ende der gemeinsam deutsch-österreichisch-ungarischen Aufmarschpläne im Osten," *Militärgeschichtliche Mitteilungen* 36, 2 (1984): 17.

82. Höbelt, "Schlieffen, Beck, Potiorek," 17; Otto, "Zum strategisch-operativen Zusammenwirken," 432; Herwig, "Disjointed Allies," 272–273.

83. Theobald von Schäfer, "Betrachtungen zum 'Bündniskrieg,'" *Wissen und Wehr* (1938): 381–382; Tunstall, *Planning for War against Russia and Serbia*, 40; DiNardo, *Breakthrough*, 6.

84. Terence Zuber, *Inventing the Schlieffen Plan: German War Planning, 1871–1914* (Oxford: Oxford University Press, 2002), 150, has an example from 1896.

85. On his friendly relations with Vienna, see Moltke's letter to his wife, September 1909, in Moltke, *Erinnerungen*, 252.

86. Gerhard Ritter, "Die Zusammenarbeit der Generalstäbe Deutschlands und Österreich-Ungarns vor dem ersten Weltkrieg," in *Zur Geschichte und Problematik der Demokratie. Festgabe für Hans Herzfeld*, ed. Wilhelm Berges and Carl Hinrichs (Berlin: Duncker & Humboldt, 1958), 537–538. See also Ritter, *Sword and the Scepter*, 2:240.

87. See Norman Stone, "V. Moltke-Conrad: Relations between the Austro-Hungarian and German General Staffs, 1909–1914," *Historical Journal* 9, 2 (1966): 206–207, n. 9.

88. Herwig, "Disjointed Allies," 278–279, stresses Aehrenthal's reluctance to enter into a formal convention. Tunstall, *Planning for War against Russia and Serbia*, 63–64, stresses his interest in less binding discussions.

89. In moments of candor, Conrad must have known better. See Dennis Showalter's comments in Herwig, *First World War*, 52–53. For a different interpretation, see Lawrence Sondhaus, *Franz Conrad von Hötzendorff: Architect of the Apocalypse* (Boston: Humanities Press, 2000), 100.

90. Seyfert, *Die militärischen Beziehungen und Vereinbarungen*, 48–49, 91–93. General Blasius Schemua, who replaced Conrad for a brief period in 1911–1912, had no permanent impact on the Austro-German relationship.

91. The younger Moltke and Conrad met for the first time in Berlin in May 1907. This marked the first direct contact between the two General Staffs in ten years. See Tunstall, *Planning for War against Russia and Serbia*, 56, 138–139. To some degree, the Germans' circumspect behavior may have been influenced by the notorious Redl affair, in which the Austrians discovered that the chief of staff of Austrian VIII Corps, Colonel Alfred Redl, was a homosexual and had been blackmailed by Russian intelligence into divulging an enormous amount of information. Although the affair ended with Redl's exposure and suicide, as well as a cover-up by Conrad, it is difficult to know whether the Germans were aware of the scope of Redl's activity. See Herwig, *First World War*, 65. The best study of the affair is Georg Markus, *Der Fall Redl* (Vienna: Amalthea Verlag, 1984). A brief, more recent examination is John R. Schindler, "Redl—Spy of the Century," *International Journal of Intelligence and Counter Intelligence* 18, 3 (Fall 2005): 483–507. Schlieffen was apparently convinced as early as 1892 that Germany's eastern plans had been compromised. See Tunstall, *Planning for War against Russia and Serbia*, 42–43. For Conrad's rather lame assurances to Moltke about the extent of the damage caused by Redl, see his letter of 18 June 1913 in Franz *Freiherr* Conrad von Hötzendorff, *Aus Meiner Dienstzeit 1906–1918*, 5 vols. (Vienna: Rikola Verlag, 1921–1925), 3:368.

92. Seyfert, *Die militärischen Beziehungen und Vereinbarungen*, 85–90.

93. Telegram from General von Prittwitz to Conrad, 18 August 1914, in Conrad, *Aus Meiner Dienstzeit*, 4:451–455. On Conrad's expectations, see Stone, "Moltke-Conrad," 226–227.

94. The Austrians were again incensed that Hindenburg did not turn south to assist them after the victory at Tannenberg. See the comments of the Austrian representative at the German High Command in Count Josef von Stürgkh, *Im deutschen Grossen Hauptquartier* (Leipzig: Paul List Verlag, 1921), 30–40. Relations between Conrad and the German military plenipotentiary in Conrad's headquarters, Freytag-Loringhoven, quickly became strained. See Conrad, *Aus Meiner Dienstzeit*, 4:491–492. The arrival of Hindenburg and Ludendorff did nothing to assuage Conrad's resentment. See ibid., 796.

95. For several examples of this, see Conrad, *Aus Meiner Dienstzeit*, 4:809–810. See also Afflerbach, *Falkenhayn*, 250.

96. Gary W. Shanafelt, *The Secret Enemy: Austria Hungary and the German Alliance, 1914–1918* (New York: Columbia University Press, 1985), 54–56, has a useful introduction to this issue.

97. Jesse Kauffman, *Elusive Alliance: The German Occupation of Poland in World War I* (Cambridge, MA: Harvard University Press, 2015), 183–184; Shanafelt, *Secret Enemy*, 39–40, 83–84, 159–161. See also Norman Stone, "The Austro-German Alliance, 1914–1918," in Neilson and Prete, *Coalition Warfare*, 26.

98. Sondhaus, *Franz Conrad von Hötzendorf*, 169. A good example of Conrad's writing style is Conrad to Arthur, Baron von Bolfras, 6 April 1915, Military Chancery of His Majesty, file 78, ÖSA/KA.

99. Afflerbach, *Falkenhayn*, 256–257. For a good idea of how much traveling Falkenhayn had to do, see Gerhard Tappen diary, 11 January 1915, BA/MA, RH

61/986. For an example of the different writing styles of Falkenhayn and Conrad, compare Conrad to Falkenhayn, 18 May 1915, BA/MA, RH 61/979, and Falkenhayn to Admiral Henning von Holtzendorff, 30 March 1916, BA/MA, RM 28/53.

100. Stürgkh, *Im deutschen Grossen Hauptquartier*, 103; Afflerbach, *Falkenhayn*, 196; Conrad, *Aus Meiner Dienstzeit*, 5"340; Tappen diary, 30 October 1914, BA/MA, RH 61/986; August von Cramon, *Unser Österreichisch-Ungarischer Bundesgenosse im Weltkrieg. Erinnerungen aus meiner vierjahrigen Tätigkeit als bevollmächtiger deutscher General beim KuK Armeekommando* (Berlin: E. S. Mittler, 1920), 22–23.

101. Sondhaus, *Franz Conrad von Hötzendorf*, 170; Bolfras to Conrad, 30 June 1915, and Conrad to Bolfras, 1 July 1915, Military Chancery of His Majesty, file 78, ÖSA/KA.

102. Sondhaus, *Franz Conrad von Hötzendorf*, 179; Karl von Kaganeck diary, 12 April 1915, BA/MA, MSg 1/2514; Gina *Grafin* Conrad von Hötzendorf, *Mein Leben mit Conrad von Hötzendorf: Sein geistiges Vernächtnis* (Leipzig: Grathlein, 1935), 132; Cramon, *Unser Österreichisch-Ungarischer Bundesgenosse im Weltkrieg*, 65–66; DiNardo, *Breakthrough*, 20.

103. Richard F. Hamilton and Holger H. Herwig, *Decisions for War, 1914–1917* (Cambridge: Cambridge University Press, 2004), 198; Shanafelt, *Secret Enemy*, 64–65; DiNardo, *Invasion*, 33; Afflerbach, *Falkenhayn*, 264–285. The Pact of London replaced the prewar Triple Entente with a formal alliance. Hence, from that date the term "Allies" properly applied to France, Great Britain, Russia, and, later, their other allied states.

104. Falkenhayn to Conrad, 13 June 1915, BA/MA, RH 61/1536; DiNardo, *Invasion*, 32–33.

105. Manfred Rauchensteiner, *Der Erste Weltkrieg und das Ende der Habsburgermonarchie 1914–1918* (Vienna: Bälau Verlag, 2013), 488; Ritter, *Sword and the Scepter*, 3:86.

106. Cramon, *Unser Österreichisch-Ungarischer Bundesgenosse im Weltkrieg*, 36–45, has interesting details. See also DiNardo, *Invasion*, 127–128; Herwig, *First World War*, 160–161.

107. Shanafelt, *Secret Enemy*, 116–117, 175; Afflerbach, *Falkenhayn*, 285. Karl's statement, in a letter to Count Czernin, is in August von Cramon and Paul Fleck, *Deutschlands Schicksalsbund mit Österreich-Ungarn* (Berlin: Verlag für Kulturpolitik, 1932), 218–221.

108. Gisbert Beyerhaus, *Einheitlicher Oberbefehl. Ein Problem des Krieges* (Munich: F. Bruckmann Verlag, 1938), 35–38.

109. The increasing reliance on Germany is traced in Shanafelt, *Secret Enemy*, 5, 46–47, 152–154, 173–174. See also Stürgkh, *Im deutschen Grossen Hauptquartier*, 60.

110. Shanafelt, *Secret Enemy*, 195–196.

111. Herwig, *First World War*, 326; Jonathan Gumz, *The Resurrection and Collapse of Empire in Habsburg Serbia, 1914–1918* (Cambridge: Cambridge University Press, 2009), 212–213.

112. On the Marne, see Cramon and Fleck, *Deutschlands Schicksalsbund*, 74–75. See also Kaganeck diary, 21 September 1914, BA/MA, MSg 1/1914.

113. It is worth pointing out that the Germans did not even inform Conrad that

Moltke had collapsed psychologically by mid-September and had been replaced by Falkenhayn. Conrad found out only by piecing together bits of information that came to him indirectly. Herwig, *First World War*, 106–107.

114. War Diary of *Süd* Army, 1 January 1915, BA/MA, PH 5 II/322; Carl Mönckeberg, *Bei Süd und Bug Armee 1915* (Stuttgart: Deutsche Verlags Anstalt, 1917), 10–11. For a detailed discussion and analysis of Conrad's first Carpathian offensive, see Graydon A. Tunstall Jr., *Blood on the Snow: The Carpathian Winter War of 1915* (Lawrence: University Press of Kansas, 2010), 66–113.

115. Oskar Tile von Kalm, *Schlachten des Weltkrieges*, vol. 30, *Gorlice* (Berlin: Oldenburg, 1930), 196–198; Austro-Hungarian VI Corps, "Vorbereitung der Schlacht bei Gorlice-Tarnow," ca. June 1915, BA/MA, RH 61/1616; Lothar Höbelt, "'So wie wir haben nicht einmal die Japaner angegriffen.' Österreich-Ungarns Nordfront 1914/15," in *Die vergessene Front. Der Osten 1914/15: Ereignis, Wirkung, Nachwirkung*, ed. Gerhard P. Gross (Paderborn: Ferdinand Schöningh, 2006), 101–105; DiNardo, *Invasion*, 42–50.

116. Stone, "Austro-German Alliance," 23–24; Shanafelt, *Secret Enemy*, 69–70; Dowling, *Brusilov Offensive*, 50; Hans von Seeckt, "Report on the KuK Army and Reorganizational Plans for the KuK Army," *Nachlass* Seeckt, BA/MA, N 247/32.

117. Hamilton and Herwig, *Decisions for War*, 157–164; Sean McMeekin, *The Berlin-Baghdad Express: The Ottoman Empire and Germany's Bid for World Power* (Cambridge, MA: Harvard University Press, 2010), 101; David R. Woodward, *Hell in the Holy Land: World War I in the Middle East* (Lexington: University Press of Kentucky, 2006), 15; Stone, *Russian Army in the Great War*, 178–179; Afflerbach, *Falkenhayn*, 336.

118. Lawrence Sondhaus, *The Great War at Sea: A Naval History of the First World War* (Cambridge: Cambridge University Press, 2014), 95–104; Herwig, *"Luxury" Fleet*, 153–154.

119. Sondhaus, *Great War at Sea*, 102–110.

120. For a modern account of the defense of Gallipoli based on Turkish sources, see Edward J. Erickson, *Gallipoli: The Ottoman Campaign* (Barnsley, UK: Pen & Sword, 2010). See also McMeekin, *Berlin-Baghdad Express*, 285. Ulrich Trumpener, "Suez, Baku, Gallipoli: The Military Dimensions of the German-Ottoman Coalition, 1914–1918," in Neilson and Prete, *Coalition Warfare*, has a very useful summary.

121. Hamilton and Herwig, *Decisions for War*, 174; Richard C. Hall, *Bulgaria's Road to the First World War* (Boulder, CO: East European Monographs, 1996), 305; DiNardo, *Invasion*, 33–34; OHL, Military Convention between Germany, Austria-Hungary and Bulgaria, 6 September 1915, BA/MA, PH 5 I/78.

122. August von Mackensen, "Kriegstage in Bulgarien," 22 November 1915, *Nachlass* August von Mackensen, BA/MA, N 39/310; DiNardo, *Invasion*, 128.

123. Mackensen, *Briefe und Aufzeichnungen*, 226; Robert A. Doughty, *Pyrrhic Victory: French Strategy and Operations in the Great War* (Cambridge, MA: Harvard University Press, 2005), 226–227; DiNardo, *Invasion*, 87.

124. Gumz, *Resurrection and Collapse of Empire*, 4–6. The quote is from Alan Palmer, *The Gardeners of Salonika* (New York: Simon & Schuster, 1965), 58.

125. KTB Army Group Mackensen, 30 August 1916, BA/MA, PH 5I/59; Reichsarchiv, *Der Weltkrieg*, 9:208; Richard L. DiNardo, "Modern Soldier in a Busby: August von Mackensen 1914–1916," in *Arms and the Man: Military History in Honor of Dennis Showalter*, ed. Michael S. Neiberg (Boston: Brill, 2011), 156.

126. Each party wanted to hold the reins, and neither would grant that to the other. See Otto, "Zum strategisch-operativen Zusammenwirken," 430–431; Seyfert, *Die militärischen Beziehungen und Vereinbarungen*, 40. Even the elder Moltke had opposed a combined command. See Theobald von Schaefer, "Betrachtungen zum Bündniskrieg," *Wissen und Wehr* 19 (1938): 376–377.

127. Beyerhaus, *Einheitlicher Oberbefehl*, 13–22. Wilhelm II also opposed a combined command. See Gordon Craig, "The World War I Alliance of the Central Powers in Retrospect: The Military Cohesion of the Alliance," *Journal of Modern History* 37, 2 (Summer 1965): 341–342. Conrad later admitted that prior to the war he saw no necessity for a unified command. See Conrad, *Aus Meiner Dienstzeit*, 4:259.

128. The precise origins of the proposal are in dispute. Rudolf Kiszling, "Bündniskrieg und Koalitionskriegsführung am Beispiel der Mittlemächte im Ersten Weltkrieg," *Wehrwissenschaftliche Rundschau* 10, 12 (1960): 635, argues that it was a German proposal. Beyerhaus, probably more correctly, attributes the idea to Arthur, Baron von Bolfras, the chief of Emperor Francis Joseph's Military Chancery. Although Francis Joseph was in favor, Conrad's opposition killed the idea. See also Herwig, *First World War*, 108–109.

129. Cramon, *Unsere Österreichisch-Ungarischer Bundesgenosse im Weltkrieg*, 10–14; Reichsarchiv, *Der Weltkrieg*, 7:369; Cramon to *OHL* Operations Section and *OHL* Operations Section to Cramon, 27 April 1915, BA/MA, RH 61/1536; DiNardo, *Breakthrough*, 42. On Falkenhayn's role in the Gorlice offensive, see Foley, *German Strategy and the Path to Verdun*, 129–140.

130. DiNardo, *Breakthrough*, 82; Rudolf Kundmann diary, 23 June 1915, Conrad Archive, ÖSA/KA, B/13; Theo Schwarzmüller, *Zwischen Kaiser and "Führer": Generalfeldmarschall August von Mackensen: Eine politische Biographie*, 2nd ed. (Paderborn: Ferdinand Schöningh, 1996), 121–122; Mackensen, *Briefe und Aufzeichnungen*, 212; Archduke Friedrich to August von Mackensen, 26 September 1915, BA/MA, RH 61/933; DiNardo, *Invasion*, 41–42.

131. Hans von Plessen diary, 22 June 1915, BA/MA, RH 61/933; Hans Meier-Welcker, *Seeckt* (Frankfurt: Bernard & Graefe Verlag für Wehrwesen, 1967), 55; Seeckt to wife, 28 June 1915, *Nachlass* Seeckt, BA/MA, N 247/57; DiNardo, *Breakthrough*, 100.

132. DiNardo, *Invasion*, 33–34; *OHL*, Military Convention between Germany, Austria-Hungary and Bulgaria, 6 September 1915, BA/MA, PH I/78.

133. See Cramon, *Unsere Österreichisch-Ungarischer Bündnisgenosse im Weltkrieg*, 22.

134. Ritter, *Sword and the Scepter*, 2:191–201, has many details.

135. Afflerbach, *Falkenhayn*, 429–430; Cramon, *Unsere Österreichisch-Ungarischer Bundesgenosse im Weltkrieg*, 69–70.

136. The Turks and Bulgarians in effect demanded a unified command under

Wilhelm II. See Cramon and Fleck, *Deutschlands Schicksalsbund*, 141–142; the full text is on 143.

137. Rudolf Kiszling, "Bündniskrieg und Koalitionskriegsführung," 638, comments on this new arrangement's role in the Romanian campaign, a glittering success. For command arrangements at the lower level, see Afflerbach, *Falkenhayn*, 466.

138. Shanafelt, *Secret Enemy*, 105; Kiszling, "Bündniskrieg und Koalitionskriegsführung," 638–639; Beyerhaus, *Einheitlicher Oberbefehl*, 33–34. See also Craig, "World War I Alliance," 343.

139. John R. Schindler, *Isonzo: The Forgotten Sacrifice of the Great War* (Westport, CT: Praeger, 2001), 246–265; Reichsarchiv, *Der Weltkrieg*, 13:276. War termination in the cases of both Romania and Russia provided occasions for bitter disagreement. Cramon, caught in the middle, has an interesting account in Cramon and Fleck, *Deutschlands Schicksalsbund*, 207–209.

140. David E. Trask, *The AEF and Coalition Warmaking 1917–1918* (Lawrence: University Press of Kansas, 1993), is a scholarly account. His *The United States in the Supreme War Council* (Middletown, CT: Wesleyan University Press, 1961) examines broader strategic issues. For some pointed comments, see Douglas Porch, "The French Army in the First World War," in *Military Effectiveness*, vol. 1, *The First World War*, ed. Allan R. Millett and Williamson Murray (Boston: Allen & Unwin, 1988), 209. More supportive of the role Foch played in 1918 is Elizabeth Greenhalgh, "General Ferdinand Foch and Unified Allied Command in 1918," *Journal of Military History* 79, 4 (October 2015): 997–1024.

141. Kaganek diary, 21 September 1914, BA/MA, MSg 1/1914; Major General Max Hoffmann, *War Diaries and Other Papers*, trans. Eric Sutton (London: Martin Secker, 1929), 1:43; Cramon and Fleck, *Deutschlands Schicksalsbund*, 102; Jakob Jung, *Max von Gallwitz (1852–1937): General und Politiker* (Osnabrück: Biblio Verlag, 1995), 64; Ludendorff to Moltke, 1 April 1915, *Nachlass* Ludendorff, BA/MA, N 77/2.

142. McMeekin, *Berlin-Baghdad Express*, 285.

143. DiNardo, *Breakthrough*, 82; Archduke Friedrich to Mackensen, 26 September 1915, BA/MA, RH 61/953; Mackensen, "Kriegstage in Bulgarien," *Nachlass* Mackensen, BA/MA, N 39/310; DiNardo, *Invasion*, 128.

144. Afflerbach, "Die militärische Planung des Deutschen Reiches," 295–297.

145. Cron, *Geschichte des deutschen Heeres*, 129–130.

146. Hans Linnenkohl, *Vom Einzelschuss zur Feuerwalze. Der Wettlauf zwischen Technik und Taktik im Ersten Weltkrieg* (Munich: Bernard & Graefe, 1990), 179–180; Hans Martens and Ernst Zipfel, *Geschichte des Ulanen-Regiments von Schmidt (1. Pommersches) Nr. 4* (Berlin: Tradition Wilhelm Kolk, 1929), 114.

147. Reichsarchiv, *Der Weltkrieg*, 14:33; Cron, *Geschichte des deutschen Heeres*, 133–134; Ludwig Wurtzbacher, "Die Versorgung des Heeres mit Waffen und Munition," in Schwarte, *Der Grosse Krieg*, 3:97–98. For a comparison with other armies, see Linnenkohl, *Vom Einzelschuss zur Feuerwalze*, 187.

148. The prewar manual, *Guidelines for Training Units about Aircraft and Means of Combating Them*, is available in James S. Corum and Richard R. Muller, eds.,

The Luftwaffe's Way of War: German Air Force Doctrine 1911–1945 (Baltimore: Nautical & Aviation Publishing Company of America, 1998), 37–45. The manual dealt primarily with airships rather than airplanes, and with regard to the latter, it considered mainly how to counter them. It was a start, however basic.

149. For a summary, see Strachan, *First World War*, 1:233.

150. John H. Morrow Jr., *The Great War in the Air: Military Aviation from 1909 to 1921* (Washington, DC: Smithsonian Institution Press, 1993), 227–228; Reichsarchiv, *Der Weltkrieg*, 14:36. The Hindenburg program is discussed in the next chapter.

151. Morrow, *Great War in the Air*, 162, 305, 310, 344–345; Lee Kennett, *The First Air War 1914–1918* (New York: Free Press, 1991), 94.

152. Cron, *Geschichte des deutschen Heeres*, 19–20.

153. Morrow, *Great War in the Air*, 104–111; Richard L. DiNardo, "German Air Operations on the Eastern Front, 1914–1917," in *Essays on World War I*, ed. Peter Pastor and Graydon A. Tunstall (Boulder, CO: East European Monographs, 2012), 66; Kennett, *First Air War*, 211–212; Reichsarchiv, *Der Weltkrieg*, 12:9, 48–49.

154. Kennett, *First Air War*, 220, is representative.

155. In September 1915 the Germans dropped more than 5,000 pounds of bombs. Only about half of them exploded. Reichsarchiv, *Der Weltkrieg*, 9:204; Major Georg P. Neumann, *Die deutschen Luftstreitkräfte im Weltkriege* (Berlin: E. S. Mittler, 1920), 242. For a summary of operations against London, see Kennett, *First Air War*, 57–60.

156. See Hubert C. Johnson, *Breakthrough: Tactics, Technology and the Search for Victory on the Western Front in World War I* (Novato, CA: Presidio, 1994), 154–156; Peter Hart, *The Great War: A Combat History of the First World War* (Oxford: Oxford University Press, 2013), 334–335.

157. DiNardo, *Breakthrough*, 50–51; General Alfred Ziethen, "Aus grosser Zeit vor zwanzig Jahren. Die Durchbruchschlacht von Gorlice," *Militär-Wochenblatt* 119, 41 (May 1935): col. 1629; German Eleventh Army, Special Order No. 28, 15 May 1915, file 11/43/4, BH/KA.

158. German Eleventh Army, Order for Aerial Reconnaissance, 6 June 1915, file 8R/11/1, BH/KA; DiNardo, "German Air Operations," 68; Bavarian 8th Reserve Division, Extract from the Campaign Experiences of the German Eastern Army, June 1915, file 8R/11/1, BH/KA.

159. Richard L. DiNardo, "The Limits of Technology: The Invasion of Serbia, 1915," *Journal of Military History* 79, 4 (October 2015): 988; Army Group Temesvár, Order for Aerial Reconnaissance, 25 September 1915, file 11/15/2, BH/KA; German Eleventh Army, Viewpoints on Reconnaissance in Serbia, 23 October 1915, file 11/15/5, BH/KA.

160. Johnson, *Breakthrough*, 70–71.

161. Ibid., 70–72; Morrow, *Great War in the Air*, 159.

162. On the effectiveness of British air support on the Somme, see Herwig, *First World War*, 203.

163. See Kuhl, *Der Weltkrieg*, 1:497; Otto von Moser, *Feldzugsaufzeichnungen als Brigade-Divisionskommandeur und als kommandierenden General 1914–1918* (Stutt-

gart: Chr. Belseresche Verlagsbuchhandlung, 1920), 211; Gallwitz, *Erleben im Westen*, 84; and Reichsarchiv, *Der Weltkrieg*, 12:36, showing the nearly universal nature of the problem with Allied close air support.

164. Morrow, *Great War in the Air*, 159, 173–174, 195–196.

165. Johnson, *Breakthrough*, 219–221, has a solid summary with useful illustrations.

166. On German strength, see Reichsarchiv, *Der Weltkrieg*, 14:29; Kennett, *First Air War*, 205; Morrow, *Great War in the Air*, 297–298. See also Johnson, *Breakthrough*, 132–135.

167. The best summary of the origin of flak is Edward P. Westermann, *Flak: German Anti-Aircraft Defenses 1914–1945* (Lawrence: University Press of Kansas, 2001), 9–27.

168. Ibid., 9–16.

169. Major (a. D.) Grosskreuz, "Flak," in *Das Ehrenbuch der Feldartillerie*, ed. Albert Benary (Berlin: Verlag Tradition Wilhelm Kolt, [ca. 1930]), 88–94.

170. Wrisberg, *Heer und Heimat*, 49–57; Wrisberg, *Wehr und Waffen*, 31–35. See also Westermann, *Flak*, 26–27.

171. James Corum, *The Roots of Blitzkrieg: Hans von Seeckt and German Military Reform* (Lawrence: University Press of Kansas, 1992), 20–22, is representative of the critical viewpoint on the German performance and its consequences.

172. Wrisberg, *Wehr und Waffen*, 159.

173. Corum, *Roots of Blitzkrieg*, 20–21; Herwig, *First World War*, 397–398.

174. Ludendorff, *Meine Kriegserinnerungen*, 462–463.

175. A surviving diagram of a storm company of Sturm-Bataillone No. 1, August 1918, is available in BA/MA, PH 10 III/23.

176. Herwig, *First World War*, 400–401, and Corum, *Roots of Blitzkrieg*, 21, have slightly differing numbers on production totals.

177. Ritter, *Kritik des Weltkrieges*, 64–65; Hermann von Kuhl, *Entstehung, Durchführung und Zusammenbruch der Offensive von 1918* (Berlin: Deutsche Verlagsgesellschaft, 1927), 81–84. The official historians of course defended the OHL. See Reichsarchiv, *Der Weltkrieg*, 14:33–34.

178. Herwig, *First World War*, 420–421.

179. Linnenkohl, *Vom Einzelschuss zur Feuerwalze*, 219–220. See also Alfred Muther, "Organisation, Bewaffnung, Munition und Munitionsverbrauch der deutschen Feldartillerie im Weltkrieg," in Benary, *Ehrenbuch der deutschen Feldartillerie*, 42. The modifications increased the ranges by about a third. See Reichsarchiv, *Der Weltkrieg*, 14:14, for a table comparing the old and new artillery pieces.

180. Linnenkohl, *Vom Einzelschuss zur Feuerwalze*, 280–281.

181. Muther, "Organisation, Bewaffnung, Munition und Munitonsverbrauch," 43.

182. Linnenkohl, *Vom Einzelschuss zur Feuerwalze*, 283; Wrisberg, *Heer und Heimat*, 58; Wrisberg, *Wehr und Waffen*, 17; Reichsarchiv, *Der Weltkrieg*, 14:33.

183. Wrisberg, *Wehr und Waffen*, 56–58.

184. Cron, *Die Organisation des deutschen Heeres*, 83.

185. Ibid., 184; Johnson, *Breakthrough*, 124; Afflerbach, *Falkenhayn*, 260–261.

The French used primitive gas projectiles, fired from rifles, in the autumn of 1914 and grenades in March 1915. See Herwig, *First World War*, 168–169; John Keegan, *The First World War* (New York: Alfred A. Knopf, 1999), 197.

186. Cron, *Geschichte des deutschen Heeres*, 184–185, has other organizational details.

187. Herwig, *First World War*, 169–171, has an excellent summary.

188. Moyer, *Victory Must Be Ours*, 120, argues that gas "wasn't very effective," either then or later. Kuhl, *Der Weltkrieg*, 1:192–193, claims that had they been prepared for a major offensive, the Germans could have advanced to Dunkirk.

189. For a review of the issues, see Tim Cook, "'Against God-Inspired Conscience': The Perception of Gas Warfare as a Weapon of Mass Destruction, 1915–1939," *War and Society* 18, 1 (May 2000): 47–69.

190. DiNardo, *Invasion*, 134; German Eleventh Army, Estimate of the Situation as of Noon, 15 June 1915, BA/MA, RH 61/1536.

191. The first *OHL* was established under Moltke, the second under Falkenhayn, and the third under the Hindenburg-Ludendorff duumvirate.

192. Lossberg, *Meine Tätigkeit im Weltkriege*, 151–152.

193. Martin Hobohm, *Soziale Heeesmisstände als Teilursache des deutschen Zusammenbruchs von 1918*, vol. 11 (first half) of *Das Werk des Untersuchungsauschusses der Verfassunggebenden Deutschen Nationalversammlung und des Deutschen Reichstages* (Berlin: Deutsche Verlagsgesellschaft für Politik & Geschichte, 1929), 252.

194. Ibid., 52–53, citing Ludendorff's order to the field, 28 November 1917, subject: Reduction of Correspondence. See also Erich Otto Volkmann, *Soziale Heeresmisstände als Mitursache des deutschen Zusammenbruchs von 1918*, vol. 11 (second half) of *Das Werk des Untersuchungsauschusses der Verfassunggebenden Deutschen Nationalversammlung und des Deutschen Reichstages* (Berlin: Deutsche Verlagsgesellschaft für Politik & Geschichte, 1929), 78–79.

195. Georg Gothein, *Warum verloren wir den Krieg?* 2nd ed. (Berlin: Deutsche Verlags-Anstalt, 1920), 223–224.

196. C. R. M. F. Cruttwell, *A History of the Great War 1914–1918*, 2nd ed. (Chicago: Academy Publishers, 1992), 107–108, argues that this was an inherent aspect of static warfare, affecting all armies to some degree.

197. Afflerbach, *Falkenhayn*, 257–258. Falkenhayn, like Allied leaders, avoided hospitals because he feared that the suffering visible there would prevent him from performing his duty. See also Paul Robinson, *Grand Duke Nikolai Nikolaevich: Supreme Commander of the Russian Army* (De Kalb: Northern Illinois University Press, 2014), 153.

198. Chef des Generalstabes des Feldheeres, M.I. Nr. 50631, 22 April 1917, signed by Ludendorff, BA/MA, PH 3/25.

199. Chef des Generalstabes des Feldheeres, M.I. No. 53000, 20 May 1917, to all Chiefs of the General Staff, the War Ministry, divisions, and so forth, signed by Ludendorff, ibid.

200. See the comments by Volkmann, a former General Staff officer, in *Soziale Heeresmisstände als Mitursache*, 80–81; and Hermann von Kuhl's review of Hans Ritter's book, "Zur 'Kritik des Weltkrieges,'" *Militär-Wochenblatt* 11 (1921): cols.

221–222. Max Bauer's denial of any such problems within the High Command seems particularly unimpressive. See Max Bauer, *Der grosse Krieg in Feld und Heimat. Erinnerungen und Betrachtungen* (Tübingen: Osiander'sche Buchhandlung, 1921), 178–179.

201. Chef des Generalstabes des Feldheeres, Secret, to all General Staff officers, M.I. No. 5, 11 July 1917, signed by Ludendorff, BA/MA, PH 3/25.

202. Groener, *Lebenserinnerungen*, 375–376.

203. This was a theme throughout Martin Hobohm's report to the postwar Reichstag committee on the causes of the collapse of 1918. Herman Kantorowicz first raised the issue of the "hatred of officers" in his 1916 pamphlet, which was published in 1919. See Herman Kantorowicz, *Offizierhass im deutschen Heer* (Freiburg: Bielefelds, 1919). Gothein, *Warum verloren wir den Krieg?* contributed importantly to the critique of the army's social system. Rudolf Krafft, *Glänzendes Elend* (Stuttgart: Verlag Robert Lutz, 1895), rediscovered after the war, became a staple of the effort to extend the critique of the officer class into the prewar era.

204. Christoph Jahr, *Gewöhnliche Soldaten. Desertion und Deserteure im deutschen und britischen Heer 1914–1918* (Göttingen: Vandenhoeck & Rupprecht, 1998), 99, reviews the literature and convincingly argues that officer deaths in both armies were 30 to 50 percent higher proportionally than enlisted deaths.

205. Ibid., 109–110; Gothein, *Warum verloren wir den Krieg?* 220–221. Even Ludendorff recognized that the quality of provisions was a factor in the gradual decline of enlisted morale. See Ludendorff, *Meine Kriegserinnerungen*, 520–521.

206. Martin Kitchen, *The German Offensives of 1918* (Charleston, SC: Tempus, 2001), 216, 220.

207. Benjamin Ziemann, "Enttäuschte Erwartung und kollektive Erschöpfung. Die deutschen Soldaten an der Westfront 1918 auf dem Weg zur Revolution," in *Kriegsende 1918. Ereignis, Wirkung, Nachwirkung*, ed. Jörg Duppler and Gerhard P. Gross (Munich: R. Oldenbourg Verlag, 1999), 173–174; Thaer, *Generalstabsdienst*, 208 (footnote); Ludendorff, *Meine Kriegserinnerungen*, 482, 491–492.

208. See the comments of Bauer, *Der grosse Krieg in Feld und Heimat*, 182. Gothein, *Warum verloren wir den Krieg?* 217–218, made the same point.

209. Thaer, *Generalstabsdienst*, 36, letter of 21 May 1915; 58, letter of 3 February 1916. See also Rupprecht, *In Treue Fest*, 2:10, 34, entries for 4 and 27 September 1916. Other comments can be found in Theodor Jochim, *Die Vorbereitung des deutschen Heeres für die grosse Schlacht in Frankreich im Frühjahr 1918*, 5 vols. (Berlin: E. S. Mittler, 1927–1930), 1:10; Ludendorff, *Meine Kriegserinnerungen*, 309; Reichsarchiv, *Der Weltkrieg*, 14:29–30.

210, Moltke to his wife, 19 September 1909, in Moltke, *Erinnerungen*, 353.

211. Stürgkh, *Im deutschen Grossenhauptquartier*, 101. See also Herwig, *First World War*, 192. After the war, even the army's defenders had to admit the inequities in granting awards to officers. See Volkmann, *Soziale Heeresmissstände als Mitursache*, 93–94.

212. This was a major element of Kantorowicz's wartime writing and later a popular book, *Offizierhass im deutschen Heer*. See the comments of Hobohm, *Soziale Heeresmissstände als Teilursache*, 100–101; Ritter, *Kritik des Weltkrieges*, 41–42.

Officers had servants (*Burschen*) who looked after their personal affairs but did not join their masters in combat. They remained behind, as Kantorowicz complained, "to protect the costly (often all too costly) personal belongings of the officers."

213. Hobohm, *Soziale Heeresmisstände als Teilursache*, 89.

214. Kitchen, *German Offensives of 1918*, 216–218, has an excellent section on this problem.

215. Jahr, *Gewöhnliche Soldaten*, 44.

216. Ibid., 24, 241.

217. Volkmann, *Soziale Heeresmissstände als Mitursache*, 63. The figures are approximate but sufficiently accurate to determine the gross numbers of executions. See also Christoph Jahr, "Bei einer geschlagenen Armee ist der Klügste, wer zuerste davonläuft. Das Problem der Desertion im deutschen und britischen Heer 1918," in Duppler and Gross, *Kriegsende 1918*, 265.

218. Volkmann, *Soziale Heeresmissstände als Mitursache*, 64–65. See also Kitchen, *German Offensives of 1918*, 163.

219. Jahr, *Gewöhnliche Soldaten*, 183–190.

220. Reichsarchiv, *Der Weltkrieg*, 14:524.

221. Jahr, *Gewöhnliche Soldaten*, 110–111, has some details on how soldiers used fake documents and other devices to hide out behind the front in France, Belgium, or Germany or even to escape to Holland or Switzerland. Bauer, *Der grosse Krieg*, 190, estimated the total number of unauthorized absences from the army at around 500,000 in April 1918. Kitchen, *German Offensives of 1918*, 163–164, concludes that desertion was not a serious problem until September 1918. His views are therefore somewhat at odds with this account.

222. Reichsarchiv, *Der Weltkrieg*, 14:523, mentions this as well as the traditional problem of Poles and Alsatians attempting to dodge military service in the despised Prussian army. See also the discussion in Hobohm, *Soziale Heeresmisstände als Teilursache*, 322.

223. Jahr, "Bei einer geschlagenen Armee," 256.

224. Ibid., 263.

225. Ibid., 259–261.

226. Both orders are cited in Hobohm, *Soziale Heeresmissstände als Teilursache*, 385–388.

227. Kuhl, *Entstehung, Durchführung und Zusammenbruch*, 75. Volkmann, *Soziale Heeresmissstände als Mitursache*, 157, estimated that between 700,000 and 1 million men were avoiding their military duties. Hobohm's research after the war found numerous orders from various sections of the front dealing with problems maintaining order in the rear, along rail lines, and so forth. See Hobohm, *Soziale Heeresmissstände als Teilursache*, 412–418.

228. Ritter, *Kritik des Weltkrieges*, 42–43, was typical of those who blamed most of the problems on poor enforcement through leniency. See also Hobohm, *Soziale Heeresmissstände als Teilursache*, 65–66, 157.

229. Goltz to Military Cabinet, 20 September 1914, BA/MA, PH 1/3, item 109.

230. Volkmann, *Soziale Heeresmisstände als Mitursache*, 34; DiNardo, *Breakthrough*, 136.

231. Hans von Zwehl, "Vom Sterben des deutschen Offizierkorps," *Militär-Wochenblatt* 106, 22 (1921): col. 24. Others argued that the total losses among the old active officer corps exceeded 50 percent. See Gothein, *Warum verloren wir den Krieg?* 217.

232. Ludendorff, *Meine Kriegserinnerungen*, 522.

233. Volkmann, *Soziale Heeresmisstände als Mitursache*, 33; Constantin von Altrock, "Zahl der Verwundungen in den Landheeren, Schutztruppen und der Marine des deutschen Reiches während des Weltkrieges 1914 bis 1918," *Militär-Wochenblatt* 106, 12 (1921): cols. 243–234.

234. Ludendorff, *Meine Kriegserinnerungen*, 310.

235. Kielmansegg, *Deutschland und der Erste Weltkrieg*, 323.

236. See Rupprecht, *In Treue Fest*, 2:88, entry of 23 January 1917; Thaer, *Generalstabsdienst*, letter of 24 August 1916; Kuhl, *Der Weltkrieg*, 2:9.

237. John Howard Lavalle, "Military Professionalism and the Realities of War: German Officer Training in the Great War" (Ph.D. diss., University of Georgia, 1997), 115–128, 156–168.

238. War Ministry to General Staff and Bavarian, Saxon, and Württemberg War Ministers et al., 5 December 1916, BA/MA, PH 2/49; Chief of the General Staff to War Minister and Military Cabinet, 24 October 1914, BA/MA, PH 1/3, 152–153.

239. Chief of Military Cabinet, *Freiherr* von Lyncker, to corps commanders, 2 August 1914, BA/MA, PH 1/3, item 1.b.

240. Wilhelm II to War Ministry, 19 September 1914, War Ministry file number Kg. Mn. No. 1288/9 14, ibid., item 105.

241. Chief of the Military Cabinet to the field units, 28 December 1914, signed by Lyncker, ibid., item 245.

242. Herbert Rosinski, *The German Army* (London: Hogarth Press, 1940), 160.

243. The following documents are in BA/MA, PH 1/3 (with page numbers noted individually): Military Cabinet to all major commands, secret, 1 September and 28 December 1914, 59, 245; Falkenhayn to Military Cabinet and High Commands, 2 August 1914, 1a; Wilhelm II to War Minister, 1 August 1914, 1; War Minister to deputy commanding generals, 3 October 1914, 129–130. On the *Feldwebelleutnant* issue, see Wrisberg, "Ausbau und Ergänzung des Heeres," 3:33.

244. Hans H. Driftmann, *Grundzüge des militärischen Erziehungs- und Bildungswesens in der Zeit 1871–1939* (Regensburg: Walhalla & Praetoria Verlag, 1979), 38.

245. Tappen diary, 7 April 1915, BA/MA, RH 61/986; DiNardo, *Breakthrough*, 29.

246. Conrad to Falkenhayn and Falkenhayn to Conrad, 2 September 1915, *AOK* Operations Bureau, Conrad-Falkenhayn Correspondence, Russia, ÖSA/KA, R512; Hindenburg to *OHL*, 11 June 1915, BA/MA, RH 61/1552.

247. Robinson, *Grand Duke Nikolai Nikolaevich*, 256; Stone, *Russian Army in the Great War*, 232.

248. Tappen diary, 16 September 1915, BA/MA, RH 61/986; *OHL*, Directive for the New Army Group of Generalfeldmarschall von Mackensen, 15 September 1915, BA/MA, PH 5 I/78.

249. DiNardo, *Invasion*, 123–124.

250. Conrad to Falkenhayn, 21 July 1915, and Falkenhayn to Conrad, 4 August 1915, *AOK* Operations Bureau, Conrad-Falkenhayn Correspondence, Russia, ÖSA/KA, R512; DiNardo, *Breakthrough*, 131; Shanafelt, *Secret Enemy*, 117. The most recent comprehensive study is Kauffman, *Elusive Alliance*.

251. The battle of Jutland is outside the scope of this study. It has produced books in sufficient number to sink a barge by sheer weight. Most studies are British focused. The best is Andrew Gordon, *The Rules of the Game: Jutland and British Naval Command* (Annapolis, MD: Naval Institute Press, 1996). For the German perspective, see Gary Staff, *Skagerrak: The Battle of Jutland through German Eyes* (Barnsley, UK: Pen & Sword, 2016); Michael Epkenhans, Jörg Hillmann, and Frank Nägler, eds., *Skagerrakschlacht: Vorgeschichte, Ereignis, Verarbeitung* (Munich: Oldenbourg, 2009). For correspondence on the matter of the Baltic islands, see Holtzendorff to Falkenhayn, 24 December 1915, Falkenhayn to Holtzendorff, 26 December 1915, Holtzendorff to Falkenhayn, 17 March 1916, and Falkenhayn to Holtzendorff, 30 March 1916, BA/MA, RM 28/53. For U-boat operations, see John Terraine, *The U-Boat Wars, 1916–1945* (New York: Putnam, 1989).

252. Foley, *German Strategy and the Path to Verdun*, 191–193; Showalter, *Instrument of War*, 133.

253. Foley, *German Strategy and the Path to Verdun*, 208; Doughty, *Pyrrhic Victory*, 274–275.

254. DiNardo, *Breakthrough*, 136; Showalter, *Instrument of War*, 166–167.

CHAPTER NINE. THE THIRD *OHL*: STRATEGIC AND TACTICAL CHANGE, 1917–1918

1. Roger Chickering, *Imperial Germany and the Great War, 1914–1918* (Cambridge: Cambridge University Press, 1998), 72–75, discusses the personalities and abilities of Hindenburg and Ludendorff. His judgment seems too negative in our view.

2. Holger Afflerbach, "Die militärische Planung des deutschen Reiches im Ersten Weltkrieg," in *Der Erste Weltkrieg. Wirkung, Wahrnehmung, Analyse*, ed. Wolfgang Michalka (Munich: Piper, 1994), 303.

3. Ibid., 306, cites the contemporary confidence in Hindenburg.

4. Albrecht von Thaer, *Generalstabsdienst an der Front und in der O.H.L. Aus Briefen und Tagebuchaufzeichnungen 1915–1919*, ed. Siegfried A. Kaehler (Göttingen: Vandenhoeck & Rupprecht, 1958), 101, letter of 3 December 1916.

5. Gerhard Ritter, *The Sword and the Scepter: The Problem of Militarism in Germany*, trans. Heinz Norden, 4 vols. (Coral Gables, FL: University of Miami Press, 1964–1973), 3:209; Manfred Nebelin, *Ludendorff: Diktator im Ersten Weltkrieg* (Munich: Siedler Verlag, 2010), 336–340.

6. L. L. Farrar, "The Strategy of the Central Powers 1914–1917," in *The Oxford Illustrated History of the First World War*, ed. Hew Strachan (Oxford: Oxford University Press, 1998), 34–35.

7. Among the better accounts are Bernd Stegemann, *Die deutsche Marinepolitik 1916–1918* (Berlin: Duncker & Humboldt, 1970); K. E. Birnbaum, *Peace Moves and U-Boat Warfare: A Study of Imperial Germany's Policy towards the United States*

April 18, 1916–January 9, 1917 (Stockholm: Almqvist & Wiksell, 1958). The German official history is Marinearchiv, *Der Krieg zur See 1914–1918*, 18 vols. (Berlin: E. S. Mittler, 1922–1966), particularly the section *Der Handelskrieg mit U-Booten*, 5 vols. (Berlin: E. S. Mittler, 1932–1966). Holger H. Herwig, *The First World War: Germany and Austria-Hungary 1914–1918*, 2nd ed. (London: Arnold Bloomsbury, 2014), 309–314; and Martin Kitchen, *The Silent Dictatorship: The Politics of the German High Command under Hindenburg and Ludendorff, 1916–1918* (New York: Holmes & Meier, 1976), have good discussions. See also Alexander Watson, *Ring of Steel. Germany and Austria-Hungary in World War I: The People's War* (New York: Basic Books, 2014), 416–424.

8. Stegemann, *Die deutsche Marinepolitik*, 20–21.

9. Theobald von Schaefer, *Generalstab und Admiralstab. Das Zusammenwirken von Heer und Flotte im Weltkrieg* (Berlin: E. S. Mittler, 1931), 21; Ritter, *Sword and the Scepter*, 3:120; Stegemann, *Die deutsche Marinepolitik*, 26; James Goldrick, *Before Jutland: The Naval War in Northern European Waters, August 1914–February 1915* (Annapolis, MD: Naval Institute Press, 2015), 145–148.

10. Lamar Cecil, *Wilhelm II*, vol. 2, *Emperor and Exile, 1900–1941* (Chapel Hill: University of North Carolina Press, 1996), 222–223; Ritter, *Sword and the Scepter*, 3:126; Herwig, *First World War*, 287–288; Holger H. Herwig, *"Luxury" Fleet: The Imperial German Navy 1888–1918*, reprint ed. (London: Ashfield Press, 1987), 164.

11. Ritter, *Sword and the Scepter*, 3:159–169; Cecil, *Wilhelm II*, 2:233. Falkenhayn had come to believe, by June 1916 at the latest, that land warfare alone would not end the war. Holger Afflerbach, *Falkenhayn. Politisches Denken und Handeln im Kaiserreich* (Munich: R. Oldenbourg, 1994), 376–382.

12. Kitchen, *Silent Dictatorship*, 112; Stegemann, *Die deutsche Marinepolitik*, 41–42.

13. David Stevenson, *The First World War and International Politics* (Oxford: Oxford University Press, 1988), 67, summarizes the relevant international treaties and declarations.

14. Stegemann, *Die deutsche Marinepolitik*, 39–40, has a summary. Holtzendorff's memorandum is now available in Dirk Steffen, ed., "The Holtzendorff Memorandum of 22 December 1916 and Germany's Declaration of Unrestricted Submarine Warfare," *Journal of Military History* 68, 1 (January 2004): 215–224.

15. Kitchen, *Silent Dictatorship*, 111–127; Ritter, *Sword and the Scepter*, 3:266ff; Afflerbach, *Falkenhayn*, 377–403; Stegemann, *Die deutsche Marinepolitik*, 41–42.

16. Herwig, *First World War*, 311–317.

17. Cecil, *Wilhelm II*, 2:242–243.

18. Most of the powerful military figures around Wilhelm II grossly underestimated the military potential of the United States. See Herwig, *First World War*, 315–316.

19. Stegemann, *Die deutsche Marinepolitik*, 57–58, 71.

20. Ritter, *Sword and the Scepter*, 3:271; Stegemann, *Die deutsche Marinepolitik*, 64–65. Herwig, *First World War*, 317–320, and Niall Ferguson, *The Pity of War* (New York: Basic Books, 1999), 282–283, have useful summaries. The Germans built about 390 submarines during the war and lost 180 to various causes, pri-

marily mines rather than depth charges. The Allies used nearly 700 aircraft and 100 airships in antisubmarine patrols. See Herwig, *First World War*, 354–355.

21. Stegemann, *Die deutsche Marinepolitik*, 60.

22. The conditional scenario emerges in Afflerbach, "Die militärische Planung des deutschen Reiches," 305. Farrar, "Strategy of the Central Powers, 1914–1917," 37–38, has a similar discussion.

23. See the comments of Farrar, "Strategy of the Central Powers, 1914–1917," 37.

24. David R. Stone, *The Russian Army in the Great War: The Eastern Front, 1914–1917* (Lawrence: University Press of Kansas, 2015), 277.

25. Joshua A. Sanborn, *Imperial Apocalypse: The Great War and the Destruction of the Russian Empire* (Oxford: Oxford University Press, 2014), 189; Dominic Lieven, *The End of Tsarist Russia: The March to World War I and Revolution* (New York: Viking, 2015), 351. When war broke out in August 1914, Tsar Nicholas II changed the name of the Russian capital from the German-sounding St. Petersburg to the more Russian-style Petrograd.

26. Herwig, *First World War*, 326.

27. Richard L. DiNardo, "Huns with Web-Feet: Operation Albion, 1917," *War in History* 12, 4 (November 2005): 396–417; Herwig, *"Luxury" Fleet*, 236–237; Stone, *Russian Army in the Great War*, 300–303. For a full-length study of Albion, see Michael B. Barrett, *Operation Albion: The German Conquest of the Baltic Islands* (Bloomington: Indiana University Press, 2008).

28. Lieven, *End of Tsarist Russia*, 358–359; Sanborn, *Imperial Apocalypse*, 232–233; Herwig, *First World War*, 372–374.

29. Chickering, *Imperial Germany and the Great War*, 79.

30. Herwig, *First World War*, 260–266, has a solid account based on newly available sources. The standard study is Gerald D. Feldman, *Army, Industry and Labor in Germany 1914–1918* (Princeton, NJ: Princeton University Press, 1966). Kitchen, *Silent Dictatorship*, has a caustic rendering of this. Chickering, *Imperial Germany and the Great War*, 79–81, is concise and balanced.

31. Herwig, *First World War*, 255–262; Feldman, *Army, Industry and Labor*, 161, 494–495; Kitchen, *Silent Dictatorship*, 68–69; Laurence V. Moyer, *Victory Must Be Ours: Germany in the Great War 1914–1918* (New York: Hippocrene Books, 1995), 203–204; Watson, *Ring of Steel*, 415.

32. Chickering, *Imperial Germany and the Great War*, 46–50. Wilhelm Deist, ed., *Militär und Innenpolitik im Weltkrieg 1914–1918*, 2 vols. (Düsseldorf: Droste Verlag, 1970), 1:63–181, has many documents on military censorship during the war.

33. The best study of German propaganda overall is David Welch, *Germany, Propaganda, and Total War, 1914–1918: The Sins of Omission* (New Brunswick, NJ: Rutgers University Press, 2000).

34. Chef des Generalstabes des Feldheeres, order to numerous agencies, 29 July 1917, subject: Guidelines for Patriotic Instruction in the Units, in Erich Ludendorff, *Urkunden der Obersten Heeresleitung über ihre Tätigkeit 1916/18*, 3rd rev. ed. (Berlin: E. S. Mittler, 1922), 271–279.

35. Martin Kitchen, *The German Offensives of 1918* (Charleston, SC: Tempus, 2001), 123, has a brief summary.

36. See, for example, a memorandum from the War Ministry to Acting Commanding Generals, 30 November 1917, subject: Guidelines for Instruction in the Homeland, in Deist, *Militär und Innenpolitik*, 2:872–878.

37. Watson, *Ring of Steel*, 485–490; Deist, *Militär und Innenpolitik*, 2:889–894.

38. Kitchen's excellent summary in *Silent Dictatorship*, 59–61, may arouse amusement or disgust, depending on the reader's mood. See also Watson, *Ring of Steel*, 489.

39. Erich Otto Volkmann, *Soziale Heeresmissstände als Mitursache des deutschen Zusammenbruchs von 1918*, vol. 11 (second half) of *Das Werk des Untersuchungsauschusses der Verfassunggebenden Deutschen Nationalversammlung und des Deutschen Reichstages*. (Berlin: Deutsche Verlagsgesellschaft für Politik & Geschichte, 1929), 52; Wilhelm Groener, *Lebenserinnerungen, Jugend, Generalstab, Weltkrieg*, ed. Friedrich *Freiherr* Hiller von Gaertringen (Göttingen: Vandenhoeck & Rupprecht, 1957), 377.

40. Hubert C. Johnson, *Breakthrough: Tactics Technology and the Search for Victory on the Western Front in World War I* (Novato, CA: Presidio, 1994), 48–51, documents this phenomenon.

41. Ernst von Wrisberg, *Heer und Heimat 1914–1918* (Leipzig: Verlag von K. F. Koehler, 1921), 84.

42. David G. Hermann, *The Arming of Europe and the Making of the First World War* (Princeton, NJ: Princeton University Press, 1996), 222–223.

43. See the popular prewar handbook Rudolf Mohr, ed., *V. Trothas Ausbildung unserer Unterführer für den Kriegsbedarf*, 3rd ed. (Berlin: E. S. Mittler, 1909), 150; and Lieutenant Weisenberger, 20th Infantry Regiment, "Entwicklungsraum der Infanterie," *Militär-Wochenblatt* 147 (1913): col. 3341.

44. Otto von Moser, *Die Ausbildung und Führung des Bataillons, des Regiments und der Brigade*, 4th ed. (Berlin: E. S. Mittler, 1914), 146. See also Hermann, *Arming of Europe*, 222–223.

45. Reichsarchiv, *Kriegsrüstung und Kriegswirtschaft* (Berlin: E. S. Mittler, 1930), 108, n. 1.

46. Figures from 1909 indicated that only about 31,000 of the 1 million men in the *Ersatz* reserve had participated in training or field exercises. See ibid., 113.

47. Bärensprung, "Gedanken über das Kriegsspiel der Reserveoffiziere," *Militär-Wochenblatt* 5 (1913): cols. 99–100.

48. For general commentary on reservist training, see Dennis Showalter, *Instrument of War: The German Army 1914–18* (New York: Osprey Publishing, 2016), 14–15. The problem was also the subject of commentary in the army's prewar literature. See Anonymous, "Zur kriegsmässigen Ausbildung der Offiziere des Beurlaubtenstandes der Infanterie," *Militär-Wochenblatt* 155 (1906): col. 3596.

49. Bärensprung, "Gedanken über das Kriegsspiel der Reserveoffiziere," 101.

50. Hermann Rahne, *Mobilmachung. Militärische Mobilmachungsplanung und Technik in Preussen und im deutschen Reich von Mitte des 19. Jahrhundert bis zum Zweiten Weltkrieg* (East Berlin: Militärverlag der deutschen demokratischer Repub-

lik, 1983), 116, argues that reserve officers "as a rule possessed sufficient military qualifications." Heiger Ostertag, *Bildung, Ausbildung, und Erziehung des Offizierkorps im deutschen Kaiserreich 1871 bis 1918* (Frankfurt: Peter Lang, 1990) 286, argues that the war showed that the reserve officers were at least equal to active officers.

51. KTB/Bavarian 11th Infantry Division, file 11/4/1, BH/KA; Richard L. DiNardo, *Breakthrough: The Gorlice-Tarnow Campaign, 1915* (Santa Barbara, CA: Praeger, 2010), 46; Richard L. DiNardo, *Invasion: The Conquest of Serbia, 1915* (Santa Barbara, CA: Praeger, 2015), 53.

52. Hartmut John, *Das Reserveoffizierkorps im Deutschen Kaiserreich 1890–1914* (Frankfurt: Campus Verlag, 1981), 141.

53. Wilhelm Groener, *Das Testament des Grafen Schlieffen. Operative Studien über den Weltkrieg* (Berlin: E. S. Mittler, 1927), 199–200, addressed these problems. For prewar warnings, see the comments of a reserve officer with eleven years of prior active duty, Captain Kretschmar, "Die Ausbildung unserere Offiziere des Beurlaubtenstandes," *Militär-Wochenblatt* 31 (1913): cols. 699–700.

54. Lieutenant Colonel von Schaumann, "Unsere Offiziere des Beurlaubtenstandes," *Militär-Wochenblatt* 63 (1913): cols. 1434–1437, 65 (1913): cols. 1478–1481; Anonymous, "Gedanken über die Ausbildung der Reserveoffizier der Infanterie bei der Truppe," *Militär-Wochenblatt* 74 (1913): col. 1685.

55. On reserve officers avoiding their annual maneuvers, see Schaumann, "Unsere Offiziere des Beurlaubtenstandes," 1478–1479.

56. John, *Das Reserveoffizierkorps*, 272–274, cites numerous contemporary sources on shortcomings. On the comparison with those of Germany's potential enemies, see Anonymous, "Die militärische Vorbildung unserer Offiziere des Beurlaubtenstandes," *Militär-Wochenblatt* 99, 7 (1914): cols. 123–124. For the public warning that these ill-trained reservists would occupy most infantry positions, see Anonymous, "Zur kriegsmässige Ausbildung der Offiziere des Beurlaubtenstandes der Infanterie," 3595–3596. One writer argued that these shortcomings were especially important at the rank of platoon leader. See Bärensprung, "Die Ausbildung der Einjährig-Freiwilligen der Infanterie," *Militär-Wochenblatt* 126 (1912): col. 2911.

57. Moser, *Ausbildung und Führung*, 189.

58. August Keim, who later lost favor for his criticisms of infantry tactics, had issued a stern warning in an article in 1890. August Keim, "Der gegenwärtige Stand der Gefechtslehre und die Ausbildung zum Gefecht," *Beiheft zum Militär-Wochenblatt* 75, 1 (1890): 10.

59. Sigismund Schlichting, *Taktische und strategische Grundsätze der Gegenwart*, 3 vols., 3rd ed. (Berlin: E. S. Mittler, 1898–1899), 3:43, 235; Joachim Hoffmann, "Die Kriegslehre des Generals von Schlichting," *Militärgeschichtliche Mitteilungen* 1 (1969): 33. See the infantry regulations, *D.V.E. 130* (1906), 79, para. 253.

60. Hugo Baron von Freytag-Loringhoven, "Das Begegnungsgefecht, kriegsgeschichtliche Betrachtungen," *Vierteljahresheft* 1 (1904): 110–111; Konstantin Hierl, "Gefechtsausdehnungen," *Vierteljahrshefte für Truppenführung und Heereskunde* 5 (1908): 295. Hierl's writings were laced with warnings about excessively dense tactical formations, particularly firing lines in the attack.

61. Anonymous, "Die sogenannte 'Angriffshetze,'" *Militär-Wochenblatt* 44 (1908): col. 1026; Editor, "Gefechtsverbindung," *Militär-Wochenblatt* 56 (1908): col. 1301; Wolf, "Welche Bewandtnis hat es mit der 'Angriffshetze'?" *Militär-Wochenblatt* 103 (1908): col. 2543.

62. Hugo Baron von Freytag-Loringhoven, "Über die Dauer von Schlachten und Gefechten," *Vierteljahshefte für Truppenführung und Heeerskunde* 2 (1905): 556–557, citing Moltke; Anonymous, "Eile Geboten," *Militär-Wochenblatt* 29 (1914): cols. 603–604.

63. A 1908 article cited numerous regulations on the need for cooperation between infantry and artillery, particularly the heavy field howitzers, in the attack. See Captain Wilhelmi, "Die schwere Feldartillerie in der Felddienst und Manöver-Ordnung, Gedanken über Kriegstüchtigkeit," *Militär-Wochenblatt* 65 (1908): cols 1527–1532. A summary of the issues surrounding the infantry attack is in Antulio J. Echevarria II, *After Clausewitz: German Military Thinkers before the Great War* (Lawrence: University Press of Kansas, 2000), 122–127.

64. Groener, *Das Testament des Grafen Schlieffen*, 198–199, was representative of the postwar criticism that the fine art of combined arms was not sufficiently practiced in peacetime, resulting in unnecessarily heavy casualties in combat. Combined-arms training became one of the hallmarks of the postwar German army.

65. Wilhelmi, "Die schwere Feldartillerie," 1527.

66. David Stevenson, *Cataclysm: The First World War as Political Tragedy* (New York: Basic Books, 2004), 60.

67. See the prescient warnings of Julius Hoppenstedt, "Die Infanterie im Kampfe der verbundene Waffen," *Militär-Wochenblatt* 90 (1912): cols. 2050–2051.

68. August Keim, *Erlebtes und Erstrebtes. Lebenserinnerungen* (Hannover: Ernst Letsch Verlag, 1925), 89–90, cites an example of how difficult it was to force units to train realistically, even if they were in the hands of a capable corps commander. Even enthusiastic supporters of the open-order tactics of the 1906 regulations recognized the difficulty of training units to use them. See Anonymous, "Die Gruppenführer," *Militär-Wochenblatt* 8 (1904): col. 158.

69. Kramer, "Angriffsschema," *Militär-Wochenblatt* 121 (1912): col. 2801; Anonymous, "Zweck und Stärke der Schützenentwicklung vor hundert Jahre und Heute," *Militär-Wochenblatt* 43 (1910): col. 1037.

70. Anonymous, "Über die Gefechtsausbildung unserer Infanterie," *Militär-Wochenblatt* 30 (1903): col. 84, complained about the differences among the twenty-three corps of that time. This article demonstrates that the problem was old and recognized and that the army allowed public criticism of its highest command positions. Nevertheless, not enough heed was paid to clear and cogent problems. For a specific example of a corps commander applying the entirely wrong tactics of cavalry to an infantry corps, see Martin Chales de Bealieu, "Erinnerungen," 3:161, *Nachlass* Chales de Bealieu, BA/MA, N 187/3.

71. Ernst von Eisenhart Rothe, "Die Infanterie," in *Ehrendenkmal der Deutschen Armee und Marine 1871–1918*, ed. Ernst von Eisenhart Rothe (Berlin: Deutscher National-Verlag, 1928), 92, has an unusually clear retrospective critique of an officer.

Dieter Storz, *Kriegsbild und Rüstung vor 1914. Europäische Landstreitkräfte vor dem Ersten Weltkrieg* (Herford: E. S. Mittler, 1992), 57–58, makes much the same point citing the prewar literature, particularly that dealing with the lessons of the Boer War.

72. Given Germany's strategic priorities in 1915, these were the western front, eastern front, and Serbia.

73. Chef des Generalstabes des Feldheeres, M.I. Nr. 3725, to subordinate commands, 8 November 1914, *Nachlass* Hauffe, BA/MA, N 11/2; Otto Mueller (Major A. D.), "Kampfmittel und Taktik der deutschen Infanterie im Weltkriege," in *Deutsche Infanterie. Das Ehrenmal der vordersten Front*, ed. Ernst von Eisenhart-Rothe, Erich von Tschischwitz, and Walther Beckmann (Zeulenroda: Verlag Bernhard Sporn, 1939), 201–216, esp. 203.

74. Helmuth Gruss, *Die deutsche Sturmbataillone im Weltkrieg, Ausbau und Verwendung* (Berlin: Junker & Dünnhaupt, 1939), 14.

75. Martin Samuels, *Doctrine and Dogma: German and British Infantry Tactics in the First World War* (New York: Greenwood, 1992), 13–14, discusses the German army's efforts to develop very light field artillery and armored shields.

76. See the comments of the anonymous author of "Bewegung und Waffenwirkung in der Taktik des Weltkrieges," *Militär-Wochenblatt* 111, 42 (1927): cols. 1537–1542, 43 (1927): cols. 1585–1592. This largely forgotten article is one of the clearest expositions of this subject.

77. Reichsarchiv, *Der Weltkrieg 1914 bis 1918*, 14 vols. (Berlin: E. S. Mittler, 1925–1944), 7:17–19, 12:26, discusses the memoranda of January 1915. Graeme Chamley Wynne, *If Germany Attacks: The Battle in Depth in the West* (1940; reprint, Westport, CT: Greenwood Press, 1976), 15–16, relies on the Reichsarchiv's vol. 7.

78. The reasons behind the decisions to mount these campaigns are discussed in the previous chapter.

79. General Alfred Ziethen, "Aus grosser Zeit vor zwanzig Jahren. Die Durchbruchschlacht von Gorlice," *Militär-Wochenblatt* 119, 41 (1935): col. 1629; DiNardo, *Breakthrough*, 50.

80. DiNardo, *Invasion*, 87.

81. DiNardo, *Breakthrough*, 66.

82. The fundamental works in English on tactical changes in the German army are Johnson, *Breakthrough*; Timothy T. Lupfer, *The Dynamics of Doctrine: The Changes in German Tactical Doctrine during the First World War*, Leavenworth Papers No. 4. (Fort Leavenworth, KS: US Army Command and General Staff College, 1981), now somewhat dated; and Wynne, *If Germany Attacks*, also dated but still of fundamental value. Martin Samuels, *Command or Control? Command, Training and Tactics in the British and German Armies 1888–1918* (London: Frank Cass, 1995), provides many details not otherwise readily available. Bruce Gudmundsson, *Stormtroop Tactics: Innovation in the German Army, 1914–1918* (New York: Praeger, 1989), is good on many individual points but lacks a firm basis in the army's regulations and surviving sources.

83. Samuels, *Command or Control?* 164, relies on G. C. Wynne, "Pattern for Limited War: The Riddle of the Schlieffen Plan, Part I," *Royal United Services Institute Journal* 102, 4 (1951): 492.

84. Wynne, *If Germany Attacks*, 19–35. Reichsarchiv, *Der Weltkrieg*, 7:56–59, discusses the battle only briefly. It was of no great strategic significance and was, by the standards of the western front, a relatively minor affair. It did, however, mark one of the many small steps and experiences in the evolution of German defensive tactics.

85. Samuels, *Command or Control?* 163–164.

86. Reichsarchiv, *Der Weltkrieg*, vol. 7, has many examples.

87. Chef d. Generalstabes d. Feldheeres, No. 7563r, (Geheim) "Gesichtpunkte für den Stellungskrieg," February 1915, 3–15, BA/MA, PH D 7/1.

88. General Staff No. 7563 (Secret) "Gesichtspunkte für den Stellungskrieg," 20 October 1915, BA/MA, PH 3/295.

89. Wynne, *If Germany Attacks*, 85; Herwig, *First World War*, 165.

90. Samuels, *Command or Control?* 167. The most comprehensive study of the French army's operations in World War I makes no mention of this. See Robert A. Doughty, *Pyrrhic Victory: French Strategy and Operations in the Great War* (Cambridge, MA: Harvard University Press, 2005).

91. Wynne, *If Germany Attacks*, 98–99, has a translation of the French order. Wynne did not have access to the High Command's draft manual of February 1915.

92. Ibid., 85. Wynne argues for its influence on the tactical specialists at the High Command.

93. The bulk of the High Command moved to Pless, in Silesia, on 7 May 1915 to be closer to the critical battles in the east and to facilitate contact with the Austro-Hungarian headquarters at Teschen. Gerhard Tappen remained chief of the Operations Sections and moved with the main body. Lieutenant Colonel Friedrich (Fritz) von Lossberg, with a staff of about a dozen junior officers, remained in Mèziéres to deal with developments on the western front. See Fritz von Lossberg, *Meine Tätigkeit im Weltkriege* (Berlin: E. S. Mittler, 1939), 131–132.

94. Samuels, *Command or Control?* 166–167.

95. Ibid., 139–140. Stein makes no mention of this in his memoirs. See Hermann von Stein, *Erlebnisse und Betrachtungen aus der Zeit des Weltkrieges* (Leipzig: K. F. Koehler, 1919).

96. Lossberg, a colonel when he moved to Third Army, remained with that command until 19 July 1916, when he became chief of the General Staff of First Army. In April 1917 he moved to Sixth Army. In June he went to Fourth Army after the Messines Ridge disaster but did not remain there long. In July Ludendorff transferred him to Second Army, which was expecting a major British offensive. He had two subsequent assignments at threatened sectors of the front after the end of the German offensives in 1918. See Lossberg, *Meine Tätigkeit*, 199–200, 214–215, 280–281, 293, 352, 359–360.

97. Samuels, *Command or Control?* 168–169, has a detailed description based on German documents captured and circulated by the British and now located in the Public Records Office.

98. Reichsarchiv, *Der Weltkrieg*, 9:102–103, citing subsequent studies by the two German field armies involved and the French official history.

99. General Staff d. Feldheeres, Nr. 7563, Geheim, "Gesichtspunkte für den Stellungskrieg," 20 October 1915, BA/MA, PH 3/295.

100. Hermann Cron, *Geschichte des deutschen Heeres im Weltkriege 1914–1918* (Berlin: Militärverlag Karl Siegismund, 1937), 23, has the details. These manuals appeared from 19 April to 8 July 1916 and had the imprint of the war minister.

101. The standard sources in English focusing on the British efforts are John Keegan, *The Face of Battle: A Study of Agincourt, Waterloo, and the Somme* (New York: Penguin, 1978); Lynn MacDonald, *Somme* (London: Michael Joseph, 1983); Martin Middlebrook, *The First Day of the Somme, 1 July 1916* (London: Allen Layne, 1971); Peter Liddle, *The 1916 Battle of the Somme: A Reappraisal* (London: L. Cooper, 1992); Peter Hart, *The Somme: The Darkest Hour on the Western Front* (New York: Pegasus Books, 2008); and William Philpott, *Three Armies on the Somme: The First Battle of the Twentieth Century* (New York: Alfred A. Knopf, 2010). More German focused, but usually at the worm's-eye level, are Christopher Duffy, *Through German Eyes: The British and the Somme 1916* (London: Weidenfeld & Nicholson, 2006), and Jack Sheldon, *The German Army on the Somme 1914–1916* (Barnsley, UK: Pen & Sword, 2005).

102. The other was the famous manual setting forth the revised offensive tactics of 1918, discussed later.

103. Afflerbach, *Falkenhayn*, 419–420, discusses the dismissal of Below's chief of staff, Grünert, and his replacement by Lossberg. Below was furious, as was his immediate superior, Crown Prince Rupprecht. This decision was highly unpopular in the army and the General Staff and probably seriously undermined Falkenhayn's moral standing. Falkenhayn's act seemed particularly inappropriate because he had just refused requests by Below and Rupprecht to reinforce Second Army. Lossberg, *Meine Tätigkeit*, 219–220, confirms the circumstances surrounding his replacement of Grünert without commenting on the controversy.

104. On the German positions, see Samuel, *Command or Control?* 171; Wynne, *If Germany Attacks*, 100–101. Konrad Krafft von Dellmensingen, *Der Durchbruch. Studie an der Hand der Vorgänge des Weltkrieges 1914–1918* (Hamburg: Hanseatische Verlagsanstalt, 1937), 72–81, generally agrees but discusses only two positions. He confirms that the second was far to the rear. On the expectations, see Hans Möller, *Fritz von Below. General der Infanterie* (Berlin: Bernard & Graefe, 1939), 48–49; Afflerbach, *Falkenhayn*, 417–418. Falkenhayn and others at the High Command seemed to welcome this opportunity to fight the British, whom he regarded as the primary enemy.

105. John Keegan, *The First World War* (New York: Alfred A. Knopf, 1999), 290–291. Hew Strachan, *European Armies and the Conduct of War* (London: Allen & Unwin, 1983), 140–144, has the higher estimate of British artillery expenditures.

106. In some places, of course, isolated trenches or sections of the wire entanglements remained intact. Keegan, *First World War*, 291–293, stressing British incompetence, perhaps overstates the extent to which trenches and barriers survived. Möller, *Fritz von Below*, 49, stresses the nearly complete destruction of the forward positions, as do most German accounts.

107. This is according to his own account: Lossberg, *Meine Tätigkeit*, 221.

108. Ibid., 249–250. See also Hart, *Somme*, 323.

109. Otto von Moser, *Feldzugsaufzeichnungen als Brigade-Divisionskommandeur und als kommandierender General 1914–1918* (Stuttgart: Chr. Belsersche Verlagsbuchhandlung, 1920), 223–224, estimated that more than 90 percent of his command's losses were due to artillery fire. He also stressed the importance of British aerial fire direction, an aspect of airpower in the First World War that has not received the attention it deserves. Lossberg, *Meine Tätigkeit*, 251, also attributed much to British aerial observation and the direction of artillery fire.

110. Lossberg, *Meine Tätigkeit*, 249–251, recorded his observations at a meeting of commanders and General Staff officers on 8 September. Max von Gallwitz, *Erleben im Westen 1916–1918* (Berlin: E. S. Mittler, 1932), 77, also recorded his efforts to thin out the front lines and use counterattacks to achieve the objectives.

111. From the infantry's point of view, this was not entirely unfavorable. Many apparently considered the shell holes, which made individual soldiers as well as small groups with machine guns nearly invisible, to be safer than trench lines, especially in light of the consequences of successful Allied aerial reconnaissance. See Hermann von Kuhl, *Der Weltkrieg 1914–1918*, 2 vols. (Berlin: Vaterländischen Verlag E. A. Weller, 1930), 1:494–495.

112. Gallwitz, *Erleben im Westen*, 93, summarizes a report of Stein, then a division commander, on these issues. Soldiers in the front shell holes (where trench lines were no longer recognizable) could not even properly prepare their "iron" rations, the emergency meals they relied on when food could not be brought forward from the company kitchens. See also Sheldon, *German Army on the Somme*, 202.

113. Gallwitz, *Erleben im Westen*, 114–116, summarizes an order sent to his subordinate units in September. He warned the commanders that too many men were disappearing from the front, some were surrendering unnecessarily, and a general decline in discipline had developed owing to officers' reluctance to punish offenders. Even officers became lax in their appearance and conduct. He warned commanders that they had failed to maintain sufficient personal contact with the forward units, a continuing problem of lengthy positional warfare, where telephones too frequently substituted for a personal presence at the front.

114. Herwig, *First World War*, 198. Other estimates vary, but Herwig's totals seem a reasonable balance.

115. Showalter, *Instrument of War*, 166. This issue receives lengthy consideration in a later section of this study.

116. Reichsarchiv, *Der Weltkrieg*, 12:32. The Operations Section of the General Staff worked to provide the army as a whole the proper lessons to be incorporated into a new doctrinal manual. Ludendorff has properly received credit for this effort, but the units would have made their views known in any case.

117. Gallwitz, *Erleben im Westen*, 107–119, 167–168, contains extracts from his army's experience, as well as that of the crown prince's army group as a whole. The latter touched off a serious dispute because of its open criticism of Gallwitz's decisions during the Somme battle. The *OHL*'s study of lessons learned is summarized in Reichsarchiv, *Der Weltkrieg*, 12:33–34.

118. Gallwitz, *Erleben im Westen*, 119.

119. The gradual development of assault unit tactics shortly thereafter began to provide the army with new methods of returning mobility to tactics. This process, at first an independent development in its own right, receives extensive treatment in a subsequent section of this study.

120. Gallwitz, *Erleben im Westen*, 107–109; Reichsarchiv, *Der Weltkrieg*, 12:33–34.

121. There is no scholarly biography of Ludendorff in English. The main studies available are Donald J. Goodspeed, *Ludendorff: Genius of World War I* (Boston: Houghton Mifflin, 1966); Robert B. Asprey, *The German High Command at War: Hindenburg and Ludendorff and the First World War* (New York: W. Morrow, 1991). See also John Daniels Buckelow, "Erich Ludendorff and the German War Effort 1916–1918: A Study in the Military Exercise of Power" (Ph.D. diss., University of California–San Diego, 1974). The two major biographies in German are Franz Uhle Wettler, *Ludendorff in Seine Zeit: Soldat-Stratege-Revolutionär, Eine Neubewerbung* (Augsburg: Kurt Vowinckel, 1996), and Nebelin, *Ludendorff*.

122. Ludendorff, *Urkunden*, 592–594, has a list of the most important regulations and related publications produced during his tenure. The reader should note that many of these were primarily updates of material originally produced under Falkenhayn, even though Ludendorff's list makes it appear that nearly all of them originated after he and Hindenburg took over. Ludendorff's war memoirs are available in English as *Ludendorff's Own Story*, 2 vols. (Freeport, NY: Books for Libraries, 1971). The German version is *Meine Kriegserinnerungen 1914–1918* (Berlin: E. S. Mittler, 1919).

123. Cron, *Geschichte des deutschen Heeres*, 24. These manuals appeared between 15 November 1916 and 1 January 1917, with the imprint of the General Staff. See also Bauer, *Der grosse Krieg*, 119.

124. Heinz-Ludger Borgert, "Landkriegführung von Schlieffen bis Guderian," in *Deutsche Militärgeschichte*, ed. Militärgeschichtliches Forschungsamt, 6 vols. (Munich: Bernard & Graefe, 1964–1979), 6:512, discusses the effort initiated by Falkenhayn. Ludendorff's *Urkunden*, 604–640, reprints a list of some of these and the full text of a slightly modified edition of the defensive manual published on 20 September 1918. Ludendorff, *Meine Kriegserinnerungen*, 307, gives credit almost exclusively to Bauer and Geyer.

125. Generalstab des Feldheeres, *Grundsätze für die Führung der Abwehrschlacht im Stellungskrieg*, pt. 8 of *Sammelheft der Vorschriften für den Stellungskrieg*, copy in BA/MA, PH D 7/26. Samuels, *Command or Control?* 178–184, describes the contents on the basis of captured and translated versions in the Public Records Office. Either he or the PRO has the title slightly wrong, as does Wynne.

126. Reichsarchiv, *Der Weltkrieg*, 12:36, footnote.

127. Ibid., 50.

128. Ludendorff, *Meine Kriegserinnerungen*, 214–215, 306.

129. *Grundsätze für die die Führung der Abwehrschlacht im Stellungskrieg*, para. 6, in Ludendorff, *Urkunden*, 604.

130. Ludendorff, *Urkunden*, 606.

131. Samuels, *Command or Control?* uses a 1 March 1917 edition captured and translated by the British in May of that year. The copy in the German military archives is slightly different, as is the edition in Ludendorff's *Urkunden*. The first edition appeared with a date of 1 December 1916. New versions with slight modifications appeared on 1 March and 10 June 1917. More important changes were incorporated into a new edition on 1 September 1917. The final iteration appeared in September 1918. See Reichsarchiv, *Der Weltkrieg*, 12:39.

132. Reichsarchiv, *Der Weltkrieg*, 12:40.

133. General Staff of the Field Army, "Die Kampfmittel in der Abwehrschlacht" (1917), 43, BA/MA, PH 3/30. Wynne, *If Germany Attacks*, 170–171, has a useful introduction.

134. Crown Prince Rupprecht of Bavaria, *In Treue Fest. Mein Kriegstagebuch*, ed. Eugen von Frauenholz, 3 vols. (Munich: Deutscher National Verlag, 1929), 2:79–80, reprints the text as part of a diary entry of 10 January 1917.

135. Samuels, *Command or Control?* 181–183.

136. The term *Eingreif Divisionen* first came into use in April 1917 in the army group of the German crown prince. See Reichsarchiv, *Der Weltkrieg*, 12:408.

137. Gallwitz, *Erleben im Westen*, 168, speaking of the March 1917 revision.

138. Bauer believed that decentralization of responsibility to the division commander was one of the manual's two main points, the other being depth. See Max Bauer, *Der grosse Krieg in Feld und Heimat. Erinnerungen und Betrachtungen* (Tübingen: Osiander'sche Buchhandlung, 1921), 119.

139. Samuels, *Command or Control?* 182–184; Wynne, *If Germany Attacks*, 252–257. Both have good summaries. Wynne apparently used the first edition of the regulations.

140. Wynne, *If Germany Attacks*, 159–168, discusses Lossberg's objections to elastic defense. Lossberg insisted on a deep but less flexible system. See also Samuels, *Command or Control?* 185–186. The Reichsarchiv, discussing the meeting in Cambrai on 8 September 1916, briefly mentioned Bauer's proposal for a "more mobile way of infantry defense," without stating who the opponents were. The Reichsarchiv noted, nevertheless, that many experienced and respected commanders and General Staff officers had expressed serious reservations. See Reichsarchiv, *Der Weltkrieg*, 12:32.

141. Samuels, *Command or Control?* 186. Ludendorff used the term "elastic" to describe the system, possibly for the first time, in an order to the field on 15 June 1918. See his *Urkunden*, 686.

142. Ludendorff's term was *Ausweichen*, meaning to give way or to dodge rather than to defend.

143. See Moser, *Feldzugsaufzeichnungen*, 245.

144. Samuels, *Command or Control?* 186–197, discusses this in detail with his customary clarity of thought.

145. Indeed, by 1918, concern for artillery was almost as prominent in the regulations as details of infantry procedures. See Ludendorff, *Urkunden*, 621–630. Herwig's brief discussion in *First World War*, 246–248, properly incorporates artillery considerations.

146. Moser, *Feldzugsaufzeichnungen*, 246–254; Samuels, *Command or Control?* 184–185.

147. Moser, *Feldzugsaufzeichnungen*, 247–249; Holger Herwig, "The Dynamics of Necessity: German Military Policy during the First World War," in *Military Effectiveness*, ed. Allan R. Millett and Williamson Murray, 3 vols. (Boston: Allen & Unwin, 1988), 1:100–101. Bruchmüller's artillery methods are the subject of a later section of this study.

148. General Staff of the Army, Ausbildungs-Lehrgänge Sedan 1917, VII Kursus (vom 11.5.–18.5.), Inhalts Verzeichnis, 9 May 1917, BA/MA, PH 3/245. See also other documents, same source and date, subjects: Verzeichnis der Teilnehmer, and Zeiteneinteilen. On the seventeenth and eighteenth courses, see General Staff of the Army, Zeiteneinteilung des 18. Übungskursus Sedan (vom 10.9.17–19.9.17) and the same document for the period 22.9.–29.9.17, BA/MA, PH 3/29 and 3/30. On the use of machine guns in the defensive battle, see Chief, General Staff of the Army, memorandum titled "Grundsätze für die Verwendung der M.G. in der Abwehrschlacht," BA/MA, PH 3/30.

149. See Hindenburg's memorandum to General Staff officers on their increased responsibilities as the nature of war changed, dated 22 November 1916, BA/MA, PH 3/26.

150. Reichsarchiv, *Der Weltkrieg*, 12:51. A limited example of the results at the corps level can be found at Generalkommando 1a [XII Corps], Nr. 1328, 9 February 1917, BA/MA, PH 6 I/299.

151. Moser, *Feldzugsaufzeichnungen*, 240, 307–309.

152. Wynne, *If Germany Attacks*, 171–184, examines the battle in great detail. Wynne considers a French offensive near Verdun in December as the first test. This discussion disregards it because the German units involved had had little time to implement the new system by then.

153. For Lossberg's own account, see *Meine Tätigkeit*, 287–288.

154. Wynne, *If Germany Attacks*, 206–254, discusses the attack and Lossberg's countermeasures in great detail. By April, the British had captured the new German regulations but, for the most part, failed to make any adjustments. The overall danger was probably never as great as it might have appeared to the Germans, since the main purpose of the attack was to divert forces from the long-planned Nivelle offensive, discussed below.

155. Kuhl, *Der Weltkrieg*, 2:85–86.

156. Reichsarchiv, *Der Weltkrieg*, uses the term in discussing the subsequent investigation by the High Command. General Falkenhausen soon moved to the position of governor-general of Belgium.

157. Ludendorff, *Meine Kriegserinnerungen*, 334.

158. See Krafft von Dellmensingen, *Der Durchburch*, 100.

159. Indeed, the continuing reservations expressed by Lossberg and Hoehn may have indirectly contributed to Falkenhausen's reluctance to rely on local counterattacks for a successful defense. See Samuels, *Command or Control?* 188, who makes the best of a plausible but by no means certain case.

160. Reichsarchiv, *Der Weltkrieg*, 12:234–237, summarizes the High Com-

mand's study. Krafft von Dellmensingen, writing after the war, concluded that the rainy weather and hesitant British leadership were the real reasons that the British failed to exploit their initial successes. See his *Der Durchbruch*, 97–98.

161. Lossberg, *Meine Tätigkeit*, 288. Wynne, *If Germany Attacks*, 182–183, suggests that Falkenhausen was too old for an energetic application of the new defensive system, but he also quotes Hermann von Kuhl's opinion that the Vimy Ridge terrain was largely unsuitable for such an elastic defense. Rupprecht, *In Treue Fest*, 2:141, notes that although Falkenhausen was old, he was still capable and energetic prior to the battle. Moser, then a corps commander, concurs in *Feldzugsaufzeichnungen*, 234. Rupprecht and Moser agree that the defeat of his army broke Falkenhausen's spirit.

162. Samuels, *Command or Control?* 187–192, discusses the battle and the German response.

163. The Germans called it the double battles on the Aisne and in Champagne. Some accounts also refer to it as the Chemin des Dames.

164. Herwig, *First World War*, 317–319, is the best available summary. Reichsarchiv, *Der Weltkrieg*, 12:306–307, has slightly different numbers.

165. C. R. M. F. Cruttwell, *A History of the Great War 1914–1918*, 2nd ed. (Chicago: Academy Publishers, 1992), 411.

166. All this is summarized in Krafft von Dellmensingen, *Der Durchbruch*, 109–114.

167. For a recent summary of Nivelle's concepts and their failure, see Doughty, *Pyrrhic Victory*, 324–354.

168. Cruttwell, *History of the Great War*, 409, notes the widespread knowledge of the offensive as early as December 1916. The Germans had good indications of the general nature of the offensive at least by the end of February. See Reichsarchiv, *Der Weltkrieg*, 12:281–288. A local German attack on 4 April 1917 captured a French order with many details of Nivelle's plan, confirming what aerial reconnaissance had already indicated.

169. Reichsarchiv, *Der Weltkrieg*, 12:282, 287, 405–407, discusses the preparations. Energetic action was required of the crown prince and his chief of staff, Count Schulenburg, because some subordinate commanders were still reluctant to adopt the new defensive system. Boehn's chief of staff, Walther Reinhardt, was also important in preparing the defense.

170. Ibid., 307–308, concluded that this was one of the most difficult areas for the attacker on the entire western front.

171. Ibid., 309–310. Keegan, *First World War*, 321ff, has a particularly picturesque account.

172. Reichsarchiv, *Der Weltkrieg*, 12:410, has the casualty figures, which Herwig, *First World War*, 329, also uses.

173. This summary is from Herwig, *First World War*, 322–324.

174. Wynne, *If Germany Attacks*, 305–307; Keegan, *First World War*, 358–359.

175. Keegan, *First World War*, 366.

176. Samuels, *Command or Control?* 195, describes these developments. Krafft von Dellmensingen, *Der Durchbruch*, 130–131, also has a useful account of the new

problem of countering limited attacks. On Lossberg's personal role in attempting to cope with the new British tactics, see Wynne, *If Germany Attacks*, 290–293.

177. Herwig, *First World War*, 332–333, summarizes the Passchendaele episode.

178. Samuels, *Command or Control?* 87–88. Samuels relies in part on Gruss, *Die deutsche Sturmbataillone*; on this point, see especially 12–15. See also Ernst Schmidt, *Argonnen*, vol. 18 of *Schlachten des Weltkrieges*. (Berlin: Gerhard Stalling, 1927), 136–137.

179. Samuels, *Command or Control?* 88; Gruss, *Die deutsche Sturmbataillone*, 15, 17, 147–148. See also Bauer, *Der grosse Krieg*, 87–88.

180. Gruss, *Die deutschen Sturmbataillone*, 17. See also Samuels, *Command or Control?* 232, on the role of Hans von Seeckt in this experimental effort.

181. Cron, *Geschichte des deutschen Heeres*, 125. See also Hermann Cron, *Die Organisation des deutschen Heeres im Weltkriege* (Berlin: E. S. Mittler, 1923), 45–46; Gruss, *Die deutsche Sturmbataillone*, 14–15, 147–148. Gudmundsson, *Stormtroop Tactics*, 27–41, has a useful section on prewar fortress warfare concepts.

182. Samuels, *Doctrine and Dogma*, 14–17; Norman Louis Kincaide, "Sturmabteilung to Freikorps: German Army Tactical and Organizational Development, 1914–1918" (Ph.D. diss., Arizona State University, 1989), 23–24.

183. Edgar *Graf* von Matuschka and Wolfgang Petter, "Organisationsgeschichte der Streitkräfte," in *Deutsche Militärgeschichte*, 2:235–236; Cron, *Geschichte des deutschen Heeres*, 125–126; Kincaide, "Sturmabteilungen to Freikorps," 26–27.

184. Gruss, *Die deutsche Sturmbataillone*, 19, citing lost archival sources.

185. Bauer, *Der grosse Krieg*, 87–88.

186. Ibid., 21.

187. Matuschka and Petter, "Organisationsgeschichte der Streitkräfte," 2:235–236.

188. Schwerin, "Das Sturmbataillone Rohr," in *Das Ehrenbuch der deutschen Pioniere*, ed. Paul Heinrici (Berlin: Verlag Tradition Wilhelm Rulf, 1937), 559–562; Gruss, *Die deutsche Sturmbataillone*, 21–27; Gudmundsson, *Stormtroop Tactics*, 44–45. Rohr survived the war and entered the Reichswehr, from which he retired as a lieutenant colonel. He died in 1929.

189. Gruss, *Die deutsche Sturmbataillone*, 44, citing archival sources now lost, particularly a tactical directive produced by Rohr's unit in May 1916.

190. Ibid., 28, 33–34.

191. Ibid., 28–31.

192. Ibid., 31–32.

193. These 1916 guidelines defined a *Sturmtrupp* as consisting of one officer or noncommissioned officer and four to eight assault engineers. The *Sturmtrupp* was thus not considered an infantry unit.

194. Gruss, *Die deutsche Sturmbataillone*, 43–46. Kincaide, "Sturmabteilung to Freikorps," 42–45, has an excellent summary, also based on Gruss.

195. Schwerin, "Das Sturmbataillon Rohr," 560.

196. Report, III Reserve Corps Ia, No. 201, "Erfahrungen aus Kämpfen der letzteren Zeit für den Angriff. Zusammengestellt aus Erfahrungen mitgeteilt vom Chef des Generalstabes des Feldheeres und aus Berichten anderer Stel-

len," 21 April 1916, BA/MA, PH 3/38. At the time, Third Reserve Corps was on the eastern front under the command of Tenth Army, indicating that the General Staff's report went to both major fronts. See Reichsarchiv, *Der Weltkrieg*, 10:534, n. 2.

197. Letter from Chief of the General Staff of the Field Army, Nr. 279595 op, to various army commands, subject: Sonderausbildung der Sturmabteilungen, 15 May 1916, BA/MA, PH 3/305. This is printed in Gruss, *Die deutsche Sturmbataillone*, 152.

198. Kincaide, "Sturmabteilungen to Freikorps," 40–42, discusses this point. See also Gruss, *Die deutsche Sturmbataillone*, 35–36.

199. Gruss, *Die deutsche Sturmbataillone*, 18–19, citing a lost report by Major Calsow.

200. Ibid., 19, 35–36, 47–48, 63.

201. Kincaide, "Sturmabteilungen to Freikorps," 66–67.

202. Heeresgruppe Kronprinz von Bayern, Abtlg. Ic, Nr. 1424 (Secret), 11 February 1916, signed by Kuhl, National Archives Records Administration, microfilm series T-78, roll 710 (hereafter cited as NARA, T-78/710).

203. Kincaide, "Sturmabteilung to Freikorps," 42.

204. Kriegsministerium to various headquarters, MJ 14180/16 A1, Secret, 8 July 1916, BA/MA, PH 3/305.

205. General Staff to various units, No. 30 002 OP, subject: Sturmbataillone, Secret, 27 June 1916, 3–5, BA/MA, PH 3/305.

206. First Army, General Staff Ia, Order No. 1841, Secret, subject: Armeebefehl, 10 December 1916, BA/MA, PH 5 II/6. This order referred to an *OHL* directive of 4 December 1916. Examples of the establishment of formal assault battalions can be found in orders of the War Ministry to various commanders, dated December 1916, NARA, T-78/710.

207. Field Marshal Erwin Rommel, *Attacks* (Vienna, VA: Athena Press, 1979), 103–105; Michael B. Barrett, *Prelude to Blitzkrieg: The 1916 Austro-German Campaign in Romania* (Bloomington: Indiana University Press, 2013), 310; KTB/Army Group Mackensen, 16 October 1916, BA/MA, PH 5 I/17; Army Group Mackensen, "The Dobrudja Campaign," pt. II, ca. December 1916, BA/MA, PH 5 I/18; Richard L. DiNardo "Modern Soldier in a Busby: August von Mackensen, 1914–1916, in *Arms and Men: Military History Essays in Honor of Dennis Showalter*, ed. Michael S. Neiberg (Boston: Brill, 2011), 161.

208. Barrett, *Prelude to Blitzkrieg*, 305. For a more favorable assessment of the Romanian performance, see Glenn E. Torrey, *The Romanian Battlefront in World War I* (Lawrence: University Press of Kansas, 2011), 254.

209. Gruss, *Die deutsche Sturmbataillone*, 56–57. See also Adolf Wild von Hohenborn, *Briefe und Aufzeichnungen des preussischen Generals als Kriegsministers und Truppenführer im Ersten Weltkrieg*, ed. Helmut Reichold (Boppard: Harald Boldt Verlag, 1986), 192.

210. Samuels, *Command or Control?* 240–241. On the War Ministry, see War Ministry to Chief of the General Staff, 31 October 1916, BA/MA, PH 3/305, 38.

211. War Minister, No. 30308/16A1, to various commands, NARA, T-78/710.

212. War Ministry to Chief of General Staff, No. 33185, 16 A1, 29 December 1916, BA/MA, PH 3/305, 75.

213. Bavarian War Ministry to rear area corps headquarters, subject: Ausbildung beim Sturmbattaillon, 10 January 1917, BA/MA, PH 3/305, 82.

214. Herwig, *First World War*, 254, has many details. As Samuels notes in *Doctrine and Dogma*, 25, Ludendorff "was simply allowing an ongoing process to continue rather than initiating any new policy." See also Kincaide, "Sturmabteilungen to Freikorps," 68–69.

215. Gruss, *Die deutsche Sturmbataillone*, 65.

216. Report, Headquarters First Army Ia, No. 1546, secret, subject: Angriffsunternehmungen, 3 November 1916, BA/MA, PH 5 II/8. This combat had taken place on the Somme.

217. Gruss, *Die deutsche Sturmbataillone*, 48, 81; Kincaide, "Sturmabteilungen to Freikorps," 71. Some of the opposition continued to spring from a reluctance to weaken the infantry battalions by transferring soldiers to special assault units.

218. Gruss, *Die deutsche Sturmbataillone*, 156–157, reprints the order of 23 December 1916.

219. Ibid., 60–62, has many details. See also Kincaide, "Sturmabteilung to Freikorps," 99–100. The order for the Rohr Battalion's numerical designation is in War Ministry order, M.I. 3815/17, A1, 7 February 1917, NARA, T-78/710.

220. Cron, *Geschichte des deutschen Heeres*, 127.

221. Gruss, *Die deutsche Sturmbataillone*, 65–72, discusses these and other developments on the eastern front.

222. Sturm Bataillon Nr. 1, Gesichtspunkte für die Art des Deinstsbetriebes bei den Kompagnien, 25.10.1916 (Neudruck 14.2.17), BA/MA, PH 5 II/6; Army Oberkommando 1, Ia, No 1847, Secret, Armeebefehl, 6 December 1916, BA/MA, PH 5 II/8.

223. Gruss, *Die deutsche Sturmbataillone*, 64.

224. Herwig, *First World War*, 249–250.

225. Gallwitz, *Erleben im Westen*, 128, 131, has examples of storm unit tactics in local attacks from the fall of 1916.

226. Nebelin, *Ludendorff*, 404.

227. Chef des Generalstabes des Feldheeres, *Anleitung für Kompanieführer* (Berlin: Reichsdruckerei, 1916), BA/MA, PH D 7/29, esp. 11, 33.

228. Ibid., 99–100, 104–105.

229. Ibid., 104–105.

230. As noted later, subsequent regulations clearly specified under which conditions the units would use traditional (if thinner) lines of skirmishers. Few points have received less attention from historians writing about tactical changes in the First World War.

231. Chef des Generalstabes des Feldheeres, *Kampaniefführer Anleitung* (*K.F.A.*) (Berlin: Reichsdruckerei, 1918), BA/MA, PH D 7/28.

232. Chef des Generalstabes des Feldheeres, *Anleitung für Kompaniefführer* (Berlin: Reichsdruckerei, 1918), 134–135.

233. Ibid., 12.

234. Ibid., 35–36, 131–132.

235. Ibid., 36.

236. Ibid., 36.

237. See the comments of Kincaide, "Sturmabteilungen to Freikorps," 217–222.

238. *Anleitung für Kompagnieführer* (1918), 132.

239. Telephone conversation between Ludendorff and Army Group, German Crown Prince, recorded in memorandum, High Command, Ia, Nr. 950 (Secret), directed to Third Army, 13 November 1916, BA/MA, PH 3/28, 211–222.

240. Möller, *Fritz von Below*, 63. See also Ludendorff, *Meine Kriegserinnerungen*, 307. The chief of the General Staff of XX Corps, Generalmajor Haxthausen, probably did most of the detailed work.

241. Chef des Generalstabes des Feldheeres, *Ausbildungsvorschrift für die Fusstruppen im Kriege* (Berlin: Reichsdruckerei, 1917), BA/MA, PH D 200/39. See Mueller, "Kampfmittel und Taktik," 216.

242. *Ausbildungsvorschrift für die Fusstruppen*, 68–69, 82–83.

243. Ibid., 85–86, 121.

244. Ibid., 95–96.

245. Ibid., 139–141.

246. Ibid., 36.

247. Cron, *Geschichte des deutschen Heeres*, 25–26. Ludendorff, *Urkunden*, 38, has a list updated through September 1918. This volume also reprints the two most important manuals.

248. Cron, *Geschichte des deutschen Heeres*, 97.

249. Ibid., 175–176.

250. Mueller, "Kampfmittel und Taktik," 216; Wilhelm Balck, *Development of Tactics—World War*, trans. Harry Bell (Fort Leavenworth, KS: General Service Schools Press, 1922), 42–44, 85–86.

251. Samuels, *Doctrine and Dogma*, 52–53, makes the case convincingly. For example, Lupfer, *Dynamics of Doctrine*, 44, refers to these methods as infiltration tactics, as do nearly all discussants of tactical adaptations in the First World War.

252. Chef des Generalstabes des Feldheeres, *Der Angriff im Stellungskrieg* (Berlin: Reichsdruckerei, 1918). This relatively brief manual was number 14 of the manuals on positional warfare. The text is available in Ludendorff, *Urkunden*, 641–666, and subsequent citations to the manual refer to this work.

253. *Der Angriff im Stellungskrieg*, in Ludendorff, *Urkunden*, 641–642. Kincaide, "Sturmabteilung to Freikorps," 185–198, has a good summary, based on Ralph H. Lutz, ed., *The Fall of the German Empire*, trans. David G. Rempel and Gertrude Rendtorff, vol. 1 of *Documents of the German Revolution* (Stanford, CA: Stanford University Press, 1932).

254. *Der Angriff im Stellungskrieg*, in Ludendorff, *Urkunden*, 642.

255. Chef des Generalstabes des Heeres, II, Nr. 7662430 p, "Ergänzungen von 1.2.1918 zum Teil 14 des Sammelheftes der Vorschriften für den Stellungskrieg," BA/MA, PH D 7/21, 16; copy in Ludendorff, *Urkunden*, 672.

256. These were assembled at *Sammelheft der Vorschriften für den Stellungskrieg*.

This thick volume is rare. A list of its contents and selections from some individual pieces can be found in Ludendorff, *Urkunden*, 592–674.

257. *Der Angriff im Stellungskrieg*, in Ludendorff, *Urkunden*, 641.

258. Ibid., 656, para. 56: "The infantry attacks using the formations given in its training regulation, A.V.F. 1918." The abbreviation A.V.F. refers to "Ausbildungsvorschrift für die Fusstruppen."

259. Ibid., 641–642.

260. Ibid., 643–645.

261. Ibid., 645.

262. Ibid., 646.

263. Ibid., 648–651.

264. Ibid., 552.

265. Ibid., 653.

266. Ibid., 654.

267. Ibid., 656–657. Wilhelm Balck, the famous tactician and author, made this clear in his postwar discussion of the infantry battles fought in 1918 and the lessons learned from them: "But we cannot do at all without the skirmish line as a battle formation; formation into shock squads is merely a makeshift." See Balck, *Development of Tactics*, 267–268.

268. *Der Angriff im Stellungskrieg*, in Ludendorff, *Urkunden*, 657–658.

269. Ibid., 657.

270. We cannot agree with Holger Herwig's assertion that "The Attack in Positional Warfare" was "the manual for Michael." See Herwig, *First World War*, 388. This manual was a guideline for preparations at high levels of tactical command, but not for the tactics themselves. See also Mueller, "Kampfmittel und Taktik," 216; Matuschka and Petter, "Organisationsgeschichte der Streitkräfte," 233.

271. *Der Angriff im Stellungskrieg*, in Ludendorff, *Urkunden*, 661–664.

272. Kincaide, "Sturmabteilung to Freikorps," 93–97, has a slightly different account, although the general outline of procedures is similar. See also *Der Angriff im Stellungskrieg*, in Ludendorff, *Urkunden*, 657; Theodor Jochim, *Die Vorbereitungen des deutschen Heeres für die Grosse Schlacht in Frankreich im Frühjahr 1918*, vol. 1, *Grundsätze für die Führung* (Berlin: E. S. Mittler, 1927), 22.

273. Dieter Storz, "Aber was hätte anders geschehen sollen? Die deutschen Offensiven an der Westfront 1918," in *Kriegsende 1918. Ereignis, Wirkung, Nachwirkung*, ed. Jörg Duppler and Gerhard P. Gross (Munich: R. Oldenbourg, 1999), 65–66, rightly stresses this point.

274. This was quite in line with the 1918 regulations on infantry training, which stated that each company commander should place storm troops in front of, in, or behind the individual attacking waves, depending on each individual case. See *Anleitung für Kompagnieführer* (1918), Anlage 5, "Anleitung zur Ausbildung von Stosstrupps," 134.

275. Kincaide, "Sturmabteilung to Freikorps," 30–31, 44–46, 93–97. Samuels, *Command or Control?* 253–255, has a good example of the attachment of heavy weapons to an assaulting regiment. See also Balck, *Development of Tactics*, 169–173, with a useful diagram.

276. A summary of these tactical formations, based on post-1918 study by one of the army's leading tacticians, may be found in Balck, *Development of Tactics*, 43–44, 165, 186, 202–203 (with diagram), 204–206, 268–269.

277. German Eleventh Army Order for Aerial Reconnaissance, 6 June 1915, file 8R 11/1, BH/KA; Army Group Temesvar, Order for Aerial Reconnaissance, 25 September 1915, file 11/15/2, BH/KA. See also Richard L. DiNardo, "German Air Operations on the Eastern Front, 1914–1917," in *Essays on World War I*, ed. Peter Pastor and Graydon A. Tunstall (Boulder, CO: East European Monographs, 2012), 68–69.

278. For a short biographical chronology of Ziethen's career, see BA/MA, MSg 109/10874; Ziethen, "Aus grosser Zeit vor zwanzig Jahren," 1629; DiNardo, *Breakthrough*, 50–55; Reichsarchiv, *Der Weltkrieg*, 8:181–182; German Eleventh Army, Report on the Fall of Przemyśl, June 1915, *Nachlass* Seeckt, BA/MA, N 247/24.

279. DiNardo, *Invasion*, 61; General der Artillerie Max von Gallwitz, *Meine Führertätigkeit im Weltkriege 1914–1918 Belgien-Osten-Balkan* (Berlin: E. S. Mittler, 1929), 389; Peter Broucek, ed., *Ein österreichischer General gegen Hitler. Feldmarschall Alfred Jansa: Erinnerungen* (Vienna: Böhlau Verlag, 2011), 302.

280. German 101st Infantry Division Brief Report on Operations of the 101st Infantry Division during the Campaign in Serbia in October and November 1915, 9 December 1915, BA/MA, PH 8 I/45; DiNardo, *Invasion*, 70; Eric Dorn Brose, *The Kaiser's Army: The Politics of Military Technology in Germany during the Machine Age, 1870–1918* (Oxford: Oxford University Press, 2001), 108; Ziethen, "Aus grosser Zeit vor zwanzig Jahren," 1630; Hermann von François, *Gorlice 1915: Der Karpathendurchbruch und die Befreiung von Galizien* (Leipzig: Verlag von K. F. Koehler, 1922), 39; DiNardo, *Breakthrough*, 54.

281. The best introduction to German artillery developments is David. T. Zabecki, *Steel Wind: Colonel Georg Bruchmüller and the Birth of Modern Artillery* (Westport, CT: Praeger, 1994). Zabecki's account is solidly founded in the archival and other primary sources available. Bruce Gudmundsson, *On Artillery* (Westport, CT: Praeger, 1993), is a broader overview of artillery.

282. Reichsarchiv, *Der Weltkrieg*, 14:99. Overall, the British and French superiority on the western front amounted to about 4,000 artillery pieces. See Count Peter Kielmansegg, *Deutschland und der Erste Weltkrieg*, 2nd ed. (Stuttgart: Klett-Cotta, 1980), 634. For the opening attack the army massed about ninety-five tubes (exclusive of mortars) of various kinds per half mile of attack frontage, a moderate density compared with the Allied offensives of 1917. See Hans Linnenkohl, *Vom Einzelschuss zur Feuerwalze. Der Wettlauf zwischen Technik und Taktik im Ersten Weltkrieg* (Munich: Bernard & Graefe, 1990), 270. Overall, the Germans had a total of about 11,000 artillery pieces in the field in early 1918. See also Alfred Muther, "Organisation, Bewaffnung und Munitionsverbrauch der deutschen Feldartillerie im Weltkrieg," in *Das Ehrenbuch der deutschen Feldartillerie*, ed. Albert Benary (Berlin: Verlag Tradition Wilhelm Kolk, ca. 1930), 37.

283. Not much is known about Pulkowski. See Zabecki, *Steel Wind*, 48–50. The Bruchmüller *Nachlass*, BA/MA, N 275/18, has some postwar correspondence on

his procedures. Reichsarchiv, *Der Weltkrieg*, 14:48, mentions the French methods. See also Linnenkohl, *Vom Einzelschuss zur Feuerwalze*, 277–279.

284. Zabecki, *Steel Wind*, 49. Pulkowski and a Major Marx established a series of courses that trained thousands of artillery officers in the new procedures. See the unstinted praise in Georg Bruchmüller, *Die deutsche Artillerie in den Durchbruchschlachten des Weltkrieges*, 2nd ed. (Berlin: E. S. Mittler, 1922), 51.

285. Bruchmüller entered the army in 1883, served in the foot artillery, and retired as a major in 1913. He returned to active duty on 5 August 1914, received honorary promotions to lieutenant colonel and colonel, and retired again, with the official rank of major, in April 1918. On his career, see his personnel file in *Nachlass* Bruchmüller, BA/MA, N 275/1. Bruchmüller, a close friend of Ludendorff, complained after the war that he had to live in relative poverty on his major's pension, even though he had commanded 15,000 guns and mortars during the war. See his "Der Feldherr Ludendorff in meinem Blickfeld," BA/MA, N 275/2, esp. 5–6. This file also contains many letters from Ludendorff to Bruchmüller. Zabecki, *Steel Wind*, 27–31, 104–105, has many details of Bruchmüller's background and lists his postwar publications. See also Samuels, *Command or Control?* 235, 249–253.

286. Zabecki, *Steel Wind*, 33–57, discusses the system in great detail. Bruchmüller wrote two books on the German artillery in general and on his system in particular: *Die deutsche Artillerie in den Durchbruchschlachten des Weltkrieges* and *Die Artillerie beim Angriff im Stellungskrieg* (Charlottenburg: Verlag Offene Worte, 1926). Also of interest is his later article "Die Artillerieführung bei den grossen deutschen Angriffen im Jahre 1918," *Wissen und Wehr* 4 (1931): 185–194, in which he stresses the advantages of his centralized system.

287. Bruchmüller, *Die deutsche Artillerie in den Durchbruchschlachten*, 25–27.

288. Johnson, *Breakthrough*, 219; Zabecki, *Steel Wind*, 53–56. See also Jochim, *Vorbereitungen*, 1:38.

289. Reichsarchiv, *Der Weltkrieg*, 14:49. Gudmundsson, *On Artillery*, 95, has a useful summary.

290. Zabecki, *Steel Wind*, 47.

291. Jochim, *Vorbereitungen*, 1:38.

292. Chef des Generalstabes des Feldheeres, II, Nr. 66815, Geh. Op., [to subordinate commands], 28 February 1918, signed by Ludendorff, BA/MA, PH 3/454, 138–141. This order, consisting of eight pages using both sides, included diagrams and detailed instructions.

293. The following account is based on Infantry Division 28, Ia/Artill. 534 op. Geh, Divisionsbefehl Nr. 2 (Artilleriebefehl), 15 March 1918, BA/MA, PH 8 I/504. On the changing nature of artillery orders, see Bruchmüller, *Die deutsche Artillerie in den Durchbruchschlachten*, 40–41.

294. Bruchmüller, *Die deutsche Artillerie in den Durchbruchschlachten*, 53.

295. Rupprecht, *In Treue Fest*, 2:383, noted that all his corps commanders objected to the High Command's directive on the rolling barrage. They wanted to give the forward divisions control over the artillery.

296. Kuhl, *Der Weltkrieg*, 1:394, noted the problems of centralized (corps) control at Verdun, at least for the long-range guns.

297. Gallwitz, *Erleben im Westen*, 164, noted the development of divisional control by early 1918. Crown Prince Rupprecht favored divisional control but had difficulty enforcing this organization in the fall of 1916. See his *In Treue Fest*, 2:7, diary entry of 2 September 1916; Reichsarchiv, *Der Weltkrieg*, 12:35–36. Gallwitz and Moser favored reliance on divisional control. See Jakob Jung, *Max von Gallwitz (1852–1937) General und Politiker* (Osnabrück: Biblio Verlag, 1995), 18, referring to Gallwitz's views even before the war. Moser, *Feldzugsaufzeichnungen*, 250, artillery officers' resistance to having divisions in command. This had been a major issue at his training course at Solesmes. See also Zabecki, *Steel Wind*, 75–76.

298. Cron, *Geschichte des deutschen Heeres*, 140–142.

299. Schwerin, "Das Sturmbataillone Rohr," 561. See also the articles by Friedrichfranz Feeser, "Infanteriegeschütze, Tankabwehr und Begleitbatterien," in Benary, *Ehrenbuch der deutschen Artillerie*, 82–86; Muther, "Organisation, Bewaffnung, Munition und Munitionsverbrauch," 46–47.

300. Jochim, *Vorbereitungen*, 1:25. Ludendorff sent numerous specific orders to the major commands demanding strict adherence to Bruchmüller's basic guidelines. See Chef des Generalstabes des Feldheeres, II, Nr. 74285 [to all commands through division level], 1 January 1918; Ludendorff to army groups and field armies, 6 February 1918; and Ludendorff to all army groups and armies, 3 March 1918, all in BA/MA, PH 3/454, 59–65, 99–100, 107–107.

301. Zabecki, *Steel Wind*, 22–23; Stone, *Russian Army in the Great War*, 294–296.

302. Herwig, *First World War*, 329–331; Zabecki, *Steel Wind*, 75; John R. Schindler, *Isonzo: The Forgotten Sacrifice of the Great War* (Westport, CT: Praeger, 2001), 254–258. For a firsthand account of some tactical actions, see Rommel, *Attacks*, 222–235.

CHAPTER TEN. THE FINAL TEST, 1918

1. Fritz von Lossberg, *Meine Tätigkeit im Weltkriege 1914–1918* (Berlin: E. S. Mittler, 1939), 136–140; Konrad Krafft von Dellmensingen, *Der Durchbruch. Studie an Hand der Vorgänge des Weltkrieges 1914–1918* (Hamburg: Hanseatische Verlagsanstalt, 1937), 36–40. The latter's study became associated with the headquarters of Sixth Army, commanded by Crown Prince Rupprecht of Bavaria.

2. On Falkenhayn's strategic views, especially his hatred of England, see Holger Afflerbach, *Falkenhayn. Politisches Denken und Handeln im Kaiserreich* (Munich: R. Oldenbourg, 1994), 452. On his growing struggle against Hindenburg and Ludendorff, see Wilhelm Solger, "Falkenhayn," in *Heerführer der Weltkrieges*, ed. Friedrich von Cochenhausen (Berlin: E. S. Mittler, 1932), 84–85, who regards the decision to reinforce the east as a major defeat for Falkenhayn. By early 1915, Hindenburg had already begun to demand Falkenhayn's removal and even threatened to resign over the issue. See Afflerbach, *Falkenhayn*, 276; Count Peter Kielmansegg, *Deutschland und der Erste Weltkrieg*, 2nd ed. (Stuttgart: Klett-Cotta, 1980), 76–77. The German crown prince, forever involved in intrigue, supported

Hindenburg, as did the pathetic and embittered Moltke. Numerous luminaries in the army and elsewhere, including Chancellor Bethmann-Hollweg, Major Max Bauer, Admiral Tirpitz, and Hans von Haeften, soon joined the campaign to unseat Falkenhayn, who survived because of his strong position with the emperor. See Holger Herwig, *The First World War: Germany and Austria-Hungary 1914–1918*, 2nd ed. (London: Arnold Bloomsbury, 2014), 134–135; Alexander Watson, *Ring of Steel. Germany and Austria-Hungary in World War I: The Peoples' War* (New York: Basic Books, 2014), 457. Most historians regard Falkenhayn's decision to deny Hindenburg's demands for massive reinforcements as correct. See the early assessment in C. R. M. F. Cruttwell, *A History of the Great War 1914–1918*, 2nd ed. (Chicago: Academy Publishers, 1992), 84–85; and a more recent concurrence in Afflerbach, *Falkenhayn*, 452.

3. It seems that Max Hoffmann and Ludendorff began to consider this at the same time. See Martin Kitchen, *The German Offensives of 1918* (Charleston, SC: Tempus, 2001), 22.

4. Reichsarchiv, *Der Weltkrieg 1914 bis 1918*, 14 vols. (Berlin: E. S. Mittler, 1925–1944), 12:543, has this exchange of views among Gallwitz, the German crown prince, and Ludendorff.

5. Ibid., 544–545.

6. Ibid., 14:50–51. The only source for this was the memoirs of Max Hoffmann, the General Staff chief in the east.

7. Norman Louis Kincaide, "Sturmabteilungen to Freikorps: German Army Tactical and Organizational Development 1914–1918" (Ph.D. diss., Arizona State University, 1989), 398–399.

8. On the contrary, Kitchen, *German Offensives of 1918*, 17, concludes that "the requirements for a defensive strategy were far more compelling than for an offensive." For the opposing view, see Watson, *Ring of Steel*, 416–417.

9. Wetzell's memorandum of May 1917 raised the possibility of failure of the submarine campaign. See Reichsarchiv, *Der Weltkrieg*, 12:549. On Ludendorff's gradual realization of this, see Kielmansegg, *Deutschland und der Ersten Weltkrieg*, 629.

10. In a memorandum dated 25 October 1917, the insightful crown prince of Bavaria proposed only limited offensives and strategic withdrawals in 1918, and he warned that the arrival of the Americans made a continued defensive just as likely to produce success as any offensive solution. In his reply of 28 October Ludendorff dismissed this line of thought and rejected the proposal for limited offensives, stating that the army had to achieve great victories before the Americans arrived. See Reichsarchiv, *Der Weltkrieg*, 14:51.

11. On this point, see Hans Meier-Welcker, "Die deutsche Führung an der Westfront im Frühsommer 1918," *Die Welt als Geschichte* 21, 3 (1961): 180–181. Meier-Welcker correctly points out that Ludendorff did not even consider a peace through compromise. Note also the sustained argument on the futility of efforts to reach a compromise in H. E. Goemans, *War and Punishment: The Causes of War Termination of the First World War* (Princeton, NJ: Princeton University Press, 2000).

12. This is the convincing conclusion of a distinguished scholar's study. See Dieter Storz, "'Aber was hätte anders geschehen sollen?' Die deutschen Offensive an

der Westfront 1918," in *Kriegsende 1918. Ereignis, Wirkung, Nachwirkung*, ed. Jörg Duppler and Gerhard P. Gross (Munich: R. Oldenbourg Verlag, 1999), 54–55.

13. Kitchen, *German Offensives of 1918*, 10–12.

14. Erich Ludendorff, *Meine Kriegserinnerungen 1914–1918* (Berlin: E. S. Mittler, 1919), 434–435.

15. Hermann von Kuhl, *Entstehung, Durchführung und Zusammenbruch der Offensive von 1918* (Berlin: Deutsche Verlagsgesellschaft für Politik & Geschichte, 1927), 52, 87–88, discusses the strategic thinking of the High Command. This is a reprint of the written testimony Kuhl prepared for the Reichstag's postwar investigation of the war. On the diplomatic basis of the decision, see Lamar Cecil, *Wilhelm II*, vol. 2, *Emperor and Exile, 1900–1941* (Chapel Hill: University of North Carolina Press, 1996), 269. Reichsarchiv, *Der Weltkrieg*, 14:14–15, relies primarily on Ludendorff's *Meine Kriegserinnerungen*, 432–435. Storz, "Die deutschen Offensive an der Westfront 1918," 56, also summarizes the prevailing opinion in the High Command, including the danger of collapse by Germany's allies. On the continuing if mistaken belief that defensive fighting was as costly as offensive combat, see Max Gallwitz, *Erleben im Westen 1916–1918* (Berlin: E. S. Mittler, 1932), 190.

16. Corelli Barnett, "A Successful Counter-stroke: 18 July 1918," in *Old Battles and New Defences: Can We Learn from Military History?* ed. Anthony Trythall (London: Brassey's, 1986), 34.

17. Crown Prince Rupprecht of Bavaria, *In Treue Fest. Mein Kriegstagebuch*, ed. Eugen von Frauenholz, 3 vols. (Munich: National Verlag, 1929), 2:268, reporting a telephone conversation with Ludendorff on 6 October 1917.

18. Krafft von Dellmensingen, *Der Durchbruch*, 140–142; Reichsarchiv, *Der Weltkrieg*, 14:51.

19. Reichsarchiv, *Der Weltkrieg*, 13:330–331, 14:51; Ernst Kabisch, *Michael. Die grosse Schlacht in Frankreich* (Berlin: Vorhut-Verlag Otto Schlegel, 1935), 32–33; Rudiger Schütz, "Einige Bemerkungen," in Duppler and Gross, *Kriegsende 1918*, 47. Herwig, *First World War*, 393–395, introduces the planning process.

20. Summaries of the 9 November memorandum can be found in Reichsarchiv, *Der Weltkrieg*, 14:52; and Krafft von Dellmensingen, *Der Durchbruch*, 141–142. Hermann von Kuhl, *Der Weltkrieg 1914–1918*, 2 vols. (Berlin: Vaterländischen Verlag E. A. Weller, 1930), 2:304, has a brief summary.

21. Krafft von Dellmensingen, no friend of Wetzell, seized on this in his account. The official history does not discuss this section of the memorandum, one of many examples of the practice of shielding Ludendorff and his entourage from criticism. Hindenburg's absence is noteworthy.

22. The two surviving accounts vary only in the details. See Kuhl, *Entstehung, Durchführung und Zusammenbruch*, 101–102; Rupprecht, *In Treue Fest*, 2:285–287. The official history, Reichsarchiv, *Der Weltkrieg*, 14:52–54, seems to rely primarily on Rupprecht's version. This may be merely a peculiarity of the authors, however, since Krafft von Dellmensingen, *Der Durchbruch*, 142, notes that a written account of Ludendorff's remarks was prepared. Kabisch, *Michael*, has some additional information on the conference. Otto Fehr, *Die Märzoffensive 1918 an der*

Westfront: Strategie oder Taktik? (Leipzig: K. F. Koehler, 1921), 9, 12–13, confirms that no transcript or summary memorandum survived. He used an archival copy of Ludendorff's written decision, discussed later.

23. Kuhl recalled that Ludendorff himself raised this alternative, but according to Rupprecht, Max Bauer did so. The official history attributes it to Ludendorff, even though its primary source seems to have been Rupprecht.

24. Fehr, *Die Märzoffensive 1918*, 13; Kuhl, *Entstehung, Durchführung und Zusammenbruch*, 102–103.

25. On these memoranda, see Kuhl, *Entstehung, Durchführung und Zusammenbruch*, 113–115; Krafft von Dellmensingen, *Der Durchbruch*, 155–161, with numerous citations and harsh criticism; Kitchen, *German Offensives of 1918*, 26. In an intervening memorandum of 19 December, Kuhl considered numerous issues to prepare for and to accompany Michael, if that proposal were adopted. Krafft discusses this memorandum, but Kuhl does not.

26. Kuhl, *Der Weltkrieg*, 2:231–232; Tim Travers, *How the War Was Won: Command and Technology in the British Army on the Western Front, 1917–1918* (London: Routledge, 1992), 24–31.

27. Kuhl, *Entstehung, Durchführung und Zusammenbruch*, 106ff, reprints the memorandum of 12 December. Krafft von Dellmensingen, *Der Durchbruch*, 150–151, reprints parts of the memorandum interspersed with bitter criticisms. Reichsarchiv, *Der Weltkrieg*, 14:63–66, has a summary.

28. Reichsarchiv, *Der Weltkrieg*, 14:66–67; Lossberg, *Meine Tätigkeit im Weltkriege*, 315–317.

29. Reichsarchiv, *Der Weltkrieg*, 14:66–67.

30. Ludendorff, *Meine Kriegserinnerungen*, 473–474, discusses his decision but does not mention the conferences at Mons and Kreuznach.

31. Of course, the chiefs discussed these ideas with the commanders and other key staff members. Rupprecht, *In Treue Fest*, 2:305, has some details about the strength available for the offensive and the shortages to be overcome.

32. The numerical designations reflected the different assignments of the field armies within the overall Michael concept, rather than full-fledged alternatives or a sequence of attacks. Thus, it is proper to refer to the first attack in March 1918 as Michael, even though many German sources refer to the parts (Michael I, II, III). See Reichsarchiv, *Der Weltkrieg*, 14:115–123. Kitchen, *German Offensives of 1918*, 272, has an excellent map.

33. Reichsarchiv, *Der Weltkrieg*, 14:68–69; Krafft von Dellmensingen, *Der Durchburch*, 115.

34. It was a cardinal principle of German theory not to tell the commanders of diversionary attacks that their attacks were merely diversions. Of course, the army group commanders and staffs knew, but usually not the divisions and lower units. This ruthless expenditure of soldiers in a secondary attack was considered the price required to ensure that diversionary attacks were pursued with sufficient effort to divert more enemy than friendly forces.

35. Ludendorff had already made his decision. On 15 January 1918 he informed

Kuhl that Rupprecht's army group would be responsible for the Michael attack. See Kitchen, *German Offensives of 1918*, 30.

36. Again, there was apparently no official written record of the discussions, which took place at Avesnes. The official history used the unpublished diaries of Kuhl and Ludendorff's postwar memoirs.

37. Reichsarchiv, *Der Weltkrieg*, 14:76–78; Ludendorff, *Meine Kriegserinnerungen*, 474.

38. Kuhl, *Der Weltkrieg*, 2:311–312. Krafft von Dellmensingen, *Der Durchbruch*, 165, correctly states that Michael, extended northward from the initial proposals, was originally supposed to be the only great attack. Kabisch, *Michael*, 35–36, also assesses the decision.

39. Kielmansegg, *Deutschland und der Erste Weltkrieg*, 633; Reichsarchiv, *Der Weltkrieg*, 14:53–54.

40. Adapted from the version in Reichsarchiv, *Der Weltkrieg*, 14:53; Storz, "Die deutschen Offensiven an der Westfront 1918," 58–59. The provision about the lack of resources for a major diversionary effort was not in the sources cited. Of course, this had been Ludendorff's basic position since the Mons conference of the previous November.

41. Erich Ludendorff, *Kriegführung und Politik*, 2nd ed. (Berlin: E. S. Mittler, 1922). Here, one must understand what German theory meant by an "operation." From Clausewitz onward, German theory used this term in very limited way, unlike modern armies. An operation was the movement of large units around a theater of war, usually leading to deployment for a battle. "Operation" meant large-scale movement, hence the belief that the breakthrough battle in positional warfare preceded the operation. A breakthrough, achieved by tactics (battles), would lead to large-scale movements (operations), which would result in decisive battles in a war of movement.

42. Rupprecht, *In Treue Fest*, 2:327, 337, diary entries of 10 February and 9 March 1918. Gallwitz also reported a meeting with Ludendorff on 25 February. Gallwitz, *Erleben im Westen*, 294.

43. Kuhl, *Der Weltkrieg*, 2:343–344.

44. Krafft von Dellmensingen, *Der Durchbruch*, 156.

45. Storz, "Die deutschen Offensiven an der Westfront 1918," 61–63, examines this issue. Wetzell claimed that more strength was available, but Kuhl denied it. For more on this issue, see below.

46. Reichsarchiv, *Der Weltkrieg*, 14:77.

47. Ibid.; Krafft von Dellmensingen, *Der Durchbruch*, 172; Dennis Showalter, *Instrument of War: The German Army 1914–18* (New York: Osprey Publishing, 2016), 255. Kuhl attributed the decision at least in part to dynastic considerations. Ludendorff's lame explanation in *Meine Kriegserinnerungen*, 475, concluded that it gave him and Hindenburg great satisfaction to involve "his royal highness the crown prince in the first great offensive battle in the West. Dynastic interests did not concern me. Although possessed of deep loyalty to the king, I am an independent man and no creature of the court." The latter is true, at least with respect to

Ludendorff's troubled relationship with Wilhelm II. See Kitchen, *German Offensives of 1918*, 34–35.

48. Reichsarchiv, *Der Weltkrieg*, 14:77–78.

49. Ibid., 78.

50. Kitchen, *German Offensives of 1918*, 38–39.

51. Kuhl, *Der Weltkrieg*, 2:309; Krafft von Dellmensingen, *Der Durchbruch*, 183; Ernst Kabisch, *Streitfragen des Weltkrieges 1914–1918* (Stuttgart: Bergers Literarisches Büro & Verlagsanstalt, 1924), 248. Even the main supporters of the offense, Crown Prince Rupprecht's staff, recognized in December that "everything depends on breaking through somewhere, anywhere. . . . A battle of material, as the English and French have attempted previously, has no prospects for success. If surprise does not succeed, and if the danger arises that the operation will turn into a battle of material, then the offensive must be halted and must be renewed at another place, to achieve a breakthrough that achieves surprise." See Reichsarchiv, *Der Weltkrieg*, 14:57.

52. Cited in Theodor Jochim, *Die Vorbereitung des deutschen Heeres für die grosse Schlacht in Frankreich in Frühjahr 1918*, 5 vols. (Berlin: E. S. Mittler, 1927–1930), 1:13.

53. Although Kuhl, *Der Weltkrieg*, 2:312–313, referred to some (Wetzell, Crown Prince Wilhelm) who argued that the goal was a favorable peace but not a dictated settlement, he concluded that Ludendorff "wanted to win as decisively as possible, as is suitable for a great commander." Max Bauer, *Der grosse Krieg in Feld und Heimat. Erinnerungen und Betrachtungen* (Tübingen: Osiander'sche Buchhandlung, 1921), 175, 177, argued that the goal was to weaken the Allies and expand the coastal bases for submarine warfare to the point that the Entente would be ready for peace.

54. Reichsarchiv, *Der Weltkrieg*, 14:87–88.

55. In discussing the goals and overall strategy of the 1918 offensive, neither the participants in Ludendorff's discussions nor the historians of the Reichsarchiv cited any documents from the High Command beyond the very brief order of 10 March 1918. Fehr, *Die Märzoffensive 1918*, 34–35, reprints the order.

56. The old analyses are still solid on these points. See Fehr, *Die Märzoffensive 1918*, 425; Kabisch, *Streitfragen des Weltkrieges*, 247.

57. See the comments in Georg Gothein, *Warum verloren wir den Krieg*, 2nd ed. (Berlin: Deutsche Verlags-Anstalt, 1920), 217.

58. Jochim, *Die Vorbereitung*, 1:10, summarizes these problems. See also Reichsarchiv, *Der Weltkrieg*, 14:29–30; Watson, *Ring of Steel*, 518–519.

59. Reichsarchiv, *Der Weltkrieg*, 14:38.

60. John Hussey, "The Movement of German Divisions to the Western Front, Winter 1917–1918," *War in History* 4, 2 (April 1997): 213–220, esp. 216–218.

61. Kuhl, *Der Weltkrieg*, 2:298; Reichsarchiv, *Der Weltkrieg*, 14:37. Kuhl's figure also included five divisions still in transit.

62. Hussey, "Movement of German Divisions," 213–220. Part of the confusion stems from how one calculates divisions that were sent to the eastern front in October and November 1917 and then returned, and how one counts the two

Landwehr divisions sent to the east. Kuhl's testimony to the Reichstag's postwar investigative committee indicated that a total of forty-two divisions had been sent to the west (forty plus the four sent and returned, minus the two *Landwehr* divisions). See Kuhl, *Entstehung, Durchführung und Zusammenbruch*, 6. Kincaide, "Sturmabteilungen to Freikorps," 182–183, accepts forty as the total transferred from the eastern and Italian fronts.

63. Tim Travers, "Reply to John Hussey: The Movement of German Divisions to the Western Front, Winter 1917–1918," *War in History* 5, 3 (July 1998): 367–370. A German infantry division had an authorized strength of 234 officers and 11,394 enlisted men. These were organized into three infantry regiments of three battalions each and artillery, engineer, logistical, and other supporting elements. Of course, few if any divisions had their full strength present at any given time, with the possible exception of the night before the beginning of a major offensive. See Kincaide, "Sturmabteilungen to Freikorps," 183–185.

64. Kuhl, *Entstehung, Durchführung und Zusammenbruch*, 7. Meier-Welcker, "Die deutsche Führung an der Westfront," 175, n. 6, accepted the figure of 200 divisions.

65. Reichsarchiv, *Der Weltkrieg*, 14:29.

66. Kuhl, *Entstehung, Durchführung und Zusammenbruch*, 61–66; Kuhl, *Der Weltkrieg*, 2:299–301.

67. Reichsarchiv, *Der Weltkrieg*, 13:398, 14:38–39. Kitchen, *German Offensives of 1918*, 17–18, concludes that the second-line units left in the Ukraine could have been useful on such tasks.

68. Rupprecht, *In Treue Fest*, 2:284, diary entry of 11 November 1917. Bolshevik political ideology soon became an issue as well, particularly as prisoners released by the Russians returned to Germany.

69. See Reichsarchiv, *Der Weltkrieg*, 14:37, and the critical comments of Meier-Welcker, "Die deutsche Führung an der Westfront," 165, n. 7.

70. Hans Kling, "Der Organisation der deutschen Infanterie im Weltkriege," in *Deutsche Infanterie. Das Ehrenmal der vordersten Front*, ed. Ernst von Eisenhart-Rothe et al. (Zeulenroda: Verlag Bernhard Sporn, 1939), 199; Kuhl, *Entstehung, Durchführung und Zusammenbruch*, 58–59.

71. Kling, "Die Organisation der deutschen Infanterie," 199.

72. Herwig, *First World War*, 395, divides the divisions into three categories: mobile, attack, and trench. This accurately draws a distinction between normal trench divisions and those, numbering about twenty-six, that received more men and equipment to participate in the initial attacks on Allied trench lines. The German army, however, made no such distinction, particularly after the opening days of the Michael attack. Instead, the contemporary accounts distinguish only between positional and mobile divisions, since the real distinction was mobility, not firepower. Kuhl distinguished between positional divisions and attack divisions, but by the latter he meant the mobile divisions, whose numbers he estimated at fifty-two. See Kuhl, *Der Weltkrieg*, 2:297; Kuhl, *Entstehung, Durchführung und Zusammenbruch*, 127. Krafft von Dellmensingen, *Der Durchbruch*, 240, made a passing reference to the distinction among divisions, but he regarded it as false

because all of them would eventually have to participate in the offensive. He, too, used the term *Angriffsdivision* as a substitute for mobile division. The official history used that term as well, continually distinguishing between positional and mobile divisions as it described the course of the campaign. The old distinction between positional divisions and those designated as counterattack (*Eingreif*) divisions had no relevance here; in any case, this was a temporary designation dependent on position in or behind the front lines.

73. Reichsarchiv, *Der Weltkrieg*, 14:41.

74. Ibid., 42. Kitchen, *German Offensives of 1918*, 19, concludes that the total was seventy-four.

75. Reichsarchiv, *Der Weltkrieg*, 14:42; Herwig, *First World War*, 384. Kincaide, "From Sturmabteilung to Freikorps," adopts the four categories used by Allied intelligence estimates. This has a certain utility, but it becomes less useful as the lower-rated divisions were rebuilt for the offensive and then as they completed the training program established to upgrade their capabilities. Kincaide's statistics have at least some validity, but they are only as accurate as the intelligence data and analyses on which they were based. The German army's evaluations of its own units are no longer available. In any case, about seventy divisions were at least partly ready for offensive combat by 21 March 1918.

76. Kincaide, "Sturmabteilungen to Freikorps," 309–310, has an introduction to the general nature of the training (physical and mental) necessary to make the transition from positional to mobile warfare.

77. Herwig, *First World War*, 384.

78. Generalstab, II/II, N. 75092, op., 9 January 1918, signed by Ludendorff, BA/MA, PH 3/454, 71.

79. Storz, "Die deutschen Offensiven an der Westfront 1918," 66–67, with emphasis on the Bavarians.

80. Chef des Generalstabes des Feldheeres, II, Nr. 6544 (secret), [to army commands], 15 February 1918, BA/MA, PH 3/454, 11–12.

81. Jochim, *Die Vorbereitung*, 1:8–9, comments on variations in trench warfare between the fronts.

82. Generalkommando VII A.K., *Richtlinien über die Ausbildung von Offizieren und Mannschaften des östlichen Kriegsschauplatzes in der westlichen Kriegführung*, 22.II.1917, BA/MA, PH 3/33, 3.

83. Ibid., 17–18.

84. Ibid., 9.

85. Ibid., 4.

86. Kincaide, "Sturmabteilung to Freikorps," 199–203, 309–310. See also Anonymous (Union of Officers), *Geschichte des Reserve-Infanterie-Regiments Nr. 35* (Berlin: Volkskraft Verlagsgesellschaft, 1935), 330–332.

87. Reichsarchiv, *Der Weltkrieg*, 14:26. The new light machine gun model LMG 08/18 first became available in large numbers in January.

88. Kuhl, *Entstehung, Durchführung und Zusammenbruch*, 97–99, summarizes the favorable conditions of artillery and small-arms weapons and munitions.

89. Kielmansegg, *Deutschland und der Erste Weltkrieg*, 635.

90. On the problems related to horses, see Reichsarchiv, *Der Weltkrieg*, 14:31–33, 41; Kielmansegg, *Deutschland und der Erste Weltkrieg*, 342–343. Storz, "Die deutschen Offensiven an der Westfront 1918," 68–69, summarizes the situation.

91. Ludendorff, *Meine Kriegserinnerungen*, 471.

92. Meier-Welcker, "Die deutsche Führung an der Westfront," 166, portrays a high command unified in its overconfidence and lacking real judgment. This is an exaggeration, since many, including Ludendorff at times, had serious doubts.

93. Reichsarchiv, *Der Weltkrieg*, 14:92–93. On Kuhl's doubts, see Michael Epkenhans, "Die Politik der militärischen Führung 1918: 'Kontinuität der Illusionen und das Dilemma der Wahrheit,'" in Duppler and Gross, *Kriegsende 1918*, 218.

94. Rupprecht, *In Treue Fest*, 2:330–331. Ludendorff apparently told the emperor that if the great breakthrough failed, the army would at least weaken the Allies with successive attacks at different locations along the front.

95. Groener to his wife, 20 January 1918, in Wilhelm Groener, *Lebenserinnerungen, Jugend, Generalstab, Weltkrieg*, ed. Friedrich *Freiherr* Hiller von Gaertringen (Göttingen: Vandenhoeck & Rupprecht, 1957), 379–380.

96. Rüdiger Schuetz, "Einführende Bemerkungen" in Duppler and Gross, *Kriegsende 1918*, 46–47.

97. According to Groener, Ludendorff recognized that the army faced a very difficult problem, the solution to which could not be predicted in advance. See Groener, *Lebenserinnerungen*, 385, diary entry of 28 February 1918. For Ludendorff's doubts, see Frederike Krüger and Michael Salweski, "Die Verantwortung der militärischen Führung deutscher Streitkräfte in den Jahren 1918 und 1945," in Duppler and Gross, *Kriegsende 1918*, 386. For a confident Ludendorff, see Albrecht von Thaer, *Generalstabsdienst an der Front und in der O.H.L. Aus Briefen und Tagebuchaufzeichnungen 1915–1919*, ed. Siegfried Kaehler (Göttingen: Vandenhoeck & Rupprecht, 1958), 164.

98. See Thaer, *Generalstabsdienst*, 164.

99. Kitchen, *German Offensives of 1918*, is the best of many.

100. Herwig, *First World War*, 389–390, has a clear account. The Michael order is in Reichsarchiv, *Der Weltkrieg*, 14:85–86; Krafft von Dellmensingen, *Der Durchbruch*, 174–175. At the time of the order (10 March), the High Command had not yet decided when the Mars and Archangel attacks would begin, but it had decided to launch the former nearly simultaneously with Michael.

101. Gerhard Ritter, *The Sword and Scepter: The Problem of Militarism in Germany*, trans. Heinz Norden, 4 vols. (Coral Gables, FL: University of Miami Press, 1970), 4:229–230.

102. Reichsarchiv, *Der Weltkrieg*, 14:79.

103. Kitchen, *German Offensives of 1918*, 46–60, has a summary of the state of the British army and its commanders in February and March 1918.

104. Reichsarchiv, *Der Weltkrieg*, 14:96, 104–105; Krafft von Dellmensingen, *Der Durchbruch*, 186–187. See also the comments of Martin Samuels, *Command or Control? Command Training and Tactics in the British and German Armies, 1888–1918* (London: Frank Cass, 1995), 247, 249.

105. Krafft von Dellmensingem, *Der Durchbruch*, 187; Reichsarchiv, *Der Weltkrieg*, 14:98.

106. Krafft von Dellmensingen, *Der Durchbruch*, 185, has some details of the artillery preparation, which followed the general outline of the Bruchmüller methods discussed previously. Hubert C. Johnson, *Breakthrough: Tactics, Technology and the Search for Victory on the Western Front in World War I* (Novato, CA: Presidio, 1994), 228, says the barrage began at 6:40, which seems to be inaccurate.

107. Storz, "Die deutschen Offensiven an den Westfront 1918," 77, rightly stresses the role of aviation on both sides in the 1918 offensive.

108. As Samuels, *Command or Control?* 265–269, points out, fog was a major factor, through probably not as much as some British generals and the British official history later claimed. The lack of visibility reduced the German artillery's effectiveness, caused infantry units to stumble upon unseen strongpoints, and reduced the ability of the advancing trench mortars to fire on defensive strongpoints. It also reduced the defenders' ability to direct fire. See Travers, *How the War Was Won*, 57; Krafft von Dellmensingen, *Der Durchbruch*, 193–194.

109. See Second Army's Order No. 27, 16 March 1918, BA/MA, PH 5 II/202, 77.

110. On the artillery in the opening days of Michael, see Samuels, *Command or Control?* 249–253.

111. Reichsarchiv, *Der Weltkrieg*, 14:106, 133; Storz, "Die deutschen Offensiven an der Westfront 1918," 72; Jochim, *Die Vorbereitung*, 1:19; Kuhl, *Der Weltkrieg*, 2:329.

112. Reichsarchiv, *Der Weltkrieg*, 14:107–114, describes Seventeenth Army's action.

113. Ibid., 196–197, has details from two corps that illustrate effective local British resistance. John Keegan, *The First World War* (New York: Alfred A. Knopf, 1999), 400–401, paints a bleak picture of the British performance on the opening day.

114. Bruchmüller was with Eighteenth Army for Michael. Ludendorff, *Meine Kriegserinnerungen*, 487, praised Bruchmüller for preparing the army's artillery for the attack, using him as an example of the importance of the individual in the conduct of war.

115. Krafft von Dellmensingen, *Der Durchbruch*, 193–194, uses very direct language in criticizing this development on the first day. Herwig, *First World War*, 395, also criticizes Ludendorff for diverting too much to the secondary portion of Michael.

116. Reichsarchiv, *Der Weltkrieg*, 14:167–168.

117. Ibid.

118. Kuhl, *Der Weltkrieg*, 2:330–331, 341, has a broad discussion that, while recognizing in retrospect the dangers of the decision, defends it on the grounds that halting either flank ran the risk that both would be halted. Storz, "Die deutschen Offensiven an der Westfront 1918," 73, regards the account of Kuhl, usually a defender of the General Staff, as critical of Ludendorff on this point. We find no basis for this conclusion, since Kuhl (ibid., 341) attributes the decision not to a mistake by Ludendorff but to the "inevitable" nature of the situation. Kuhl's ear-

lier account, *Entstehung, Durchführung und Zusammenbruch,* 131–132, discussed the decision without any criticism of Ludendorff's logic. Herwig, *First World War,* 395–396, notes the importance of the change in emphasis.

119. On the British and French overreaction to the initial German advances, see Kuhl, *Der Weltkrieg,* 2:334–336.

120. On the near panic at British headquarters, see Travers, *How the War Was Won,* 54–56, 66–71; on command methods generally, see ibid., 81–83.

121. Generalstab des Heeres, Operationsabteilung [press release], 24 March 1918, signed by Ludendorff, BA/MA, PH 3/54. This file has about fifteen of these reports, issued at the twice-daily High Command situation briefings that were usually given by lower-ranking General Staff officers.

122. Herwig, *First World War,* 394.

123. Ibid., 396.

124. Storz, "Die deutschen Offensiven an der Westfront 1918," 74–75, has a summary. See also Elizabeth Greenhalgh, *Victory through Coalition: Britain and France during the First World War* (Cambridge: Cambridge University Press, 2005), 192–195.

125. Kitchen, *German Offensives of 1918,* 90–91. Kitchen's subsequent account contains many examples of less than complete cooperation.

126. Ibid., 103. For a reassessment of Haig's role in Foch's appointment, see Elizabeth Greenhalgh, "Myth and Memory: Sir Douglas Haig and the Imposition of Allied Unified Command in March 1918," *Journal of Military History* 68, 3 (July 2004): 771–820.

127. Reichsarchiv, *Der Weltkrieg,* 14:134.

128. Ibid., 197–199, has these and other details.

129. Ibid., 197–198, 221; Kitchen, *German Offensives of 1918,* 88; Ludendorff, *Meine Kriegserinnerungen,* 483.

130. This summary is based on Reichsarchiv, *Der Weltkrieg,* 14:195–196, 213–215, 220–229; Kuhl, *Der Weltkrieg,* 2:331–332.

131. Only one officer in Ludendorff's inner circle, Max Hoffmann, realized that the game was up and peace would be necessary. See Ritter, *Sword and the Scepter,* 4:233.

132. This summary is based on Reichsarchiv, *Der Weltkrieg,* 14:244–245; Kuhl, *Der Weltkrieg,* 2:333; Rupprecht, *In Treue Fest,* 2:371–372.

133. Storz, "Die deutschen Offensiven an der Westfront 1918," 78. Ludendorff's *Meine Kriegserinnerungen* refers to the attack under the "Armentieres" name.

134. Kitchen, *German Offensives of 1918,* 97.

135. Reichsarchiv, *Der Weltkrieg,* 14:266. Ludendorff, *Meine Kriegserinnerungen,* stated that the goal of the attack was merely to seize the high ground north of the Lys River. His account of this battle, which he falsely tried to present as an integral part of Michael, is among the weakest in his memoirs. Kuhl openly asked, "What could one expect from this attack?" He then noted that the high ground mentioned in Ludendorff's memoirs "had no value to the High Command." See Kuhl, *Der Weltkrieg,* 2:346. Kuhl wrote a memorandum (4 April 1918) to the effect that he hoped this would bring a decisive victory, "since we cannot continue in

this manner" due to losses, munitions, horses, and so forth. See Reichsarchiv, *Der Weltkrieg*, 14:266.

136. The air force, for example, had about 500 aircraft available to support both armies. Some adjustments were made in artillery support, including slowing the rate of the rolling barrage and increasing firing on strongpoints and machine gun positions, particularly by mortars.

137. Reichsarchiv, *Der Weltkrieg*, 14:270.

138. Cruttwell, *History of the Great War*, 516.

139. Kitchen, *German Offensives of 1918*, 98.

140. The following summary is based on Reichsarchiv, *Der Weltkrieg*, 14:272ff; Cruttwell, *History of the Great War*, 517ff, unless otherwise noted.

141. Kitchen, *German Offensives of 1918*, 105.

142. Ibid., 115.

143. Reichsarchiv, *Der Weltkrieg*, 14:281–282, has an unusually critical commentary.

144. Kuhl, *Entstehung, Durchführung und Zusammenbruch*, 154.

145. Reichsarchiv, *Der Weltkrieg*, 14:300.

146. See Storz, "Die deutschen Offensiven an der Westfront 1918," 78.

147. Groener, *Lebenserinnerungen*, 432, painted a grim picture of the Georgette attack, emphasizing insufficient forces and lack of preparation, although he did not link these directly to the tactical system of 1918, which assumed both.

148. Reichsarchiv, *Der Weltkrieg*, 14:300. This, of course, meant looting instead of advancing.

149. Cruttwell, *History of the Great War*, 529.

150. See Ludendorff, *Meine Kriegserinnerungen*, 483.

151. Reichsarchiv, *Der Weltkrieg*, 14:329–330.

152. Chef des Generalstabes des Feldheeres, Ia/II Nr. 7745, geh. Op., 17 April 1914, BA/MA, PH 3/55.

153. See Storz, "Die deutschen Offensiven an der Westfront 1918," 82–83.

154. Gallwitz, *Erleben im Westen*, 319, stated that he welcomed a renewed offensive because of the situation in Germany, where, he anticipated, the conflict over the reform of Prussia's three-class voting system would soon intensify.

155. See the well-developed argument by Frederike Krüger and Michael Salewski, "Die Verantwortung der militärischen Führung deutscher Streitkräfte in den Jahren 1918 und 1945," in Duppler and Gross, *Kriegsende 1918*, 387.

156. Wetzell's estimate (19 April 1918) that these were the only divisions available is cited in Reichsarchiv, *Der Weltkrieg*, 14:313. Wetzell's real preference remained the old proposal of an attack near Verdun.

157. Kuhl, *Entstehung, Durchführung und Zusammenbruch*, 158, citing the High Command's order of 1 May 1918. See also Reichsarchiv, *Der Weltkrieg*, 14:316–317, 328, 413–414.

158. Ludendorff, *Meine Kriegserinnerungen*, 516.

159. The following account of Blücher and Gneisenau is based on Reichsarchiv, *Der Weltkrieg*, 14:311–411, unless otherwise noted. Subsidiary attacks had

their own code names, Goerz and Yorck; here, these are subsumed in the larger designs.

160. Kitchen, *German Offensives of 1918*, 128–136, has a clear discussion.

161. Storz, "Die deutschen Offensiven an der Westfront 1918," 83.

162. See Cruttwell, *History of the Great War*, 524–525.

163. Travers, *How the War Was Won*, 100–103.

164. Storz, "Die deutschen Offensiven an der Westfront 1918," 85–86.

165. Robert A. Doughty, *Pyrrhic Victory: French Strategy and Operations in the Great War* (Cambridge, MA: Harvard University Press, 2005), 455. Doughty's treatment of the French side is the best available in English.

166. See Cruttwell, *History of the Great War*, 526–527.

167. See Laurence V. Moyer, *Victory Must Be Ours: Germany in the Great War, 1914–1918* (New York: Hippocrene Books, 1995), 248. Herwig, *First World War*, 405–406, harshly criticizes Ludendorff's decision to expand the offensive.

168. In addition to the Reicharchiv's account, see Kuhl, *Der Weltkrieg*, 2:359–360.

169. See Keegan, *First World War*, 406–407.

170. Kitchen, *German Offensives of 1918*, 154. Kitchen's narrative has many details of the battles and a good account of the deep anxiety on both sides. As was the case during many battles in this war, both sides could see danger, disappointment, and failure in the same actions.

171. The official German account, Reichsarchiv, *Der Weltkrieg*, 14:392, gave the following totals for losses: German, 98,000; French, 103,000; English, 29,000; American, 2,400 (thus an Allied total of about 135,000).

172. Reichsarchiv, *Der Weltkrieg*, 14:397–406; Kitchen, *German Offensives of 1918*, 164–168.

173. Helmuth Gruss, *Die deutsche Sturmbataillone im Weltkrieg, Ausbau und Verwendung* (Berlin: Junker & Dünnhaupt, 1939), 120–127. Herwig, *First World War*, 416, errs when he states that Ludendorff approved disbanding all the storm battalions and that this was accomplished.

174. Kitchen, *German Offensives of 1918*, 166.

175. Reichsarchiv, *Der Weltkrieg*, 14:414.

176. Ibid., 415–416, citing a memorandum by Wetzell of 6 June 1918.

177. Ludendorff, *Meine Kriegserinnerungen*, 514–515. He apparently hoped to achieve sufficient success in the Marneschutz attack to force Foch to transfer both French and British forces away from Flanders. See Reichsarchiv, *Der Weltkrieg*, 14:423; Kuhl, *Der Weltkrieg*, 2:378. Kuhl, in his usual postwar effort to defend Ludendorff, also argued that the Marne salient threatened the flank of a renewed German attack in Flanders and that the Germans had to either eliminate it or conduct a general withdrawal.

178. Reichsarchiv, *Der Weltkrieg*, 14:415, 429.

179. Ibid., 423, 531–533; Meier-Welcker, "Die deutsche Führung an der Westfront," 172.

180. Reichsarchiv, *Der Weltkrieg*, 14:429–430. By this time (22 June), Luden-

dorff was clearly caught up in his own private offensive fury and was blind to the increasingly difficult situation of many of the infantry units as well as the strategic consequences of continued fruitless attacks.

181. Ibid., 445, n. 1, based on a 1930 communication by Schulenburg. See also Herwig, *First World War*, 404; Manfred Nebelin, *Ludendorff: Diktator im Ersten Weltkrieg* (Munich: Siedler Verlag, 2010), 435. Contrary to some accounts, Ludendorff did not state that individual soldiers should be expected to attack regardless of whether they had influenza.

182. Reichsarchiv, *Der Weltkrieg*, 14:443–444, records the reservations of several senior officers.

183. Ibid., 429–432, discusses these proposals.

184. On the general preparations, see Ludendorff, *Meine Kriegserinnerungen*, 533–534.

185. Third Army Command, Ia, Nr. 5873, op., "Armeebefehl für den Einsatz von Sturmtruppen bei Reims," 28 June 1918, BA/MA, PH 6 I/334, 85.

186. In some sections, engineers and infantry units had moved forward to construct bridges and secure crossings at the beginning of the artillery barrage. The following account is based on Reichsarchiv, *Der Weltkrieg*, 14:446–465, unless otherwise noted.

187. They also had ample indications that an offensive in this area was imminent. See Kitchen, *German Offensives of 1918*, 180.

188. Doughty, *Pyrrhic Victory*, 465–470. So poor was security that even the headquarters guards knew the kaiser planned to come to the front for the offensive. These enlisted men also knew the location and date of the attack. See Reichsarchiv, *Der Weltkrieg*, 14:441, n. 4. Georg Bruchmüller, *Die deutsche Artillerie in den Durchbruchschlachten des Weltkrieges*, 2nd ed. (Berlin: E. S. Mittler, 1922), 29, stressed the importance of this loss of surprise.

189. German Seventh Army's commander of engineers, General Unverzagt, lost his life at one of these bridgeheads. On the improved French defensive methods, see Storz, "Die deutschen Offensiven an der Westfront 1918," 92–93; Kuhl, *Der Weltkrieg*, 2:381–383.

190. Herwig, *First World War*, 406–407, briefly describes the battle and Ludendorff's flights of fancy.

191. David T. Zabecki, *Steel Wind: Colonel Georg Bruchmüller and the Birth of Modern Artillery* (Westport, CT: Praeger, 1994), 95–96.

192. Kuhl, *Der Weltkrieg*, 2:381.

193. Doughty, *Pyrrhic Victory*, 470–471. Herwig, *First World War*, 407–409, has a good summary. Ludendorff, *Meine Kriegserinnerungen*, 537, has a truncated version. Kuhl, *Der Weltkrieg*, 2:393–394, has a good account, as well as a map of the western front. Kuhl (ibid., 394) was perhaps the first to argue that 18 July 1918, not 8 August (the "black day of the German army") was the real milestone of the war.

194. Doughty, *Pyrrhic Victory*, 474–475, discusses Foch's "strategy of opportunism" for the remainder of 1918.

195. Thaer, *Generalstabsdienst*, 222; Krüger and Salewski, "Die Verantwortung des militärischen Führung," 392.

196. Kitchen, *German Offensives of 1918*, 184ff, has many well-constructed examples of the constant state of emergency facing the *OHL* and the army group commanders.

197. For a useful summary of these final offensives, see Travers, *How the War Was Won*, 110–156.

198. Cecil, *Wilhelm II*, 2:294–295; Watson, *Ring of Steel*, 556. The role of the army's common soldiers in the fall of Wilhelm II is covered in Scott Stephenson, *The Final Battle: Soldiers of the Western Front and the German Revolution of 1918* (Cambridge: Cambridge University Press, 2009), 67–108.

199. For example, Kuhl, *Der Weltkrieg*, 2:341.

200. Meier-Welcker, "Die deutsche Führung an der Westfront," 180; Ritter, *Sword and the Scepter*, 4:231.

201. See Kielmansegg, *Deutschland und der Erste Weltkrieg*, 631–632; Kabisch, *Streitfragen des Weltkrieges*, 271–276, with a lengthy discussion of the postwar literature; Niall Ferguson, *The Pity of War* (New York: Basic Books, 1999), 316–317, to name a few.

202. The most convincing study of this remains Travers, *How the War Was Won*, 50–65, 89–90. See also Storz, "Die deutschen Offensiven an der Westfront 1918," 75–76. The Germans were aware that the British were attempting to copy their methods. See an order of 28th Division, 16 March 1918, BA/MA, PH 8 I/504.

203. Paddy Griffith, *Battle Tactics of the Western Front: The British Army's Art of Attack, 1916–1918* (New Haven, CT: Yale University Press, 1994), 90–91, 127–128, 193–196. Note also the comments of Shelford Bidwell and Dominick Graham, *Coalitions, Politicians and Generals: Some Aspects of Command in the World Wars* (London: Brassey's, 1993), 53.

204. Krafft von Dellmensingen, *Der Durchbruch*, 277ff. On the lack of speed as a decisive factor, see Anonymous, "Bewegung und Waffenwirkung in der Taktik des Weltkrieges," *Militär-Wochenblatt* III, 43 (1927): cols. 1590–1591.

205. Travers, *How the War Was Won*, 86–88, 99.

206. Samuels, *Command or Control?* 272–273, argues for the "breakout" consideration. Jochim, *Die Vorbereitung*, 22–23, argues that the lack of cavalry was the reason for failure. John Terraine also raised this possibility, which Samuels, *Command or Control?* 274, strongly denies.

207. See Reichsarchiv, *Der Weltkrieg*, 14:198–199. Storz, "Die deutschen Offensiven an der Westfront 1918," 77–78; Meier-Welcker, "Die deutsche Führung an der Westfront," 170.

208. On the overall logistical situation, see Samuels, *Command or Control?* 274–275. Cruttwell, *History of the Great War*, 513–514, discounts the significance of looting, although he agrees that there were many examples of this and other breakdowns in discipline.

209. Thaer, *Generalstabsdienst*, 184; Ludendorff, *Meine Kriegserinnerungen*, 209–210; Epkenhans, "Die Politik der militärischen Führung," 221.

210. Moyer, *Victory Must Be Ours*, 244, 292; Kincaide, "Sturmabteilung to Freikorps," 264, 268; Krafft von Dellmensingen, *Der Durchbruch*, 208; Samuels, *Command or Control?* 264. Martin Middlebrook's calculations are not entirely

convincing, or lower, but they still indicate very heavy losses on the first day; see Samuels, *Command or Control?* 264. Travers, *How the War Was Won*, 108, has a discussion of German casualties by month.

211. Reichsarchiv, *Der Weltkrieg*, 14:424, citing a memorandum by Kuhl.

212. Count Edgar von Matuschka and Wolfgang Petter, "Organisationsgeschichte der Streitkräfte," in *Deutsche Militärgeschichte*, ed. Militägeschichliches Forschungsamt (Munich: Bernard & Graefe, 1964–1979), 2(2):229; Reichsarchiv, *Der Weltkrieg*, 14:522–523, 608.

213. Kincaide, "Sturmabteilung to Freikorps," 372–373.

214. Herwig, *First World War*, 421.

215. Cruttwell, *History of the Great War*, 522.

216. Versions of this statement can be found throughout the literature on the First World War. For further critical analysis of Ludendorff's approach, see Herwig, *First World War*, 406.

217. Holger Herwig, "Dynamics of Necessity," in *Military Effectiveness*, ed. Allan R. Millett and Williamson Murray, 3 vols. (Boston: Allen & Unwin, 1988), 1:103, cites several of these, including Generals Leeb, Lossberg, and Thaer.

218. 12th Infantry Division, Ia, No. 182, Secret, Angriffsstudie Nr. 3 über Michael-Angriff und Marsangriff, 12 March 1918, BA/MA, PH D 8 I/12, 81.

219. Jehuda L. Wallach, *The Dogma of the Battle of Annihilation: The Theories of Clausewitz and Schlieffen and Their Impact on the German Conduct of Two World Wars* (1967; reprint, Westport, CT: Greenwood Press, 1986), 187.

220. Krafft von Dellmensingen, *Der Durchbruch*, 156–157. Kuhl's memorandum can be found in Kuhl, *Entstehung, Durchführung und Zusammenbruch*, 113.

221. Erich Ludendorff, *Mein militärischer Werdegang* (Munich: Ludendorffs Verlag, 1935), 88.

222. Michael Geyer, "German Strategy in the Age of Machine Warfare, 1914–1945," in *Makers of Modern Strategy*, ed. Peter Paret (Princeton, NJ: Princeton University Press, 1986), 552; Corelli Barnett, *The Swordbearers: Supreme Command in the First World War* (New York: William Morrow, 1965), 282.

223. Dennis Showalter, *Tannenberg: Clash of Empires* (Hamden, CT: Archon Books, 1991), 344.

224. Jochim, *Die Vorbereitung*, 1:19.

225. Rupprecht, *In Treue Fest*, 2:372.

226. Ludendorff, *Meine Kriegserinnerungen*, 474.

CONCLUSIONS

1. James McRandle and James Quirk, "The Blood Test Revisited: A New Look at German Casualty Counts in World War I," *Journal of Military History* 70, 3 (July 2006): 680.

2. Gordon A. Craig, *Germany 1866–1945* (New York: Oxford University Press, 1978), 39–40.

3. Lamar Cecil, *Wilhelm II*, vol. 2, *Emperor and Exile, 1900–1941* (Chapel Hill: University of North Carolina Press, 1996), 211; Holger Afflerbach, "Wilhelm II as Supreme Warlord in the First World War," in *The Kaiser: New Research on Wilhelm*

II's Role in Imperial Germany, ed. Annika Mombauer and Wilhelm Deist (Cambridge: Cambridge University Press, 2004), 204.

4. For a discussion of German naval war plans, see James Goldrick, *Before Jutland: The Naval War in Northern European Waters, August 1914–February 1915* (Annapolis, MD: Naval Institute Press, 2015), 73–74.

5. Geoffrey Wawro, *The Austro-Prussian War: Austria's War with Prussia and Italy in 1866* (Cambridge: Cambridge University Press, 1996), 273; Dennis Showalter, *The Wars of German Unification* (London: Arnold, 2004), 273–275; Hajo Holborn, "The Prusso-German School: Moltke and the Rise of the General Staff," in *Makers of Modern Strategy from Machiavelli to the Nuclear Age*, ed. Peter Paret (Princeton, NJ: Princeton University Press, 1986), 293–294; Michael Howard, *The Franco-Prussian War*, reprint ed. (London: Routledge, 1988), 65–66.

6. For a recent defense of Joffre, see Robert A. Doughty, "'Papa' Joffre and the Great War," *Journal of Military History* 79, 4 (October 2015): 959–980.

7. Graydon A. Tunstall, *Blood on the Snow: The Carpathian Winter War of 1915* (Lawrence: University Press of Kansas, 2010), 212; Manfred Rauchensteiner, *Der Erste Weltkrieg und das Ende der Habsburgermonarchie 1914–1918* (Vienna: Böhlau Verlag, 2013), 312–318.

8. Alexander Watson, *Ring of Steel. Germany and Austria-Hungary in World War I: The People's War* (New York: Basic Books, 2014), 466–467; Rauchensteiner, *Der Erste Weltkrieg*, 614–620; Gary W. Shanafelt, *The Secret Enemy: Austria-Hungary and the German Alliance, 1914–1918* (Boulder, CO: East European Monographs, 1985), 88–91.

SELECTED BIBLIOGRAPHY

ARCHIVAL SOURCES
Austria
Österreichischer Staatsarchiv-Kriegsarchiv, Vienna
Germany
Bundesarchiv Koblenz
Bundesarchiv-Kriegsarchiv, Munich
Bundesarchiv/Militärchiv, Freiberg
United States
National Archives and Records Administration, College Park, MD

OFFICIAL GERMAN DOCTRINAL AND OTHER PUBLICATIONS
Generalinspektion des Ingenieur- und Pionierkorps und der Festungen. *Kriegser-fahrungen über Feldbefestigungen.* Berlin: Reichsdruckerei, June 1915.
Generalinspektion des Militär-Erziehungs-und Bildungswesens (Prussia). *Leit-faden für den Unterricht in der Taktik auf den königlichen Kriegsschulen.* Berlin: E. S. Mittler, published nearly annually. The 1912 version was the 17th edition.
General Staff. *Anhaltspunkte für den Generalstabsdienst. (nur für den Dienstge-brauch).* Berlin: Reichsdruckerei, 1915. (This is the famous "red book," also known as the "red donkey." It had a vacant place for insertion of the *Taschen-buch,* cited below).
———. *Der deutsch-französische Krieg 1870–71.* 3 vols. Berlin: E. S. Mittler & Sohn, 1874.
———. *Taschenbuch des Generalstabsoffiziers. Geheim.* Berlin: Reichsdruckerei, 1914.
General Staff, Field Army. *Allgemeines über Stellungsbau 15. 8. 1917.* Berlin: Reichs-druckerei, 1917.
———. *Anleitung für Kompagnieführer.* Berlin: Reichsdruckerei, 1916.
———. *Ausbildungsvorschrift für die Fusstruppen im Kriege.* 2nd Entwurf. Berlin: Reichsdruckerei, January 1918.
———. *Der Angriff in der Stellungskrieg 1.1.1918, Ergänzung 1. 2. 1918.* Berlin: Reichs-druckerei, 1918.
———. *Grundsätze für die Führung der Abwehrschlacht im Stellungskriege vom 1.9.1917.* 14 parts. Berlin: Reichsdruckerei, 1917.
———. *Kompagnie-Führer-Anleitung.* 4th Entwurf. Berlin: Reichsdruckerei, Sep-tember 1918.
———. *Richtlinien über die Ausbildung von Offizieren und Mannschaften des östli-chen Kriegsschauplatzes in der westlichen Kriegführung* [29 November 1917]. Copy in Bundesarchiv/Militärchiv, PH 3/33.
———. *Sammelheft der Vorschriften für den Stellungskrieg für Alle Waffen 1916–1918.* Berlin: Reichsdruckerei, 1916–1918.

General Staff, 7th Section. "Die Entwicklung der deutschen Infanterie im Welt-krieg 1914–1918." *Militärwissenschaftliche Rundschau* 3 (1938): 376–419.

Kriegsministerium (Prussia). *D.V.E. No. 40. Bestimmungen über Generalstabsrei-sen, 14 April 1908.* Berlin: E. S. Mittler, 1908.

———. *D.V.E. Nr. 41. Dienstordnung der Kriegsschulen 10 Dezember 1906.* Berlin: E. S. Mittler, 1906.

———. *D.V.E. Nr. 53. Grundzüge der höhere Truppenführung vom 1 Januar 1910* (Nur für den Dienstgebrauch). Berlin: Reichsdruckerei, 1910.

———. *D.V.E. Nr. 130. Exerzier-Reglement für die Infanterie, 29 Mai 1906.* Berlin: E. S. Mittler, 1906. In English: *Drill Regulations for the Infantry, German Army,* trans. Francis J. Behr. Washington, DC: US Government Printing Office, 1907.

———. *D.V.E. Nr. 219. Mobilmachungsplan für das Deutsche Heer von 9 Oktober 1913 Geheim.* Berlin: Reichsdruckerei, 1913.

———. *D. V. E. Nr. 267. Felddienst-Ordnung.* Berlin: E. S. Mittler, 1908.

———. *D.V.E. Nr. 270. Bestimmungen für die grössere Truppenünbun-gen-Manöver-Ordnung.* Berlin: E. S. Mittler, 1914.

———. *Feldbefestigungsvorschrift (F.B.).* Berlin: E. S. Mittler, 1893.

Reichsarchiv. *Der Weltkrieg 1914 bis 1918.* 14 vols. Berlin: E. S. Mittler, 1925–1944.

———. *Kriegsrüstung und Kriegswirtschaft. Anlagen zum ersten Band.* Berlin: E. S. Mittler, 1930.

Reichsluftfahrtministerium. *Die Militärluftfahrt bis zum Beginn des Weltkrieges 1914.* 2 vols. Berlin: E. S. Mittler, 1941.

BOOKS, ARTICLES, AND DISSERTATIONS

Absolon, Rudolf. *Die Wehrmacht im Dritten Reich.* 6 vols. Boppard: Harald Boldt Verlag, 1969–1995.

Adams, R. J. Q., ed. *The Great War: Essays on the Military, Political and Social His-tory of the First World War.* College Station: Texas A&M University Press, 1990.

Afflerbach, Holger. *Falkenhayn. Politisches Denken und Handeln im Kaiserreich.* Munich: R. Oldenbourg, 1994.

———. "Kronprinz Rupprecht von Bayern im Ersten Weltkrieg." *Militärgeschicht-liche Zeitschrift* 75 (2016): 21–54.

———. "Wilhelm II as Supreme Warlord in the First World War." *War in History* 5, 4 (November 1998): 427–449.

Alger, John I. *The Quest for Victory: The History of the Principles of War.* Westport, CT: Greenwood Press, 1982.

Alten, Georg von. *Handbuch für Heer und Flotte.* 10 vols. Berlin: Deutsche Verlag-shaus Bong, 1909.

Altrock, Constantin von. "Zahl der Verwundungen in den Landheeren, Schutz-truppen und der Marine des deutschen Reiches während des Weltkrieges 1914 bis 1918." *Militär-Wochenblatt* 12 (1921): cols. 243–246.

———, ed. *Vom Sterben des deutschen Offizierkorps.* 2nd ed. Berlin: E. S. Mittler, 1922.

Anders, [Captain]. "Zur Kriegsmässigkeit unserer Übungen." *Militär-Wochenblatt* 148 (1911): cols. 3408–3410.

Anonymous [C. v. K.]. "Zusammenwirken von Infanterie und Artillerie." *Militär-Wochenblatt* 99, 1 (1914): cols. 1210–1214.

———. *Das alte Heer, von einem Stabsoffizier.* Charlottenburg: Verlag der Welt-bühne, 1920.

———. "Die militärische Vorbildung unserer Offiziere des Beurlaubtenstandes." *Militär-Wochenblatt* 7 (1914): cols. 121–128.

———. "Die sogenannte 'Angriffshetze.'" *Militär-Wochenblatt* 44 (1908): cols. 1026–1031.

———. *Die Truppenführung.* Berlin: R. Eisenschmidt, 1914.

——— [Union of Officers]. *Geschichte des Reserve-Infanterie-Regiments Nr. 35.* Berlin: Volkskraft Verlagsgesellschaft, 1935.

Ardenne, v. "Angriffskraft dichter und loser Schützenlinien." *Militär-Wochenblatt* 36 (1909): cols. 808–810.

———. "Langsames Feuer dichter Schützenlinien?" *Militär-Wochenblatt* 65 (1909): cols. 1481–1482.

Aron, Raymond. *Clausewitz: Philosopher of War*, trans. Christine Booker and Nor-man Stone. Englewood Cliffs, NJ: Prentice-Hall, 1985.

Association of Former Officers of the Regiment. *Das 1. Masurische Infanterie-Regiment Nr. 146 1897–1919.* Berlin: Verlag Tradition Wilhelm Kolk, 1929.

Astore, William J., and Dennis Showalter. *Hindenburg: Icon of German Militarism.* Washington, DC: Potomac Books, 2005.

Balck, Wilhelm. *Development of Tactics—World War*, trans. Harry Bell. Fort Leav-enworth, KS: General Service Schools Press, 1922.

———. "Die Lehren des Burenkrieges für den Gefechtstätigkeit der drei Waffen." *Beiheft zum Militär-Wochenblatt* 7 (1904): cols. 254–297.

———. "Gefechtsaufgaben bei Infanteriebesichtigungen." *Militär-Wochenblatt* 24 (1913): cols. 539–543; 25 (1913): cols. 563–567.

———. "Nachtübungen, Ausbildung und Besichtigung." *Militär-Wochenblatt* 45 (1911): cols. 1027–1032, 48 (1911): cols. 1053–1057, 49 (1911): cols. 1078–1083.

———. "Regiments- und Brigadeübungen der Infanterie." *Militär-Wochenblatt* 102 (1913): cols. 2291–2299.

———. *Taktik.* 6 vols. Berlin: R. Eisenschmidt, 1908–1912.

———. "Über Nachtschiessen der Infanterie." *Militär-Wochenblatt* 94 (1913): cols. 2123–2131.

Bald, Detlev. *Militärische Verantwortung in Staat und Gesellschaft. 175 Jahre Gener-alstabsausbildung in Deutschland.* Koblenz: Bernard & Graefe, 1986.

Bärensprung, von. "Die Ausbildung der Einjährig-Freiwilligen der Infanterie." *Militär-Wochenblatt* 126 (1912): cols. 2911–2918.

———. "Gedanken über das Kriegspiel der Reserveoffiziere." *Militär-Wochenblatt* 4 (1913): cols. 75–78, 5 (1913): cols. 99–103.

Barrett, Michael B. *Operation Albion: The German Conquest of the Baltic Islands.* Bloomington: Indiana University Press, 2008.

———. *Prelude to Blitzkrieg: The 1916 Austro-German Campaign in Romania.* Bloomington: Indiana University Press, 2013.

Bartel, Horst, and Ernst Engelberg, eds. *Die grosspreussisch-militaristische Reichs-gründung 1871*. 2 vols. East Berlin: Akademie Verlag, 1971.

Bassford, Christopher. *Clausewitz in English: The Reception of Clausewitz in Britain and America 1815–1945*. New York: Oxford University Press, 1994.

———. "John Keegan and the Grand Tradition of Trashing Clausewitz: A Polemic." *War and Society* 1, 3 (1994): 317–366.

Bauer, Max. *Der grosse Krieg in Feld und Heimat. Erinnerungen und Betrachtungen*. Tübingen: Osiander'sche Buchhandlung, 1921.

Beck, Ludwig. *Studien*, ed. Hans Speidel. Stuttgart: K. F. Koehler, 1955.

Benary, Albert, ed. *Das Ehrenbuch der deutschen Feldartillerie*. Berlin: Verlag Tradition Wilhelm Kolk, ca. 1930.

Berendt, General of Artillery Richard von. "Aus grosser Zeit vor zwanzig Jahren: Der Feldzug in Serbien." *Militär-Wochenblatt* 13 (1935): cols. 523–527.

Berges, Wilhelm, and Carl Hinrichs, eds. *Zur Geschichte und Problematik der Demokratie. Festgabe für Hans Herzfeld*. Berlin: Duncker & Humboldt, 1958.

Bergh, Max van den. *Das deutsche Heer vor dem Weltkriege*. Berlin: Sanssouci Verlag, 1934.

Bernhardi, Friedrich von. *Denkwürdigkeiten aus meinem Leben*. Berlin: E. S. Mittler, 1927.

———. "Der Kampf der drei Waffen und die Organisation der Kavallerie." *Militär-Wochenblatt* 69 (1910): cols 1643–1648, 70 (1910): cols. 1680–1683, 71 (1910): cols. 1698–1700.

———. "Die Artillerie beim Infanterieangriff. Eine Entgegnung." *Militär-Wochenblatt* 83 (1912): cols 1895–1901, 84 (1912): cols. 1924–1929.

———. "Die Elemente des modernen Krieges." *Beiheft zum Militär-Wochenblatt* (1898): 429–459.

———. *On War of Today*, trans. Karl von Donat. 2 vols. New York: Dodd, Mead, 1914.

———. "Über Angriffsweise Kriegführung." *Beiheft zum Militär-Wochenblatt* 4 (1905): cols. 125–151.

———. *The War of the Future in Light of the Lessons of the World War*, trans. F. A. Holt. London: Hutchinson, 1920.

Beseler, Hans. "Beitrag zur Ausbildung der Einjährig-Freiwilligen." *Militär-Wochenblatt* 131 (1906): cols. 3045–3051.

———. "Graf Schlieffen. Gesammelte Schriften." *Militär-Wochenblatt* 77 (1913): cols. 1745–1749, 78/80 (1913): cols. 1837–1845, 81 (1913): cols. 1873–1876, 82 (1913): cols. 1886–1892.

———. "Krieg und modernes Verkehrswesen." *Preusssiche Jahrbücher* 151 (February 1913): 387–409.

———. "Über Millionenheere." *Deutsche Revue* 37 (February 1912): 207–213.

———. *Vom Soldatenberufe*. Berlin: E. S. Mittler, 1904.

Beyerhaus, Gisbert. *Einheitlicher Oberbefehl. Ein Problem des Weltkrieges*. Munich: F. Bruckmann Verlag, 1938.

Bidwell, Shelford, and Dominick Graham. *Fire-Power: British Army Weapons and Theories of War 1904–1945*. Boston: George Allen & Unwin, 1982.

Birnbaum, Karl E. *Peace Moves and U-Boat Warfare: A Study of Imperial Germany's Policy towards the United States April 18, 1916–January 9, 1917*. Stockholm: Almqvist & Wiksell, 1958.

Blackbourn, David. *The Long Nineteenth Century: A History of Germany, 1780–1918*. New York: Oxford University Press, 1998.

Blaschke, Richard. *Carl von Clausewitz*. Berlin: Junker & Dünnhaupt Verlag, 1934.

Blau, E. G. "Die ältere Moltke und Schlieffen." *Wissen und Wehr* 1 (1934): 824–834.

Blau, Erich-Gunter. *Die operative Verwendung der deutschen Kavallerie im Weltkrieg 1914–1918*. Vol. 1, *Freidensvorbereitung*. Munich: C. H. Beck'sche Verlagsbuchhandlung, 1934.

Blume, Wilhelm von. "Die Probleme des Krieges." *Militär-Wochenblatt* 152 (1908): cols. 3547–3555.

———. "Operationslinie." *Militär-Wochenblatt* 143 (1905): cols. 3269–3271, 104 (1906): cols. 2409–2412.

———. "Selbstätigkeit der Führer im Kriege." *Beiheft zum Militär-Wochenblatt* 10 (1896): cols. 479–534.

Blumenthal, Count Alfred von, ed. *Tagebücher des Generalfeldmarschalls Graf von Blumenthal aus den Jahren 1866 und 1870/71*. Stuttgart: J. G. Cotta'sche Buchhandlung Nachfolger, 1902.

Boeck, Friedrich von der. "Das Verhalten der Infanterie im Gefecht gegen Kavallerie." *Militär-Wochenblatt* 67 (1908): cols. 1569–1576.

———. "Zur Frage der Infanterietaktik (Erwiderung)." *Militär-Wochenblatt* 16 (1903): cols. 438–443.

Boehn, Hubert von. *Generalstabsgeschäfte. Ein Handbuch für Offiziere aller Waffen*. Potsdam: Verlag von Eduard Döring, 1862.

Boemke, Manfred, Roger Chickering, and Stig Förster, eds. *Anticipating Total War: The German and American Experiences 1871–1914*. Cambridge: Cambridge University Press, 1999.

Boetticher, Friedrich von. *Schlieffen*. Göttingen: Musterschmidt Verlag, 1957.

Boguslawski, A. von. *Betrachtungen über Heerwesen und Kriegführung*. Berlin: R. Eisenschmidt, 1897.

———. *Die Entwicklung der Taktik von 1793 bis zur Gegenwart*. Berlin: Luckhardt, 1869.

———. "Grundsätze, Schlagwort und Phantasie." *Militär-Wochenblatt* 73 (1903): cols. 1779–1785, 74 (1903): cols. 1810–1816.

———. *Strategische Erörterungen betreffend die von General von Schlichting vertretenen Grundsätze*. Berlin: R. Eisenschmidt, 1901.

Borgert, Hans L. *Grundzüge der Landkriegführung von Schlieffen bis Guderian*. Munich: Bernard & Graefe, 1979.

Brabant, Artur. *Generaloberst Max Freiherr von Hausen. Ein deutscher Soldat*. Dresden: Buchdruckerei der Wilhelm & Bertha v. Baentesch Stiftung, 1926.

Bradley, Dermot, and Ulrich Marwedel, eds. *Militärgeschichte, Militärwissenschaft und Konfliktforschung*. Osnabrück: Biblio Verlag, 1977.

Brandt, Heinrich von, ed. *Aus dem Leben des Generals der Infanterie z. D. Heinrich von Brandt*. 3 vols. Berlin: E. S. Mittler, 1868.

Bronsart von Schellendorff, Paul. *Der Dienst des Generalstabes*. 2 vols. Berlin: E. S. Mittler, 1875–76.

———. *Geheimes Kriegstagebuch 1870–1871*, ed. Peter Rassow. Bonn: Athenäun Verlag, 1954.

Brose, Eric Dorn. *The Kaiser's Army: The Politics of Military Technology in Germany during the Machine Age, 1870–1918*. Oxford: Oxford University Press, 2001.

Broucek, Peter, ed. *Ein österreichischer General gegen Hitler. Feldmarschalleutnant Alfred Jansa: Erinnerungen*. Vienna: Böhlau Verlag, 2011.

Bruchmüller, Georg. *Die Artillerie beim Angriff im Stellungskrieg*. Charlottenburg: Verlag Offene Wort, 1926.

———. "Die Artillerieführung bei den grossen deutschen Angriffen im Jahre 1918." *Wissen und Wehr* 4 (1931): 185–194.

———. *Die deutsche Artillerie in den Durchbruchschlachten des Weltkrieges*. 2nd ed. Berlin: E. S. Mittler, 1922.

Bry, Gerhard. *Wages in Germany: 1871–1945*. Princeton, NJ: Princeton University Press, 1960.

Buchfinck, Ernst. "Der Meinungskampf um den Marnefeldzug." *Historische Zeitschrift* 152, 2 (1935): 286–300.

———. "Feldmarschall Graf von Haeseler 19. 1. 1836–26. 10. 1919." *Wissen und Wehr* 1 (1936): 3–9.

———. "General Albert von Boguslawski. Ein Gedenkblatt zu seinem 100. Geburtstag: 24. 12. 1834–1934." *Wissen und Wehr* 12 (1934): 816–824.

Bucholz, Arden. *Hans Delbrück and the German Military Establishment: War Images in Conflict*. Iowa City: University of Iowa Press, 1985.

———. *Moltke and the German Wars, 1864–1871*. New York: Palgrave, 2001.

———. *Moltke, Schlieffen and Prussian War Planning*. New York: Berg, 1991.

Buhle, P. [Major a. D.]. "Hindenburg." *Wissen und Wehr* 8 (1934): 499–503.

———. "Von der Marschgeschwindigdkeit." *Militär-Wochenblatt* 19 (1925): cols. 660–661.

Bülow, Prince Bernhard von. *Denkwürdigkeiten*. 4 vols. Berlin: Ullstein, 1931.

Burchardt, Lothar. *Friedenwirtschaft und Kriegsvorsorge. Deutschlands wirtschaftliche üstungsbestrebungen vor 1914*. Boppard am Rhein: Harald Boldt Verlag, 1962.

Buttar, Prit. *Germany Ascendant: The Eastern Front, 1915*. Oxford: Osprey, 2015.

Büttner, Ursula, ed. *Das Unrechtregime. Internationale Forschung über den Nationalsozialismus*. Hamburg: Hans Christians Verlag, 1986.

Caemmerer, Rudolf von. "Der Kampf um die Schlichtingsche Lehre." *Militär-Wochenblatt* 22 (1902): cols. 571–580, 25 (1902): cols. 649–653, 26 (1902): cols. 680–686, 28 (1902): cols. 766–769.

———. *The Development of Strategical Science during the 19th Century*, trans. Karl von Donat. London: Hugh Rees, 1905.

———. "Über den 'Freifeldangriff 1905.'" *Militär-Wochenblatt* 5 (1905): cols. 93–100.

———. "Zur Frage der Infanterietaktik." *Militär-Wochenblatt* 8 (1903): cols. 241–25l, 9 (1903): cols. 268–273, 10 (1903): cols. 299–306.

———. "Zwei Bemerkungen zu Moltkes Strategie im Jahre 1866." *Militär-Wochenblatt* 156 (1905): cols. 3603–3608.

Cardinal von Widdern, Georg. *Handbuch für Truppenführung und Stabsdienst.* 3rd ed. Gera: Verlag v. A. Reisewitz, 1884.

Cecil, Lamar. *Wilhelm II.* 2 vols. Chapel Hill: University of North Carolina Press, 1989, 1996.

Chickering, Roger. *Imperial Germany and the Great War, 1914–1918.* Cambridge: Cambridge University Press, 1998.

Chickering, Roger, and Stig Förster, eds. *Great War, Total War: Combat and Mobilization on the Western Front 1914–1918.* Cambridge: Cambridge University Press, 2000.

Citino, Robert M. *The German Way of War: From the Thirty Years' War to the Third Reich.* Lawrence: University Press of Kansas, 2005.

Clausewitz, Carl von. *Historical and Political Writings,* ed. and trans. Peter Paret and Daniel Moran. Princeton, NJ: Princeton University Press, 1992.

———. *On War* [1832], trans. Michael Howard and Peter Paret. Princeton, NJ: Princeton University Press, 1976.

———. *Vom Kriege,* ed. Werner Hahlweg. 19th ed. Bonn: Ferdinand Dümmlers Verlag, 1980.

Clemente, Steven E. "Mit Gott! Für König und Kaiser." Ph.D. diss., University of Oklahoma, 1989.

Cochenhausen, Friedrich von, ed. *Eine Sammlung Wehrpolitischer Aufsätze.* Hamburg: Hanseatische Verlagsanstalt, 1933.

———. *Heerführer des Weltkrieges.* Berlin: E. S. Mittler, 1939.

———. *Von Scharnhorst zu Schlieffen 1806–1906. Hundert Jahre preusssich-deutscher Generalstab.* Berlin: E. S. Mittler, 1933.

Coetzee, Marilyn Shevin. *The German Army League: Popular Nationalism in Wilhelmine Germany.* New York: Oxford University Press, 1990.

Conrad von Hötzendorf, Franz Baron. *Aus Meiner Dienstzeit 1906–1918.* 5 vols. 6th ed. Vienna: Rikola Verlag, 1921–1925.

Conrad von Hötzendorf, Gina Grafin. *Mein Leben mit Conrad von Hötzendorf: Sein geistiges Vernächtnis.* Leipzig: Grathlein, 1935.

Cook, Tim. "'Against God-Inspired Conscience': The Perception of Gas Warfare as a Weapon of Mass Destruction, 1915–1939." *War and Society* 18, 1 (May 2000): 47–69.

Corum, James S., and Richard R. Muller. *The Luftwaffe's Way of War: German Air Force Doctrine 1911–1945.* Baltimore: Nautical & Aviation Publishing Company of America, 1998.

Craig, Gordon A. *The Battle of Königgrätz: Prussia's Victory over Austria, 1866.* 1964. Reprint, Westport, CT: Greenwood Press, 1975.

———. *The Politics of the Prussian Army 1640–1945.* New York: Oxford University Press, 1956.

———. "The World War I Alliance of the Central Powers in Retrospect: The Military Cohesion of the Alliance." *Journal of Modern History* 37 (1965): 336–344.

———, ed. *War, Politics and Diplomacy: Selected Essays.* New York: Praeger, 1966.

Cramon, August von. *Unser Österreich-Ungarischer Bundesgenosse im Weltkriege.* Berlin: E. S. Mittler, 1920.

Cramon, August von, and Paul Fleck. *Deutschlands Schicksalsbund mit Österreich-Ungarn*. Berlin: Verlag für Kampfpolitik, 1932.

Cron, Hermann. *Die Organisation des deutschen Heeres im Weltkriege*. Berlin: E. S. Mittler, 1923.

———. *Geschichte des deutschen Heeres im Weltkriege 1914–1918*. Berlin: Militärverlag Karl Siegismund, 1937.

Cruttwell, C. R. M. F. *A History of the Great War 1914–1918*. 2nd ed. Chicago: Academy Publishers, 1992.

Deichmann, Paul. *Der Chef im Hintergrund. Ein Leben als Soldat von der preussischen Armee bis zur Bundeswehr*. Oldenburg: Gerhard Stalling, 1970.

Deines, Adolf von. "Ein Kriegsministerieller Erlass gegen die willkürliche Abänderung und Vervollständigung der von höchster Stelle ausgehenden Vorschriften." *Militär-Wochenblatt* 21 (1914): cols. 429–430.

Deist, Wilhelm. *Militär, Staat und Gesellschaft*. Munich: R. Oldenbourg, 1991.

———. *Militär und Innenpolitik im Weltkrieg 1914–1918*. 2 vols. Düsseldorf: Droste Verlag, 1970.

———. "Zur Institution des Militärbefehlshabers und Obermilitärbefehlshabers im ersten Weltkrieg." *Jahrbücher für die Geschichte Mittel-und ostdeutschlands* 13/14 (1965): 222–240.

———, ed. *The German Military in the Age of Total War*. Warwickshire, UK: Berg Publishers, 1985.

Delbrück, Hans. "Strategie und Taktik in der Offensive von 1918." *Militär-Wochenblatt* 11 (1925): cols. 361–363.

Demeter, Karl. *Das deutsche Offizierkorps in Gesellschaft und Staat 1650–1945*. 4th rev. ed. Frankfurt: Bernard & Graefe, 1965.

Dilthey. *Militär-Dienst Unterricht für Freiwillige*. Berlin: E. S. Mittler, 1887.

DiNardo, Richard L. *Breakthrough: The Gorlice-Tarnow Campaign, 1915*. Santa Barbara, CA: Praeger, 2010.

———. "The Falsest of Truisms: Who Writes History?" *World History Connected* 12, 1 (February 2015), http://worldhistoryconnected.press.illinois.edu/12.1/forum_dinardo.html.

———. "Huns with Web-Feet: Operation Albion, 1917." *War in History* 12, 4 (November 2005): 396–417.

———. *Invasion: The Conquest of Serbia, 1915*. Santa Barbara, CA: Praeger, 2015.

———. "The Limits of Encirclement: The Invasion of Serbia, 1915." *Historian* 78, 3 (Fall 2016): 486–503.

———. "The Limits of Technology: The Invasion of Serbia, 1915." *Journal of Military History* 79, 4 (October 2015): 981–996.

———. "Southern by the Grace of God but Prussian by Common Sense: James Longstreet and the Exercise of Command in the U.S. Civil War." *Journal of Military History* 66, 4 (October 2002): 1011–1032.

DiNardo, Richard L., and Daniel J. Hughes. "Germany and Coalition Warfare in the World Wars: A Comparative Study." *War in History* 8, 2 (April 2001): 166–190.

Doepner, Friedrich. "Hat Graf Bruehl Clausewitz verfaelscht?" *Wehrwissehschaftliche Rundschau* 32, 5 (May 1983): 245–247.

———. "Karl Eduard Pönitz, 1795–1858." *Zeitschrift für Heereskunde* 52, 340 (November–December 1988): 140–143.

———. "Technik und Tradition in der deutschen Armee vor 1914." *Europäische Wehrkunde* 30, 10 (October 1983): 496–499.

Dorondo, David R. *Riders of the Apocalypse: German Cavalry and Machine Warfare, 1870–1945.* Annapolis, MD: Naval Institute Press, 2012.

Doughty, Robert A. "French Strategy in 1914: Joffre's Own." *Journal of Military History* 67, 2 (April 2003): 427–454.

———. "'Papa' Joffre and the Great War." *Journal of Military History* 79, 4 (October 1915): 959–980.

———. *Pyrrhic Victory: French Strategy and Operations in the Great War.* Cambridge, MA: Harvard University Press, 2005.

Dowling, Timothy C. *The Brusilov Offensive.* Bloomington: Indiana University Press, 2008.

Dreetz, Dieter. "Zur Unerfüllbarkeit der personellen Ersatzforderungen der deutschen militärischen Führung für das Feldheer im Ersten Weltkrieg." *Revue Internationale d'Histoire Militaire* 63 (1985): 51–60.

Driftmann, Hans H. *Grundzüge des militärischen Erziehungs-und Bildungswesens in der Zeit 1871–1939.* Regensburg: Walhalla & Praeteoria Verlag, 1979.

Duffy, Christopher. *Through German Eyes: The British and the Somme, 1916.* London: Weidenfeld & Nicholson, 2006.

Dukes, Jack R., and Joachim Remak, eds. *Another Germany: A Reconsideration of the Imperial Era.* Boulder, CO: Westview Press, 1988.

Duppler, Jörg, and Gerhard P. Gross, eds. *Kriegsende 1918. Ereignis, Wirkung, Nachwirkung.* Munich: R. Oldenbourg Verlag, 1999.

Dupuy, Trevor N., et al., eds. *International Military and Defense Encyclopedia.* 6 vols. New York: Brassey's, 1993.

Echevarria, Antulio J., II. *After Clausewitz: German Military Thinkers before the Great War.* Lawrence: University Press of Kansas, 2000.

———. "Borrowing from the Master: Uses of Clausewitz in German History Literature before the Great War." *War in History* 3, 3 (1996): 274–292.

———. *Clausewitz's Center of Gravity: Changing Our Warfighting Doctrine—Again!* Carlisle, PA: US Army Strategic Studies Institute, 2002.

Ehlert, Hans, Michael Epkenhans, and Gerhard P. Gross, eds. *The Schlieffen Plan: International Perspectives on the German Strategy for World War I,* trans. David T. Zabecki. Lexington: University Press of Kentucky, 2014.

Ehlert, Hans, et al., eds. *Der Schlieffenplan. Analysen und Dokumente.* Paderborn: Ferdinand Schöningh, 2006.

Eisenhart-Rothe, Ernst von, ed. *Ehrendenkmal der Deutschen Armee und Marine 1871–1918.* Berlin: Deutscher National-Verlag, 1928.

Elster, Hanns Martin. *Kriegsminister, General-Feldmarschall, Ministerpräsident Graf Albrecht von Roon. Sein Leben und Wirken.* Berlin: Verlag Karl Siegismund, 1938.

Elze, Walter. *Das Deutsche Heer von 1914.* 1939. Reprint, Osnabrück: Biblio Verlag, 1968.

Endres, Franz Karl. "Wie bestrebt sich Napoleon, wie Moltke die Einheitlichkeit der Heerführung zu gewährleisten?" *Jahrbücher für die deutsche Armee und Marine* (1910): 42–54, 162–178.

English, John, et al., eds. *The Mechanized Battlefield.* London: Pergamon-Brassey's 1985.

Epkenhans, Michael. "Military-Industrial Relations in Imperial Germany, 1870–1914." *War in History* 10, 1 (January 2003): 1–26.

———. "Neuere Forschungen zur Geschichte des Ersten Weltkrieges." *Archiv für Sozialgeschichte* 38 (1998): 458–487.

Epkenhans, Michael, Jörg Hillmann, and Frank Nägler, eds. *Skagerrakschlacht: Vorgeschichte, Ereignis, Verarbeitung.* Munich: Oldenbourg, 2009.

Epstein, Robert M. *Napoleon's Last Victory and the Emergence of Modern War.* Lawrence: University Press of Kansas, 1994.

Erickson, Edward J. *Gallipoli: The Ottoman Campaign.* Barnsley, UK: Pen & Sword, 2010.

Esch, Max von der. "Frontausdehnung und Tiefengliederung." *Militär-Wochenblatt* 53 (1909): cols. 1213–1219.

Estorff, Eggert von. "Der Burenkrieg und seine taktischen Lehren nach Deutscher und Englischer Auffassung." *Militär-Wochenblatt* 111 (1910): cols. 2588–2591.

Estorff, von [Colonel]. "Gefechtsausdehnungen." *Militär-Wochenblatt* 24 (1914): cols. 478–479.

———. "Taktische Lehren aus dem Russisch-japanischen Feldkriege im Lichte unserer neuesten Vorschriften." *Militär-Wochenblatt* 36 (1908): cols. 810–820, 57 (1908): cols. 1317–1325, 79 (1908): cols. 1849–1854, 80 (1908): cols. 1871–1876, 108 (1908): cols. 2537–2542, 109 (1908): cols. 2561–2566, 119 (1908): cols. 2795–2802, 120 (1908): cols. 2823–2829.

———. "Vorführen der Reserven zum Sturm." *Militär-Wochenblatt* 30 (1908): cols. 673–677.

Evans, Richard J., ed. *Society and Politics in Wilhelmine Germany.* London: Croom Helm, 1978.

Falkenhausen, Friedrich *Freiherr* von. "Angriff und Verteidigung." *Vierteljahrshefte für Truppenführung und Heereskunde* 4 (1906): 383–414.

———. *Ausbildung für den Krieg.* 2 vols. Berlin: E. S. Mittler, 1902.

———. *Flankenbewegung und Massenheer. Der Gedanke von Leuthen in Anwendung auf die Gegenwart.* Berlin: E. S. Mittler, 1911.

———. *Kriegführung und Wissenschaft.* Berlin: E. S. Mittler, 1913.

———. "Kriegsmässige Ausbildung." *Militär-Wochenblatt* 139 (1911): cols. 3193–3196.

———. "Vortruppen." *Vierteljahrshefte für Truppenführung und Heereskunde* 2 (1905): 663–693.

Falkenhausen, Hugo *Freiherr* von. "Exerzieren und Fechten." *Vierteljahrshefte für Truppenführung und Heereskunde* 4 (1907): 464–487.

Falkenhayn, Erich von. *The German General Staff and Its Decisions, 1914–1916*. New York: Dodd, Mead, 1920.

Fehr, Otto. *Die Märzoffensive 1918 an der Westfront. Strategie oder Taktik?* Leipzig: K. F. Koehler, 1921.

Feldman, Gerald D. *Army, Industry and Labor in Germany 1914–1918*. Princeton, NJ: Princeton University Press, 1966.

Ferguson, Niall. *The Pity of War*. New York: Basic Books, 1999.

Fischer, Fritz. *Germany's Aims in the First World War*. New York: W. W. Norton, 1967.

———. *Krieg der Illusionen. Die deutsche Politik von 1911 bis 1914*. 2nd ed. Düsseldorf: Droste, 1969.

———. *World Power or Decline: The Controversy over Germany's Aims in the First World War*, trans. Lancelot L. Farrar, Robert Kimber, and Rita Kimber. New York: W. W. Norton, 1974.

Foerster, Wolfgang. *Aus der Gedankenwerkstatt des Deutschen Generalstabes*. Berlin: E. S. Mittler, 1931.

———. "Das Bild des modernen Feldherrn: Ein Wort der Abwehr und Verständigung." *Wissen und Wehr* 4 (1939): 243–256.

———. "Einige Bemerkungen zu Gerhard Ritters Buch 'Der Schlieffenplan.'" *Wehrwissenschaftliche Rundschau* 7, 1 (1957): 37–44.

———. *Graf Schlieffen und der Weltkrieg*. 2nd ed. Berlin: E. S. Mittler, 1925.

Foley, Robert. *German Strategy and the Path to Verdun: Erich von Falkenhayn and the Development of Attrition, 1870–1916*. Cambridge: Cambridge University Press, 2005.

———. "Preparing the German Army for the First World War: The Operational Ideas of Alfred von Schlieffen and Helmuth von Moltke the Younger." *War and Society* 22, 2 (October 2004): 1–25.

Förster, Gerhard. *Totaler Krieg und Blitzkrieg*. East Berlin: Deutscher Militärverlag, 1967.

Förster, Roland G., ed. *Generalfeldmarschall von Moltke. Bedeutung und Wirkung*. Munich: R. Oldenbourg, 1991.

Förster, Stig. "Der deutsche Generalstab und die Illusion des kurzen Krieges 1871–1914. Metakritik eines Mythos." *Militärgeschichtliche Mitteilungen* 54 (1995): 61–95.

———. *Der doppelte Militarismus. Die deutsche Heeresrüstungspolitik zwischen Status-Quo-Sicherung und Aggression 1890–1913*. Stuttgart: Franz Steiner Verlag, 1985.

———. "Facing 'People's War': Moltke the Elder and Germany's Military Options after 1871." *Journal of Strategic Studies* 10, 2 (June 1987): 209–230.

———, ed. *Militärische Verantwortung in Staat und Gesellschaft. 175 Jahre Generalstabsausbildung in Deutschland*. Koblenz: Bernard & Graefe, 1986.

Förster, Stig, and Jörg Nagler, eds. *On the Road to Total War: The American Civil War and the German Wars of Unification 1870–71*. Cambridge: Cambridge University Press, 1997.

Francois, Hermann von. "Der Grenzschutz im Osten im August 1914 und seine Reibungen." *Wissen und Wehr* 10 (1929): 341–356.

———. *Gorlice 1915: Der Karpathendurchbruch und die Befreiung von Galizien*. Leipzig: Verlag von K. F. Koehler, 1922.

———. *Marneschlacht und Tannenberg. Betrachtungen zur Deutschen Kriegführung der ersten sechs Kriegswochen*. Berlin: August Scherl, 1920.

Fransecky, Eduard von. *Denkwürdigkeiten des preussischen Generals der Infanterie Eduard von Fransecky*, ed. Walter von Bremen. Berlin: Boll & Pickardt, 1913.

Frauenholz, Eugen von. *Das Gesicht der Schlacht. Taktik und Technik in der deutschen Kriegsgeschichte*. Stuttgart: Union Deutscher Verlagsgesellschaft, 1937.

———. *Das Heerwesen des XIX Jahrhunderts*. Munich: C. H. Beck, 1941.

———. "Friedrich der Grosse-Napoleon-Moltke. Probleme der Kriegführung im XVIII und XIX Jahrhundert." *Wissen und Wehr* 4 (1930): 193–218.

———. *Im Banne der Persönlichkeit. Aus der Lebenserinnerungen des Generals der Infanterie a. D. E. von Eisenhart Rothe*. Berlin: Verlag Oskar Franz Hübner, 1931.

Frauenholz, Eugen von, et al., eds. *Deutsche Infanterie. Das Ehrenmal der vordersten Front*. Zeulenroda: Verlag Bernhard Sporn, 1939.

Freytag-Loringhoven, Hugo Baron von. *Betrachtungen über den Russisch-Japanischen Krieg*. 2 vols. Berlin: E. S. Mittler, 1913.

———. "Das Begegnungsgefecht, kriegsgeschichtliche Betrachtungen." *Vierteljahrshefte für Truppenführung und Heereskunde* 1 (1904): 110–132.

———. *Die Grundbedingungen kriegerischen Erfolgen. Beiträge zur Psychologie des Krieges im 19. und 20. Jahrhundert*. Berlin: E. S. Mittler, 1914.

———. *Die Heerführung Napoleons in ihrer Bedeutung für unsere Zeit*. Berlin: E. S. Mittler. 1910.

———. *Die Heerführung Napoleons und Moltkes. Eine vergleichende Studie*. Berlin: E. S. Mittler, 1897.

———. "Die Macht der Gewohnheit ein Hemmnis kriegerischen Erfolges." *Vierteljahrshefte für Truppenführung und Heereskunde* 6 (1909): 379–412.

———. "Die Russen in den Kriegen der Vergangenheit." *Vierteljahrshefte für Truppenführung und Heereskunde* 2 (1905): 223–267.

———. "Eine Zeit des Rückganges in der Kriegskunst." *Vierteljahrshefte für Truppenführung und Heereskunde* 2 (1905): 597–608.

———. *General-Feldmarschall Graf von Schlieffen*. Leipzig: Historia Verlag Paul Schraepler, 1920.

———. *Krieg und Politik in der Neuzeit*. Berlin: E. S. Mittler, 1911.

———. *Menschen und Dinge wie ich sie in meinem Leben sah*. Berlin: E. S. Mittler, 1923.

———. "Studien über Clausewitz." *Vierteljahrshefte für Truppenführung und Heereskunde* 1 (1904): 135–176, 364–374, 535–578.

———. "Über die Dauer von Schlachten und Gefechten." *Vierteljahrshefte für Truppenführung und Heereskunde* 2 (1905): 547–557.

Friedjung, Heinrich. *Der Kampf um die Vorherrschaft in Deutschland*. 2 vols. Stuttgart: Cotta, 1901–1902.

Friedrich Karl, Prince von Preussen. *Denkwürdigkeiten aus seinem Leben*, ed. Wolfgang Foerster. 2 vols. Stuttgart: Deutsche Verlags-Anstalt, 1910.

Friedrich, Emperor, III. *Das Kriegstagebuch von 1870/71*, ed. Heinrich Otto Meissner. Berlin: Verlag von K. S. Koehler, 1926.

Fritsch, [Lieutenant Colonel]. "Wird Man im Kriege auf Luftschiffen und Flugzeuge von unten Schiessen." *Militär-Wochenblatt* 141 (1913): cols. 3193–3197.

Fuller, J. F. C. *A Military History of the Western World.* 3 vols. New York: Funk & Wagnalls, 1954–1956.

Gallie, W. B. *Philosophers of Peace and War: Kant, Clausewitz, Marx, Engels and Tolstoy.* Cambridge: Cambridge University Press, 1978.

Gallwitz, Max von. *Erleben im Westen 1916–1918.* Berlin: E. S. Mittler, 1932.

———. *Meine Führertätigkeit im Weltkriege 1914/1916.* Berlin: E. S. Mittler, 1929.

Gat, Azar. *The Development of Military Thought: The Nineteenth Century.* Oxford: Clarendon Press, 1992.

———. *Fascist and Liberal Visions of War: Fuller, Liddell Hart, Douhet and Other Modernists.* Oxford: Clarendon Press, 1998.

———. *The Origins of Military Thought: From the Enlightenment to Clausewitz.* Oxford: Clarendon Press, 1989.

Gayl, Egon *Freiherr* von. *General von Schlichting und sein Lebenswirk.* Berlin: Verlag von Georg Stilke, 1913.

Gebsattel, Ludwig *Freiherr* von. *Generalfeldmarschall Karl von Bülow.* Munich: J. F. Lehmanns Verlag, 1929.

Geiss, Immanuel, ed. *Julikrise und Kriegsausbruch: Eine Dokumentensammlung.* 2 vols. Hannover: Verlag für Literatur und Zeitgeschehen, 1963–1964.

Geyer, [Major]. "Lehren für den Kampf um Festungen aus den Ereignissen des Weltkrieges auf dem westlichen Kriegsschauplatz." *Wissen und Wehr* 6 (1925): 441–456, 499–512.

Geyer, Michael. *Deutsche Rüstungspolitik 1860–1980.* Baden-Baden: Suhrkampf, 1984.

Giese, Franz. *Geschichte des Reserve-Infanterie-Regiments 227 im Weltkrieg 1914/18.* Privately published, 1931.

Gleich, G. von. *Die alte Armee und ihre Verirrungen.* 2nd ed. Leipzig: Verlag von K. F. Koehler, 1919.

Goemans, H. E. *War and Punishment: The Causes of War Termination in the First World War.* Princeton, NJ: Princeton University Press, 2000.

Goldrick, James. *Before Jutland: The Naval War in Northern European Waters, August 1914–February 1915.* Annapolis, MD: Naval Institute Press, 2015.

Goltz, Colmar *Freiherr* von der. *The Conduct of War: A Short Treatise on Its Most Important Branches and Guiding Rules*, trans. Major G. F. Leverson. London: Kegan Paul, 1908.

———. *Denkwürdigkeiten*, ed. Friedrich *Freiherr* von der Goltz and Wolfgang Foerster. Berlin: E. S. Mittler, 1929.

———. *Krieg- und Heerführung.* Berlin: R. von Decker's Verlag, 1901.

———. *The Nation in Arms*, trans. Philip Ashworth. London: W. H. Allen, 1906.

———. "Welche Weg hat die kriegsmässige Ausbildung der Infanterie einzuschlagen?" *Militär-Wochenblatt* 1 (1905): cols. 18–21.

Gordon, Andrew. *The Rules of the Game: Jutland and British Naval Command*. Annapolis, MD: Naval Institute Press, 1996.

Görlitz, Walter, ed. *The Kaiser and His Court: The Diaries, Note Books and Letters of Admiral Georg Alexander von Müller, Chief of the Naval Cabinet 1914–1918*, trans. Mervyn Savill. New York: Harcourt, Brace & World, 1961.

Gossler, Konrad von. *Über den Misserfolg strategischer Operationen*. Stuttgart: Deutsche Verlags-Anstalt, 1911.

Gothein, Georg. *Warum verloren wir den Krieg?* 2nd ed. Berlin: Deutsche Verlags-Anstalt, 1920.

Greenhalgh, Elizabeth. "General Ferdinand Foch and Unified Allied Command in 1918." *Journal of Military History* 79, 4 (October 2015): 997–1024.

———. *Victory through Coalition: Britain and France during the First World War*. Cambridge: Cambridge University Press, 2005.

Greiner, Helmuth. "Der Zusammenbruch 1918. Bemerkungen zum Werke des Untersuchungsausschlusses." *Wissen und Wehr* 6 (1925): 321–336.

Griffith, Paddy. *Battle Tactics of the Western Front: The British Army's Art of Attack, 1916–1918*. New Haven, CT: Yale University Press, 1994.

———. *Forward into Battle: Fighting Tactics from Waterloo to Vietnam*. Chichester, UK: Antony Bird, 1981.

Groener, Wilhelm. *Das Testament des Grafen Schlieffen. Operative Studien über den Weltkrieg*. Berlin: E. S. Mittler, 1927.

———. *Der Feldherr wider Willen. Operative Studien über den Weltkrieg*. 2nd ed. Berlin: E. S. Mittler, 1931.

———. *Der Weltkrieg und seine Probleme. Rückschau und Ausblick*. Berlin: Verlag Georg Stilke, 1920.

———. "Die Liquidation des Weltkrieges." *Preussische Jahrbücher* 179 (1920): 36–61, 172–194, 337–348.

———. *Lebenserinnerungen, Jugend, Generalstab, Weltkrieg*, ed. Friedrich *Freiherr* Hiller von Gaertringen. Göttingen: Vandenhoeck & Rupprecht, 1957.

Groote, Wolfgang von, ed. *Grosse Soldaten der europäische Geschichte*. Bonn: Athenäum Verlag, 1961.

Gross, Gerhard P. *The Myth and Reality of German Warfare: Operational Thinking from Moltke the Elder to Heusinger*, ed. David T. Zabecki. Lexington: University Press of Kentucky, 2016.

———, ed. *Die vergessene Front. Der Osten 1914/15: Ereignis, Wirkung, Nachwirkung*. Paderborn: Ferdinand Schöningh, 2006.

Gruss, Helmuth. *Die deutsche Sturmbataillone im Weltkrieg, Ausbau und Verwendung*. Berlin: Junker & Dünnhaupt, 1939.

Gudmundsson, Bruce I. *On Artillery*. Westport, CT: Praeger, 1993.

———. *Stormtroop Tactics: Innovation in the German Army, 1914–1918*. New York: Praeger, 1989.

Gumz, Jonathan. *The Resurrection and Collapse of Empire in Habsburg Serbia, 1914–1918*. Cambridge: Cambridge University Press, 2009.

Haarbrücker, E. "Die technischen Nachrichtenmittel im Dienste der Kavallerie." *Militär-Wochenblatt* 90 (1908): cols. 2114–2118.

Hackel, Othmar, ed. *Militärgeschichte in Deutschland und Oesterreich vom 18. Jahrhundert bis in die Gegenwart.* Bonn: E. S. Mittler, 1985.

Hahlweg, Werner. *Carl von Clausewitz. Soldat-Politiker-Denker.* Göttingen: Musterschmidt Verlag, 1969.

Hahnke, Wilhelm von. "Zum Schlieffen-Plan und Moltke-Aufmarsch 1914." *Militär-Wochenblatt* 2 (1925): cols. 44–48.

Hall, Richard C. *Bulgaria's Road to the First World War.* Boulder, CO: East European Monographs, 1996.

Hamilton, Richard F., and Holger H. Herwig, eds. *Decisions for War, 1914–1917.* Cambridge: Cambridge University Press, 2004.

———. *War Planning 1914.* New York: Cambridge University Press, 2010.

Hanika, Johann. "Das lenkbare Luftschiff im Dienste des Krieges." *Militär-Wochenblatt* 60 (1908): cols. 1381–1385, 61 (1908): cols. 1411–1418, 62 (1908): cols. 1435–1439.

Hart, Peter. *The Great War: A Combat History of the First World War.* Oxford: Oxford University Press, 2013.

———. *The Somme: The Darkest Hour on the Western Front.* New York: Pegasus Books, 2008.

Hartmann, E. "Der militärische Wert der Flugzeuge." *Militär-Wochenblatt* 87 (1911): cols. 2016–2021.

Hartmann, Julius von. *Lebenserinnerungen, Briefe und Aufsätze.* 2 vols. Berlin: Verlag von Gebrüder Paetel, 1882.

Hauser, Oswald, ed. *Zur Problematik Preussen und Das Reich.* Köln: Bölau Verlag, 1984.

Haycock, Ronald, and Keith Neilson, eds. *Men, Machines and War.* Waterloo, ON: Wilfrid Laurier University Press, 1988.

Headrick, Daniel R. *The Invisible Weapon: Telecommunications and International Politics 1851–1945.* New York: Oxford University Press, 1991.

Hein, Günter W. *Das kleine Buch vom deutschen Heere.* Leipzig: Verlag von Lipsius & Tischer, 1901.

Heinricci, Paul, ed. *Das Ehrenbuch der deutschen Pioniere.* Berlin: Verlag Tradition Wilhelm Kolk, 1937.

Hermann, David G. *The Arming of Europe and the Making of the First World War.* Princeton, NJ: Princeton University Press, 1996.

Hermann, Helmuth. "Die Erkrankung des Generalobersten Helmuth von Moltke." *Militär-Wochenblatt* 10 (1926): cols. 331–335.

Herre, Franz. *Moltke. Der Mann und sein Jahrhundert.* Stuttgart: Deutsche Verlags-Anstalt, 1984.

Herrguth, Jürgen. *Deutsche Offiziere an öffentlichen Hochschulen.* Munich: Bernard & Graefe, 1979.

Hertzberg, Wilhelm von. "Betrachtungen über die Grundsätze eines neuen Exerzier-Reglements für die Kavallerie." *Militär-Wochenblatt* 129 (1908): cols. 3001–3007, 131 (1908): cols. 3066–3070.

————. "Charakter." *Militär-Wochenblatt* 168 (1913): cols. 3817–3822.

Herwig, Holger H. "Admirals versus Generals: The War Aims of the Imperial German Navy, 1914–1918." *Central European History* 5, 3 (September 1972): 208–233.

————. "Disjointed Allies: Coalition Warfare in Berlin and Vienna, 1914." *Journal of Military History* 54, 3 (July 1990): 265–280.

————. *The First World War: Germany and Austria-Hungary 1914–1918.* 2nd ed. London: Arnold Bloomsbury, 2014.

————. "From Tirpitz to Schlieffen Plan: Some Observations on German Military Planning." *Journal of Strategic Studies* 9, 1 (March 1986): 53–63.

————. *The German Naval Officer Corps: A Social and Political History, 1890–1918.* Oxford: Clarendon Press, 1973.

————. "Germany and the 'Short-War' Illusion: Toward a New Interpretation?" *Journal of Military History* 66, 3 (July 2002): 681–694.

————. *"Luxury" Fleet: The Imperial German Navy 1888–1918.* Reprint ed. London: Ashfield Press, 1987.

————. *The Marne, 1914: The Opening of World War I and the Battle that Changed the World.* New York: Random House, 2009.

Heuss, [Second Lieutenant]. "'Weiterwerfen,' von Befehlen." *Militär-Wochenblatt* 85 (1908): cols. 1998–1999.

Hierl, Konstantin. "Die Bedeutung der krigegeschichtlichen Studiums der Napoleonischen Epoche." *Beiheft zum Militär-Wochenblatt* 4 (1902): 193–213.

————. "Gefechtsausdehnungen." *Vierteljahrshefte für Truppenführung und Heereskunde* 5 (1908): 285–310.

Hindenburg, Paul von Beneckendorff und von [Hermann Mertz von Quirnheim]. *Out of My Life by Marshal von Hindenburg*, trans. F. A. Holt. 2 vols. New York: Harper & Brothers, 1921.

Hittle, J. D. *The Military Staff: Its History and Development.* 3rd ed. Harrisburg, PA: Stackpole, 1961.

Höbelt, Lothar. "Schlieffen, Beck Potiorek und das Ende der gemeinsamen deutschen-österreichisch-ungarischen Aufmarschpläne im Osten." *Militärgeschichtliche Mitteilungen* 36, 2 (1984): 7–30.

Hobohm, Martin. *Soziale Heeresmissstände als Teilursache des deutschen Zusammenbruchs von 1918.* Vol. 11 (first half) of *Das Werk des Untersuchungsauschusses der Verfassunggebenden Deutschen Nationalversammlung und des Deutschen Reichstages.* Berlin: Deutsche Verlagsgesellschaft für Politik & Geschichte, 1929.

Hoehn, [Bavarian Generalmajor]. *Führungstechnik der Artillerie (Feldartillerie und Schwere Artillerie) im Feldkriege.* 2nd ed. Munich: Theodor Riedel's Buchhandlung, 1910.

Hoenig, Fritz August. *Inquiries into the Tactics of the Future*, trans. Carl Reichmann. London: W. H. Allen, 1898.

Hoeppner, General of Cavalry Ernest von. *Germany's War in the Air: The Development and Operations of German Military Aviation in the World War.* Reprint ed. Nashville, TN: Battery Press, 1994.

Hoffmann, Joachim. "Die Kriegslehre des Generals von Schlichting." *Militärges-chichtliche Mitteilungen* 1 (1969): 5–35.

Hoffmann, Max. *Die Aufzeichnungen des Generalmajors Max Hoffmann*, ed. Karl Friedrich Nowak. 2 vols. Berlin: Verlag für Kulturpolitik, 1929.

Hoffmann, Otto von. *Lebenserinnerungen des königlich preussischen Generalleut-nants Otto von Hoffmann*, ed. Col. V. Hoffmann. Oldenburg: Schulzsche Hof-Buchhandlung & Hof-Buckdruckerei, 1907.

Hohenlohe-Ingelfingen, *Prinz* Krafft zu. *Aus meinem Leben*. 4 vols. Berlin: E. S. Mittler, 1907.

———. *Letters on Strategy*. 2 vols. London: Kegan Paul, Trench, Trübner, 1898.

Holleben, General Paul von. "Wissenschaftliche Grundlage für den Offizier." *Jahrbücher für die deutsche Armee und Marine* (1902): 461–475.

Holmes, Terence. "Asking Schlieffen: A Further Reply to Terence Zuber." *War in History* 10, 4 (2003): 464–479.

———. "The Real Thing: A Reply to Terence Zuber's 'Terence Holmes Reinvents the Schlieffen Plan.'" *War in History* 9, 1 (2002): 111–120.

———. "The Reluctant March on Paris: A Reply to Terence Zuber's 'The Schlief-fen Plan Reconsidered.'" *War in History* 8, 2 (2001): 208–232.

Hoppenstedt, Julius. "Die Artillerie im Kampfe der verbundenen Waffen." *Mil-itär-Wochenblatt* 69 (1912): cols. 1581–1585, 74 (1912): cols. 1619–1626, 75 (1912): cols. 1653–1655, 76 (1912): cols. 1699–1672.

———. "Die Infanterie im Kampfe der verbundenen Waffen." *Militär-Wochenblatt* 89 (1912): cols. 2019–2022, 90 (1912): cols. 2049–2054.

———. *Taktik und Truppenführung in Beispielen*. Dritter Teil: *Aufklärung, Marschsi-cherung, Vorposten*. Berlin: E. S. Mittler, 1903.

Horne, John, ed. *State, Society and Mobilization in Europe during the First World War*. New York: Cambridge University Press, 1997.

Horne, John, and Alan Kramer. *German Atrocities, 1914: A History of Denial*. New Haven, CT: Yale University Press, 2001.

Howard, Michael. "Men against Fire: Expectations of War in 1914." *International Security* 9, 1 (Summer 1984): 41–57.

———, ed. *Clausewitz*. Oxford: Oxford University Press, 1983.

———. *Studies in War and Peace*. New York: Viking Press, 1970.

———. *The Theory and Practice of War*. Bloomington: Indiana University Press, 1975.

Huber, Ernst R. *Deutsche Verfassungsgeschichte seit 1789*. 4 vols. Stuttgart: Kohl-hammer, 1957–1969.

Hughes, Daniel J. "Abuses of German Military History." *Military Review* 66, 12 (December 1986): 66–76.

———. *The King's Finest: A Social and Bureaucratic Profile of Prussia's General Of-ficers, 1871–1914*. New York: Praeger, 1987.

———. "Schlichting, Schlieffen, and the Prussian Theory of War in 1914." *Jour-nal of Military History* 59, 2 (April 1995): 257–277.

Hull, Isabel V. *Absolute Destruction: Military Culture and the Practices of War in Imperial Germany*. Ithaca, NY: Cornell University Press, 2005.

Hülsen, Walther von. "Die Schützenformen im Angriff." *Militär-Wochenblatt* 124 (1910): cols. 2883–2887, 125 (1910): cols. 2905–2909, 126 (1910): cols. 2927–2931, 127 (1910): cols. 2942–2951, 128 (1910): cols. 2975–2979.

———. "Feuerüberlegenheit." *Militär-Wochenblatt* 29 (1909): cols. 639–645.

———. "Feuer und Bewegung im Angriffe." *Militär-Wochenblatt* 152 (1906): cols. 3515–3519.

———. "Noch Einmal. Kampfkräftige Schützenlinie." *Militär-Wochenblatt* 56 (1910): cols. 1351–1354.

———. "Yorksche Ausbildung." *Vierteljahrshefte für Truppenführung und Heereskunde* 4 (1906): 70–77.

———. "Zahl und Raum im Kampfe der forderen Linien." *Militär-Wochenblatt* 155 (1906): cols. 3589–3595.

Hussey, John. "The Movement of German Divisions to the Western Front, Winter 1917–1918." *War in History* 4, 2 (April 1997): 213–220.

Hutten-Czapski, Count Bogdan von. *Sechzig Jahre Politik und Gesellschaft.* 2 vols. Berlin: E. S. Mittler, 1936.

Immanuel, Friedrich. "Der Angriff der deutschen, französischen, russischen Infanterie nach den neuesten Vorschriften." *Militär-Wochenblatt* 33 (1911): cols. 733–737, 34 (1911): cols. 759–762, 35 (1911): cols. 784–788.

———. "Der offensive Geist in unserer neuen Felddienst-Ordnung." *Militär-Wochenblatt* 71 (1908): cols. 1664–1667.

———. *Handbuch der Taktik.* 2 vols. Berlin: E. S. Mittler, 1910.

———. "Marschgewohnung." *Militär-Wochenblatt* 68 (1912): cols. 1561–1567.

———. *Siegen und Niederlagen im Weltkriege. Kritische Betrachtungen.* Berlin: E. S. Mittler, 1919.

Jackman, Steven D. "Shoulder to Shoulder: Close Control and 'Old Prussian Drill' in German Offensive Infantry Tactics, 1871–1914." *Journal of Modern History* 68 (January 2004): 73–104.

Jäger, Herbert. *German Artillery of World War One.* Ramsbury, UK: Crowood Press, 2001.

Jähns, Max. *Feldmarschall Moltke.* Berlin: Ernst Hoffman, 1900.

———. *Militärgeschichtliche Aufsätze,* ed. H. Schottelius and Ursula von Gersdorff. Osnabrück: Biblio Verlag, 1970.

Jahr, Christoph. *Gewöhnlich Soldaten. Desertion und Deserteur im deutschen und britischen Heer 1914–1918.* Göttingen: Vandenhoeck & Rupprecht, 1998.

Janson, Rudolf von. "Das militärische Ausbildungsjahr der Infanterie." *Beiheft zum Militär-Wochenblatt* 3 (1901): 121–141.

———. "Der Kampf gegen die Ueberlegenheit." *Militär-Wochenblatt* 3 (1901): cols. 56–63, 4 (1901): cols. 88–96.

———. *Duties of the General Staff,* trans. Harry Bell. 2nd ed. Leavenworth, KS: Army Service School, 1901.

———. "Lose Gedanken über Uebungen mit gemischter Waffen." *Militär-Wochenblatt* 62 (1908): cols. 1425–1429.

Janssen, Karl Heinz. "Der Wechsel in der Obersten Heeresleitung 1916." *Vierteljahrshefte für Zeitgeschichte* 7, 4 (October 1959): 337–371.

Jany, Kurt. *Geschichte der Preussischer Armee vom 15. Jahrhundert bis 1914.* 2nd ed. 4 vols. Osnabrück: Biblio Verlag, 1967.

Jäschke, Gotthard. "Zum Problem der Marne-Schlacht von 1914." *Historische Zeitschrift* 190 (1960): 311–348.

Jeismann, Karl-Ernst. *Das Problem des Präventivkriegs im europäischen Staaten- system mit besonderem Blick auf die Bismarckzeit.* Freiburg: Verlag Karl Albert, 1957.

Jochim, Theodor. "Der Herbstfeldzug 1914." *Wissen und Wehr* 2 (1929): 81–106.

———. "Der Marnefeldzug 1914 nach dem amtlichen Kriegswerke des Reichsar- chives." *Wissen und Wehr* 9 (1926): 513–527, 10 (1926): 592–611.

———. *Die Operationen und rückwärtigen Verbindungen der deutschen 1. Armee in der Marneschlacht 1914.* Berlin: E. S. Mittler, 1933.

———. *Die Vorbereitung des deutschen Heeres für die grosse Schlacht in Frankreich in Frühjahr 1918.* 5 vols. Berlin: E. S. Mittler, 1927–1930.

John, Hartmut. *Das Reserveoffizierkorps im Deutschen Kaiserreich 1890–1914.* Frank- furt: Campus Verlag, 1981.

Johnson, Hubert C. *Breakthrough: Tactics, Technology and the Search for Victory on the Western Front in World War I.* Novato, CA: Presidio, 1994.

Johnson, J. H. *Stalemate! The Great Trench Warfare Battles of 1915–1917.* London: Arms & Armor Press, 1995.

Jomini, Baron Antoine. *The Art of War.* Reprint ed. Westport, CT: Greenwood Press, 1971.

Jung, Jakob. *Max von Gallwitz (1852–1937) General und Politiker.* Osnabrück: Bib- lio Verlag, 1995.

Jünger, Ernst. *Copse 125: A Chronicle from the Trench Warfare of 1918,* trans. Basil Creighton. 1930. Reprint, New York: Howard Fertig, 1988.

———. *Storm of Steel: From the Diary of a German Storm-Troop Officer on the West- ern Front,* trans. Basil Creighton. Garden City, NY: Doubleday, Doran, 1929.

Jüstrow, Karl. *Feldherr und Kriegstechnik.* Oldenburg: Gerhard Stalling, 1933.

Kabisch, Ernst. *Michael. Die grosse Schlacht in Frankreich.* Berlin: Vorhut-Verlag Otto Schlegel, 1935.

———. *Streitfragen des Weltkrieges 1914–1918.* Stuttgart: Bergers Literarisches Büro & Verlagsanstalt, 1924.

Kaiser, Klaus-Dieter. "Die Eingliederung der ehemals selbständigen Nord- deutschen Truppenkörper in die preussische Armee in den Jahren nach 1866." Ph.D. diss., Free University of Berlin, 1972.

Kallee, [Major]. "Über Umfassung." *Beiheft zum Militär-Wochenblatt* 6 (1890): 187–214.

Kalm, Oskar Tile von. *Schlachten des Weltkrieges.* Vol. 30, *Gorlice.* Berlin: Olden- burg, 1930.

Kauffman, Jesse. *Elusive Alliance: The German Occupation of Poland in World War I.* Cambridge, MA: Harvard University Press, 2015.

Keegan, John. *The First World War.* New York: Alfred A. Knopf, 1999.

Keim, August. "Angewandte Taktik." *Militär-Wochenblatt* 119 (1903): cols. 2820– 2825.

———. "Der gegenwärtige Stand der Gefechtslehre und die Ausbildung zum Gefecht." *Beiheft zum Militär-Wochenblatt* 1 (1890): 1–22.

———. *Erlebtes und Erstrebtes. Lebenserinnerungen.* Hannover: Ernst Letsch Verlag, 1925.

———. "Kriegslehre und Kriegführung." *Beiheft zum Militär-Wochenblatt* 1 (1889): 1–22.

———. "Taktik." *Militär-Wochenblatt* 76 (1908): cols. 1785–1788.

Kelly, Patrick J. "Strategy, Tactics and Turf Wars: Tirpitz and the Oberkommando der Marine, 1892–1895." *Journal of Military History* 66, 4 (October 2002): 1033–1060.

Kennedy, Paul, ed. *Grand Strategies in War and Peace.* New Haven, CT: Yale University Press, 1991.

———. *The War Plans of the Great Powers, 1880–1914.* London: Allen & Unwin, 1979.

Kennett, Lee. *The First Air War 1914–1918.* New York: Free Press, 1991.

Kessel, Eberhard. "Die Tätigkeit des Grafen Waldersees als Generalquartiermeister und Chef des Generalstabs der Armee." *Die Welt als Geschichte* 14, 2 (1954): 181–211.

———. *Militärgeschichte und Kriegstheorie in neuer Zeit, Ausgewählte Aufsätze,* ed. Johannes Kunisch. Berlin: Duncker & Humboldt, 1987.

———. *Moltke.* Stuttgart: K. F. Koehler Verlag, 1957.

———. "Napoleonische und Moltkesche Strategie." *Wissen und Wehr* 20 (1939): 171–181.

———. "Um Problem des Wandels der Kriegskunst vom 18. Zum 19. Jahrhundert." *Wissen und Wehr* 20 (1939): 100–110.

Kielmansegg, Peter Count. *Deutschland und der Erste Weltkrieg.* 2nd ed. Stuttgart: Klett-Cotta, 1980.

Kiesling, Bernhard. "Das Schema des Freifeldangriffs." *Militär-Wochenblatt* 154 (1912): cols. 3555–3560, 155 (1912): cols. 3575–3581.

Kiesling, Eugenia C. "*On War:* Without the Fog," *Military Review* 63, 5 (September–October 2001): 85–87.

Kiliani, Emanuel von. "Die Operationslehre des Grafen von Schlieffen und ihre deutschen Gegner." *Wehrkunde* 10 (1961): 71–76, 133–138.

Kincaide, Norman Louis. "Sturmabteilung to Freikorps: German Army Tactical and Organizational Development 1914–1918." Ph.D. diss., Arizona State University, 1989.

Kiszling, Rudolf. "Bündniskrieg und Koalitionskriegführung am Beispiel der Mittelmächte im Ersten Weltkrieg." *Wehrwissenschaftliche Rundschau* 10, 12 (1960): 633–641.

Kitchen, Martin. *The German Offensives of 1918.* Charleston, SC: Tempus, 2001.

———. *The German Officer Corps, 1890–1918.* Oxford: Clarendon Press, 1968.

———. *The Silent Dictatorship: The Politics of the German High Command under Hindenburg and Ludendorff, 1916–1918.* New York: Holmes & Meier, 1976.

———. "The Traditions of German Strategic Thought." *International History Review* 1, 2 (April 1979): 163–190.

Kluck, Alexander von. *The March on Paris and the Battle of the Marne 1914*. London: Edward Arnold, 1920.

———. *Wanderjahre-Krieg-Gestalten*. Berlin: Verlag R. Eisenschmidt, 1929.

Köhler, Max. *Der Aufstieg der Artillerie bis zum Grossen Kriege*. Munich: Hugo Meiler, 1938.

Kohut, Thomas A. *Hermann von Tresckow. General der Infanterie und General-Adjutant Kaiser Wilhelms I*. Berlin: E. S. Mittler, 1911.

———. *William II and the Germans: A Study in Leadership*. New York: Oxford University Press, 1991.

Krafft, Rudolf. *Glänzendes Elend*. Stuttgart: Verlag Robert Lutz, 1895.

Krafft von Dellmensingen, Konrad. *Der Durchbruch. Studie an Hand der Vorgänge des Weltkrieges 1914–1918*. Hamburg: Hanseatische Verlagsanstalt, 1937.

———. "Schlieffen-Moltke der Jüngere-Bülow." *Militär-Wochenblatt* 2 (1925): cols. 35–44.

Kraft, Heinrich. *Der Anteil der 11. Bayer. Inf. Div. an der Durchbruchsschlacht von Gorlice-Tarnow*. Munich: C. H. Beck'sche Verlagsbuchhandlumg, 1934.

Kraft, Heinz. *Staatsräson und Kriegführung im Kaiserlichen Deutschland 1914–1916*. Göttingen: Musterschmidt Verlag, 1980.

Krebs, Karl. "Der preussische Generalstab und der Geist der Reformzeit." *Wehrwissenschaftliche Rundschau* 7, 4 (1957): 203–215.

Kretschmann, [Major]. "Die Eisenbahnlage auf dem rechten Heeresflügel während der Marneschlacht 1914." *Militär-Wochenblatt* 20 (1921): cols. 421–424.

Kretschmar, [Captain]. "Der Kampf der Infanterie gegen Maschinengewehre." *Militär-Wochenblatt* 103 (1913): cols. 2320–2324.

Kretschmar, Felix. "Die Ausbildung unserer Offiziere des Beurlaubtenstandes." *Militär-Wochenblatt* 31 (1913): cols. 699–701.

Krieg, Thilo. *Wilhelm von Doering, königlich preussischer Generalmajor*. Berlin: E. S. Mittler, 1898.

Kuhl, Hermann von. *Der deutsche Generalstab in Vorbereitung und Durchführung des Weltkrieges*. Berlin: E. S. Mittler, 1920.

———. *Der Marnefeldzug 1914*. Berlin: E. S. Mittler, 1921.

———. *Der Weltkrieg 1914–1918*. 2 vols. Berlin: Vaterländischen Verlag E. A. Weller, 1930.

———. "Die Ergebnisse des Untersuchungsauschusses über den Zusammenbruch der Offensive 1918." *Militär-Wochenblatt* 2 (1925): cols. 242–252.

———. "Die Schlacht an der Marne 1914." *Militär-Wochenblatt* 8 (1921): cols. 159–160.

———. *Entstehung, Durchführung und Zusammenbruch der Offensive von 1918*. Berlin: Deutsche Verlagsgesellschaft, 1927.

———. "Zur Beurteilung unserer Heerführer im Weltkriege." *Preussische Jahrbücher* 184, 3 (April–June 1921): 289–299.

Kuhl, Hermann von, and Walter von Bergmann. *Movements and Supply of the German First Army during August and September, 1914: A Treatise*. Fort Leavenworth, KS: Command and General Staff School Press, 1929.

Lange, Karl. *Marneschlacht und deutsche Oeffentlichkeit 1914–1939*. Düsseldorf: Bertelsmann Universitätsverlag, 1974.

Lavalle, John Howard. "Military Professionalization and the Realities of War." Ph.D. diss., University of Georgia, 1997.

Lee, John. *The Warlords: Hindenburg and Ludendorff*. London: Weidenfeld & Nicholson, 2005.

Lehmann, Konrad. "Conrad von Hötzendorf und die deutsche Oberste Heeresleitung im ersten Kriegshalbjahre." *Archiv für Politik und Geschichte* 10/11 (1926): 521–556.

Lehmann, Konrad, and Eggert von Estorff. *Dienstunterricht des Offiziers. Anleitung zur Erteilung des Mannschaftsunterrichts in Beispielen*. Berlin: E. S. Mittler, 1909.

Lehmann, Max. *Scharnhorst*. 2 vols. Leipzig: Verlag von S. Hirzel, 1886–1887.

Lenski, Franz von. *Aus den Leutnantsjahren eines alten Generalstabsoffiziers: Erinnerungen an den Rhein und die Reichshauptstadt aus den 80er und 90 Jahren des 19. Jahrhunderts*. Berlin: Bath, 1922.

———. *Lern- und Lehrjahre in Front und Generalstab*. Berlin: Bernard & Graefe, 1939.

Lessel, Emil von. *Böhmen, Frankreich, China 1866–1901. Erinnerungen eines preussischen Offizier*, ed. Walter Hubatsch. Cologne: G. Grote'sche Verlagsbuchhandlung, 1981.

Lettow-Vorbeck, Oscar von. *Der Feldzug in Böhmen 1866*. 2nd ed. Berlin: E. S. Mittler, 1910.

———. *Geschichte des Krieges von 1866 in Deutschland*. Vol. 1. Berlin: E. S. Mittler, 1896.

Lichtenstern, Reisner *Freiherr* von. "Über den Frontenangriff der Infanterie auf freier Fläche." *Militär-Wochenblatt* 57 (1902): cols. 1531–1536.

———. "Zur Feuergeschwindigkeit." *Militär-Wochenblatt* 67 (1903): cols. 1649–1655.

Liddell Hart, Basil H. *History of the First World War*. Reprint ed. London: Cassell, 1970.

Liddle, Peter H. *Passchendaele in Perspective: The Third Battle of Ypres*. London: Leo Cooper, 1997.

Liebert, Eduard von. *Aus Einem bewegten Leben*. Munich: J. F. Lehmanns Verlag, 1925.

Liebmann, Curt. "Die deutsche Gefechtsvorschriften von 1914 in der Feuerprobe des Krieges." *Militärwissenschaftliche Rundschau* 2 (1937): 456–487.

———. "Die Entwicklung der Frage eines einheitlichen Oberbefehls im Weltkriege." *Wissen und Wehr* 1 (1928): 1–36, 2 (1928): 65–99.

Lieven, Dominic. *The End of Tsarist Russia: The March to World War I and Revolution*. New York: Viking, 2015.

Lindenau, Wolf von. "Was lehrt uns der Burenkrieg für unseren Infanterieangriff." *Beiheft zum Militär-Wochenblatt* 3 (1902): 133–175.

Linnebach, Karl, ed. *Deutsche Heeresgeschichte*. Hamburg: Hanseatische Verlagsanstalt, 1935.

Linnenkohl, Hans. *Vom Einzelschuss zur Feuerwalze. Der Wettlauf zwischen Technik und Taktik in Ersten Weltkrieg*. Munich: Bernard & Graefe, 1990.

Liss, Ulrich. "Der Nachrichtendienst in den Grenzschlachten im Westen im August 1914." *Wehrwissenschaftliche Rundschau* 12, 3 (March 1962): 140–160, 12, 5 (May 1962): 270–287.

———. "Graf Schlieffens letztes Kriegsspiel." *Wehrwissenschaftliche Rundschau* 15, 3 (March 1965): 162–166.

Loeffler, Captain. "Taktische Fragen." *Vierteljahrshefte für Truppenführung und Heereskunde* 1 (1904): 398–407.

Lossberg, Friedrich von. *Meine Tätigkeit im Weltkriege.* Berlin: E. S. Mittler, 1939.

Ludendorff, Erich. *Kriegführung und Politik.* 2nd ed. Berlin: E. S. Mittler, 1922.

———. *Meine Kriegserinnerungen.* Berlin: E. S. Mittler, 1919.

———. *Mein militärischer Werdegang.* Munich: Ludendorffs Verlag, 1935.

———. *Urkunden der Obersten Heeresleitung über ihre Tätigkeit 1916/18.* 3rd rev. ed. Berlin: E. S. Mittler, 1922.

Lueerssen. "Feldartillerie im Zusammenwirken mit Infanterie 1870/71 und heute." *Militär-Wochenblatt* 141 (1910): cols. 3273–3277.

Lupfer, Timothy T. *The Dynamics of Doctrine: The Changes in German Tactical Doctrine during the First World War.* Leavenworth Papers No. 4. Fort Leavenworth, KS: US Army Command and General Staff College, 1981.

Mackensen, August von. *Mackensen. Briefe und Aufzeichnungen der Generalfeldmarschalls aus Krieg und Frieden,* ed. Wolfgang Foerster. Leipzig: Bibliographisches Instituts, 1938.

Mantey, von [Colonel a. D.]. "Betrachtungen über den deutschen Aufmarsch 1914." *Wissen und Wehr* 4 (1926): 234–250.

———. "Betrachtungen über die Grenzschlachten im August 1914. Eine kriegsgeschichtliche Studie." *Wissen und Wehr* 7 (1926): 385–406, 8 (1926): 460–485.

Marcks, Erich [Major]. "Clausewitz' Lehre vom Kriege." *Wissen und Wehr* 5 (1930): 259–276.

Markus, Georg. *Der Fall Redl.* Vienna: Amalthea Verlag, 1984.

Martens, Hans, and Ernst Zipfel. *Geschichte der Ulanen-Regiments von Schmidt (1. Pommersches) Nr. 4.* Berlin: Tradition Wilhelm Kolk, 1929.

Marwedel, Ulrich. *Carl von Clausewitz. Persönlichkeit und Wirkungsgeschichte seines Werkes bis 1918.* Boppard: Harald Boldt Verlag, 1978.

Marx, [Lieutenant General a. D.]. "Graf Haeseler als Erzieher. Erinnerungen und Betrachtungen an seinem 100. Geburtstag." *Wissen und Wehr* 1 (1936): 10–31.

Maurer, John H. *The Outbreak of the First World War: Strategic Planning, Crisis Decision Making and Deterrence Failure.* Westport, CT: Praeger, 1995.

May, Ernst R., ed. *Knowing One's Enemies: Intelligence Assessment before the Two World Wars.* Princeton, NJ: Princeton University Press, 1984.

McMeekin, Sean. *The Berlin-Baghdad Express: The Ottoman Empire and Germany's Bid for World Power.* Cambridge, MA: Harvard University Press, 2010.

McRandle, James, and James Quirk. "The Blood Test Revisited: A New Look at German Casualty Counts in World War I." *Journal of Modern History* 70, 3 (July 2006): 667–702.

Meckel, Jacob. *Allgemeine Lehre von der Truppenführung im Kriege.* 3rd ed. Berlin: E. S. Mittler, 1890.

Meier-Welcker, Hans. "Die deutsche Führung an der Westfront im Frühsommer 1918." *Die Welt als Geschichte* 21, 3 (1961): 164–184.

———. *Seeckt.* Frankfurt: Bernard & Graefe Verlag für Wehrwesen, 1967.

Meisner, H. O. *Der Kriegsminister.* Berlin: Hermann Reinshagen Verlag, 1940.

Mertz von Quirheim, Hermann. *Der Führerwille in Entstehung und Durchführung, erläutert an den Vorgängen beim gemeinsamen Oberbefehl in den Reichslanden August–September 1914.* Oldenburg: Gerhard Stalling, 1932.

Mette, Sigfried. *Vom Geist deutscher Feldherren. Genie und Technik 1800–1918.* Zurich: Scienta, 1938.

Meyer, Thomas, ed. *Helmuth von Moltke 1848–1916. Dokumente zu seinem Leben und Wirken.* 2 vols. Basel: Perseus Verlag, 1993.

Michalka, Wolfgang, ed. *Der Erste Weltkrieg. Wirkung, Wahrnehmung, Analyse.* Munich: Piper, 1994.

Militärgeschichtliches Forschungsamt, ed. *Beiträge zur Militär-und Kriegsgeschichte.* 6 vols. Stuttgart: Deutsche Verlags-Anstalt, 1962.

———. *Deutsche Militärgeschichte.* 6 vols. Munich: Bernard & Graefe, 1964–1979.

———. *Operatives Denken und Handeln in deutschen Streitkräften im 19. und 20. Jahrhundert.* Bonn: E. S. Mittler, 1988.

Millett, Allan R., and Williamson Murray, eds. *Military Effectiveness.* 3 vols. Boston: Allen & Unwin, 1988.

Mohr, [Major]. "Heranarbeiten im Feldkriege und das Eingraben im Gefecht." *Militär-Wochenblatt* 18 (1908): cols. 397–402.

Mohr, Rudolf, ed. *V. Trothas Ausbildung unserer Unterführer für den Kriegsbedarf.* 3rd ed. Berlin: E. S. Mittler, 1909.

Möller, Hanns. *Fritz von Below. General der Infanterie.* Berlin: Bernard & Graefe, 1939.

Mollin, Volker. *Auf dem Wege zur "Materialschlacht": Vorgeschichte und Funktionen des Artillerie-Industrie-Komplexes im Deutschen Kaiserreich.* Pfaffenweiler: Centaurus Verlag, 1986.

Moltke, Count Helmuth von. *Ausgewählte Werke,* ed. Ferdinand von Schmerfeld. 4 vols. Berlin: Reimar Hobbing, 1925.

———. *Gesammelte Schriften und Denkwürdigkeiten.* 8 vols. Berlin: E. S. Mittler, 1892–1918.

———. *Moltke on the Art of War: Selected Writings,* ed. and trans. Daniel J. Hughes. Novato, CA: Presidio, 1993.

———. *Moltkes Militärische Werke.* 17 vols. Berlin: E. S. Mittler, 1892–1918.

Moltke, Helmuth von. *Erinnerungen, Briefe, Dokumente 1877–1916,* ed. Eliza von Moltke. Stuttgart: Der Kommende Tag Verlag, 1922.

———. *Helmuth von Moltke 1848–1916. Dokumente zu seinem Leben und Wirken,* ed. Thomas Meyer. 2 vols. Basel: Perseus Verlag, 1993.

Mombauer, Annika. *Helmuth von Moltke and the Origins of the First World War.* Cambridge: Cambridge University Press, 2001.

———. *The Origins of the First World War: Controversies and Consensus.* London: Pearson Education, 2002.

————. "A Reluctant Military Leader? Helmuth von Moltke and the July Crisis of 1914." *War in History* 6, 4 (1999): 417–446.

Mombauer, Annika, and Wilhelm Deist, eds. *The Kaiser: New Research on Wilhelm II's Role in Imperial Germany.* Cambridge: Cambridge University Press, 2004.

Mönckeberg, Carl. *Bei Süd und Bug Armee 1915.* Stuttgart: Deutsche Verlags Anstalt, 1917.

Moncure, John. *Forging the King's Sword: Military Education between Tradition and Modernization: The Case of the Royal Prussian Cadet Corps, 1871–1918.* New York: Peter Lang, 1993.

Morgen, Curt von. *Meiner Truppen Heldenkämpfe. Aufzeichnungen.* Berlin: E. S. Mittler, 1920.

Morrow, John H., Jr. *Building German Airpower, 1909–1914.* Knoxville: University of Tennessee Press, 1976.

————. *The Great War in the Air: Military Aviation from 1909 to 1921.* Washington, DC: Smithsonian Institution Press, 1993.

Moser, Otto von. *Ausbildung und Führung des Bataillons, des Regiments und der Brigade.* 4th ed. Berlin: E. S. Mittler, 1914.

————. *Die obersten Gewalten im Weltkrieg.* Stuttgart: Chr. Belser, 1931.

————. *Feldzugsaufzeichnungen als Brigade-Divisionskommandeur und als kommandierender General 1914–1918.* Stuttgart: Chr. Belsersche Verlagsbuchhandlung, 1920.

————. "Zu den Deckblätter für das Infanterie-Exerzier-Reglement vom August 1909." *Militär-Wochenblatt* 11 (1910): cols. 228–232.

Moyer, Laurence V. *Victory Must Be Ours: Germany in the Great War 1914–1918.* New York: Hippocrene Books, 1995.

Mueller, Harald. "Zu den Anfängen der militärischen-Absprachen zwischen Deutschland und Österreich-Ungarn im Jahre 1882." *Zeitschrift für Militärgeschichte* 7 (1968): 206–215.

Mueller, Klaus-Jürgen, ed. *The Military and Politics in Society in France and Germany in the Twentieth Century.* Oxford: Berg, 1995.

Mueller, Lieutenant. "Über Gefechtsverluste." *Vierteljahrshefte fuer Truppenfuehrung und Heereskunde* 2 (1905): 429–451.

Mueller-Brandenburg, Hermann. *Von der Marne zur Marne. Militärische Schlaglichter auf den Zusammenbruch.* Berlin: Verlag für Sozialwissenschaft, 1919.

Müller, Hermann. *Die Entwicklung der Feldartillerie.* 3 vols. Berlin: E. S. Mittler, 1892–1894.

Müller-Loebnitz, Wilhelm. *Die Führung im Marne-Feldzug 1914.* Berlin: E. S. Mittler, 1939.

————. "Graf Schlieffen und der Geist deutscher Feldherrntums." *Wissen und Wehr* 11 (1938): 804–811.

————. *Von Schlieffen bis Ludendorff.* Leipzig: Ernst Oldenburg Verlag, 1925.

Muncy, Lysbeth Walker. *The Junker in the Prussian Administration under William II, 1888–1914.* Providence, RI: Brown University Press, 1944.

Murray, Williamson, MacGregor Knox, and Alvin Bernstein, eds. *The Making of Strategy: Rulers, States and War*. Cambridge: Cambridge University Press, 1994.

Muth, Jörg. *Command Culture: Officer Education in the US Army and the German Armed Forces, 1901–1940, and the Consequences for World War II*. Denton: University of North Texas Press, 2011.

Nagel, Fritz. *Fritz: The World War I Memoirs of a German Lieutenant*, ed. Richard A. Baumgartner. Huntington, WV: Der Angriff Publications, 1981.

Nebelin, Manfred. *Ludendorff: Diktator im Ersten Weltkrieg*. Munich: Siedler Verlag, 2010.

Neiberg, Michael S., ed. *Arms and the Man: Military History Essays in Honor of Dennis Showalter*. Boston: Brill, 2011.

Neilson, Keith, and Roy A. Prete, eds. *Coalition Warfare: An Uneasy Accord*. Waterloo, ON: Wilfrid Laurier University Press, 1983.

Neumann, Major Georg P. *Die deutschen Luftstreitkräfte im Weltkriege*. Berlin: E. S. Mittler, 1920.

Nicolai, Walther. *Nachrichtendienst. Presse und Volksstimmung im Weltkrieg*. Berlin: E. S. Mittler, 1920.

Obermann, Emil. *Soldaten, Burger, Militaristen. Militär und Demokratie in Deutschland*. Stuttgart: J. G. Cotta'sche Buchhandlung Nachfolger, [ca. 1955].

Ohnesorge, [Generalmajor a. D]. "Die Legende von der Ueberlegenheit der französischen Artillerie gegenüber der deutschen im Jahre 1914." *Militär-Wochenblatt* 2 (1926): cols. 44–47.

Olden, Rudolf. *Hindenburg. Oder der Geist der preussischen Armee*. 1935. Reprint, Hildesheim: Gerstenberg, 1982.

Örtzen, Karl Ludwig von. "Älter und Ueberalterung." *Wissen und Wehr* 10 (1932): 530–554.

———. "Generalfeldmarschall Helmuth Graf v. Moltke und der Generalstab, vom Weltkriege ausgesehen." *Wissen und Wehr* 9 (1934): 585–624.

Osten-Sacken und Bei Rhein, Ottomar Baron von der. *Preussens Heer von seinen Anfängen bis zur Gegenwart*. 3 vols. Berlin: E. S. Mittler, 1914.

Ostertag, Heiger. *Bildung, Ausbildung und Erziehung des Offizierkorps im deutschen Kaiserreich 1871 bis 1918*. Frankfurt: Peter Lang, 1990.

Östreich, Gerhard. *Neostoicism and the Early Modern State*, ed. Brigitta Östreich and H. G. Koenigsberger. London: Cambridge University Press, 1982.

Otto, Helmut. "Entstehung und Wesen der Blitzkriegsstrategie des deutschen Imperialismus vor dem ersten Weltkrieg." *Zeitschrift für Militärgeschichte* 6 (1967): 400–414.

———. *Schlieffen und der Generalstab*. East Berlin: Deutscher Militärverlag, 1966.

———. "Zum strategisch-operativen Zusammenwirken des deutschen und österreichisch-ungarischen Generalstabes bei der Vorbereitung des ersten Weltkrieges." *Zeitschrift für Militärgeschichte* 2 (1963): 423–440.

Palmer, Alan. *The Gardeners of Salonika*. New York: Simon & Schuster, 1965.

Paret, Peter. *Clausewitz and the State*. Oxford: Oxford University Press, 1976.

———. "Education, Politics and War in the Life of Clausewitz." *Journal of the History of Ideas* 29, 3 (July–September 1968): 394–408.

————, ed. *Makers of Modern Strategy from Machiavelli to the Nuclear Age*. Princeton, NJ: Princeton University Press, 1986.

Parkinson, Roger. *Clausewitz: A Biography*. New York: Stein & Day, 1971.

Pastor, Peter, and Graydon A. Tunstall, eds. *Essays on World War I*. Boulder, CO: East European Monographs, 2012.

Pearton, Maurice. *Diplomacy, War and Technology since 1830*. Lawrence: University Press of Kansas, 1984.

Petrenz, [Major], et al. *Reserve-Infanterie-Regiment Nr. 3*. Oldenburg: Verlag von Gerhard Stalling, 1926.

Pflanze, Otto. *Bismarck and the Development of Germany*. 3 vols. Princeton, NJ: Princeton University Press, 1961–1990.

Philpott, William. "Britain and France Go to War: Anglo-French Relations on the Western Front, 1914–1918." *War in History* 2, 1 (1995): 43–64.

————. *Three Armies on the Somme: The First Battle of the Twentieth Century*. New York: Alfred A. Knopf, 2010.

Pönitz, Karl. *Militärische Briefe eines Verstorbenen an seine noch Lebenden Freunde historischen, wissenschaftlichen und humoristischen Inhalts*. 3 vols. Adorf: Verlagsbureau, 1841–1845.

Porch, Douglas. *The March to the Marne: The French Army 1871–1914*. Cambridge: Cambridge University Press, 1981.

Poten, Bernard. *Geschichte des Militär-Erziehungs- und Bildungswesens*. 4 vols. Berlin: A. Hofmann, 1889–1897.

Pratt, Edwin A. *The Rise of Rail-Power in War and Conquest 1833–1914*. Philadelphia: J. B. Lippincott, 1916.

Preussen, Friedrich Karl von. *Statistisches Handbuch für den preussischen Staat*, ed. Königlich Statistisches Bureau. Berlin: Verlag des Koeniglisches Statischen Bureaus, 1888.

Priesdorff, Kurt von, ed. *Soldatisches Führertum*. 10 vols. Hamburg: Hanseatisches Verlagsanstalt, 1936–1942.

Prussia, Grosser Generalstab. *Geschichte der deutsch-französische Krieg 1870–71*. 5 vols. Berlin: E. S. Mittler, 1874–1881.

Rabenau, von. *Die deutsche Land-und Seemacht und die Berufspflichten des Offiziers*. Berlin: E. S. Mittler, 1914.

Rahne, Hermann. *Mobilmachung. Militärische Mobilmachungsplanung und Technik in Preussen und im deutschen Reich vom Mitte des 19. Jahrhunderts bis zum Zweiter Weltkrieg*. East Berlin: Militärverlag der deutschen demokratischen Republik, 1983.

Randewig, [First Lieutenant]. "Die deutsche Funkaufklärung in der Schlacht bei Tannenberg." *Wissen und Wehr* 3 (1932): 128–141.

Rauchensteiner, Manfred. *Der Erste Weltkrieg und das Ende der Habsburgermonarchie 1914–1918*. Vienna: Böhlau Verlag, 2013.

Reinhardt, Walther. *Wehrkraft und Wehrwille. Aus seinem Nachlass mit einer Lebensbeschreibung*, ed. Ernst Reinhardt. Berlin: E. S. Mittler, 1932.

Rich, Norman. *Friedrich von Holstein: Politics and Diplomacy in the Era of Bismarck and Wilhelm II*. 2 vols. Cambridge: Cambridge University Press, 1965.

Richter, Johann. "Änderungen des Exerzier-Reglements für die Feldartillerie." *Militär-Wochenblatt* 102 (1912): cols. 2324–2325.

———. "Aus den Gefechtslehren der Feldartillerie Deutschlands, Östereich-Ungarns, Frankreichs und Russlands." *Militär-Wochenblatt* 107 (1913): cols. 2391–2397, 108 (1913): cols. 2419–2423.

———. Übungen zur Forderung des Zusammenwirkens zwischen Infanterie und Artillerie." *Militär-Wochenblatt* 42 (1910): cols. 1011–1018.

Ritter, Gerhard. *The Sword and the Scepter: The Problem of Militarism in Germany*, trans. Heinz Norden. 4 vols. Coral Gables, FL: University of Miami Press, 1964–1973.

Ritter, Hans. *Kritik des Weltkrieges. Das Erbe Moltkes und Schlieffens im grossen Kriege.* 2nd rev. ed. Leipzig: K. F. Koehler, 1921.

Robinson, Paul. *Grand Duke Nikolai Nikolaevich: Supreme Commander of the Russian Army.* De Kalb: Northern Illinois University Press, 2014.

Rohkrämer, Thomas. *Der Militarismus der "kleinen Leute." Die Kriegervereine in Deutschland 1871–1914.* Munich: R. Oldenbourg, 1990.

Röhl, John C. G. *The Kaiser and His Court: Wilhelm II and the Government of Germany.* 1987. Reprint, Cambridge: Cambridge University Press, 1994.

Rohne, Heinrich. "Die Artillerie bei Infanterieangriff." *Militär-Wochenblatt* 47 (1912): cols. 1039–1045, 48 (1912): cols. 1072–1078.

———. "Die Entwicklung der modernen Feldartillerie." *Vierteljahrshefte für Truppenführung und Heereskunde* 1 (1904): 481–531.

———. "Maschinengewehre und Geschütz." *Militär-Wochenblatt* 31 (1913): cols. 697–700.

———. "Neue Gedanken über die Verwendung der Feldartillerie." *Militär-Wochenblatt* 161 (1911): cols. 3727–3731.

———. "Nochmals: Die Artillerie beim Infanterieangriff." *Militär-Wochenblatt* 94 (1912): cols. 2151–2156.

———. "Über die Artilleriewirkung im ostasiatischen Krieg." *Militär-Wochenblatt* 84 (1908): cols. 1963–1968, 85 (1908): cols. 1993–1998, 86 (1908): cols. 2012–2018.

———. "Zum Problem des Infanterieangriffs." *Militär-Wochenblatt* 7 (1912): cols. 131–137.

Rohr, [Captain]. "Infanteristisches." *Militär-Wochenblatt* 68 (1904): cols. 1702–1706.

Rohwer, Jürgen, ed. *Neue Forschungen zum Ersten Weltkriege.* Koblenz: Bernard & Graefe, 1985.

Rommel, Field Marshal Erwin. *Attacks.* Vienna, VA: Athena Press, 1979.

Roon, Count Albrecht von. *Denkwürdigkeiten aus dem Leben des Generalfeldmarschalls Kriegsministers Grafen von Roon*, ed. Count Waldemar von Roon. 3 vols. Breslau: Verlag von Eduard Treuwendt, 1897.

Rosinski, Herbert. *The German Army.* London: Hogarth Press, 1940.

———. "Scharnhorst to Schlieffen: The Rise and Decline of German Military Thought." *Naval War College Review* 29, 1 (January 1976): 83–103.

Rücker, W. "Ein Beitrag zur Schulung der Unterführer." *Militär-Wochenblatt* 149 (1910): cols. 3488–3492, 150 (1910): cols. 3510–3515.

Rumschöttel, Hermann. *Das bayerische Offizierkorps 1860–1914.* Berlin: Duncker & Humboldt, 1973.

Rupprecht, Crown Prince of Bavaria. *In Treue Fest. Mein Kriegstagebuch,* ed. Eugen von Frauenholz. 3 vols. Munich: Deutscher National Verlag, 1929.

Rüstow, Wilhelm. *Die Feldherrnkunst des neunzehnten Jahrhunderts. Zum Selbststudium und für den Unterricht an höheren Militärschulen.* 2nd ed. Zurich: Druck & Verlag von Friedrich Schulthess, 1867.

Samuels, Martin. *Command or Control? Command Training and Tactics in the British and German Armies, 1888–1918.* London: Frank Cass, 1995.

———. "Directive Command and the German General Staff." *War in History* 2, 1 (March 1995): 22–42.

———. *Doctrine and Dogma: German and British Infantry Tactics in the First World War.* New York: Greenwood, 1992.

Sanborn, Joshua A. *Imperial Apocalypse: The Great War and the Destruction of the Russian Empire.* Oxford: Oxford University Press, 2014.

Schaefer, Theobald von. "Betrachtungen zum 'Bündniskrieg.'" *Wissen und Wehr* 19 (1938): 373–392.

———. *Generalstab und Admiralstab. Das Zusammenwirken von Heer und Flotte im Weltkrieg.* Berlin: E. S. Mittler, 1931.

Scharfenort, Louis von. *Die königlich preussische Kriegsakademie.* Berlin: E. S. Mittler, 1910.

Schaumann, [Lieutenant Colonel] von. "Unsere Offiziere des Beurlaubtenstandes." *Militär-Wochenblatt* 63 (1913): cols. 1434–1437.

Scheibert, J., ed. *Illustrirtes Deutsches Militär-Lexikon.* Berlin: Verlag von W. Pauli's, 1897.

Scherff, Wilhelm von. *Der Schlachtenangriff im Lichte der Schlichting'sche 'Taktischen Grundsätze' und der Boguslawski'schen 'Betrachtungen.'* Berlin: Verlag von R. Eisenschmidt, 1898.

———. *Die Lehre vom Kriege auf der Grundlage seiner neuzeitlichen Erscheinungsformen. Ein Versuch.* Berlin: E. S. Mittler, 1897.

———. *Unsere heutige Infanterie-Taktik. Spiegel der Augustkämpfe 1870 um Metz.* Berlin: Militär-Verlag R. Felix, 1893.

Schering, Walter. *Carl von Clausewitz. Geist und Tat, Das Vermächtnis des Soldaten und Denkers.* Stuttgart: Alfred Kroner Verlag, 1941.

———. "Clausewitz' Lehre von Zweck und Mittel." *Wissen und Wehr* 9 (1936): 606–631.

———. *Die Kriegsphilosophie von Clausewitz.* Hamburg: Hanseatische Verlagsanstalt, 1935.

Schindler, John R. *Isonzo: The Forgotten Sacrifice of the Great War.* Westport, CT: Praeger, 2001.

———. "Redl—Spy of the Century?" *International Journal of Intelligence and Counter Intelligence* 18, 3 (Fall 2005): 483–507.

———. "Steamrolled in Galicia: The Austro-Hungarian Army and the Brusilov Offensive, 1916." *War in History* 10, 1 (2003): 27–59.

Schlichting, Sigismund von. "Antwort auf Herrn Oberst v. Lettows Kritik." *Militär-Wochenblatt* 79 (1901): cols. 79–88.

———. *Moltkes Vermächtnis*. Munich: Verlag der Allgemeinen Zeitung, 1901.

———. *Moltke und Benedek. Eine Studie über Truppenführung zu den 'Taktischen und strategischen Grundsätze der Gegenwart.'* Berlin: E. S. Mittler, 1900.

———. "Taktische und strategische Grundsätze der Gegenwart." *Beiheft zum Militär-Wochenblatt* 4 (1896): 193–229.

———. *Taktische und strategische Grundsätze der Gegenwart*. 3 vols. 3rd ed.Berlin: E. S. Mittler, 1898–1899.

———. "Über das Infanteriegefecht." *Beiheft zum Militär-Wochenblatt* 1 (1879): 36–68.

———. *Über Truppenführung aus dem Jahre 1887*. Schwedt: Felix Freyhoff, 1888.

Schlieffen, Alfred Count von. *Alfred von Schlieffen's Military Writings*, ed. and trans. Robert T. Foley. London: Frank Cass, 2003.

———. *Dienstschriften des Chefs des Generalstabes der Armee Generalfeldmarschalls Graf von Schlieffen*, ed. General Staff. 2 vols. Berlin: E. S. Mittler, 1937–1938.

———. *Generalfeldmarschall Graf Alfred Schlieffen. Briefe*, ed. Eberhard Kessel. Göttingen: Vandenhoeck & Rupprecht, 1958.

———. *Generalfeldmarschall Graf Alfred v. Schlieffen. Gesammelte Schriften*, ed. General Staff. 2 vols. Berlin: E. S. Mittler, 1913.

Schmidt, Ernst. *Schlachten des Weltkrieges*. Vol. 18, *Argonnen*. Berlin: Gerhard Stalling, 1927.

Schmidt, G. "Die Entwicklung des Flugwesens in dem Jahrsfrist 1908 bis 1912 und ihre militärische Bedeutung." *Militär-Wochenblatt* 34 (1913): cols. 764–770.

Schmidt-Bückeburg, Rudolf. *Das Militärkabinett der preussischen Könige und deutscher Kaisers. Seine geschichtliche Entwicklung und staatsrechtliche Stellung 1787–1918*. Berlin: E. S. Mittler, 1932.

Schneider, Paul. *Die Organisation des Heeres*. Berlin: E. S. Mittler, 1931.

Schniewindt, [Lieutenant General]. "Die Nachrichtenverbindungen zwischen den Kommandobehörden während des Bewegungskrieges 1914." *Wissen und Wehr* 3 (1929): 129–152. Translated in *Signal Corps Bulletin* 74 (September–October 1933): 1–26.

Schnitter, Helmut. *Militärwesen und Militärpublizistik. Die militärische Zeitschriftenpublizistik in der Geschichte des bürgerlicher Militärwesens in Deutschland*. East Berlin: Deutscher Militärverlag, 1967.

Schönaich, Baron Paul von. *Mein Damaskus. Erlebnisse und Bekenntnisse*. Berlin-Hessenwinkel: Verlag der neuen Gesellschaft, 1926.

Schulte, Bernd-Felix. *Die deutsche Armee 1900–1914. Zwischen Beharren und Verändern*. Düsseldorf: Droste Verlag, 1977.

Schuurman, Bart. "Clausewitz and the 'New Wars' Scholars." *Parameters* 40, 1 (March 2010): 89–100.

Schwarte, Max, ed. *Der grosse Krieg 1914–1918*. 10 vols. Leipzig: Johann Ambrosius Barth, 1921.

———. *Die militärischen Lehren des Grossen Krieges.* 2nd ed. Berlin: E. S. Mittler, 1923.

Schwarzmüller, Theo. *Zwischen Kaiser und "Führer." Generalfeldmarschall August von Mackensen. Eine politische Biographie.* 2nd ed. Paderborn: Ferdinand Schöningh, 1996.

Schwerin, Count von. *Der Adjutantendienst bei den Truppen aller Waffen bei Garnisonskommandos und Bezirkskommandos.* 2nd ed. Berlin: E. S. Mittler, 1909.

Schwertfeger, Bernard. *Die grossen Erzieher des deutschen Heeres. Aus der Geschichte der Kriegsakademie.* Potsdam: Rütter & Loening Verlag, 1936.

Seeckt, Hans von. *Aus meinem Leben 1866–1917.* Leipzig: Hase & Kohler, 1938.

Senger und Etterlin, Ferdinand M. von. "Cannae, Schlieffen und die Abwehr." *Wehrwissenschaftliche Rundschau* 13, 1–2 (January–February 1963): 26–43.

Seyfert, Gerhard. *Die militärischen Beziehungen und Vereinbarungen zwischen dem deutschen und dem österreichischen Generalstab vor und bei Beginn des Weltkrieges.* Leipzig: Buckdruckerei Johannes Moltzen, 1934.

Shanafelt, Gary W. *The Secret Enemy: Austria-Hungary and the German Alliance, 1914–1918.* New York: Columbia University Press, 1985.

Sheldon, Jack. *The German Army on the Somme 1914–1916.* Barnsley, UK: Pen & Sword, 2005.

Showalter, Dennis E. "Army and Society in Imperial Germany: The Pains of Modernization." *Journal of Contemporary History* 18 (1983): 583–618.

———. "From Deterrence to Doomsday Machine: The German Way of War 1890–1914." *Journal of Military History* 64, 3 (July 2000): 679–709.

———. "German Grand Strategy: A Contradiction in Terms?" *Militärgeschichtliche Mitteilungen* 48, 2 (1990): 65–102.

———. "Goltz and Bernhardi: The Institutonalization of Originality in the Imperial German Army." *Defense Analysis* 3, 4 (1987): 305–318.

———. *Instrument of War: The German Army 1914–1918.* New York: Osprey Publishing, 2016.

———. "Prussian Cavalry 1806–1871: The Search for Roles." *Militärgeschichtliche Mitteilungen* 14, 1 (1976): 7–22.

———. *Railroads and Rifles: Soldiers, Technology and the Unification of Germany.* 1975. Reprint, Hamden, CT: Archon Press, 1986.

———. *Tannenberg: Clash of Empires.* Hamden, CT: Archon Books, 1991.

———. *The Wars of German Unification.* London: Arnold, 2004.

Simon, Walter M. *The Failure of the Prussian Reform Movement, 1807–1819.* Ithaca, NY: Cornell University Press, 1955.

Snyder, Jack. *The Ideology of the Offensive: Military Decision Making and the Disasters of 1914.* Ithaca, NY: Cornell University Press, 1984.

Sondhaus, Lawrence. *Franz Conrad von Hötzendorf: Architect of the Apocalypse.* Boston: Humanities Press, 2000.

———. *The Great War at Sea: A Naval History of the First World War.* Cambridge: Cambridge University Press, 2014.

Speck, William. *Das Königlich Preussische Reserve-Infanterie Regiment 84.* Zeulenroda: Bernhard Sporen Verlag, 1937.

Staabs, Hermann von. *Aufmarsch nach zwei Fronten. Auf Grund der Operations-pläne von 1871–1914*. Berlin: E. S. Mittler, 1925.

Stadelmann, Rudolf. *Moltke und der Staat*. Krefeld: Scherpe Verlag, 1950.

———. *Scharnhorst, Schicksal und geistige Welt*. Wiesbaden: Limes Verlag, 1952.

Staff, Gary. *Skagerrak: The Battle of Jutland through German Eyes*. Barnsley, UK: Pen & Sword, 2016.

Steffen, Dirk. "The Holtzendorff Memorandum of 22 December 1916 and Germany's Declaration of Unrestricted U-Boat Warfare." *Journal of Military History* 68, 1 (January 2004): 215–224.

Stegemann, Bernd. *Die Deutsche Marinepolitik 1916–1918*. Berlin: Duncker & Humboldt, 1970.

Stein, Hermann von. *Erlebnisse und Betrachtungen aus der Zeit des Weltkrieges*. Leipzig: K. F. Koehler, 1919.

Steinberg, Jonathan. *Bismarck: A Life*. Oxford: Oxford University Press, 2011.

Stephenson, Scott. *The Final Battle: Soldiers of the Western Front and the German Revolution of 1918*. Cambridge: Cambridge University Press, 2009.

Stevenson, David. *Armaments and the Coming of War: Europe 1904–1914*. Oxford: Clarendon Press, 1996.

———. *Cataclysm: The First World War as Political Tragedy*. New York: Basic Books, 2004.

———. *The First World War and International Politics*. Oxford: Oxford University Press, 1988.

Stockhausen, Major. "Über des Herabwerfen von Sprengkörpern aus Luftschiffen und Flugzeugen." *Militär-Wochenblatt* 155 (1902): cols. 3589–3591.

Stoker, Donald. *Clausewitz: His Life and Work*. New York: Oxford University Press, 2014.

Stone, David R. *The Russian Army in the Great War: The Eastern Front, 1914–1917*. Lawrence: University Press of Kansas, 2015.

Stone, Norman. *The Eastern Front 1914–1917*. New York: Charles Scribner's Sons, 1975.

———. "V. Moltke-Conrad: Relations between the Austro-Hungarian and German General Staffs, 1909–1914." *Historical Journal* 9, 2 (1966): 201–228.

Storz, Dieter. *Kriegsbild und Rüstung vor 1914. Europäische Landstreitkräfte vor dem Ersten Weltkrieg*. Herford: E. S. Mittler, 1992.

Stosch, Albrecht von. *Denkwürdigkeiten des Generals und Admirals Albrecht von Stosch*, ed. Ulrich von Stosch. Stuttgart: Deutscher Verlags-Anstalt, 1904.

Strachan, Hew. *European Armies and the Conduct of War*. London: Allen & Unwin, 1983.

———. *The First World War. Vol. 1, To Arms*. Oxford: Oxford University Press, 2001.

———, ed. *The Oxford Illustrated History of the First World War*. Oxford: Oxford University Press, 1998.

Stürgkh, Josef Count von. *Im deutschen Grossen Hauptquartier*. Leipzig: Paul List Verlag, 1921.

Sumida, Jon Tetsuro. "A Concordance of Selected Subjects in Carl von Clause-witz's *On War*." *Journal of Military History* 78, 1 (January 2014): 271–331.

———. *Decoding Clausewitz: A New Approach to* On War. Lawrence: University Press of Kansas, 2008.

Tappen, Gerhard. *Bis zur Marne 1914. Beiträge zur Beurteilung der Kriegführung bis zum Abschluss der Marne-Schacht*. Oldenburg: Gerhard Stalling, 1920.

Taylor, A. J. P. *War by Time Table: How the First World War Began*. New York: American Heritage Press, 1969.

Teitler, G. *The Genesis of the Professional Officers' Corps*. London: Sage Publications, 1977.

Terraine, John. *The U-Boat Wars, 1916–1945*. New York: Putnam, 1989.

Teske, Hermann. *Colmar Freiherr von der Goltz. Ein Kämpfer für den militärischen Fortschritt*. Göttingen: Musterschmidt, 1957.

Thaer, Albrecht von. *Generalstabsdienst an der Front und in der O.H.L. Aus Briefen und Tagebuchaufzeichnungen 1915–1919*, ed. Siegfried A. Kaehler. Göttingen: Vandenhoeck & Rupprecht, 1958.

Thiele, Fritz. *Zur Geschichte der Nachrichtentruppe: 1899–1924*. Berlin: Preuss, 1925.

Thiele, Lieutenant Colonel. "Führung und Nachrichtenverbindungen." *Jahrbuch für Wehrpolitik und Wehrwissenschaften* (1939): 61–72.

Torrey, Glenn E. *The Romanian Battlefront in World War I*. Lawrence: University Press of Kansas, 2011.

Trautmann, Frederic, trans. and ed. *A Prussian Observes the American Civil War: The Military Studies of Justus Scheibert*. Columbia: University of Missouri Press, 2001.

Travers, Timothy, and Christian Archer, eds. *How the War Was Won: Command and Technology in the British Army on the Western Front, 1917–1918*. London: Routledge, 1992.

———. *The Killing Ground: The British Army, the Western Front and the Emergence of Modern Warfare 1900–1918*. London: Allen & Unwin, 1987.

———. *Men at War: Politics, Technology and Innovation in the Twentieth Century*. Chicago: Precedent Publishing, 1982.

Trumpener, Ulrich. "War Premeditated? German Intelligence Operations in July 1914." *Central European History* 9, 1 (March 1976): 58–85.

Trythall, Anthony, ed. *Old Battles and New Defences: Can We Learn from Military History?* London: Brassey's, 1986.

Tuchman, Barbara. *The Guns of August*. New York: Macmillan, 1962.

Tunstall, Graydon A., Jr. *Blood on the Snow: The Carpathian Winter War of 1915*. Lawrence: University Press of Kansas, 2010.

———. *Planning for War against Russia and Serbia: Austro-Hungarian and German Military Strategies, 1871–1914*. Boulder, CO: Social Science Monographs, 1993.

Tyng, Sewell. *The Campaign of the Marne 1914*. New York: Longman, Green, 1935.

Uhle-Wettler, Franz. *Ludendorff in Seiner Zeit: Soldat–Stratege–Revoutionär. Eine Neubewertung*. Augsburg: Kurt Vowinckel Verlag, 1996.

Van Creveld, Martin. *Command in War*. Cambridge, MA: Harvard University Press, 1985.

———. *Supplying War: Logistics from Wallenstein to Patton*. Cambridge: Cambridge University Press, 1977.

Venorh, Wolfgang. *Ludendorff. Legende und Wirkichkeit*. Frankfurt: Ullstein, 1993.

Verdy du Vernois, Julius von. *Strategie*. 3 vols. Berlin: E. S. Mittler, 1902–1904.

———. *Studien über den Krieg*. 3 vols. Berlin: E. S. Mittler, 1892–1902.

Verhey, Jeffrey. *The Spirit of 1914: Militarism, Myth and Mobilization in Germany*. Cambridge: Cambridge University Press, 2000.

Villacres, Edward J., and Christopher Bassford. "Reclaiming the Clausewitzian Trinity." *Parameters* 25, 3 (Autumn 1995): 9–19.

Vogel, [Lieutenant]. "Der Angriff und die Krise in der Schlacht." *Militär-Wochenblatt* 18 (1908): cols. 387–392, 19 (1908): cols. 416–421.

Vogt, Adolf. *Oberst Max Bauer. Generalstabsoffizier im Zwielicht*. Osnabrück: Biblio Verlag, 1974.

Vogt, Hermann. *Das Buch vom deutschen Heer*. Bielefeld: Velhagen & Klasing, 1886.

Volckheim, Ernst. *Die deutschen Kampfwagen im Weltkriege*. Berlin: E. S. Mittler, 1923.

Volker, Ullrich. "Das deutsche Kalkül in der Julikrise 1914 und die Frage der englischen Neutralität." *Geschichte in Wissenschaft und Unterricht* 34, 2 (1983): 79–97.

Volkmann, Erich Otto. *Soziale Heeresmissstände als Mitursache des deutschen Zusammenbruchs von 1918*. Vol. 11 (second half) of *Das Werk des Untersuchungsauschusses der Verfassunggebenden Deutschen Nationalversammlung und des Deutschen Reichstages*. Berlin: Deutsche Verlagsgesellschaft für Politik & Geschichte, 1929.

Wachter, von. "Dünne und dichte Schützenlinie." *Militär-Wochenblatt* 60 (1910): cols. 1423–1428.

Wagner, Reinhold. *Grundlagen der Kriegstheorie*. Berlin: E. S. Mittler, 1912.

Wagner, Rudolf. *Hinter den Kulissen des Grossen Hauptquartier*. Berlin: Adalbert Schultz Verlag, 1931.

Waldersee, Alfred Count von. *Denkwürdigkeiten des Generalfeldmarschalls Alfred Grafen von Waldersee*, ed. H. O. Meisner. 3 vols. Berlin: Deutsche Verlags-Anstalt, 1925.

Wallach, Jehuda L. *Das Dogma der Vernichtungsschlacht: die Lehren von Clausewitz und Schlieffen und ihre Wirkungen in zwei Weltkriegen*. Frankfurt: Bernard & Graefe, 1967.

———. *The Dogma of the Battle of Annihilation: The Theories of Clausewitz and Schlieffen and Their Impact on the German Conduct of Two World Wars*. 1967. Reprint, Westport, CT: Greenwood Press, 1986.

———. *Kriegstheorien. Ihre Entwicklung im 19. und 20. Jahrhundert*. Frankfurt: Bernard & Graefe, 1972.

———. *Uneasy Coalition: The Entente Experience in World War I*. Westport, CT: Greenwood Press, 1993.

Wartensleben-Carow, Hermann Count von. *Hermann Graf von Wartensleben-Carow. Eine Lebensbild 1826–1921*, ed. Countess Elisabeth von Wartensleben. Berlin: E. S. Mittler, 1923.

Watson, Alex. "'For Kaiser and Reich': The Identity and Fate of the German Volunteers, 1914–1918." *War in History* 12, 1 (2005): 44–74.

Watson, Alexander. *Ring of Steel. Germany and Austria-Hungary in World War I: The People's War*. New York: Basic Books, 2014.

Watter, Count von [Generalleutnant a. D.]. "Gegen die Legende von der Unterlegenheit der deutschen Feldartillerie gegenüber der französischen zu Kriegsbeginn." *Militär-Wochenblatt* 34 (1926): cols. 1250–1252.

Wawro, Geoffrey. *The Austro-Prussian War: Austria's War with Prussia and Italy in 1866*. Cambridge: Cambridge University Press, 1996.

———. *The Franco-Prussian War: The German Conquest of France in 1870–1871.* Cambridge: Cambridge University Press, 2003.

———. *A Mad Catastrophe: The Outbreak of World War I and the Collapse of the Habsburg Empire*. New York: Basic Books, 2014.

Weisenberger, [Second Lieutenant]. "Entwicklungsräume der Infanterie." *Militär-Wochenblatt* 147 (1913): cols. 3341–3342.

Welch, David. *Germany, Propaganda and Total War, 1914–1918: The Sins of Omission*. New Brunswick, NJ: Rutgers University Press, 2000.

Westermann, Edward P. *Flak: German Anti-aircraft Defenses 1914–1945*. Lawrence: University Press of Kansas, 2001.

Wetzell, Georg. *Der Bündniskrieg. Eine militärpolitisch operativ Studie des Weltkrieges*. Berlin: E. S. Mittler, 1937.

———. "Der 'Bündniskrieg' und die Kritik." *Militär-Wochenblatt* 28 (1938): cols. 1745–1754, 1812–1818.

Wheeler-Bennett, John. *Wooden Titan: Hindenburg in Twenty Years of German History 1914–1934*. New York: William Morrow, 1936.

White, Charles. *The Enlightened Soldier: Scharnhorst and the Militärische Gesellschaft in Berlin, 1801–1805*. New York: Praeger, 1989.

Wild von Hohenborn, Adolf. *Briefe und Aufzeichnungen des preussischen Generals als Kriegsminsters und Truppenführer im Ersten Weltkrieg*, ed. Helmut Reichold. Boppard: Harald Boldt Verlag, 1986.

Wilhelm I. *Militärische Schriften weiland Kaiser Wilhelms des Grossen Majestät*, ed. Prussia Kriegsministerium. 2 vols. Berlin: E. S. Mittler, 1897.

Wilhelm, Rolf. *Das Verhältnis der süddeutschen Staaten zum Norddeutschen Bund 1867–1870*. Husum: Matthiesen Verlag, 1978.

Wilhelmi, Captain. "Die schwere Feldartillerie in der Felddienst und Manöver-Ordnung, Gedanken über Kriegstüchtigkeit." *Militär-Wochenblatt* 93, 1 (1908): cols. 1527–1532.

Williamson, Samuel R., and Peter Pastor, eds. *Essays on World War One: Origins and Prisoners of War*. New York: Social Science Monographs, 1983.

Wilson, Trevor. *The Myriad Faces of War: Britain and the Great War, 1914–1918*. Cambridge: Polity Press, 1986.

Winter, Denis. *Haig's Command: A Reassessment*. New York: Viking, 1991.

Woodward, David R. *Hell in the Holy Land: World War I in the Middle East*. Lexington: University Press of Kentucky, 2006.

Wrisberg, Ernst von. *Heer und Heimat 1914–1918*. Leipzig: Verlag von K. F. Koehler, 1921.

———. *Wehr und Waffen 1914–1918*. Leipzig: Verlag von K. F. Koehler, 1921.

Wynne, Graeme Chamley. *If Germany Attacks: The Battle in Depth in the West*. 1940. Reprint, Westport, CT: Greenwood Press, 1976.

Zabecki, David T. *Steel Wind: Colonel Georg Bruchmüller and the Birth of Modern Artillery*. Westport, CT: Praeger, 1994.

Zabel, Jürgen-Konrad. *Das preusssiche Kadettenkorps. Militärische Jugenderziehung als Herrschaftsmittel im preussischen Militärsystem*. Frankfurt: Haag & Herchen, 1978.

Zanthier, [Colonel z. D.]. "Führerausbildung." *Beiheft zum Militär-Wochenblatt* 5 (1900): 141–180.

Zedlitz-Trützschler, Count Robert von. *Zwölf Jahre am deutschen Kaiserhof: Aufzeichnungen*. Stuttgart: Deutsche Verlags Anstalt, 1924.

Ziethen, General Alfred. "Aus grosser Zeit vor zwanzig Jahren. Die Durchbruchschlacht von Gorlice." *Militär-Wochenblatt* 119, 41 (May 1935): cols. 1627–1632.

Zöberlein, Hans. *Das Glaube an Deutschland. Ein Kriegserleben von Verdun bis um Umsturz*. Munich: Zentralverlag der NSDAP, 1935.

Zoellner, Eugen. *Schlieffens Vermächtnis*. Berlin: E. S. Mittler, 1938.

Zuber, Terence. *Inventing the Schlieffen Plan: German War Planning, 1871–1914*. Oxford: Oxford University Press, 2002.

———. "The Schlieffen Plan Reconsidered." *War in History* 6, 3 (1999): 262–305.

———. "Terence Holmes Reinvents the Schlieffen Plan." *War in History* 8, 4 (2001): 468–476.

———. "Terence Holmes Reinvents the Schlieffen Plan—Again." *War in History* 10, 1 (2003): 92–101.

Zwehl, Hans von. *Generalstabsdienst im Frieden und im Kriege*. Berlin: E. S. Mittler, 1923.

———. *Maubege, Aisne-Verdun. Das VII Reserve-Korps im Weltkriege von seinem Beginn bis Ende 1916*. Berlin: Verlag Karl Curtius, 1921.

———. "Vom Sterben des deutschen Offizierkorps." *Militär-Wochenblatt* 2 (1921): cols. 23–26, 39 (1922): cols. 839–842.

INDEX

Given the scope of the work, the authors decided that the index should be limited mainly to people. Where necessary, some concepts central to German military theory, doctrine, and planning have been included as well as a few important place names.